THE TARGUMS

OF

ONKELOS AND JONATHAN BEN UZZIEL

ON THE PENTATEUCH.

LEVITICUS, NUMBERS, AND DEUTERONOMY.

THE TARGUMS

OF

ONKELOS AND JONATHAN BEN UZZIEL

ON THE PENTATEUCH;

WITH THE FRAGMENTS OF THE

JERUSALEM TARGUM.

FROM THE CHALDEE.

BY

J. W. ETHERIDGE, M.A.

TRANSLATOR OF THE NEW TESTAMENT FROM THE PESCHITO SYRIAC.

LEVITICUS, NUMBERS, AND DEUTERONOMY.

"THIS provision, (the Paraphrase,) made by men, was directed by the Ruler of Providence, in His love for the remnant of His people, to afford us stay and staff in His Toran. His laws and precepts, till the time of the Redemption shall arrive, when He will raise from the dust the fallen tabernacle of David, and say to the daughter of Zion, Awake, arise."

MENDELSSOHN.

LONDON:

LONGMAN, GREEN, LONGMAN, ROBERTS,
AND GREEN.

——

1865.

GLOSSARY

OF HIERATIC AND LEGAL TERMS

IN THE

PENTATEUCH;

ON THE BEST AUTHORITIES, CHRISTIAN AND RABBINICAL.

THE biblical title of the Mosaic writings most usually
employed is HA TORAH, "the Law;" from *yarah*, "to
teach," or "direct:"—"the Law of the Lord," to
assert its true origin and authority; and "the Law of
Moses," to denote the mediatorial agency by which it
was given to mankind. The common conventional title,
"the Pentateuch," is a combination of the Greek words,
τεῦχος, "a volume," and πέντε, "five;" "the Five-
fold Book;" which corresponds with the Rabbinical
appellation of *Chamishah Chumeshe hattorah*, "the Five
Fifths of the Law." Whether this division was made
by the author, or the entire work was composed by him
in one continuous treatise, cannot be fully ascertained.
The five books, as we now classify them, are not distinguished in the original Hebrew by any other specific
titles than the initial words. Thus Genesis, from its
first word, is called *Bereshith*, "In the beginning;"
Exodus, *Ve Elleh Shemoth*, "These are the names;"
Leviticus, *Vaiyikra*, "And he called;" Numbers, *Vai-
dabber*, "And he spoke," with the current title of
Bemidbar, "In the wilderness;" while Deuteronomy
takes its name from the first two words, *Elleh Hadde-*

barim, " These are the words," or *Sepher Debarim,* "the Book of the Words."

The general contents of the Pentateuch are,—1. Historical ; 2. Legislative. In Genesis the Historical details are given in successive sections called *Toledoth,* αἱ γενέσεις, histories, especially of the origin of persons or things, from *yalad,* " to create," or " bring forth." Thus we have the *toledoth* of the heavens and the earth, from the first verse of the first chapter of Genesis, to the sixth verse of the second chapter. These are followed by the *toledoth* of Adam, chap. v. 1 ; of Noah, vi. 9 ; of the first nations, 10, and the first empire, 11 : after which come the *toledoth* of Abraham, Isaac, Jacob, and Joseph, to the end. In the following books the history, no longer biographical, takes a broader character, and describes the development of the Hebrew nation as such, from the Exodus to the death of Moses. The greater portion of the Pentateuch, however, from the middle of the second to the end of the fifth book, is a digest of the Laws of the Jewish Dispensation, ethical, ritualistic, and secular. The last book condenses both the history and the legislation, by a summary which culminates in a marvellous grandeur of prophecy, whose words of warning and benedictions of grace become, for all time, a Divinely spoken attestation to the Torah as a Revelation from God.

This is all that needs to be said here on the structure of the work at large ; my design in these introductory pages being restricted to the simple object expressed at the head,—a brief explication of the terminology of the Pentateuch, and not a hermeneutic study of its several parts, for which I refer the student to the learned volumes of Graves and Macdonald, Baehr and Fairbairn, Havernick, Hengstenberg, and the commentators in general. Nor have I entered even on the question of the authenticity of the works of the Hebrew legislator, about which we have had within the last three years many able treatises, contributing to set that most important truth upon a foundation not more sure than it was before, but more evidently sure to us. The genuineness of the Mosaic writings, the credibility of their contents, and the Divine inspiration which is their source, are now more firmly believed in than ever; a result which all who reverence the Bible as the Word of God must rejoice in, however they may deplore the painful circumstances which gave occasion to the controversy, or the wavering of too many, shaken by scepticism, through the influence of one-sided objections, who would have stood firm had they sought and found the support which always comes to the sincere and impartial inquirer with the full knowledge of the truth.

In the arrangement of these terms and phrases of the Pentateuch, to avoid the dryness of a mere alphabetic vocabulary, I have grouped them under the various subjects to which they relate, with a slight tissue of connecting remarks, which may serve at once to render them a little more readable, and conduce to their elucidation.

I. THE DIVINE NAMES

THE holy Pentateuch opens with a sentence which combines the majesty and simplicity of a Divine oracle: "In the beginning Elohim created the heavens and the earth;" a sentence whose few but sublime words throw the first beam of light on the otherwise inscrutable mystery of existence, and lead us up to the fountain and cause of created being, in God, its Author and End.

I. The name ELOHIM is the plural form of *El* or

Eloha, the ground-form of which some think they find in the Hebrew root *alah,* "to swear," *i. q.,* a God in covenant: some, that it lies in the cognate Arabic root *alaha,* "to worship," or "adore," from which are formed alike the Arabian name of *Allah* and the Hebrew *Eloha,* the Being who alone is adorable · but others, deriving it from the abstract noun *El,* or *Ul,* consider *Elohim* to be an appellation of the Omnipotent; the name of a Being whose will concentrates all power in itself. *El Elohim* in their view is equivalent to ὁ Θεὸς ἰσχυρός, or Παντοκράτωρ, "the Almighty God."

Yet to Him who is of necessity One, is here given, and by His own dictate, a plural appellation. This phenomenon, which occurs in a multitude of places in the Old Testament, is explained as being a mere adaptation to the usual style of royalty ;—*pluralis majestatis, vel excellentiæ.* According to this view it does not indicate a plurality of Persons in the Deity, but the multiform and all-comprising perfection of the One God ; the index of physical and moral majesty in their highest expression. When, therefore, we read such words as, "Elohim said, Let us make man in Our Image ;" (Gen. i. 26 ;) or, "Behold, the man is become as one of Us ;" (Gen. iii. 22 ;) the formula is to be understood after the manner in which we read the plural in a proclamation of one of the kings of the earth. But the insufficiency of this explanation is apparent in the fact, that Elohim is used not only with plural pronouns in the first person, as in the texts quoted, but with plural adjectives, (*Elohim kerobim,* "near Gods," Deut. iv. 7; *chayim,* "living Gods," Jer. x. 10; *kedoshim,* "holy Gods," Joshua xxiv. 19,) and in concord with plural verbs in the third person. (Gen. xx. 13 : *Hithu Elohim othi,* "The Gods caused me to wander." Gen. xxxv. 7 : *Niglu elaif ha-Elohim,* "The

Gods were revealed to him." See also Gen. xxxi. 53.)[1] When we read in some royal proclamation such words as, "We have decreed," the form of the pronoun being usual on the lips of a king makes no hindrance to our perception that the words are those of an individual; but when we read, "The kings have decreed," we are obliged, by the common sense of language, to understand more kings than one. But such is the combination of the nominative and the verb in the texts just cited. The Bible, did it contain no other intimation on the mystery of the Triune Nature, by combining this plural name of the Deity with a singular verb, as in Gen. i. 1, or with another Divine name in the singular, as " Jehovah Elohim," or *El Elohim*, would not fail to suggest the conception of a nature in which simplicity or unity of essence is characterized by a plurality of Persons.

The modern Jewish theologians, in their wish to keep at the greatest distance from the peculiar doctrines of Christianity, have diverged in some instances, and this among them, from the belief of their ancient predecessors. The Jewish people, at the Christian epoch, and for a long time after it, though steadfast as any of their descendants in the doctrine of the Divine unity, were nevertheless habituated to the idea of a personal plurality in Him whose name is Elohim. Considering the four Christian Gospels merely as authentic contemporary history, we have in them important documentary evidence of the state of public opinion and religious belief among that people eighteen hundred years ago. In reading the various discourses and colloquies which have a record on those pages, can we suppose that when Jesus Christ told the people of the willingness of

---

[1] We could refer to the plural form in Eccles xii 1 " Remember thy Creators :' but the reading there is precarious, as many good MSS. have the singular.

"the Father" to give "the Holy Spirit" to those
who ask Him, He used terms which were not already
familiar to them? So when He spoke with Nicodemus
of "the Spirit" as the Regenerator, and of God so
loving the world as to give His only begotten Son for
its redemption, or when the Baptist discoursed of the
love which the Father hath for the Son, did these
sacred appellations fall for the first time upon their
ears? In truth the formula *Ab, Ben, ve Ruach ha
Kadosh*, "Father, Son, and Holy Spirit," was theirs
before it was ours. It developed the sense of what
they read in their Scriptures of One who is the Father,
(Mal. ii. 10 ;) of One who is the Son; (Prov. xxx. 4;)
and of One who is the Spirit of Holiness. (Psalm li. 11 ;
cxxxix. 7 ; Isaiah xlviii. 16.) They had a term which
corresponds to our technical word "Trinity," namely,
Shilosh, and in Aramaic *Talithutho ;* and in some of
their earliest post-biblical literature the doctrine intimated by that term has a categorical expression as distinct
as any that are found in the creeds of the church.[2]

[2] I may refer, for examples, to the passages in the Zohar, where the
Shema, or confession of the Divine Unity, (Deut. vi. 4,) is explained
upon Trinitarian principles. "Hear, O Israel Jehovah our God is one
Jehovah. By the first name in this sentence, Jehovah, is signified God
the Father, the Head of all things. By the next words, our God, is
signified God the Son, the fountain of all knowledge ; and by the
second Jehovah is signified God the Holy Ghost, proceeding of them
both. To all which is added the word One, to signify that these three
are Indivisible. But this mystery shall not be revealed until the
coming of Messiah." So the *Trisagion*, or angels' song, in Isai. vi. is
expounded in the same way. "Holy, holy, holy Lord God of Sabaoth.
Isaiah, by repeating Holy three times, does as much as if he had said,
Holy Father, Holy Son, and Holy Spirit ; which three Holies do make
but one only Lord God of Sabaoth." The sacred dogma itself is thus
laid down "Come and see the mystery. There are three degrees (in
Elohim) ; and each degree is by itself [*balchudi*] · nevertheless [*aph al-
baq*] all are one ; all united in unity, and this inseparable from that."
(*Zohar*, cap. 3. Compare the *Jezirah*, i. 35) The Zohar gives a

II. JEHOVAH, יהוה. In this holy and awful Name, as the revealed appellation of the Self-Existing, All-Sufficient, and Unchangeable Being, we possess the germ and principle of all true theology. The Hebrew divines call it, by emphasis, *Ha Shem*, THE NAME; with the reverential epithets of *Shema Rabba*, "the Great Name;" *Shem shel arba othioth*, "the Name of Four Letters;" (the Greek *Tetragramma*;) *Shem ha-etsem*, "the very Name;" *Shem hammeyochad*, "the one, singular, or peculiar Name;" and *Shem hammephorash*, "the Name of Manifestation," as making the Divine Nature known; (from *pharash*, "to explain;") or, in the meaning which that verb bears in Aramaic of being separate or distinguished,—"the Name which is especially sacred."

The reverence and godly fear with which this Divine title is regarded, have among the Jews for two thousand years made it a name for the thought, rather than the tongue; and the silence of so many ages, in the disuse of it as a vocable, has been followed by the absolute loss of its true pronunciation. The averseness to the use of the Name by the voice was at an early period strengthened by the view taken of the third commandment, as not only forbidding perjury and blasphemy, but also the light and indiscriminating pronunciation of the Holy Name in common conversation; and by conclusions from the case in Levit. xxiv. 11–16, where the sin of the man was thought to have consisted not only in his blaspheming the Name, but in pronouncing it. See the Targums on the place. The influence of this feeling showed itself in the habit of refraining from the

curious, but of course defective, illustration from the human voice, which is *one* thing, though formed by the union of *three* elements,—warmth, vapour, and air. The passage, which contains some good dogmatic definitions, may be found on p 18 of the Sulzbach edition, and p. 43 of that of Amsterdam.

common use of the Name, except in worship, and in
pious salutations; (*Berakoth*, iii. 5;) and then of
restricting the utterance of it to the lips of the
priest in the public services of religion.   Thus, in
pronouncing the trinal blessing, (Num. vi.,) the priest
"might make utterance of the Name according to its
writing." (*Shem hammephorash ki-kethabo.—Talmud,
Sotah*, vii. 6; *Tamid*, vii. 2.)   When the high priest
pronounced it in the service of the day of Atonement,
the people fell prostrate on the ground. (*Mishna, Yoma,*
vi. 2.)   So that hitherto the use of it was not absolutely forbidden, but the abuse only.   But the exag-
geration of the sentiment led at last to the final cessation of the use itself.   After the time of the high
priest Shemeon Hazaddik, it ceased to be spoken.
It was heard in the temple for the last time from his
mouth.   Henceforward whoever should attempt to pronounce it was to have no part in the world to come.
(*Sanhedrin*, x. 1.)   The consequence has been an utter
oblivion of the orthoëpy of the Name, not only in its
oral sound, but in its grammatical vocalization; a defect
which has caused not a little embarrassment as to the
precise composition and import of the appellation.   The
four antique consonants remain, like an immutable
symbol of the Divine Being; but the manner in which
they are vocalized, from the peculiar nature of the
Hebrew language, will greatly modify the signification.
And perhaps no name has been subjected to so many
experiments for some past time as the sacred one before
us, for which the following modes of expression have
been severally contended for:—YeHeVeH, YeHVeH,
YaHVeH, YaHaVaH, YaHaVeH, YeHoVaH.   After
these we cease to wonder at the diversities in the Greek
and other ethnic forms of the name; as Ἀια, Ἰαω, Ἰαβε,
Ἰευω, Διος, *Jovis*, and *Jova*.

But amid all these variations as to the mode in which it should be syllabled, the real meaning of the name is not seriously obscured. The basis of it stands sure, in the Hebrew verb *hayah*, "to be;" a verb of which there are two forms, *hayah* and *havah*, the latter being the more ancient. It is that which appears in the name Jehovah; a circumstance which should be taken into account in examining one of the questions of the day on the antiquity of the name.

Now, of the preterite *hayah* or *havah*, "He was," the third person future, masculine, is *Yihyeh*, or *Yihveh*, "He will be;" a form of the verb which certainly gives that of the title YHVH. In this point of view, as predicating futurity of existence, it is held to express, in the third person, "He will be;" that which the Almighty affirmed of Himself (Exod. iii. 14) in the first person, *Ehyeh*, "I will be." But the futurity of existence here proclaimed is not that of one who is only to be hereafter; it is the permanent existence of a Being who now Is, and who ever has Been. For the form *Yihveh* is held to be equivalent with *Ye-havah*, the prefix of the future combined with the preterite root, to indicate the permanence of One who has ever existed. He who Was and Is, is He who Will Be. The punctuation of the Name as Yehovah is an attempt to express the fulness of this truth, in admitting the three elements of the verb "to Be." Thus *Yehe*, "He will be;" *Hoveh*, "He is;" *Havah*, "He was." So in the Apocalypse the Deity is named as ὁ ἦν, καὶ ὁ ὢν, καὶ ὁ ἐρχόμενος, (Rev. iv. 8,) "He who was, and who is, and who is to come," or "to be, still;" in Hebrew, *Hu haveh, hu hoveh, vehu yehveh*. Hence the name Yehovah has always been considered as the peculiar and incommunicable title of the Being who is self-existent, all-sufficient, and unchangeable. In the Tetragramma there is a concentration of all the Divine attributes; for He who is the self-existent must be self-sufficient, and therefore infinitely blessed, benevolent, and just; omniscient, because spiritual in His nature, and everywhere present, as existing absolutely, boundless in power as in presence; immutable, inhabiting eternity.

The Masorites punctuated the name Jehovah with the vowels of אֲרֹנָי *Adonai*; thus, יְהֹוָה. But when the two titles, Jehovah and Adonai, occur in the Bible in apposition, the former is pointed with the vowels of אֱלֹהִים, as in Hab. iii. 19 : יֱהֹוִה אֲרֹנָי.

The authors of the Septuagint Version, under the influence of the Palestinian feeling with regard to the Holy Name, do not give it a literal expression, but render it by ὁ Κύριος, "the Lord;" and Yehovah Elohim by Κύριος ὁ Θεός. The old Syriac Version for Yehovah employs the title *Morio*, "the Lord." The Syrians considered this name with its four letters M.R.I.A. to correspond with the Hebrew Tetragram, יהוה; and the letters themselves as the initials of words symbolical of the Divine Nature; the first, *m*, standing for *morutho*, "dominion;" the second, *r*, for *rabbutho*, "majesty," or "greatness;" the third and fourth, *i, a,* for *aithutho*, "essential being." *Morio*, "The Lord," is distinguished from the common form of *Mar*, "a lord," and is never used but as an appellation of the Deity. In the Chaldee Targums *Yehovah* is always expressed by *Yeya*.

III. EHEYEH ASHER EHEYEH. Exod. iii. 14 · "And God said to Moses, I AM THAT I AM. Thus shalt thou say to the children of Israel, I AM hath sent me to you." 15: "And God said yet to Moses, Thus shalt thou say to the children of Israel, Jehovah the God of your Fathers hath sent me to you. This is My Name for ever, and this is My Memorial for all generations." It will be seen that *Jehovah* in the fifteenth verse is used synonymously with *Eheyeh asher Eheyeh* in the fourteenth; and that in the latter title is to be found the Divine exposition of the former one. Grammatically *Eheyeh* is the first person singular future of *hayah*, "he was,"—"I Will Be:" but some good Hebrew divines believe that the word, as here used, consists of the preterite *hayah*, "he was," with the first person prefix א, the initial and representative of the pronoun *Anochi*, I—אֶהְיֶה *E-heyeh;* as if He had said, "I Am He who hath been;" or, "I, who have been, Am He who Is." This, then, like the Tetragramma, is an incommunicable Name of the Unchangeable because Self-Existent One; or, as Maimonides interprets the Divine words, "the Being who is BEING, that is, a Being who must of necessity Be; for that which exists of necessity must have existed evermore." And to the same effect the exposition given by the metaphysical theologian Rabbi Joseph Albo: "I Am the Cause of My own Being, and the First Cause of all other: for all other being is, not because it is, but because I AM."

The Almighty made here this announcement of His unchangeableness, to give greater stress to His now revealed purpose to deliver Israel from bondage, and to redeem them into the liberty of His people. "I Am for ever; and therefore am able to fulfil My promises." So, in the sixth chapter of Exodus, the Name of the Immutable Jehovah, though known already in an imperfect manner by the patriarchs, is now to be known for the first time as that of Israel's COVENANT GOD, whose purposes, though they require the lapse of ages and millenniums for their full unfoldment, are the purposes of One with whom a thousand years are as a day.

The Septuagint translates *Eheyeh* by, 'Εγώ εἰμι ὁ ὤν, "I am the Existent." Onkelos leaves the Hebrew untranslated; but the Palestinian Targum attempts a paraphrase : " He who spake, and the world was ; who spake, and all things were. And He said, This shalt thou say to the sons of Israel, I Am He who Is, and who Will Be, hath sent me unto you." The Jerusalem Targum has,—" And the Word of the Lord said to Mosheh, He who spake to the world, Be, and it was ; and who will speak to it, Be, and it will be. And He said, Thus shalt thou speak to the sons of Israel, Eheveh hath sent me unto you."

IV. El Shaddai. (Gen. xvii. 1.) There are two leading opinions on the ground and meaning of this name. One, that it is derived from the noun *dai,* " plenitude " or " abundance," and, combined with the personal prefix *sh,* (the abbreviation of *asher,* " who,") denotes the all-sufficiency of God, *El sh'dai.* But the more generally received derivation makes it come from *shad,* " power," " force," especially that which is over- whelming, (*shadad,*) irresistible, like the hurricane, or the rising tide of the ocean. *El Shaddai* is " the Almighty God," " the Omnipotent." *Shaddai* is the *pluralis majestatis ;* and in most of the texts in which it occurs is no doubt rightly rendered by " the Almighty." The Septuagint translates it sometimes by Θεός; (Gen. xlix. 25 ;) sometimes by ὁ Ἱκανός, " the Sufficient ;" (Ruth i. 20, 21 ;) but more com- monly by Παντοκράτωρ, " the Almighty." Onkelos retains the Hebrew ; the Syriac has *El Shaddai Aloha ;* and the Samaritan Version, in Gen. xvii. 1, *Anah Chiulah Sapukah,* " I am the Mighty, the Sufficient." It may be remarked that the first revelation of this name to Abraham is joined with a command to walk before God and to be perfect; a command which fallen humanity can only obey by the effectual grace of the All-Sufficient Being who gives it. Compare Isai. xl. 28, 31.

V. ADONAI, "The Lord;" (Gen. xv. 8;) either from *dūn*, "to judge," and so expressing the rectoral dominion of God, or from *adon*, (pointed *eden*,) "a basis," "foundation;" a title of the Divine Supporter and therefore Proprietor and Lord of all creation. [In Deut. xxxii. 4 God is called *Ha Tsūr*, "the Rock," as the foundation and strength of created existence.] The form *Adonai* is considered to be the *pluralis excellentiæ*. It must be distinguished from *Adoni*, "my lord," the common title given to a superior.

VI. HELYON or ELYON, the Most High; from *halah* or *alah*, "to ascend," or "excel:" the Great Supreme, God over all. Gen. xiv. 22: *El Helyon koneh shammayim va-arets*, "God the most High, possessor of the heavens and earth." Onkelos, *El Illaah.* Jonathan, *Eloha Illaha.* Samaritan Version, "The Most Mighty." Septuagint, ὕψιστος, *Altissimus.*

Note. MEMRA DA YEYA. Though this designation, peculiar to the Chaldee Targums, may not be classed with the Divine names as given in the Hebrew Scriptures, yet as it is often used in the paraphrases as an equivalent for some one of them, it ought not to be omitted in the present conspectus. We have already offered some observations upon it in the Introduction to our first volume; and only add here a short supplement, by way of giving clearer definement and stronger corroboration to the doctrine there laid down.

The term *Memra* is used in a variety of acceptations. It is what the grammarians call *verbum* πολύσημον, "a word of several meanings." 1. *Memra* has the sense of a mere articulate word or spoken declaration. In such places it generally wants the final aleph: *memr*, "a word," *sermo*, *oratio*, like *pithgama* or *milla* in Chaldee. 2. It is used with the import of an emphatic pronoun. Thus, *memri*, "my word," equivalent to "I myself;" *memreka*, "thou thyself;" *memrieh*, "he himself." Example: "There is a covenant between me and thee." *Kayema bein memri uvein memrika*. So Gen. xxvi. 3: "I will be with thee." Targ.: *Ve yehe memri be sahduk*: "And My word," *i. e.*, I Myself, "will be thy helper." 3. As a personal appellation, intensifying the idea of personality. It is then *Memra da Yeya*, "the Word of the Lord," *i. e.*, the Lord Himself. Exod. xix. 17: "And Moses led forth the people to meet with God." Targum: *Likdamoth Memra da Yeya*, "to meet with the Word of the Lord." So Exod. iii. 11, 12, 14; Gen. i. 27; xxviii. 21.

But, 4.—and here is the point in question—It is used, we affirm, not only as a proper name, but as the proper name of one Person in the Godhead, as distinguished from another, so as to indicate in some degree the Targumist's perception of the mystery of a Personal Subsistence in the Divine nature, who is God with God, a second Person in the yet undivided Being of the One Jehovah. For the proof we adduce the following examples.

(1.) Gen. xvi. 7: *Hebrew text:* "And the Angel of the Lord found her by a fountain of water in the wilderness.......And he said, Hagar, whence camest thou, and whither wilt thou go? And she said, I flee from the face of my mistress. And the Angel of the Lord said to her, Return.......I will multiply thy seed exceedingly, that it shall not be numbered for multitude.......And she called the name of Jehovah who spake to her, Thou God seest me: for she said, Have I also here looked after Him who seeth me? Wherefore

the well was called *Beer laharoi*, A well to the Living
One who seeth me."

Targum of Palestine: "And the Angel of the Lord
found her at the fountain of waters in the desert.......
And he said, Hagar,.. whence comest thou, and
whither dost thou go? And she said, From before my
mistress have I fled. And the Angel of the Lord said
to her, Return....Multiplying I will multiply thy sons,
and they shall not be numbered for multitude.......And
she gave thanks before the Lord, whose Memra spake
to her, and thus said, Thou art He who livest and art
Eternal; who seest, but art not seen: for she said,
Here is revealed the glory of the Shekinah of the Lord
after a vision." [*Jerusalem Targum:* "And Hagar
gave thanks and prayed in the Name of the Memra of
the Lord, who had been manifested to her, saying,
Blessed be Thou, Eloha, the Living One of Eternity,
who hast looked upon my affliction.......Wherefore she
called the well, The well at which the Living and
Eternal One was revealed."]

Here Hagar sees God, and the Memra, in one. But
in the Memra she sees the Angel of the Lord, *i. e.*, one
who is sent. A person cannot be described as sending
himself: but God sends the Memra: the Memra is
therefore God, but God in a second personality.

(2.) Exod. xxxiii. 21: "And the Lord said, Behold,
there is a place by Me, and thou shalt stand upon a
rock. And it shall come to pass, while My glory
passeth by, that I will put thee in a cleft of the rock,
and will cover thee with My hand, while I pass by."

Targ. Palest.: "Thou shalt stand upon the rock:
and it shall be that when the glory of My Shekinah
passeth before thee, I will put thee in a cavern of the
rock, and I will overshadow thee with My Memra, until
the time that I have passed by." The distinction here

is plain. The Memra overshadows Moses while Jehovah passes by.

(3.) Num xxiii. 4 : *Hebrew text:* "And God met
Bileam." *Targ. Palest. :* "And the Memra from
before the Lord met Bileam." *Conf.* Onkelos *in loc.*
and the margin.

(4.) Of the Angel whom the Lord promises Moses
(Exod. xxiii. 20) to send before the people to be their
guide and protector through the wilderness, He says,
"Observe him, and obey his voice : .. ..for My Name
is in him :" *ki Shemi bekirbo,* "*quia Nomen Meum in
interiori ejus est ;*" and therefore some of the rabbins
identify the Angel with Shaddai. See Jarchi *in loco.*
In this view, "My Name is in him," is equivalent with
"My Nature or Essence is in him." He is the Divine
Angel; *Malak habberith,* "the Angel of the Covenant;" *Malak haggoel,* "the Angel the Redeemer."
But in the Targums this Angel is identified with the
Memra. Thus, in Deut. xxxi. 6, Moses, referring to
the promise of the heavenly Guide, bids the Israelites
cast away all fear of their enemies ; where the Targum
reads, "Fear them not : for the Memra of the Lord thy
God will be the Leader before thee." And in Joshua
v. 14, 15, the Being who had the appearance of a man,
as He spake with the Hebrew captain, but whose presence made the ground on which He stood "holy
ground," says to him, (according to the Targum,) "I
am the Angel sent from the presence of God.......And
Joshua fell upon his face, and adored." "This Angel,"
says Moses Ben Nachman, "is the Angel Redeemer, of
whom it is written, 'For My Name is in him.' He is
the Angel who said to Jakob, 'I am the God of
Bethel ;' He it is of whom it is said, 'God called to
Moses out of the bush.'......For it is written, 'Jehovah
brought us up out of Egypt ;' and elsewhere, 'He

sent His Angel, and brought us up out of Egypt.'
Again it is written, 'And the Angel of His Presence saved them;' that Angel, namely, who is the
Presence of God, of whom it is said, 'My Presence
shall go with thee, and I will give thee rest.' Finally,
this is the Angel of whom the prophet speaks, ' He
whom ye seek shall suddenly come to His temple, even
the Angel of the Covenant whom ye delight in.'" In
the passage quoted here by the Rabbi, from Isaiah lxiii.
8, 9, the Targum of Jonathan ben Uzziel identifies the
Angel with the Memra, sent to redeem and to save.
The comment of Philo is equally remarkable : " God,
as the Shepherd and King, conducts all things according to law and righteousness, having established over
them" τὸν ὀρθὸν αὐτοῦ λόγον, πρωτόγονον υἱόν, " His
true Word (and) Only Begotten Son, who, as the
Viceroy of the great King, protects and ministers to
this sacred flock. For it is said, Behold, I am: I will
send My angel before thy face to keep thee in the
way." (De Agricult., Opp., i., 308.)

Taking these passages into consideration, it seems
difficult to arrive at any other conclusion than that the
doctrine of the Targum on this subject is the same as
that of St. John : " In the beginning was the Word,
and the Word was with God, and the Word was God."
Onkelos and Jonathan ben Uzziel are witnesses to such
a faith existing in the pre-apostolic times; and Philo of
Alexandria, when discoursing with such amplitude upon
the Logos, writes not as a mere Platonic philosopher,
but as a believer in the traditional theology of his fore-
fathers. The germ of this article of their faith they
found in their canonical Scriptures. See the texts in
our Introduction to the first volume of this work, p. 24.

II. NOTICES OF THE MESSIAH IN THE PENTATEUCH.

THE first promise given by God to fallen man was the promise of a Saviour. It speaks of Him as "the seed of the woman,"—*zarah*, her "offspring" Eva saw in the birth of her first son a pledge of the fulfilment of the promise, and said, "I have obtained a man from the Lord." Onkelos: "I have obtained the Man from before the Lord." Syriac. "I have obtained the Man of the Lord:" *Kanith Gabro la-Morio.* For the scriptural comments on the promise and its antecedents, compare John viii. 44; 1 John iii. 8; 1 Cor. xv. 47. This first promise, though veiled in enigma, was plain enough to banish despair and kindle new hope: it sank deep into the human breast, and the children of Adam carried it with them in all their wanderings. It is well called the *Proto-Evangelium,* the Primary Gospel. It was comparatively obscure; for we expect not the splendour of the meridian hour to come at early dawn: but, as time passed, new revelations contributed to clear it up,

> "While light on light, and ray on ray,
> Successive brighten d into day"

Even in the Pentateuch we witness such a progression.

1. The first promise merely declared that the Destroyer of the serpent should be a man.

2. In the prophecy of Noah, (Gen. ix. 26, 27,) there is a presumptive implication, that of the three races who were to descend from that patriarch, the expected One would spring from that of Shem.

3. Among the Shemitic nations, that which would have Abraham for their ancestor was to be the favoured people, who should claim Him as their kinsman. (Gen. xii. 1–3; xviii. 18; xxii. 18;—*bezareka,* "in thy seed."

Compare Gen. xxvi. 4; Acts iii. 25; Gal. iii. 8, 9, 16, 18.) Then,

4. Of the tribes into which the Abrahamic nation was divided, Judah's would be that from which the Lord was to arise: Gen. xlix. 10; where *Shiloh* is a name of the Messiah. Some modern Jewish interpreters make it, indeed, the name of the *place* so called, and put it in the dative, rendering *ad ki yavo Shiloh,* "until," or "even though, they come to Shiloh." But this does violence to the very grammar of the words. *Shiloh* is the nominative, and the verb *yavo* is in the singular, "he shall come." The Targums translate *Shiloh* by "the King Messiah;" and the Palestine one describes Him as "a son of Jehudah." The Talmud (Sanhedrin) takes the same view. So does Abravanel in his commentary on the text; and that found in the Zohar lays down the same doctrine, with the addition that the letter i, yod, (the initial of Jehovah,) in the name, indicates that the Messiah will be a Divine person. The name Shiloh signifies "the Maker of Peace."

5. As a Priest, the Messiah is typified in Aharon, who had the title of *Kohen ha Mashiach,* "the Anointed Priest."

6. As a Prophet, in Moses, Deut. xviii. 15–18. The Jewish application of this prediction to the succession of prophets at large is utterly opposed to the terms of the text, all of them in the singular number. "*A* prophet, from the midst of *thee," kamoni,* "like *myself,* will the Lord thy God raise up unto thee: *him* shall ye hear." So also in the Divine promise: "*A* prophet," *kamoka,* "like *thee* will I raise up; and I will put My word in *his* mouth, and *he* shall speak," &c. But it is also written that "among all the prophets that followed Moses, no one was like him;" and as the great national deliverer, the mediator of an alliance with God, a legis-

lator who established a dispensation of religion, and as the head of the body ecclesiastical, no prophet could arise like Moses, till He came who is the Wisdom and the Word of God. (John i. 17, 18; Luke ix. 29–36; Acts iii. 22.)

7. As a King, he is symbolized by the star and the sceptre in the prophecy of Balaam, Num. xxiv. 17–24. Onkelos: "When a king shall arise from Jacob, and the Messiah become great in Israel." So, too, Eben Ezra, who says that many Hebrew commentators agree in explaining it of the Messiah. In the great revolt of the Jews in Hadrian's time, their leader, the pretended Messiah Barkokab, derived his prestige from that assumed name of "the Son of the Star," in allusion to this very prophecy; fulfilled typically and partially by David's victories over Edom and Moab; but only really and Divinely in the world-saving victory and blessed reign of Him "who is the Root and Offspring of David, and the bright and morning Star."

III NAMES OF HEATHEN GODS IN THE PENTATEUCH.

Elohim acherim. Onkelos, *Elaha ocharan.* Θεοὶ ἕτεροι. (Exod. xx. 3.)

Baal or *Bahal,* Chal. *Behel,* or, the guttural omitted, *Bel;* most commonly used with the article, Ha-Baal, to distinguish the name of the god from the ordinary term *baal,* "a lord," or "master." (Num. xxii. 41; Deut. iv. 3.) Baal was the sun-god of the Phenicians, Canaanites, and Babylonians, and was worshipped as the productive power of nature. The plural *Baalim* denotes either the images of the god, or the various properties attributed to him. The name *Baal* is sometimes put not only for the sun, but also for the planet Jupiter, and is then joined with *Gad*, the designation of that star in the oriental astronomy. So, too, in the Zabian mythology Jupiter takes the name of Bel.

Ashtoreth (the Astarte of the Greeks) was the feminine producing power of nature. As the masculine power was recognised and adored in the sun, so the moon was the symbol of *Ashtoreth*. The name *Ashtoroth Karnaim* in Gen. xiv. 5, "the two horned *Ashtoreths*," carries evident reference to the moon as she appears in the early nights of the month. As Baal is connected with the planet Jupiter, so *Ashtoreth*, among the Syro-Phenicians, had a similar relation to that of Venus.

Peor, Pehor, or *Baal Pehor:* LXX., Βεελφεγώρ: worshipped by the Moabites and Midianites with licentious practices. (Num. xxv. 1–9; Deut. iv. 3.) The Rabbins give an obscene meaning to the name *Peor;* but others, as Gesenius, derive it from an old verb, still retained in Ethiopic, signifying to "serve" or "worship."

Chemosh, Kemosh, Χαμώς, (Num. xxi. 29,) is considered to be another name for the idol *Pehor*. The etymology is hopeless. A black star was used as the symbol of Chemosh, which seems to give him a connexion with the planet Saturn.

Molok, or *Ha-Molek,* literally "the ruling one," from *malak,* "to reign;" and so rendered in the Septuagint by the appellatives ὁ ἄρχων and βασιλεύς, as well as by the retained Hebrew name, with the spelling of Μόλοχ. From the similar meaning of the name with that of *Baal,* "a sovereign," or "lord," Molek is regarded as another epithet for the same deity,—the Ruler of Existence; but as manifesting his dominion in the destruction of life, a phase of character opposite to that of *Habaal,* the Sovereign Producer. Hence the worship of Molek was solemnized with fatal rites. The parent surrendered the life of his offspring, and burned his own child as a holo-

caust. (Lev. xviii. 21 ; xx. 1-5 ; Jer. xix. 5 ; Ezek. xvi.
20.) The names of *Malcham* and *Milkom* (Amos v. 26;
1 Kings xi. 5 ; Zeph. i. 5 ; Acts vii. 43) are variations of
Molek. In the astro-religious system of the Phœnicians
the gloomy planet Saturn, " *stella nocens*," [3] was looked
upon as his representative.

Seirim, or *Sehirim*, "satyrs;" (Lev. xvii. 7;)
literally, "hairy ones," "goats." Onkelos and Syriac,
Sheidin, "demons." LXX., μάταιοι, "vanities."

Shedim, "demons." (Deut. xxxii. 17.) So also
Onkelos, Septuagint, and Syriac. The Arabic Version
has *Sheateen*, "Satans."

Besides these proper or descriptive names of the
Gentile deities in the Pentateuch, there are several others
employed as epithets of execration or contempt.

Elilim, from *ĕlil*, "of nought, vain, false, of nothing
worth."

Hebilim, from *hebel*, "a breath or vapour ; something light or vain." (Deut. xxxii. 21.)

Toeboth, "abominations." (Deut. xxxii. 16.) *Zarim*,
the same.

Gillulim : (Deut. xxix. 17 :) probably from *galal*,
" dung ; " hence the name is rendered in the margin by
" dungy gods;" Vulgate, *sordes*.

Shikutsim, "abominations," (*ibid*.,) from *shakats*,
" to be filthy or loathsome."

The visible representation of a god, a material idol, is
designated in the Pentateuch by

Pesel, " a graven or carved image ; " (Exod. xx. 4 ,)
from *pasal*, "to cut or hew." Onkelos, *tselam*, "a
resemblance." The most common name in the Targums for idols is *taavath*, or *taavan*.

Temunah : (Exod. xx. 4 :) Onkelos, *demuth*, "similitude," which well represents the meaning of the Hebrew. LXX., ὁμοίωμα.

Semel, "a likeness," (similitude,) and *Tabnith*, "a form or model,"—both in Deut. iv. 16. Onkelos, *Tsura*, "a type;" γλυπτός, "a sculpture, or shaped form."

Matsebah, "a statue," from *Natsab*, "to stand firmly." (Deut. vii. 5.) Onkelos, *Kama*. This may be a denomination not only of an idol in human or other form, but also of an anointed stone or pillar of the well known class called *Bætylia*.

Chammanim, "sun images;" Lev. xxvi. 30, where Onkelos has *chanisnesekun*, "your monuments to the sun." "*Delubra, statuæ solares, soli dicatæ*."— CASTEL. "Temples of the sun."—EBEN EZRA. The German Jewish commentators, Mendelssohn, &c., prefer "sun columns, or obelisks."

Eben maskith, lapis speculationis. Onkelos, *eben segida*, "a stone for adoration;" LXX., λίθος σκοπός, "a conspicuous stone," a hieroglyphical monument; rendered in some texts, "a stone of devices." (Lev. xxvi. 1.)

Massekah, "a molten image," from *nasak*, "to melt or cast." Onkelos, *mattekah*. (Deut. xxvii. 15.)

Teraphim. (Gen. xxxi. 19.) The obscurity which hangs over the true meaning of this word may be judged of by the multiplicity of derivations assigned to it. 1. That, by a change in the first letter, it is equivalent to *Seraphim*, and may denote images of bright or burnished brass. 2. That it comes from *tseraph*, "to melt;" (whence *tsoreph*, "a goldsmith;") and signifies "molten images." 3. It comes from *rapha*, "to heal," and describes talismans used as charms for curing or averting diseases. 4. From *taraph*, (in Hiphil,) "to feed, nourish" (like the Greek τρέφειν). The Teraphim, in this view, were some kind of objects, the presence of which in a house was thought to insure support and plenty. 5. Some Rabbins make it a term of contempt, from *turaph*, "shamefulness," and others, 6. With the same idea, derive it from *raphaim*, "weak things," like the dead. 7. Another opinion assigns it to the Syriac *teraph*, "to ask of, inquire;" in which respect the Teraphim were domestic oracles. The only certainty is, that they were household idols, like the *lares* and *penates*. Onkelos renders the word by *tselmanaya*, "images;" the Septuagint, εἴδωλα; and the Persic translator, by "astrolabes."

The priesthood of these heathen deities are called in the Hebrew Bible by the name *Kemarim*; from *kamar*, "to burn;" Chald., *kumara*. In addition to the priests of the heathen altar, we read in the Pentateuch and elsewhere of a class or classes of hierophants whose profession lay among the mystical rites which were supposed to open to mortals an intercourse with the spiritual world. They are noticed under the following names :—

Mekashephim. (Deut. xviii. 10.) *Mekasheph*, "a magician or sorcerer;" from *kashaph*, originally, "to offer prayer," but degenerated to idolatrous incantations. Onkelos renders the noun by *charash*; and the Septuagint, φαρμακός. Such as used herbs and drugs, the blood of victims and the bones of the dead, for their operations, burning them on an altar or tripod. So the magicians, Exod. vii. 11, did their wonders, by their *lehatim*, "flames." (Rashi; Maimonides; Eben Ezra; who derive the word from *lahat*, "to burn;" while others make it come from *lūt*, "to hide or conceal," and render *lehatim* by "their occult artifices." Onkelos: *belachashehun*, "by their incantations.")

Chartumim, (from *cheret*, "an engraving tool, an iron pen, or style,") "interpreters of hieroglyphics," ἱερογραμματεῖς. More generally, "interpreters of dreams, casters of nativities, astrologers." (Exod. vii. 11.)

Hakamim, or *Chakamim*, "sages; men of science;" from *chakam*, "to be skilful." The same class of persons as the *Chartumim*. LXX., "sophists." The name was given to the physicians and scientific attendants in the royal court, like the Arabian *hakims*. (Exod. vii. 11.)

Yiddeonim, from *yada*, "to know:" "wise men, wizards, soothsayers." (Deut. xviii. 11, Lev. xix. 31; Exod. xxii. 18.)

Menachashim, "augurs;" from the root *nachash*, indicating the use of serpents in some manner in their operations. So the verb *nachash* in Pihel is "to divine or augur." (Deut. xviii. 10.)

Meonen, "an augur who divines by the drift of clouds, the flight of birds, &c." (Deut. xviii. 10.)

Doresh el hammethim, "a necromancer, an inquirer of or from the dead." Deut. xviii. 11: Ἐπερωτῶν τοὺς νεκρούς

Kosem Kesamim, "a diviner by divination," from *kasam*, "to divine;" one who made auguries by *lots;* μαντευόμενος μαντείαν. (Deut. xviii. 10.)

Chober chaber, "a user of spells;" (Deut. xviii. 11;) from *chabar*, "to bind together;" one who practised magic by knotted things or the conjunction of words Compare VIRGIL, *Ecl.* viii. 77.

Shoel ob, "a consulter with evil spirits." (Deut. xviii. 11.) *Ob* or *Aub* is "a bottle or bag," primarily; also, "the stomach," yet is applied to a necromancer, who professes to call up the dead for consultation. From the primary meaning of the term the *shoel ob* has been thought to be a mere ventriloquist, simulating the voice of an unseen being supposed to be present. The Greek rendering of *ob* is "a Pythonist." I believe *aub* is Coptic for "a serpent."

There is a significant epithet used several times in the

Targums on the Pentateuch, in reference to many of the artists mentioned above; that of *ladin*, "impostors."

IV. THE SACRED PLACE.

WHILE the flame of the Shekinah diffused its beams over the eastern gate of Eden, the children of Adam had the visible token that God had not forsaken the earth, nor left them to the utter desolation of apostasy; and when, in after days, the Sanctuary arose at His bidding in the wilderness, the same token of mercy re-appeared in the Place where His law was enshrined, His Name revealed, and His purposes of mercy set forth in types and foreshadows of the great Redemption, whose blessings are to become the heritage of all the families of the earth at the full unfoldment of His kingdom, when the "great voice out of heaven" will be heard, saying, "Behold, the Tabernacle of God is with men, and He will dwell with them, and they shall be His people, and God Himself shall be with them and be their God."

I. THE HOLY TABERNACLE, though the work of man's hands, was made according to a Divinely revealed archetype, in Hebrew a *tabenith*, (from the root *banah*, "to build,") a model for building, an exemplar, disclosed to the eyes of Moses in the mount. (Exod. xxv. 40.) For *tabenith* Onkelos has *demuth*, "likeness," and the Septuagint *typos*.

The materials were supplied by the voluntary contributions of the people, and constituted a national oblation, *terumah*, "a thing uplifted, and offered to God:" Onkelos, *aphrashutha*, "a separation," *i.e.*, of those portions of their property for the sacred purpose.

II. GENERAL NAMES FOR THE TABERNACLE. 1. *Ko-desh*, or *Kadash*, "the Holy." 2. *Mikdash*, "sanctuary." 3. *Ohel*, "the tent;" LXX., σκηνή. 4. *Mishkan*, "the dwelling;" Chal., *mashkena*, from *shakan*, "to dwell." 5. *Ohel ha Eduth;* Targ., *Mashkan zimna*, "the Tabernacle of ordinance, or appointment;" from Chal., *zeman*, "*paravit, præparavit, destinavit;*" Syriac, *Mashkan zabno*; LXX., Σκηνὴ τοῦ μαρτυρίου. 6. *Ohel Moed*, "the Tabernacle of meeting," *conventus.* 7. *Ha Beth*, "the House." 8. *Mishkan Kebod Yehovah*, "the Dwelling of the Glory of the Lord."

III. Terms relating to the form of the Tabernacle.

1. The Court,[4] *Chatsar ha mishkan;* Chal., *Darath mashkena;* αὐλή, *atrium;* Syr., *Dorotho;* the enclosure or area in which the Tabernacle stood. It was open to the sky; the surroundings were formed by wooden pillars, *amudim*, στύλοι, with silver-plated capitals, *roshim*, based in sockets, *adonim*, "supporters," Chal., *samka*, of brass. To these columns were appended silver hooks, *vavim*, through which passed the silver rods, *chashukim*, overspread with the hangings, *kelahim*, Chal., *seradin*, ἱστία, curtains of *shesh mashezor*, "fine twined linen," fastened to the ground by *yetudoth*, "pins of brass." The length of the court was one hundred cubits, about fifty-eight yards, with twenty pillars on each side; the breadth, fifty cubits, with ten pillars; the height, five cubits. At the east end was the gate of the court, *shaar ha chatser;* Chal., *tera-daretha;* πύλη τῆς αὐλῆς. It had four columns, over which was spread a hanging, *masak*, Chal., *perasa*, κάλυμμα, of twenty cubits, wrought with threads of blue, purple, scarlet, and white.

2. The Tabernacle itself stood somewhat beyond the middle of the court; in form, oblong; length from east to west, thirty cubits; breadth from north to south, ten cubits; and height, ten cubits.

The walls were constructed of boards, *kerashim*, Chal.,

[4] See Exodus xxxvi., &c.

dapaya, of the acacia tree, *ets shittim*,[5] ξύλον ἄσηπτον, "incorruptible wood," forty-eight in number; twenty on the north, twenty on the south side, six on the west, with one additional at two of the corners. The boards were ten cubits in length, a cubit and a half broad, and a half cubit thick. They were plated with gold. They stood upright, secured to the earth by having each two tenons, *yadoth*, fastening into two sharp-pointed silver *adonim* or "supporters," which entered the surface of the ground. The boards were united by bars, or poles, *berichim*, running transversely through golden rings, *tebaoth*, fastened on the outside of the boards. On the eastern end of the tabernacle there were no boards. The east end was covered with a veil or hanging, *masak*, Sept., ἐπίσπαστρον, of blue, red, crimson, and twined linen, embroidered; a tapestry of ten cubits square, suspended on five columns of gold-coated acacia wood, with brasen supporters.

Over this outward framework there were four integuments. (1.) The interior sides were covered by ten curtains, *yerioth*, Onkelos, *yerihan*, Sept., αὐλαῖαι, each twenty-eight cubits long and four cubits broad; the material, fine twined byssus, *shesh mashezor*, with in-wrought figures of cherubim in blue, purple, and scarlet. These curtains were joined with each other by fifty purple loops, *lelaoth*, Onkelos, *anulin*, Sept., ἄγκυλαι, and fifty golden hooks, *keresim*, Onk., *phurephin*. This interior covering has the name of *Ha Mishkan*, "the Tabernacle." (2.) The second, called "the Tent," *Ohel*, Chal., *Pherasa*, consisted of curtains woven of goats' hair, *yerioth izzim*, spread over the outside of the first curtains. (3.) Over this was a third covering, of

---

[5] A tree of the genus Acacia, either the *Acacia gummifera* or the *A. Seyal*, both of which have abounded in the valleys of the Arabian wilderness.

rams' skins dyed red, *oroth eilim meaddamim ;* Onkelos, *mashkey dedikrey mesankey,* "skins of rams reddened ;" and, (4.) The whole was surmounted by a fourth defence, composed of "badgers' skins," *oroth techashim ;*[6] Onkelos, *mashkey de-sasgona,* "skins of purple." These last two integuments of the Tabernacle have the common name of *ha mikeseh,* "the covering."

3. The INTERIOR of the structure consisted of two compartments, having a different relative degree of sacredness,—the Holy, and the Most Holy. The first has the name of *Ha Kodesh,* "the Holy," "the Sanctuary;" Onkelos, *kudesha ;* Sept., τὰ ἅγια, (in the New Testament, σκηνὴ πρώτη, Heb. ix. 2.) It was twenty cubits long and ten cubits high. The second, *Kodesh ha kadashim,* "the Holy of Holies," Onk., *Kodesh kudshaya,* ἁγία τῶν ἁγίων, was a perfect square, of ten cubits in length, breadth, and height. It was divided and concealed from the sanctuary by a magnificent veil or curtain, *ha paroketh,* Onk., *paruktha,* Sept., καταπέτασμα, fabricated in blue, purple, scarlet, and fine twined linen, with cherubic figures, and suspended on four columns overlaid with gold.

IV. APPARATUS OF THE TABERNACLE. The sacred building itself stood, not exactly in the middle of the court, but twenty cubits distant from the northern, southern, and western sides of it; so that the larger space of fifty cubits might lie between the gate of the court on the east, and the first veil or door of the tabernacle.

In this larger space of the Court stood,

1. The Altar of Burnt Sacrifice, *misbeach ha olah,* Chal., *madbecha de-altha ;* Sept., θυσιαστήριον; three cubits high, and five in length and breadth, formed of

[6] What animal was called by this name is perfectly uncertain whether the badger, the jackal, or the seal.

boards, *luchoth*, of acacia, and covered with brass.
Being portable, it was hollow; but, when stationary for
service, was filled with earth to the upper rim. The
four corners projected upwards, like horns, *karnoth*, τὰ
κέρατα, to which the living animal might be bound,
(Psalm. cxviii. 27,) and serving also to prevent the
dead carcase from falling off. A border, or ledge, *kar-
kob*, went round the top; with which was connected a
network of brass, *resheth nechosheth*, to receive fragments of fuel, &c., which fell away from the burning
mass. At the four corners strong rings, *tabaoth*, were
fixed, through which went the staves employed for the
carriage of the altar.

The utensils for the work done at the altar were,
shovels, *yayim*, for collecting the ashes; pots, *siroth*,
for carrying them away; bowls, or basins, *mizrakoth*,
for receiving the blood which was to be sprinkled;
forks, or tongs, *mizlagoth*, for manipulating the parts of
the sacrifice in the fire; and brasen shovels, *machtoth*,
" fire-pans."

2. The Laver, *kiyor*, Chal., *kiyora*, λουτήρ, a large
vase, probably semicircular, standing on a *ken*, or
basis. This receptacle for the water needed by the
priests for their ablutions was founded with the finest
brass, (Exod. xxxviii 8,) such as ancient mirrors were
made of, and admitted of a fine polish, which rendered
the surface of the laver available as a mirror in which
the priests could see their own resemblance. It stood
between the altar and the curtain of the sanctuary.

Within the Holy Place were,

1. The Candelabrum, *menorah*, from *ner*, "a
light;" Onkelos, *menartha*; ἡ λυχνία: the material,
pure gold; in weight a talent. From its base, *yerek*,
rose a perpendicular shaft or stem, *kaneh*, from which
projected six carved branches, *kanim*, three on each

side, reaching in height to the top of the stem. The candelabrum had a height of three cubits, and a breadth from the extremities of the opposite branches of two cubits. On the six branches and on the top of the shaft were lamps, seven in all, supplied every evening with olive oil. Three, or, according to others, one lamp, ever burned; the rest were lighted at evening, and extinguished in the morning. The branches were adorned with the forms of almond and pomegranate flowers, and apples, or some ornament of a spherical shape. The utensils were, the snuffers, *malkachim*, and the fire-pans, *machtoth*. The candelabrum stood within the south-western side of the sanctuary.

2. The Table, *shulchan*, Onk., *phatora*, Sept., τράπεζα, made of acacia, a cubit and a half high, two cubits long, and one broad; the whole plated with gold. The top of the table was surrounded with a border (*zer*) of gold; and below the top, or leaf, was a wooden band, *misgereth*, about four inches broad, with a border. Four *tabaoth zahab*, or "rings of gold," were fastened to the legs, for the transport of the table. It stood in the sanctuary on the north side.

Upon this table were placed twelve unleavened cakes, *chaloth*, in two rows, six in each. Over the cakes incense was burned, probably in a censer, to signify that they were consecrated, offered and set before God. Hence the name *lechem ha panaim*, "bread of the Presence." They were renewed every Sabbath, and always on the table, *lechem tamid*, "the perpetual bread." They are sometimes called *lechem le azkarah*, Chal., *lechem le adkara*, "the bread of memorial;" a token of gratitude for daily bread, and an expression of trust in the God of Providence. They were a memorial furnished by the people, and therefore twelve loaves, after the number of the tribes.

The table was provided with a service of utensils: *kearoth*, "dishes," *acetabula*, in which the bread was brought and taken away; bowls, *kaphoth*, for the frankincense burned over the bread; *kesoth* and *menakioth*, "cans" and "cups" for libations connected with the burning of the frankincense; all of gold.

3. The Altar of Incense, *mizbeach mikter ketoreth;* Onkelos, *midbecha le-aktera alohi ketorath busemin,* "the altar on which to burn sweet incense: ' so also *mizbeach ha penimi,* "the inner altar," because within the sanctuary. The Septuagint terms it θυσιαστήριον θυμιάματος; the Syriac, *madelcho de maatar etro,* "the altar fuming perfume." It was two cubits high and one in length and breadth, constructed of acacia wood, plated with pure gold, *mizbeach ha zahab,* "the golden altar." It had a wreath, *zer,* and *karnoth,* or " horns," of the same.

The Incense, *ketoreth,* was compounded of four ingredients: (1.) *Nataph, i. e.,* storax; (2.) *Shekeleth, i. e.,* onycha; (3.) *Chelbenah samim,* sweet galbanum; (4.) *Lebonah zaka,* "pure frankincense." Onkelos: (1.) *Natupha;* (2.) *Tuphera;* (3.) *Chelbentha busesin;* (4.) *Lebuntha dakyetha.* The Peschito Syriac the same. Septuagint: (1.) Σтακτή; (2.) Ὄνυχα; (3) Χαλβάνη ἡδυσμοῦ; (4) Λίβανος διαφανής. These, it should be added, were mixed with salt, Exod. xxx. 35, *memullach,* "salted;" where Onkelos reads *mearah,* "mixed," *i. e.,* with salt, as the emblem of incorruptness.

Other ingredients were subsequently added in the temple practice. Maimonides enumerates myrrh, cassia, spikenard, saffron, costus, cinnamon, sweet bark, salt, amber, and a combustible root or herb he calls *maalath asam,* "the smoke-raiser." (*Keley ha Mikdash,* ii., sect. 3.) Such multiplications were unwarrantable:

but the Rabbins defend them by a tradition that they were ordained to Moses on Mount Sinai.

Incense was offered, at daybreak, (*yoma* iii., 1, 5,) and after the evening sacrifice. It was the emblem of acceptable worship, and especially of prayer which presses heavenward. (Psalm cxli. 2.)

In burning incense the priest used a censer, *machtah*, (from *chathah*, "to take fire or coals" from hearth or altar,) Chal., *machtitha*, LXX., πυρεῖον, "a burner," θυίσκη, θυμιατήριον, "thurible for incense;" a vessel of metal; form not certainly known. In the daily service it was carried by the priest into the holy place and set upon the golden altar, and was probably shaped like a chalice, with a base for standing upon the altar. But the censer which the high priest held in his hand on the day of atonement must have been furnished with a chain or handle. The censer used in the daily service was of brass; that carried by the high priest within the veil was of gold.

Beyond the veil, in the Holy of Holies, stood the emblematic Throne of God; that is to say, the Ark and Mercy-seat, overshadowed by the wings of the cherubim.

1. The Ark, *aron*, Chal., *arona;* termed also *aron ha eduth*, "the ark of the testimony," κιβωτὸς τοῦ μαρτυρίου; and *aron ha berith*, "the ark of the covenant, κιβωτὸς τῆς διαθήκης; was an oblong coffer, or chest, made of acacia wood, and plated with gold within and without, with an exterior border round the top, of pure gold. The length was two cubits and a half, the breadth one cubit and a half, and the height the same as the breadth. Like the two altars, it had rings with staves for transportation.

Within the ark were deposited the *sheney luchoth abanim*, the "two tables of stone," inscribed with the *eduth*, or "testimony" of the moral law. Before it stood the urn of manna, and the blossomed rod of

Aharon, and on one side the manuscript of the law.
(Deut. xxxi. 26.)

2. The Mercy-Seat. In some commentaries and books on the Jewish ritual the mercy-seat is described as being "the lid of the ark;" but that is a mistake. The ark had its own lid, of acacia wood plated with gold; but in the Divine directory, Exod. xxv. 17, the mercy-seat is spoken of as an object distinct from the ark, and formed of gold only. The lid covered the ark; but the mercy-seat covered the lid; verse 21, "Thou shalt put the mercy-seat," *al ha-aron milmaelah*, " UPON the ark ABOVE." So, on the day of atonement, the high priest is directed to sprinkle the blood, not on the surface of the lid of the ark, but upon the front of the mercy-seat toward the east. In size, it was precisely of the same length and breadth as the ark, so as to fit within the rim which surrounded the lid, and, according to the Talmud, (*succah* 5,) was a hand-breadth in thickness.

The name by which it is commonly designated is *ha-kapporeth*, Chaldee, *kappurtha*, Sept., ἱλαστήριον, "the propitiatory." The Hebrew name comes from *kaphar*, "to cover;" in Pihel, "to atone for," and "to forgive." In the Hebrew Bible forgiveness is called "the covering of sin." (Psalm xxxii. 1.) The mercy-seat is the place of meeting between a reconciled God and redeemed man. (Exod. xxv. 22; Hebrews iv. 16; Num vii. 89.)

3. United with, and fabricated of the same massive gold as, the mercy-seat, were two symbolical figures called *Kerubim*, Chal., *Kerubaia*; one at each end, standing in a bending attitude, as if looking into the ark. Everything relating to these objects is veiled in mystery. No intimation is given about their forms or lineaments, except that their wings overspread the mercy-seat. In the more graphic descriptions of the

Cherubim seen by Ezechiel, (chap. i. and x.,) and by St. John, (Rev. iv.,) they are represented with the four faces of the ox, the lion, the eagle, and the man; but from Exod. xxv. 20 it may be inferred that those upon the ark had only the human visage; which seems to authorize the idea of Eben Ezra, that they had the appearance of "winged men." Among the opinions about the meaning of these mystic forms, one is, that they were emblems of the Divine Presence; and another, that they set forth a representation of redeemed humanity. The name *Cherub* has been variously derived. Some consider the word the same as the Hebrew *ki rob*, "like the mighty;" some think it to be the Chaldee *ki rabia*, "like a young man;" others, the Syriac *kerub*, "great or powerful."

4. "The King eternal, immortal, invisible, whom no man hath seen, or can see," was mercifully pleased, under both the patriarchal and Mosaic dispensations, to make His Presence known by a visible splendour, an intense light, or effulgence, to which is given the name of *Ha-kebod Yehovah*, "the Glory of the Lord," Chaldee, *Yekara da Yeya*; Sept., δόξα Κυρίου; Syr., *Shubcho da-morio*. (Lev. ix. 23.) Such a Theophany was given in the Holy of Holies, above the ark, between the cherubim. (Psalm lxxx. 1; 1 Sam. iv. 4; Exod. xxv. 22.) So did the Divine Being condescend to reveal His purpose to *dwell* in the sanctuary: and on His account the name of The *Shekinah* is applied to the visual glory. The word *shekinah* does not, indeed, occur in the Hebrew Bible, but is used by the Jewish theologians, as a derivative from the biblical word *shakan*, "to dwell," to denote the presence and inhabitation of the God of Israel in the Tabernacle, and subsequently in the Temple. The Targumist frequently uses the word, but under the form of *shekintha*.

That the Tabernacle, as a whole, had a symbolical character, has been, with but few exceptions, the constant belief both of Jews and Christians. The sacred structure was an outward sign of the presence of God among His people, a shrine for His law ; a centre of communication with Himself in His own way of appointment. In this point of view the Tabernacle may be called a Theocratic Sacrament But, from strong intimations in the New Testament Scriptures, we learn to contemplate it also as a typical adumbration of the Incarnate Person and mediatorial work of Him who is the end of the law for righteousness unto every one who believeth; of the Word, who was made flesh and ἐσκήνωσεν ἐν ἡμῖν, "*tabernacled* among us, and we beheld His *glory*" (John i. 14.) When this principle is accepted, we find all the Tabernacle ritual brighten into a meaning worthy of its Divine Author. In the laver, with its cleansing element, the perpetual light of the golden candelabrum, the sacred bread, the altar flaming with sacrifice, the sprinkled blood, the incense which betokened availing intercession, and the High Priest who offered it, we see " the shadows of the good things to come," the passing emblems of what the Gospel unfolds to us in the immutable realities of a redemption through which all men may draw near unto God.

Note. Beside the holy Tabernacle, we read of another, called the *ohel moed*, " the tent of meeting ." (Exod. xxxiii. 7 :) a large tent where Moses gave audience to the people in cases requiring instruction Chal., *mishkan beth ulphano*, "the tabernacle of the house of instruction."

V. SACRED PERSONS.

PRIESTHOOD, *kehunnah*, (Exod. xl. 15,) in Chaldee, *kahanuth*, ἱερατεία, "the office of a priest;" *kohen*, ἱερεύς. The verb *kahan* is only used in the derivative, and does not occur in its radical form in the Hebrew Bible. Gesenius says that "in Arabic it denotes to prophesy, to foretell, as a soothsayer; and among the heathen Arabs the substantive bore that signification; also that of a mediator, or middle person who interposed in any business; which seems to be its radical meaning, as prophets and priests were regarded as mediators between men and the Deity. In the earliest families of the race of Shem, the offices of priest and prophet were undoubtedly united, so that the word originally denoted both; and at last the Hebrew idiom kept one part of the idea, and the Arabic another." [7]

In one respect the entire Hebrew people might have been considered a sacerdotal race, as being chosen and set apart from the Gentile world; the visible church of the only God, and His worshippers and witnesses, to whom belonged the glory and the adoption, the covenant and the service of God, and to whom were intrusted, for the world's future benefit, the oracles of Divine revelation. On this account they had the designation of *kedoshim*, "consecrated ones," called of God to be *mamleketh kohanim*, "a kingdom of priests." (Exod. xx. 6.) But the official priesthood, the ministration of the altar, was restricted to the family of Aharon of the tribe of Levi, *Leviyim*.

All the men of that tribe had an ecclesiastical character, and formed, in a subsidiary manner, a sacerdotal body, intrusted with a variety of offices connected with

---

[7] The heathen priests are called in the Bible by the name of *kumarim*.

the services of the altar, and the religious interests of the people. They entered on those duties at the age of thirty, (in the later temple times at twenty,) and were superannuated when fifty years old. At twenty-five they appear to have begun their novitiate or probation: (Num. viii. 24, 25:) at thirty they were regularly inducted, by ablution, sacrifice, and the *semicha*, or imposition of hands. (Num. viii. 5–22.)

They had the charge of the Tabernacle and its contents. In the nomadic years, prior to the settlement in Canaan, the carriage of its several parts from one station to another fell to their care. They superintended the supplies for the altar, &c., and were stewards of the sacerdotal revenues. They attended the priests at the altar, and sometimes slew the victims; and in the temple services performed the office of choristers. In addition to these functions they discharged the duties of teachers, and instructed the people in the knowledge and duties of religion.

Instead of a territorial district in the land of Canaan, like the other tribes, that of Levi had a compensation, in the grant of forty-eight cities situated in various parts of the country, the tithes of the land, and remunerative gifts of the people.

Connected with the service of the Tabernacle there was a class of inferior servitors who were not Levites. They had the name of *Nethinim*, " given ones ; " (from *nathan*, " to give ; ") men granted to the Levites as helpers, as the Levites themselves had been granted to Aharon and his sons for helpers ; (Num. viii. 19 ;) Onkelos, *Mesirim*, from *masar*, " to deliver over. On the temple Nethinim see Ezra viii. 20, where for *Nethinim* the Peshito reads *Yehibin*, " given ones."

The priests had the same term of service as the Levites. They were consecrated to their office by—a.

Washing. (Exod. xxix. 4.) *b.* Sacrifice. (Verses 10–12.) *c* The application of the sacrificial blood and the anointing oil to their persons and vestments. (Exod. xxix. 20, 21.) The blood was applied to their ears, hands, and feet, to remind them to hear, to act, and to walk, or conduct themselves, according to the word of God. *d.* By placing certain portions of the offering upon their hands. (Exod. xxix. 22–25.) This act was called the *milluim,* "the consecration," literally "the filling," *i. e.,* the hands of the priest with the sanctified portions. *e.* By investing them with the sacerdotal vestments, *bigdey kodesh,* "the garments of holiness:" *viz.,* 1. A cotton or linen garment reaching from the loins to the knees, *miknese-bad.* 2. A coat or tunic of linen, *ketoneth-shesh,* reaching to the ankles. 3. A girdle, *abnet,* a handbreath wide, ornamented with flowers in purple, blue, and scarlet, worn twice round the waist, the ends hanging down to the ankles, or thrown over the left shoulder. 4. A linen mitre, or cap, *migbaah,* from *gabia,* " calyx," which gives perhaps the idea of its form ; LXX., κιδαρις. The priests wore no sandals when engaged in the Tabernacle.

They took their various duties there by allotment.

1. In the court: *a.* To attend to the fire on the altar. (Lev. vi. 13.) *b.* To sacrifice the victim. *c.* To sprinkle the blood. (Lev. i. 5–11.) *d.* To wave the offering. (Lev. xiv. 24.) *e.* To burn what was to be consumed. (Lev. ii. 2.) *f.* To cleanse the altar from ashes, &c. (Lev. vi. 9–11.)

2. In the holy place: *a.* To fill the seven lamps with oil. *b.* To burn incense morn and even. (Luke i. 9.) *c.* To change the shew-bread.

3. Besides these they had various duties relating to the religious, domestic, and national affairs of the people. *a.* To pronounce between persons and things

as ceremonially clean or unclean. (Lev. xiii. 14; Luke
xvii. 14.) *b.* To bind or release from vows, as the
Nazirite. (Num vi.) *c.* To judge in cases of alleged
adultery. (Num. v.) *d.* To teach the people the
law. (Lev. x. 11; Mal. ii. 7.) *e.* To take charge of the
consecrated gifts. *f.* To sound the silver trumpets at festivals. (Num. x. 2, 8.) *g.* To attend the army in time
of war. (Num. x. 9.)

Believers in the New Testament are taught to regard
the Mosaic priesthood, corporately, as a typical representation of a higher one, that of Jesus Christ. In the
acts performed by them at the altar and in the Holy
Place were foreshadowed the real and effectual work of
His mediation who is at once the altar, the victim, and
the priest. But it was in the person of the HIGH PRIEST
that this Divine idea received its fullest typical development. In the fulfilment of his solemn offices this
minister of the tabernacle made with hands became the
impersonation of "our Great High Priest, the Minister
of the sanctuary and of the true tabernacle, which the
Lord hath pitched, and not man; who, not by the blood
of goats and calves, but by His own blood hath entered
into the Holy Place, having obtained eternal redemption
for us." (Heb. viii. and ix) With this typical reference
the Hebrew pontiff bears the name not only of *kohen ha
rosh*, and *kohen ha gadol*, but of KOHEN HA MASHIACH.

The first of the Levitical race who was invested with
this surpassing dignity was Aharon; the last was
Phannias ben Samuel, who perished at the destruction
of Jerusalem. Legitimately the successor of Aharon
was to be of his own lineage, the eldest son having the
first or hereditary right; but this order was in the last
times not unfrequently infringed.

1. The consecration of the high priest was performed
with the same ceremonies as those observed at that of

the common priests, with the difference that he was first clothed in his robes, and the sacred oil was poured upon his head. Hence he is called *ha kohen ha Mashiach,* "the anointed priest."

[The material of the holy consecrating oil—*shemen mishchath kodesh,* Onkelos, *meshach rebuth kudesha*—was a compound of—*a.* Pure myrrh, *mar deror ;* Onk., *mera dakia ; σμύρνα ἐκλεκτή. b.* Sweet cinnamon, *kinneman besem, κίνναμον εὐώδης. c. Calamus, keneh besem, κάλαμος εὐώδης,* or *ἀρωματικός. d.* Cassia, *kiddu,* Onk., *ketsiatha, ἴρις. e.* Olive oil, *shemen zayith,* Onk., *meshach zetha, ἔλαιον ἐξ ἐλαίων .*—in the proportions given in Exod. xxx. 23. It was used exclusively for the anointing rite, and was emblematic of the gifts and graces of the Holy Spirit.]

2. The vestments of the high priest, *bigdey kodesh,* Onk., *lebushey kudesha, στολαὶ ἀγίαι,* consisted of two sets of robes · the one of simple white linen, *bigdey habad,* Onk., *lebushey butsa,* tunic, girdle, and mitre; the white colour being symbolical of purity. (Rev. xix. 8.) In this dress he officiated in the former part of the Day of Atonement. (Lev. xvi. 23.) The other set of robes were distinguished for their magnificence, *bigdey zahab,* "golden garments," *bigdey le-kabod u-le-tiphareth,* "vestments of glory and of beauty."

(1.) The *meil,* Chal., *meila,* a robe of azure colour, *ὑάκινθος,* the emblem of what is heavenly, serene, and pure; worn over the white vesture, (*ketoneth tashbets,*) it combined the idea of purity and heavenly elevation. This flowing mantle was embroidered with pomegranates, *rimmonim,* probably both the flowers and the fruit; they are considered emblematically to denote the *love* of God; and between the pomegranates small bells of gold, whose musical tones were heard as the high priest walked within the sanctuary. (Psalm lxxxix. 15.)

(2.) The *ephod;* (from *aphad*, "to bind, or gird on;") a short vest, ἐπωμίς, Vulg., *superhumerale;* woven, of gold, blue, *tekeleth*, red, *argaman*, crimson, *tolaath sheni*,[8] and fine twined linen, *shesh mashezar*;[9] material and colours identical with those employed in the linings and veil of the tabernacle, and no doubt with a similar ideal meaning.   While blue denotes the colour of the heavens, and white is that of innocence and sanctity, crimson, which fire and blood have in common, is thought to symbolize life; and red, to stand for dignity, majesty, and royal power.   The ephod was clasped on the shoulder-pieces of the robe by two large onyx stones set in gold, on which were engraven the names of the twelve tribes; the high priest being thus designated the Representative of the whole Israelitish people.   The ephod was con-fined at the extremity by a girdle or band composed of the same materials and colours.

(3.) Upon the bosom of the ephod was the breastplate, *choshen ha mishpat;* Onkelos, *choshen dina*, "the instrument of judgment, or decision;" Sept., λογεῖον τῶν κρίσεων; Vulgate, *rationale;* Syriac, *phariso dedino*, "the thorax of judgment."   It was a parallelogram of two spans in length and one in breadth, but doubled or folded so as to have a breadth and length of one span, or about ten inches: the material the same as the ephod, but on the external front were inset four rows of precious stones, three in a row.   i. Sardius, topaz, carbuncle. ii. Emerald, sapphire, diamond.   iii. Ligure, agate, amethyst.   iv. Beryl, onyx, jasper.[1]   On these twelve stones were engraved the names of the tribes, so that

---

[8] Vermilion. *Tolaath ha-sheni*, from *tolaath*, a worm or insect used for dyeing, and the Arab. *sheney*, "to shine." Others derive it from the Hebrew *sheney*, "two," *i. e.*, twice dyed.

[9] *Shesh*, " linen;" *mashezar*, "twined."

[1] I give the names of the jewels as in the common version. The reader is referred to the note at p. 537 of our translation of the Pales-

the high priest bare them on his heart when he went in
to appear before God. The breastplate was fastened to
the ephod by golden cords inserted into golden rings on
its upper corners, running into the sockets of the two
onyx stones on the shoulders, and by rings at the two
inferior corners, through which ran a blue ribbon. By
these things the breastplate was bound inseparably to
the ephod.

(4.) On his head the high priest wore a turban,
mitsnepheth, from *tsanaph*, " to wind or wrap round ; "
LXX., μίτρα; upon which was fastened by blue ribbons
a plate or diadem of gold, with the engraved inscription,
KODESH LA YEHOVAH, " HOLINESS UNTO THE LORD."

(5.) Connected, though to us in some uncertain way,
with the breastplate, were the Urim and Thummim, the
means or instruments of decision or judgment, in doubt-
ful matters of importance to the public interests of the
nation. *Urim* is the plural form of the noun אור *ur*, " fire,
or light," and *Tummim* the plural of תם *thom*, or *tắm*,
"fulness or completion, integrity, uprightness, truth,"
from *tamam*, " to be complete, or in full number, to be
perfect." The ordinary rendering of Urim and Thummim is, "Lights and Perfections." Onkelos merely
Aramaizes the terms, *Uraia ve-tummaia*. The LXX.
give them by τὴν δήλωσιν καὶ τὴν ἀλήθειαν, " manifestation and truth ; " the other Greek versions by Aquila,
Symmachus, and Theodotion, by τοὺς φωτισμοὺς καὶ
τὰς τελειότητας, " illuminations and perfections ; " the
Syriac, by *nahiro ve shalmo*, "resplendence and completion ; " the Samaritan version, by " elucidations and
certainties;" and the Vulgate, by *doctrinam et veritatem ;*
the Arabic, by " holiness and truth."[2]

tinian Targum on Exodus, for a tabular view of the textual variations in
their names.

[2] The German translators render the terms variously : LUTHER,
Licht und Recht ; so MICHAELLIS, BELLERMAN, *Die vollkommen Feuri*

As to the manner in which responses were obtained by the Urim and Thummim, *silente Scriptura nihil pro certo statuatur.* There are several conjectures, more or less plausible, but conjectures only. *Er. gr* . 1. Two tablets, representing an affirmative or a negative, inserted within the folds or pouch of the breastplate, and used in the manner of drawing lots. 2. That the priest dressed in the ephod stood before the veil, and heard the answer pronounced by a voice from within. 3. The verbal answer could be spelled out by the priest, as one letter after another became illuminated. (See the Palestinian Targum on Exod. xxviii. 30.) 4. The wearing of the breastplate had a moral influence on the mind of the priest, which predisposed him to receive the answer by an inward dictate of the Holy Spirit. 5. The Urim and Thummim were identical with the twelve jewels. We see in Exod. xxviii. 30 that the Urim and Thummim were to be put upon the breastplate : what was put upon it but the jewels? They were therefore the Urim and Thummim, and were ordained to make, instrumentally, the perfect revelation, *Tummim,* by their lights, *Urim.* Now as the Divine response, unlike the more diffuse oracles given in after days by the Holy Spirit to the prophets, was vouchsafed to the high priest in a simple affirmative or negative, Yes or No, it is conjectured that the affirmative answer might have been given by the increased refulgence of the jewels, and the negative by the withholdment of it. On the general subject compare Exod. xxviii. 30 ; Lev. viii. 8 ; Exod. xxxv. 27 ; Ezek. xxviii. 14 ; 1 Sam. xxiii. 2 ; and the instances in Num.

gen. GESENIUS, *Offenbarung und Wahrheit,* "revelation and truth " KOSTER, *Aufklärung und Entscheidung,* "enlightenment and decision " BAEHR, *Vollständige Erleuchtung,* "complete illumination " ZÜLLIG, *Geschliffene und ungeschliffene (Diamenten,)* "polished and unpolished (diamonds)," taking the Hebrew word *tam* in the sense of " what is simple, in its natural state, uncultured."

xxvii. 18–31; Joshua vii. 13, 21; Judges i. 1; xx. 18, 28; 1 Sam. xiv. 40–43; 1 Sam. xxiii. 9–12; xxviii. 6.

Among the typical persons of the Old Testament the high priest stands pre-eminently as a representative of the Messiah, 1. As the minister of atonement at the altar; 2. The intercessor before the throne; 3. The infallible counsellor with whom is the oracle of God; and, 4. As the comforter, who bears upon his lips the effectual benediction. (Numbers vi.)

VI. SACRED THINGS.

SACRIFICES. The principle of piacular sacrifice has obtained in the religions of all nations, as a token of repentant confession of sin, and a sign of hope in the pardoning mercy of God. But as the surmises of mere nature would have deterred mankind from a practice which, as destructive of a life that the Creator only could give, would augment His displeasure rather than secure His favour, it is reasonable to believe that the rite must have been adopted, not as a human expedient, but in obedience to a revelation of the Divine will. This conclusion is strengthened by the fact that the rite of sacrifice was appointed by God Himself in the Mosaic cultus, but not then first appointed by Him. Before the time of Moses He had enjoined it on Abraham. (Gen. xv.) He had manifested His approval of it when offered by the earlier patriarchs, as by Noah, amid the solitudes of the postdiluvian world, (Gen. ix.,) and by Abel, at the gate of Paradise. (Gen. iv.; Heb. xi.)

The general name for sacrifices in the Pentateuch is *Zebachim*. *Zebach*, Chal., *Debach*, is a victim slain at the altar, from *zabach*, "to kill or immolate." *Korban, mettannah, terumah, masseeth*, are designations for any kinds of offerings, bloody or unbloody.

The Mosaic sacrifices have been variously classified, but the most simple and comprehensive order is that in which they are arranged under the two heads of the EXPIATORY and the EUCHARISTIC.

I. The first class includes the sacrifices proper. In them the life of the victim was offered for the life of the sinner, and its blood was shed as an atonement for guilt.

These piacular sacrifices were of three kinds. 1. The OLAH, *kalil*, or "whole burnt offering," because wholly consumed, and sent up, by the action of fire, in the flame and smoke of the altar. *Olah*, Chal., *alatha*, comes from *alah*, "to ascend;" LXX., ὁλοκαύτωμα, "holocaust," a term which refers to the entire consumption of the victim. 2. The CHATTAAH, or "sin offering;" the same word signifying "sin;" Chal., *chattatha*; Sept., ἁμαρτία, *i. e.*, περὶ ἁμαρτίας. 3. The ASHAM, or "trespass offering," from *ashmah*, "to be guilty;" Chal., *ashama*; Sept., θυσία σωτηρίου, "the sacrifice of salvation;" Vulg., *hostia pro delicto*; Sept., περὶ πλημμελείας. While the difference between sin and trespass offerings is textually marked in the Levitical law, the distinction between the offences for which they were offered is not so clearly given. Some think that "sins," in the technical phraseology of the ceremonial law, are violations of prohibitory statutes; *i. e.*, doing something which the law forbids to do. "Trespasses," on the other hand, are violations of imperative statutes; *i.e.*, neglecting to do those things which are commanded.

These piacular sacrifices are sometimes called *kippurim*, Chal., *kippuraia*, LXX., καθάρισμοι, "expiations or atonements." On the question about the manner in which they were expiatory, or on the real relation between their presentation and the forgiveness of sin, there are two opposite doctrines.

1. There was that in the nature of the sacrifice itself

which could efficaciously atone for sin. But the divines who take this view are not agreed as to the principle upon which the offerings became expiative. *a.* Some have thought that the virtue of the sacrifice consisted in this,—that a certain material possession was given up by the offerer for the sake of gaining a spiritual blessing. *b.* Others consider the sacrifice in the light of a fine, by the payment of which the offender is set right with his judge; while, *c.* Others, holding that evil rests in that which is material or sensual, and regarding blood as the representation of the sensual or evil principle, see in the shedding and presentation of blood at the altar a physical atonement for moral evil or sin. *d.* Yet in direct opposition to this theory another opinion considers the vital blood to have been propitiatory because it was pure, and represented the acknowledgment of the offerer's obligation to have been himself pure, and his desire to become so.

2. The second doctrine is, that the Mosaic sacrifices had not, nor could have, any intrinsic or atoning power in themselves; but derived their value from their having been Divinely appointed as means to lead the mind of the offerer to a real expiation, of which they were the symbols. They were types of the atoning sacrifice of the Lamb of God who taketh away the sin of the world, emblems of His great sacrifice whose "soul was made an offering" (*asham*) "for sin," (Isai. liii. 10,) and who "redeemed us unto God by His blood:" Heb. ix. 3–28; x. 10–14; Matt. xxvi. 28; Mark xiv. 24; Luke xxii. 20; 1 Cor. xi. 24, 25; Heb. xii. 24; 1 Peter i. 2; (Exod. xxiv. 8;) John i. 29, 36; xix. 36, 37; 1 Cor. v. 7; 1 Peter ii. 24; (Isai. liii. 5–12;) 2 Cor. v. 21; Eph. v. 2; Rom. viii. 23–25; vii. 25; 1 John ii. 2; iv. 10. "The Law," says St. Chrysostom, "was the Gospel in anticipation: the Gospel is the Law in fulfilment."

For the ritual of sacrifices, *vide* the first seven chapters of Leviticus. The expurgatory ordinance of the "red heifer," *parah admah*, Targum, *tortha simketha*, Sept., δάμαλις πυρρά, (*vacca rufa, quasi coloris ignei,*) Numbers xix., comes under the denomination of the *oloth*, or "burnt sacrifices," but combines with the propitiatory a purifying effect. This twofold virtue is unfolded in reality in and through the sacrifice of Christ (Hebrews ix. 11–14.)

II. The other class of Levitical oblations were EUCHARISTIC:—*Zibchey Thodah*, "sacrifices of praise."

1. The SHELAMIM, or "peace offerings," LXX, σωτήριον, εἰρηνικά. These were of the kinds of oblations called "bloody," consisting of the slaughtered bodies of clean and perfect sacrificial animals; certain parts of which were consumed on the altar, but the rest partaken of as a feast upon a sacrifice by the offerer and his guests. Thus the Targum always renders *shelamim* by *nekesath kedeshaia*, "consecrated victims." In their death, and the destruction of parts of them on the altar, were set forth the means of reconciliation; and in the participation of them by the offerer, the enjoyment of that reconciliation in peace with God. Under the *shelamim* may be ranged also the sacrifices by which covenants were confirmed.

2. MINCHOTH. The *mincha* (apparently derived from *nuach*, "to rest," as the husbandman reposes after the toils of harvest [3]) is expressed in the English Bible by "meat offering," and in the Jewish German one by "*Mehl oder Speise-opfer;*" in the Peschito by *kurbano da semida*, "the oblation of flour;" Targum, *minchatha;* Sept., δῶρον, δόσις, *munus.* The various materials of the *mincha* are specified in the second chapter of Leviticus. They were anointed with oil, the sign of conse-

---

[3] Or, because received graciously, with *content.*

cration, and offered with frankincense, the symbol of worship, and with salt, as a covenant token. Some portions were burned, and the remainder assigned to the priests.

An oblation of this kind was presented, (1.) As an expression of gratitude, *zebach hattudah*, Chal., *nesach todetha*, θυσία τῆς αἰνέσεως, (Lev. vii. 12,) εὐχαριστία. (2.) As the accompaniment of a vow, offered with prayer for some deliverance or blessing; *neder*, Chal., *nidra*, εὐχή; or, (3.) As a voluntary gift, *nedabah*, Chal., *nedabtha*, ἑκουσιασμός.

Among such oblations were, (1.) The sheaf or *homer* of barley, δράγμα, offered on the second day of Pascha. (Lev. xxiii. 10) (2.) The two wave-loaves, *lechem tenupha shetayim*; Onkelos, *lechem aramutha tarteen geritsan ,* two uplifted cakes offered at Pentecost on the completion of harvest. (Lev. xxiii. 17.) (3.) The trespass offering of the poor, who could not afford an animal, but who were permitted to offer flour instead. (Lev. v. 11.)

Portions of the *shelamin, minchoth,* and other oblations, were lifted up by the priest towards heaven. This made the thing so offered a *terumah,* (from *ram,* "to elevate,") Onkelos, *arama,* "an elevation," Sept., ἀφόρισμα. It was an act of adoration which acknowledged God above as the supreme Giver of all good things. Again, the consecrated oblation was waved, on the outstretched hands of the priest, backward and forward, hither and thither, as toward the four points of the horizon, in acknowledgment of the universal providence of Him who giveth food to all flesh. It then took the name of *tenupha,* (from *naph,* "to stretch out,") Onkelos, *aphrashutha,* "a separation," something held forth as devoted; LXX., ἀφαίρεμα, *quod aufertur, vel in donarium separatur.*

With a burnt-offering, in addition to the victim, a

D

mincha of flour was offered, accompanied with oil and wine in equal proportion. The wine was poured out round the altar, as a libation; English Version, "a drink offering;" Hebrew, *nesek*, from *nusak*, "to pour out;" Onk., *niseka*; Sept., σπονδή, *libamen*. For the evangelic import compare Matthew xxvi. 27, 28.

3. BIKKURIM. "The earth is the Lord's, and the fulness thereof; the world, and they that dwell therein." He is the Creator and Preserver of our being, and the Giver of all our good. It is meet and right and our bounden duty to make acknowledgment of this. One way by which the Israelitish people gave confession of the Divine Proprietorship, their sense of dependence upon God, and their gratitude for His mercies, was by the presentation of their firstfruits to the Lord; and that with the full assurance that the oblation would be accepted, because it had been appointed by Himself. (Exod. xxii. 29; Lev. xix. 23–25; Num. xv. 20; xviii. 12, 13; Deut. xviii. 4; xxvi. 2–11.)

Such an offering was called *reshith*, "a firstling," from *rosh*,[4] "the head," the chief or best of its kind; ἀπαρχή, *primitiæ, præstantissimum;* and *bikkurim*, "first products," from *bakar*, "to be early," πρωτογεννήματα, Syriac, *rish-allaltho*, "the first of the produce." The names of *terumah* and *tenupha*, already explained, are given also to some of the firstlings, because lifted up and waved at the altar. More strictly, the name *bikkurim* was applied to the fruits, &c., when presented in their natural state, *primitivi fructus;* and that of *terumah*, to produce no longer raw, but prepared.

1. The firstborn son was to be consecrated to God. In the patriarchal time the priesthood was invested in him who had the right of primogeniture. When the Levitical order was established, the firstborn of all the

---

[4] Another derivation is from the Arabic, *shathath,* ' to separate."

families of the tribes was presented to the Lord, but redeemed from the duties of the priesthood by a commutative fine, not exceeding five shekels. In this rite there was also a commemoration of the sparing mercy of God to Israel in the night when the firstborn of the Egyptians were destroyed. (Exod. xiii. 13 ; Num. xviii. 14–16; Luke ii. 27.)

2. The firstlings of the flock and herd were offered as sacrifices, part of them burned, and the rest appropriated to the priests. (Lev. xxvii. 26.) Of animals not fit for the altar, the firstlings were to be slain, but not sacrificed. But they might be redeemed from death by the sacrifice of a lamb in their stead, or by the payment of a price, *ad valorem*. (Lev. xxvii. 13.)

3. Agrarian produce was acknowledged as the gift of God by the oblation of the firstfruits. On two occasions every year this was done representatively by the nation at large. (1.) At Passover, the barley being then ready for the sickle, a public service took place on the second day of the feast ; a sheaf reaped in a field near the city was carried in solemn procession to the house of God ; and the grain, with oil and frankincense, waved before the Lord of the world. (2.) At Pentecost, the harvest being then completed, the loaves made of the new corn were presented as a wave offering in the same manner.

4. These were public or national eucharists for the bounties of Providence ; but all proprietors were individually bound to present their first produce, whether of the field and garden, the wool of the flock, or the honey of the hive, in the proportion, as a *minimum*, of one sixtieth. This might be done either by a pilgrimage to the holy place, or by bringing the oblation to the priest resident in the proprietor's neighbourhood. The fruit was brought in a basket, and presented with a

formula of words prescribed in the twenty-sixth chapter
of Deuteronomy.

5. Tithes, *maaser*, δεκάτη In the ideal meaning
attached to numbers, *ten* is considered as the number of
fulness and sufficiency as to worldly things, just as *seven*
is the exponent of perfectness in things sacred. So
ashar in Hebrew is "to be rich or full" In this view
the tenth has been held in all time as the fit proportion
of a man's worldly goods to be given to God. This
practice is not first inculcated in the Mosaic law : it
obtained as well in the primeval religion of the patriarchs, (Gen. xiv. 20; xxviii. 22,) and among the religious institutes of the Gentiles at large. (HERODOTUS,
Melpom., 152; DIOD. SIC., xx., 14.) After the firstfruits, a tenth of the produce constituted the great or
first tithe. Another tenth, called "the second tithe,"
was presented at the temple, but enjoyed by the offerers.
This was done two years successively ; but in the third
year such tithes might be consumed at home, in acts of
hospitality to the poor. (Deut. xiv. 28, 29 ; xxvi. 12–
15.) The Levites themselves paid tithes. (Num. xviii.
25–32)

6. While some things consecrated might be redeemed,
those that were given absolutely, by an especial devotement, could not. These came under the denomination
of *cherem*. (Lev. xxvii.)

VII. HOLY SEASONS.

THE whole life of the chosen people of God was to be
consecrated to Him who gave it ; and among the appointments designed to promote this end was the recur-
rence of stated seasons of religious solemnities, by which
the years of their personal history were hallowed and
made happy. These occasions were termed *chaggim*,
"feasts ;" *moadey-Jehovah*, "the festivals of the Lord,"

αἱ ἑορταὶ Κυρίου, Onk., *moadaya da Yeya.* The term *moadey-Jehovah* was only given to such days on which holy assemblies, *mikra kodesh,* were held, and a meeting, *moed,* with God took place. The festivals commemorated the dealings of God with them and their fathers; they kept before the people the great truths of their religion; they promoted and sanctified their social intercourse, and strengthened the sentiment of their common nationality.

Several additional feasts are mentioned in subsequent parts of the Bible, ordained only by ecclesiastical authority; but those Divinely appointed in the Pentateuch may be arranged in two classes,—the Sabbatical, and the Historical, or commemorative festivals.

I. In the former class are included,

1. The Seventh Day, *Shabbath la-Jehovah,* "the Sabbath of the Lord;" *yom hashshevihi Shabbath Shabbathon,* "the seventh day, a Sabbath of Repose;" (Exod. xx. 10; Lev. xxiii. 3;) σαββάτων ἀνάπαυσις. [The Christian Church claims also an interest in the Sabbath, as a weekly season of repose from the toils of this world, and a sacred opportunity for advancing our preparation for a better one. Recognising the moral nature of the institution, attested by its place in the requirements of the Decalogue, the canon of morality for every nation and every age, and the reference to it in the annals of the Genesis, where it stands historically recognised as ordained and observed so long before the rise of the Mosaic dispensation, she learns to reverence the Sabbath as an ordinance for all humanity, "made for MAN," and therefore coeval and continued with the human race; blessed of God at the first; still blessed, and a fruitful means of blessing to the individual, the family, and the nation by whom it is rationally and religiously observed.]

2. The Feast of Trumpets, *shabbathon, zekeron teruah,* "a rest, a memorial of sounding;" Onk., *nechacha, dvkeran yabala;* ἀνάπαυσις, μνημοσύνη σαλπίγγων, "a rest, a memorial of trumpets." A festival which came in with the new moon of the seventh month, Tishri. This was the *Rosh hashanah,* the commencement of the civil year. It was ushered in by religious solemnities commemorative of the mercy of Him who is "our Help in ages past, our Hope for years to come." It should be observed, however, that it has been disputed whether the distinction between the ecclesiastical and civil year is not a post-Mosaic one. Some, too, think they discern in the festival of the seventh month's new moon a type of the future renovation of Israel. The moon is the scriptural emblem of the Church; the darkened moon, of a Church in apostasy. The new moon, as she turns again to the sun, brightens once more under his beams. (Isai. lx. 1, 20.)

3. The Sabbatical Year; once in seven years, when there should be *Shabbath Shabbathon la-arets,* "a Sabbath of Repose to the land;" Onkelos, *neyach shemittha le-arah,* "a repose of remission to the land." This also has been regarded as a type of the repose to be enjoyed by the earth in the seventh age, the Sabbath of time. The assurance of an adequate supply for the wants of the people, notwithstanding the cessation of agriculture in the seventh year, by the superabundant harvest yielded in the sixth, is one of the material guarantees of the Divine legation of Moses. (Lev. xxv. 1–7, 17, 20; Deut. xv. 1–10.)

4. After the lapse of seven sabbatical, or forty-nine, years came, on the tenth day of Tishri, the Great Year of Redemption and release: *Yobel,* or, *Shenath ha Yobel,* Onkelos, *Yobela,* "the year of Jubilee," ἔτος τῆς ἀφέσεως, "the year of remission," ἀφέσεως

σημασία, "the signal of release or liberation." The primary object of this institution was the readjustment of such interests of personal liberty, and landed or any real property, as had been disturbed in the past interval of years. And this gives the best meaning to the term " Jubilee," as coming from *hobil,* "to cause to bring back, or recall;" though others, going back to the root of the word in *yabal,* "to flow like water" with fulness and impetuosity, refer it to the flowing, swelling note of the trumpet which ushered in the year. Lev. xxv. 9: "Thou shalt make the" *shophar teruah,* "the sounding peal of the trumpet to pass through the land; it shall be *Yobel* to you."

It is disputed whether the Jubilee was celebrated in the forty-ninth year or that which followed. The Divine ordinance certainly defines the fiftieth to be the year. (Lev. xxv. 11.)

At this " time of restitution" the Hebrew bondsman returned free to his own family, and real property which had been mortgaged reverted to its hereditary owners. The conditions and regulations are given in Leviticus xxv. Loans, too, were released in the Sabbatical year; (Deut. xv. 2, 9;) a privilege which was no doubt extended to the debtor in the greater one of the Jubilee.

All Christians see in the Jubilee a foreshadow of the "good things to come." It spoke, with a perpetual prophecy, of that " acceptable year of the Lord" which the Saviour of mankind declared that He Himself had been sent to preach. (Luke iv.) The Jubilean note was the prelude to that of the Gospel trumpet which proclaims the world redeemed, and calls upon the captive to cast aside his chains, and to go forth, made free from sin. As the Jubilee trumpet went through the land, so must the sound of the Gospel be made to be-heard through all the peopled earth, that the nations "may be turned from darkness to light, and from the power of Satan unto God, to receive remission of sins, and an inheritance among the sanctified." So too, with regard to the fate of Israel, there comes a day when "the great trumpet shall be blown, and they shall come which were ready to perish in the land of Assyria, and the outcasts in the land of Egypt, and shall worship the Lord in the holy mount at Jerusalem." (Isai. xxvii. 13; Matt. xxiv. 31.) And, finally, we read of the trumpet that will sound when time has run the cycle of its ages, and the captivity of the grave be ended, and the risen dead, who are "counted worthy to obtain that world," will be put in possession of the "incorruptible inheritance which passeth not away." (1 Cor. xv. 52; Job xix. 25, 26; Matt. xxv. 34.) These are the Sabbatical Feasts of the Lord.

II. Of the COMMEMORATIVE Festivals, the precedence belongs to

1. The Passover; as founded on an event which forms the epoch of the national history of the Hebrew people,—their exodus from Egypt, and the initiation of their ecclesiastical year. (Exod. xii. 2.) The appellations, *Pesach*, Onkelos, *Pascha*, signify "a passing over, a sparing, or protection;" *Pesach la Yehovah*, "the Lord's Passover;" Onk., *Pascha kedem Yeya*, "the Passover before the Lord;" (Exod. xii. 11;) Sept., Πάσχα Κυρίου. This name specifies the Passover in its strict sense; the night-feast itself; *a.* Preceded by the selection, on the tenth of Nisan, of the lamb, or kid, *seh*, Onkelos, *immar*, πρόβατον, which was to be faultless, *tamim*, Onk., *shelim*, τέλειον; a male, *zakar*, of the year, *ben shanah*, either *min hakkebashim*, from the lambs, or *min ha izzim*, from the goats. *b.* The putting away of all leavened bread, *chomets*, Onk., *cha-*

miia, ζύμη. *c*. The immolation of the victim, as a sacrifice, *zebach ha pesach*, on the fourteenth of Nisan at evening; [literally, *beyn ha-arbayim*, "between the two evenings;" Onkelos, *beyn shemshaya*, "between the suns;" Peschito, *b'amarobai shemisho*, "at the passing over of the sun:" all these forms of expression, as well as a similar one among the Arabians, being idioms for "the afternoon," or the interval between the passing of the sun from the meridian and his final disappearance below the horizon. Among the Hebrew commentators, Kimchi, Raschi, and, before them, Saadja Gaon coincide in this view. The Talmud more narrowly defines "the first evening" as the time when the heat of the day begins to abate, towards the close of the afternoon, about three hours before sunset, at which latter "the second evening" begins.] *d*. Some of the blood, on the first Passover in Egypt, was sprinkled with a bunch of hyssop on the *mezuzoth*, "two side-posts," and on the *mashekoph*, or "lintel" of the door. *e*. It was roasted entire, on two spits thrust through it, the one lengthwise, the other transversely passing the longitudinal one near the fore legs; the two spits taking thus the form of a cross. *f*. It was eaten as a family meal with suitable guests. *g*. It was eaten with unleavened bread, *matssoth*, and with *merorim*, "bitter herbs," the tokens of the affliction they had endured in the house of bondage.

The festival was prolonged during the week, with the modified name of the Feast of Unleavened Bread, *Chag hammatssoth*, ἑορτὴ τῶν ἀζύμων. (Exod. xiii. 6, 7.) The term Passover is given to the entire feast, and in common parlance to eat the unleavened cakes was to "eat the passover." (Deut. xvi. 3. Compare Luke xxii. 1, and John xviii. 28; where "passover" does not mean the supper, which had transpired on the pre-

ceding night, but the unleavened cakes, which could
not be eaten by those who were ceremonially defiled;
a remark which serves to obviate an alleged contradiction in the Gospels.)   On the second of the seven days,
the corn harvest being ready for the sickle, the sheaf as
the first fruits was reaped, and presented as a wave
offering before the Lord.   See on the *minchoth*.

The Passover in its mystical aspects was, (1.) A commemoration of the great national deliverance at the
Exodus.   (2.) A sacrament of renewed allegiance to
God, as their Theocratic King; or a yearly ratification
of the covenant between Jehovah and His people.   (3.)
A type of Redemption by the Messiah.   The Christian
Church, by inspired authority, regards the paschal lamb
as an image of the Lamb of God who taketh away the
sin of the world; the Victim slain to redeem us from
the bondage of corruption into the glorious liberty of
the children of God; and the sheaf, springing from the
grain seed which had died in the earth, and presented
to God, as a type of His resurrection, who was delivered for our offences to death and the grave, and
raised up for our justification.   The sheaf was presented "on the morrow after the Sabbath," (Lev. xxiii.
15,) "the first day of the week." (Luke xxiv. 1.)   On
that day Jesus rose.   Behold the fulfilment of the
Paschal type !   "Christ our Passover is sacrificed for
us." (1 Cor. v. 7.)   "Now is Christ risen from the
dead, and become the First Fruits of them that slept."
(1 Cor. xv. 20.)   (4.) The Jews contemplate the
Passover as a prophetic signal of their future release
and restoration to Canaan.   They see that this pro-
spective deliverance is associated in the prophecies with
the memory of that from Egypt, as a Divine pledge of
its accomplishment.   Thus Micah vii. 11–20: "In
that day thy walls are to be built.   In that day the

decree" (which had consigned thee to captivity) " shall be put afar off. In that day they shall come to thee from Assyria, and from the cities, and from sea to sea, and from mountain to mountain.......Feed thy people with thy rod, which have dwelt solitarily in the wood ; let them feed in the midst of Carmel, in Bashan and in Gilead, as in the days of old. *According to*" (*or as in*) "*the days of thy coming out of Egypt will I show unto him marvellous things.* The nations will see, and be confounded in all their might ; they shall be afraid of the Lord our God, and shall fear because of Thee. Who is a God like unto Thee, that pardoneth iniquity, and passeth by the transgression of the remnant of His inheritance ? He retaineth not His anger for ever, because He delighteth in mercy. He will turn again, He will have compassion upon us; and Thou wilt cast all their sins into the depths of the sea. Thou wilt perform the truth unto Jacob, and the mercy to Abraham, which Thou hast sworn unto our fathers from the days of old."

This prophetic bearing is not lost sight of in the grand Paschal ritual now, and for ages past, in use among the Jews. From a recitative—too long to be quoted in full —which occurs in that service, we will render the following illustrative sentences :—

"At Passover the faithful sang a hymn : And the Lord saved on that day. At the Pesach in Egypt.

At Passover a voice shall be heard from on high : Israel shall be saved in the Lord with eternal salvation. At the Pesach to come.

At Passover the redeemed went out with an uplifted hand, and Israel saw the hand. At the Pesach in Egypt.

At Passover with the greatness of His glorious power

the Lord will put forth His hand the second time.
At the Pesach to come.

At Passover the multitude of His armies with goodly
wealth walked on dry ground in the midst of the sea.
At the Pesach in Egypt.

At Passover the Lord will wave His hand with a tempestuous wind, and will dry up the tongue of the
Egyptian sea.[5]   At the Pesach to come.

At Passover came the sharp storm, ordained (to overwhelm) the camp of the Egyptians, with the fiery
pillar and the cloud.   At the Pesach in Egypt.

At Passover will be new wonders upon those of old,
"blood and fire and pillars of smoke."[6]   At the
Pesach to come.

At Passover he was arrayed to destroy His foes: but
the sons of Israel went out with an uplifted hand.
At the Pesach in Egypt.

At Passover will the cup of salvation and peace (be
ours:) for (He hath said), With joy shall ye be led
forth and with peace.[7]   At the Pesach to come.

At Passover he completed to destroy the Anamim;[8] for
there was not a house where there was not one dead.
At the Pesach in Egypt.

At Passover the nations will imagine vainly to strive
(with the Messiah:) and this will be the plague.
At the Pesach to come.

At Passover the Lord opened all the (closed) gates (of
the Egyptians:) but passed over the doors (of Israel).
At the Pesach in Egypt.

The Great One and the Ruler hath given the Passover
for a sign of protection and deliverance, escape and
salvation.   At the Pesach to come.

At the Passover the peculiar people were confirmed to be

---

[5] Isaiah xi.   [6] Joel ii.   [7] Isaiah lv. 12.   [8] Egyptians

free : for the Lord fought for them against the Egyptians. At the Pesach in Egypt.

A Passover is yet to be for the redemption of the captives : and the Lord will go forth and fight against the nations.[9] At the Pesach to come.

At Passover He darkened to His enemies the shining lights : but all the sons of Israel had light. At the Pesach in Egypt.

At Passover there shall be favour by the Word of Him who formed thee : Arise, shine, for thy light cometh. At the Pesach to come.

At Passover they praised Him for His strength and for His might : for the Lord had redeemed His people. At the Pesach in Egypt.

At Passover will the praise of His power be set forth : Our Redcemer, the Lord of Hosts is His Name. At the Pesach to come."

(Congregation and reader together.)

" At the Passover He will add salvation to salvation : He will remember His covenant to save the people brought nigh to Him in love. Who is like Thee among the mighty, O Lord ? Who is like Thee, glorious in holiness, awful in praises, doing marvels ? Thy children saw Thy Majesty, Thou Divider of the sea before Moses ! "[1]

2. The seven weeks after Pascha were occupied with the labours of harvest, on the conclusion of which the second of the annual pilgrim festivals took place. This was the *chag ha-shabuoth*, " the Feast of Weeks," Onkelos, *chagga de shabuaya*, ἑορτὴ ἑβδομάδων. Commencing on the fiftieth day from the second day of the Pass-

[9] Zech. xiv 16.

[1] MACHSOR, *Seder Pesach*, Service for the Seventh Night.

over week, (Lev. xxiii. 15,) this anniversary among the
later Jews took the name of the Pentecost, *chamishim yom*,
(verse 16,) ἡμέρα τῆς πεντηκοστῆς; also the Feast of
Harvest or Ingathering, and the Day of the Firstfruits.
(Num. xxviii.) Its observance combined, (1.) The
commemoration of the bounty of Providence in the
harvest ingathered, of which the public token was the
wave-offering of the two loaves made of the new corn;
and, (2.) As man liveth not by bread only, but by every
word of the Lord, their thanksgiving for the revelation
of His Law at Mount Sinai.

It was at this Feast of Weeks at Jerusalem, attended
by the men of the home land of Israel, and by devout
proselytes of many Gentile nations, that the Christian
Pentecost was inaugurated, (Acts ii.,) when the Divine
Spirit wrote the Law again, not on tables of stone, but
on the living heart. "Whereof the Holy Ghost is a
witness to us: for after that He had said before, This
is the covenant that I will make with them after those
days, saith the Lord: I will put my laws into their hearts,
and in their minds will I write them: and their sins
and iniquities will I remember no more." Then too
was ushered in that Feast of Ingathering, which the
church has, or should have, celebrated ever since in
a perpetual Harvest of Souls. The three thousand of
the first Pentecost were the First Fruits presented to
the Lord of that consummation to be witnessed, when
"all Israel shall be saved, with the fulness of the
Gentiles."

3. The Feast of Tabernacles (*chag ha sukkoth*, Onkelos,
chagga de metalya, "the feast of shades or bowers," Sept.,
ἑορτὴ σκηνῶν, St. John and Josephus, σκηνοπηγία)
commenced on the 15th of Tishri, and continued seven
days. As indicated by the name, it was intended to
commemorate the tabernacle life of their fathers in the

wilderness; in doing which, every family took their
meals each day in a temporary booth, awning, or summer
bower,[2] either in the garden or upon the flat roof of
the house. The vintage and fruit harvest being now
completed, the public thanksgiving for the mercies of
the past year contributed to the cheerful tone of the
season.

The observances of the Feast of Tabernacles had a
peculiar grandeur. At the temple altar the sacrifices
were on an unusual scale, as laid down in Numbers xxix.,
where it will be seen that in addition to the other victims
prescribed the bullocks offered during the seven days
amounted to seventy; an oblation which the Jews
regarded as a sacrifice offered on behalf of the nations of
the world at large.

A procession moved each day round the altar court,
holding in their hands the *lulab* and the citron, and
chanting the Hosannah passages of Psalm cxviii. On
the seventh day the procession was repeated seven times.
The *lulab*, which was a wreath or bunch of small branches
bound together, and carried in the hand *instar sceptra*,
consisted, if we read rightly Lev. xxiii. 40, of, 1. The
branches of the palm, *kappoth temarim*, Onk., *lulabin*,
Syr., *lebarotho de dekelo*, Sept., κάλλυντρα φοινίκων.
2. Branches of the myrtle, *anaph ets aboth*, *i. e.*, the
" bough of a bushy tree," (Sept., κλάδους ξύλου δασεῖς,
ramos ligni densos,) which the Jews consider as a term
for the myrtle, by which Onkelos and the Syriac translators render it. 3. Willows of the brook, *arbey nachal*,
Onk., *arbin di nechal*, Sept., ἰτέαι, *salices*.

There are poetical, if not mystical, ideas associated
with these images. The myrtle is the emblem of justice.
See the Targum on Esther ii. 7, where we read, "The

---

[2] See the Palestine Targum on Lev. xxiii., and the Mishna, treatise
Sukkah.

just are compared to the myrtle." The willow is the emblem of affliction; the palm, of victory. In the Apocalypse St. John beholds the just made perfect, waving the palm, without the willow.

In the illuminated court of the temple "the Psalms of Degrees" were chanted by an immense choir of Levites : and on the seventh or Great Day of the Feast was the solemnity of the libation of water, drawn in a golden vase from the fountain of Siloam, and poured out by the priest at the altar, the whole assembly joining in the Song of Salvation given in the twelfth chapter of Isaiah. It appears from *Bereshith Rabba* and the Jerusalem Talmud that the Jews regarded the water as an emblem of the pure and purifying Law, the giving of which they celebrated with what they called *simchath-Torah*, "the rejoicing for the Law :" but further, that the joy then cherished in their bosoms predisposed them for the reception of the Holy Spirit ; so that Siloah's well became to them like a means of receiving the grace of the Divine Spirit. But our Saviour, in the solemn words proclaimed by Him on the Great Day of the last Feast of Tabernacles before His death, announced the privilege of those who believe in Him to have the purifying Spirit within themselves, an interior fount of life (John vii. 37.)

In the prophecy of Zechariah, chap. xiv. 16, it is intimated that when Jerusalem in her future days of blessing shall become the joy of the earth, the people of God will go up thither from time to time, and from many lands, to celebrate a festival which, from its joyful character, will bear a resemblance to, and is indeed called by the name of, the Feast of Tabernacles.

But the passing generations of the good who are strangers and pilgrims upon earth, with no continuing city, but tenants for a time of the frail, fading tabernacle of the body, are looking for and hastening on to a city of habitation whose Maker and Builder is God. Their pilgrimage ends when "the holy, who do His commandments," enter the gates of those blessed abodes. We transfer, in faith and hope, to the eternal Jerusalem what is written of the best days and best blessings of the earthly one. "Look upon Zion, the city of our solemnities: thine eyes shall behold Jerusalem a quiet habitation; thine eyes shall see the King in His beauty, in the land afar off."

Thus much for the Festivals: the only FAST prescribed in the Pentateuch is that on the Day of Atonement; when the sins of the whole people were spread before God in penitential confession, accompanied by the sacrifices which set forth the great means of expiation. This august solemnity transpired five days before the Feast of Tabernacles, that is to say, on the tenth day of the month Tishri, which took on that account the appellation of *Taenith Gadol,* "the Great Fast," and *Yom Kippur,* "the Day of Expiation," or simply but emphatically YOMA, "the Day." In this great transaction every Israelite was bound to take a part. (Lev. xxiii. 27–29.) The twenty-four hours constituting the day, from the evening, just after sunset, or, as it was held, as soon as three stars could be counted in the sky, till the following evening at the same time, were marked by a rigid fast:[3] no food, no fire, no bathing, no work: the people went barefoot, and all

---

[3] "*Before the Lord who sitteth above the circle of the heavens may our streaming tears, like a flood on the earth, wash out the handwriting of our sins*

"*We stand all day before the Lord of the whole world, from the rising of the morn, until the coming forth of the stars.*"

MOSES ABEN EZRA. *Neila for the Day of Atonement.*

was silence and humiliation. At home each member of the family was occupied in the Word of God, in self-examination, and in solitary prayer; till as many as could find standing-room in the neighbourhood of the temple engaged in the long service at which the high priest officiated in person. For the ritual itself compare Leviticus xvi. 1–34; xxiii. 26–32; Numbers xxix. 7–11. The principal terms connected with it have been already defined. The only one which now calls for remark is the epithet given to the goat upon which fell the lot to live, while its companion fell under the doom of death. The animal which was sent away alive is designated *Azazel*. The Divine directory, Lev. xvi. 8, reads, "And Aharon shall cast lots upon the two goats; one lot for the Lord, and the other lot for Azazel. And Aharon shall bring the goat upon which the Lord's lot fell, and offer him for a sin-offering," literally *ve-asahu chattah*, "and shall make him to be sin." (Compare 2 Cor. v. 21.) "But the goat on which the lot fell for Azazel, he shall set before the Lord alive, to propitiate upon him," *le shalach otho la azazel ha midbarah*, "to send him for," or to, "Azazel, towards the wilderness." There is, it must be confessed, an air of mystery over the expressions, which seems to excuse the conflict of opinions—I may say, fancies—which have early and late divided the word-critics of the Bible upon the signification of the name Azazel. We will mention the principal.

I. It is an appellation of the Divine Being. Thus the Syriac version of the text gives the name as *Azaza-el*, "the Mighty God." In the Latin translation of the Peschito there is a gloss to the same effect: "*La Azaza-el, i. e., Deo Fortissimo.*" But it must be seen that if this interpretation be the true one, the casting of lots would be a useless formality, as each goat would equally fall to the Deity, either as "the Lord," or as "the Mighty God."

2. It was the name of a *place*, to which the living goat was led away. See here Onkelos and the Palestinian Targums on Lev. xvi. 8, and Rashi's commentary on the text.

3. It is a personal name, not for the Almighty, but for Satan, or one of the fallen angels. The name Azalzel does occur in that way in the Book of Enoch, and in rabbinical writings, as in Menachem on Leviticus; and the *Boraitha* of Eliezer, where the four most powerful demons are named Sammael, Azazel, Azael, and Machazeel. But though in the oriental demonology the name might have been applied to Satan, it does not follow that the evil being had anything to do with the scape-goat on the day of atonement; either in the animal being made his representative, or in its being sent to him. In the former case the sins of Israel were confessed, so to speak, over the head of the devil; in the second, the infernal spirit is elevated in the transaction to a co-partnership with the Almighty: both the one notion and the other are too repugnant to our perceptions of propriety to be admissible.

4. A fourth and, as it appears to us, a far more eligible opinion is, that which, deriving it from *az*, "a goat," and *azal*, a verb which signifies "to go away," makes the name Azazel descriptive of the fate of the living goat, as antithetical to that of the animal that had fallen under the doom of death. The one died at the altar; the other goes forth to its native wilderness alive. Viewing the solemnities of the Day of Atonement in their evangelical aspects, this meaning of the name has the greater recommendation. It has also the authority of the Septuagint, which translates Azazel by ὁ ἀποπομπαῖος, "the dismissed one;" from ἀποπέμπω,

"to send away." The animals, though two in number, are yet but parts of one provision for a symbolic atonement for sin; and conjointly represent the expiatory work of the One Redeemer, who, in bearing away the sin of the world, was delivered to *death* for our offences, and raised to *life* for our justification. So this mystical goat dies, and yet lives · but as a single animal could not exhibit the two phases of the truth to be set forth in the type, two were appointed; the one to die, the other to go away alive. "We have redemption in His blood, even the remission of sins." "As far as the east is from the west, so far hath He removed our transgressions from us."

VIII. MISCELLANEOUS TERMS
RELATING TO THE CIVIL AND RELIGIOUS LIFE OF THE HEBREW PEOPLE

I. *Torah, Torath Yehovah;* from *yarah,* "to instruct:" the entire body of Divine precepts which form the life of righteousness; Targum, ORAITHA *da Yeya;* Syr., Peschito, *Nomuseh de Morio;* Sept., ὁ νόμος τοῦ Κυρίου.

Berith, Habberith, "the covenant;" *dibree habberith :* Onk., *yath pithgamee keyama,* "the words of the covenant." (Exod. xxxiv. 28.)

Asereth haddebarim, "the ten words;" Onk., *asera pithgamin,* οἱ δέκα λόγοι, "the Decalogue." (Exod. xxxiv. 28.)

Mitsvah, "a commandment," plur., *mitsvoth;* root, *tsava,* "to set;" (so, law, *lex, legis,* is, etymologically, "that which is laid down ,") Sept., ἐντολή.

Hok, plur., *hukkim,* (the H, *cheth,* strong guttural,) "a statute, a fixed appointment, a decree;" Onk., *keyam ;* Sept., πρόσταγμα.

Pikkudim, "prescriptions, rules," δικαιώματα.

Mishpat, pl., *mishpatim* or *shephatim*, "a judicial decision," from *shaphat*, "to distinguish, determine;" Onk., *dinaya*, pl., Sept., δικαίωμα.

Din, Chal *dina*, "a judgment, a matter to be adjudged;" δίκη.

Edah, "testimony;" *Eduth*, "an ordinance;" emphatically, the Law on the tablets.

Mishmaroth, "things to be observed;" from *shamar*, "to keep watch over."

II. *Ketubah*, "marriage contract." *Mekadesh*, also *Kedushin*, "Betrothment," from *kadash*, "to set apart."

Eres, "marriage vow," from *aras*, "to betroth." *Mochar*, "dowry." (Gen. xxix. 18, 27.)

Kallah, "a bride," (because crowned?) *Chatan*, "a bridegroom." *Choten*, "a wife's father." *Cham*, "a husband's father."

Pelegesh, "a concubine," plur., *pilagshim*, a secondary wife; married, but not with the ceremonies of the usual marriage. The name given to the various wives in a family cursed with polygamy was *zeroth*, "troubles, adversaries, or rivals," (1 Sam. i. 6,) because, as R. David Kimchi informs us in his note on that text, they are most commonly causes of trouble, jealousy, and vexation to each other.

Yabam, a brother who was to marry the childless widow of his deceased relative. *Yeboom*, the espousals of a *yabam*. (Deut. xxv.)

Chalitsa, the ceremony of taking off the shoe, if the brother should refuse the *yeboom*. (Deut. xxv. 9.)

Get, plur., *gittin*, "a writing of divorce."

Nin, "offspring, posterity," from *nūn*, "to flourish." *Zera*, the same as *nin*.

Bekor, "the firstborn," πρωτότοκος. *Bekorah*, "primogeniture."

Ben, "a son;" Chal., *Bar*.　*Bath*, "a daughter."

Yonek, "a sucking infant."　*Gamul*, the same.　*Taph*, (collective noun,) "little ones, children, a family."　*Yeled*, "a child, boy."　*Nahar*, "a youth;" fem., *naarah*. *Elem*, "a marriageable youth."

Almanah, "a widow."　*Yatom*, "an orphan."

Mishpacha, "a family," as a sub-division of a *Shebet*, "tribe."

Beth-Ab, or *Aboth*, "a number of families related."

III. *Aloof*, an Edomite "duke," leader, a chief; root, *aluph*; (Gen. xxxvi. 40;) Onk., *Rabba*; Sept., ἡγεμών, "a chief of a tribe," φυλάρχης.

Nasi, "a prince, magistrate."　*Rosh beth aboth*, "a chief of the house of the fathers."　*Roshee shebatim*, "heads of tribes."

Amarkella, (Chaldee, found only in the Targums,) "a chief." According to Rashi the word means "a treasurer."

Shoter, "an overseer."　*Shophet*, "a judge;" root, *shaphat*.

Sar, "a captain;" root, *sarar*, "to rule."　*Saree alaphim, meoth, chamishim, asaroth*, "captains of thousands, hundreds, fifties, and tens."

Kahal, a church," *ecclesia*.　*Sod*, "an assembly," *comitia*.

Edah, "a congregation;"　*Zikney ha edah*, "the elders of the congregation;"　*Nesiey ha edah*, "the princes of the same;" (Num. xi. 16,) the seventy elders; regarded by the Jews as the primary germ of the Sanhedrim.

Baal, "a master."　*Baalah*, "a mistress."　*Ebed*, "a servant."　*Shiphahath*, "a maid-servant."

Gar, "a stranger;" from *gūr*, "to sojourn."

Shebuah, "an oath."　*Temurah*, "an exchange, commutation, compensation, the thing exchanged."　*Kopher nephesh*, or *piddion nephesh*, "indemnification," or commutation for punishments incurred by injuring others. (Exod. xxi.)

Goel, from *gaal, redemit, vindicavit*, "a redeemer or avenger;" the right to redeem possessed by the nearest of kin; Chal., *Geal*. (Num. xxxv. 19; Lev. xxv. 25; compare Ruth iii. 12, 13.)

PUNISHMENTS.—*Gemul, tagmul*, "retribution." *Pekudah*, "visitation."

Bekoreth, "scourging;" from *bakar*, "an ox;" because inflicted with the ox-tail; others, from *bakar, visitare*.

Sekilah, regimah, "stoning;" from *sakal*, and *ragam, lapidare*.

Serepha, "burning,"—either the dead body, or branding the living one.

Hereg, "beheading." *Chenek*, "strangling." *Teliya*, "hanging" the dead body for exposure.

Kareth, "cutting off from the people;" excommunication, sometimes bodily death. (Lev. xxiii. 29.)

Nidui, cherem, shammatha, the three degrees of excommunication.

IV. *Yekehath*, "obedience." *Shemiah*, or *Mishmah*, "hearkening to," in the sense of obeying; root, *shema*, "to listen."

Asham, "a sin." *Chattaah*, "transgression," from *chata*, "to slide, stumble, or miss the mark." *Pesha*, "revolt, sedition;" root, *pasha*, "to rebel." *Tahor*, "clean," Chal., *dakia, καθαρός*. *Tumé*, "unclean," Chal., *mesaah, ἀκάθαρτος*. Clean and unclean, as a condition of the human body, or the species of an animal, as judged of by the standard of the Levitical law. *Toah*, "apostasy" from God; root, *taah*, "to wander." *Abar*, "to transgress a limit." *Avon*, "iniquity, moral dis-

tortion;" root, *avah*, "to be perverse, deal perversely."
Sarah, "a deviation from the law;" root, *sūr*, "to turn
away, decline from." *Evel, avlah,* "iniquity, injustice;"
root, *aval*. *Shegaga*, "an error, inadvertency," root,
shagag or *shagah*, "to err." *Shegiah*, "a sin of ignorance." *Sheker*, "prevarication, falsity;" from *shakar*,
"to lie." *Nebalah*, "wickedness, folly;" root, *nabal.*
Zimmah, "crime, mischief;" root, *zamam*, "to devise
or purpose evil." *Remiah*, "remissness, unfaithfulness;"
root, *ramah*, in Piel, "to deceive." *Maal*, "faithless-
ness;" root, *maal*, "to deal treacherously." *Risha* and
reshah, "guilt, wickedness;" root, *rasha*, "to be guilty,
liable to punishment." In the Targums *choba, chobtha,*
from *chob, peccavit, debitor fuit*. *Beliyaal*, "worthless-
ness," from *beli*, "without," and *yaal*, "usefulness."
Ben-beliyaal, ish beliyaal, "a worthless man," Onk., "a
son of wickedness;" Sept., παράνομος.

V. *Teshubah*, "conversion;" root, *shūb*, "to return."
Charata, (Chaldee,) "penitence." *Vidui*, "confession;"
root, *yada*, "to know," Piel, "to make known."

Kippurim, "amends, atonement;" root, *kaphar*, in
Piel, "to expiate."

Emunah, "faith;" root, *aman*, "to stand firm, to be
true;" in Hiphil, *heĕmin*, "to confide in, lean upon."
Betach, "trust, confidence;" root, *batach*, "to confide
in, to be quiet."

Selicha, "pardon;" root, *salach*, to forgive." *Zedakah*,
"justification or righteousness;" root, *zadak*, "to be
right." Of Abraham it is written, (Gen. xv. 6,) *Vehee-
min ba-Yehovah, vaiyachshebeha*[4] *lo Zedakoh*: "And
he believed in the Lord, and He counted it to him for
righteousness." Compare Rom. iv. 3, as quoted from the
Septuagint. Onkelos, *Vehemin be Memra da Yeya ve*

---

[4] Root, *chashab*, "to think, judge, account, or reckon as anything."

chashlah leh lizeko: "And he believed in the Word of the Lord, and He accounted it to him for justification."

Tikevah, "hope, expectation;" root, *kavah,* "to wait for."

Ahabah, ahava, "love," root, *ahab,* "to love or delight in."

Chesed, "kindness;" *Rachamim,* "tender mercies;" root, *racham,* "to love."

Ratson, "benevolence;" root, *ratsah, placere. Emeth,* "truth, veracity."

Kodesh, Kedushah, "holiness;" root, *kadash,* "to be sacred," Hiphil, "to sanctify."

Teshuah, "salvation;" also *Yesha,* root, *yasha,* "to save, deliver, succour."

Yesharah, "rectitude, uprightness;" root, *yasha;* from which, as is commonly thought, comes the name *Jeshurun,* given in the Pentateuch to Israel; though others connect it with the Arabic root *yasara,* "to prosper, be wealthy," like the Hebrew *ashar,* "to be blessed."

Hithhalek eth ha-Elohim, "to walk with God." (Gen. v. 24.) *Hithhalek lipnei,* "to walk before Him." (Gen. xvii. 1.) *Hithhalek acheri,* "to walk after, be obedient to." (Deut. viii. 19.) *Halek im bekeri,* "to walk contrary to, be rebellious against God." (Lev. xxvi. 40.)

Neder, "a vow;" a voluntary engagement, or sacred promise, made either as an acknowledgment of benefits received, or as a means of obtaining them. (Gen. xxviii. 22.) Onkelos, *keyam;* Sept., εὐχή. *Nedarim* were either affirmative, in the devotement of the person or one's property to God, or negative, in the vow of abstinence from things in themselves lawful. Such was the vow of the Nazir. (Lev. xxv.; Num. vi. 2.) "A certain man came to me[5] from the south, intending to take the

---

[5] Simeon ha Zadik, high priest.

E

vow of a Nazarite: he was beautiful in countenance, and
his hair waved in graceful locks. My son, I said, what
moves thee to destroy thy hair? He replied, I am a
shepherd to my father in my native place. I went to
draw water from the fountain, and looking at the reflec-
tion of my own face in the water, vanity seized me, and
became a temptation to hinder my future happiness.
Wretch, said I then to myself, art thou proud of that
which is not thine, and which must soon be dust and
ashes? So now I swear that I go not hence until these
locks be cut off. And I arose, and kissed his head, and
said, May such Nazarites increase in Israel!" (*Talmud*.)

Tephillah, "prayer;" root, *phallel*, in Hithpa. in the
sense of *speravit*; προσευχή; Onk., *Tepilla*. *Bakkasha*,
"supplication;" root, *bakash*, "to seek earnestly, strive
for." *Sheēlah*, "a petition;" root, *shaal*, "to ask."

Berakah, "blessing, benediction;" root, *barak*, "to
pronounce a blessing;" Onk., *Birketha*; εὐλογία.

Forms of Benediction. *Meborah Adonai*, "Be thou
blessed of the Lord." *Birekath Adonai aleka*, "The
blessing of the Lord be upon thee." *Adonai immeka*,
"The Lord be with thee" *Shalom leka*, "Peace be
with thee."

The Divine Benediction. Hebrew text, *Yebarekka,
Yehovah veyishmereka*, "The Lord bless thee, and keep
thee." *Yaer Yehovah panaif eleyka, vichunneka*, "The
Lord make His face to shine upon thee, and be gracious
unto thee." *Yissa Yehovah panaif eleyka, veyasem leka
shalom*, "The Lord lift up His countenance upon thee,
and confer upon thee peace." (Num. vi. 24.) Compare
the passage in the Targums of Onkelos and Palestine.

In the edifying service for the Day of Atonement in
the Hebrew Machsor, this most holy benediction is
employed with a devotional comment on each word, con-

sisting of some illustrative text from the Scriptures. Thus :—

1. *May He bless thee :* "The Lord who made heaven and earth bless thee out of Zion."

The Lord : "O Lord our Lord, how excellent is Thy Name in all the earth !"

And keep thee : "Preserve me, O God ; for in Thee do I put my trust."

2. *Make shine :* "God be gracious unto us, and bless us, and cause His face to shine upon us."

The Lord : "The Lord, the Lord God, merciful and gracious, long-suffering, and abundant in goodness and truth."

His Face : "Turn Thee unto me, and be gracious unto me ; for I am alone and afflicted."

Unto thee : "Unto Thee, O Lord, do I lift up my soul."

And be gracious unto thee : "Behold, as the eyes of servants look unto the hand of their masters, and the eyes of a maiden to the hand of her mistress, so our eyes wait upon the Lord our God, until He be gracious unto us."

3. *May He lift up :* "He shall receive a blessing from the Lord, and righteousness from the God of his salvation, and find grace and good understanding in the eyes of God and man."

The Lord : "O Lord, have mercy on us ; we have trusted in Thee : be Thou our strength every morning ; our salvation in the time of trouble."

His Face : "O Lord, hide not Thy face from me : in the day of my distress incline Thine ear unto me."

Unto thee : "Unto Thee do I lift up mine eyes, O Thou who dwellest in the heavens."

And give : "And they shall put My Name upon the children of Israel, and I will bless them."

Thee: "Thine, O Lord, is the greatness, and the power, and the glory, and the victory, and the majesty; for all that is in the heaven and in the earth is Thine: Thine is the kingdom, O Lord, and Thou art exalted as Supreme above all."

Peace: " Peace to him that is afar off, and to him that is near, saith the Lord, and I will heal him."

END OF THE GLOSSARY.

THE TARGUM OF ONKELOS

ON

THE BOOK VAIYIKRA

OR

LEVITICUS.

SECTION OF THE LAW XXIV.

VAIYIKRA

I. AND the Lord called unto Mosheh, and the Lord spake with him from the tabernacle of ordinance, saying: Speak with the sons of Israel, and say to them: When one of you will bring an offering before the Lord of the cattle, of oxen or of sheep, you shall offer your oblations. If his oblation be a burnt offering of the oxen, (it shall be) a male, unblemished; he shall offer him at the door of the tabernacle of ordinance; he shall offer him for acceptance before the Lord. And he shall lay his hand upon the head of the burnt offering, that it may be acceptable for him to propitiate on his behalf. And he shall sacrifice the young bullock before the Lord; and the sons of Aharon the priest shall bring the blood, and sprinkle the blood round about upon the altar which is at the door of the tabernacle of ordinance. And he shall take away (the skin) of the burnt offering, and divide it, by its members. And the sons of Aharon the priest shall put fire upon the altar, and lay the wood in order upon the fire. And the priests, the sons of Aharon, shall arrange the limbs and the head and the fat

on the wood upon the fire which is on the altar. But
his inwards and his legs he shall wash with water; and
the priest shall burn the whole upon the altar an entire
burnt offering, an oblation to be received with acceptance before the Lord.

And if his oblation be from the flock, of the sheep or
the young of the goats for a burnt offering, he shall
bring a perfect male. And he shall sacrifice him at the
north side of the altar before the Lord; and the priests
the sons of Aharon shall sprinkle his blood round about
upon the altar. And he shall divide him by his members, and his head and his feet; and the priest shall lay
them upon the wood which is on the fire upon the altar.
But the inwards and the legs he shall wash with water,
and the priest shall bring the whole and burn (it) upon
the altar: it is a whole burnt offering, an oblation to be
received with acceptance before the Lord.

But if the burnt offering of his oblation before the
Lord be from fowl, he shall bring his oblation from the
turtles or the young of a pigeon. And the priest shall
offer it upon the altar, and wring off its head, and burn
upon the altar, and pour its blood by the side of the
altar: and he shall remove its crop with its food, and
throw it on the east side of the altar, at the place where
they empty the ashes. And he shall cleave it through
its wings, (but) divide (it) not, and the priest shall burn
it at the altar upon the wood that is on the fire: it is a
burnt offering, an oblation that shall be received with
acceptance before the Lord.

II. But if a man bring an oblation of a mincha[6] before the Lord, his oblation shall be of meal, and he shall
pour oil upon it, and put frankincense thereon, and
bring it to the priests the sons of Aharon; and the
priest shall take from it his handful of the meal with

---

[6] *Mincha*, a bloodless oblation.

---

its oil, and all its frankincense, and burn the memorial of
it at the altar; an oblation to be received with favour
before the Lord. And that which remaineth of the
mincha shall be Aharon's and his sons'; it is most holy
among the oblations of the Lord. And when thou
bringest the oblation of a mincha baked in the oven, it
shall be of meal cake unleavened, mingled with oil, with
unleavened wafers anointed with oil. And if the mincha be (prepared) in a pan, thy oblation shall be of meal
mingled with oil; unleavened shall it be. And thou
shalt break it in pieces, and pour oil thereon; it is a
mincha. But if thy oblation be a mincha from the gridiron, thou shalt make it of meal with oil. And the mincha which is made of these thou shalt bring before the
Lord, and present it to the priest, and he will offer it at
the altar. And the priest shall separate its memorial
from the mincha, and burn upon the altar an oblation
to be received with favour before the Lord. And that
which remaineth of the mincha shall be Aharon's and
his sons': it is most holy among the oblations of the
Lord. No mincha which you offer before the Lord may
be made with leaven; for no leaven or honey shall you
burn with any oblation before the Lord. In the oblation of first fruits you may offer them before the Lord,
but not burn them at the altar, that they may be accepted
with favour. And every offering of thy mincha thou
shalt salt with salt; and thou mayest not withhold the
salt of the covenant of thy God from upon thy mincha;
upon every oblation thou shalt offer salt. And when
thou offerest the mincha of first fruits before the Lord,
green ears[7] dried with fire, broken and soft, shalt thou
offer as the mincha of thy first fruits. And thou shalt
put oil on it, and lay frankincense thereon: it is a mincha; and the priest shall burn its memorial of its broken

[7] Samaritan Vers, "without the husk."

grain and of its oil with all the frankincense, an oblation before the Lord.

III. And if his oblation be a victim of the sanctified things;[8] if from oxen, whether male or female, he shall offer it perfect before the Lord. And he shall lay his hand upon the head of his oblation at the door of the tabernacle of ordinance; and the priests the sons of Aharon shall sprinkle the blood round about upon the altar. And of the oblation of the sacred victim the fat that covereth the inwards, even all the fat that is upon the inwards, and the two kidneys and the fat which is upon them on the sides, and the caul that is upon the liver with the kidneys, he shall remove. And the sons of Aharon shall burn it at the altar, with the burnt offering which is on the wood upon the fire, an oblation[9] to be received with grace before the Lord. But if his oblation of a consecrated victim before the Lord be from the flock, whether male or female, he shall offer it perfect. If his oblation be a lamb, he shall present it before the Lord, and lay his hand upon the head of his oblation, and slay it before the tabernacle of ordinance; and the sons of Aharon shall sprinkle its blood upon the altar round about. And of his oblation of the consecrated victim before the Lord, its fat, the entire tail close by the backbone, he shall remove; the fat which covereth the inwards, even all the fat which is upon the inwards, and the two kidneys and the fat which is upon them upon the sides, and the caul that is over the liver, with the kidneys, he shall take away; and the priest shall burn it at the altar; it is the meat (*lechem*, bread) of an oblation before the Lord.

But if his oblation be from the young goats, he shall

---

[8] *Kedeshaia*, the Chaldee term for the Hebrew *shelamim* rendered in the English Bible, " peace offerings."

[9] Sam. Vers., "a sweet-smelling oblation."

present it before the Lord, and lay his hand upon its head, and slay it before the tabernacle of ordinance; and the sons of Aharon shall sprinkle its blood upon the altar round about. And of his oblation he shall offer as an oblation before the Lord the fat which covereth the inwards, and all the fat which is upon the inwards, and the two kidneys, and the fat which is upon them on the sides; but the caul that is over the liver with the kidneys he shall take away. And the priest shall burn them at the altar: it is the meat of an oblation to be received with acceptance; all the fat (shall be offered) before the Lord. It is an everlasting statute unto your generations, and in all your dwellings, that neither the fat nor the blood shall be eaten.

IV. And the Lord spake with Mosheh, saying: Speak with the sons of Israel, saying: When a man sinneth through ignorance of any of the precepts of the Lord, as to that which should not be done, and acteth contrary to one of them: if the high priest sin after the manner of the people's sin, let him bring before the Lord for the sin that he hath sinned a young bullock without blemish for his sin. And he shall bring the bullock to the door of the tabernacle of ordinance before the Lord, and lay his hand upon the bullock's head, and slay the bullock before the Lord. And the high priest shall take of the blood of the bullock and carry it into the tabernacle of ordinance. And the priest shall dip his finger in the blood, and sprinkle (some) of the blood seven times in the presence of the Lord before the veil of the sanctuary. And the priest shall put some of the blood upon the horns of the altar of sweet incense before the Lord in the tabernacle of ordinance, and all the (remaining) blood of the bullock he shall pour out at the foundation of the altar of burnt sacrifice which is at the door of the tabernacle of ordinance. And all the fat of the bullock

of the sin offering he shall separate from it; the fat
which covereth the inwards, and all the fat which is upon
the inwards, and the two kidneys, and the fat which is
upon them that is by the flanks; and the caul that is
upon the liver, together with the kidneys, he shall remove, as it was separated from the bullock of the consecrated victims, and the priest shall offer it upon the
altar of burnt sacrifice. But the skin of the bullock and
all his flesh, with his head, and with his legs, and his
inwards, and his food, he shall carry forth,[1] even the
whole bullock, without the camp unto a clean place, to a
place for the pouring out of ashes, and burn him upon
wood in the fire; at the place for the pouring out of
ashes shall he be burned.

And if the whole congregation (*kenishta*) of Israel
shall mistake, and the thing be hid from the eyes of the
assembly, (*kehala*), and they shall have done (somewhat
against) one of all the commandments of the Lord which
it is not right to do, and have become guilty; when the
sin that they have sinned is known, the assembly shall
offer a young bullock for a sin offering, and bring him
before the tabernacle of ordinance. And the elders of
the congregation shall lay their hands upon the head of
the bullock in the presence of the Lord, and kill the
bullock before the Lord. And the high priest shall
bring of the blood of the bullock into the tabernacle of
ordinance; and the priest shall dip his finger in the
blood, and sprinkle seven times in the presence of the
Lord before the veil. And some of the blood he shall
put upon the horns of the altar that is before the Lord
in the tabernacle of ordinance, and all (the rest of the)
blood he shall pour out at the foundation of the altar of
burnt sacrifice which is at the door of the tabernacle of
ordinance. And all the fat he shall separate from him,

---

[1] Heb. text, *vehotsi*, " he shall cause to be carried forth."

and sacrifice at the altar. And he shall do with the
bullock as he did with the bullock of the sin offering, so
shall he do with him; and the priest shall atone for
them, and it shall be forgiven them. And he shall carry
forth [2] the bullock without the camp, and burn him as
he burned the former bullock : it is a sin offering for
the congregation.

Should a ruler sin and do (contrary to) any of the
commandments of the Lord his God what is not right
to do, through ignorance, and be guilty; when his sin
becomes known to him in what he hath transgressed, he
shall bring his oblation, a kid of the goats, a male,
unblemished ; and he shall lay his hand upon the head
of the goat, and kill him at the place where the burnt
sacrifice is slain before the Lord ; it is a sin offering.
And the priest shall take of the blood of the sin offering
with his finger, and put it upon the horns of the altar of
burnt sacrifice, and pour out the blood at the foundation of
the altar of burnt sacrifice. And he shall burn all the
fat at the altar, as the fat of the sanctified oblation (is
burned) ; and the priest shall atone on his behalf for his
sin, and it shall be forgiven him.

And if one of the people of the land inadvertently sin in
doing contrary to any of the commandments of the Lord
what is not right to do, and become guilty ; when his sin
is known to him, in what he hath sinned, he shall bring
his oblation, a female kid of the goats, unblemished, for
the sin that he hath sinned. And he shall lay his hand
on the head of the sin offering, and kill the sin offering
at the place of burnt sacrifice ; and the priest shall take of
the blood with his finger, and put it upon the horns of the
altar of burnt offering, and pour out all the blood at the
foundation of the altar. And he shall remove all the fat,
as he took away the fat from the consecrated offerings, and

[2] See note on p. 82.

the priest shall burn it at the altar, to be received with
acceptance before the Lord ; and the priest shall atone
for him, and it shall be forgiven him. But if he present
a lamb for his sin offering, he shall bring a female
unblemished, and lay his hand upon the head of the
sin offering, and kill the sin offering at the place where
the burnt sacrifice is killed.   And the priest shall take
of the blood of the sin offering with his finger, and put it
upon the horns of the altar of burnt sacrifice, and pour
out all the blood at the foundation of the altar. And he
shall remove all the fat, as he removed the fat of the
lamb of the sanctified oblations, and the priest shall burn
it at the altar with the oblations of the Lord ; and the
priest shall atone for him, for the sin that he hath
sinned, and it shall be forgiven him.

V. And if a man sin, and (one) hear the voice (which
demands) swearing that he is a witness, or that he hath
seen or known, if he will not show it, he shall bear his
sin.   Or if a man shall have touched anything unclean,
whether the carcase of an unclean beast, or the carcase
of unclean cattle, or the carcase of an unclean reptile,
and it be hidden from him, he shall be defiled and
guilty.   Or if he shall touch the uncleanness of a man,
any uncleanness which defileth him, and it be hidden
from him ; but (afterwards) becometh aware of it and is
guilty ;—or if a man swear, declaring with his lips, for
evil or for good, according to whatever the man shall
declare by oath, and (the truth) be hidden from him,
and he (afterwards) have knowledge thereof, he is
guilty of one of these.   And it shall be that when (he
knoweth that) he is guilty in one of these (things) he
shall confess that he hath sinned thereby ; and shall
bring his sin offering before the Lord for the sin that
he hath sinned ; a she-lamb from the flock, or a kid of
the goats, for a sin offering ; and the priest shall atone

for him and for his sin. But if his hands be not sufficient to offer a lamb, let him bring for the sin that he
hath sinned two turtle doves, or two young pigeons
before the Lord, one for the sin offering, and one for the
burnt sacrifice. And he shall bring them to the priest,
and he shall offer the sin offering first, and wring off its
head near to the spine, but he shall not divide (the
bird). And he shall sprinkle the blood of the sin offering upon the side (wall) of the altar, and pour out the
remainder of the blood at the base of the altar; it is a
sin offering. And the second he shall make a burnt
sacrifice, according to the proper (rite); and the priest
shall make atonement for the sin that he hath sinned,
and it shall be forgiven him. But if (neither) two turtle doves nor a pair of young pigeons pertain to him, he
shall bring, as his oblation for the sin that he hath
sinned, the tenth of three sein of flour for a sin offering;
he shall not put oil upon it, nor put frankincense upon
it, for it is a sin offering. And he shall bring it to the
priest, and the priest shall take a handful of it as the
memorial thereof, and burn it at the altar with the
oblations of the Lord: it is a sin offering. And the
priest shall make atonement for him, for the sin that he
hath sinned in any one of these (things), and it shall be
forgiven him: and to the priest it shall be, as the
mincha.

And the Lord spake with Mosheh, saying: When a
man hath indeed falsified, but hath sinned inadvertently
concerning things consecrated to the Lord, he shall
bring for his trespass offering before the Lord a ram
without blemish from the flock by its value in silver
shekels, in the shekel of the sanctuary, for a trespass
offering. And that which he had defaulted of the holy
thing he shall make good, and add a fifth thereupon, and
give it to the priest; and the priest shall make atone-

ment for him with the ram of the trespass offering, and
it shall be forgiven him.

And if a man sin and do against any of the commandments of the Lord that which is not right to do,
and know not, and sin, he shall bear his sin. But he
shall bring a lamb unblemished from the flock according to the estimation for a trespass offering (or according to the estimation of the trespass) unto the priest;
and the priest shall atone for his error which he hath
committed unwittingly, and it shall be forgiven him.
It is a trespass offering for the sin that he hath sinned;
he shall offer the trespass offering before the Lord.

VI. And the Lord spake with Mosheh, saying: If a
man sin and falsify with falsehood [3] before the Lord, and
deal falsely with his neighbour in a thing deposited, or
in fellowship of hands, or by rapine or violence against
his neighbour; or if he have found that which had been
lost and deny it, and swear falsely, by any one of all
these which a man doeth and sinneth therein; it shall
be that when he hath (so) transgressed and become
guilty, he shall return what he hath robbed by robbery,
or taken away by violence, or the deposit which was
deposited with him, or the lost thing that he had found:
or all that about which he had sworn falsely, he shall
make it good in the capital, and add one fifth thereon;
unto him to whom it belongeth shall he give it on the
day of his (offering for) guilt. And the trespass offering that he shall bring before the Lord (must be) a ram
unblemished from the flock according to the estimation
of the trespass, unto the priest. And the priest shall
make atonement for him before the Lord, and it shall be
forgiven him for any one of all (these) in which he may
have acted to be guilty thereby.[4]

[3] Sam. Vers., " defraud with falsehood."
[4] May have injured with guilt.

SECTION XXV.

VAIYIKRA TSAV.

AND the Lord spake with Mosheh, saying: Instruct
Aharon and his sons, saying: This is the law of the
Burnt Offering. It is burnt offering, because burned
upon the altar all night until morning, and the fire of
the altar shall be burning in it. And the priest shall
dress himself with vestments of linen, and wear drawers
of linen upon his flesh; and he shall separate the ashes
which the fire hath consumed with the burnt offering
upon the altar, and set them beside the altar. And he
shall take off his vestments, and dress himself with other
garments, and carry forth the ashes without the camp
unto a clean place. But the fire upon the altar shall be
burning on it, and never be extinguished; and the
priest shall burn wood on it from morning to morning, and lay the burnt offering in order upon it, and
burn upon it the fat of the sanctified oblations. The
fire shall be ever burning on the altar, it shall not be
extinguished.

And this is the law of the Mincha which the sons of
Aharon shall offer in the presence of the Lord before
the altar. And he shall separate therefrom his handful
of the flour of the mincha and of its oil, and all the
frankincense that is upon the mincha, and burn it at the
altar as its memorial to be accepted with favour before
the Lord. And the remainder of it may Aharon and
his sons eat, unleavened shall it be eaten in the holy
place, in the court of the tabernacle of ordinance shall
they eat it. It shall not be baked with leaven. I have
given it as their portion of my oblations; it is most
sacred, as the sin offering and as the trespass offering.
All the males of the children of Aharon may eat it.

(This) is an everlasting statute [5] for your generations concerning the oblations of the Lord: every one who toucheth them shall be holy.

And the Lord spake with Mosheh, saying, This is the oblation of Aharon and his sons which they shall present before the Lord on the day when they anoint him. The tenth of three seahs of flour for a mincha perpetually, a half in the morning, and a half at eventide. It shall be made in a pan with oil; while soft it shall be brought a baken mincha offered in pieces [6] to be accepted with favour before the Lord. And of his sons, the priest who shall be anointed in his stead shall perform it. (This is) an everlasting statute before the Lord: it shall be burned entirely, and every mincha of the priest shall be entirely (burned); it is not to be eaten.

And the Lord spake with Mosheh, saying: Speak with Aharon and with his sons, saying, This is the law of the sin offering: In the place where the burnt offering is killed, there shall the sin offering be killed before the Lord; it is most sacred. The priest who maketh atonement with its blood shall eat it; in the holy place it shall be eaten, in the court of the tabernacle of ordinance. Every one who toucheth the flesh thereof must be holy. And if he drop some of its blood upon a vestment, that which is bedropped shall be purified in the holy place. But the earthen vessel in which it was sodden shall be broken; and if it be sodden in a vessel of brass, (that) shall be scoured and washed in water. Any man of the priests may eat thereof: it is most sacred. But no sin offering whose blood is brought into the tabernacle of ordinance to make atonement in the sanctuary may be eaten, but shall be burned with fire.

[5] Sam Vers, " It is an everlasting portion "
[6] Sam. Vers., "thou shalt divide it in pieces "

VII. And this is the law of the Trespass Offering, it
is most holy.   In the place where they kill the burnt
offering, there shall they kill the trespass offering and
sprinkle its blood round about; and all the fat of it shall
be offered, with the tail and the fat which covereth the
inwards. And the two kidneys and the fat which is upon
them, upon the inwards, and the caul that is upon the liver,
with the kidneys, he shall take away.   And the priest
shall burn them at the altar, an oblation before the
Lord; it is a trespass offering.   Every man of the priests
may eat thereof in the holy place; it is most sacred.
As the sin offering, so the trespass offering; they have
one law; to the priest who maketh atonement therewith
shall it be.   And when the priest offereth a man's burnt
sacrifice, the skin of the sacrifice that the priest offereth
shall be his.   And every mincha that is baken in the
oven, or made in the pan, or upon the baking pan, to
the priest who offereth it shall it belong.   And every
mincha sprinkled with oil, and that which is not sprinkled,
shall belong to all the sons of Aharon, to the one man
as to his brother.

And this is the law of the Sanctified Oblations [7] which
he shall offer before the Lord.   If he present it as a
thanksgiving, he shall offer as the sacrifice of thanksgiving unleavened cakes sprinkled with oil, and unleavened wafers anointed with oil, and baken biscuits of
flour sprinkled with oil.   With the cakes he may offer
his oblation of leavened bread for his sanctified oblation
of thanksgiving.   And of it he shall offer one of all the
separated oblations before the Lord: (the remainder)
shall belong to the priest who sprinkleth the blood of
the sanctified oblations.   And the flesh of his consecrated thank offering shall be eaten on the day that it is
offered, none of it shall be covered over till the morning.

[7] Peace offerings

But if the offering of his oblation be a vow, or a voluntary gift, it may be eaten (partly) on the day that his sacrifice is offered, and that which remaineth of it may be eaten on the day after it; but what remaineth of the flesh of the sacrifice on the third day shall be burned with fire. If the flesh of his consecrated sacrifice be indeed eaten on the third day, it shall not be accepted from him who offered it, neither shall it be reckoned to him; it is an abomination,[8] and the man who ate of it shall bear his sin. And if flesh that is consecrated touch any thing unclean, it shall not be eaten, but be burned with fire. Every one who is clean by sanctification to eat the consecrated flesh may eat the flesh that is consecrated. But the man who eateth of the flesh of sacrifices consecrated before the Lord with his uncleanness upon him, that man shall be destroyed from his people. And the man who toucheth any thing unclean, whether the uncleanness of man or the uncleanness of beast, or of any unclean reptile, and eateth of the flesh of sacrifices consecrated before the Lord, that man shall perish from his people.

And the Lord spake with Mosheh, saying: Speak with the sons of Israel, saying: You may not eat the fat of the ox or sheep or goat. But the fat of a dead carcase and the fat of an animal torn by a wild beast may be used in any manner of work, but of it you shall not eat. For whosoever eateth the fat of an animal that they offer as an oblation before the Lord, the man who eateth shall perish from his people. Nor in any of your habitations may you eat the blood of fowl or of beast: every man who eateth any kind of blood, that man shall be destroyed[9] from his people.

---

[8] Sam. Vers , " a rejected thing."

[9] Or, "shall cease from." Sam Vers., "shall be rooted out." Heb. text, "be cut off from," "be excommunicated."

And the Lord spake with Mosheh, saying : Speak
with the sons of Israel, saying : Whosoever offereth his
sanctified victim before the Lord, let him bring the
oblation of his sanctified victim (himself) before the Lord,
his own hands shall bring the oblations of the Lord :
let him bring the fat with the breast, that the breast may
be lifted up an uplifting before the Lord.   And the
priest shall burn the fat at the altar ; but the breast
shall be for Aharon and his sons.   And the right shoulder (also) of your sanctified victims you shall give for
a separation unto the priest.   He of Aharon's sons who
offereth the blood and the fat of the sanctified victims
shall have the right shoulder for a portion.   For the
uplifted breast and the shoulder of separation of the
sacrifices of the Beni Israel I have given to Aharon
the priest and to his sons by an everlasting statute [1]
from the sons of Israel.

This is the anointing of Aharon, and the anointing of
his sons and of the Lord's oblations, in the day that they
present them to minister before the Lord, which the
Lord commanded to give them in the day that they consecrate them from the sons of Israel, an everlasting
statute unto your generations.   This is the law of the
burnt offering, of the mincha, and of the sin-offering,
and of the trespass offering, and of the oblation of the
sanctified victims which the Lord commanded Mosheh
in Mount Sinai, on the day when he commanded the
sons of Israel to offer their oblations before the Lord in
the wilderness of Sinai.

VIII. And the Lord spake with Mosheh, saying :
Bring Aharon near, and his sons with him, with the
vestments, and the oil of consecration, and the bullock
for the sin offering, and the two rams, and the basket of
unleavened (cakes) ; and let all the congregation gather

[1] Sam. Vers., " for a perpetual portion."

together at the gate of the tabernacle of ordinance.   And
Mosheh did as the Lord commanded him, and the congregation was gathered together at the gate of the tabernacle of ordinance.   And Mosheh said to the congregation, This is the thing which the Lord hath commanded
to be done.

And Mosheh brought Aharon and his sons near, and
washed them with water; and he put upon him the vestment, and girded him with the girdle, and dressed him
with the robe, and set upon him the ephod, and bound
him with the band of the ephod, and ordained him therewith; and set upon him the breastplate, and put in the
breastplate the uraia and the thummaia.   And he set the
mitre upon his head, and placed on the mitre, on the
forehead of his face, the plate of gold, the diadem of
Holiness, as the Lord had commanded Mosheh.

And Mosheh took the consecrating oil, and anointed
the tabernacle and all that was in it, and sanctified them.
And he sprinkled of it upon the altar seven times, and
anointed the altar and all its vessels, and the laver and
its base, to sanctify them.   And he poured the oil of
consecration upon Aharon's head, and anointed him to
consecrate him.

And Mosheh brought the sons of Aharon near, and
dressed them in the vestments, and girded them with
girdles, and appointed them with mitres, as the Lord
had commanded Mosheh.   And he brought the bullock
near for the sin offering, and Aharon and his sons laid
their hands upon the head of the bullock which was the
sin offering.   And Mosheh took the blood, and put it
upon the horns of the altar round about, with his finger,
and purified the altar, and the blood he poured out at
the base of the altar, and consecrated it to make atonement upon it.   And he took all the fat which was upon
the inwards, and the caul of the liver, and the two

kidneys with their fat; and Mosheh burned them at the
altar. But the bullock, with his skin, and his flesh, and
his food, he burned with fire without the camp, as the
Lord commanded Mosheh. And he brought the ram
for the burnt offering, and Aharon and his sons laid
their hands upon the head of the ram, and he killed it,
and Mosheh sprinkled the blood upon the altar round
about. And the ram he divided by his members; and
Mosheh burned the head and the members with the fat.
And the inwards and the legs he washed with water:
and Mosheh burned all the ram at the altar: it was a
whole burnt offering to be received with acceptance, an
oblation before the Lord, as the Lord had commanded
Mosheh. And he brought the second ram of the oblations; [2] and Aharon and his sons laid their hands on the
head of the ram, and he killed it; and Mosheh took of
its blood, and put it upon the tip of Aharon's right ear,
and upon the thumb of his right hand, and upon the
toe of his right foot. And he brought the sons of
Aharon, and Mosheh put of the blood upon the tip of
their right ear, and upon the finger of their right hand,
and upon the toe of their right foot; and Mosheh
sprinkled the blood upon the altar round about. And he
took the fat and the tail, and all the fat which is upon
the inwards, and the caul of the liver, and the two kidneys
and their fat, and the right shoulder: and from the
basket of unleavened cakes that was before the Lord he
took one unleavened cake, and one cake of bread (anointed
with) oil, and one wafer, and set them upon the fat and
upon the right shoulder, and put the whole upon Aharon's
hands and upon the hands of his sons, and uplifted them,
an elevation before the Lord. And Mosheh took them
from off their hands, and burned (them) at the altar upon
the burnt offering: they were offerings to be received

---

[2] Sam. Vers., "of the completion."

with acceptance, an oblation before the Lord. And Mosheh took the breast, and uplifted it, an elevation before the Lord: of the ram of the oblations it was the portion of Mosheh, as the Lord had commanded Mosheh. And Mosheh took of the oil of consecration, and of the blood that was upon the altar, and sprinkled upon Aharon, upon his vestments, and upon his sons, and upon his sons' vestments with him, [and sanctified Aharon and his garments, and his sons and his sons' garments with him.][3]

And Mosheh spake to Aharon and to his sons: Boil the flesh at the gate of the tabernacle of ordinance, and eat it there with the bread which is in the basket of oblations, as I was commanded, saying, Aharon and his sons shall eat it. And that which remaineth of the flesh and of the bread, you shall burn in the fire. And from the door of the tabernacle of ordinance ye shall not go forth (for) seven days, until the day that the days of your oblation be completed; for seven days shall your oblations be offered, as hath been done this day, (as) the Lord commanded to be done to make atonement for you. And at the door of the tabernacle of ordinance ye shall dwell seven days and nights, and watch the watches of the Word of the Lord, that you die not; for so am I commanded. And Aharon and his sons did all the things which the Lord had commanded by the hand of Mosheh.

SECTION XXVI.
SHEMINI.

IX. AND on the eighth day Mosheh called Aharon and his sons and the elders of Israel. And he said unto Aharon, Take to thee a calf, a young bullock from the

_____

[3] The clause in brackets is not found in some copies.

herd, for a sin offering, and a ram for a burnt offering
unblemished, and offer before the Lord. And with the
sons of Israel he spake, saying, Take a kid of the goats
for a sin offering, and a calf, and a lamb of the year,
unblemished, for a burnt offering; and a bullock and a
ram for a hallowed offering, to sacrifice before the Lord;
and a mincha of flour sprinkled with oil: for this day
will the glory of the Lord be revealed to you.

And what Mosheh had commanded they brought
before the tabernacle of ordinance, and all the congregation approached and stood before the Lord. And Mosheh
said, This is the thing that the Lord hath commanded
to be done, and the glory of the Lord shall be revealed
to you.

And Mosheh said to Aharon, Approach the altar, and
make thy sin offering and thy burnt sacrifice, and make
atonement for thyself and for the people, and perform
the oblation of the people, and make atonement for them,
as the Lord commanded. And Aharon drew near to
the altar, and slew the calf for the sin offering for himself.
And the sons of Aharon brought the blood to him, and
he dipped his finger in the blood, and put it upon the
horns of the altar, and poured out the blood at the base
of the altar. But the fat, and the kidneys, and the caul
of the liver of the sin offering he burned at the altar, as
the Lord commanded Mosheh. And the flesh and the
skin he burned in the fire without the camp.

And he killed the whole burnt offering; and the sons
of Aharon brought the blood to him, and he sprinkled it
upon the altar round about. And they brought to him
the whole burnt offering by its members with the head,
and he burned upon the altar. And he washed the
inwards and the legs, and burned with the offering at
the altar.

And he brought the oblation of the people, and took

the kid for the sin offering of the people, and killed it,
and made atonement with its blood, as before. And he
brought the whole burnt offering, and performed in the
manner proper. And he took the mincha, and filled his
hand with it, and burned it upon the altar beside the
morning sacrifice. And he slew the bullock and the
ram for the hallowed oblations of the people; and the
sons of Aharon brought the blood to him, and he sprinkled
the blood round about. Also the fats of the bullock
and of the ram, the tail, and the covering of the inwards,
with the kidneys, and the caul of the liver; and they
placed the fats upon the breast, and burned the fats at
the altar. And the breast with the right shoulder
Aharon uplifted, an elevation before the Lord, as the
Lord commanded Mosheh.

And Aharon lifted up his hands over (to) the people
and blessed them, and came down from performing the
sin offering, and the burnt sacrifice, and the hallowed
oblations. And Mosheh and Aharon entered the tabernacle of ordinance, and came forth and blessed the
people; and the glory of the Lord was revealed unto all
the people: and fire came forth from before the Lord,
and consumed upon the altar the burnt sacrifice and
the fats and all the people saw, and gave praise, and
fell upon their faces.

X. But the sons of Aharon, Nadab and Abihu, took
each man his censer and put fire in them, and put sweet
incense upon it, and offered (or brought) before the
Lord strange fire which He had not commanded them.
And fire came out from before the Lord and consumed
them, and they died before the Lord.

And Mosheh said unto Aharon, This is that which the
Lord spake, saying, In them who approach Me I will be
sanctified, and in the face of all the people will I be
glorified. And Aharon was silent.

And Mosheh called to Mishael and to Elzaphan, the sons of Uzziel the uncle of Aharon, and said to them, Come nigh, and carry your brethren from before the sanctuary without the camp. And they came nigh, and carried them in their vestments out of the camp, as Mosheh had spoken.

And Mosheh said to Aharon and to Elazar and to Ithamar his sons, Make not bare your heads, nor rend your garments, lest you die, and wrath be upon all the congregation; but let your brethren and all the house of Israel bewail the burning which the Lord hath kindled; and go not forth from the door of the tabernacle of ordinance, lest you die; for the anointing oil of the Lord [4] is upon you. And they did according to the word of Mosheh.

And the Lord spake unto Aharon, saying: Drink not wine nor strong drink, neither thou nor thy sons with thee, when you enter into the tabernacle of ordinance, that you die not. It is an everlasting statute unto your generations, for the distinguishment between the holy and the common, and between the unclean and the clean; and that you may teach the sons of Israel all the statutes which the Lord hath spoken to them through Mosheh.

And Mosheh spake with Aharon and with Elazar and with Ithamar his sons who were left: Take the mincha which remaineth of the oblations of the Lord, and eat it unleavened at the side of the altar, because it is most holy. It shall be eaten in the holy place; for it is thy portion, and the portion of thy sons of the oblations of the Lord; for so have I been commanded. But the breast of the uplifting and the shoulder of the separation you may eat on (any) clean place, and thy sons and thy daughters with thee; for it is thy portion, and the portion of thy sons, which hath been given of the hallowed

---

[4] Sam. Vers., "the oil of excellency."

sacrifices of the children of Israel. The shoulder of the
separation and the breast of the uplifting they will bring
with the oblation of the fat things to uplift, an elevation
before the Lord: and they shall be thine and thy sons'
with thee by an everlasting statute, as the Lord hath
commanded.

But Mosheh made inquiry[5] for the goat of the sin
offering; and, behold, it had been burned; and he was
angry with Elazar and Ithamar the sons of Aharon who
were left, saying: Why have you not eaten of the sin
offering in the holy place, because it is most holy; and
He hath delivered it unto you for pardoning mercy upon
the sin of the congregation to make atonement for them
before the Lord? Behold, the blood of it was not
brought in within the sanctuary: eating you should have
eaten it within the holy (precinct), as I had commanded.
And Aharon said to Mosheh, Behold, this day they have
brought their sin offering and their burnt offering before
the Lord; but such griefs as these having come upon
me, if I had eaten of the sin offering to-day, would it
have been right before the Lord? And Mosheh heard,
and it was pleasing in his eyes. [6]

XI. And the Lord spake with Mosheh and to Aharon,
saying to them: Speak with the children of Israel, saying: These are the animals which you may eat of all the
beasts which are upon the earth. Every one that parteth
the sole and divideth the paw (or hoof) and that
bringeth up the cud among cattle, that you may eat.
But these you shall not eat,—of them that bring up the
cud or of them that divide the hoof—the camel, because
he bringeth up the cud, but divideth not his hoof, he is
unclean to you. And the coney, because he bringeth
up the cud, but doth not divide the hoof, is unclean to

---

[5] " Requiring, required."

[6] Compare the Palestinian Targum on the place.

you. And the hare, because he bringeth up the cud, but the hoof divideth not, shall be unclean to you. And the swine, because he parteth the sole, and divideth the hoof, but cheweth not the cud, he shall be unclean to you. You shall neither eat their flesh nor touch their carcases; they are unclean to you.

And these you may eat of all that are in the waters; every one that hath fins and scales in the waters, in the seas, and in the rivers, of them you may eat. But any one that hath not (both) fins and scales in the seas and in the rivers; every (such) reptile of the waters, and every living animal in the waters, shall be unto you an abomination. An abomination shall they be to you; of their flesh you shall not eat, and their carcases you shall abhor; whatsoever hath not (both) fins and scales in the waters is to be an abomination to you.

And these shall you hold in abomination among the birds; you shall not eat them, they are an abomination: the eagle, and the sea eagle, and the osprey, and the kite, and the vulture, after his kind; and every raven after his kind; and the ostrich, and the night bird, and the gull, and the hawk, after his kind; and the owl, and the diver for fish, and the ibis, and the swan, and the green bird, and the stork, and the pica, after his kind, and the moorcock, and the bat. Every winged thing that creepeth, (or) walketh upon four,[7] is an abomination to you. Yet these you may eat, of every creeping thing that flieth, that walketh upon four which hath joints above its feet wherewith to leap upon the ground. Of such as these you may eat, the locust after his kind, and the bald locust, and the serpent-killer after his kind, and the grasshopper after his kind;[8] but every

[7] Animals with wings, having more than two feet, as insects.—MEN-DELSSOHN.

[8] The names in the Hebrew text are *arbeh, saleam, chargol,* and *chagab.* Onkelos renders them by *goba, rashona, chargola,* and *chagaba.* They

other creeping thing that flieth having four feet is to be
an abomination to you. And by these you will be unclean; every one who toucheth their carcases shall be
unclean until the evening. And whosoever carrieth a
carcase of them, shall wash his clothes and be unclean
until the evening; every beast that divideth the hoof.
but is not cloven-footed, and that bringeth not up the
cud, is to be unclean to you; whosoever toucheth them
shall be unclean. And every (animal) that goeth upon
its paws, of all beasts that go upon four, shall be unclean
to you; whoever toucheth their carcases shall be unclean
until the evening. And whoever carrieth their carcase
shall wash his clothes and be unclean until the evening;
to you they are unclean.

And these shall be to you unclean among the reptiles
which creep upon the ground;—the weasel, and the
mouse, and the crocodile after his kind, and the field
mouse (or ferret,) and the chameleon, and the newt, and
the lizard, and the mole. These are unclean to you of
all that creep; every one who toucheth them in their
dead state shall be unclean until evening. And upon
whatever any of them may fall in their dead state it
shall be unclean; whether a vessel of wood, or raiment,
or skin, or sack, everything whatever in which work is
done, must be put into water, and it shall be unclean
until the evening, and must be purified. And whatever
earthen vessel into which any of them may fall, all that
is within (it) is polluted, and you shall break it. Any
food for eating, upon which water (from such vessel) is
poured, shall be unclean, and all liquor which was for

refer probably to four of the ten species of locusts, though it seems
impossible to identify them specifically The Mishna gives four marks
by which a clean locust may be known: "Of locusts, all the kinds are
clean which have four feet, four wings, and four leaping legs, and whose
wings cover the greatest part of the body "—*Cholin*, c. 3.

drinking in any (such) vessel shall be unclean. And anything upon which a part of their dead bodies may have fallen shall be unclean; oven or cooking pan, they shall be broken, they are unclean and shall be unclean to you. Nevertheless, a fountain or a pit, the place of a collection of waters, (into which they may have fallen,) shall be clean; but he who toucheth their dead bodies shall be unclean. And if a part of their carcase fall upon any seeding seed which is to be sown, it is clean; but if water be put upon the seed, and a part of their carcase fall thereupon, it is unclean to you.

And if any one of the cattle of which you eat die, whosoever toucheth its carcase shall be unclean until the evening. And he who eateth of its carcase shall wash his clothes, and be unclean until the evening. And he who may carry its carcase shall wash his clothes, and be unclean until the evening. And every reptile that creepeth upon the ground is abominable, it shall not be eaten. Whatsoever goeth upon its belly, and whatever goeth upon four, anything that hath many feet, and every reptile that creepeth upon the ground, you shall not eat, for they are an abomination.[9] Ye shall not make yourselves abominable with your animals by any reptile that creepeth, nor make yourselves unclean, nor be polluted by them, lest by them you be made unclean. For I am the Lord your God; sanctify yourselves and be holy, for I am Holy; that you may not contaminate your souls with any reptile which creepeth upon the ground; for I am the Lord who brought you up from the land of Mizraim to be unto you a God; and you shall be holy, for I am Holy.

This is the law of the cattle, and of the fowl, and of

---

[9] This, the forty-second, is the middle verse of the Pentateuch. The Masorites affirm the exact middle to be the *vau holem* in the word *gahvon*, 'belly.''

every living animal that moveth in the waters, and of
every living thing that moveth on the ground, for
making a distinction between the unclean and the clean,
between the animal that may be eaten, and the animal
that may not be eaten.

SECTION XXVII.

TAZRIA

XII. AND the Lord spake with Mosheh, saying:
Speak with the children of Israel, saying: A woman,
when she hath conceived and borne a male child, shall
be unclean seven days; according to the days for the removal of her uncleanness, (or, her seclusion from her
uncleanness,) she shall be unclean. And on the eighth
day he shall be circumcised in the flesh of his foreskin;
and she shall continue thirty and three days in the purification of blood; no sacred thing may she touch, nor
may she come into the sanctuary, until the days of her
purification be completed. But if she bear a female
child, she shall be unclean fourteen days, according to
(the law of) her separation; and sixty and six days she
will remain for the purification of the blood. And when
the days of her purification are complete, for the son or
for the daughter, let her bring a lamb of its year for a
burnt offering, and a young pigeon or a turtle dove for
a sin offering, unto the door of the tabernacle of ordinance, unto the priest, who shall offer it before the
Lord, and make atonement for her, and she shall be
cleansed from the uncleanness of her blood. This is the
law for her who beareth male or female. But if she find
not her hand sufficient for (the providing of) a lamb,
let her take two turtle doves, or two young pigeons;

one for the burnt offering, and the other for the sin offering, and the priest shall make atonement for her, and
she shall be clean.

XIII. And the Lord spake with Mosheh and with
Aharon, saying: A man, in the skin of whose flesh there
may be an abscess, or pustule, or brightness, and it be
in the skin of his flesh like a stroke of the leprosy, shall
be brought unto Aharon the priest, or to one of his
sons the priests. And the priest shall see the plague
in the skin of the flesh, and if the hair in the affected
spot be turned white, and the appearance of the plague
be deeper than the skin of his flesh, it is the plague of
leprosy; and the priest shall inspect him and make (pronounce) him to be unclean. But if a bright spot be in
the skin of his flesh, and the appearance be not deeper
than the skin, and the hair be not turned white, the
priest shall shut up the stricken (man) seven days.
And on the seventh day the priest shall inspect him,
and if the plague stands as it did, if the plague hath not
increased in the skin, let the priest shut him up a second
seven days. And the priest shall look upon him on the
second seventh day; and, behold, if the plague hath become obscure, and the plague hath not spread in the
skin, the priest shall make him to be clean; it is a sore,
and he shall wash his clothes and be clean.

But if the diseased spot increase again in the skin
after having been seen by the priest for his cleansing, he
shall be brought a second time to the priest. And the
priest inspecting, and, behold, the soreness hath increased in the skin, the priest shall make him to be unclean; it is the leprosy.

When the plague of leprosy is in a man, let him be
brought to the priest. And the priest shall inspect him,
and, behold, if the abscess is white in the skin, and it
hath turned the hair white, and the sign of quick flesh

be in the abscess, it is an old leprosy in the skin of the
flesh, and the priest shall make him unclean, but shall
not shut him up (to ascertain his uncleanness), for he is
unclean.   And if the leprosy increasing shall increase in
the skin, and the leprosy cover the whole skin of the
plague (struck man) from his head unto his feet, wherever the eyes of the priest may look, the priest shall observe, and, behold, (if) the leprosy covereth all his flesh,
the plagued shall be (considered) clean ; the whole of
him is turned white, he is clean.   But in the day that
quick flesh appeareth in him he shall be unclean ; and
the priest shall observe the quick flesh, and make him
to be unclean.   The quick flesh is unclean, it is the
leprosy.   But if the quick flesh turn to be white, he
shall come to the priest ; and the priest shall observe,
and, behold, if the plague is turned white, the priest shall
make the plagued to be clean ; he is clean.

And if a man have in him, in his skin, an ulcer, and
it hath healed, but in the place of the ulcer there come
a white abscess, or a bright spot, reddish-white, let him
show it to the priest, and the priest shall inspect, and,
behold, if the appearance of it be deeper than the skin,
and the hair be turned white, the priest shall make him
to be unclean ; it is the plague of leprosy increasing
in the ulcer.   But if the priest look on it, and, behold,
the hair is not white, nor (the depth) lower than the
skin, and it hath become obscure, the priest shall seclude
him seven days ; and if increasing it increaseth in the
skin, the priest shall make him to be unclean ; it is the
plague.   But if the spot abideth in its place, and increaseth not, it is a description of an ulcer, and the priest
shall make him clean.

Or, if a man hath in his skin a burning wound, and
there be the sign of a glowing wound whitish-red or
(altogether) white, the priest shall look upon it, and, be-

hold, if the hair be white in the bright spot, and the appearance be deeper than the skin, it is leprosy increasing in the wound, and the priest shall make him unclean; it is the plague of leprosy. But if the priest see it, and, behold, the hair is not white in the spot, and it is not deeper than the skin, and is becoming obscure, the priest shall seclude him seven days. And the priest shall look upon him on the seventh day; if, increasing, it increaseth in the skin, the priest shall make him to be unclean; it is the plague of leprosy. But if the spot abideth in its place, and doth not increase in the skin, but hath become obscure, it is (only) a burning sore, and the priest shall make him to be clean, for it is the sign of an inflammation.

And if a man or a woman have a plague on the head, or in the beard, the priest shall inspect the plague, and, behold, if the appearance is deeper than the skin, and there is in it a thin reddish hair, the priest shall make him unclean; it is a scar (or scurvy), it is leprosy in the head or the beard. And if the priest observe the plague of the scurvy, and, behold, its appearance is not deeper than the skin, and the hair in it is not black, the priest shall seclude him who hath the plague of the scurvy seven days. And the priest shall inspect the plague on the seventh day; and, behold, if the scurf hath not increased, and there is no reddish hair in it, and the appearance of the scurf be not deeper than the skin, he must shave around the scurfed spot; but the spot itself he must not shave; and the priest shall shut him up (who hath) the scurf a second seven days. And the priest shall look upon the scurf on the seventh day, and, behold, if the scurf is not increased in the skin, and its appearance is not deeper than the skin, the priest shall make him clean; and he shall wash his clothes and be clean. But if the scurf increase in the skin after that he hath been (prononnced) clean, the priest shall inspect him, and, behold, if the scurf be increased in the skin, the priest need not seek for the reddish hair; he is unclean. But if the scurf abide as it was, and black hair have sprung up in it, the scurf hath healed, he is clean, and the priest shall make him to be clean.

And if a man or a woman have in the skin of their flesh bright white spots, then the priest shall look, and, behold, if the spots in the skin of their flesh be dim white, it is a freckle growing in the skin; he is clean.

And if a man's hair fall off from his head, he is bald, but he is clean. And if the hair of his head fall off toward his face, he is partly bald, but is clean. But if in the baldness or partial baldness there be a whitish red scar, it is leprosy growing in the baldness or partial baldness. Then the priest shall look, and, behold, if the plague spot be whitish red in the baldness or the partial baldness, as the appearance of leprosy in the skin of the flesh, the man is a leper, he is unclean; and the priest shall verily make him to be unclean; his plague is in his head.

And the leper in whom is the plague,—his clothes shall be rent, and his head bared; and, like the mourner, he shall be covered unto his lip, and shall cry: Be not made unclean! Be not made unclean! All the days that the plague is upon him shall he be unclean; he is unclean; he shall dwell apart, his habitation shall be without the camp.

The garment which hath the plague of leprosy in it, whether it be in a garment of woollen or of linen, whether in the warp or in the woof of linen or of woollen, or in leather, or anything made of skin. if the plague be green or red in the garment or in the skin, whether in the warp, or in the woof, or in anything of skin, it is a plague of leprosy, and must be showed to the priest. And the priest shall look at the plague, and shut it up seven days. And he shall look at the plague on the seventh day; if the plague hath increased in the garment, whether in the warp or in the woof, or in a skin, or anything made of skin for work, it is a plague of consuming leprosy, it is unclean. And he shall burn the garment, whether it be in warp or woof, of wool, or of linen, or anything (made) of skin, which hath the plague in it; for it is a consuming leprosy; he shall burn it in fire. But if the priest look, and, behold, the plague hath not increased in the garment, whether in warp or woof, or in anything of skin; then the priest shall direct, and they shall wash that wherein is the plague, and he shall shut it up a second seven days. And the priest shall look after that they have washed the plague, and, behold, if (the state of) the plague hath not changed from what it was, and the plague hath not increased, it is (nevertheless) unclean; thou shalt burn it with fire, it is a fretting leprosy, whether in its smoothness or its roughness (*i. e.*, its right or wrong side). And if the priest look, and, behold, the plague hath become obscure after they have washed it, he shall tear it out of the garment, or out of the skin, or out of the warp, or of the woof. And if it reappear in the garment, in warp or woof, or increase in any vessel of skin, thou shalt burn in fire that which hath the plague in it. And the garment, or warp, or woof, or anything of skin which hath been washed, and the plague hath gone from it, shall be dipped the second time, and shall be clean. This is the law for the plague of leprosy in a garment of woollen or linen, in the warp or the woof, or anything of skin, to make it to be clean or unclean.

SECTION XXVIII.

METSORA.

XIV. AND the Lord spake with Mosheh, saying:
This shall be the law for the leper on the day of his
purification: He shall be brought to the priest, and
the priest shall go forth out of the camp, and the priest
shall look, and, behold, if the leper be healed of his
leprosy, then the priest shall direct that there be brought
for him who is to be cleansed two birds, alive, clean, and
wood of the cedar and scarlet (wood) and hyssop. And
the priest shall direct that one of the birds be killed in
an earthen vessel with spring water. And he shall take
the living bird with the cedar wood, and the scarlet, and
the hyssop, and dip them and the living bird in the
blood of the bird that had been killed over the spring
water. And he shall sprinkle it on him who is to be
cleansed from leprosy seven times, and he shall be clean:
and the living bird he shall send forth upon the face of
the field   And he who is cleansed shall wash his
clothes, and shave off all his hair, and wash himself clean
with water, and afterward he may come into the camp;
but he shall dwell without his tent seven days. And on
the seventh day he shall (again) shave off all the hair of
his head, and his beard and his eyebrows, the whole of
his hair shall he shave off, and wash his clothes, and
wash his flesh with water, and he shall be clean. And
on the eighth day let him take two (he) lambs unblemished, and one ewe lamb of the year unblemished,
and three tenths of flour sprinkled with oil for a mincha,
and one loga of oil. And the priest who maketh him
clean shall make the man who is cleansed to stand with
them before the Lord at the door of the tabernacle of

ordinance. And the priest shall take one lamb and offer him for a trespass offering, and the loga of oil, and shall uplift them an elevation before the Lord. And he shall slay the lamb on the place where the sin offering is killed, and the burnt offering, (namely,) in the holy place; for as the sin, so the trespass, offering is the priest's: it is most sacred. And the priest shall take some of the blood of the trespass offering, and the priest shall put it upon the tip of the right ear of him who is cleansed, and upon the thumb of his right hand, and upon the toe of his right foot. And the priest shall take of the log of oil and pour it on the priest's left hand. And the priest shall dip the finger of his right hand in the oil which is upon his left hand, and shall sprinkle of the oil with his finger seven times before the Lord. And of the rest of the oil which is upon his hand the priest shall put upon the tip of the right ear of him who is cleansed, and upon the thumb of his right hand, and upon the toe of his right foot, upon the blood of the trespass offering. And the remainder of the oil which is upon the priest's hand he shall put upon the head of him who is cleansed, and the priest shall make atonement for him before the Lord. And the priest shall perform the sin offering, and make atonement for him who is cleansed from his defilement, and afterwards shall he kill the burnt offering. And the priest shall sacrifice the burnt offering with the mincha at the altar, and the priest shall make atonement for him, and he shall be clean.

But should he be a poor man, and his hand have not (so much) pertaining (to him), let him take one lamb for the trespass offering for the elevation to atone for him, and one-tenth of flour sprinkled with oil for the mincha, and a loga of oil and two turtle doves or two young pigeons which his hand may possess; and one shall be the sin offering, and one the burnt offering. And he

shall bring them on the eighth day of his purification
unto the priest, at the door of the tabernacle of ordinance before the Lord. And the priest shall take the
lamb of the trespass offering, and the log of oil, and the
priest shall uplift them, an elevation before the Lord.
And he shall kill the lamb of the trespass offering, and
the priest shall take of the blood of the trespass offering,
and put it upon the tip of the right ear of him who is
cleansed, and on the finger of his right hand, and on the
toe of his right foot. And of the oil the priest shall
pour (some) upon the priest's left hand ; and the priest
shall sprinkle with his finger of the oil that is in his left
hand seven times before the Lord. And the priest shall
put of the oil which is in his hand upon the tip of the
right ear of him who is cleansed, and on the finger
of his right hand, and on the toe of his right foot, upon
the spot of the blood of the trespass offering. And the
remainder of the oil which is in the priest's hand he
shall put upon the head of him who is cleansed, to propitiate for him before the Lord. And he shall offer
(perform) one of the turtle doves, or of the young
pigeons, which his hand may possess, the one for a sin
offering, and one for a burnt offering, with the mincha ;
and the priest shall make atonement for him who is
cleansed, before the Lord. This is the law for him in
whom hath been the plague of leprosy, whose hand hath
not had sufficiency for (the sacrifices of) his purification.

And the Lord spake with Mosheh and to Aharon,
saying : When you have entered the land of Kenaan,
which I will give unto you for a possession ; and I have
put the plague of leprosy upon a house in the land of
your possession , and he who owns the house shall come
and show to the priest, saying, There is a plague, as it
appeareth to me, in the house : the priest shall direct

that they turn out (all that is in) the house before the
priest goeth in to inspect the plague; that all that is in
the house be not (condemned as) unclean; and afterward the priest shall enter to survey the house. Then
he shall look at the plague; and, behold, if the plague
be in the walls of the house in seams, green or red, and
they appear to be deeper than the (surface of the) wall,
then the priest shall go out from the house to the door
of the house, and shut up the house seven days. And
the priest shall return on the seventh day, and look, and,
behold, if the plague hath increased in the walls of the
house, then the priest shall order that they take down
the stones of the house in which the plague is, and cast
them without the town into an unclean place. And
they shall scrape the house within round about, and
throw the plaster (dust) which they have scraped off
without the town, into an unclean place. And they
shall take other stones, and insert them in the place of
the former stones, and shall take other plaster and
cover the house. And if the plague return and increase
in the house after that the stones have been taken down,
and after they have scraped the house, and after it hath
been plastered (anew); then the priest shall enter, and,
behold, if the plague hath increased in the house, it is a
corroding leprosy in the house, it is unclean. And they
shall break down the house, the stones of it, the timber,
and all the mortar of the house; and he shall carry
them[1] (have them carried) without the town unto an
unclean place. And whoso goeth into the house all the
days that it is shut up, shall be unclean until the evening. And he who may sleep in the house shall wash
his clothes, and he who eateth in the house shall wash
his clothes. But if the priest, having entered, shall look,
and, behold, the plague hath not increased in the house

[1] Sam. Vers., "they shall destroy."

after the house hath been plastered, the priest shall make (pronounce) the house to be clean, for the plague hath been cured. And he shall take, to purify the house, two birds, and cedar wood, and scarlet, and hyssop. And he shall kill the one bird in a vessel of pottery with spring water, and take the cedar wood, and the hyssop, and the scarlet, and the living bird; and dip them in the blood of the bird which had been killed and in the spring water, and sprinkle the house seven times. And he shall purify the house with the blood of the bird, and with the spring water, and with the living bird, and with the cedar wood, and with the hyssop, and with the scarlet.   But he shall send forth the living bird out of the town, upon the face of the field, and make atonement for the house, and it shall be clean.

This is the law for every plague of leprosy and of scorbutics, and for leprosy in clothing, and in a house: and for abscess, and scar, and inflamed spot: to teach on what day it is unclean, and on what day it is purified. This is the law for the leprosy

XV. And the Lord spake with Mosheh and to Aharon, saying: Speak with the sons of Israel, and say to them: When any man hath a defluxion by the running of his flesh, he is unclean. And this shall be his uncleanness by his defluxion, when his defluxion floweth from his flesh, or his flesh hath ceased from its flowing, it is (the cause) of his uncleanness. Every bed whereon he lieth who hath the defluxion shall be unclean; and anything whereon he sitteth shall be unclean.   And whoever toucheth his bed shall wash his clothes, bathe himself in water, and be unclean until the evening. And he who sitteth on a thing whereon he who hath the issue hath sat shall wash his clothes, and bathe in water, and be unclean until the evening.   And he who toucheth the flesh of him who hath the issue shall wash his clothes, and bathe in water, and be unclean until evening. And if he who hath the issue spit upon one who is clean, he shall wash his clothes, and bathe in water, and be unclean until evening. And any saddle (or carriage) that he who hath the issue may ride upon shall be unclean; and whoever toucheth any things that have been under him shall be unclean until evening; and he who carrieth them shall wash his clothes, and bathe in water, and be unclean until evening. And whomsoever he who hath the issue toucheth, and hath not rinsed his hands in water, shall wash his clothes, and bathe in water, and be unclean until evening. And every vessel of earthenware which he who hath the issue may have touched shall be broken, and every vessel of wood shall be rinsed in water.

And when he who hath had a defluxion shall be cleansed of his issue, he shall number to himself seven days for his purification, and wash his clothes, and bathe his flesh in spring water, and be clean. And on the eighth day let him take two turtle doves, or two young pigeons, and bring before the Lord at the door of the tabernacle of ordinance, and give them to the priest. And the priest shall perform (the offering of) them; one for the sin, and one for the burnt, offering; and the priest shall make atonement for him before the Lord, for his issue. And if seed of copulation go out from a man, he shall wash all his flesh with water, and be unclean until evening. And any garment or any skin on which may be seed of copulation, shall be washed in water, and be unclean until evening. The woman with whom a man shall lie with seed of copulation, they shall bathe themselves with water, and be unclean until evening.

If a woman have a defluxion of blood in her flesh, seven days shall be for her separation, and whoso

toucheth her shall be unclean until evening. And
every thing on which she lieth in her separation shall
be unclean, and any thing that she sitteth upon shall
be unclean. And any one who toucheth her bed shall
wash his clothes, and bathe in water, and be unclean
until evening; and any one who toucheth a thing upon
which she hath sat shall wash his clothes, and bathe in
water, and be unclean until evening. And if it be on
her bed, or any thing on which she hath sat, when he
hath touched it, he shall be unclean until the evening.
And if a man lie with her, and her separation be upon
him, he shall be unclean seven days, and any bed whereon
he lieth shall be unclean.

And if a woman hath a defluxion of blood many days
beyond the time of her separation, if it run beyond (the
time) of her separation, all the days of the issue of her
uncleanness shall be as the days of her separation; she
shall be unclean. Any bed on which she lieth all the
days of her defluxion shall be as the bed of her separation, and every thing on which she sitteth shall be
unclean as the uncleanness of her separation. And
whoso toucheth them shall be unclean, and shall wash
his clothes, and bathe in water, and be unclean until
evening.

But if she be cleansed from her defluxion, then let
her number to herself seven days, and afterward she is
clean. And on the eighth day let her take for herself
two turtle doves, or two young pigeons, and bring them
to the priest at the door of the tabernacle of ordinance.
And the priest shall make the one a sin offering, and
one a burnt offering, and the priest shall atone before
the Lord for the issue of her uncleanness. And (thus)
shall you separate the children of Israel from their
uncleanness, that they die not, by defiling My Tabernacle
which is among them. This is the law for him who

hath an issue, or whose seed goeth from him, and who
is defiled therewith; and of her who hath an issue of
separation; and of him who hath a flowing issue, of the
male and of the female, and of him who lieth with her
who is unclean.

SECTION XXIX.

ACHAREY.

XVI. AND the Lord spake with Mosheh after the
two sons of Aharon were dead, who offered the strange
fire before the Lord, and died; and the Lord said unto
Mosheh, Speak with Aharon thy brother, that he may
not enter at any time into the Holy Place within the
veil before the mercy-seat which is upon the ark, that
he die not; for in the cloud will I reveal Myself over
the mercy-seat.

With this shall Aharon enter the holy place: With a
young bullock for a sin offering, and a ram for a burnt
offering. With the holy linen vesture shall he be
clothed, and linen drawers shall be upon his flesh, and
with the linen girdle shall he be bound, and the linen
mitre shall be upon his head: these are holy garments;
and he shall wash his flesh in water, and then put
them on.

And of the congregation of the sons of Israel let him
take two kids of the goats for a sin offering, and one
ram for a burnt offering. And Aharon shall offer the
bullock of the sin offering for himself, and make atonement for himself and for the men of his house.

And he shall take the two goats, and make them to
stand before the Lord, at the door of the tabernacle of
ordinance. And Aharon shall put lots upon the two

goats; one lot for the Name of the Lord, and one lot
for Azazel.[2] And Aharon shall offer the goat whose
lot came up for the Name of the Lord, and make him a
sin offering; and the goat whose lot came up for Azazel
he shall make to stand alive before the Lord, to make
an atonement upon him, and to send him away to Azazel, to the desert.

And Aharon shall offer the bullock for his own sin,
and make atonement for himself and for the men of his
house; and he shall kill the bullock for the sin offering
which is for himself. And he shall take a censer full of
coals of fire from off the altar before the Lord, and his
handful of sweet incense beaten small, and carry (them)
within the veil. And he shall put the sweet incense
upon the fire before the Lord, and the cloud of incense
will envelope the mercy-seat which is over the testimony,
that he may not die. And he shall take of the blood of
the bullock, and sprinkle it with his finger upon the
face of the mercy-seat eastward, and before the mercy-
seat he shall sprinkle seven times of the blood with his
finger.

And he shall kill the goat for the sin offering of
the people, and enter, with its blood, within the veil,
and do with his blood as he had done with the blood of
the bullock, and sprinkle it upon the mercy-seat and
before the mercy-seat. And he shall (thus) make atonement for the holy place on account of the uncleanness
of the children of Israel, and the rebellion of all their
sin. And so shall he do for the tabernacle of ordinance
which remaineth with them in the midst of their uncleanness. But no man shall be in the tabernacle of
ordinance (at the time of) his entering to make atone-

---

[2] To be sent to Azazel, a steep rough mountain, (RASHI,) not far
from Mount Sinai (EBEN EZRA). See the Talmud in *Joma*, 67. Compare the Glossary, pp. 66–68.

ment in the holy place until his coming out: and he shall atone for himself, and for the men of his house, and for all the congregation of Israel.

And he shall go forth to the altar which is before the Lord, and make atonement for it; and take of the blood of the bullock and of the goat's blood, and put upon the horns of the altar round about; and of the blood he shall sprinkle upon it with his finger seven times, and cleanse it and sanctify it from the uncleanness of the children of Israel.

And when he hath completed to atone for the holy place, and for the tabernacle of ordinance, and for the altar, then shall he bring the living goat. And Aharon shall lay his two hands upon the head of the live goat, and confess over him all the iniquities of the children of Israel, and all their rebellions, and all their sins, and put them upon the head of the goat, and send him away, by the hand of an appointed man, to go into the desert. And the goat shall bear upon him all their iniquities into a land not inhabited; and he shall send the goat away into the desert.

And Aharon shall go into the tabernacle of ordinance, and put off the linen robes which he wore on going into the Holy Place, and shall lay them there aside. And he shall wash his flesh with water in the Holy Place, and put on his garments, and come forth to offer his burnt sacrifice, and the burnt sacrifice of the people, and make atonement for himself and for the people. And the fat of the sin offering he shall burn at the altar.

But he who led away the goat unto Azazel shall wash his clothes, and bathe his flesh in water, and afterwards go into the camp. And the bullock of the sin offering whose blood was carried in to make atonement in the Holy Place, he shall take forth out of the camp, and they shall burn their skins and their flesh and their food with fire. And he who burned them must wash his clothes, and bathe his flesh with water, and may then enter into the camp.

And this shall be to you for an everlasting statute: in the seventh month, on the tenth day of the month, you shall afflict (humble) your souls,[3] and do no work, whether the native-born or the stranger that dwelleth among you. For on that day he shall make atonement for you, to cleanse you from all your sins, that you may be cleansed from all your sins before the Lord. A Sabbath it shall be to you, and you shall humble your souls. It is an everlasting statute.

And the priest whom he shall anoint, and who shall offer his oblation, to minister instead of his father, shall make the atonement, and dress himself with the vestments of fine linen, even the consecrated vestments. And he shall make atonement for the Holy of Holies, and for the tabernacle of ordinance and for the altar he shall atone, and for all the people of the congregation shall he atone. And this shall be to you an everlasting statute for the expiation of all the children of Israel from all their sins once in the year. And he did as the Lord commanded Mosheh.

XVII. And the Lord spake with Mosheh, saying: Speak with Aharon, and with his sons, and with all the sons of Israel, and say to them: This is the word which the Lord hath commanded, saying: Any man of the house of Israel who shall kill bullock or lamb or goat in the camp, or who shall kill (such as sacrifices) without the camp, and bring it not to the door of the tabernacle of ordinance, that it may be offered an oblation in the presence of the Lord before the tabernacle of the Lord, blood shall be reckoned to that man; he hath shed blood, and that man shall be destroyed from his

[3] Sam. Vers., "by fasting."

people. In order that the sons of Israel may bring their victims which they (formerly) sacrificed upon the face of the field, before the Lord at the door of the tabernacle of ordinance, unto the priest, and offer them as consecrated oblations in the presence of the Lord.

And the priest shall sprinkle the blood upon the altar of the Lord at the door of the tabernacle of ordinance, and burn the fat to be received with acceptance before the Lord. And they shall no more sacrifice their victims unto demons after which they have wandered : this shall be an everlasting statute to you unto your generations.

And say thou to them, Whatever man of the house of Israel, or the stranger who sojourneth among you, who sacrificeth a burnt offering or a consecrated victim, and bringeth it not to the door of the tabernacle of ordinance, that it may be performed before the Lord, that man shall be destroyed from his people. And what man soever of the house of Israel or of the strangers who sojourn among you, who shall eat any blood, I will set my anger[4] upon the man who shall have eaten blood, and will destroy him[5] from among his people. Because the life of flesh is in the blood, and I have given it to you upon the altar to make atonement for your souls ; for it IS THE BLOOD THAT ATONETH FOR THE SOUL. Therefore have I said to the children of Israel, Let no man of you eat blood, nor let the strangers who sojourn among you eat blood ; and whatever man of the sons of Israel, or of the strangers who sojourn among you, that hunteth venison of beast or bird which may be eaten, let him pour out its blood and cover it in the earth (or in the dust) ; for the life of all flesh is its blood ; it is for its life ; and I have said to the children of Israel, You shall not eat the blood of any flesh, for the life of all

---

[4] Sam. Vers , "I will stir up my wrath."   [5] "I will extirpate him."

flesh is its blood; every one who eateth of it shall be destroyed.

And every one who eateth of a carcase (that hath died of itself) or hath been torn, whether he be native born or of the strangers, let him wash his clothes, and bathe in water, and be unclean until the evening, and (then) shall he be clean. But if he wash not, nor bathe his flesh, he shall bear his transgression.

XVIII. And the Lord spake with Mosheh, saying: Speak with the sons of Israel, and say unto them: I am the Lord your God: You shall not do according to the people of the land of Mizraim in which you dwelt, nor after the works of the people of the land of Kenaan, whither I am bringing you, shall you do, neither shall you walk in their laws. My judgments shall you perform, and keep My statutes to walk in them; I am the Lord your God. And you shall keep My statutes and My judgments, which if a man do he shall live by them an everlasting life. I am the Lord.

No man shall come nigh to any of his own flesh to uncover the nakedness; I am the Lord. The nakedness of thy father, or the nakedness of thy mother, thou shalt not uncover. She is thy mother; thou shalt not uncover her nakedness. The nakedness of thy father's wife thou shalt not uncover, it is thy father's nakedness. The nakedness of thy sister, the daughter of thy father, or the daughter of thy mother, who hath been begotten of thy father by another wife, or of thy mother by another husband, their nakedness thou shalt not uncover. The nakedness of thy son's daughter, or the daughter of thy daughter, thou shalt not uncover; for they are thy nakedness. The nakedness of the daughter of thy father's wife who hath been begotten of thy father, who is thy sister, thou shalt not uncover. The nakedness of thy father's sister thou shalt not uncover;

she is of kin to thy father. The nakedness of thy
mother's sister thou shalt not uncover; for she is of kin
to thy mother. The nakedness of thy father's brother
thou shalt not uncover; unto his wife thou shalt not
come near; she is the wife of thy father's brother. The
nakedness of thy daughter-in-law thou shalt not
uncover; she is thy son's wife, thou shalt not uncover
her nakedness. The nakedness of thy brother's wife
thou shalt not uncover; it is thy brother's nakedness.
The nakedness of a woman and of her daughter thou
shalt not uncover; thou shalt not take the daughter of
her son nor the daughter of her daughter to uncover her
nakedness, they are near of kin, it is a device of wickedness. And a wife with her sister thou shalt not take to
cause her tribulation by uncovering her nakedness over
her in her life (time). And unto a woman in the separation of her uncleanness shalt thou not come near to
uncover her nakedness. Nor with the wife of thy
neighbour shalt thou carnally lie to defile her. And of
thy children thou shalt give none to transfer them to
Molek, (or, to make them pass through to Molek,)
neither shalt thou profane the Name of the Lord thy
God: I am the Lord. And with the male thou shalt
not lie as with the woman; it is an abhorrent thing.
Nor with any beast shall be thy lying down to defile
thyself with it; neither shall a woman stand before a
beast to permit him to prevail with her; it is confusion.[6]
Ye shall not pollute yourselves with any of these; for
with all these have the peoples defiled themselves whom
I am about to drive away from before you. And the
land (itself) is contaminated; and I will visit the guilt
that is upon it, and the land shall vomit forth the
inhabitants. But you shall keep My statutes and My
judgments, and commit none of these abominations,

---

[6] Sam. Vers, "it is indignation."

neither the native born nor the sojourners who sojourn
among you;—for all these abominations have been done
by the men of the land who have been before you, and
the land hath been polluted;—that the land vomit you
not out when ye defile it; as it will have cast out the
people who were before you. For whoso committeth
any of these abominations, the souls that do them shall
be destroyed from among their people. And you shall
observe the keeping of My word, that you do not
(according to) the abominable usages which have been
done before you, nor be corrupted by them. I am the
Lord your God.

SECTION XXX.

KEDOSHIM.

XIX And the Lord spake with Mosheh, saying:
Speak with all the congregation of the sons of Israel
and say to them, You shall be holy; for I, the Lord
your God, am holy. A man shall reverence his mother
and his father, and you shall keep the day of My Sabbath: I am the Lord your God Turn not after idols,
nor make molten things (for worship): I am the Lord
your God. And when you offer the sacrifice of consecrated things before the Lord, make the sacrifice thereof
with your own free will. On the day that it is sacrificed
it may be eaten, and on the following day; but that
which remaineth on the third day shall be burned with
fire. If indeed it be eaten on the third day, it (the
oblation) is rejected, and shall not be accepted. And
whoever eateth it shall bear his guilt; for he hath profaned that which was consecrated, and that man shall be
destroyed from his people.

And when you reap the harvest of your land, thou

shalt not wholly reap the corners of thy field, and the
gleanings of thy harvest thou shalt not gather. Neither
in thy vineyard shalt thou (entirely) ingather, nor collect the remainder of thy vineyard; thou shalt leave
them for the poor, and for the stranger : I am the Lord
thy God.   You shall not steal, nor prevaricate, nor be
false, a man with his neighbour.   Neither swear by My
Name unto falsehood, nor profane the Name of thy
God : I am the Lord.

Thou shalt not overbear thy neighbour, nor be coer-
cive : the hire of the hireling shall not abide with thee
till the morning.   Thou shalt not curse him who cannot
hear, nor put a stumblingblock before him who cannot
see, but shalt fear thy God : I am the Lord.   You shall
not deal falsely in judgment, nor accept the face of the
poor, nor honour the face of the great; in truthfulness
shalt thou judge thy neighbour.   Thou shalt not make
false accusations against thy people, neither stand
against thy neighbour's blood : I am the Lord.   Thou
shalt not hate thy brother in thy heart : reproving,
reprove thou thy neighbour, and contract not sin on
his account.   Thou shalt not be revengeful, nor keep
enmity against the children of thy people, but love thy
neighbour as thyself.   I am the Lord.

You shall observe My statutes. Thy cattle thou shalt
not make to gender with various kinds, nor sow thy
field with various kinds, nor let a garment of a mixture
of woollen and linen come upon thee.   And if a man
lie carnally with a woman, and she be a handmaid
betrothed unto (another) man, and with redemption of
money not redeemed, nor having freedom given to her
by an instrument of writing, the stripe shall be upon
her; they shall not be put to death, for she was not
free.[7]   But he shall bring his trespass offering before

[7] Compare chap. xx. 10.

G 2

the Lord, at the door of the tabernacle of ordinance, a ram for a trespass offering. And the priest shall make atonement with the ram of the trespass offering before the Lord for the sin that he hath sinned, that the sin he hath sinned may be forgiven him.

And when you have entered upon the land, and have planted any (kind) of tree for eating, the fruit of it shall be put away (from you); three years shall it be set aside to be destroyed; it shall not be eaten. But in the fourth year all the fruit shall be consecrated for thanksgiving before the Lord; and in the fifth year you shall eat the fruit of it, that the fruit may be added (increased) to you. I am the Lord your God.

You shall not eat anything with the blood. You shall not use enchantments,[8] nor augury by the clouds. You shall not shave the hair on your head in a circle,[9] nor destroy the hair of thy beard, nor make a cutting for the dead in thy flesh; nor imprint signatures upon you: I am the Lord. Thou shalt not profane thy daughter to make her to become a fornicatress, lest the land become whorish, and the land be filled with the ways of wickedness. The days of Sabbaths, which are Mine, observe ye, and hold in reverence the house of My sanctuary. I am the Lord. Turn not after deceivers, nor inquire by diviners to pollute yourselves with them: I am the Lord your God.

Thou shalt rise up before one who is a teacher in the law, and pay honour to the presence of the aged, and fear thy God. I am the Lord. And if a stranger sojourn with you in the land, you shall not oppress him. As one born among you shall be the stranger who sojourneth among you, and thou shalt love him as thy-

---

[8] Peschito, " You shall not augur by a winged animal," i. e., by the flight of birds.

[9] See HERODOTUS, iii., 8

self, because you were sojourners in the land of Mizraim:
I am the Lord your God. You shall commit no falsity
in judgment, in rule, (or line,) in weight, or in measure.
Balances of truth, weights of truth, a measure in truth,
and hins of truth you shall have. I am the Lord your
God, who have brought you out from the land of Mizraim;
and you shall keep all My statutes, and all My judgments,
and do them: I am the Lord.

XX. And the Lord spake with Mosheh, saying,
Speak unto the sons of Israel: Whatever man of the
sons of Israel, or of the strangers who sojourn in Israel,
giveth his offspring unto Molek,[1] with killing shall he
be killed; the people of the house of Israel shall stone
him with stones. And I will show My displeasure
against that man, and will destroy from among his
people, because he hath given his offspring unto Molek,
to defile My sanctuary and to profane My holy Name.
And if the people of the house of Israel turn away (or
hide) their eyes from that man when he giveth his
offspring to Molek, that they may not have to put him
to death, I will give forth My anger against that man,
and against his abettors, and will destroy him, and all
who go after him, to wander after Molek, from among
their people. And the man who turneth away after
impostors and diviners to wander after them, I will
set My displeasure upon that man, and will cut him off
from among his people. But you shall be sanctified,
and be holy; for I am your God. And you shall observe
My statutes, and do them: I am the Lord who sanctify
you. For the man who curseth his father or his mother
shall be surely put to death; he hath cursed his father,
he is guilty of death. And the man who committeth
adultery with his neighbour's wife shall be surely put to
death; the adulterer and the adulteress. And the man

---

[1] Molek, the Ruler = Baal.

who lieth with his father's wife, uncovering his father's
nakedness, shall be surely put to death; both of them
are guilty of death. And a man who lieth with his
daughter-in-law, both of them shall be slain: they
have wrought confusion, they are guilty of death. And
a man who lieth with a man as with a woman, both of
them have wrought abomination: they are to be surely
put to death, of death they are guilty. And when a man
taketh a wife along with her mother, it is wickedness;
both he and they shall be burned with fire; such wickedness shall not be among you. And if a man lie with a
beast, he shall be surely put to death, and you shall kill
the beast. And if a woman approach to a beast to
submit to it, the woman shall be put to death, and the
beast; they shall verily be killed; of death they are
guilty. And a man who shall take his sister, the
daughter of his father, or the daughter of his mother,
and see her nakedness, and she see his nakedness, it is
an ignominy, and they shall be destroyed before the eyes
of the children of their people: he hath uncovered the
nakedness of his sister, he shall receive (the punishment
of) his guilt. And a man who lieth with a woman who
is unclean, and uncovereth her nakedness, he hath
uncovered her shame, and she hath uncovered the
uncleanness of her blood: both of them shall be cut off
from among their people. Neither shalt thou uncover
the nakedness of thy mother's sister, nor of thy father's
sister; for he will have uncovered that of his near kin;
they shall receive for their sin. And if a man lie with
the wife of his father's brother, he hath uncovered the
nakedness of his father's brother; they shall receive for
their guilt, without children shall they die. And if a
man take his brother's wife,[2] a thing to be kept aloof

---

[2] The deceased brother having left children. The law in Deut. xxv. 5
refers to the case of a childless widow.

from, (*merachaka,*) he hath uncovered the nakedness of his brother, they shall be childless. But keep you all My statutes and all My judgments, and do them, that the land into which I bring you to dwell may not cast you out. You shall not walk in the laws of the peoples whom I drive away from before you; for they have committed all these things, and My Word hath abhorred them. But I have said to you, Ye shall inherit this land, and I will give it to you to possess it, a land producing milk and honey. I am the Lord your God who have separated you from the peoples. And you shall make distinction between animals clean and unclean, and between fowls unclean and clean, and not make your souls abominable by beast, or by fowl, or by any thing that creepeth on the ground which I have separated (as to be) unto you unclean. And you shall be holy before Me; for I the Lord am holy, aud I have separated you from the nations to be worshippers before Me. A man or a woman with whom are impostures or divinations shall be verily put to death; with stones they shall be stoned, they are guilty of death.

SECTION XXXI.

EMOR.

XXI. AND the Lord spake with Mosheh, saying: Speak unto the priests, the sons of Aharon, and say to them: Let no one be defiled among his people on account of the dead: yet for his kin, who is nigh to him, for his mother, and for his father, and for his son, and for his daughter, and for his brother, and for his sister, a virgin who is near to him, who hath no husband, for her he may be defiled. But a chief among his people (the high priest) shall not defile himself, to make himself profane. They shall not make baldness on their heads, nor cut away the hair of their beards, nor scarify their flesh with marks. They shall be holy before their God, and shall not profane the Name of their God; for they offer the oblations of the Lord their God, and they shall be holy. They shall not take to wife a woman who is a harlot, or one who is corrupted, nor may they take a woman who hath been put away from her husband; for (the priest is to be) holy before his God. Thou shalt consecrate him, for he is to offer the oblation of thy God: he shall be sacred to thee; for I the Lord, who sanctify you, am Holy. And if the daughter of a man who is a priest profane herself by becoming an harlot, she hath profaned the sanctity of her father; she shall be burned with fire.

And the (high) priest who hath been consecrated from his brethren, upon whose head hath been poured the oil of consecration, and who, at the offering of his oblation, is arrayed with the (holy) robes, shall not make bare his head, nor rend his garments. Nor shall he enter unto any dead body, nor defile himself for his father or his mother. And he shall not go out from the sanctuary nor defile the sanctuary of his God; for the crown of the[3] anointing oil of his God is upon him. I am the Lord. And he shall take a wife in her virginity; a widow, or a divorced person, or a corrupt harlot, these he shall not take; but a virgin from his people shall he take for a wife. And his offspring he shall not profane among his people; for I the Lord do sanctify him.

And the Lord spake with Mosheh, saying: Speak with Aharon, saying: A man of the generations of thy sons who hath any blemish on him shall not approach to offer the oblation of his God. For no man in whom is a blemish may come nigh; a blind man, or lame, or flat-

---

[3] Sam Vers, "of the excellency."

nosed, or disproportioned;[4] or a man who hath a broken foot, or a broken hand, or who is crookbacked, or dwarfish,[5] or who hath a white spot in his eye,[6] or the scurvy, or ringworm, or who hath ruptured testicles. No man of the offspring of Aharon the priest who hath a blemish may approach to offer the oblations of the Lord ; having a blemish in him he shall not draw near to present the oblation of his God : yet of the sanctified oblations of his God, even of the most holy, he may eat : only he shall not enter within the veil, nor approach the altar, because he hath a blemish ; that he profane not My sanctuary ; for I am the Lord who sanctify them. And Mosheh spake with Aharon, and with his sons, and with all the sons of Israel.

XXII. And the Lord spake with Mosheh, saying . Speak with Aharon and with his sons, and let them keep separate from [7] the consecrated things of the children of Israel, that they profane not the Name of My Holiness which they (are to) sanctify before Me : I am the Lord. Say to them, Any man of all the sons of your generations who shall touch the hallowed things which the children of Israel consecrate before the Lord, having his uncleanness upon him, that man shall perish before Me : I am the Lord. Any man of Aharon's offspring who hath leprosy or an unclean effusion shall not eat of the consecrated things until he be clean ; and whosoever toucheth any unclean animal, or a man whose seed goeth from him, or a man who toucheth any reptile that maketh him unclean, or a man who maketh him unclean by any of his uncleanness, the man who toucheth him shall be unclean until the evening, and may

---

* Pesch. Syriac here, " or who hath the ear slit."

⁵ Or, " whose eyebrows have fallen off "—*Ibid.*

⁶ Or, "having sightless eyes," or "having white spots in his eyes."—*Ibid*

⁷ " At the time of their uncleanness."—RASHI.

not eat of things consecrated unless he wash his flesh
with water. But when the sun hath gone down, and he
shall have purified himself, he may afterward eat of the
hallowed things, for it is his food.

A carcase which hath been torn he may not eat, to
defile himself therewith: I am the Lord. But let
them keep the keeping of My word, lest they bring
guilt upon themselves, and die for it, because they have
profaned it: I am the Lord who sanctify them. No
stranger shall eat of that which is consecrated, neither a
sojourner with a priest, or a hireling, may eat of the
consecrated thing. But if the priest buy a person with
a purchase of his money, he may eat of it, and he who
hath been born in his house, they may eat of his bread.
And the daughter of a priest, if she be married to a
stranger, may not eat of things set apart and hallowed.
But if the priest's daughter be a widow, or divorced,
and, having no child, hath returned to her father's
house, as in her youth, she may eat of her father's
meat; but no stranger shall eat thereof.

And if a man eat some consecrated thing through
ignorance, he shall add a fifth unto it, and give the
consecrated thing unto the priest. And let them not
profane the hallowed things of the children of Israel
which are set apart before the Lord, nor bring upon
themselves iniquities and sins, when they eat in uncleanness the things that are holy. I am the Lord, who
sanctify them.

And the Lord spake with Mosheh, saying · Speak with
Aharon, and with his sons, and with all the children of
Israel, and say to them: When any man of the sons of
Israel, or of the sojourners in Israel, will offer the oblation of any of their vows or any of their freewill oblations which they may offer before the Lord for a burnt
sacrifice, that it may be acceptable from you, (let it be)

a male without blemish, of the bullocks, or of the lambs,
or of the goats. But whatever hath a blemish in it you
shall not offer, for it will not be acceptable for you.
And if a man present a consecrated victim before the
Lord, as a vow set apart, or a freewill offering of the
herd or of the flock, it must be perfect, to be acceptable;
there shall be no blemish in it. Blind, or broken, or
mutilated, or having imposthumes, or ulcers, or blotches,
these you shall not offer before the Lord, nor of them
present an oblation upon the altar before the Lord.
But a bullock or a lamb that hath anything superfluous
or deficient you may make a free will offering,[8] but for
a vow it will not be acceptable. And that which is
crushed, or rent, or worn out, or emasculated, you shall
not offer before the Lord, nor do it [9] in your land. Nor
from (the hand of) a son of the Gentiles may you offer
an oblation to your God of any of these, because their
corruption is in them, a blemish is in them ; they will
not be acceptable for you.

And the Lord spake with Mosheh, saying : When a
bullock, or lamb, or goat, is brought forth, it shall be
seven days with its dam, and on the eighth day and
thenceforward it will be acceptable to be offered as an
oblation before the Lord. Whether it be a cow or ewe,
ye shall not immolate (both) her and her offspring on
one day. And when you present a thank-offering before
the Lord, offer it so as to be acceptable for you. It is
to be eaten on that day, nothing shall remain of it till
the morning. I am the Lord. And you shall observe
My commandments, and do them. I am the Lord.
Nor shall you profane My holy Name, for I will be

---

[8] The meaning, according to the Rabbins, is, that the animal itself was
not to be brought, but the value of it in money, to be applied to the
repairs of the sanctuary, &c.

[9] Pesch. Syr , " nor sacrifice it."

hallowed among the sons of Israel. I am the Lord who
sanctify you, who have led you forth from the land of
Mizraim to be unto you Eloha : 1 am the Lord.

XXIII. And the Lord spake with Mosheh, saying:
Speak with the sons of Israel, and say to them ⸱ The
FESTIVALS of the Lord which you shall convoke as holy
convocations, these are My festivals. Six days thou shalt
do work, but on the seventh day is the rest of the Shabbath ; a holy convocation, (in it) you shall do no work.
It is a Sabbath before the Lord in all your dwellings.

These are the festivals of the Lord, holy convocations
which you shall convoke in their seasons. In the first
month, on the fourteenth of the month, between the
suns, is the Pascha before the Lord, and on the fifteenth
day of this month is the feast (*chagga*) of unleavened
cakes before the Lord; seven days you shall eat unleavened bread. In the first day you shall have a holy
convocation ; no laborious work shall you do ; but you
shall offer an oblation before the Lord seven days ; in
the seventh day there shall be a holy convocation ; no
laborious work may you do

And the Lord spake with Mosheh, saying : Speak with
the sons of Israel, and say to them : When you have
entered into the land that I will give unto you, and you
reap its harvest, you shall bring an omera of the first of
your harvest unto the priest, and he shall uplift the
omera before the Lord to be accepted for you : after the
day of the festivity (*yoma taba*) shall the priest uplift it.
And you shall perform on the day of your elevation of
the omera (the sacrifice of) an unblemished lamb of the
year, as a burnt offering before the Lord. And the
mincha thereof shall be two-tenths of flour mingled with
oil, an oblation to be accepted before the Lord ; and its
libation, wine, the fourth of a hin. Neither bread, nor
parched corn, nor green ears shall you eat until this day

when you bring the oblation of your God ; an everlasting statute unto your generations in all your dwellings.

And count to you, after the festival day, from the day that you brought the omera of the elevation, seven weeks, complete shall they be. Until the (day) after the seventh week number fifty days, and (then) offer a new mincha before the Lord. Bring from your dwellings two loaves for an elevation, two cakes, of two-tenths of flour shall they be, baked with leaven, as first fruits before the Lord. And with the bread you shall offer seven unblemished lambs of the year, one young bullock, and two rams; they shall be a burnt offering before the Lord, with their mincha and their libation, to be received with acceptance before the Lord. And you shall make one of the goats (a sacrifice) for a sin offering, and two lambs of the year for consecrated offerings. And the priest shall uplift them with the bread of the first fruits an elevation before the Lord ; with the two lambs they (the loaves) shall be consecrated before the Lord for the priest. And on this same day you shall proclaim (that) it shall be a holy convocation to you. Ye shall do no work of labour. (This is) an everlasting statute in all your dwellings unto your generations.

And when you reap the harvest of your land, thou shalt not entirely finish the corner of thy field in thy reaping, nor shalt thou gather up the gleanings of thy harvest ; for the poor and for the stranger thou shalt leave them : I am the Lord your God.

And the Lord spake with Mosheh, saying : Speak with the sons of Israel, saying : In the seventh month[1] you shall have a (season of) Rest ; a memorial of the Trumpet, a holy convocation, no work of labour shall you do, but offer an oblation before the Lord.

And the Lord spake with Mosheh, saying : But on the

---

[1] *Tishri*, September.

tenth day of this seventh month shall be the Day of Atonement (*Yoma de Kippuraia*, the Day of Expiations) ; a holy convocation you shall have, and afflict (or humble) your souls,[2] and offer the oblation before the Lord. And no work [3] may you do on that same day, for it is the Day of Atonement, to make an atonement for you before the Lord your God. For every man who will not humble himself [4] on that same day, shall be cut off from his people. And any man who doeth any work on that same day, I will destroy that man from among his people. No work shall you do : an everlasting statute unto your generations, in all your dwellings. A Sabbath of rest shall it be to you, and ye shall humble your souls, on the ninth of the month at evening : from evening to evening you shall rest your rest.[5]

And the Lord spake with Mosheh, saying : Speak with the sons of Israel, saying : On the fifteenth day of this seventh month (shall be) the Feast of Bowers,[6] seven days before the Lord. On the first day a holy convocation ; no work of labour may you do. Seven days you shall offer oblations before the Lord, on the eighth day you shall have a holy convocation, and offer an oblation before the Lord. You shall be gathered together ; no work of labour may you do.

These are the Festivals of the Lord which you shall proclaim to be holy convocations, to offer an oblation before the Lord, a burnt sacrifice, and a mincha, and a consecrated offering, and libations (according to) the directory of the day, on its day. Beside (or except) the Sabbaths of the Lord, and beside your gifts, and beside

[2] Sam Vers , "by fasting"

[3] Not even the preparation of food , the fast being absolute.

[4] Sam Vers., "will not fast"

[5] *Tenuchun neyachakun.* Heb , *Tishebethu shabbatekem.*

[6] Or "shades ; " *Chaga di-metalaia.* Heb , *chag ha-sukkoth,* "feast of booths, or tabernacles."

all your vows, and beside all your freewill offerings
which you present before the Lord. Also on the fifteenth
day of the seventh month, when you have gathered in
the produce of the ground, you shall solemnize a feast
of the Lord seven days. On the first day there shall be
rest, and on the eighth day rest. And you shall take to
you on the first day the fruit of the orange (or citron)
tree,[7] and branches of palms,[8] and myrtles, and willows
of the brook, and rejoice before the Lord your God
seven days. And solemnize it, a feast before the Lord,
seven days in the year; it is an everlasting statute unto
your generations; in the seventh month shall you
solemnize it. In bowers shall you dwell seven days;
every one who is native born in Israel shall dwell (or
sit) in the bowers : that your generations may know
that I made the children of Israel to dwell under the
shadow of clouds when I brought them forth from the
land of Mizraim. I am the Lord your God. And
Mosheh declared the order of the Festivals of the Lord,
and taught them to the sons of Israel.

XXIV. And the Lord spake with Mosheh, saying,
Instruct the sons of Israel to bring to thee oil of olives,
pure (and) beaten, to give light, to make the lamps burn
continually. Outside of the veil of the testimony in the
tabernacle of ordinance, shall Aharon order it from
evening till morning before the Lord continually, an
everlasting statute unto your generations. Upon the
pure candelabrum shall he order the lamps before the
Lord continually. And thou shalt take flour, and prepare twelve cakes; two tenths shall be for one cake.
And thou shalt place them in two rows (orders), six in
an order, upon the pure table before the Lord. And
thou shalt put pure frankincense upon (each) order, and
it shall be for Bread of Memorial, (*Lechem leadkara*,) an

---

[7] Heb., "the tree hadar." Onkelos, *ilana ethrogia*　　[8] *Lulabin.*

oblation before the Lord.   From Sabbath day to Sabbath
day he shall order it before the Lord continually, from
the offerings of the children of Israel, an everlasting
statute.   And it shall be for Aharon and for his sons,
that they may eat it in the holy place; for it is most
sacred to him of the oblations of the Lord by an everlasting statute.

And the son of a woman, a daughter of Israel, but
he was the son of a Mizraite man, went out among the
children of Israel; and the son of the Israelite woman,
and a man, a son of Israel, had contention in the camp.
And the son of the woman the daughter of Israel gave
expression to the Name, and execrated.   And they
brought him unto Mosheh.   And the name of his
mother was Shelomith, the daughter of Dibree, of the
tribe of Dan.   And they bound him in the house of
confinement, until it should be explained to them by the
decree of the Word of the Lord.   And the Lord spake with
Mosheh, saying: Bring forth him who hath imprecated
without the camp, and let all who heard lay their hands
upon his head, and let all the congregation stone him.
And speak thou with the sons of Israel, saying: Whatever man imprecateth before his God shall bear his
guilt, and he who (so) expresseth the Name of the Lord,
dying shall die, and all the congregation shall stone
him, as well the stranger as the native born; when he
hath made (blasphemous) expression of the Name, he
shall be put to death.

And the man who killeth any soul of man shall die,
being put to death.   And he who killeth the life of a
beast shall make it good, life for life.   And if a man
inflict a blemish on his neighbour, as he hath done, so it
shall be done to him: bruise for bruise, eye for eye,
tooth for tooth, as he hath inflicted a blemish upon a
man, it shall be done to him.   And he who killeth a

beast shall make it good; but he who killeth a man
shall be put to death.   One judgment shall you have,
for the stranger as for the native born shall it be; for I
am the Lord your God.   And Mosheh spake with the
sons of Israel, and they brought out the blasphemer
without the camp, and stoned him with stones; and the
sons of Israel did as the Lord commanded Mosheh.

SECTION XXXII.

BEHAR SINAI.

XXV. AND the Lord spake with Mosheh in the
mountain of Sinai, saying: Speak with the children of
Israel, and say to them: When you have entered into
the land that I will give you, the land shall have rest by
an intermission (*shemet shemittha*) before the Lord.   Six
years thou shalt sow thy field, and six years prune thy
vineyard, and gather in its fruit; but in the seventh
year the land shall have a respite of rest (*neach shemittha*), a respite before the Lord; thou shalt not sow
thy field nor prune thy vineyard.   The after crop of thy
harvest thou shalt not reap, neither make vintage of the
grapes which thou mayest have left, it shall be a year of
remission to the land.   Yet the remission of the land [9]
shall be to thee for food, to thee, and to thy servant,
and to thy handmaid, and to thy hireling, and to the
sojourner who dwelleth with thee.   And for thy cattle,
and for the beasts that are in thy land, shall all the
produce of it be for meat.

And number to thee seven (such) years of Release,

---

[9] The produce of the land during the time of remission.—RASHI, EBEN
EZRA. For the whole year it was common property, and not the owner's
exclusively.

which are seven times seven years; and the days of the seven years of release shall be to thee (in all) forty and nine years. And thou shalt make the sound of the trumpet to pass forth, in the seventh month on the tenth of the month, on the day of the expiations shall you make (the sound of) the trumpet to pass through all your land. And you shall sanctify the year of the fifty years, and proclaim liberty in all the land to all its inhabitants; it is and it shall be a jubilee to you; and each man shall return to his inheritance, and each to his family shall return. A jubilee shall that year of fifty years be to you. Ye shall not sow nor reap the after crop, nor make vintage of the remainder, for it is a jubilee; it shall be sacred to you; of the growth of the field you may eat. In the year of this jubilee a man shall return to his inheritance.

And when thou sellest a sale to thy neighbour, or buyest of thy neighbour's hand, you shall not impose, a man upon his brother. For the number of the years after the (last) jubilee thou shalt buy of thy neighbour; for the number of the years of the produce he shall sell to thee: according to the multitude of the years thou shalt increase the price, and according to the fewness of the years thou shalt diminish the price; for he selleth thee the amount of the fruits. And you shall not impose, a man upon his neighbour; but thou shalt fear thy God, for I am the Lord your God. And you shall perform My statutes, and keep My judgments, and do them, and dwell in the land in security. And the land shall yield her fruitage, and you shall eat unto the full, and dwell upon it in security. And if you say, What shall we eat in the seventh year; behold, we are not to sow, nor to gather in our fruit? I will command My benediction upon you in the sixth year, and it shall produce for three years. And you shall sow in the eighth year, and eat of the old produce unto the ninth year: until the fruit come in, you shall eat of the old.

But you may not sell the ground absolutely : for the land is Mine, for you are guests and sojourners before Me ; and in all the land of your inheritance you shall let the ground have redemption.

When thy brother hath become poor, and shall have sold his possession, his redeemer who is of kin to him may come and release that which his kinsman has sold. And if he have no one to release it, and it pertaineth to his hand to find sufficient means for its redemption ; then let him reckon the years of its sale, and restore the full amount to the man who bought it, that he may return to his possession. But if his hand find not sufficiency to give him, the (property) sold shall be in the hand of the buyer until the year of Jubilee, and shall go out in the Jubilee, and return to his possession.

And if a man sell a dwelling house in a town surrounded with a wall, he may redeem it within the full year of the sale of it ; within that time shall be its redemption. But if it be not repurchased when the whole year is completed, the house that is in the walled town shall belong absolutely to him who bought it for his generations ; it shall not go out at the Jubilee. But the houses of the villages which have no wall round about them shall be accounted as the field of the land ; they may be redeemed, or shall go out at the Jubilee.

And the cities of the Levites, the houses of the cities of their inheritance, may be always redeemed by the Levites (or, be a perpetual redemption for the Levites). And (so of him) who purchaseth of the Levites, the purchased house in the city of their possession shall go out at the Jubilee ; for the houses of the cities of the Levites are their inheritance among the sons of Israel. But a field in the suburbs of their cities may not be sold; for it is an everlasting possession for them.

And if thy brother hath become poor, and his hand waver with thee, then thou shalt strengthen him, and he shall be a guest and a sojourner with thee. Thou shalt not take from him any usuries,[1] nor interest (increase), but shalt fear thy God, and let thy brother live with thee. Thou shalt not give him thy money for usury,[1] nor thy food for increase. I am the Lord your God, who brought you out from the land of Mizraim, to give you the land of Kenaan, and to be your God.

And if thy brother hath become poor with thee, and hath sold himself to thee, thou shalt not make him do the works of slaves, but as a hired man and an inmate shall he be with thee; until the year of Jubilee shall he serve with thee: then shall he go out from being with thee, he and his children with him, and return to his family and to the inheritance of his fathers. For they are My servants, whom I brought out from the land of Mizraim; they shall not be sold as the selling of bondmen. Thou shalt not make him serve with rigour, but shalt fear thy God. Thy bondmen and thy handmaids thou shalt have from the Gentiles who are about thee; from them thou mayest obtain bondmen and handmaids. And also from the sons of the uncircumcised strangers who sojourn with you, of them and of their children who are with you which are born in the land, you may obtain a possession, and may make them an inheritance for your children after you to inherit them for a possession to serve them perpetually; but among your brethren the sons of Israel no man shall make his brother labour with hardness. And if the hand of an uncircumcised sojourner with thee wax strong, and thy brother with thee become poor and sell himself to the uncircumcised

---

[1] Sam. Vers., "From him thou shalt not take double."

sojourner with thee, or to an Aramite of the race of the stranger, after that he is sold he may have redemption; one of his brethren may redeem him. Either his father's brother, or the son of his father's brother, may redeem him; or any one of kin to the flesh of his family may redeem him; or if his hand be able, he may redeem himself. And he shall reckon with his purchaser from the year that he sold himself, unto the year of Jubilee, and the money of his payment shall be according to the number of the years, according to the days of an hireling shall it be with him. If the years be yet many, according to them shall he give the price of his redemption; or if but few years remain unto the year of Jubilee, he shall compute with him, and according to the years shall give for his redemption. As a hireling year by year shall he be with him; he shall not work him with rigour before thine eyes. But if he be not redeemed within those years, he shall go out at the year of Jubilee, he and his children with him. For the sons of Israel are My servants; they are servants whom I brought out of the land of Mizraim: I am the Lord your God.

XXVI. You shall make to you no idols, nor image, nor set up for you a statue; nor a stone for worship shall you make on your land to worship upon it, for I am the Lord your God. The days of my Sabbaths you shall keep, and reverence the house of my sanctuary: I am the Lord.

SECTION XXXIII.

BECHUKKOTHAI.

IF you walk in My statutes, and observe My commandments and perform them, then will I give you

rains in their season, and your land shall yield her produce, and the tree of the field its fruit. And for you
the threshing shall reach unto the vintage, and the vintage shall reach unto the shooting forth of the seed ; and
you shall eat your bread with sufficiency, and dwell safely
in your land. And I will give peace in the land, and
you shall inhabit, and no one (be among you) who dis-
turbeth. And I will make the evil beast to cease from
the land, neither shall they who destroy with the sword
pass through on your land. And you shall chase your
adversaries, and they shall fall before you by the sword.
And five of you shall chase a hundred, and a hundred of
you put a myriad to flight, and your adversaries shall fall
before you by the sword. For I will have regard to you[2]
in my Word, to do you good, and will add to you, and
multiply you, and establish My covenant with you. And
you shall eat the old of the old, and shall turn out
the old before the new. And I will set My Tabernacle
among you, and My Word shall not reject you. And I
will make My Shekinah to dwell among you, and I will
be to you Eloha, and you shall be a people before Me.
I am the Lord your God who brought you out from the
land of Mizraim, that you should not be bondmen to
them ; and I brake off the yoke of the Gentiles from
you, and brought you into liberty.[3]

But if you will not be obedient to My Word, nor
perform all these commandments ; and if you despise My
statutes, and your soul abhor My judgments, so as not
to do all My commandments, by your making My covenant of no effect, (or, by your changing My covenant,) I
also will do this unto you : I will visit you with trouble, wasting, and burning, with darkness of eyes, and
exhaustion of soul ; and ye shall sow your seed in vain,

[2] Sam Vers, " I will be propitious. '
[3] Sam. Vers, " brought you into covenant with Me "

for your enemies shall eat it. And I will reveal My anger against you, and you shall be broken before your enemies; they that hate you shall reign over you, and ye shall flee when no one pursueth you. And if yet with these ye will not obey My Word, I will add sevenfold chastisement upon your sins. And I will break the glory of your power, and will make the heavens above you obdurate as iron, to give no rain, and the ground beneath you hard as brass in yielding no fruit; and your strength shall be put forth in vain, for your ground will not yield its produce, nor the tree of the earth its fruit. And if you will walk on frowardly before Me, and will not turn again to obey My Word, I will add to bring upon you a stroke sevenfold (heavier) according to your sins. And I will send the beast of the wilderness against you, and it shall devour you, and consume your cattle, and diminish you, and make your ways desolate. And if through these (calamities) ye will not be corrected by My Word, but will walk before Me with hardness (of heart), I also will proceed with you in hardness,[4] and will smite you, even I, sevenfold for your sins. And I will bring upon you those who kill with the sword, who shall take vengeance upon you in punishment for your transgressions against the words of the law. And you will congregate in your cities; but I will send forth the pestilence among you, and you shall be delivered into the hands of your enemies. When I shall have broken for you the support of food, ten women will prepare your bread in one oven, and return your bread by weight, and you will eat, but will not be satisfied. And if with this you will not be obedient to My Word, but will walk before me with obstinacy, I will proceed with you with strengthened anger, and will chastise you, even I, sevenfold for your sins. And ye shall eat the flesh of your

<hr>

[4] Sam. Vers., "relentlessly."

sons, and the flesh of your daughters will you eat. And
I will destroy your high places, and cut down your
images, and will throw your carcases upon the carcases of your idols, and My Word shall abhor you.
And I will make your cities a waste, and lay waste
your sanctuary, and accept no more the offering of your
congregation. And I will make your country a wilderness, and your enemies who will dwell in it shall spread
desolation upon it. And I will disperse you among the
nations, and draw out after you them who kill with the
sword, and your country shall be a desert and your cities
a waste. Then shall the land enjoy her repose all the
days in which it shall be a desert, and you be in the
land of your enemies : so shall the land repose, and enjoy her remission : all the days of its desolateness it
shall rest ; because it did not rest in your times of intermission, when you were inhabitants upon it. And to
the heart of those of you who are left in the land of
their enemies will I send brokenness, and they shall flee
at the sound of a falling leaf; they shall flee as flying
from before those who kill with the sword, and fall,
while no man pursueth. They shall thrust, one man
against his brother, as (fugitives) from before them who
destroy with the sword, while no one is pursuing, and
ye shall have no power against your adversaries ; and ye
shall perish among the nations, and the land of your
enemies shall consume you. And they who are left of
you shall pine away in your sins, in their adversaries'
land, and for their sins, also, the evil deeds of their
fathers which their own hands hold fast, shall they pine
away.[5]

But, if they will confess their sins, and the sins of
their fathers, and their falseness with which they have
acted falsely before My Word, and that they have walked

[5] Sam. Vers , " they shall be crucified."

before me in obduracy, (while) I also have dealt against
them with sharpness, and brought them into the land of
their enemies; when then their stout heart shall be
broken, and they concur with (the punishment of) their
sins, I will remember my covenant with Jacob, and my
covenant with Izhak, and also my covenant with Abraham will I remember, and I will remember the land.
But the land shall be left by them, and shall enjoy her
repose while made desolate for them, and they shall receive (the punishment of) their sins; curses instead of
blessings will I have brought upon them who had cast
away My judgments, and whose soul had abhorred My
statutes.　Yet, even in the land of their enemies I will
not strike them down, nor cast them away to consume
them utterly, and to make My covenant with them to
change; for I am the Lord their God.　But I will remember the former covenant with them whom I brought
out of the land of Mizraim in the eyes of the nations,
that I might be their God.　I am the Lord.

These are the statutes and judgments and laws which
the Lord appointed between His Word and the sons
of Israel, in the mountain of Sinai, by the hand of
Mosheh.

XXVII. And the Lord spake with Mosheh, saying:
Speak with the sons of Israel, and say to them : When
a man setteth apart a votive offering, (it shall be) by
estimation of the life before the Lord.　If it be the
valuation for a male from twenty years to sixty years
old, the valuation shall be fifty shekels of silver, in the
shekel of the sanctuary.　And if a female, the valuation
shall be thirty shekels.　And if the age be from five
years to twenty years, the valuation for a male shall be
twenty shekels, and for a female ten shekels.　And if the
age be from a month unto five years, the valuation for a
male shall be five shekels of silver, and for a female

three shekels of silver shall be the valuation. But if
(the age) be sixty years and upwards, for a male the
valuation shall be fifteen shekels, and for a female ten
shekels. But if he be too poor (for the sum of) his
valuation, then he shall stand before the priest, and the
priest shall make valuation for him upon the word of
that which the hand of him who maketh the vow may
possess; so shall the priest make his estimate.

And if it be an animal of which (some portion) will
be offered an oblation before the Lord, all that he giveth
of it before the Lord shall be sacred; he shall not alter
it or change it, good for bad, or bad for good; and if
he will indeed change animal for animal, both it and
that for which it is changed shall be sacred. And if it
be any unclean animal, of which none may be offered an
oblation before the Lord, he shall present the animal before the priest, and the priest shall value it, whether
good or bad; according to the estimate of the priest so
shall it be. And if he will redeem it, then he shall add
the fifth upon its value.

And when a man shall sanctify his house, to be consecrated before the Lord, the priest shall value it, whether
good or bad; as the priest shall value it, so shall it stand.
And if he who had consecrated it will redeem his house,
then let him add the fifth of the price of its value upon
it, and it shall be his.

And if a man consecrate a field of his possession before the Lord, its valuation shall be according to (the
quantity of) its seed; if sown with barley, a measure[6]
shall be (valued at) fifty shekels of silver. If he consecrate his field from the year of Jubilee, it shall stand
according to its value. But if he consecrate his field
after the year of Jubilee, the priest shall reckon the
money with him according to the years which remain

---

[d] *Kor.* Heb , *Chomer* = seventy-five gallons.

until the (next) year of Jubilee, and it shall be abated from the valuation. But if he will redeem the field that he had consecrated, let him add to it a fifth of its valuated price, and it shall be confirmed to him. But if he will not redeem the field, or if he have sold the field to another man, it shall not be redeemed any more: but the field, when it would have gone out at the Jubilee, shall be consecrated before the Lord as a field devoted (*hekel cherema*); the possession of it shall be to the priest. And if a man will consecrate before the Lord a field which he hath bought, and which is not of the fields of his inheritance, then the priest shall reckon the sum (receipt) of its value until the year of Jubilee, and he shall give the price of it in that day, a holy thing before the Lord. In the year of Jubilee the field shall return unto him who sold it, to whom the possession of the land had belonged. And every valuation shall be in the shekel of the sanctuary, twenty maheen before the Lord.

Moreover, the first-born among cattle which is to be a firstling before the Lord, no man may consecrate, whether ox or sheep; it is the Lord's already. And if it be an unclean animal, then he shall redeem it according to its valuation, and add one fifth thereto: or if it be not redeemed, then it shall be sold according to its valuation. Nevertheless, no devoted thing which a man shall have devoted before the Lord of all that he hath of man or of beast and of the field of his possession may be sold or redeemed; every devoted thing is most sacred before the Lord. No devoted one who is devoted (or accursed) of men, (as the criminal doomed to death,) shall be redeemed; being slain, he shall be killed.

And all the tythe of the land, whether of the seed of the land or of the fruit of the tree, is the Lord's; it is sacred before the Lord. But if a man will redeem any of his tythe, a fifth shall he add upon it. And every tything of oxen or sheep, whatever passeth under the tything rod, shall be sacred before the Lord. He shall not choose between the good and bad, neither shall he change it. But if he will commute it, both it and that for which it was exchanged shall be consecrate, and not be redeemed.

These are the commandments which the Lord commanded Mosheh for the children of Israel, in the mountain of Sinai.

END OF THE TARGUM OF ONKELOS ON THE BOOK
VAIYIKRA.

THE TARGUM OF PALESTINE

COMMONLY ENTITLED

THE TARGUM OF JONATHAN BEN UZZIEL,

ON THE

BOOK OF LEVITICUS.

SECTION OF THE TORAH XXIV.

TITLE VAIYIKRA.

I. AND it was when Mosheh had completed to
erect the tabernacle that Mosheh reasoned and judged
in his heart, and said: To Mount Sinai, whose excellency is the excellence only of an hour, and its holiness
the holiness but of three days, I could not ascend till
the time that the word was spoken to me; but the excellence of this the tabernacle of ordinance is an eternal
excellency, and its holiness an everlasting holiness,
therefore is it right that I should not enter within it
until the time that I am spoken with from before the
Lord. Then did the word[1] of the Lord call unto
Mosheh, and the Word[2] of the Lord spake with him
from the tabernacle of ordinance, saying:

[JERUSALEM TARGUM. And it was when Moshch had
completed to erect the tabernacle, to anoint it, and sanctify it, and all its vessels, that Mosheh reasoned in his
heart, and said: Within Mount Sinai, whose majesty

---

[1] *Dibbura,* "oracle."   [2] *Memra.*

was the majesty of an hour, and its holiness the holiness
of an hour, I might not ascend till the time which was
bidden me from before the Lord; nor into the tabernacle of ordinance, whose majesty is an eternal majesty,
and its holiness an everlasting holiness, is it right for
me to enter till the time that I am bidden from before
the Lord And the Word of the Lord called to Mosheh;
for the Word of the Lord was altogether with him, from
the tabernacle of ordinance, saying:]

Speak with the sons of Israel, and say to them : If
a man of you,—but not of the rebellious worshippers of
idols,—bring an oblation before the Lord, (it must be)
from the clean cattle, from the oxen or from the sheep;
but not from the wild beasts may you offer your oblations. If his oblation be a burnt offering of oxen, he
shall bring a male unblemished to the door of the tabernacle of ordinance, and offer him to be accepted for himself before the Lord. And he shall lay his right hand
with firmness upon the head of the sacrifice, that it may
be acceptable from him to propitiate on his behalf. And
the slayer shall kill the ox at the place of slaughter before the Lord, and the sons of Aharon the priest shall
bring the blood in vessels, and sprinkle the blood which
is in the basins round about the altar that is at the door
of the tabernacle of ordinance. And he shall take away
the skin from the sacrifice, and divide him according to
his members. [JERUSALEM. And he shall skin the
holocaust, and divide him by his members.] And the
sons of Aharon the priest shall put fire upon the altar,
and lay wood in order upon the fire; and the priests the
sons of Aharon shall lay the members in order and the
heart and the covering of the fat upon the wood that is
on the fire upon the altar. And he shall wash the inwards and his legs with water; and the priest shall offer
the whole upon the altar of burnt offering, an oblation

to be accepted with grace before the Lord. [JERUSALEM. And he shall wash.] And if his oblation be of the flock, whether of the lambs or of the young goats, he shall bring a male unblemished. And the slayer shall kill it at the foot of the altar on the north side, before the Lord, and the priests the sons of Aharon shall sprinkle the blood that is in the basins upon the altar round about. And he shall divide it by its members, its head and its body, and the priest shall set them in order on the wood which is upon the fire on the altar. And the inwards and his legs he shall wash with water, and the priest shall offer the whole and burn it at the altar of burnt sacrifice; it is an offering to be received with grace before the Lord.

And if his oblation before the Lord be of birds, he shall bring his oblation from the turtle doves or the young of pigeons; but of the turtle doves he shall bring the largest, and of the pigeons the young ones. And the priest shall offer it upon the altar, and shall wring off its head, and burn upon the altar, and press out its blood at the side of the altar. And he shall remove its gullet and the contents thereof, and throw it by the eastern side of the altar in the place where they burn the cinders. [JERUSALEM. And the priest shall bring it to the side of the altar, and twist off its head, and lay it in order upon the altar, and press out its blood at the bottom of the altar. And he shall remove its ventricle with the dung, and throw it by, on the east of the altar at the place where the cinders are emptied.] And he shall cut it between its wings, but not to sever the wings from it; and the priest shall burn it at the altar upon the wood which is on the fire: it is a sacrifice, an oblation to be received with favour before the Lord. [JERUSALEM. And he shall cut it through its wings, but not to dissever; and the priest shall lay it in order upon the altar, on the wood that is upon the fire.]

II. But when a man will offer the oblation of a
mincha before the Lord, his oblation shall be of meal
flour, and he shall pour oil upon it, and put incense
thereon, and bring it to the priests the sons of Aharon ;
and he shall take from thence his hand full of the meal
and of the best of the oil, with all the frankincense ; and
the priest shall burn the goodly memorial at the altar,
an oblation to be accepted with grace before the Lord.
And what remaineth of the mincha shall be Aharon's
and his sons', most holy among the oblations of the
Lord.   And when thou wilt offer the oblation of a
mincha of that which is baked in the oven, it shall be
cakes of flour, unleavened and mixed with oil, and wafers
unleavened, which are anointed with oil. [JERUSALEM.
And wafers unleavened.]   And if thy oblation of a
mincha be from the pan, it shall be of flour mingled with
oil, unleavened shall it be.   He shall break it in pieces,
and pour oil thereupon.   It is a mincha. [JERUSALEM.
And he shall break it in pieces, and pour oil thereon.]
And if thy oblation be a mincha from the gridiron, it
shall be made of flour broiled with oil.   And the mincha
which hath been made with the flour and the oil thou
shalt bring in before the Lord, and the man who
bringeth it shall present it to the priest, and the priest
shall take it to the altar.   And the priest shall separate
from the mincha a memorial of praise, and burn it at
the altar, an oblation to be accepted with grace before
the Lord.   And what remaineth of the mincha shall be
for Aharon and his sons, it is most holy among the
oblations of the Lord.   But no mincha which thou
offerest to the Lord shalt thou make with leaven ; for
neither leaven nor honey mayest thou offer as an oblation before the Lord.

When thou offerest an oblation of first fruits before
the Lord, the bread of the first fruits thou mayest bring

leavened, and the dates in the season of first fruits, and
the fruit with its honey thou mayest bring, and the
priest may eat them; but they shall not burn them at
the altar as an oblation to be received with favour.
And every oblation of thy mincha thou shalt salt with
salt; thou shalt not withhold the salt of the covenant of
thy God from thy mincha, because the twenty and four
gifts of the priests are appointed with a covenant of
salt; therefore salt shalt thou offer with all thy oblations. And if thou wilt present a mincha of first fruits
before the Lord, (ears of wheat) roasted by fire, roasted
flour and meal of barley shalt thou offer as a mincha of
thy first fruits. And thou shalt put olive oil upon it,
and lay frankincense thereon; it is a mincha. And
the priest shall burn its memorial of praise from the
meal and from the best of the oil, with all the frankincense, an oblation before the Lord.

III. And if his oblation be of the sanctified victims,[3]
if from thy cattle he offer, whether male or female,
he shall offer it perfect. And he shall lay his right
hand firmly on the head of his oblation, and the slayer
shall kill it at the door of the tabernacle of ordinance,
and the priests the sons of Aharon shall sprinkle the
blood upon the altar round about. And of the sanctified victim, his oblation before the Lord, he shall offer
the covering of fat which covereth the inwards, even all
the fat which is upon the inwards. And the two kidneys,
and the fat which is upon them, that is, upon the
folding, and the caul that is upon the liver with the
kidneys, he shall remove. And the sons of Aharon shall
offer it on the altar with the sacrifice that is on the wood
which is upon the fire, an oblation to be received with
favour before the Lord. And if his oblation of a consecrated offering before the Lord be from the flock,

[3] Peace offerings. See Glossary.

H 5

whether male or female, his oblation shall be perfect.
If he present a lamb for his oblation, he shall bring it
before the Lord; and lay his right hand firmly on the
head of his oblation, and the slayer shall kill it before
the tabernacle of ordinance, and the sons of Aharon
shall sprinkle its blood upon the altar round about.
And of the offering of his consecrated oblation he shall
offer the best of its fat, and remove the whole of the
tail, close to the spine, the covering of fat which
covereth the inwards, even all the fat that is upon the
inwards. [JERUSALEM. And the fat and the entire breast
to the chine he shall remove, and the fat which covereth
the inwards.] And the two kidneys and the fat which
is upon them, upon the foldings, and the caul that is
over the liver, together with the kidneys, he shall take
away. And the priest shall sacrifice it at the altar, the
meat of an oblation before the Lord.

And if his oblation be from the young goats, he shall
bring it before the Lord, and lay his right hand upon
its head, and the slayer shall kill it before the tabernacle of ordinance, and the sons of Aharon shall sprinkle
its blood upon the altar round about. And of his oblation before the Lord he shall offer the covering of fat
which covereth the inwards, even all the fat that is upon
the inwards. And the two kidneys and the fat which
is upon them (and) on the foldings, and the caul which
is over the liver, along with the kidneys, he shall take
away. And the priest shall sacrifice them at the altar,
the meat of an oblation to be received with favour. All
the fat (shall be offered) before the Lord. It is an everlasting statute unto all your generations, that neither
the fat nor the blood shall be eaten in any of your
dwellings, but upon the back of the altar it shall be
sacrificed unto the Name of the Lord.

IV. And the Lord spake with Mosheh, saying: Speak

with the sons of Israel, saying : When a man hath sinned
inadvertently against any of the commandments of the
Lord (in doing) what ought not to be done, and he
hath done it against any one of them : if the high
priest who is consecrated with oil hath sinned,—as
when he hath offered a sin offering for the people not
according to the rite,—he shall bring for his sin a young
bullock unblemished before the Lord for a sin offering.
He shall bring in the bullock to the gate of the tabernacle of ordinance, to the presence of the Lord, and lay
his right hand upon the head of the bullock, and the
slayer shall kill the bullock before the Lord.   And the
high priest who is anointed with oil shall take of the
blood of the bullock, and carry it into the tabernacle of
ordinance ; and the priest shall dip his fingers in the
blood, and sprinkle the blood seven times in the presence
of the Lord before the veil of the sanctuary.   [JERUSA-
LEM. And the priest shall dip his fingers, and sprinkle
some of the blood seven times.]   And the priest shall
put some of the blood upon the horns of the altar of
sweet incense that is before the Lord in the tabernacle
of ordinance, and all the rest of the blood of the bullock
he shall pour out at the foundation of the altar of burnt
sacrifice which is at the gate of the tabernacle of ordinance.   And all the fat of the bullock of the sin offering he shall separate from him, the covering of fat which
covereth the inwards, even all the fat which is upon the
inwards.   And the two kidneys, and the fat which is
upon them, upon the folding, and the caul that is upon
the liver, with the kidneys, he shall remove.   As it was
separated from the bullock of the consecrated sacrifice,
so shall (these things) be separated from the lambs and
from the goats, and the priest shall burn them upon the
altar of burnt offering.   And all the skin of the bullock,
and his flesh with his head and with his legs, and his

inward parts and his dung, the whole of the bullock he shall carry forth into a clean place without the camp, to a place where the cinders are poured out, and shall burn him with wood in the fire, at the place where cinders are poured out shall he be burned.

And if the whole congregation of Israel have erred, and the thing hath been hidden from the sight of the congregation in doing inadvertently against one of the commandments of the Lord what was not right to be done, and (thus) have sinned; and the sin which they have sinned be made known to them, the congregation shall offer a young bullock as a sin offering, and shall bring him before the tabernacle of ordinance. And twelve of the elders of the congregation, the counsellors (*amarkelin*) appointed over the twelve tribes, shall lay their hands firmly upon the head of the bullock, and the slayer shall kill the bullock before the Lord. And the high priest shall carry some of the blood of the bullock into the tabernacle of ordinance. And the priest shall dip his finger into the blood, and sprinkle some thereof seven times in the presence of the Lord before the veil; and he shall put some of the blood upon the horns of the altar that is before the Lord within the tabernacle of ordinance, and all the (residue of the) blood he shall pour out at the foundation of the altar of burnt offering which is at the door of the tabernacle of ordinance. And all the fat he shall separate from him, and burn at the altar. And he shall do with the bullock as he did with the bullock for the sin of the high priest, so shall he do with him. And the priest shall atone for them, and it shall be forgiven them. And the bullock shall be carried forth without the camp and be burned, as the former bullock of the high priest was burned, that through it the sin of Israel may be forgiven It is a sin offering for the congregation.

At what time the ruler of his people shall have
sinned, and done against any of the commandments of
the Lord his God that which ought not to have been
done, and he hath sinned through ignorance; if his sin
that he hath sinned be made known to him, he shall
bring for his oblation a kid of the goats, a male,
unblemished; and he shall lay his right hand firmly
upon the head of the goat, and the slayer shall kill him
at the place of the sacrifice of the burnt offering before
the Lord. It is a sin offering. And the priest shall take
of the blood of the sin offering upon his finger, and put it
on the horns of the altar of burnt sacrifice, and he shall
pour out the blood at the foundation of the altar of burnt
sacrifice. And all the fat he shall burn at the altar, as
was the fat of the sanctified oblations; and the priest
shall atone for him on account of his sin, and it shall
be forgiven him.

And if a man of the people of the land sin through
ignorance in doing (against) one of the commandments
of the Lord what was not right to do, and he hath
sinned; if his sin that he hath sinned be made known
to him, he shall bring for his oblation an unblemished
female of the goats for the sin that he hath sinned; and
he shall lay his right hand on the head of the sin offering, and kill the sin offering at the place of burnt
sacrifice; and the priest shall take of the blood with
his fingers, and put it on the horns of the altar of burnt
sacrifice, and pour out all the blood at the foundation
of the altar. And he shall remove all her fat, as the
fat of the consecrated sacrifices was taken off, and the
priest shall burn it at the altar, to be received with
acceptance before the Lord; and the priest shall atone
for him, and he shall be forgiven.

But if he bring a lamb as his offering for sin, he
shall bring a female, unblemished; and lay his right

hand on the head of the sin offering, and kill it as an oblation for sin, at the place of burnt sacrifice. And the priest shall take of the blood of the sin offering, and put it upon the horns of the altar of burnt sacrifice, and pour out all the blood at the foundation of the altar. And all the fat he shall remove, as the fat of the lamb of the sanctified victims was removed, and the priest shall burn it at the altar with the oblations of the Lord, and the priest shall make atonement for him on account of the sin that he hath sinned, and it shall be forgiven him.

V. When a man shall have sinned, and heard the voice of the oath of execration, or have been himself a witness, or shall have seen that one of the world hath transgressed against the words of an oath, or shall have known that his companion hath sworn or imprecated vainly, if he show it not, he shall bear his sin. Or if a man touch anything unclean, whether the carcase of an unclean beast, or a carcase of unclean cattle, or the carcase of an unclean reptile, and it be hidden from him, and he, being unclean, shall touch any consecrated thing, he is guilty. Or if he touch the uncleanness of a man, even whatever uncleanness that defileth him, and it be hidden from him, and he touch anything consecrated,—after that it is discovered by him, and he knoweth that he is defiled and not clean, he shall be guilty. Or if a man shall swear to make declaration with his lips to do evil or good [JERUSALEM. To do evil or good] upon any matter upon which a man may affirm, whether of the present or the future, that he can make declaration by oath, and he falsify therein, and it be hidden from him, but afterward it be discovered to him, and he know that he hath falsified, and he repent not; though he hath become guilty in any one of these, if he shall have (thus) sinned in any one of these four

things, but afterwards repent, he shall make confession
of the sin by which he hath sinned. And he shall
bring the oblation of his trespass offering to the Presence of the Lord for the sin that he hath sinned, a
female lamb of the flock, or a kid of the goats, for a sin
offering; and the priest shall atone for him (that he
may be absolved) from his sin. But if his hand find
not sufficiency to bring a lamb, let him bring, as an
offering for the trespass that he hath committed, two
large turtle doves or two young pigeons before the
Lord; one for a sin offering, and one for a burnt sacrifice. And he shall bring them to the priest, who shall
offer that which he may choose for the sin offering
first · and he shall wring its head near to the spine,
but not separate its head from the neck; and he shall
sprinkle some of the blood upon the side of the altar, and
pour out the remainder of the blood at the foot of the
altar: it is a sin offering. And of the second bird he shall
make a burnt sacrifice, according to the rite, with the
bird which he had chosen for the sin offering, and not
according to the rite for the bullock, or the lamb, or
the young goat. And the priest shall expiate him from
the sin that he hath sinned, and it shall be forgiven
him. But if his hand find not sufficiency to bring two
large turtle doves or two young pigeons, let him bring
as an oblation for sin a tenth part of three sein of flour
for a sin offering; but let him not put oil thereon nor
frankincense, for it is a sin offering. And he shall
bring it to the priest, and the priest shall take a handful for a commendable memorial thereof, and burn it at
the altar with the oblations of the Lord: it is a sin
offering. And the priest shall atone for his sin that he
hath sinned, and it shall be forgiven him. And the
remainder shall be a mincha to the priest.

And the Lord spake with Mosheh, saying: When a

man falsifieth with falsity and sinneth, though with inadvertence, in making misuse of the holy things of the Lord, he shall bring the oblation for his trespass to the presence of the Lord, an unblemished ram from the flock, with an estimation in silver according to the value of the holy thing which hath been misappropriated, in shekels, after the shekels of the sanctuary, for a trespass offering. And the misuse of the holy thing by which he sinned, (the perversion of what was) sanctified, he shall make good, and shall add the fifth of its value unto it, and bring it to the priest who shall atone for him with the ram of the trespass offering, and it shall be forgiven him.

If a man sin, and do against any one of all the commandments of the Lord that which is not right to do, though he knew it not, he hath sinned, and shall bear his guilt; but (when he hath discovered it), let him bring a ram unblemished from the flock according to his estimation for a trespass offering unto the priest, and the priest shall atone for him for the ignorance with which he erred ignorantly and sinned, and it shall be forgiven him. It is an oblation for trespass. Whosoever hath become guilty, a trespass oblation let him bring, an oblation for trespass unto the Name of the Lord, for the sin that he hath sinned.

VI. And the Lord spake with Mosheh, saying When a man sinneth and falsifieth with falsehoods unto the Name of the Word of the Lord, or denieth to his neighbour the deposit which hath been deposited with him, whether in partnership of hands, or by rapine, or reckless dealing with his neighbour; [JERUSALEM. Or shall be contumacious (or slanderous) with his neighbour;] or if he find a thing that hath been lost and denieth it, and sweareth falsely about any one of all these by which a man in doing them shall become

guilty, he who shall thus transgress, and sin, and swear,
shall restore what he hath robbed with robbery or
injured by injury, or the deposit that was deposited
with him, or the lost thing which he had found, or
whatsoever about which he had sworn with falsehood,
he shall make good in the capital, and shall add a fifth
of its value thereto, and deliver it to its owner on the
day that he maketh penance for his sin.　And he shall
bring an oblation for his trespass to the presence of the
Lord; a male unblemished from the flock, according to
its estimation for the trespass, (shall he bring) unto the
priest.　And the priest shall atone for him before the
Lord, and it shall be forgiven him concerning any one
of all these which he may have done and become guilty.

SECTION XXV.

VAIYIKRA TSAV

AND the Lord spake with Mosheh, saying, Instruct
Aharon and his sons, saying, This is the law of the
burnt offering which is brought to make atonement for
the thoughts (errors) of the heart: it is a burnt offering which is made in (the manner of) the burnt offering at Mount Sinai, and abideth upon the place of
burning on the altar all the night until the morning.
for the fire of the altar shall be burning in it.　And the
priest shall dress himself in vestments of linen, and
put drawers of linen upon his flesh; [JERUSALEM.
Drawers;] and shall separate the ashes which the fire
(maketh) in consuming the burnt offering upon the
altar, and shall place them at the side of the altar.
And he shall take off his vestments and put on other

garments, and carry forth the ashes without the camp
into a clean place. But the fire upon the altar shall
burn upon it unextinguished, and the priest shall lay
wood upon it from morning to morning, at four hours
of the day, and shall set in order the burnt offering
upon it, and burn upon it the fat of the sanctified oblations. The fire shall be ever burning upon the altar;
it shall never be extinguished.

And this is the law of the Mincha, which the priests,
the sons of Aharon, shall offer in the presence of the
Lord before the altar. And he shall separate his handful of the flour of the mincha, of the best thereof, with
all the frankincense which is upon the mincha, and
burn it at the altar to be received with favour, as a
memorial of praise before the Lord. And that which
remaineth of it shall Aharon and his sons eat; unleavened shall they eat it in the holy place, in the court of
the tabernacle of ordinance shall they eat it. Their
portion of the residue of the mincha of My oblations
given to them shall not be baked with leaven; it is
most sacred, as the sin offering and as the trespass
offering. Every man of the sons of Aharon may eat of
it. This is an everlasting statute for your generations
concerning the oblations of the Lord: every one who
toucheth them must be sanctified.

And the Lord spake with Mosheh, saying: This is
the oblation of Aharon and of his sons, which they are
to offer before the Lord on the day that they anoint
him, that he may possess the inheritance of the high
priesthood. A tenth of three seahs of fine flour for a
mincha, one half in the morning and a half at eventide. Thou shalt make it upon a pan, mixed with olive
oil shalt thou offer it; in divided pieces shalt thou offer
the mincha, to be received with acceptance before the
Lord. [JERUSALEM. Fried shalt thou offer it; broken

in pieces shalt thou offer the mincha, a sweet savour of
acceptableness unto the Name of the Lord.]   And the
high priest who is anointed with oil, (and also when
(any one) of his sons who are constituted priests (is
consecrated) in his place,) shall perform this : it is an
everlasting statute before the Lord : the whole shall be
set in order and burned.   For every mincha of the
priest shall be wholly set in order and consumed : it
shall not be eaten.

And the Lord spake with Mosheh, saying : Speak
with Aharon and with his sons, saying : This is the law
of the sin offering which is to be killed in the place
where the burnt offering is killed; it shall be slain as a
sin offering before the Lord; it is most sacred.   The
priest who maketh atonement with blood may eat of it
in the holy place; it shall be eaten in the court of the
tabernacle of ordinance; whosoever toucheth the flesh of
it must be sanctified.   And if any one let some of its
blood fall upon a garment, (the garment so) bedropped
shall be washed in the holy place.   And every earthen
vessel in which (the flesh of it) is boiled shall be broken,
lest that which is common be boiled in it; or if it be
boiled in a vessel of brass, it shall be scoured with
potter's earth and washed in waters.   Every man of the
priests may eat thereof; it is most sacred.   But no sin
offering whose blood is carried into the tabernacle of
ordinance to make atonement in the sanctuary may be
eaten; it must be burned with fire.

VII. And this is the law of the Trespass Offering; it
is most holy.   In the place where they kill the burnt
sacrifice they shall kill the trespass offering, and the
blood thereof shall he sprinkle upon the altar round
about.   And he shall offer all the fat thereof, and the
tail, and the fat which covereth the inwards; and the
two kidneys, and the fat which is upon them, and upon

the inwards.   And the caul that is upon the liver and
upon the kidneys shall he take away; and the priest
shall burn them at the altar, an oblation before the
Lord: it is a trespass offering.   Every man of the
priests may eat of it, in the holy place shall it be eaten :
it is most sacred.   As the rite of the sin offering, so is
the rite of the trespass; there is one law for them : the
priest who maketh atonement with its blood shall have
it.   And when the priest offereth another man's burnt
sacrifice, the skin of the burnt sacrifice which he offereth
shall be the priest's.   And every mincha which is baked
in the oven, and every one that is made in a pot, or in a
frying pan, or upon a dish, the priest who offereth it
shall have it for his own.   And every mincha mixed
with oil, or which is dry, shall be for any of the sons of
Aharon, a man as his brother.

And this is the law of the Sanctified Victims which
they may offer before the Lord.   If he offer it for a
thanksgiving, let him offer with the oblation of thanks
unleavened cakes mingled with olive oil, and unleavened
wafers anointed with olive oil, and flour fried with a
mixture of olive oil. [JERUSALEM. One rule.] Upon
the cakes he shall offer his oblation of leavened bread
with the hallowed sacrifice of thanksgiving.   And of it
he shall present one as a separation before the Lord;
the priest who sprinkleth the blood of the hallowed
sacrifice shall have it.   And the flesh of his hallowed
sacrifice of thanksgiving shall be eaten on the day when
it is offered; none of it may be laid up (or covered up)
until the morning.

But if his hallowed sacrifice be a vow or a free-will
gift, the sacrifice may be (partly) eaten on the day when
it is offered, and the remainder may be eaten on the day
following at evening.   And what remaineth of the flesh
of the hallowed sacrifice on the third day shall be burned

in fire. If, eating, he will eat of the flesh of his hallowed
sacrifice on the third day, it shall not be accepted of him
who offered it, nor reckoned to him for righteousness ;
it will be a profane thing, [JERUSALEM. It will be a
profane thing,] and the man who eateth of it shall bear
his sin. And if the flesh of things hallowed touch any
uncleanness, it must not be eaten, but be burned in
fire ; but (as to) flesh that is consecrated, every one who
is clean by sanctification may eat the hallowed flesh.
But the man who eateth of the flesh of the hallowed
sacrifice that is offered before the Lord with his uncleanness upon him, that man shall be destroyed from among
his people. The man also who toucheth any unclean
thing, whether the uncleanness of man, or of unclean
beasts, or any unclean reptile, and eateth of the flesh of
the hallowed sacrifices offered before the Lord, that man
shall be cut off from his people.

And the Lord spake with Mosheh, saying: Speak
with the sons of Israel, saying: You may not eat any
fat of oxen, or sheep, or goats ; but the fat of an animal
which corrupteth in the hour of sacrifice, or which dieth
a dead thing by death, or the fat of a beast that is torn,
may be used in any work ; but the fat of an animal that
is in a right (condition) shall be burned upon the altar,
and shall in no wise be eaten. For he who eateth (the
fat) of an animal that is fit to be offered as an oblation
before the Lord, that man who eateth the fat shall be cut
off from his people. In none of your dwellings shall
you eat the blood whether of bird or of beast. Every
man who eateth the blood of any living thing, that man
shall be cut off from his people.

And the Lord spake with Mosheh, saying: Speak
with the sons of Aharon, saying : Whosoever presenteth
his hallowed sacrifice before the Lord, shall himself bring
the oblation of his hallowed sacrifice unto the presence

of the Lord. His hands shall bring the oblations of
the Lord which he would set apart as his hallowed
sacrifice, the fat, the fatness that is upon the breast, and
the breast cut out with two ribs here and two ribs there
at the top, shall he bring to be uplifted, an elevation
before the Lord. [JERUSALEM. His own hands shall
bring in the oblation of the Lord. the fat which is upon
the breast he shall give it, and the breast, to wave it a
wave offering before the Lord.] And the priest shall
burn the fat upon the altar, and the breast shall be for
Aharon and for his sons. [JERUSALEM. The breast.]
And the right shoulder of your hallowed sacrifice from
the side unto the extremity (*deroa*, arm) you shall give
as a separation unto the priest. He of the sons of
Aharon who offereth the blood and the fat of the hallowed
sacrifice shall have the right shoulder as his portion.
For the uplifted breast and the shoulder of separation
have I taken of your hallowed sacrifice, and given them
to Aharon the priest and to his sons by an everlasting
statute, from the children of Israel. This pertaineth to
the consecration of Aharon and to the consecration of
his sons over all the Levites their brethren, that they
may eat of the Lord's oblations in the day that they
present them to minister before the Lord; which the
Lord commanded to be given them in the day of their
consecration from among the sons of Israel, by an everlasting statute to your generations.

This is the law of the burnt offering which is brought
to atone for the thoughts of the heart; of the mincha,
of the sin offering, of the trespass offering, and of the
peace offering, or the hallowed sacrifices which the Lord
commanded Mosheh in Mount Sinai, in the day that
he commanded the sons of Israel to offer their oblations
before the Lord in the tabernacle that he made unto
him in the wilderness of Sinai.

VIII. And the Lord spake with Mosheh, saying: Bring near Aharon who is afar off on account of the work of the calf; and take the vestments that I commanded thee, and the oil of consecration, and the bullock, and the two rams, with the basket of unleavened cakes. And let all the congregation gather together at the gate of the tabernacle of ordinance.

And Mosheh did as the Lord commanded, and the congregation assembled on the twenty and third of the days of the month of Adar, at the gate of the tabernacle of ordinance. And Mosheh said to the congregation: This is the thing which the Lord hath commanded to be done. And Mosheh took Aharon and his sons, and washed them with water. And he set in order upon him the vestment, and girded him with the girdle, and clothed him with the mantle robe, and put upon him the ephod, and bound him with the band of the ephod, and ordained him therewith. And he set the breast-plate upon him, and ordered in the breastplate the uraia and the tummaia. And he put the mitre upon his head, and set upon the mitre over his forehead the plate of gold, the diadem of holiness, as the Lord commanded Mosheh. And Mosheh took the oil of con-secration, and anointed the tabernacle, and sanctified it. And he sprinkled upon the altar seven times, and sanc-tified the altar and all its vessels, and the laver and its foundation to sanctify them. And he poured of the oil of consecration upon Aharon's head, and anointed him after he had invested him, to sanctify him.

And Mosheh brought near Aharon and his sons, and clothed them with vestments, and girded them with girdles, and decked them with mitres, as the Lord com-manded Mosheh. And he brought the bullock for the sin offering, and Aharon and his sons laid their right hands upon the head of the bullock, for their sin

offering. And Mosheh killed the bullock : and Mosheh
took the blood and put it upon the horns of the altar
round about with his finger, and anointed the altar (to
expiate it) from all double-mindedness, constraint, and
force, from the thoughts of his heart, should any one of
the princes of the sons of Israel have taken his separation from his brethren by violence, and brought it for
the work of the tabernacle,[4] or lest any one was found
among the children of Israel who had it not in his
heart to bring for the work, but heard the voice of the
crier, and was constrained, and brought without willingness ; therefore cleansed he it with the blood of the
bullock, and poured the rest of the blood at the foot of
the altar, and sanctified it to make atonement thereon.
And he took all the fat that was on the inwards, and
the caul of the liver, and the two kidneys with their fat,
and Mosheh burned them at the altar. But the bullock, and the skin, and his flesh, and his offal, he burned
in fire without the camp, as the Lord commanded
Mosheh.

And he took the ram for the burnt offering, and
Aharon and his sons laid their right hand upon the head
of the ram. And he killed the ram ; and Mosheh
sprinkled the blood upon the altar round about. And
he divided the ram after its parts, and Mosheh burned
the head and the parts and the fat. And the inwards
and the feet he washed with water ; and Mosheh burned
the ram at the altar, a burnt sacrifice to be received with
acceptance, an oblation before the Lord, as the Lord
commanded Mosheh. And he brought the second ram,
the ram of completion which completed all ; and
Aharon and his sons laid their hand upon the head of
the ram. And he killed the ram, and Mosheh took of
its blood, and put it upon the extremity of Aharon's ear,

---

[4] Exod. xxv. Numbers vii.

the middle cartilage of the right ear, and upon the
middle joint [5] of his right foot.　And he brought the
sons of Aharon, and Mosheh put of the blood upon the
middle cartilage of their right ears, and upon the middle
joint of their right feet, and Mosheh poured out all
the remaining blood upon the altar round about.　And
he took the fat, and the tail, and all the fat which was
upon the inwards, and the caul of the liver, and the two
kidueys, and their fat, and the right shoulder; and from
the basket of unleavened cakes which was before the
Lord he took one unleavened cake of bread mixed with
oil, and one wafer, and put it upon the fat and upon
the right shoulder, and laid the whole in order upon
Aharon's hands, and upon the hands of his sons,
and he lifted them up, an elevation before the Lord.
And Mosheh took them from off their hands, and burned
(them) upon the altar with the burnt sacrifice; a completing offering were they to complete all, to be received
with acceptance before the Lord.　And he took the
breast, and uplifted it, an elevation before the Lord: of
the oblation-ram that was the separated portion of
Mosheh, as the Lord commanded Mosheh.

And Mosheh took the consecrating oil, and of the
blood which was upon the altar, and sprinkled upon
Aharon, and upon his vestments, and on his sons, and
on their vestments with him; and sanctified Aharon and
his vestments, and his sons and their vestments with
him.

And Mosheh said to Aharon and to his sons, Boil
the flesh of the oblations in pots at the door of the
tabernacle of ordinance, and there shall you eat it with
the bread which is in the basket of oblations, according
to the precept which was spoken; Aharon and his sons
shall eat it.　And what remaineth of the flesh, and of

* Or, "member," *pirka.*

I

the bread, you shall burn with fire.   And from the door
of the tabernacle you shall not go forth seven days, until
the day that your consecration be completed, (because
in seven days is the tabernacle set up and taken in
pieces,) and your oblation be offered.   (So did he, and
ordained the order of the oblations on that day.)   Likewise the Lord hath commanded to be done by you after
the days of consecration, to make atonement for you.
And at the door of the tabernacle of ordinance you shall
reside day and night seven days, and watch the vigils of
the Word of the Lord, that you may not die, for thus
it hath been commanded.   And Aharon and his sons
did all the things which the Lord had commanded by
the hand of Mosheh.

SECTION XXVI.

SHEMINI

IX.   On the eighth day of the anointing of Aharon and
his sons, and the eighth day of that consecration, being
the first day of the month of Nisan, when Mosheh had
erected the tabernacle, he took it not down, neither
ministered any longer at the altar; but Mosheh called
Aharon and his sons, and the elders of the sanhedrin of
Israel.   And he said to Aharon, Take thou a calf, the
young of a bullock, for a sin offering, that Satan may
not accuse thee concerning the calf that thou madest at
Horeb; and take a ram for the burnt sacrifice, that
there may be a memorial for thee of the righteousness
of Izhak whom his father bound as a ram on the
mountain of worship, both of them shall be perfect, and
bring them before the Lord.   And to the children of
Israel spoke he, saying: Take for yourselves a kid of the

goats, because Satana resembles him, lest he recount against you the accusation concerning the kid of the goats, which the sons (tribes) of Jakob killed, (Gen. xxxvii. 31,) and offer him for a sin offering; and a calf, because ye worshipped the calf, (Exod. xxxii. 4,) and a lamb of the year, that there may be for you a memorial of the righteousness of Izhak, whom his father did bind as a lamb, both of them perfect, for a burnt offering; with a bullock and a lamb, for a hallowed oblation to sacrifice before the Lord, that He may be gracious to you; and a mincha mingled with oil of the olive. For this day will the glory of the Lord's Shekinah be revealed unto you.

And Aharon and his sons, and all the sons of Israel, hastened and took what Mosheh commanded, and presented them in front of the tabernacle of ordinance; and the whole congregation drew near, and lifted up their heart fully before the Lord.

And Mosheh said, This is the thing which you must do. Put away the imagination of evil from your hearts, and there will speedily (at once) be revealed to you the glory of the Shekinah of the Lord. But when Aharon saw at the corner of the altar the form of the calf, he was afraid to approach to its side. Mosheh, therefore, said to him, Take courage, and go near to the altar, fearing not, and offer thy sin offering, and make atonement for thyself and for the people, and perform the oblation of the people, and make atonement for them, as the Lord hath commanded. And Aharon approached to the altar with resolution,[6] and slew the calf for his own sin offering. And the sons of Aharon brought the blood to him, and he dipped his finger in the blood of the young bullock, and put it upon the horns of the altar, and the rest of the blood he poured out at the foundation of the altar, and sanctified it for the making of atonement upon it.

6 Or, "promptitude."

And the fat, and the kidneys, with the caul of the liver
of the sin offering, he burned at the altar, as the Lord
had commanded Mosheh. But the flesh and the skin
burned he with fire without the camp.

And he killed the burnt offering, and the sons of
Aharon brought the blood to him, and he sprinkled it
upon the altar round about. And they brought the
burnt offering to him by its divisions, and the head, and
he burned (them) upon the altar. And he washed the
inwards and the fat, and burned the burnt offering, at
the altar.

And they brought the oblation of the people. And
he took the goat for the people's sin offering and killed
it, and made atonement with the blood of the goat, as
he had made atonement with the blood of the calf of
the sin offering for himself, which he had offered before.
And they brought the burnt offering, and he performed
it, after the rite of the burnt offering which he had
offered for himself. And they brought the mincha, and
he filled his hands therefrom, and took of it a portion
for its memorial, and burned upon the altar, beside the
morning sacrifice. And he killed the bullock and the
ram of the hallowed oblations (peace offering) of the
people, and the sons of Aharon brought the blood to
him, and he sprinkled it upon the altar round about .
and the fat of the bullock, and of the ram, the tail, and
that which covereth the inwards, and the two kidneys,
and the caul of the liver; and he laid the fat upon the
breast, and burned the fat upon the altar. But the
breast and the right shoulder Aharon uplifted, an elevation before the Lord, as the Lord commanded Mosheh.
And Aharon stretched out his hands towards the people
and blessed them, and came down from the altar with
joy, after he had finished to perform the sin offering and
the burnt offering and the hallowed oblation. But

when, after the oblations had been performed, the
Shekinah did not reveal itself, Aharon was ashamed, and
said to Mosheh, It may be that the Word of the Lord
hath no pleasure in the work of my hands.   Then went
Mosheh and Aharon into the tabernacle of ordinance,
and prayed for the people of the house of Israel, and
came forth and blessed the people, and said, May the
Word of the Lord receive your oblations with favour,
and remit and forgive your sins.

Then, instantly the Glory of the Lord's Shekinah
revealed itself to all the people: and the Fire came
forth from the Presence of the Lord, and consumed
upon the altar the sacrifice and the fat.   And all the
people saw, and gave praise, and bowed in prayer upon
their faces.   [JERUSALEM.   And bowed in prayer upon
their faces.]

X. But the sons of Aharon, Nadab and Abihu, took
each man his censer, and put fire therein, and laid sweet
incense upon it, and offered before the Lord strange fire
taken from (under) the hearth-pots, which had not been
commanded them.   [JERUSALEM.   Outside fire.]   And a
flame of fire came out from before the Lord (as) with
anger, and divided itself into four streams, (or lines,)
and penetrated their nostrils, and burned their lives
(souls) without destroying their bodies; and they died
before the Lord.

And Mosheh said, This is that which the Lord spake
with me in Sinai, saying : In them who come near before
Me I will have the tabernacle to be sacred, that, if they
be not heedful in the service of the oblations, I will
burn them with flaming fire from before Me, that in the
sight of all the people I may be glorified.   And Aharon
heard, and was silent; and he received a good reward
for his silence.

And Mosheh called unto Mishael and to Elzaphan,

the sons of Uzziel the Levite, the relative of Aharon, and said to them, Take your brethren from the sanctuary, and carry them without the camp. And they came nigh, and carried them with hooks of iron in their garments, and buried them without the camp, as Mosheh had directed.

And Mosheh said to Aharon, and to Elasar and to Ithamar, his sons, Unbare not your heads, neither rend your garments, lest you die by the burning fire, and there be wrath upon all the congregation; but be silent, and justify the judgment upon you, and let all your brethren of the house of Israel bewail the burning which the Lord hath kindled. And from the door of the tabernacle of ordinance go not forth lest you die; for the oil of the Lord's consecration is upon you. And they did according to the word of Mosheh.

And the Lord spake with Aharon, saying, Drink neither wine nor anything that maketh drunk, neither thou nor thy sons with thee at the time when ye are to enter into the tabernacle of ordinance, as thy sons did who have died by the burning of fire. It is an everlasting statute for your generations; and for the distinguishing between the sacred and the common, and between the unclean and the clean, and for teaching the children of Israel all the statutes which the Lord hath spoken to them by the hand of Mosheh.

And Mosheh spake with Aharon, and Elasar and Ithamar, his sons, who were left from the burning: Take the mincha that remaineth of the Lord's oblations, and eat it unleavened at the side of the altar, because it is most sacred: and you may eat it in the holy place; for it is thy portion and the portion of thy sons of the oblations of the Lord: for so have I been commanded. But the breast of the uplifting and the shoulder of the separation you may eat in (any) clean place, thou and

thy sons with thee, because it is thy portion and the
portion of thy sons which hath been given from the
hallowed sacrifices of the children of Israel. The
shoulder of the separation and the elevated breast with
the fats of the oblations they shall bring to be uplifted
an elevation before the Lord, and they shall then be thine
and thy sons' with thee, by an everlasting statute, as the
Lord commanded.

And on this day three goats shall be offered; the
goat for the beginning of the month, (or, new moon,) the
goat of the people's sin offering, and the goat for the
sin offering which Nachson bar Aminadab hath brought
for the dedication of the altar. And Aharon and his
sons went and burned those three. (But) Mosheh came
and inquired for the goat of the people's sin offering;
he sought it, but, behold, it had been burned, and he
was angry with Elasar and Ithamar, the sons of Aharon
who were left, and said, Why have you not eaten the
sin offering in the holy place? forasmuch as it is most
sacred, and hath been given to you for absolving the sin
of the congregation, to make atonement for you before
the Lord; and, behold, none of its blood hath been
carried in within the sanctuary. You should have
indeed eaten it in the holy place, as I have been
instructed. And Aharon said to Mosheh, Behold, this
day the sons of Israel have brought the oblation of
their sin offering and their burnt sacrifice before the
Lord; but a stroke hath befallen me, in those my two
sons. Of the second tythe is it not commanded, Thou
shalt not eat of it while mourning? How much more,
then, of the sin offering? If I had eaten of the sin
offering this day with my two sons who are left, would
it not have been an error, so that they too might have
been burned by a judgment, for doing that which was
not pleasing before the Lord? And Mosheh heard, and

it was approvable before him, and he sent out a crier through the camp, saying, I am he from whom the rite hath been hidden, and Aharon my brother hath brought its remembrance to me.

[JERUSALEM. They have brought their sin offerings and their burnt sacrifice before the Lord ; and I have been instructed that these of the sin offering are more weighty than those of the second tythes, of which it is not allowed to the mourner to eat; and to me hath been a great sorrow this day through the death of my two sons Nadab and Abihu : and consider, if, while mourning over them, I were to eat to-day of the sin offering, I should do what would not be pleasing or right before the Lord. When Mosheh had heard, and the word was pleasing in his sight, he sent out a herald through all the camp of Israel, and said, I am he from whom the rite had been hidden; but Aharon my brother hath taught it unto me. And because Mosheh humbled himself, he received thereupon a great reward. For Mosheh heard, and the word was pleasing before him.]

XI. And the Lord spake with Mosheh and with Aharon, bidding them and the sons of Aharon admonish the children of Israel to taste their food in purity, and to separate on account of uncleanness eighteen kinds of food to be rejected. Speak with the children of Israel, saying : These are the animals which are fit to you for food, of every beast which is upon the earth. Whatsoever divideth the hoof and is cloven-footed, and that which hath horns bringing up the cud among the beasts, that you may eat. But you may not eat of the kinds that (only) bring up the cud, nor (of them which only) divide the hoof, because (they are) born of the unclean. The camel, because he bringeth up the cud, but divideth not the hoof; he is unclean to you. And the coney, because he bringeth up the cud, but divideth not the hoof,

is unclean to you.   And the hare, because he bringeth
up the cud, but divideth not the hoof, is unclean to you.
And the swine, because he divideth the hoof, and is cloven-
footed, but cheweth not the cud, is unclean to you.   Of
their flesh you shall not eat, nor touch their carcase ; they
are abominable to you.   And these you may eat, of all that
are in the waters : every one that hath fins and scales in
the seas and in the rivers, these you may eat.   But any one
that hath not fins and scales in the seas and in the rivers,
and of anything that is in the sea that crawleth, shall
be an abomination to you, and an abomination shall
their jelly and their sauce be to you ; of their flesh you
shall not eat, and their carcase you shall have in abhorrence, and from the use of them you must keep aloof.
Every one that hath neither fins nor scales in the waters
shall be an abomination to you.

And these kinds of birds must be abominated : those
not a finger long, or that have no vesicle (*zephaq*), or
whose crop (*kurkeban*, ingluvies) peeleth not away,[7] are
not to be eaten, they are abomination ; the eagle, the
black eagle, and the osprey, and the kite, and the vulture
after his kind, and every raven after his kind, and the
ostrich, and the night raven, and the gull, and the hawk
after his kind, and the snatcher of fish from the sea,
and the ibis, and the bustard, and the cuckoo, and the
woodpecker, and the white stork, and the black, after
his kind, and the woodcock, and the bat.

And every flying reptile that goeth upon four, the fly
species, the wasp (or hornet) species, and the bee species
shall be an abomination to you : nevertheless of the
honey of the bee you may eat.   So also of these you
may eat, of every flying reptile that goeth upon four ;

---

[7] Every bird which hath a crop, and of which the internal coat of
the stomach may be readily peeled off, is of the clean species.—MISHNA
Cholin, c. iii , § 6.

every one that hath joints above his feet to leap therewith upon the ground. Of these kinds of them you
may eat: the wingless locust after his kind, and the
bald locust after his kind, the serpent-killer after his
kind, and the karzeba, which is the palmerworm, after
his kind. But all flying reptiles which have four feet
are to be an abomination to you; and by them you
would be defiled: whosoever toucheth their carcase shall
be unclean until evening. Whoever carrieth any of
their carcase must wash his clothes and be unclean until
evening. All cattle which divide the hoof, but are not
cloven-footed nor throw up the cud, are to be unclean
to you, any one who toucheth them shall be unclean.
Every one that goeth upon his paws of all animals that
walk upon four shall be unclean to you. Whoever
toucheth their carcase shall be unclean until evening.
Whoever beareth their carcase shall wash his clothes
and be unclean until evening; unclean are they to
you.

And these also to you are such as defile; the blood, the
skin, and the flesh of every reptile that creepeth upon
the ground: the weasel, the mouse, black, red, and
white, and the toad, after his kind; and the sucking
serpent, and the chameleon, and the lizard, and the snail,
and the salamander. These eight kinds are unclean to
you among all reptiles: whoever toucheth them, their
skin or their blood, shall be unclean until the evening.
And whatever upon which any part of their dead body
may fall, as their members when separated from them,
shall be unclean; every vessel of wood, or garment, or
leather, or sack, anything in which work is done, in four
measures of water it shall be dipped, and be unclean for
use until evening, when it shall be purified. And any
earthen vessel into which any of them may fall, any
vessel in which they may be, shall be unclean and be

broken; all food for eating upon which (such) water
cometh shall be unclean, and any fluid which is used for
drinking in any such vessel shall be unclean. And any
thing upon which a part of their carcase may fall shall
be unclean, whether ovens or pans they shall be broken,
they are defiled and shall be unclean to you. [JERU-
SALEM. The ovens and pans shall be broken.] But
fountains and cisterns, the place of the collection of
running waters, shall be clean: but he who toucheth the
carcase of any of those things (that may have fallen)
into the water shall be unclean. And if any part of
their carcase fall in the way upon seed that is to be
sown, that which is sown dry shall be clean; but if the
carcase of any of them fall upon water that is put upon
the seed when so wetted, the seed is unclean to you.
And if the limb of any clean beast that you may eat be
torn and it die, whosoever toucheth its carcase shall be
unclean until the evening. He who eateth of its carcase
shall wash his clothes, and be unclean until the evening;
and he who carrieth its carcase shall wash his clothes,
and be unclean till evening.

And every reptile that creepeth on the ground is an
abomination, it shall not be eaten. And whatever goeth
upon its belly, and whatever animal crawleth upon four,
from the serpent unto the caterpillar which hath many
feet, of any reptile that creepeth upon the ground you
may not eat, for they are an abomination. [JERUSALEM.
Whatsoever writhes upon its belly among all animals.]
You shall not contaminate your souls by any reptile that
creepeth, nor defile yourselves with them, lest by them
you make yourselves unclean. For I am the Lord
your God; therefore sanctify yourselves, and be holy,
for I am Holy, and defile not your souls by any reptile
that creepeth upon the ground: for I am the Lord who
have brought you up free from the land of Mizraim,

that I may be a God to you; and you may be holy, for
I am Holy.

This is the decree of the law concerning beasts, and
birds, and every living animal that creepeth upon the
ground; for making distinction between the unclean
and the clean; between the animal whose flesh may be
eaten, and the animal whose flesh may not be eaten.

SECTION XXVII.

TAZRIA

XII. And the Lord spake with Mosheh, saying:
Speak with the sons of Israel, saying: When a woman
hath conceived and borne a male child, she shall be
unclean seven days, as the days of the removal of her
uncleanness shall she be unclean. But on the eighth
day she shall be loosed, and her child shall be circumcised in the flesh of his foreskin. And thirty and three
continuous days she shall have for the purification of
the whole blood; but she must not touch things sacred,
nor come into the sanctuary until the time when the
days of her purification be completed. And if she hath
borne a daughter, she shall be unclean fourteen continuous days according to (the law of) her separation; and on
the fifteenth she shall be released; but sixty and six continuous days shall she have for the (full) purification of
the blood.

And when the days of her purification are completed
for the son or the daughter, she shall bring a lamb of
its year for a burnt offering, and a young pigeon or a
turtle dove for a sin offering, unto the priest at the door
of the tabernacle of ordinance; and the priest shall offer·

it before the Lord and make atonement for her; then
shall she be purified from either source of (her) blood.
This is the law of the purification of her who hath borne
a son or a daughter.

But if she find not her hand sufficient to bring a
lamb, let her bring two turtle doves or two young
pigeons; one for the burnt offering, and one for the
sin offering, and the priest shall make atonement for
her, and she shall be clean.

XIII. And the Lord spake with Mosheh, saying: If
a man have in the skin of his flesh a rising tumour or a
white spot, [JERUSALEM. A tumour, or sore, or white
spot,] and it be in the skin of his flesh (as) the plague
of leprosy, let him be brought unto Aharon the priest,
or to one of the priests his sons. And the priest shall
look at the plague in the skin of the flesh,—and if the
hair of the stricken place be turned to whiteness, and
the appearance of the plague be deeper (than the surface), and be whiter than the skin of his flesh, like
snow, it is the plague of leprosy; and the priest having
inspected him shall make him to be unclean.

But if the bright spot be white like chalk in the
skin of his flesh, and the appearance of it be not deep,
with whiteness like snow rather than skin, the hair, too,
not being turned to whiteness like chalk, the priest
shall shut up him who is plagued seven days; and the
priest shall inspect him on the seventh day, and, behold,
if the plague stand as it was, and have not gone on
wider in the skin, the priest shall shut him up a second
seven days. And the priest shall inspect him the
second seventh day; and, behold, if the plague hath
become darker, and hath not gone wider in the skin,
the priest shall make him to be clean; it is an obstinate sore, and he shall wash his clothes and be clean.

But if the inveterate sore widen in the skin after he

had been shown to the priest who had pronounced him
clean, let him a second time be seen by the priest.
And the priest shall look; and, behold, if the widening
of the inveterate sore hath gone on in the skin, the
priest shall make him unclean; for it is the leprosy.

When the plague of leprosy is upon a man, let him
be brought to the priest. And the priest shall observe;
and, behold, if there be a white tumour rising on the
skin like pure wool, and the hair be turned to whiteness as the white of an egg, and the sign of quick flesh
be in the tumour, it is an inveterate leprosy in the skin
of his flesh; and the priest shall adjudge and pronounce him unclean, but not shut him up, for he is
(known to be) unclean. Yet if the leprosy increasing
increaseth in the skin, and the leprosy covereth all the
skin of his flesh, from his head even to his feet, in
whatever part the eyes of the priest may look on, in
deliberating between cleanness and uncleanness, the
priest shall consider; and, behold, if the leprosy covereth all his flesh, the plagued man shall be (pronounced)
to be clean: all of him is turned to whiteness, he is
clean. But in the day that live flesh appeareth in him
he is unclean. And the priest shall observe the live
flesh, and make him to be unclean; on account of the
live flesh in him he is unclean; it is leprosy. Or if the
live flesh be turned and changed into whiteness, he
shall be brought to the priest; and the priest shall
observe, and, behold, the plague is turned white, and
the priest shall adjudge the plague to be clean; he is
clean.

And if a man have in his skin an ulcer, and it hath
healed; but in the place of the ulcer there hath come a
white rising tumour, or a bright fixed spot, (in colour)
white mixed with red; he shall be seen by the priest.
And the priest shall look; and, behold, if the appear-

ance of it be deeper than the skin, and it becometh
white, and the hair is turned white, the priest shall
make him to be unclean; for it is a plague of leprosy
which increaseth in the ulcer. And if the priest look,
and, behold, the hair in it is not whitened, and the
whiteness (of the spot) is not in appearance deeper than
the skin, and that it hath become dim, then must the
priest shut him up seven days. [And the priest shall
look on the seventh day;] and if it hath gone on
widening in the skin, the priest shall make him to be
unclean; for it is the plague of leprosy. But if the
spot abideth in its place, and hath not gone on widening
in the skin, but hath become fainter, it is an inflamed
blotch; and the priest shall make him to be clean; it
is a burning scar.

Or if there be in a man's skin a hot burning, and in
the burning wound a spot of white mixed with red,
or white only; the priest shall look upon it: and,
behold, the hair is turned white as chalk, and its
appearance is deeper than the skin becoming white as
snow; it is leprosy growing in the burning spot; and
the priest shall make him unclean, it is the plague of
leprosy. But if the priest look on it, and, behold, the
hair on the burning place be not white, and it be not
deep, nor becoming whiter than the skin, though it
may be dim; then the priest shall shut him up seven
days. And the priest shall see him on the seventh
day; and if it hath gone on widening in the skin, the
priest shall make him unclean; it is the plague of
leprosy. But if the priest look on it, and, behold, the
hair on the burning place is not white, and it is not
deep, nor whiter than the skin, though it may be dim;
then the priest must shut him up seven days. And
the priest shall see him on the seventh day; and if it
hath gone on widening in the skin, the priest shall

make him unclean, for it is the plague of leprosy. But if the inflamed spot abide in its place, and go not on to widen in the skin, and it be dim (in appearance), it is a burning spot; and the priest shall make him to be clean, for it is a burning wound.

And if a man or a woman have a plague upon the head, or in the beard, the priest shall look upon the plague; and, behold, if the appearance is deeper and whiter than the skin, and yellow hair be in it, in sight like a thin thread of gold, the priest shall make him unclean; it is a scurvy, a leprosy in the head or the beard. But if the priest view the scurfed plague, and, behold, if the appearance of it be not deeper nor whiter than the skin, and there be no black hair in it, the priest shall shut up him who hath the scurfed plague seven days. And the priest on the seventh day shall look upon the plague; and, behold, if the plague hath not gone on in breadth, and no yellow hair like gold be in it, and the appearance of the scurf is not deeper than the skin, he shall cut away the hair which surrounds the scar, but the scurfed part he must not shave; and the priest shall shut him who hath the scurf, seven days. Then shall the priest look upon the scurf on the seventh day; and, behold, if the scar hath not gone on in breadth in the skin, and its appearance is not deeper nor becoming whiter than the skin, the priest shall make him to be clean; and he shall wash his clothes and be clean.

But should the breadth of the scar go on in the skin after his purification, the priest shall inspect it: and, behold, if the breadth hath increased, the priest need not look narrowly after the yellow hair; for he is unclean. But if the scar abideth, (without widening,) and black hair hath sprung up in it, the scar hath healed; he is clean, and the priest shall make him to be clean.

And if a man or a woman have in the skin of their flesh bright white spots, the priest shall look, and, behold, if the spots in the skin of their flesh are a greyish white, it is a bright freckle growing in the skin; he is clean.

And if a man's hair fall off from his head, he is bald, but he is clean. And if the hair fall away from the brow of his face, he is partly bald, but he is clean. But if his baldness or partial baldness hath in it a white plague mixed with red, it is a leprosy growing in his baldness or partial baldness. And the priest shall look upon it, and, behold, if the spot of the plague be white mixed with red in his baldness, or partial baldness, like the appearance of leprosy in the skin of the flesh, he is a leprous man, he is unclean, and the priest shall verily make him to be unclean, for the plague is on his head.

And the leper in whom is the plague shall have his clothes rent, and his hair shall be taken off, going to the shearer's, and his lips shall be covered; and he shall be clothed like a mourner, and crying, as a herald, he shall say, Keep off, keep off from the unclean! All the days that the plague is in him he shall be unclean, for unclean he is, he shall dwell alone by himself, to the side of his wife he must not come nigh, and his habitation shall be without the camp.

And a garment in which is the plague of leprosy, whether a garment of wool or a garment of linen, whether in the warp or in the woof, in linen or in woollen, or in a skin, or in anything made of skin: if the plague be green or red in the garment, or in the skin, whether in the warp or in the woof, or in anything of leather, it is the plague of leprosy, and must be shown to the priest. And the priest shall look upon the plague, and shall shut it up seven days: and he shall look upon the plague on the seventh day, and if the plague hath

become wider in the garment, whether in the warp or
woof, or in the skin, or anything made of skin, it is a
manifest plague of leprosy, it is unclean.[8] But if the
priest look, and, behold, the width of the plague hath not
advanced in the garment, in warp or woof, or anything
of skin, let the priest direct that they wash the material
which hath the plague in it, and shut it up a second
seven days. And the priest shall look after they have
washed the plague, and, behold, the (condition of the)
plague hath not altered from what it was, and the plague
hath not advanced in its size, it is unclean, thou shalt
burn it in the fire, for the leprosy is deep in its bare-
ness (or in its outward side). And if the priest observe,
and, behold, the plague hath become dim, then shall he
tear it out of the garment, or from the leather, or out
of the warp or the woof. But if it re-appear in the
garment, or in the warp or woof, or in anything of skin,
and maketh increase, thou shalt burn such material
which hath the plague in it. And the garment, or the
warp or woof, or anything of skin, which thou shalt
wash, and the plague depart from it, shall be washed a
second time, and it shall be clean.

This is the law for the plague of leprosy in a garment
of woollen or of linen, or the warp or the woof, or anything of skin, to make it to be clean or to be unclean.

SECTION XXVIII.

METSORA.

XIV. AND the Lord spake with Mosheh, saying:
This shall be the law for the leper: on the day of his

[8] The fifty-second verse is wanting.

purification he shall be brought to the priest. And the
priest shall go forth out of the camp, and look, and
behold, the leper hath been healed of his leprosy. Then
the priest shall direct that he who is to be cleansed take
two birds, alive and clean, and wood of the cedar, and
scarlet (wool), and hyssop. And the priest shall instruct
the killer to kill one of the birds in an earthen vessel
with spring water. Let him take the living bird with
the cedar wood, and the scarlet, and the hyssop, and dip
them and the living bird in the blood of the bird that
had been killed, and in the spring water. And let him
sprinkle it upon the face of him who is to be cleansed
of the leprosy seven times, and cleanse him; and send
forth the living bird over the face of the field. And it
will be that if that man is again to be stricken with
leprosy, the living bird will come back to his house on
that day, and may be held fit to be eaten. But the bird
that had been killed the priest shall bury in the presence
of the leper. And he who is cleansed shall wash his
clothes, and shave off all his hair, and wash himself in
water, and be clean; and afterward he may enter the
camp, but shall dwell without his tent, the house of his
habitation, and come not to the side of his wife for
seven days. And on the seventh day he shall again
shave off all the hair of his head, of the beard, and
of the eyebrows, even all his hair shall he shave, and
dip his clothes, and wash his flesh in water, and he is
clean.

And on the eighth day let him take two lambs unblemished, and one ewe lamb of the year unblemished;
and three-tenths of flour for the mincha mingled with
olive oil, and one log of olive oil. And the priest who
purifieth the man who is to be cleansed shall make him
stand with the lambs before the Lord at the door of the
tabernacle of ordinance. And the priest shall take one

lamb, and offer him as an oblation for trespass, with the
log of oil, and uplift them an elevation before the Lord.
And the slayer shall kill the lamb in the place where the
sin offering is killed, and the burnt offering, in the holy
place; because, as the sin offering, so the trespass offering is the priest's; it is most sacred. And the priest
shall take of the blood of the trespass offering, and
shall put it upon the middle point of the right ear of
him who is to be cleansed, and upon the middle joint of
his right hand, and on the middle joint of his right foot.
And the priest, with his right hand, shall take (some)
from the log of oil, and pour it upon the priest's left
hand; and the priest shall dip his right hand finger in
the oil which is in his left hand, and sprinkle the oil
with his finger seven times. And of what remaineth of
the oil that is in his hand the priest shall put some upon
the cartilage of the right ear of him who is to be
cleansed, and upon the middle finger of his right hand,
and on the middle toe of his right foot upon the spot
whereon he had first put the blood of the trespass offering. And that which yet remaineth of the oil that is
in the priest's hand he shall put upon the head of him
who is to be cleansed, and the priest shall make atonement for him before the Lord. And the priest shall
perform the oblation of the sin offering, and make atonement for him who is to be cleansed from his defilement;
and afterwards shall he kill the burnt offering. And
the priest shall offer the burnt offering with the mincha
at the altar, and the priest shall make atonement for him,
and he will be clean.

But if he be a poor man, and his hand have not sufficiency, let him take one lamb for the trespass offering
to be an elevation to make atonement for him, and one
tenth of flour mingled with olive oil for the mincha, and
a log of olive oil. And two large turtle doves, or two

young pigeons, of the sufficiency of his hand, and let one be for the sin and one for the burnt offering. And he shall bring them on the eighth day for his purification unto the priest, at the door of the tabernacle of ordinance. And the priest shall take the lamb for the trespass offering, and the log of oil, and uplift them, an elevation before the Lord. And the slayer shall kill the lamb of the trespass offering, and the priest shall take the blood of the trespass offering, and put it upon the middle cartilage of the right ear of him who is to be cleansed, and on the middle joint of his right hand, and on the middle joint of his right foot. And the priest shall pour some of the oil with his right hand into the priest's left hand, and the priest with the finger of his right hand shall sprinkle of the oil that is in his left hand seven times before the Lord. And the priest shall put of the oil that is in his hand on the middle cartilage of the right ear of him who is to be cleansed, and on the middle joint of his right hand, and on the middle joint of his right foot, upon the spot whereon he first put the blood of the trespass offering. And what remaineth of the oil that is upon the priest's hand he shall put upon the head of him who is to be cleansed, to atone for him before the Lord. And the priest shall perform (the offering of) one of the large turtle doves, or of the pigeons of which his hand had sufficiency. That which his hand was sufficient to bring, let him bring, one for the sin, and one for the burnt offering, with the oblation of the mincha, and let the priest make atonement for him who is to be cleansed before the Lord. This is the decree of instruction for him in whom is the plague of leprosy. If there be not sufficiency in his hands to bring the greater oblations, let him bring of these oblations which are easier (and) which are here explained, on the day of his purification.

And the Lord spake with Mosheh and with Aharon, saying, When you have entered upon the land of Kenaan, which I will give you for a possession, and a man who hath builded a house by rapine finds that I have put the plague of leprosy in the house of the land of your inheritance; and he who owneth the house shall come to the priest, saying, There is a plague, as it appeareth to me, in the house then the priest shall direct that they make the house empty before the priest cometh to inspect the house, that all that is in the house may not be (condemned as) unclean; and after that the priest shall go in to inspect the house. And the priest shall look, and, behold, if the plague be like (the colour of) two beans crushed with stones, and goeth lower than the four walls, green or red, and its appearance be deeper than the walls; the priest shall go out from the house to the door of the house, and shut up the house seven days. And the priest, returning on the seventh day, shall look, and, behold, if the breadth of the plague hath increased in the wall of the house, then the priest shall direct that they break out the stones which have the plague in them, and throw them without the city into an unclean place. And they shall scrape the inside of the house round about, and throw the dust which they have scraped off without the city into an unclean place. And they shall take other stones, and insert them in the place of the (former) stones, and let other mortar be taken, and the house be replastered. [JERU-SALEM. And they shall plaster the house.] But if the plague return and increase in the house, after the stones have been broken out, and after the house hath been scraped, and after that it hath been replastered, then the priest shall come and look, and, behold, (if) the breadth of the plague hath increased in the house, it is a plain leprosy in the house, it is unclean. Then shall they

destroy that house, and its stones, and its timber, and
all the plaster of the house, and he shall remove it
without the city to an unclean place. And whoever
goeth into the house in the days that it is shut up, shall
be unclean until evening. And whoever sleepeth in the
house shall wash his clothes, and whoever eateth in the
house shall wash his clothes.

But if, having gone in, the priest looketh, and, behold,
the breadth of the plague hath not increased in the
house, after the house hath been plastered, then the
priest shall make the house to be clean, for the plague
hath healed. And he shall take, for the purification of
the house, two turtle doves and cedarwood and scarlet
and hyssop; and the slayer shall kill one turtle dove in
a vessel of earthenware with spring water; and he shall
take the cedarwood and the hyssop and the scarlet and
the living bird, and dip them in the blood of the bird
that had been killed and in the spring water, and
sprinkle the house seven times. And he shall purify
the house with the blood, with the living bird, and with
the cedarwood, and with the hyssop, and with the
scarlet. And the living bird he shall send forth out of the
town upon the face of the field, and shall atone for the
house, and it shall be clean. But if it is to be that the
house will be again struck with leprosy, the bird on that
day will return, and may be fit for food. But the bird
that was killed shall the priest bury in the presence of
the owner of the house. This is the decree of instruction in the law for every plague of leprosy and scorbutus,
and for leprosy in apparel, or in a house; and for
tumours, scars, and inflamed blotches. [JERUSALEM.
And for tumours, scars, and inflamed blotches.] That
the priest may teach the people to discern between the
day of darkness in which they may not be able to see
the plague, and the day of light; and between a man

who is unclean and a man who is clean. This shall be the decree of instruction for the leprosy.

XV. And the Lord spake with Mosheh and with Aharon, saying: Speak with the sons of Israel, and say to them: A man, whether young or old, who hath a defluxion from his flesh, when he hath seen it three times, is unclean. And this shall be his uncleanness,— the appearance of the colour of white in his defluxion inflaming the defluxion of his flesh; or when his flesh hath stopped from his defluxion, it is his uncleanness. Every bed on which one who hath such defluxion lieth shall be unclean; and every thing on which such an one sitteth shall be unclean. And the man who toucheth his bed shall wash his clothes, and wash himself in forty seahs of water, and shall be unclean until evening. And whoever may sit upon a thing whereon such an one who hath an issue hath sat, let him wash his clothes, and bathe in forty seahs of water, and be unclean until evening. And whoever may touch the flesh of one having an issue, let him wash his clothes, and bathe in forty seahs of water, and be unclean until evening. And if he who hath an issue spit upon any one who is clean, let him wash his clothes, and bathe in forty seahs of water, and be unclean until evening. And every girdle or saddle upon which he who hath an issue rideth shall be unclean. And whoever toucheth any thing that hath been under him shall be unclean until evening; and he who carrieth them shall wash his clothes, and bathe in forty seahs of water, and be unclean until evening. And whoever toucheth him who hath the issue, and washeth not his hands in water, shall be unclean; if he be a man, he shall wash his clothes, and bathe in forty seahs of water, and be unclean until the evening. And any vessel of earthenware whose inside may have been touched by him who hath the issue shall be broken; and any vessel of wood shall be washed in water.

But if he who hath had the issue shall have ceased from it, he shall number to himself seven days for his purification, and wash his clothes, and bathe his flesh in spring water, to be clean. And on the eighth day let him take for himself two large turtle doves, or two young pigeons, and bring them before the Lord at the gate of the tabernacle of ordinance, and deliver them to the priest. And the priest shall make one a sin offering and one a burnt offering, and the priest shall atone for him before the Lord, and he shall be cleansed from his issue. But if a man sin through ignorance and seed goeth from him, let him wash all his flesh in forty seahs of water, and be unclean until evening. And any garment or skin on which seed may be shall be washed in water, and be unclean until evening; and secondly, a woman with whom a man lieth shall wash in forty seahs of water, and be unclean until evening. And if a woman hath an issue of blood, red or dark, yellow as saffron, or water of clay, or as red wine mixed with two parts of water, she hath an uncleanness of blood in her flesh; she shall dwell apart seven days; any one who toucheth her shall be unclean until evening. Whatever such an one shall lie upon during the time of her separation shall be unclean; and whatever such an one sitteth upon during the time of her separation shall be unclean. And whoever toucheth her bed shall wash his clothes, and bathe himself with forty seahs of water, and be unclean until evening. And whoever toucheth any thing upon which such an one hath sat shall wash his clothes, and bathe in forty seahs of water, and be unclean until evening. And if the effusion of her body be upon her bed, or on a thing upon any part of which she sitteth, what time any one toucheth it, he shall be

K

unclean until evening. If a man lie with her in the
time of her separation, he shall be unclean seven days;
and any bed upon which he lieth shall be unclean. But
a woman who hath a defluxion of blood three days
beyond the time of her separation, or when it floweth
after the days of her separation, all the days of the
uncleanness of her defluxion shall she be unclean; he
who lieth with her shall be unclean. And any bed
upon which such an one lieth all the days of her
defluxion shall be as the bed which was accounted hers
during the time of her separation, and any thing upon
which such an one sitteth shall be unclean as the uncleanness of her separation. And whoever toucheth those
(things) shall be unclean, and shall wash his clothes, and
bathe in forty seahs of water, and be unclean until the
evening.

But when she is cleansed from her issue, let her
number to herself seven days, and afterwards wash in
forty seahs of water, and be clean. And on the seventh
day, let her take for herself two turtle doves, or two
young pigeons, and bring them to the priest, at the
door of the tabernacle of ordinance; and the priest shall
make one a sin offering, and the other a burnt offering;
and the priest shall make atonement before the Lord
on account of the defluxion of her uncleanness. So
shall you separate the children of Israel from their uncleanness, and make them to be separate from their
wives at the time of their seclusion, and to give not
occasion that they die for their uncleanness in defiling
My tabernacle, where the glory of My Shekinah dwelleth
among them.

This is the decree of instruction for him who hath a
defluxion, and for him whose seed goeth forth and defileth him; and for her who is unclean in the time of
her separation, and for any one who hath an issue,

whether male or female, and for a man who lieth with
the unclean. All these shall be advised of their uncleanness, and, when purified, shall bring the oblations
that make atonement for them.

SECTION XXIX.

ACHAREY MOTH.

XVI. AND the Lord spake with Mosheh, after that
the two sons of Aharon the high priest had died (or, the
priests the two elder sons of Aharon had died) at the
time of their offering extraneous fire (*aisha baria*) before
the Lord; died they by the flaming fire. [JERUSALEM.
The two sons of Aharon, in their offering extraneous
fire.] And the Lord said unto Mosheh: Speak with
Aharon thy brother, that he enter not at any time into
the holy place within the veil before the mercy-seat;
for the cloud of the glory of My Shekinah is revealed
over the place of the mercy-seat.

This shall be the rite (*mida*) for the entering of
Aharon into the holy place. With a young bullock,
having no mixture, for the sin offering, and a ram for
the burnt offering. With the vestments of fine linen,
the holy robe, shall he be dressed, and linen drawers shall
be upon his flesh, and with the girdle of fine linen shall he
be bound, and the mitre of fine linen shall be ordained
for his head. These are the holy garments; but with
the golden robes he shall not enter, that there be not
brought to memory the sin of the golden calf; and at
the time when he is to enter he shall wash his flesh in
forty seahs of water, and attire himself with them.

And from the congregation of the sons of Israel let
him take two kids of the goats, without mixture, for a
sin offering, and one ram for a burnt offering. And

Aharon shall offer the bullock of the sin offering which (hath been purchased) with his own money, and make an atonement with words of confession [9] for himself and for the men of his house. And he shall take the two goats, and cause them to stand before the Lord, at the door of the tabernacle of ordinance. And Aharon shall put upon the goats equal lots; one lot for the Name of the Lord, and one lot for Azazel: and he shall throw them into the vase, and draw them out, and put them upon the goats. And Aharon shall bring the goat upon which came up the lot for the Name of the Lord, and make him a sin offering. And the goat on which came up the lot for Azazel he shall make to stand alive before the Lord, to expiate for the sins of the people of the house of Israel, by sending him to die in a place rough and hard in the rocky desert which is Beth-hadurey.

And Aharon shall bring the bullock which is for himself, and make atonement with confession of words for himself, and for the men of his house, and kill the bullock for his sin offering.

And he shall take a censer full of coals burning with fire from off the altar from before the Lord, and with his hand full of sweet incense, beaten small, he shall enter within the veil. And he shall put the sweet incense upon the fire before the Lord, and the cloud of the fuming incense shall envelope the mercy-seat that is over the testimony, that he may not die by the flaming fire before the Lord. And he shall take of the blood of the bullock, and sprinkle with his right finger upon the face of the mercy-seat eastward, and before the mercy-seat he shall sprinkle the blood seven times with his right finger.

Then shall he kill the goat of the sin offering which is (purchased with) the money of the people, and carry

[9] Or, "with confession of words.   *be-ishteoth milaya.*

in of the blood of the goat within the veil, and do with
the blood of the goat as he did with the blood of the
bullock, and sprinkle it upon the mercy-seat, and before
the mercy-seat. And he shall make atonement for the
holy place, with confession of words for the uncleanness
of the children of Israel, and for their rebellions, and
for their sins ; and so shall he do for the tabernacle of
ordinance which remaineth with them in the midst of
their uncleanness. But let no one be in the tabernacle
of ordinance at the time of his going in to make atonement in the holy place for the sins of Israel, until the
time of his coming out ; and so shall he make atonement for himself, and for the men of his house, and for
all the congregation of Israel.

And he shall withdraw, and come forth from the
holy place, unto the altar which is before the Lord,
and make atonement upon it with confession of words,
and take of the blood of the bullock and of the
blood of the goat, mingled together, and put it upon
the horns of the altar round about. And he shall
sprinkle upon it from the blood with his right finger
seven times, and cleanse it, and sanctify it from the
defilements of the children of Israel.

And when he hath completed to make atonement for
the holy place, and for the tabernacle of ordinance, and
for the altar, with confession of words, he shall bring
near the living goat. And Aharon shall lay his hands
(upon him) in this order, his right hand upon his left,
upon the head of the living goat, and confess over him
all the iniquities of the children of Israel, and all their
rebellions, and all their sins, and shall put them, with
an oath uttered and expressed with the Great and
glorious Name, upon the head of the goat, and send
(him) away by the hand of a man prepared from the
year foregoing, to take him into a rocky desert which is

Beth-hadurey; and the goat shall bear upon him all their sins into a desert place; and the man shall send forth the goat to a rocky desert; and the goat will go up on the mountains of Beth-hadurey, and a tempestuous wind from the presence of the Lord will carry him away, and he will die.

And Aharon shall enter the tabernacle of ordinance, and take off the robes of fine linen with which he was attired at the time of his going into the holy place, and shall lay them aside there. Then shall he wash his flesh in the sanctuary, and afterward attire himself, and withdraw, and come forth, and perform his burnt offering and the burnt offering of the people, and make atonement for himself and for his people. And the fat of the sin offering he shall burn at the altar.

And he who led away the goat to Azazel shall wash his clothes, and bathe his flesh in forty seahs of water, and afterward he may enter the camp. But the bullock for the sin offering, and the goat for the sin offering, whose blood was brought into the sanctuary to make atonement, shall be carried away upon carriages[10] by the hands of young men who are priests; and they shall bear them without the camp, and burn them with fire, their skin, their flesh, and their dung. And he who burneth them shall wash his clothes, and bathe his flesh in forty seahs of water, and afterwards he may enter the camp.

And this shall be to you for an everlasting statute: in the seventh month, it is the month Tishri, on the tenth day of the month, you shall humble your souls, (abstaining) from food, and from drinks, and from the use of the bath, and from rubbing,[1] and from sandals, and from the practice of the bed: nor shall you do any work, neither the native-born nor the stranger who dwel-

---

[10] *Aslin*, "bars."   [1] Castel, 2152.

leth among you. For on this day he shall make ATONE-
MENT for you to cleanse you from all your sins; and you
shall confess your transgressions before the Lord, and
shall be clean. It is a Sabbath of rest to you: no work
of business shall you do, but shall humiliate your souls.
[JERUSALEM. But in it you shall fast for your souls.]
It is an everlasting statute.

And the priest who is anointed, and who hath offered
his oblation to minister instead of his father, shall be
clothed in the robes of fine linen, even the consecrated
robes. And he shall make atonement for the Holy of
Holies, and for the tabernacle of ordinance, and for the
altar; and for the priests, and for all the people of the
congregation, shall he atone, with confession of words.
And this shall be to you for an everlasting statute, to
expiate the children of Israel from all their sins, once in
the year. And Aharon did as the Lord commanded
Mosheh.

XVII. And the Lord spake with Mosheh, saying:
Speak with Aharon and with his sons, and with the sons of
Israel, and tell them: This is the word which the Lord
hath commanded, saying: A man of the house of Israel,
young or old, who shall kill as a sacrifice a bullock, or
lamb, or goat in the camp, or who killeth it without the
camp, and bringeth it not to the door of the tabernacle of
ordinance to offer it an oblation before the Lord, before
the tabernacle of the Lord, the blood of slaughter shall
be reckoned to that man, and it shall be to him as if
he had shed innocent blood, and that man shall be destroyed from his people. In order that the sons of
Israel may bring their sacrifices which they have [here-
tofore] killed on the face of the field, they may [hence-
forth] bring them before the Lord, at the door of the
tabernacle of ordinance, unto the priest, and sacrifice
their consecrated victims before the Lord. And the

priest shall sprinkle the blood upon the altar of the
Lord, at the door of the tabernacle of ordinance, and
burn the fat, to be received with acceptance before the
Lord.   Neither shall they offer any more their sacrifices
unto idols which are like unto demons, after which they
have wandered.   This shall be an everlasting statute to
them, unto their generations.

And thou shalt tell them : A man, whether young or
old, of the house of Israel, or of the strangers who
sojourn among you, who shall sacrifice a burnt offering,
or consecrated oblation, and bring it not to the door of
the tabernacle of ordinance, to be made an oblation
before the Lord, that man shall be destroyed from his
people.

A man also, whether young or old, of the house of
the family of Israel, or of the strangers who sojourn, in
dwelling among them, who shall eat any blood, I will
cause employment to turn away (or cease) from that
man who eateth any blood, and will destroy him from
among his people.   Because the subsistence of the life
of all flesh is in the blood, and I have given it to you
for a decree, that you shall bring the blood of the
victim unto the altar to make atonement for the blood
of your lives, because the blood of the victim is to atone
for the guilt of the soul.   Therefore have I said to the
sons of Israel, Beware lest any man among you eat the
blood.   Neither shall the strangers who sojourn by
dwelling among you eat the blood.   And any man,
whether young or old, of the house of the stock of
Israel, or of the sojourners who sojourn by dwelling
among you, who hunteth venison of beast or fowl proper
to be eaten, shall pour out its blood when it is killed ;
and if what he hath killed be not destroyed (or
strangled ?), let [the blood] be covered with dust.
Because the subsistence of the life of all flesh is its

blood; it is its life; and I have told the sons of Israel,
You shall not eat the blood of any flesh; for the subsistence of the life of all flesh is its blood: whosoever
among you eateth it shall be destroyed. And any man
who shall eat flesh which hath been thrown away on
account of having been strangled (or corrupted), or
the flesh of that which hath been torn, (any man,)
whether native or sojourner, shall wash his clothes, and
bathe in forty seahs of water, and be unclean until
evening, when he shall be clean; but if he be perverse
and will not wash, nor bathe his flesh, he shall bear his
transgression. [JERUSALEM. And if he will not cleanse
nor purify his flesh, he shall bear his transgression.]

XVIII. And the Lord spake with Mosheh, saying:
Speak with the sons of Israel, and say to them, I am the
Lord your God. After the evil work of the people of the
land of Mizraim, among whom you have dwelt, you shall
not do; so likewise, after the evil work of the people of the
land of Kenaan, whither I am bringing you, ye shall
not do, neither shall you walk according to their laws;
but you shall perform the orders of My judgments, and
observe My statutes to walk in them: I am the Lord
your God. And you shall keep My statutes, and the
order of My judgments, which if a man do he shall live
in them, in the life of eternity, and his portion shall be
with the just: I am the Lord.

No man, either young or old, shall come nigh to any
of the kindred of his flesh to dishonour (their) nakedness by carnality, or by the knowledge of their nakedness.
I am the Lord. The nakedness of thy father, or the
nakedness of thy mother, thou shall not dishonour. A
woman shall not lie with her father, nor a man with his
mother; she is thy mother; thou shalt not discover her
nakedness. The nakedness of thy father's wife thou
shalt not dishonour, for it is the nakedness of thy

father. The nakedness of thy sister, the daughter of thy
father, or the daughter of thy mother, (or of her) whom
thy father begat by another wife, or of thy mother,
whom thy mother bare by thy father or by another
husband, thou shalt not dishonour. The nakedness of
thy son's daughter, or the daughter of thy daughter,
thou shalt not dishonour, because they are as thy own
nakedness. The nakedness of thy father's wife's daughter, who hath been begotten of thy father, she is thy
sister, thou shalt not dishonour. The nakedness of thy
father's sister thou shalt not dishonour; she is of kin
to thy father's flesh. The nakedness of thy mother's
sister thou shall not dishonour; for she is of kin to thy
mother's flesh. The nakedness of thy father's brother
thou shalt not dishonour, nor come nigh to his wife
carnally; she is the wife of thy father's brother. The
nakedness of thy daughter-in-law thou shalt not dishonour; she is the wife of thy son, thou shalt not dishonour her nakedness. The nakedness of thy brother's
wife thou shalt not dishonour in the life-time of thy
brother, or after his death, if he have children; for it is
the nakedness of thy brother. The nakedness of a
woman and of her daughter thou shalt not dishonour,
neither shalt thou take her son's daughter, or the
daughter of her daughter, to dishonour their nakedness;
for they are of kin to her flesh; it is corruption.
Neither shalt thou take a wife in the lifetime of her
sister, to aggrieve her by dishonouring her nakedness,
over her, all the days of her life. And unto the side of a
woman in the time of the separation of her uncleanness
thou shalt not draw nigh to dishonour her nakedness.
Nor unto the side of thy neighbour's wife shalt thou come
to defile her. And of thy offspring thou shalt not give
up any to lie carnally with the daughters of the Gentiles,
to perform strange worship; nor shalt thou profane the

Name of thy God: I am the Lord. [JERUSALEM.
Neither shall ye profane the Name of your God : thus
speaketh the Lord.]   Nor with a male person shalt thou
lie as with a woman ; it is an abhorrent thing.   Neither
shalt thou lie with any beast to corrupt thyself therewith ; nor shall any woman approach before a beast for
evil pleasure ; it is confusion.   Defile not yourselves by
any one of all these ; for by all these have the peoples
defiled themselves whom I am about to drive away from
before you.   And the land hath been defiled, and I have
visited the guilt upon it, and the land delivereth itself
of its inhabitants.   But you, O congregation of Israel,
observe My statutes, and the order of My judgments,
and commit not one of these abominations, neither (you
who are) native born, or the strangers who sojourn
among you.   For these abominable things have been
done by the men of the land who have been before you,
so that the land hath been polluted : lest, when you
pollute the land, it cast you forth, as it will have delivered itself of the people that were before you.   [JERU-
SALEM. And the land cast you not forth.]   For whoever committeth any one of these abominations, the
souls who do so shall be destroyed from among their
people.   Observe you (then) the keeping of My Word,
in being careful to avoid the practice of these abominable rites, which have been practised in the land before
you, and the defilement of yourselves by them : I am
the Lord.

SECTION XXX.

KEDOSHIM.

XIX. AND the Lord spake with Mosheh, saying :
Speak with the whole congregation of the sons of Israel,

and say to them: Ye shall be holy, for I the Lord your
God am Holy. Let every man revere his mother and
his father, and keep the days of My Sabbaths: I am the
Lord your God. Go not astray after the worship of
idols, nor make gods for yourselves that are molten: I
am the Lord your God. And when you sacrifice the
consecrated victims before the Lord, you shall make the
sacrifice acceptable. On the day that it is sacrificed you
may eat of it, and on the day following; but what
remaineth on the third day shall be burned with fire.
But if it be indeed eaten on the third day, it is profaned,
and shall not be accepted. And he who eateth it shall
receive (the penalty of) his sin; for he hath profaned the
holy of the Lord, and that man shall be destroyed from
among his people.

And in the time that you reap the harvest of your
land you shall not finish one corner [2] that is in the
circuit of thy field, and the (full) ingathering of thy
harvest thou shalt not collect. Neither mayest thou
shake out thy vines; (the whole of) their bunches, and
the remnant of thy vines thou shalt not gather: thou
shalt leave them for the poor and for the strangers at
the time of their collection: I am the Lord your God.
[JERUSALEM. And when you reap the harvest of your
land, thou shalt not altogether finish gathering what is
in your fields, and the (full) collection of your harvest
you shall not gather in; neither shake your vines of all
their clusters, nor collect the fallen grapes of your vines.]

Sons of Israel, My people, you shall not steal, nor
prevaricate, nor do fraudulently one man with his
neighbour. Sons of Israel, My people, let no one of
you swear by My Name in vain, to profane the Name
of thy God: I am the Lord. Thou shalt not be
oppressive (hard) upon thy neighbour, nor take away

[2] Heb, *peah*, " corner." Targ, *umana*, " nook, or edge."

by force, nor let the hire of the hireling be remaining all
night at thy side until the morning. Thou shalt not curse
one who heareth not, nor set a stumbling-block before
the blind, but shalt fear thy God : I am the Lord.
Thou shalt not act falsely in the order of judgment,
neither accept the face of the poor, nor honour the face
of the great ; but in truthfulness shalt thou judge thy
neighbour. Thou shalt not go after the slanderous
tongue,[3] which is cruel as a sword that killeth with its
two edges in uttering false accusations to afflict thy
people. Thou shalt not hinder the acquittal of thy neighbour in witnessing against him in the judgment : I am
the Lord. [JERUSALEM. My people of the house of
Israel, follow not the slanderous tongue[3] against your
neighbour, nor be silent about thy neighbour's blood,
what time in the judgment thou knowest the truth : so
speaketh the Lord.]

Speak not bland words with your lips, having hatred
to your brother in your hearts ; but reproving you shall
reprove your neighbour ; and though it make you
ashamed, you shall not contract sin on account of him.
Be not revengeful, nor cherish animosity against the
children of thy people ; but thou shalt love thy neighbour himself, as that though there be (cause of) hatred
with thee thou mayest not do (evil) to him : I am the
Lord.

You shall keep My statutes. Thy cattle shall not be
made to gender with various kinds, neither sow thy
field with mixed seeds, nor put upon thee a garment of
divers materials, (as) wool and linen. And if a man lie
carnally with a woman, and she be an (Israelitish) handmaid (about to be) made free, and betrothed to a free
man, but her redemption not altogether completed by
(the payment of) the money, or the written instru-

---

[3] "The triple tongue." See Introduction, vol. i., p. 12.

ment of liberation not having been given to her, let
inquisition be made for judgment: she is liable to be
chastised, but he is not.   But it shall not be considered
a matter of putting to death, because she was not
altogether free. (Deut. xxii. 22–24.)   And the man
who lay with her must bring his trespass offering to the
door of the tabernacle of ordinance, a ram for a trespass
offering.   [JERUSALEM.   They have rebelled, they are
guilty.]   And the priest shall make atonement with
the ram of his trespass offering before the Lord, for his
sin that he hath sinned; and the sin that he hath sinned
shall be forgiven.

And when you have come into the land, and have
planted any tree that may be eaten of, you shall verily
circumcise the fruit of it; three years shall it be to you
for rejection, to be destroyed; it shall not be eaten.
And in the fourth year all the fruit of it shall be consecrated, (a token of) praise before the Lord delivered for
the priest (or, to be redeemed from the priest).   But in
the fifth year thou mayst eat the fruit of it; for produce
will be increased to you from the heavens: I am the
Lord your God.

You shall not eat the flesh of any sacrifice while the
blood remaineth in the veins.   You shall not be observers
of auguries, after the sanhedrin of the speculators.   You
shall not round off the (hair on) the sides of your
heads, nor shave the corners of your beards.   And a
corrupting incision for the soul of the dead thou shalt
not make in thy flesh, neither set upon yourselves an
inscription by the incutting of any figurated sign: I am
the Lord.   You shall not profane your daughters to
give them up to fornication: neither delay to give your
daughters unto husbands in their proper ages, lest they
go astray by fornication after the people of the land, and
the land be filled with whoredom.

The days of My Sabbaths you shall keep, and go unto
My sanctuary with reverence : I am the Lord. Go not
astray after those who inquire of impostors, or bring up the
dead, or interrogate the bone of Jeddua : [4] neither be
ye inquirers with them, to pollute yourselves thereby :
I am the Lord your God. You shall rise up before the
aged who instruct in the law ; and honour the presence
of the wise, and fear thy God : I am the Lord.

And if a stranger becometh a sojourner, and settleth
among you in your land, you shall not molest him with
hard words : but the stranger who sojourneth among
you shall be (treated) as the native born, and thou shalt
love him as thyself : thou shalt not deal with him as if
thou didst hate him ; for ye were sojourners in the land
of Mizraim : I am the Lord your God.

You shall not deal falsely in the ordering of
judgment ; in the admeasurement of summer and
winter ; in weight and measure, in heaping up, or in
sweeping off : [5] but balances of truth, weights of truth,
measures of truth, and tankards of truth, shall yours
be. I am the Lord your God who brought you
redeemed from the land of Mizraim : and you shall
observe all My statutes, and all the ordinations of My
judgments, and do them : I am the Lord.

XX. And the Lord spake with Mosheh, saying :
And with the sons of Israel speak thou, to say : A man
of the family of the sons of Israel, whether young or
old, who shall make (an offering) of his offspring unto
Molek to be burned in the fire, shall be verily put to
death : the people of the house of Israel shall punish
his guilt by the infliction of stones ; and I will cause a

---

[4] *Sanhedrin*, vii., 7

[5] " In the heaper up, (shovel,) and the smoother off, " *michka*, an
instrument of wood for smoothing off the surface of a measure of any
dry material, so as to make it exactly full, and no more.

reverse, to make prosperity to cease with that man, and will cut him off from among his people; because he gave his offspring in strange worship to pollute My sanctuary, and to profane My holy Name. And if the people of the house of Israel hiding hide, their eyes from that man, when he giveth his offspring unto strange worship, that they might not kill him, then will I appoint a reverse, to make a controversy against that man, and against his family who protect (cover) him, to chastise (them) with afflictions; and him will I destroy, and all who follow him to wander after strange worship, from among their people.

And the man who turns aside to inquire of the impostors, or to seek to bring up the dead, or to inquire by the bone of Jeddua, to go astray after them, I will appoint a reverse to punish that man, and will destroy him by a plague from among his people. But sanctify yourselves, and be holy in your bodies, that your prayers may be received with acceptance: I am the Lord who sanctify you. And observe My statutes and perform them: I am the Lord who sanctify you.

For the young man or the old man who curseth his father or his mother by the revealed Name, shall be verily put to death by the casting of stones; because he hath cursed his father or his mother, he is guilty of death. And the man who by adultery defileth the wife of (another) man, or who committeth adultery with the wife of his married neighbour, shall be verily put to death, by strangulation, with the hard towel in the tender part (?): and, on account of a betrothed person, by the casting of stones. both the adulterer and the adulteress (shall die). And a man who lieth with his father's wife, whether his own mother or another wife, and who hath dishonoured the nakedness of his father, shall be verily put to death: both of them are guilty of death by the casting of stones. And if a man lieth with his daughter-in-law, both of them shall be put to death; they have wrought confusion, they are guilty of death by the casting of stones. And if a man lie with a man as with a woman, they have wrought abomination; both of them shall die by the stoning of stones. And if a man take a wife and her mother, it is fornication; let them be burned with fire with melted lead in their mouth, that fornication may not be among you. And a man who lieth with a beast shall be surely put to death with the stoning of stones, and the beast shall be slain with spikes. And if a woman approacheth the side of any beast that it may have to do with her, they shall be slain; the woman by the casting of stones, and the beast by the slaughter of spikes, they shall die; for they are deserving of death. And if a man lie with his sister, his father's daughter, or the daughter of his mother, and he dishonour her nakedness, it is depravity: for I showed mercy with the first ones, on behalf of the peopling of the world by them, while as yet I had not promulged the law in the world: but after the law hath been declared in the world, every one who committeth these things shall be destroyed by mortality, and the children of their people shall witness their punishment; for he who hath dishonoured the nakedness of his sister shall be guilty of death. And a man who lieth with a woman who is unclean, and dishonoureth her nakedness, they shall both of them be destroyed by a plague from among their people. Nor shalt thou dishonour the nakedness of thy mother's sister nor thy father's sister; for he hath dishonoured the flesh of his near kin: they shall receive the penalty of their guilt in dying. And if a man lie with the wife of his father's brother, he hath dishonoured the nakedness of his father's brother: they shall receive their punishment; they shall be consumed by mortality; without children shall they die. And if a man take the wife of his brother during his life, it is an abomination : he hath dishonoured the nakedness of his brother; without children shall they be.

But you, the congregation of Israel, shall observe all My statutes, and all the ordinations of My judgments, and do them; that the land into which I am to bring you to dwell in it may not cast you out : and walk not after the laws of the peoples whom I drive away from before you; for they have committed all these abhorrent things, and My Word hath abhorred them. But I have told you to beware of these horrors, that you may inherit their land; and I will give it you to possess it, a land producing milk and honey. I am the Lord your God who have separated you from the nations. And you shall make distinction between the animal which is fit to be eaten, and that which it is improper to eat; and between the fowl which it is improper to eat, and that which is fit to be eaten. Defile not your souls by (eating of) the animal that is torn by a wild beast, or the bird torn by the falcon, or anything that creepeth upon the ground, which I have separated from you for their uncleanness. And you shall be holy before me; for holy am I, the Lord, who have chosen you, and separated you from the nations to be worshippers before Me. And the man or the woman who hath in them (the spirit of) divination or necromancy shall die by the casting of stones; for they are guilty of death.

SECTION XXXI.

EMOR.

XXI. AND the Lord spake to Mosheh, saying: Speak unto the priests, the men of the children of Aharon, that they keep themselves apart from defilement, and thus shalt thou say to them : For a man who is dead, (the priest) shall not defile himself among his people ; but for a woman who is of kin to his flesh, for his mother, and for his father, and for his son, and for his daughter, and for his brother, and for his sister, a virgin who is nigh to him, and who hath neither been betrothed, nor married to a husband, for her he may defile himself.　The husband shall not defile himself on account of his wife, except so far as it is right for him ; but for a relative of those who do the work of his people he may defile himself.　They shall not mark themselves between their eyes, nor set a mark upon their heads, nor cut away the corners of their beards, nor make any incision in their flesh : but they shall be holy before their God, and shall not profane the name of their God ; [JERUSALEM. They shall not profane ;] for the oblations of their God they do offer, and they must be holy in their bodies.　They shall not take to wife a woman who hath gone astray by fornication, [JERUSALEM. A woman a fornicatress, or profane,] or who was born illegitimate, nor a woman who hath been put away, whether from her husband or the husband's brother, may they take ; for he is to be holy before his God.　Thou shalt sanctify him unto the priesthood ; for the oblation itself of thy God he is to offer : he shall be holy to thee, and thou shalt not make him profane : I, the Lord who sanctify you, am holy.　And if the betrothed daughter of a man of the priesthood

profane herself, by going astray in fornication ; if, while
she is yet in her father's house, she is guilty of fornication, she shall be burned with fire.

And the high priest who hath been anointed over his
brethren, and upon whose head the anointing oil was
poured, and who offered his oblation to be arrayed in
the (holy) robes, shall not make his head bare, nor
either rend or tear his garment in the hour of grief.
Nor unto any person who is dead shall he go in, nor
for his father or his mother make himself unclean.   And
he shall not go forth from the sanctuary, or profane the
sanctuary of his God ; for the anointing oil of his God
is upon him : I am the Lord.   And he shall take a
wife who is in her virginity ; but a widow, or a divorced
person, or one who was born of depraved parents, or
who hath gone astray by fornication, such as these he
shall not take ; but a virgin proper shall he take to wife
from the daughters of his people.   Neither shall he
profane his offspring among his people ; for I the Lord
do sanctify him.

And the Lord spake with Mosheh, saying : Speak
with Aharon, saying : No man of thy sons in the families
of their generations who hath a blemish in him shall be
qualified to offer the oblation of his God : for no man
who hath a blemish in him shall offer.   A man who is
blind or lame, or stricken in his nostrils, or mutilated in
his thigh, or a man who hath a broken foot, or a broken
hand, or whose eyelids droop so as to cover his eyes, or
who hath no hair on his eyelids ; or who hath a suffu-
sion of whiteness with darkness in his eyes ; or who
hath the dry scurvy, or who is full of the blotches of
Egypt, or whose testicles are swollen or shrunk, (JERU-
SALEM. Or one whose eyelids cover his eyes, or hath no
hair on his eyelids, or who is overgrown, or a dwarf, or
blear-eyed, or filled with scurvy or with blotches, or who

is wanting in the testicles,] no man, a priest of the race
of Aharon the priest who hath in him any such blemish,
shall be qualified to offer the oblations of the Lord.
He hath a blemish, and it is not meet for him to offer
the oblation of his God. Nevertheless he may support
himself with the residue of the oblations of his God
which remaineth of the most holy and of the holy
(offerings) ; only he must not enter within the veil, nor
approach the altar ; for a blemish is in him, and he shall
not profane My sanctuary; for I the Lord do sanctify
them. And Mosheh spake with Aharon and with his
sons, and with all the sons of Israel.

XXII. And the Lord spake with Mosheh, saying :
Speak with Aharon and with his sons, that they keep
apart from the consecrated things of the children of
Israel, and profane not the Name of My Holiness (in
whatever) they hallow before Me: I am the Lord.
Say to them, Take heed in your generations :—Whatever man of all your sons who shall offer things hallowed,
which the children of Israel have consecrated before the
Lord, having his uncleanness upon him, that man shall
be destroyed with a stroke of death before Me: I am
the Lord. Any man, young or old of the offspring of
Aharon, who is a leper, or hath a running issue, shall
not eat of things consecrated till he be clean : and whoever toucheth any uncleanness of man, or one from
whom uncleanness hath proceeded, or who toucheth any
reptile that maketh unclean, or (the corpse of) a dead
man which maketh unclean, or any of the uncleanness
of his life, the man being a priest who toucheth such
shall be unclean until the evening, and may not eat of
the holy things, except that he wash his flesh in forty
seahs of water. And when the sun hath set and he be
fit, he may afterward eat of the holy things; for they
are his food. But of a dead carcase, or (that which hath

been) killed (by violence), he may not eat to defile himself therewith. I am the Lord. But the sons of Israel
shall observe the keeping of My Word, that they may
not bring sin upon themselves, nor die for it by the
flaming fire; because they have profaned it: I am the
Lord who sanctify them.

No stranger or profane person shall eat of a consecrated thing, (neither) a son of Israel who is an inmate of
the priest, nor any hireling, may eat of the hallowed
thing. But if the priest buy a man a stranger with
the price of his money, he may eat of it, and such as
have grown up in his house may eat of his bread. And
the daughter of a priest, if she be married to a man a
stranger, may not eat of things set apart by consecration.
But if the daughter of a priest be a widow, or be divorced,
and having no child by him hath returned to her father's
house, and hath not been wedded to a brother-in-law,
(Deut. xxv. 5,) she, being as in the days of her youth,
and not being with child, may eat of her father's meat,
but no stranger shall eat thereof. And if a man of
Israel eat that which is consecrated unknowingly, let
him add a fifth part of its value to it, and give the (price
of the) holy thing unto the priest. Let them not profane the sacred things of the children of Israel which
are set apart unto the Name of the Lord, nor let the sin
of their trespass be found upon them, by eating in
uncleanness their consecrated things; for I am the
Lord who do sanctify them.

And the Lord spake with Mosheh, saying: Speak
with Aharon, and with his sons, and with all the children of Israel :—A man, whether young or old, of the
house of the family of Israel, or of the strangers who
are in Israel, who shall offer his oblation of any of their
vows, or their free will offerings which they present
before the Lord for a burnt sacrifice, to be acceptable

for you, it shall be perfect, a male of the bullocks, of
the lambs, or of the young goats. But anything that
hath a blemish you shall not offer; for that will not be
acceptable from you. And if a man will offer a consecrated victim before the Lord to fulfil a vow, or as a
free will offering, from the herd, or from the flock, it
must be perfect to be acceptable; no blemish shall be
in it. Whatever is blind, or broken-boned, or stricken
in the eyelids, or whose eyes are stricken with a mixture
of white and dark, or one filled with scurvy or the
blotches of murrain, you shall not offer before the Lord,
nor present an oblation of them on the altar before the
Lord. A bullock or a ram that hath superfluity or
deficiency of the testicles, you may make a free will
offering, but for a vow it will not be acceptable. That
which is crushed, or ruptured, or diseased, or enervated,
you shall not offer to the Name of the Lord; and in
your land you shall not emasculate. And from the
hand of a son of the Gentiles you shall not offer the
oblation of your God of any of these, because their corruption is in them; a blemish is in them, they are profane, they shall not be acceptable for you.

And the Lord spake with Mosheh, saying (to the
effect that): What time thou callest to our mind the
order of our oblations, as they shall be offered year by
year, being our expiatory offering for our sins, when on
account of our sins (such sacrifices are required), and we
have none to bring from our flocks of sheep, then shall
a bullock be chosen before him, in memorial of the
righteousness of the elder who came from the east, the
sincere one who brought the calf, fat and tender, to Thy
Name. A sheep is to be chosen, secondly, in memory
of the righteousness of him who was bound as a lamb on
the altar, and who stretched forth his neck for Thy
Name's sake, while the heavens stooped down and con-

descended, and Izhak beheld their foundations, and his
eyes were blinded by the high things; on which account
he was reckoned to be worthy that a lamb should be
provided for him as a burnt offering.   A kid of the goats
is to be chosen likewise, in memorial of the righteousness of that perfect one who made the savoury meat of
the kid, and brought it to his father, and was made
worthy to receive the order of the blessing: wherefore
Mosheh the prophet explaineth, saying: Sons of Israel,
my people, When a bullock, or a lamb, or a kid is
brought forth according to the manner of the world, it
shall be seven days after its dam, that there may be
evidence that it is not imperfect; and on the eighth day
and thenceforth, it is acceptable to be offered an oblation to the Name of the Lord.   Sons of Israel, my
people, as our Father in heaven is merciful, so shall you
be merciful on earth: neither cow, nor ewe, shall you
sacrifice along with her young on the same day.   And
when you offer a sacrifice of thanksgiving to the Name
of the Lord, you shall offer so as to be accepted.   It
shall be eaten on that day, none shall remain till the
morning: I am the Lord.   And you shall observe My
commandments to do them.   I am the Lord who give
a good reward to them who keep My commandments
and My laws.   Nor shall you profane My Holy Name,
that I may be hallowed among the children of Israel.
I am the Lord who sanctify you, having brought you
forth redeemed from the land of Mizraim, that I may
be to you Eloah: I am the Lord.

[JERUSALEM. In the time that thou remindest us of
the order of the oblations as they are to be offered year
by year; our offerings are to make atonement for our
sins.   But when our sins have given occasion, and we
have not wherewith to bring from our flocks of sheep,
a bullock is to be chosen before Me, to recall to remem-

brance the elder of the east, sincere altogether, who brought to Thy Name a calf tender and good, which he gave to the young man, who hasted to dress it, and to bake unleavened cakes; and the angels did eat, and he was accounted worthy to receive the announcement that, behold, Sarah should give birth to Izhak. A lamb is to be chosen, secondly, to call to remembrance the righteousness of the prince who suffered himself to be bound upon the altar, and stretched forth his neck for Thy Name's sake; when .the heavens stooped down and condescended, and Izhak beheld their foundations, and his eyes were blinded by the high things (or, from the heights), on which account he was held worthy that a lamb should be provided in his stead for a burnt offering. A kid of the goats also is to be chosen, to call to remembrance the righteousness of that perfect one who put on the skins of the kids, and made savoury meat, and brought of his viands unto his father, and gave wine to him to drink; on account of which he was held worthy to receive the orders of blessings from Izhak his father, that the twelve sacred tribes should arise to Thy Name. Behold, then, how Mosheh, the prophet of the Lord, expoundeth, and saith, Sons of Israel, my people, When a bullock, or a lamb, or a goat is brought forth, it shall be seven days after its dam; on the eighth day and thenceforth it shall be fit to be offered as an oblation to the Name of the Lord.]

XXIII. And the Lord spake with Mosheh, saying: Speak with the sons of Israel, and say to them, The orders of the time of the Festivals of the Lord, which you shall proclaim as holy convocations,—these are the orders of the time of My festivals. Six days shalt thou do work, and the seventh day (shall be) a Sabbath and a rest, a holy convocation. No manner of work may you do; it is a Sabbath to the Lord in every place of your habitations.

These are the times of the Festivals of the Lord, holy convocations which you shall proclaim in their times : In the month of Nisan, on the fourteenth day of the month, between the suns (shall be) the time for the sacrifice of the Pascha to the Name of the Lord. And on the fifteenth day of this month the feast of unleavened cakes to the Name of the Lord. Seven days you shall eat unleavened bread. On the first day of the feast a holy convocation shall be to you ; ye shall do no work of labour, but offer the oblation to the Name of the Lord seven days; in the seventh day of the feast shall be a holy convocation ; you shall do no work of labour.

And the Lord spake with Mosheh, saying : Speak with the sons of Israel, and say to them : When you have entered into the land which I give you, and you reap the harvest, you shall bring the sheaf of the first fruits of your harvest unto the priest ; and he shall uplift the sheaf before the Lord to be accepted for you. After the first festal day of Pascha (or, the day after the feast-day of Pascha) on the day on which you elevate the sheaf, you shall make (the sacrifice of) a lamb of the year, unblemished, a burnt offering unto the Name of the Lord : and its mincha, two-tenths of flour, mingled with olive oil, for an oblation to the Name of the Lord, to be received with acceptance ; and its libation, wine of grapes, the fourth of a hin. But neither bread nor parched corn (of the ripe harvest) nor new ears may you eat until this day, until the time of your bringing the oblation of your God : an everlasting statute unto your generations in all your dwellings.

And number to you after the first feast day of Pascha, from the day when you brought the sheaf for the elevation, seven weeks; complete they shall be. Until the day after the seventh week you shall number fifty days, and shall offer a mincha of the new bread unto the Name of the Lord. From the place of your dwellings you are to bring the bread for the elevation; two cakes of two-tenths of flour, which must be baked with leaven, as first fruits unto the Name of the Lord. And with that bread you are to offer seven lambs of the year, unblemished, and a young bullock without mixture (of colour), the one for a sin offering, and two lambs of the year for a sanctified oblation. And you shall make (a sacrifice) of a young goat without mixture, the one for a sin offering, and two lambs of the year for a sanctified oblation. And the priest shall uplift them with the bread of the first fruits, an elevation before the Lord, with the two lambs; they shall be holy to the Name of the Lord, and shall be for the priest. And you shall proclaim with life and strength that self-same day, that at the time of that day there shall be to you a holy convocation: you shall do no work of labour: it is an everlasting statute in all your dwellings for your generations.

And when you reap the harvest of your ground, you shall not finish one corner that is in thy field at thy reaping, nor shalt thou gather the gleanings of thy harvest, but leave them for the poor and the strangers: I am the Lord thy God.

And the Lord spake with Mosheh, saying: Speak with the children of Israel, saying: In Tishri, which is the seventh month, shall be to you a festival of seven days, a memorial of trumpets, a holy convocation. No work of labour may you do, but offer an oblation before the Lord unto the Name of the Lord. And the Lord spake with Mosheh, saying: But on the tenth day of this seventh month is the Day of Atonement; a holy convocation shall it be to you, and you shall humble

your souls, (abstaining) from food, and from drink, and
from the use of the bath, and from anointing, and the
use of the bed, and from sandals; and you shall offer
an oblation before the Lord, and do no work on this
same day; for it is the Day of Atonement, to make atonement for you before the Lord your God. For every
man who eateth in the fast, and will not fast that same
day, shall be cut off by death from among his people.
[JERUSALEM. For every soul who hideth himself from
fasting, and fasteth not on the day of the fast of his
atonement.] And every man who doeth any work on
that same day, that man will I destroy with death from
among his people. No work of labour may you do:
an everlasting statute for your generations, in all your
dwellings. It is a Sabbath and time of leisure for you
to humble your souls. And you shall begin to fast at
the ninth day of the month at even time; from that
evening until the next evening shall you fast your fast,
and repose in your quietude, that you may employ the
time of your festivals with joy. [JERUSALEM. From
evening to evening you shall fast your fast, and repose
in your quietude, that you may employ the time of your
festivals with joy.]

And the Lord spake with Mosheh, saying: Speak with
the sons of Israel: In the fifteenth day of this seventh
month shall be the Feast of Tabernacles, seven days
unto the Name of the Lord. On the first day of the
feast is a holy convocation; no work of labour may you
do. Seven days you shall offer an oblation to the Name
of the Lord, you shall gather together to pray before the
Lord for rain; no work of labour may you do. These
are the times of the order of the Lord's festivals which
you are to convoke for holy convocations, to offer an
oblation to the Name of the Lord, a burnt sacrifice and
a mincha, sanctified offerings and libations, the rite of a

day in its day; beside the days of the Lord's Sabbaths, beside your gifts, and beside your vows, and beside your free-will offerings which you bring before the Lord. But on the fifteenth of the seventh month, at the time when you collect the produce of the ground, you shall solemnize a festival of the Lord seven days. On the first day, rest; and on the eighth day, rest. And of your own shall you take on the first day of the feast, the fruits of praiseworthy trees, citrons, and lulabin, and myrtles, and willows that grow by the brooks; and you shall rejoice before the Lord your God seven days. [JERUSALEM. Citrons and lulabs.] And you shall solemnize it before the Lord seven days in the year, by an everlasting statute in your generations shall you observe it in the seventh month. In tabernacles of two sides according to their rule, and the third a handbreadth (higher), that its shaded part may be greater than that into which cometh the sunshine,[6] to be made for a bower (or shade) for the feast, from different kinds (of materials) which spring from the earth and are uprooted: in measure seven palms, but the height within ten palms. In it you shall sit seven days;[7] the males in Israel, and children who need not their mothers, shall sit in the tabernacles, blessing their Creator whenever they enter thereinto. That your generations may know how, under the shadow of the cloud of glory, I made the sons of Israel to dwell at the time that I brought them out redeemed from the land of Mizraim. And Mosheh declared the time of the orders of the Lord's festivals, and taught them to the sons of Israel.

XXIV. And the Lord spake with Mosheh, saying: Command the children of Israel that they bring, of their own, pure beaten olive oil for the light, that the lamps

---

[6] Vide *Mishna*, order ii, treatise 17, *Sukkah*.

[7] One meal at least each day in the bower.

may burn continually, on the day of Sabbath, and on the day of work; outside of the veil of the testimony for evermore, because the Shekinah dwelleth in Israel: in the tabernacle of ordinance shall Aharon order it from evening till morning before the Lord continually, by an everlasting statute unto your generations.

And thou shalt take flour, and bake thereof twelve cakes, according to the twelve tribes; two tenths shall be one cake. And thou shalt set them in two orders (rows), six in one order, and six in the other upon the table in its purity, as it is ordained before the Lord. And thou shalt put upon the orders pure frankincense, that it may be an oblation of memorial bread before the Lord. From Sabbath day to Sabbath day he shall order it anew before the Lord continually from the children of Israel. This shall be an everlasting statute. And it shall be for Aharon and for his sons, and they shall eat it after they have taken it from off the table in the holy place; for it is most sacred to him of the oblations of the Lord by an everlasting statute.

But a wicked man, a rebel against the God of heaven, had come out of Mizraim, the son of the Mizraite man who had killed the man of Israel in Mizraim, and had gone in unto his wife, who conceived and bare a son among the children of Israel. And while the Israelites were dwelling in the wilderness, he had sought to spread his tent in the midst of the tribe of the children of Dan; but they would not permit him, because in the arrangements of Israel every man dwelt with his family by the ensigns of the house of their fathers. And they contended together in the camp, and the son of the Israelitess with a man of Israel, who was of the tribe of Dan, went to the house of judgment; and when they had come out from the house of judgment, where he had been condemned, the son of the daughter of Israel expressed and

reviled the great and glorious Name of Manifestation
which he had heard at Sinai, and defied and execrated ;
and the name of his mother was Shelomith, the daughter
of Dibree, of the tribe of Dan. [JERUSALEM. And the
son of the woman of Israel reviled the Manifested Name,
and defied.]

This is one of four judgments which were brought in
before Mosheh the prophet, who decided them by the
dictate of the Word, who is above. They were judgments about money and about life. In the judgments
on money Mosheh was prompt; but in the judgment
on life he was deliberate (or slow by delay). And to
each (party) Mosheh said, I have not heard: that he
might teach the chiefs of the Sanhedrin of Israel, who
were to arise after him, to be prompt in judgments
respecting money, but slow in judgments that affected
life; and not to be ashamed to inquire for counsel in
cases that should be too hard for them, forasmuch as
Mosheh, Rabban of Israel, had need to say, I have not
heard. Therefore they shut him up in the house of
confinement till the time that it should be explained to
them by the decree of the Word of the Lord.

[JERUSALEM. This is one of four judgments that
were brought before Mosheh our Rabbi. In two of
them was Mosheh slow by delay, and in two of them
was Mosheh expeditious. With the blasphemer who
blasphemed the Holy Name with scoffings, and with the
gatherer of sticks who profaned the Sabbath, Mosheh
had delay, because they were judgments that affected
life; but in the case of unclean persons who could
not perform the Pascha in its time, and in that of the
daughters of Zelophehad, Mosheh could be prompt,
because they were judgments on temporal matters. But
to those he would say, I have not heard: to teach the
judges who were to arise after Mosheh to be slow in

judgments on life, and to be expeditious in judgments
of Mammon; and not to be ashamed to say, I have not
heard; for Mosheh our Rabban said, I have not heard.
And they shut him up in confinement, while as yet it
had not been explained to them from before the Lord
with what judgments they were to deal with him.]

And the Lord spake with Mosheh, saying: Bring
forth the blasphemer without the camp, and let the
witnesses who heard his blasphemy, and the judges, lay
their hands upon his head, and let the whole congregation stone him with stones. And speak thou with the
sons of Israel, saying: A man young or old who shall
blaspheme the known Name of his God shall bear his
sin. Whosoever expresseth and revileth the Name of
the Lord shall verily be put to death; all the congregation shall cast stones upon him, whether he be a
sojourner or native-born, when he hath blasphemed the
Name that is Alone, he shall die.

And if a man destroy the life of any one of the
children of Israel, he shall verily be put to death by the
sword. And he who destroyeth the life of an animal
shall make it good, a living animal for a living one.
And a man who inflicteth a blemish on his neighbour,
whatsoever he hath done it shall be done unto him: the
value of a fracture for a fracture; the value of an eye
for an eye; the value of a tooth for a tooth; whatsoever
blemish he inflicteth upon the man, the same shall be
rendered unto him. [JERUSALEM. Fracture shall be
recompensed by fracture, an eye shall be recompensed
by an eye, a tooth for a tooth, the blemish he hath
given to the man it shall be given unto him.] He who
killeth a beast shall restore it; but he who slayeth a
man shall be slain. One judgment shall you have for
the stranger and for the native; for I am the Lord your
God. And Mosheh spake with the sons of Israel, and

they brought forth the blasphemer without the camp,
and stoned him with stones; and the sons of Israel
did it, by laying their hands upon, leading him away,
hanging, and burying him, as the Lord had commanded
Mosheh.

SECTION XXXII.

BEHAR SINAI.

XXV. AND the Lord spake with Mosheh in the
mountain of Sinai, saying: Speak with the children of
Israel, and say to them : When you have entered into
the land that I will give to you, then shall the ground
rest for a rest before the Lord. Six years you shall sow
your fields, and six years prune your vineyards and
gather in the fruit; but in the seventh year there shall
be a rest of remission to the earth, that she may rest
before the Lord; you shall not sow your fields, nor
prune your vineyards. The after crop which remaineth
from your harvests you may not reap, nor of your later
grapes make a vintage; a year of remission it shall be
unto the earth ; but the remission [8] of the ground shall
be to you for food, to thee, to thy servant, and to thine
handmaid, and to thy hireling, and to the stranger who
dwelleth with thee; and for thy cattle and for the
animals that are in thy land shall be the produce of it
(also).

And thou shalt number to thee seven Sabbaths of
years, seven times seven years, and they shall be to thee
the sum of the days of seven Sabbaths (or remissions,
shemittin) of years, forty and nine years. And thou

---

[8] The produce yielded spontaneously during the time of remission to
be enjoyed in common. So Rashi, Eben Ezra, and Bar Nachman

shalt make the voice of the trumpet to sound a jubilee;
in the seventh month, on the tenth day of the month,
on the Day of the Expiations thou shalt make the voice
of the trumpet of Liberty to pass through all your land.
And you shall sanctify that year, the fiftieth year, and
proclaim liberty in the land of Israel to all the inhabitants; Jubela shall it be to you, and you shall return
every man to his inheritance, and every man unto his
family, you shall return.   The year of Jubela shall that
fiftieth be to you: ye shall not sow, nor reap the after
crop, nor make vintages of the grapes which have been
let alone.   For that Jubela shall be sacred to you, the
produce of the field shall you eat.   Iu this year of
Jubela you shall return every man unto his inheritance.

And when you sell sales to your neighbours, or you
buy disposable (or moveable) goods from the hand of
your neighbours, it is not allowable for a man to defraud
his neighbour.   Sons of Israel, My people, if you sell a
field or a vineyard, according to the sum of the number
of years after the Jubela you shall buy of your neighbour; according to the number of years for gathering
the produce they shall sell it to you; according to the
greatness of the amount of the years shall the price be
enlarged; and according to the smallness of the amount
of the years the price shall be diminished, because he sells
to thee the amount of the fruitage to be ingathered.
And you shall not overreach one man his neighbour by
hard words, but fear your God: I am the Lord your
God.   And you shall perform My statutes, and observe
the order of My judgments and do them, that you may
dwell upon the land securely.   And the land will yield
her produce, and you shall eat and be satisfied, and
dwell upon the land in security.

But if you say, What shall we eat in the seventh
year; behold, we sow not, nor ingather even the after

crop of our provision? I will command My blessing upon you from my treasures of goodness, which are in the heaven of My Presence, in the sixth year, and it will create produce that will suffice for three years. But you shall sow in the eighth year, and eat of the old produce of the sixth year until the ninth year; until the time of the incoming of the new produce, shall you eat of the old.

And the land of Israel shall not be sold absolutely, for the land is Mine; for you are sojourners and guests with Me. And in all the land of your possession you shall let the ground have redemption.

And if thy brother hath become poor and hath sold his possession, his redeemer who is near of kin to him may come and redeem the sale of his brother. But if a man have no one who is qualified to redeem that which he hath sold, and it befall to his own hand to find the price of its redemption, then let him count the sum of the years of its sale, and give the amount to the man who bought it, and return to his possession. But if his hand meet not with the price that he should give him, then the property sold shall (remain) in the hand of him who bought it until the year of Jubela, and shall then go out without money, and he shall return to his possession.

And if a man sell a dwelling-house, in a town surrounded by a wall, it may have redemption until the completing of the year from its sale: from time to time shall be its redemption. But if it be not redeemed at the completing of the full year, the house that is in a walled town shall be confirmed absolutely to him who bought it, unto his generations: it shall not go out at the Jubela. But houses in villages which have no walls round about them, are to be accounted as tents which are spread upon the fields of the earth; they may be

redeemed, and they shall go out at the Jubela. But the
cities of the Levites, the houses of the cities of their
possession may be always redeemable by the Levites.
And when one hath purchased of the Levites the house
that was sold in the cities of their possession, it shall go
out at the Jubela; for the houses of the Levites are
their inheritance among the children of Israel. But a
field in the suburbs of their cities shall not be sold, for
it is an everlasting possession for them. [JERUSALEM.
But a field in the suburbs of their cities shall not be
sold, because a possession].

And if thy brother hath become poor, and his hand
wavereth with thee, then thou shalt strengthen and do
him good, as a guest and a sojourner he shall be
nourished with thee. My people of the house of Israel,
you shall not take usuries or remunerations (in his case),
but thou shalt fear thy God, and let thy brother have
nourishment with thee. My people of the house of
Israel, you shall not lend him for usury, nor give (him)
your provisions for increase. [JERUSALEM. Thy money
thou shalt not lend him for usuries, nor give thy food
for increase]. I am the Lord your God, who redeemed
and brought you out redeemed from the land of Mizraim,
to give unto you the land of Kenaan, and to be unto
you Eloha

If thy brother with thee shall have become poor, and
have sold himself unto thee, thou shalt not make him
serve according to the laws of the service of bondmen;
but as a hired man and as a sojourner shall he serve with
thee, until the year of Jubela shall he serve thee. Then
shall he go out from thee at liberty, he and his children
with him, and return to his family, and to the heritage
of his fathers shall he return. For they are My servants
whom I brought forth redeemed from the land of Mizraim; they shall not be sold according to the laws of

the sale of bondmen. Neither may you make him
serve with rigour, but thou shalt fear the Lord thy God.
But your bondmen and your handmaids which you may
have, of the handmaids of the Gentiles, of them you may
purchase bondmen and handmaids.

Moreover, of the children of the uncircumcised
strangers who sojourn among you, of them you may buy,
and of their families that are with you, which they have
begotten in your land; but not from the Kenaanaee;
and they shall be yours for possession. And you may
leave them to your children after you, to inherit as a
perpetual possession; them you shall make to serve:
but of your brethren of the sons of Israel no man
(may enslave) his fellow; them shall you not make to
serve with rigour.

And if the hand of the uncircumcised sojourner with
you wax strong, and thy brother with him become poor,
and sell himself to the uncircumcised stranger who is
with thee, or to the stock of a strange religion, to serve
him or to worship with him who is of the generation of
strangers; when it is known to you that he hath been sold,
forthwith redemption shall be his; one of his brethren
shall redeem him; either the brother of his father or
the son of his father's brother may redeem him; or a
kinsman of the flesh of his family may redeem him; or
by his own hand being made strong, or by the hand of
the congregation, he may be redeemed. And he shall
account with the uncircumcised person who had bought
him, from the year that he was sold until the year of
Jubela, and the price of his re-purchase shall be according to the number of the years; according to the days
of an hireling shall it be with him. If yet there be
many years, according to their number he shall give for
his redemption of the money that he was bought for.
But if few years remain till the year of Jubela, he shall

compute with him, and according to the amount of the
years give for his redemption. As a hireling by the
year shall he be with him, and his master shall not make
him to serve with rigour while thou see it. But if he
be not redeemed within those years, he shall go out free
at the year of Jubela, he and his children with him.
For the sons of Israel are Mine, to obey My laws, My
servants are they whom I brought out redeemed from
the land of Mizraim. I am the Lord your God.

XXVI. You shall not make to you idols or images,
nor erect for you statues to worship, neither a figured
stone[9] shall ye place in your land to bow yourselves
toward it. [JERUSALEM. Nor a stone for an idol.]
Nevertheless a pavement sculptured with imagery you
may set on the spot of your sanctuary, but not to worship
it: I am the Lord your God. The days of My Sabbaths you shall keep, and walk to the house of My
sanctuary in My fear; I am the Lord.

SECTION XXXIII.

BECHUKKOTHAI

If you will go forward in the statutes of My law, and
keep the orders of My judgments, and perform them,
then will I give you the rains for your lands in your
seasons, the early and the late, and the land shall yield
the fruits of increase, and the tree on the face of the
field shall be prosperous in its fruit. And with you the
threshing shall reach to the vintage, and the vintage
unto the springing of the seed, and you shall eat your
bread and be satisfied, and dwell securely in your land.

[9] Glossary, p. 23.

And I will give peace in the land of Israel, that you may
repose, and there be none to disturb; and I will make
the power of the wild beast to cease from the land of
Israel, and the unsheather of the sword shall not pass
through your land. And you shall chase your adversaries, and they will fall before you broken with the
sword. And five of you will chase a hundred, and a
hundred of you put a myriad to flight, and your adversaries shall fall before you, broken with the sword. For
I will turn from the wages of the Gentiles, to fulfil to
you the recompense of your good works, and I will
strengthen you, and multiply you, and establish My
covenant with you. And you shall eat the old that is
old without having the corn-worm, and the old from
before the new produce shall ye turn out of your barns.
And I will set the Shekinah of My Glory among you,
and my Word shall not abhor you, but the Glory of My
Shekinah shall dwell among you, and My Word shall be
to you for a redeeming God, and you shall be unto My
Name for a holy people. I am the Lord your God, who
brought you out redeemed from the land of Mizraim,
that you should not be bondmen to them, and brake
the yoke of their bondage from off you, and brought
you out from among them, the children of liberty, and
led you forth with an erect stature.

But if you will be unwilling to hear the instructions
of the doctrine of My law, and to perform all these
precepts with your free choice; and if you despise My
statutes, and hate in your soul the orders of My judgments, to do not all My precepts, but your purpose be to
abolish My covenant; this also will I do to you: I will
draw out against you the smiting pestilence, the flame
and the fever, to consume your eyes, and to exhaust life;
and ye shall sow your seed in vain, for it shall not
spring up, and that which groweth of itself shall your

enemies devour. And I will appoint a reverse to your
affairs, and you shall be broken before your foes, and
they who hate you shall rule over you; and you will
flee when no one pursueth you. And if after these
chastisements ye be not willing to obey the doctrines of
My law, I will add to punish you with seven plagues,
for the seven transgressions with which you have sinned
before Me. And I will break down the glory of the
strength of your sanctuary, and will make the heavens
above you obdurate as iron, to yield no moisture, nor
send you dew or rain, and the ground beneath you to be
like brass to put forth (only) to destroy its fruit. And
your strength shall be consumed in vain, for your land
shall not yield what you bestow upon it, and the tree
upon the face of the field shall drop its fruit. And if
you still walk perversely with Me, and will not hearken
to the doctrine of My law, I will add to bring upon you
(yet) seven plagues, for the seven transgressions with
which ye have sinned before Me; and I will send
against you the strength of the wild beast, to make you
childless, and to destroy your cattle without, and to
diminish you within, and your highways shall be desolate.

And if by these chastisements ye will not be corrected
before Me, but will walk before Me perversely, I will
Myself also remember you adversely in the world, and
will destroy you, even I, with seven plagues, for seven
transgressions with which ye have sinned before Me.
And I will bring against you a people unsheathing the
sword to take vengenance upon you, for that you will
have abolished My covenant; and when you are gathered
together from the wilderness into your cities, I will send
the pestilence among you, or deliver you to die by the
hand of your adversaries. And when I shall have
broken for you the staff of all the subsistence of food,

then ten women may bake your bread in one oven on account of its scarcity, and measure and divide it to you diminished in weight, and you will eat and not be satisfied.

But if by no one correction ye will hearken to the instruction of My law, but will walk perversely before Me, I will also remember you adversely in the world, and will chastise you, even I, with seven plagues, for the seven transgressions with which ye have sinned before Me. And ye shall eat the flesh of your sons, and the flesh of your daughters. Mosheh the prophet hath said, How heavy will have been the guilt, and how bitter those sins, that caused our fathers to eat the flesh of their sons, and the flesh of their daughters, because they kept not the commandments of the law! [JERUSALEM. How evil that guilt, and how bitter those sins, which caused our fathers in Jerusalem to eat the flesh of their sons and their daughters!] And I will destroy your high places, and overthrow your diviners and your enchanters, and your carcases will I cast away with the carcases of your idols, and My Word shall abhor you. And I will make your cities desert places, and desolate your sanctuary; nor will I receive with acceptance the odour of your oblations. And I, even I, will lay your country waste, that the spirit of quietness may not be upon it; so that your enemies who will dwell in it shall be confounded. And you will I disperse among the nations; for I will stir up against you a people who draw the sword, and your country shall be devastated, and your cities be solitary. Behold, then shall the land enjoy the years of its Sabbaths all the days that it is forsaken of you, and you are wanderers in the land of your enemies. All the days that it is forsaken by you it shall rest, because it was not at rest in the years of the times for repose when you were dwellers upon it.

And unto those of you who remain will I bring brokenness of their hearts in the land of their enemies, and the sound of a leaf falling from the ttee shall put them to flight ; and they shall flee as those who flee from the sword, and fall, while no man pursueth. And they shall thrust each man his brother, as before them who draw the sword, though none pursue ; and you shall have no power of resistance to stand before your adversaries. And you shall perish among the nations, and be consumed with pestilence in the land of your enemies. And those who remain of you shall fail (melt away) for their sins in the land of your enemies, and also for the evil sin of your fathers which they held fast in their hands : like them shall they melt away.

But (when) in the hour of their ueed they shall confess their sins, and the sins of their fathers, with their falseness with which they have acted falsely against My Word ; and that they have acted frowardly also with Me, so that I have remembered them adversely in the world, and brought them into captivity in the land of their enemies ; behold, then will their proud heart have been broken, and they will make confession of their sins, and I will remember in mercy the covenant which I confirmed with Jakob at Bethel, and the covenant which I covenanted with Izhak at Mount Moriah, and the covenant which I covenanted with Abraham, between the divided portions, I will remember, and the land of Israel will I remember in mercy. But the land shall (first) be relinquished and forsaken by you ; and enjoy the repose of her remissions all the days that it shall be deserted by you. And they will receive retribution for their sins : curses instead of blessings will come upon them, measure for measure : because they shunned the orders of My judgments, and their souls revolted from the covenant of My law.

Yet for all this I will have mercy upon them by My
Word, when they are captives in the land of their
enemies, I will not spurn them away in the kingdom of
Babel; nor shall My Word abhor them in the kingdom
of Madai, to destroy them in the kingdom of Javan, or
to abolish My covenant with them in the kingdom of
Edom;[1] for I am the Lord in the days of Gog.[2]
[JERUSALEM. And I will remember in mercy the covenant which I established with Jakob at Bethel; and
the covenant which I confirmed with Izhak at Mount
Moriah, and the covenant I confirmed with Abraham
between the divided parts I will remember in mercy;
and the land of Israel will I remember in mercy. Yet
the land shall be forsaken by you, and shall enjoy the
repose of her remission (times) all the days that she is
deserted of you. And they shall be broken for their
sins; with measure for measure, and orders for orders,
because they spurned the order of My judgments. Yet
for this, when dwellers in the land of their enemies, I
will not spurn them away in the kingdom of Babel, nor
abhor them in the kingdom of Madai, nor destroy them
in the kingdom of Javan, (Greece,) to abolish My covenant with them in the kingdom of Edom; for He (will
be) the Lord your God in the days of Gog.] And I
will remember with them the covenant which I confirmed before Me with their fathers in the time that I
brought them out redeemed from the land of Mizraim;
when all the nations beheld all the mighty acts which I
wrought for them, that I might be their God; I, the
Lord.

These are the statutes and the orders of the judgments and decrees of the law, which the Lord appointed
between His Word and the sons of Israel, in the
mountain of Sinai, by the hand of Mosheh.

[1] Rome.   [2] Ezek. xxxix., Zech. xiv.

XXVII. And the Lord spake with Mosheh, saying:
Speak with the children of Israel, and say to them:
When a man willeth to set apart the separation of a
vow, in the valuing of the life unto the name of the
Lord, then his valuation for a male from twenty years
old unto sixty years, fifty shekels, in the shekel of the
sanctuary, shall be his valuation: but if for a female,
his valuation shall be thirty shekels. And if it be a
child from five years until twenty years, his estimation
for a male shall be twenty shekels; and for a female,
ten shekels. But for a child of a month old until five
years, his estimation for a male shall be five silver
shekels, and for a female, three silver shekels. Moreover, for a man of sixty years and upwards, his estimation shall be fifteen shekels, and for a female, ten
shekels. But if he be too poor for (such) a rate of his
estimation, he shall stand before the priest; and the
priest shall make an estimation for him, according to
the ability of his hand, so shall the priest estimate for
him.

And if it be an animal, of such as are offered as an
oblation before the Lord, whatever he giveth of it
before the Lord shall be sacred. He shall not alter it,
nor change it, that which is perfect for that which hath
blemish, or that in which there is blemish for the
perfect: but if by changing he will exchange animal
for animal, both that and the one that is changed shall
be consecrate. [JERUSALEM. And he shall not change
it, good for bad, or bad for good: but if changing he
will exchange animal for animal, both that and his
changed one shall be sacred.] But if it be an unclean
animal, of such as are not offered as an oblation before
the Lord, he shall make the animal stand before
the priest. And the priest shall value it, whether
good or bad; as the priest shall value, so shall

it be.　But if he would redeem it, let him add a
fifth of its price upon that of its valuation. [JERU-
SALEM. And if it be some unclean animal of such as
are not offered as an oblation to the name of the Lord,
let the priest order it, whether good or bad; according
to the priest's valuation shall it be.......And let him
add a fifth of its price above its valuation.]

　　When a man would consecrate his house, as a consecrated thing before the Lord; the priest shall value
it, whether good or bad; according as the priest shall
estimate, so shall it stand. [JERUSALEM. A sanctified
thing unto the name of the Lord: then the priest shall
order: as the priest hath ordered it shall be.]　And if
he who hath consecrated would redeem his house, let
him add a fifth of the price of its valuation thereunto,
and it shall be his. [JERUSALEM. And if he who hath
made sacred..... a fifth of the price of its valuation
upon it, and it shall be his.]

　　And if a man would dedicate (a portion) of the field
of his inheritance before the Lord, the valuation of it
shall be according to the measure of its seed: a space on
which may be sown a kor (seventy-five and a half pints)
of barley (shall be considered) worth fifty shekels of
silver.　If he will dedicate the ground from the year of
Jubela, it shall stand according to its valuation.　But
if he will dedicate his field after the year of Jubela, the
priest shall compute with him the sum of the money
according to the proportion of years that remain unto
the next Jubela year, and shall abate it from the valuation.　[JERUSALEM. And if a man would separate (a
portion) of a field of his inheritance unto the Name of
the Lord, its valuation shall be according to its sowing,
a chomer of barley seed.......And if he separate his
field from the year of Jubela, according to its value it
shall stand.]　And if he would redeem the field that he

had consecrated, let him add one fifth of the money
upon its valued price, and it shall be confirmed to him.
[JERUSALEM. And if he would redeem that field which
had been consecrated, let him add a fifth of the silver
shekels above its estimation, and it shall be his.]   But
if he will not redeem the field, but sell it to another
man, it shall not be redeemed again : the field, when it
goeth out at the Jubela, shall be sacred before the
Lord; as a field separated for the priest it shall be his
inheritance. [JERUSALEM. It shall be a sanctified thing
unto the Lord, as a field of separation.]   And if he
would consecrate before the Lord a field which he hath
bought, and which is not of the land of his inheritance,
then the priest shall compute with him the amount of
the price of its valuation until the year of Jubela; and
he shall give its value on that day, as a consecrated
thing before the Lord.   In the year of Jubela the
field shall return to him from whom he bought it,
to him who had the inheritance of the land.   And
every valuation shall be in shekels of the sanctuary :
twenty mahin are a shekel. [JERUSALEM. And if
he would consecrate a purchased field unto the Name
of the Lord, then the priest shall compute with him the
value of the separation unto the year of Jubela, and he
shall give the separation of the value on that day, a
holy thing unto the Name of the Lord.   At the year of
Jubela the field shall revert to him from whom he had
bought it, to him who had the inheritance of the land.
And every estimation shall be according to the shekels
of the sanctuary.]

Moreover, the firstling among cattle which is separated to the Name of the Lord, whether ox or lamb, a
man cannot separate (as a votive gift), because it (already
belongeth) to the Name of the Lord.   And if it be an
unclean animal, then he shall redeem it according to its

valuation, and add a fifth of the price to it; but if he will not redeem it, then it shall be sold at the price of its valuation. [JERUSALEM. But the firstling among cattle, whether ox or lamb, which is separated before the Lord, belongeth (already) to the Name of the Lord. But if it be of an unclean animal, then let him redeem it according to its valuation, and add a fifth of its price unto it. And if it be not redeemed, it shall be sold according to its value.

Nevertheless, no devoted thing which a man shall separate before the Lord of anything that is his, of man, or beast, or field of his inheritance, shall be sold or redeemed ; every (devoted) separation is most sacred before the Lord. [JERUSALEM. Only no devoted thing that a man shall separate to the Name of the Lord of anything that he hath of child or cattle; every separation is most sacred to the Name of the Lord.] Every separation which shall be separated of man[3] shall not be redeemed with money, but with burnt offerings, and with sanctified victims, and with supplication for mercy before the Lord, because such are to be put to death. [JERUSALEM. Every one of the children of men set apart(or devoted) shall not be redeemed ; dying, he shall be put to death.]

And all the tythe of the land, of the seed of the ground, or the fruits of the tree, is the Lord's, and is most sacred before the Lord. But if a man will redeem any (part) of his tythes, he shall add a fifth part of its value thereunto. And every tythe of oxen and sheep, whatever passeth under the (tything) rod, the tenth shall be consecrated before the Lord. He shall not scrutinize between the good and the bad, nor exchange it; but if

---

[3] Every man who is devoted to death , the criminal guilty of murder , the Canaanites, also, at the the taking of Jericho, &c.

changing he will exchange it, both it and that for which
it is changed shall be sacred, and not be redeemed.

These are the precepts which the Lord prescribed
unto Mosheh, and of which not one must be trifled with
(or, innovated upon); and He prescribed them to be
shown unto the children of Israel at Mount Sinai.
[JERUSALEM. Verse 30 : It pertaineth to the Name of
the Lord; it is holy unto the Name of the Lord. 31 :
But if a man will redeem any portion of his tythe, let
him add upon it a fifth part of its price; and every
tythe of ox and sheep, whatever passeth under the rod,
a tenth shall be holy unto the Name of the Lord. He
shall not scrutinize between good and bad, nor exchange
it ; but if he will change it, then shall both it and that
for which it is changed be sacred, and not be redeemed.
These are the Commandments.]

END OF THE PALESTINIAN TARGUM ON VAIYIKRA.

THE TARGUM OF ONKELOS

ON

THE BOOK BEMIDBAR

OR

NUMBERS.

———

SECTION OF THE TORAH XXXIV.

TITLE BEMIDBAR.

I. AND the Lord spake with Mosheh in the wilderness of Sinai, in the tabernacle of ordinance, on the first of the second month, in the second year of their coming out from the land of Mizraim, saying: Take the sum [1] of all the congregation of the children of Israel after their kindreds, and after the house of their fathers, with the number of their names, every male by their capitations: from a son of twenty years and upwards, every one who can go forth to war in Israel, thou and Aharon number them by their hosts. And with you let there be a man of each tribe, a man who is chief of the house of his fathers. And these are the names of the men who shall stand with you. Of Reuben, Elizur bar Shedeur; of Shemeon, Shelumiel bar Zuri-Shaddai; of Jehudah, Nachshon bar Ammadab; of Issakar, Nethanel bar Zuar; of Zebulon, Eliab bar Chelon; of the Beni-Joseph, —of Ephraim, Elishama bar Amihud; of Menasheh, Gam-

[1] *Chushban*, "reckoning, account."

M

hel bar Pheda-Zur; of Benyamin, Abidan bar Gideoni;
of Dan, Achiezer bar Ami-Shaddai; of Asher, Phagiel
bar Akran; of Gad, Eljasaph bar Dehuel; of Naphtali,
Achira bar Enan. These were the called ones of the
congregation, princes of the tribes of their fathers, chiefs
of the thousands of Israel were they.

And Mosheh and Aharon took these men who were
expressed by their names; and they assembled all the
congregation on the first of the second month, and they
declared their pedigrees according to the house of their
fathers, with the number of their names from twenty
years old and upwards, by their polling. As the Lord
commanded Mosheh, he numbered them in the wilderness of Sinai

And the sons of Reuben the firstborn of Israel, by
their generations and their families, according to the
house of their fathers, with the number of their names,
by their polls; every male from twenty years old and
upward, all going forth in the host: of the tribe of
Reuben were numbered forty and six thousand and five
hundred. Of the sons of Shemeon, by their generations
and their families and the house of their fathers, were
numbered, by the number of their names, according to
their polls, every male from twenty years old and upwards, every one going forth in the host; of the tribe
of Shemeon, were numbered fifty and nine thousand and
three hundred. Of the sons of Gad, the generations of
the families of the house of their fathers, according to
the number of their names from twenty years old and
upwards, every one going forth in the host; of the tribe
of Gad, were numbered forty and five thousand and six
hundred and fifty. Of the sons of Jehudah, the generations of the families of the house of their fathers, by the
number of their names, from twenty years old and upwards, every one going forth in the host; of the tribe

of Jehudah, were numbered seventy and four thousand
and six hundred. Of the sons of Issakar, the generations of the families of the house of their fathers, by
the number of their names, from twenty years old and
upwards, every one going forth in the host; of the
tribe of Issakar, were numbered fifty and four thousand
and four hundred. Of the tribe of Zebulon, the generations of the families of the house of their fathers, by
the number of their names, from a son of twenty years
and upward, every one going forth in the host; of the
tribe of Zebulon, were numbered fifty and seven thousand and four hundred. Of the sons of Joseph, the
generations of the Beni Ephraim by the kindreds of the
house of their fathers, in the number of their names,
from a son of twenty years and upwards, every one
going forth in the host; of the tribe of Ephraim, forty
thousand and five hundred. The generations of the
Beni Menasheh by the kindreds of the house of their
fathers, in the number of their names, from a son of
twenty years and upwards, every one going forth in the
host; of the tribe of Menasheh, were numbered thirty
and two thousand and two hundred. The generations
of the sons of Benyamin, by the kindreds of the house
of their fathers, in the number of their names, from a
son of twenty years and upward, every one going forth
in the host; of the tribe of Benyamin, were numbered
thirty and five thousand and four hundred. The generations of the Beni Dan, by the kindreds of the house of
their fathers, in the number of their names, from a son
of twenty years and upward, every one going forth in
the host; of the tribe of Dan, were numbered sixty and
two thousand and seven hundred. Of the generations
of the Beni Asher, by the kindreds of the house of their
fathers, in the number of their names, from a son of
twenty years and upward, every one going forth in the

host; of the tribe of Asher, were numbered forty and
one thousand and five hundred. The generations of
the sons of Naphtali, by the kindreds of the house of
their fathers, in the number of their names, from a son
of twenty years and upwards, every one going forth in
the host; of the tribe Naphtali, were numbered fifty
and three thousand and four hundred.

These were the numbered ones whom Mosheh and
Aharon, and the twelve men, the princes of Israel, did
number, severally, according to the house of their
fathers   And all those who were numbered of the Beni
Israel according to the house of their fathers, from a son
of twenty years and upward, every one going forth in
the host of Israel; all the numbered ones were six
hundred and three thousand and five hundred and
fifty. But the Levites, by the tribe of their fathers,
were not numbered among them.

And the Lord had spoken with Mosheh, saying:
Only the tribe of Levi thou shalt not number, nor take
the account of them among the sons of Israel. But
thou shalt appoint the Levites over the tabernacle of
the testimony, and over all its vessels, and over all that
belongeth to it: and they shall carry the tabernacle
and all its vessels, and serve it; and they shall encamp
round about the tabernacle. And when the tabernacle
is to go forward, the Levites shall take it apart; and
when the tabernacle is to be stationary, the Levites
shall set it up; but the stranger who cometh nigh shall
be put to death.

And the sons of Israel shall encamp every man upon
his own dwelling-place, and every man by his standard,
according to their hosts. But the Levites shall dwell
round about the tabernacle of the testimony, that there
may not be wrath upon the congregation of the sons of
Israel; and the Levites shall watch the watching of the

tabernacle of testimony. And the sons of Israel did according to all that the Lord commanded Mosheh, so did they.

II. And the Lord spake with Mosheh and with Aharon, saying : Every man (shall encamp) by his standard, by the ensign of the house of their fathers shall the sons of Israel encamp. Over against the tabernacle of ordinance shall they encamp round about.

The standard of the camp of Jehudah shall they pitch, according to their hosts, eastward toward the sunrise : and the chief of the sons of Jehudah is Nachshon bar Aminadab.[2] And his host, and the number of them, seventy and four thousand and six hundred. And they who pitch next by him shall be the tribe of Issakar ; and the chief of the sons of Issakar, Nethanel bar Zuar ; and his host, and the numbered of it, fifty and four thousand and four hundred. The tribe of Zebulon, and the chief of the sons of Zebulon, Eliab bar Chelon. And his host, and the numbered of them, fifty and seven thousand and four hundred. All that were numbered of the camp of Jehudah, a hundred and eighty and six thousand and four hundred, by their hosts : they shall go forward in front.

The standard of the camp of Reuben (shall be) to the south, by their hosts : and the chief of the Beni Reuben, Elizur bar Shedeur. And his host, and the numbered of it, forty and six thousand and five hundred. And they who pitch by him shall be the tribe of Shemeon ; and the chief of the Beni Shemeon, Shelumiel bar Zuri-Shaddai ; and his host, and the numbered of them, fifty and nine thousand and three hundred. And the tribe of Gad, and the chief of the Beni Gad, Eljasaph bar Dehuel ; and his host, and the numbered of them, forty and five thousand six hundred and fifty.

---

[2] Matt. i. 3, 4; Luke iii 32, 33.

All who were numbered of the camp of Reuben, a hundred and fifty and one thousand four hundred and fifty, by their hosts: they shall go forward secondly.

But the tabernacle of ordinance shall be taken forward with the camp of the Levites, in the midst of the camp: as they encamp, so shall they go onward, every man in his place, by their standard.

The standard of the camp of Ephraim, by their hosts, shall be to the west · and the chief of the Beni Ephraim, Elishama bar Ammihud. And his host and their numbered ones, forty thousand and five hundred. And they who shall be next by him shall be the tribe of Menasheh: and the chief of the Beni Menasheh, Gamliel bar Phedazur. And his host, and the numbered thereof, thirty and two thousand and two hundred. And the tribe of Benyamin, and the chieftain of the sons of Benyamin, Abidan bar Gideoni: and his host, and the numbered thereof, thirty and five thousand and four hundred. All the numbered of the camp of Ephraim were a hundred and eight thousand and one hundred, by their hosts: and they went forward thirdly.

The standard of the camp of Dan (shall be) to the north, by their hosts; and the chieftain of the Beni Dan, Achiezer bar Ammi-Shaddai. And his host, and the numbered thereof, sixty and two thousand and seven hundred. And those who encamp by him shall be the tribe of Asher; and the chieftain of the Beni Asher, Phagiel bar Akran. And his host, and the numbered of it, forty and one thousand and five hundred. And the tribe of Naphtali, and the chief of the Beni Naphtah, Achira bar Enan: and his host, and the numbered thereof, fifty and three thousand and four hundred. All who were numbered of the camp of Dan, a hundred and fifty and seven thousand and six hundred: they shall go hindmost by their standards.

These are they who were numbered of the sons of Israel, by the house of their fathers; all who were numbered in the camps by their hosts, six hundred and three thousand five hundred and fifty. But the Levites were not numbered among the sons of Israel, as the Lord commanded Mosheh. And the sons of Israel did according to all which the Lord commanded Mosheh: so did they encamp by their standards, and so went they forward every man by his family, and by the house of his fathers.

III. And these are the generations of Aharon and Mosheh in the day that the Lord spake with Mosheh in the mountain of Sinai. And these are the names of the sons of Aharon. His firstborn, Nadab; and Abihu, Elazar, and Ithamar. These are the names of the sons of Aharon, the priests, who were consecrated that their oblations might be offered, (and that they might) minister. But Nadab and Abihu died before the Lord; in their offering the strange fire before the Lord in the wilderness of Sinai: and they had no children. And Elazar and Ithamar ministered before Aharon their father.

And the Lord spake with Mosheh, saying: Bring the tribe of Levi near, and appoint them before Aharon the priest, that they may minister with him. And they shall keep the watch and the charge of all the congregation by the tabernacle of ordinance to perform the service of the tabernacle. And they shall keep all the vessels of the tabernacle of ordinance, and the charge of the sons of Israel to perform the service of the tabernacle. And thou shalt give the Levites unto Aharon, and to his sons; they are delivered and given to him from the sons of Israel. And thou shalt appoint Aharon and his sons, that they may keep their priesthood; but the stranger who cometh near shall be put to death.

And the Lord spake with Mosheh, saying: And I, behold, I have brought near the Levites from among the sons of Israel instead of every firstborn that openeth the womb of the sons of Israel; and the Levites shall minister before Me. For every firstborn is Mine; on the day that I slew every firstborn in the land of Mizraim, I sanctified before Me every firstborn in Israel from man to animal; they are Mine: I am the Lord.

And the Lord spake with Mosheh in the wilderness of Sinai, saying: Number the sons of Levi, after the house of their fathers, by their families; every male from a month old and upward shalt thou number them. And Mosheh numbered them according to the word of the Lord, as he had been commanded.

And these were the sons of Levi by their names: Gershon and Kehath and Merari. And these are the names of the Beni Gershon after their families: Lebni and Shemei. And the Beni Kehath after their families: Amram and Izhar, Hebron and Uzziel. And the Beni Merari by their families, Mahali and Mushi; these are the families of the Levites after the house of their fathers.

Of Gershon were the family of Libni and the family of Shemei; these are the families of Gershon. Those that were numbered of them, every male from the son of a month and upward, the number of them was seven thousand and five hundred. The families of Gershon shall encamp behind the tabernacle, westward: and the Rab of the house of the fathers of Gershon, Eljasaph bar Lael. And the charge of the Beni Gershon in the tabernacle of ordinance (shall be) the tent and its covering, and the hanging of the door of the tabernacle of ordinance; and the curtains of the court, and the hanging of the gate of the court which is by the tabernacle, and by the altar round about, and the cords of it, for all its service.

And of Kehath was the family of Amram, and the family of Izhar, and the family of Hebron, and the family of Uzziel: these are the families of Kehath. According to the number of all the males, from the son of a month and upward, eight thousand and six hundred, keeping the charge of the sanctuary. The families of the Beni Kehath shall encamp by the side of the tabernacle, southward. And the Rab of the house of the fathers of the Kehath families (shall be) Elizaphan bar Uzziel. And their charge shall be the ark, and the table, and the candelabrum, and the altar, and the vessels of the sanctuary with which they minister, and the tent, (or hanging, Sam. Vers., "covering,") and all (that pertaineth to) the service thereof. And the chief (armarkella) who is appointed over the chiefs (rabbins) of the Levites is Elazar bar Aharon the priest: under his hand shall they be appointed who have the charge of the keeping of the sanctuary.

Of Merari, the families of Mahli and the families of Mushi. And the numbers of them, according to the numbers of all the males, from the son of a month and upwards, six thousand and two hundred. And the Rab of the house of the fathers of the Merari families, Zuriel bar Abichael; and they shall encamp on the side of the tabernacle northward. And the charge [3] for the custody of the sons of Merari shall be the boards of the tabernacle, and its bars, and its pillars, and its sockets, and all its vessels, and whatever (pertaineth) to its service; and the pillars of the court round about, and their sockets, their pins, and their cords. But they who encamp before the tabernacle eastward, even before the tabernacle of ordinance toward the sunrise, shall be Mosheh, and Aharon and his sons, keeping charge of the sanctuary, to watch over the children of Israel; and

---

[3] Sam. Vers., "business."

the stranger who cometh near shall be put to death.
All who were numbered of the Levites whom Mosheh
and Aharon numbered by the word of the Lord, by
their families, every male, from the son of a month and
upward, twenty and two thousand.[4]

And the Lord spake unto Mosheh, Number all the
firstborn males of the children of Israel, from the son of
a month upward, and the number of their names.
And thou shalt take the Levites before me,—I am the
Lord,—instead of all the firstborn of the sons of Israel;
and the cattle of the Levites instead of all the firstlings
of the cattle of the Beni Israel. And Mosheh numbered, as the Lord commanded him, all the firstborn of
the sons of Israel. And all the firstborn males, by the
number of their names, from the son of a month and
upward by their numbers, were twenty and two thousand two hundred and seventy and three.

And the Lord spake with Mosheh, saying: Take the
Levites instead of all the firstborn of the Beni Israel,
and the cattle of the Levites instead of their cattle; and
the Levites shall minister before Me: I am the Lord.
And of the redeemed ones of the two hundred and
seventy and three of the sons of Israel who are more
than the Levites, thou shalt take of each five shekels,
by poll, in the shekel of the sanctuary shalt thou take;
twenty mahin are a shekel. And thou shalt give the
silver of the redeemed who exceed them to Aharon and
his sons. And Mosheh took the silver of the redeemed
who were more than the redeemed by the Levites. Of
the firstborn of the Beni Israel he took the silver, a
thousand and three hundred and sixty-five shekels, in

---

[4] On the difficulties connected with these numbers, see "Bishop
Colenso's Objections to the Pentateuch, examined by Dr. ABRAHAM
BENISCH" London. 1863. Also "An Examination of Bishop Colenso's
Difficulties,' by the late Dr. M'CAUL. London. 1864.

the shekel of the sanctuary. And Mosheh gave the silver of the redeemed ones to Aharon and to his sons, by the Word of the Lord, as the Lord had commanded Mosheh.

IV. And the Lord spake with Mosheh and with Aharon, saying: Take the reckoning of the Beni Kehath from among the sons of Levi by the house of their fathers, from thirty years and upward, unto fifty years; all that come to the host, to do the work of the tabernacle of ordinance. And this (shall be) the service of the Beni Kehath in the tabernacle of ordinance,—the Holy of Holies. And Aharon and his sons shall enter in, what time the camp is to proceed; and they shall unloose the veil that is hung, and cover therewith the ark of the testimony, and put over it a covering of hyacinthine skins, and overspread it with a wrapper, wholly purple, having inset its staves. And upon the table of the presence bread they shall spread a wrapper of purple, and on it put the bowls and mortars, and the measures and cups for libations, and the bread that is ever on it; and overspread it with a wrapper of scarlet, and cover it with a covering of hyacinth skins, having inset its staves. And they shall take a purple wrapper, and cover the candelabrum of the light, and its lamps, and its tongs, and its snuff dishes, and all the vessels of the service by which they serve it; and put it and all its vessels into a covering of hyacinthine skins, and set it upon a bar. And upon the golden altar they shall spread a purple wrapper, and cover it with a covering of hyacinth skins, and fix its staves And they shall take all the vessels of the ministry with which they minister in the sanctuary, and put them in a cloth of purple, and cover them with a covering of hyacinth skins, and set them upon bars.

And they shall collect the cinders from the altar, and

spread upon it a wrapper of crimson, and put thereon all its vessels by which they minister upon it; censers, fleshhooks, shovels, and basins; all the vessels of the altar; and spread over it a covering of hyacinthine skins, and inset its staves.   And when Aharon and his sons have completed to cover up the sanctuary, and all the vessels of the sanctuary in the moving of the camp, the sons of Kehath shall go in to carry (them), but they shall not touch the holy things (themselves), lest they die; but these are the burden of the sons of Kehath in the tabernacle of ordinance.

And that delivered unto Elazar bar Aharon the priest (shall be) the oil for the light, and the aromatic incense, and the continual mincha, and the anointing oil, (with) the charge of all the tabernacle, and whatever belongeth to the sanctuary and its vessels.

And the Lord spake with Mosheh and with Aharon, saying : Cut not off the tribe of the family of Kehath from among the Levites;[5] but do this to them, that they may live and not die, in their approach to the Holy of Holies · Let Aharon and his sons go in, and appoint each man his service and his burden.   But they shall not go in to see, when the vessels of the sanctuary are covered, lest they die.

SECTION XXXV.

NASO.

AND the Lord spake with Mosheh, saying : Take the account of the sons of Gershon also, after the house of their fathers, by their families; from thirty years and upwards to fifty years shalt thou number them, of all

---

[5] Do not occasion their death.

who come by companies to perform service in the tabernacle of ordinance. This is the service of the family of Gershon, to serve and to carry. And they shall carry the curtains of the tabernacle, and the tent of the tabernacle of ordinance, its covering, and the covering of hyacinth which is over it above, and the hanging for the door of the tabernacle of ordinance; and the curtains of the court, and the hanging that is at the entrance of the court, which is by the tabernacle and by the altar round about, and their cords, and all the instruments of their service; and with all that is delivered to them they shall perform their service. By the word of Aharon and his sons shall be all the service of the Beni-Gershon, with all their burdens, and all their employment; and you shall appoint them in charge with all their burdens. This is the service of the family of the Beni-Gershon in the tabernacle of ordinance, and their charge shall be under the hand of Ithamar bar Aharon the priest.

The sons of Merari number thou after the families of their father's house; from a son of thirty years and upward unto fifty years, shalt thou number them, of all who come by companies to perform the service of the tabernacle of ordinance. And this is the charge of their burthen of all the service in the tabernacle of ordinance; the boards of the tabernacle, and its bars, and its pillars, and their bases; and the columns of the court round about, their bases, pins, and cords of all the instruments of all their service; and by their names you shall number the instruments of the charge of their burthen. This is the ministry of the family of the Beni-Merari, after all their service in the tabernacle of ordinance under the hand of Ithamar bar Aharon the priest.

And Mosheh and Aharon and the chiefs of the congregation numbered the sons of Kehath, by their families, and by the house of their fathers; from a son

of thirty years and upward to fifty years; every one
who came with the band to the service in the tabernacle
of ordinance.   And they who were numbered of them
by their families, were two thousand seven hundred and
fifty.   These are the numbered of the family of Kehath,
every one serving in the tabernacle of ordinance, whom
Mosheh and Aharon numbered upon the Word of the
Lord, by the hand of Mosheh.

And the numbered of the sons of Gershon after the
families of their father's house, from thirty years and
upwards to fifty years, every one who cometh with the
band to the service of the tabernacle of ordinance, even
those who were numbered of them by their families of
their father's house, were two thousand six hundred
and thirty.   These are the numbered of the Beni-
Gershon, every one who did service in the tabernacle of
ordinance, whom Mosheh and Aharon numbered by the
mouth of the Word of the Lord.

And the numbered of the Beni-Merari, by the families
of their father's house, from thirty years and upward to
fifty years, all who come by bands to serve in the tabernacle of ordinance, even they who were numbered by
their families, were three thousand and two hundred.
These are they who were numbered in the families of
the Beni-Merari, whom Mosheh and Aharon numbered
by the mouth of the Word of the Lord, by the hand of
Mosheh.   All the numbered ones of the Levites whom
Mosheh and Aharon and the chiefs of Israel numbered,
by their families, and by the house of their fathers, from
thirty years and upward to fifty years, all who came to
minister the ministry of the service, and the work of
carrying in the tabernacle of ordinance, even the numbered of them were eight thousand five hundred and
eighty.   Upon the Word of the Lord they were numbered by the hand of Mosheh; every man according to

his service and his burthen they were numbered, as the Lord commanded Mosheh.

V. And the Lord spake with Mosheh, saying: Command the sons of Israel to send away from the camp every one who is leprous, and every one who hath an issue, and every one who is defiled with the pollution of the life of man: from male to female you shall send them away, that they defile not their camps; for My Shekinah dwelleth among you. And the sons of Israel did so; as the Lord spake with Mosheh, so did the sons of Israel.

And the Lord spake with Mosheh, saying: When a man or a woman hath committed any of the sins of mankind to prevaricate prevarication before the Lord, and that man hath become guilty; they shall make confession of the sin which they have committed, and restore the principal of (the property of) the trespass, and add a fifth part thereto, and give to him against whom the sin was committed; but if the man (hath deceased, or) hath no kinsman unto whom the trespass should be returned, let the trespass be restored before the Lord unto the priest, besides the ram of atonement which shall be offered to atone for him. And all separated things of all the consecrations of the sons of Israel which are offered by the priest are his. And the consecrated tenths of every man shall be his, and whatsoever a man giveth unto the priest shall be his.

And the Lord spake with Mosheh, saying: Speak with the sons of Israel, and say to them: If a man's wife go astray and prevaricate against him prevarication, and a man lie with her, and it be hidden from her husband's eyes, and she be contaminated, and there be no witness against her, and she be not convicted (or apprehended); but the spirit of jealousy come upon him, and he be jealous of his wife that she hath been

defiled; or the spirit of jealousy come upon him, and
he become jealous of his wife, though she be not defiled;
then shall the man bring his wife to the priest, and
bring her offering for her, a tenth part of three seins of
barley flour; he shall pour no oil thereon, nor put
frankincense upon it, because it is a mincha of jealousy,
a mincha of remembrance, bringing sins to remembrance.   And the priest shall bring her near, and make
her stand before the Lord.   And the priest shall take
water from the laver in an earthen vessel.   And the
priest shall take from the dust which is on the floor of
the tabernacle, and put it into the water.   And the
priest shall make the woman stand before the Lord, and
shall uncover the woman's head, and put the mincha of
remembrance, the mincha of jealousy, upon her hands;
and in the priest's hand shall be the bitter waters of
cursing.[6]

And the priest shall adjure her, and say to the
woman If no man hath lain with thee, and if thou
hast not gone astray to uncleanness (with another)
instead of thy husband, be thou unhurt (*zakaah*, innocent, clean) from these bitter waters of cursing.   But
if thou hast gone astray (to another) instead of thy
husband, and art defiled; and another man hath lain
with thee, besides thy husband, the priest shall adjure
the woman by the oath of the curse; and the priest
shall say to the woman : The Lord set thee for a curse
and an execration in the midst of thy people, by the
Lord making thy thigh to be corrupt, and thy bowels
to swell.   And these waters of cursing shall enter thy
inside, to make thy bowels to swell, and thy thigh to
become corrupt.

And the woman shall say, Amen, Amen !

And the priest shall write these maledictions upon a

[6] Sam. Vers., "the waters of proof, or probation."

book,[7] and shall wash them out with the bitter waters. And he shall make the woman to drink the bitter waters of cursing; and the waters of the curse shall enter into her unto bitterness.

And the priest shall take from the woman's hand the mincha of jealousy; and wave the mincha before the Lord, and offer it upon the altar. And the priest shall take with a full hand from the mincha the memorial of it, and burn it upon the altar; · and afterward the woman shall drink the water.

And when he hath made her drink the water, it shall be that if she hath been defiled and hath wrought perverseness with her husband, the waters of the execration will enter into her with bitterness, and her bowels will swell, and her thigh become corrupt : and the woman shall be for an execration among her people.

But if the woman hath not been defiled, but is innocent, they shall enter harmlessly, and she shall conceive with conception.

This is the law of jealousy, when a woman hath gone astray from her husband, or when the spirit of jealousy passeth upon a man, and he become jealous of his wife. He shall make the wife stand before the Lord; and the priest shall do for him (according to) all this law. And the man shall be innocent from guilt,[8] but the woman shall bear her sin.

VI. And the Lord spake with Mosheh, saying : Speak with the children of Israel, and say to them : When a man or a woman would be separated by a vow of the Nazira, to be devoted before the Lord; he shall abstain from wine, (whether) new or old; vinegar of new wine or vinegar of old wine he may not drink; neither of anything expressed from grapes may he

---

[7] "Parchment," Mishna.

[8] The husband will not be guilty, though the guilty wife may die from the effects of the water.

drink; nor of grapes, either fresh or dried, may he eat.
All the days of his nazirate he may not eat of aught
that is produced by the vine (wine tree), from its kernels to its expressed juice. All the days of his nazir-
vow a razor shall not pass upon his head; until the
days be fulfilled which he should devote before the
Lord, he shall be consecrate; he shall let the hair of
his head grow all the days of his vow before the Lord;
he shall come near no dead person: for his father or
his mother, for his brother or his sister, should they
die, he shall not make himself unclean; because the
consecration[9] of Eloha is upon his head: all the days
of his nazirhood shall he be consecrate before the Lord.

And if any one with him die suddenly (to him)
unawares, and he defile the head of his vow, let him
shave his head on the day of his purification, on the
seventh day let him shave it: and on the eighth day
let him bring two turtle-doves or two young pigeons
unto the priest, to the door of the tabernacle of ordinance. And let the priest make one a sin offering, and
one a burnt offering, to atone for him; for that he had
sinned by the dead; and let him consecrate his head
(anew) on that day. And he shall devote before the
Lord the days of his nazirhood, and bring a lamb of
the year for a trespass offering: but the former days
have been in vain, because he hath defiled his vow.

And this is the law of the Nazirite on the day that
the days of his vow are fulfilled. He shall be brought
to the door of the tabernacle of ordinance; and shall
present his oblation before the Lord, a lamb of the
year, one unblemished, for a burnt offering, and one ewe
lamb of the year, unblemished, for a sin offering; and
one ram unblemished for a consecrated oblation; and

---

[9] Or, "the crown." So also the Sam Vers. Peschito, *kelila*, "the
diadem"

a basket of unleavened bread, cakes of flour mingled
with oil, and unleavened wafers anointed with oil, their
minchas and their libations. And the priest shall present them before the Lord; and make the sin offering
and the burnt offering, and the ram he shall make a
consecrated oblation before the Lord with the basket
of unleavened cakes; and the priest shall make the
mincha, and the libation therewith.

And let the Nazirite, at the door of the tabernacle of
ordinance, shave his consecrated head; and take the
hair of his consecrated head and lay it upon the fire
which is under the cauldron, for the peace offerings.
And the priest shall take the boiled shoulder of the
ram, and one of the unleavened cakes from the basket,
and one unleavened wafer, and put (them) upon the
hands of the Nazirite after the shaving of his consecration. And the priest shall uplift them, an elevation
before the Lord. It shall be dedicated to the priest,
with the breast of the elevation, and the shoulder of the
separation; and after that the Nazirite may drink wine.

This is the law of the Nazirite, who hath vowed his
oblation before the Lord, for his consecration, besides
those which may come to his hand; according to the
vow which he hath vowed, so shall he do according to
the law of his consecration.

And the Lord spake with Mosheh, saying: Speak
with Aharon and with his sons, saying: Thus shall you
bless the children of Israel, and shall say unto them:

The Lord bless thee and keep thee. The Lord make
His Shekinah to shine upon thee, and be merciful to
thee. The Lord turn away His displeasure from thee,
and bestow upon thee peace.[1]

And they shall bestow the benediction of My Name
upon the sons of Israel, and I will bless them.

[1] Glossary, page 74.

VII. And it was on the day when Mosheh had completed to set up the tabernacle, and to anoint it, and to
consecrate it, and all its vessels, and had anointed and
sanctified them, that the princes of Israel, heads of the
house of their fathers, the chiefs of the tribes, who had
been appointed over them who were numbered, came
near, and brought their oblations before the Lord.
Six covered waggons and twelve oxen; a waggon for
two of the princes, and an ox for each one: and they
brought them before the tabernacle.

And the Lord spake to Mosheh, saying: Take (the
waggons) from them, that they may be for the work of the
service of the tabernacle of ordinance; and thou shalt give
them to the Levites, to each man according to the need of
his work.[2] And Mosheh took the waggons and the oxen,
and gave them to the Levites. Two waggons and four
oxen gave he to the sons of Gershon, according to the
need of their work, and four waggons and eight oxen
he gave to the sons of Merari, according to the need of
their work, by the hand of Ithamar bar Aharon the
priest. But to the sons of Kehath he gave not, because
they had the work of the sanctuary, and carried upon
their shoulders.

And the princes offered at the dedication (*chanucha*)
of the altar on the day that they anointed it, and the
princes presented their oblations before the altar. And
the Lord said to Mosheh, One prince shall offer, on each
day of the dedication of the altar.

And he who offered his oblation on the first day was
Nachshon bar Aminadab, of the tribe of Jehudah. And
his offering was, one bowl of silver, a hundred and
thirty shekels was its weight; one silver vase, seventy
shekels in weight, in shekels of the sanctuary; both of

[2] Contrast with the recent discovery of the "higher" critics, that
the priest had to carry the carcase of an ox upon his own back.

them filled with flour, mingled with oil, for a mincha;
one pan (censer) weighing ten shekels; it was of gold,
filled with fragrant incense; one young bullock, one ram,
one lamb of the year for a burnt offering; one kid of the
goats for a sin offering; and for consecrated oblations,
two oxen, five rams, five goats, five lambs of the year.
This was the oblation of Nachshon bar Aminadab.

On the second day offered Nethanel bar Zuar, prince
of the tribe of Issakar. He offered his oblation,—one
silver bowl, a hundred and thirty shekels was its weight;
one silver vase, its weight seventy shekels, in the shekels
of the sanctuary; both of them filled with flour sprinkled
with oil for a mincha; one pan weighing ten shekels;
it was of gold, full of fragrant incense; one young
bullock, one ram, one lamb of the year for a burnt
offering, one kid of the goats for a sin offering; and
for a sacrifice of consecrated things, two oxen, five rams,
five goats, five lambs of the year. This was the oblation
of Nethanel bar Zuar.

On the third day, the prince of the Beni Zebulon,
Eliab bar Chelon. His offering, one silver bowl, its
weight one hundred and thirty shekels; one silver vase,
its weight seventy shekels in the shekels of the sanctuary; both of them filled with flour mingled with oil
for a mincha; one pan weighing ten shekels; it was of
gold, and filled with fragrant incense; one young bullock,
one lamb of the year for a burnt offering, one kid of the
goats for a sin offering; and for consecrated offerings,
two oxen, five rams, five goats, five lambs of the year.
This was the oblation of Eliab bar Chelon.

On the fourth day the prince of the sons of Reuben,
Elizur bar Shedeur. His offering, one silver bowl, one
hundred and thirty shekels its weight, one silver vase,
weighing seventy shekels in the shekels of the sanctuary,
both of them filled with flour sprinkled with oil for a

muncha'; one pan weighing ten shekels; it was of gold,
and filled with fragrant incense; one young bullock,
one ram, one lamb of the year for a burnt offering, one
kid of the goats for a sin offering; and for the consecrated oblation, two oxen, five rams, five goats, five
lambs of the year. This was the oblation of Elizur bar
Shedeur.

On the fifth day the prince of the Beni Shemeon,
Shelumiel bar Zurishaddai. His offering, one silver
bowl, one hundred and thirty shekels was its weight,
one silver vase, weighing seventy shekels in the shekels
of the sanctuary, both of them filled with flour mingled
with oil for a muncha; one pan weighing ten shekels;
it was of gold, filled with fragrant incense; one young
bullock, one ram, one lamb of the year for a burnt
offering, one kid of the goats for a sin offering; and
for consecrated oblations two oxen, five rams, five goats,
five lambs of the year. This was the oblation of Shelumiel bar Zurishaddai.

On the sixth day the prince of the sons of Gad,
Eljasaph bar Dehuel. His offering, one silver bowl, its
weight one hundred and thirty shekels, one silver vase,
weighing seventy shekels in shekels of the sanctuary,
both filled with flour sprinkled with oil for a muncha;
one pan weighing ten shekels of gold, full of fragrant
incense; one young bullock, one ram, one lamb of the
year for a burnt offering, one kid of the goats for a sin
offering; and for consecrated oblations, two oxen, five
rams, five goats, five lambs of the year. This was the
oblation of Eljasaph bar Dehuel.

On the seventh day the prince of the sons of Ephraim,
Elishama bar Ammihud. His offering, one silver bowl
weighing one hundred and thirty shekels, one silver
vase weighing seventy shekels in shekels of the sanctuary, both of them filled with flour sprinkled with oil

for a mincha; one pan weighing ten shekels of gold,
filled with fragrant incense; one young bullock, one
ram, one lamb of the year, for a burnt offering; one kid
of the goats for a sin offering; and for consecrated
oblations, two oxen, five rams, five goats, five lambs of
the year. This was the oblation of Elishama bar
Ammihud.

On the eighth day the prince of the Beni Menashe,
Gamliel bar Phedazur. His offering, one silver bowl,
weighing one hundred and thirty shekels, one silver vase,
weighing seventy shekels in shekels of the sanctuary,
both of them filled with flour sprinkled with oil for a
mincha; one pan weighing ten shekels of gold, filled
with fragrant incense; one young bullock, one ram,
one lamb of the year, for a burnt offering; one kid of
the goats for a sin offering; and for consecrated oblations, two oxen, five rams, five goats, five lambs of the
year. This was the oblation of Gamliel bar Phedazur.

On the ninth day the prince of the sons of Benyamin,
Abidan bar Gideoni. His oblation, one silver bowl, weighing one hundred and thirty shekels, one silver vase,
weighing seventy shekels in shekels of the sanctuary,
both of them filled with flour sprinkled with oil for a
mincha; one pan weighing ten shekels of gold, filled
with fragrant incense; one young bullock, one ram, one
lamb of the year, for a burnt offering; one kid of the
goats for a sin offering; and for consecrated oblations,
two oxen, five rams, five goats, five lambs of the year.
This was the oblation of Abidan bar Gideoni.

On the tenth day the prince of the sons of Dan,
Achiezer bar Amishaddai. His oblation, one silver bowl,
weighing one hundred and thirty shekels, one silver
vase, weighing seventy shekels in shekels of the sanctuary, both of them filled with flour sprinkled with oil
for a mincha; one pan weighing ten shekels of gold,

filled with fragrant incense; one young bullock, one
ram, one lamb of the year, for a burnt offering; one
kid of the goats for a sin offering; and for consecrated
oblations, two oxen, five rams, five goats, five lambs of
the year. This was the oblation of Achiezer bar Amishaddai.

On the eleventh day the prince of the Beni Asher,
Phagiel bar Akran. His oblation, one silver bowl,
weighing one hundred and thirty shekels, one silver
vase, weighing seventy shekels in shekels of the sanctuary, both of them filled with flour sprinkled with oil
for a mincha; one pan weighing ten shekels of gold,
filled with fragrant incense; one young bullock, one
ram, one lamb of the year, for a burnt offering; one kid
of the goats for a sin offering; and for consecrated
oblations two oxen, five rams, five goats, five lambs of the
year. This was the oblation of Phagiel bar Akran.

On the twelfth day, the prince of the Beni Naphtali,
Achira bar Enan. His oblation, one silver bowl, weighing one hundred and thirty shekels, one silver vase,
weighing seventy shekels in shekels of the sanctuary,
both of them filled with flour sprinkled with oil
for a mincha; one pan weighing ten shekels of gold,
filled with fragrant incense; one young bullock, one
ram, one lamb of the year, for a burnt offering; one kid
of the goats for a sin offering, and for consecrated
oblations two oxen, five rams, five goats, five lambs of
the year. This was the oblation of Achira bar Enan.

This was the dedication of the altar, on the day that
they anointed it. By the princes of Israel (were offered)
twelve silver bowls, twelve silver vases, twelve golden
censers; one hundred and thirty shekels was the weight
of one silver bowl, and seventy that of one silver vase:
all the silver vessels weighed two thousand four hundred
shekels in shekels of the sanctuary. The golden censers

were twelve, full of fragrant incense, weighing each ten shekels; the weight of the censers was, in shekels of the sanctuary, all the gold of the censers one hundred and twenty (shekels). All the bullocks for the burnt offering were twelve bullocks, rams twelve, lambs of the year twelve, and their minchas. And for the sin offering twelve kids of the goats. And all the oxen for consecrated victims were twenty-four oxen, rams sixty, goats sixty, lambs of the year sixty. This was the Dedication of the Altar after they had anointed it.

And when Mosheh had gone into the tabernacle of ordinance to speak with Him, then heard he the Voice of Him who spake with him from above the Mercy Seat over the Ark of the Testimony, between the two Kerubaia; and He spake unto him.

SECTION XXXVI.

BEHAALOTHECA.

VIII. AND the Lord spake with Mosheh, saying. Speak with Aharon, and say to him: When thou dost kindle the lamps upon the face of the candelabrum, the seven lamps shall be burning (together). And Aharon did so: on the face of the candelabrum he made the lamps burn, as the Lord commanded Mosheh. And this work of the candelabrum was of beaten gold, from its shaft to its lilies, beaten (gold) according to the pattern which the Lord had showed to Mosheh, so had he made the candelabrum.

And the Lord spake with Mosheh, saying: Bring near the Levites from among the sons of Israel, and purify them. And thus shalt thou do to them to purify

N

them. Sprinkle upon them the water of purification,
and make the razor to pass over all their flesh, and let
them wash their vestments, and they shall be clean.
And let them take a young bullock, and his mincha of
flour, sprinkled with oil; and a second bullock, a
young bullock shalt thou take, for the sin offering.
And bring the Levites before the tabernacle of ordinance, and assemble all the congregation of the children
of Israel.

And thou shalt bring the Levites before the Lord;
and the sons of Israel shall lay their hands upon the
Levites; and Aharon shall offer the Levites[3] as an
elevation before the Lord from the sons of Israel,
that they may perform the service of the Lord.   And
the Levites shall lay their hands upon the head of the
bullocks, and make the one for a sin offering, and the
other for a burnt offering, before the Lord, to make an
atonement for the Levites.   And thou shalt set the
Levites before Aharon, and before his sons, and offer
them up (as) an elevation before the Lord.   And thou
shalt thus separate the Levites from among the sons of
Israel, that the Levites may minister before Me.   And
afterward shall the Levites enter, to minister (in) the
tabernacle of ordinance, for thou wilt have purified
them, and offered them up as an elevation.   For by a
separation are they separated unto Me from among the
sons of Israel, instead of every firstborn who openeth the
womb of all the children of Israel have I taken them
to be) before Me.   For Mine are all the firstborn of
the children of Israel, of man and of beast: in the day
that I slew all the firstborn in the land of Mizraim did
I sanctify them before Me.   And I have taken the
Levites instead of all the firstborn of the sons of Israel.

[3] Literally, "shall elevate an elevation."   The elevation not always
done bodily.

And the Levites I have given as a gift[4] unto Aharon and to his sons, from among the sons of Israel, to minister the service for the children of Israel in the tabernacle of ordinance, and to make atonement for the children of Israel, that death may not be among the children of Israel when the children of Israel come nigh to the sanctuary.

And Mosheh and Aharon, and all the congregation of the sons of Israel, did unto the Levites according to all that the Lord commanded Mosheh for the Levites; so did the sons of Israel to them. And the Levites were purified, and they cleansed their raiment, and Aharon offered them (as) an elevation before the Lord; and Aharon made an atonement for them to purify them. And afterwards the Levites went in to perform their service in the tabernacle of ordinance before Aharon and before his sons; as the Lord had commanded Mosheh concerning the Levites, so did they unto them.

And the Lord spake with Mosheh, saying: This is (the law) of the Levites: from a son of five-and-twenty years and upward he shall come with the bands in their service (in the) tabernacle of ordinance, and from fifty years old he shall return from the company of the ministers, and work no longer; but minister with his brethren at the tabernacle of ordinance in keeping the custody; yet the service he shall not perform: so shalt thou do with the Levites in their charge.

IX. And the Lord spake with Mosheh, in the wilderderness of Sinai, in the second year of their going forth from the land of Mizraim, in the first month, saying: Let the children of Israel perform the Pascha in its time. On the fourteenth day of this month, between the suns, they shall perform it in its time according to all the rites of it, and according to all the form of it,

4 Lit, "delivered ones . those made over" Heb., *Nethinim.*

n 2

shall they do it. And Mosheh spake with the sons of
Israel to perform the Pascha. And they performed the
Pascha in Nisan, on the fourteenth day of the month,
between the suns, in the wilderness of Sinai ; according
to all that the Lord had commanded Mosheh, so did the
children of Israel.

But there were men who were unclean by defilement,
(having touched) the body of a (dead) man, and they
could not make the Pascha on that day, and they came
before Mosheh and before Aharon that day, and the
men said to him : We are unclean, by the defilement of
the life of a man, and are, therefore, restrained from
offering the oblation of the Lord in its time among the
sons of Israel. And Mosheh said to them, Wait, till I
shall have heard what will be commanded from before
the Lord about your case   And the Lord spake with
Mosheh, saying : Speak with the sons of Israel, saying :
If any man be unclean by the defilement of the life of a
man, or be in the way, afar off from you or from your
dwellings, he shall perform the Pascha before the Lord
in the second month,[5] on the fourteenth day, between the
suns, they shall perform it ; with unleavened (bread) and
with bitter (herbs) shall they eat it : they shall not
leave of it till the morning, and a bone of it shall not
be broken ; according to all the rites of the Pascha shall
they perform it.   But the man who is clean, and is not
upon a journey, and forbeareth to perform the Pascha,
that man shall be cut off from his people : because he
hath not offered the Lord's oblation in its time, that
man shall bear his guilt.   And if a stranger sojourn
with you, and will perform the Pascha before the Lord,
according to the rites of the Pascha, and according to
the forms thereof, so shall he do : one statute shall you
have, for the stranger, and for the native of the land.

[5] The regular time was the first month.

And on the day that the Tabernacle was erected the
Cloud covered the Tabernacle of the Testimony; and at
evening there was upon the Tabernacle as the vision of
Fire, until the morning. So was it continually; the
Cloud covered it (by day), and the appearance of the Fire
in the night. And according as the Cloud was uplifted
above the Tabernacle, the sons of Israel afterward went
on; and at the place where the Cloud rested, there did
the sons of Israel encamp. By the Word of the Lord
the sons of Israel journeyed, and by the Word of the
Lord they encamped; all the days that the Cloud rested,
they remained. However long the time the Cloud was
upon the Tabernacle, (however) many the days, the sons
of Israel kept the watch of the Word of the Lord, and
journeyed not. And if the Cloud was over the Tabernacle
a number of days, according to the Word of the Lord
they remained, and by the Word of the Lord they went
forward. Or if the Cloud was (over the Tabernacle only)
from the evening till the morn, and the Cloud was uplifted in the morning, they went forward; whether (in
the) days or nights the Cloud was uplifted, they went forward; whether it was two days, or a month, or a longer
season, (time by time,) the Cloud was in staying upon
the Tabernacle to remain thereon, the children of Israel
remained, and went not forward; but at the lifting up
of it they proceeded. By the Word of the Lord they
abode, and by the Word of the Lord they proceeded;
they observed the watch of the Word of the Lord, upon
the Word of the Lord through Mosheh.

X. And the Lord spake with Mosheh, saying: Make
thee two trumpets of silver, beaten shalt thou make
them, and they shall be for thee to convoke the
assembly, and to move forward the host. And they
shall blow with them, and bring all the congregation
together unto thee, at the door of the tabernacle of

ordinance. And if they blow with but one, the chiefs,
the heads of thousands of Israel, shall gather together
to thee. When you blow with a full note, (or alarm,)
the host that encampeth eastward shall go forward,
and when you blow with the second alarm, the hosts
that encamp southward shall go on; an alarm [6] shall
they blow for their journeys. But when the congregation is to be gathered together, you shall blow, but not
with the alarm. And the sons of Aharon, the priests,
are to blow with the trumpets; and this shall be to you
a perpetual statute for your generations.

And when you enter upon the battle fight for your
country, with the oppressors who oppress you, ye shall
blow the alarm with the trumpets, that your remembrance may come for good before the Lord your God,
(and) that you may be delivered from them who hate
you.

And on the day of your rejoicing, and on your
solemnities, and at the beginning of your months, ye
shall blow with the trumpets over your burnt offerings,
and over your consecrated victims; and they shall be
for a memorial before your God : I am the Lord your
God.

And it was in the second year, in the second month,
on the twentieth day of the month, that the Cloud was
uplifted from above the Tabernacle of the Testimony,
and the children of Israel went forward upon their
journeys from the wilderness of Sinai ; and the Cloud
rested in the wilderness of Pharan. And they went
forward at the first by the Word of the Lord through
Mosheh. In the first place the standard of the camp of
the Beni Jehudah went forward by their hosts; and
over the host was Nachshon bar Aminadab. And
over the host of the tribe of the Beni Issakar, Nethanel

---

[6] Trumpet notes *Tekoha, Shevorim, Teruha*

bar Zuar. And over the host of the tribe of the Beni Zebulun, Eliab bar Chelon.

And the tabernacle was taken down, and the sons of Gershon went forward, and the sons of Merari, carrying the tabernacle.

And the standard (or order) of the camp of Reuben went forward by their hosts, and over its host was Elizur bar Shedeur: and over the host of the tribe of the Beni Shemeun was Shelumiel bar Zurishaddai. And over the host of the Beni Gad was Eljasaph bar Dehuel. And the sons of Kehath went forward, carrying the sanctuary, and (the Gershonites and sons of Merari) set up the tabernacle against they came.

And the standard of the camps of the Beni Ephraim went forward by their hosts, and over his host was Elishama bar Amihud. And over the host of the tribe of the Beni Menasheh was Gamliel bar Phedazur. And over the host of the tribe of the Beni Benyamin, Abidan bar Gideoni.

And the standard of the camps of the Beni Dan went forward collecting each camp according to their hosts; and over his host was Achiezer bar Amishaddai. And over the host of the tribe of the Beni Asher, Phagiel bar Akran; and over the host of the tribe of the Beni Naphtali, Achira bar Enan. These arc the journeys of the sons of Israel, and according to their hosts they went forward.

And Mosheh said unto Hobab bar Reuel, the Midian-ite, the father-in-law of Moshch, We are journeying to the place of which the Lord hath said, I will give it unto you: come thou with us, and we will do thee good; for the Lord hath spoken, to bring good upon Israel. But he said to him, I will not go (with you), but to my country and to my kindred will I go. And he said, Leave us not, I beseech thee; for thou knowest how we should encamp in the wilderness; and the great things that will be done for us thou wilt see with thine eyes. And it shall be that if thou wilt go with us, with the good by which the Lord shall do us good, will we do good to thee.

And from the mountain on which the glory of the Lord had been revealed they went forward, journeying three days; and the ark of the Lord's covenant went before them, three days' journey, to provide for them a place of encampment. And the Cloud of Glory of the Lord overspread them by day as they went forth from their encampments. And when the ark went forward, Mosheh said: Reveal thyself, O Lord, that Thine enemies may be scattered, and Thy adversaries may flee before thee. And when it rested, he said. Return, O Lord, and dwell in Thy glory among the multitudes of the thousands of Israel.

XI. But the people were discontented (or, were fomenting evil) before the Lord; and it was heard before the Lord, and His anger was strongly moved, and a fire was kindled against them from before the Lord, and it consumed the outskirts of the camp. And the people cried unto Mosheh, and Mosheh prayed before the Lord, and the fire was subdued. And Mosheh called the name of that place Enkindlement; because the fire had been kindled against them from before the Lord.

And the mixed multitude who were among them demanded with demand; and the children of Israel also turned, and wept, and said: Who will feed us with flesh? We remember the fish which we ate in Mizraim freely, the cucumbers and melons, the cresses and onions and garlick. But now our soul longeth, yet there is nothing before our eyes but manna. Now the manna was like the seed of coriander, and its appearance as the appearance of bedilcha. And the people went about and gathered; and he who would ground it in mills, or he who would beat it in the mortar, and they dressed it in the pan, and made cakes of it, and its taste was like the taste of a confection of oil. And when the dew came down upon the camp at night, the manna descended upon it.

And Mosheh heard the people lamenting with their families, a man at the door of his tent. And the displeasure of the Lord grew very strong, as in the eyes of Mosheh it was evil. And Mosheh said before the Lord, Wherefore hast Thou done painfully to Thy servant, and why have I not found mercy before Thee, that Thou hast put the burden of all this people upon me? Am I father to all this people, or are they my children, that Thou hast said to me, Carry them in thy strength, as the nurse carrieth the suckling, unto the land which Thou hast covenanted to their fathers? Whence shall I have flesh to give to all this people? for they lament to me, saying: Give us flesh to eat. I am not able to bear all this people alone, because it is too heavy for me. And if Thou do thus with me, kill me, I pray, if I have found mercy before Thee, that I may not see my wretchedness. And the Lord said to Mosheh, Gather unto Me seventy men of the elders [7] of Israel, whom thou knowest to be elders of the people, and the overseers [8] thereof, and bring them to the tabernacle of ordinance, and let them stand there with thee; and I will reveal Myself, and will speak with thee there; and I will make enlargement [9] of the Spirit that is upon thee, and put it upon them, that they may bear with thee the burden of the people, and thou mayest not sustain it by thyself alone. And

---

[7] Sam Vers., "the sages.'   [8] Sam Vers, "scribes."

[9] Heb, 'I will take away of the Spirit " LXX, *idem.* Syr, "I will diminish from the Spirit "

say thou to the people, Prepare yourselves for the
morrow, and you shall eat flesh; for that you have
lamented before the Lord, saying : Who will give us flesh,
that we may eat? for it was better with us in Mizraim;
and I will give you flesh, and you shall eat.   Not one
day shall you eat (it), nor two days, nor five days, nor
ten days, nor twenty days; but for a month of days,
until you loathe it, and it be an offence to you;
because you have felt dislike to the Word of the Lord,
whose Shekinah dwelleth among you; and before whom
you have wept, saying : Why came we out of Mizraim?

But Mosheh said, The people among whom I am are
six hundred thousand footmen; and Thou hast said, I
will give them flesh to eat for a month of days.   Shall
the oxen and sheep be slaughtered for them, to satisfy
them, or all the fish of the sea be gathered that they
may be satisfied?   And the Lord said to Mosheh : Is
the Word of the Lord restrained?   Now shalt thou see
whether My saying come to pass with thee or not.

And Mosheh went forth, and told the people the
words of the Lord, and gathered together seventy men
of the elders of the people, and set them round about
the tabernacle.   And the Lord was revealed in the
Cloud, and spake with him, and he made enlargement
of the Spirit that was upon him, and imparted to the
seventy men, the elders; and it came to pass that when
the Spirit of prophecy rested upon them they prophesied,
and ceased not.   But two men remained in the camp,
the name of the one Eldad, and the name of the second
Medad; and the Spirit of prophecy rested upon them;
and, though they were in the writings, they had not
come out of the camp; but they prophesied in the
camp.   And a young man ran, and showed to Mosheh,
and said : Eldad and Medad do prophesy in the camp.
And Jehoshua bar Nun, the minister of Mosheh from

his youth, answered and said, Ribbom Mosheh, put them in bond.   But Mosheh said, Art thou jealous for my sake ?[1]   I would that all the people of the Lord did prophesy, and that the Lord would confer the Spirit of prophecy upon them.   And Mosheh returned to the camp, he and the elders of Israel.   And the wind proceeded from before the Lord, and the quails flew abroad from the sea, and it bare them upon the camp as (the breadth of) a day's journey here, and a day's journey there, round about the camp, and as at a height of two cubits over the face of the ground.   And the people were up all that day, and all the night, and all the day after it, and collected the quails; he who collected least (gathered together) ten heaps; and they spread them abroad, round about the camp.

While yet the flesh was between their teeth, and they had not yet finished, the displeasure of the Lord was manifested strongly against the people, and the Lord inflicted death among the people with a very great mortality.   And he called the name of that place, The Graves of the Demanders;[2] because there they buried the people who demanded.   From the Graves of the Demanders the people journeyed to Hatseroth, and they were in Hatseroth.

XII. And Miriam and Aharon spake against Mosheh, because of the fair woman [3] whom he had taken, because the fair woman who had been sent away he had taken. And they said, Hath the Lord spoken only with Mosheh?   Hath He not spoken with us also?   And it was heard before the Lord.   [But the man Mosheh was very humble,[4] more than all the men who were

---

[1] " Art thou jealous with my jealousy ?"

[2] Heb., *Kibroth Hattaavah,* "the Graves of Desire."

[3] *Ittha Shaphutha.* Heb., *Ha-isha ha Kushith,* "the woman the Ethiopian."

[4] Or, "bent down" Comp. verses 14, 15

upon the face of the earth.] And the Lord spake
suddenly with Mosheh, and to Aharon and to Miriam:
Come forth, you three, to the tabernacle of ordinance;
and those three went forth. And the Lord was revealed
in the pillar of the Cloud, and stood at the door of the
tabernacle: and He called Aharon and Miriam, and they
two came forth. And He said, Hear now My words.
If there be prophets with you, I the Lord will reveal
Myself (to them) in visions, in dreams will I speak with
them. But not so (with) My servant Mosheh; over all
My house faithful is he. Speaker with speaker will I
speak with him; in apparition, and not in similitudes;
and he shall behold the likeness of the glory of the
Lord. And how is this, that you have not been afraid
to speak against My servant, against Mosheh? And
the displeasure of the Lord was strong against them,
and He went up. And the Cloud went up from over
the tabernacle. And, behold, Miriam was white as snow;
and Aharon looked upon Miriam, and, behold, she was
leprous. And Aharon said to Mosheh, My lord, I
entreat that thou wouldst not lay this sin upon us, in
that we have acted foolishly, and have transgressed.
Let not this one, I entreat, be separated from among
us, for she is our sister. Pray, now, over this dead flesh
which is in her, that she may be healed. And Mosheh
prayed before the Lord, saying: O God, I beseech Thee,
heal her now. But the Lord said to Mosheh, If her
father, correcting, had corrected her, ought she not to
have been ashamed seven days? Let her be shut up
seven days without the camp, and afterward be admitted.
And Miriam was shut up without the camp seven days;
and the people journeyed not until Miriam was brought
in. And afterward the people journeyed from Hatseroth, and encamped in the wilderness of Pharan.

SECTION XXXVII.

SHELACH.

XIII. AND the Lord spake with Mosheh, saying:
Send thou men, that they may explore the land of
Kenaan, which I will give to the children of Israel: one
man for each tribe of their fathers shall you send, each
one a ruler among them. And Mosheh sent them from
the wilderness of Pharan, according to the Word of the
Lord. All those men were heads of the children of
Israel; and these are their names: For the tribe of
Reuben, Shamua bar Zakur; for the tribe of Shemeon,
Shaphat bar Hori; for the tribe of Jehudah, Kaleb bar
Jephuneh; for the tribe of Issakar, Igal bar Joseph;
for the tribe of Ephraim, Hoshea bar Nun; for the tribe
of Benyamin, Phalti bar Raphu; for the tribe of Zebulon, Gediel bar Sodi; for the tribe of Joseph, the tribe
of Menasheh, Gaddi bar Susi; for the tribe of Dan,
Ammiel bar Gemali; for the tribe of Asher, Sethor bar
Mikael; for the tribe of Naphtali, Nachbi bar Vapsi; for
the tribe of Gad, Geüel bar Machi: These are the names
of the men whom Mosheh sent to explore the land.

And Mosheh called Hoshea bar Nun Jehoshua   And
Mosheh sent them away to explore the land of Kenaan.
And he said to them, Go up hither by the south, and
ascend to the mountain, and see the country what it is,
and the people who dwell upon it, whether they be
strong or weak, few or many; and what the land is in
which they dwell, whether good or bad; and what the
cities they inhabit, whether open, or walled in; and
whether the land is rich or poor; whether it hath trees
or not: and you, be of good courage, and bring of the

fruits of the land. And the days were the days of the first grapes.

And they went up, and explored the country, from the wilderness of Zin unto Rechob, to come unto Hamath. And they went up by the south, and came to Hebron; and there were Achiman, Sheshai, and Talmai, sons of the giants; (and Hebron was built seven years before Tanis of Mizraim.) And they came to the Stream of Grapes, and cut down there a branch, with one cluster of grapes, and carried it on a staff between two; and (they took also) of the pomegranates, and of the figs. That place was called the Stream of Grapes,[5] on account of the grapes (*athkela*) which the sons of Israel cut down from thence. And they returned from the exploration of the country at the end of forty days.

And they went and came to Mosheh, and to Aharon, and to all the congregation of the children of Israel at the wilderness of Pharan, at Rekam, and returned the word to them, and to all the congregation, and showed them the fruit of the land. And they recounted to him, and said: We came to the land whither thou didst send us, and truly it doth produce milk and honey, and this is the fruit of it. But very mighty are the people who inhabit the land, and the cities are fortified and very great; and we saw, also, the sons of the giants there. The Amalkaah dwell in the land of the south, and the Hittaah and Jebusaah and Amoraah dwell in the mountain, and the Kenaanaah dwell by the sea, and upon the bank of the Jordan.

And Kaleb quieted the people for Mosheh, and said: Going, let us go up and possess it, for we are able to (do) it: but the men who had gone up with him said, We are not able to go up against the people, for they are stronger than we. And they gave forth an evil

[5] *Nachela de athkela.* Heb., *Nachal Eshkol.*

report (name) about the land which they had explored to the children of Israel, saying : The country which we have passed through to search it, is a land that killeth its inhabitants; and all the people whom we saw in it are men of stature; and there we saw the giants, the sons of Anak, which are of the giants; and we looked, in our own sight, as locusts, and so were we in their eyes.

XIV. And all the congregation lifted up and gave (forth) their voice; and all the people wept that night. And all the children of Israel murmured against Mosheh and Aharon; and the whole congregation said to them, O that we had died in the land of Mizraim, or that we had died in this wilderness! And why is the Lord bringing us to this land, that we may fall by the sword, and our wives and our children become a prey ? Would it not be better for us to return into Mizraim ? And they said, a man to his brother, Let us appoint a chieftain, and go back into Mizraim.

And Mosheh and Aharon fell upon their faces before all the assembly of the sons of Israel. And Jehoshua bar Nun, and Kaleb bar Jephuneh, who were of the explorers of the land, rent their clothes. And they spake to all the congregation of the sons of Israel, saying : The land, which we passed through to explore it, is a good land, most exceedingly. If the Lord hath pleasure in us, even He will bring us into this land, and give us the land which produceth milk and honey. Only be not rebellious against the Word of the Lord, nor be afraid of the people of the land, for they are delivered into our hand; their strength is departed from them, and the Word of the Lord is our helper: fear them not. But all the congregation said that they would stone them with stones.

And the Glory of the Lord was revealed at the

tabernacle of ordinance, unto all the children of Israel.
And the Lord said to Mosheh, How long will this
people provoke Me, and how long will they disbelieve
in My Word, for all the signs which I have wrought
among them? I will smite them with the pestilence
and consume them; and will make of thee a people
greater and stronger than they. But Mosheh said
before the Lord, And the Mizraee will hear of it;—
for Thou didst bring up by Thy power this people from
among them, and they will tell unto the inhabitants of
this land; for they have heard that Thou, O Lord, dost
dwell in Thy Shekinah among this people, whose eyes
behold the glorious Shekinah of the Lord, and that Thy
Cloud overshadoweth them, and that in the pillar of the
Cloud Thou conductest them in the day, and in the
pillar of Fire by night. Now if Thou shalt kill this
people as one man, the nations who have heard the
fame of Thy power will speak, saying: Because there
was not strength (enough) before the Lord to bring
this people into the land which He covenanted to them,
He hath killed them in the desert. And now I beseech,
let power be magnified from before the Lord, as Thou
hast thus spoken, saying: The Lord is far from anger,
and great in performing goodness and truth: forgiving
iniquity and rebellion and sins, pardoning them who
return unto His law · but acquitting not them who will
not turn, (but) visiting the sins of the fathers upon the
rebellious children unto the third and unto the fourth
generation. Pardon, I beseech, the sins of this people
according to the amplitude of Thy goodness, and as
Thou hast forgiven [6] this people from Mizraim until
now.

And the Lord said, I have pardoned according to
thy word. Yet, as I live, with the glory of the

---

[6] Sam. Vers., " as thou hast borne this people."

Lord shall all the earth be filled. Because all these
men who have seen My glory, and the signs I wrought
in Mizraim and in the desert, but have tempted before
Me these ten times, and have not been obedient to My
Word,—if they shall see the land which I covenanted
to their fathers, nor shall any see it who have provoked
before Me. But My servant Kaleb, for that there was
in him another spirit, and that he hath wholly followed (in) My fear, him will I bring into the land
whither he went, and his children shall possess it.—
Now the Amalkaah and the Kenaanaah dwelt in the
valley.—To-morrow, turn you and get you to the wilderness by the way of the Sea of Suph.

And the Lord spake with Mosheh and unto Aharon,
saying: How long shall this evil congregation be murmuring against Me? The murmuring of the sons of
Israel which they murmur against Me is heard before
Me. Say to them, As I live, saith the Lord, even as ye
have spoken before Me, so will I do to you. In this
wilderness shall your carcases fall, and all who are
numbered of you, of all your numbers, from one of
twenty years and upward who have murmured against
me—if you shall come into the land in which I
covenanted in My Word to cause you to dwell, except
Kaleb bar Jephuneh, and Jehoshua bar Nun. But your
children, of whom you said they were for a prey, will I
bring in, and they shall know the land which you have
abhorred. But your carcases shall fall in this wilderness; and your children shall go about in the wilderness forty years, and shall bear your iniquities until
your carcases be laid in the wilderness. According to
the number of the days in which you explored the land,
forty days, a day for a year, a day for a year, you shall
receive for your sins, even forty years, and you shall
know (the consequence of) your murmuring against

me.[7] I, the Lord, have made the decree in My Word, —if I will not do unto all this evil congregation who have gathered together against Me; in this wilderness shall they find their end, and here shall they die.

And the men whom Mosheh sent to search the land, and who returned to make all the congregation murmur against him, by bringing forth an evil name upon the land, those men who brought out the evil name upon the land died by the plague before the Lord. But Jehoshua bar Nun and Kaleb bar Jephuneh lived, of those men who went to explore the land.

And Mosheh told these words to all the children of Israel, and the people bewailed 'greatly. And they arose in the morning to go up to the top of the mountain, saying: Behold, we will go up to the place of which the Lord hath spoken; for we have sinned. But Mosheh said, Wherefore do you transgress against the decree of the Word of the Lord? But it will not prosper. Go not up, for the Shekinah of the Lord is not among you, and be not broken before your enemies. For the Amalkaah and the Kenaanaah are there before you, and you will fall by the sword; for, because you have turned away from the service of the Lord, the Word of the Lord will not be your helper. Yet they would commit the wickedness of going up to the summit of the mountain, though the ark of the Lord's covenant, and Mosheh, removed not from the midst of the camp. And the Amalkaah and the Kenaannah who dwelt in the mountain came down and smote them, and pursued them unto Hormah.

---

[7] Heb text, *Eth tenuath*, "My vengeance." Samaritan text, "Ye shall know My vengeance." Sam Vers, "the compensation." Sept., "the fury of My anger." Syriac, "You shall know what (follows) upon your murmuring before Me"

XV. And the Lord spake with Mosheh, saying:
Speak with the children of Israel, and say to them:
When you shall (at last) have come into the land which
I will give you, and you will make an oblation before
the Lord, a burnt offering, or a consecrated sacrifice for
the release of a vow, or in a free will offering, or in
your solemnities to render an acceptable service before
the Lord, from the herd or from the flock; let him
who offereth his oblation before the Lord bring for a
mincha a tenth of flour sprinkled with the fourth of a
hina of oil. And wine for a libation the fourth of a
hina shall he make upon the burnt offering, or hallowed
sacrifice, for one lamb: or for a ram he shall make a
mincha of two tenths of flour sprinkled with the third
of a hina of oil; and wine for the libation thou shalt
bring the third of a hina, to be received with acceptance before the Lord. And when thou makest a
bullock a burnt offering, or a hallowed sacrifice for the
release of a vow, or hallowed sacrifices before the Lord,
let him bring with the bullock a mincha of three tenths
of flour sprinkled with a half hina of oil; and wine
shalt thou bring for the libation the half of a hina, an
oblation to be received with acceptance before the Lord.
So shalt thou do for one bullock, or one ram, or one
lamb from the lambs, or from the kids. According to
the number that you perform so shall you do with each,
according to their number. All native born (Hebrews)
shall do these things to offer an oblation to be received
with favour before the Lord. And if a sojourner who
sojourneth with you, or whoever among you in your
generations will make an oblation to be received with
favour before the Lord, as you do, so shall he do. One
congregation and one rite shall be for you and for the
sojourners who sojourn; it is an everlasting statute; as
you are, so shall the sojourner be before the Lord: one

law and one judgment shall be for you and for the sojourners who dwell with you.

And the Lord spake with Mosheh, saying: Speak with the sons of Israel, and say to them, When you have come into the land into which I will bring you, and when you eat of the bread of the land, you shall set apart a separation before the Lord. Of the first of your food you shall set apart a cake for a separation, as the separation of the threshing-floor, so shall you set it apart; of the first of your bread (dough) you shall give the separation before the Lord in your generations.

And should you be in ignorance, and not do all these commandments of which the Lord hath spoken with Mosheh, even all which the Lord commanded you by the hand of Mosheh from the day that the Lord commanded and thenceforward in your generations, it shall be that if anything be hid from the eyes of the congregation and you do ignorantly, then all the congregation shall make a burnt offering of one young bullock, to be received with acceptance before the Lord, with his mincha and his libation, according to the proper manner, and one kid of the goats for a sin offering: and the priest shall make atonement for all the congregation of the sons of Israel, and it shall be forgiven them, for it was ignorance, but they shall bring their oblation before the Lord on account of their ignorance. And it shall be forgiven to all the congregation of the children of Israel, and to the sojourners who sojourn among them; for all the people (were) in ignorance. And if one sin ignorantly, he shall bring a female kid of the year for a sin offering; and the priest shall make atonement for the man who hath erred in his sin through ignorance before the Lord, to atone for him, and it shall be forgiven him. For the native born of the sons of Israel, and for the sojourner who sojourneth among you, one law shall there be for you, for him who acteth in ignorance. But the man who doeth presumptuously,[8] whether of the native born, or of the sojourners, he provoketh the Lord to anger, and that man shall perish from among his people: because he hath despised the word of the Lord, and hath made His commandment vain, that man shall be utterly destroyed, his sin is upon him.

And while the children of Israel were in the wilderness, they found a man stealing wood on the day of the Sabbath, and they who had found him stealing wood brought him to Mosheh and Aharon, and to all the congregation. And they bound him in the house of custody; for it had not been explained to them what they should do to him. And the Lord said unto Mosheh, The man shall be surely put to death; all the congregation shall stone him with stones without the camp. And all the congregation brought him forth without the camp, and stoned him with stones, and he died; as the Lord commanded Mosheh.

And the Lord spake to Mosheh, saying: Speak with the children of Israel, and bid them that they make them fringes[9] upon the borders of their garments throughout their generations, and that upon the fringes on the borders they put a ribbon of hyacinth. And they shall be to you for fringes, that you may look upon it, and remember all the commandments of the Lord, and do them, and not wander after the imagination of your heart, or after the sight of your eyes, after which you have gone astray. That you may remember and do all My precepts, and be saints before your God. I am the Lord your God who brought you forth from the land of Mizraim to be to you Eloha: I am the Lord your God.

[8] Lit., " who acteth with uncovered head."
[9] *Kervspedin*. Heb., *tsitsith*. compare the Greek in Matt. ix. 20.

SECTION XXXVIII.

KORACH.

XVI. But Korach bar Izhar bar Kahath bar Levi, and Dathan and Abiram the sons of Eliab, and On bar Pelath of the Beni Reuben, made a division. And they rose up in the presence of Mosheh with (other) men of the sons of Israel, two hundred and fifty, chiefs of the congregation, who at the time of the convocation had been men of name.[1] And they gathered together against Mosheh, and against Aharon, and said to them, You are too great;[2] for the whole of the congregation are all of them holy, and the Lord's Shekinah dwelleth among them : wherefore then are you lifted up above the church of the Lord ?

And Mosheh heard, and fell upon his face. And he spake with Korach, and with all the congregation, saying : In the morning the Lord will make known who it is who pertaineth to Him, and who hath been consecrated to approach to His presence, and whosoever He shall appoint shall go near unto His service. This do : Take you censers, Korach and all his congregation ; and put fire in them, and put sweet incense upon it before the Lord to-morrow: and the man whom the Lord will choose, he shall be holy. You have too much,[3] sons of Levi.

And Mosheh said to Korach, Hear now, sons of Levi · Is it a little thing with you that the God of Israel hath separated you from the congregation of Israel to bring you near before Him to perform the service of the Lord's

---

[1] Heb., "called to the council, men of name." Syr., "who were at the time called men of name."

[2] *Sagi lekun* Heb text, *Rab lakem*, "Too much for you." Syriac, " Is it not sufficient for you that all the congregation are consecrated ? "

[3] Or, " are too great," *Sagi lekun.*

tabernacle, and to stand before the congregation to minister to them? But He hath brought thee nigh, and all thy
brethren the sons of Levi with thee . and seek you now
the High Priesthood also? Therefore thou and all thy
company have gathered together against the Lord. And
Aharon, what is he, that you murmur against him?

And Mosheh sent to call Dathan and Abiram, the
sons of Eliab; but they said, We will not come up. Is
it a trifle that thou hast brought us from a land making
milk and honey to kill us in the desert, that thou mayest
domineer and rule over us? Neither hast thou brought
us into the land that maketh milk and honey, to give us
an inheritance of fields and vineyards: wilt thou blind
the eyes of these men? We will not come up.

And Mosheh was greatly angered, and said before
the Lord, Receive not Thou their offering: I have not
taken one ass from them, neither have I injured one of
them. And Mosheh said to Korach, Be thou and all
thy company prepared before the Lord, thou and they
and Aharon to-morrow. And take every man his censer,
and put sweet incense upon them, each man to offer
before the Lord (with) his censer. And they took every
man his censer, and set fire in it, and put sweet incense
thereon, and stood at the door of the tabernacle of ordinance, with Mosheh and Aharon. And Korach assembled with him all the company at the door of the tabernacle of ordinance.

And the glory of the Lord was revealed to all the
congregation; and the Lord spake with Mosheh and to
Aharon, saying: Separate yourselves from among this
company, and I will consume them at once. But they
fell upon their faces, and said, O God, the God of the
spirits of all flesh, shall one man sin, and thou be wroth
with all the congregation? And the Lord spake with
Mosheh, saying: Speak with the congregation, saying:

Get you up from among the tents of Korach, Dathan,
and Abiram.   And Mosheh arose and went unto
Dathan and Abiram, and the elders of Israel followed
him.   And he spake with the congregation, saying:
Remove now from the tents of these guilty men, and
touch not anything that is theirs, lest you be stricken
with all their sins.   And they gat up from the tents of
Korach, Dathan, and Abiram round about; and Dathan
and Abiram came out, and stood at the door of their
tents, with their wives, and their sons, and their families.

And Mosheh said: By this shall you know that the
Lord hath sent me to do all these works, because (I do
them) not of my own will: If these men die the death
of all men, and the visitation of all men be visited upon
them, the Lord hath not sent me.   But if the Lord
create a creation, and the earth open her mouth, and
swallow them up, and all that is theirs, and they go
down alive into Sheul, then you will know that these
men have caused anger before the Lord.

And it was, when he had finished to speak all these
words, that the ground under them clave asunder, and
the earth opened her mouth, and swallowed them up,
and the men of their houses; and all the men of Korach,
and all their substance, they, and all who were theirs,
went down alive into Sheul; and the earth closed upon
them, and they perished from among the congregation.

And all Israel who stood round about them fled
from their cry; for they said, Lest the earth swallow us.
And fire came out from before the Lord, and consumed
the two hundred and fifty men who had offered the
sweet incense.

And the Lord spake with Mosheh, saying: Speak to
Elazar bar Aharon the priest, that he take out the
censers from among the burnings, and throw away the
fire, for they are consecrated.   The censers of those

guilty men who sinned against their souls, let him make
of them beaten plates, to cover the altar, for they had
offered them before the Lord, and they are consecrated;
and they shall be for a sign unto the children of Israel.
And Elazar the priest took the golden censers, with
which they who were burned had offered, and beat them
abroad, for a covering for the altar, to be a memorial to
the sons of Israel, that no strange man who is not of
the seed of Aharon shall approach to burn sweet
incense before the Lord, and that he be not as Korach
and his company, as the Lord had said to him by the
hand of Mosheh.

But on the day which followed, all the congregation
of the sons of Israel murmured against Mosheh and
against Aharon, saying: You have caused the death of
the Lord's people And it was, while the congregation
gathered against Mosheh and against Aharon, that they
looked toward the tabernacle of ordinance; and, behold,
the cloud covered it, and the glory of the Lord was
revealed. And Mosheh and Aharon went up before the
tabernacle of ordinance; and the Lord spake with
Mosheh, saying: Separate yourselves from the midst of
this congregation, that I may now consume them. But
they fell upon their faces. And Mosheh said to Aharon:
Take the censer, and put fire upon it from the altar, and
lay on sweet incense, and go quickly to the congregation, and make atonement for them; for anger hath
gone forth from before the Lord, the plague hath begun.
And Aharon took, as Mosheh had said, and ran into
the midst of the congregation, and, behold, the plague
had begun among the people; and he put on sweet incense and made atonement for the people. And he stood
between the dead and the living, and the plague ceased.

But they who died of the plague were fourteen
thousand and seven hundred, beside those who died on

account of the matter of Korach. And Aharon returned to Mosheh, unto the door of the tabernacle of ordinance, and the plague ceased.

XVII. And the Lord spake with Mosheh, saying: Speak with the sons of Israel, and take from them severally a rod, according the house of their fathers, twelve rods, and write thou the name of each man upon his rod. And upon the rod of Levi thou shalt write the name of Aharon; for one rod (only) there shall be for (each) chief of their father's house. And thou shalt lay them up in the tabernacle of ordinance before the testimony, where I will appoint My Word to be with thee. And it shall be that the rod of the man whom I will choose shall bud; and I will make to cease from before Me the murmuring of the sons of Israel, with which they have murmured against you. And Mosheh spake with the sons of Israel; and all their chiefs gave to him, every chief one rod, according to the house of their fathers, twelve rods. And Aharon's rod was among their rods. And Mosheh laid up the rods before the Lord in the tabernacle of the testimony.

And it came to pass on the following day, that Mosheh went into the tabernacle of the testimony; and, behold, the rod of Aharon of the house of Levi had germinated, and produced branches, and had blossomed, and ripened almonds. And Mosheh brought out all the rods from before the Lord unto all the sons of Israel, and they recognised and took every man his rod.

And the Lord said to Mosheh: Take back Aharon's rod before the testimony, to be kept for a sign unto the rebellious people, that their murmurings before Me may come to an end, and they die not. And Mosheh did as the Lord commanded, so did he.

And the children of Israel spake to Mosheh, saying:

Behold, some of us are slain with the sword; and, behold, some are swallowed up by the earth; and, behold, some perish with the plague. Whoever, approaching, approacheth the tabernacle of the Lord dieth; behold, we are consumed with death.

XVIII. And the Lord said to Aharon : Thou and thy sons, and the house of thy fathers with thee, shall make reconciliation on account of transgressions (against) the sanctuary; and thou and thy sons with thee shall make atonement for the sins of your priesthood. And thy brethren also of the tribe of Levi, the tribe of thy father, bring with thee, and let them be added with thee, to serve thee; but thou and thy sons with thee (shall minister) before the tabernacle of the testimony. And they shall keep thy charge, and the charge of all the tabernacle; but to the vessels of the sanctuary and of the altar they (the Levites) shall not approach, that neither they nor you may die. And they shall be joined with thee, and keep charge of the tabernacle of ordinance for all the service of the tabernacle, and a stranger shall not come near you. And they shall keep charge of the sanctuary and of the altar, that there may be no more wrath upon the sons of Israel. And, behold, I have taken your brethren, the Levites, from among the sons of Israel ; as a gift are they given to you before the Lord, to perform the service of the tabernacle of ordinance. But thou, and thy sons with thee, take charge of your priesthood, for every thing about the altar and within the veil you shall fulfil the service ; the ministry of the priesthood I have given you as a gift, and the stranger who cometh near shall die.

And the Lord said to Aharon : Behold, I have given to thee the charge of My separated things; of all that are consecrated by the sons of Israel unto thee have I given them, and to thy sons, on account of the anoint-

ing, by an everlasting statute. This shall be thine of
the most holy things which remain from the fire, of all
their oblations, and of all their minchas, and of all their
sin offerings, and of all their trespass offerings which
they render before Me; they are most sacred to thee
and to thy sons. In the sanctuary thou mayest eat
thereof, every male may eat it, to thee it shall be consecrated.

And this is thine: the separated things of their
minchas, of all the elevations of the sons of Israel, to thee
have I given them, and to thy sons, and to thy daughters
with thee, by an everlasting statute:[3] every one who is
clean in thy house may eat thereof all the best of the
oil,[4] and all the best of the wine,[5] and the wheat, the
first fruits of them which they present before the Lord,
unto thee I have given them. The first fruits of all that
is on their land which they present before the Lord shall
be thine; every one in thy house who is clean may eat
thereof. Every thing devoted in Israel shall be thine.
Whatever openeth the womb of all flesh which they
offer before the Lord, of man, or of beast, shall be for
thee; but thou shalt surely redeem the firstborn of
man, and the firstling of an unclean animal thou shalt
redeem; and his redemption shall be at the age of one
month; thou shalt redeem with the price of five shekels,
in the shekel of the sanctuary it is ten meahs: but the
firstling of an ox, or of a sheep, or of a goat, thou
mayest not redeem, they are consecrated; thou shalt
sprinkle their blood upon the altar, and burn their fat,
an oblation to be accepted before the Lord. But their
flesh shall be for thee, as the breast of the elevation,
and the right shoulder, they shall be thine. All the

[3] Sam. Vers., "for a perpetual portion."
[4] Sam Vers., "of the new oil."
[5] Sam. Vers., "the dry juice, or the old."

consecrated separations which the sons of Israel set
apart before the Lord, I have given to thee and to thy
children with thee by an everlasting covenant; an everlasting covenant of salt it is before the Lord, with thee,
and thy children with thee.

And the Lord said to Aharon: In their land thou
wilt not have possession, nor will thine be a portion
among them; the gifts that I have given thee, they are
thy portion and thy inheritance among the children of
Israel. And to the sons of Levi, behold, I have given
all the tenths in Israel for a possession, on account of
the service[6] with which they serve in the ministry of
the tabernacle of ordinance. But the children of Israel
must no more come nigh to the tabernacle of ordinance,
to contract guilt and to die. But the Levites shall perform the service of the tabernacle of ordinance, and
shall bear their iniquity; a statute for ever unto your
generations. And among the sons of Israel they shall
not possess an inheritance; for the tenths of the children
of Israel which they set apart before the Lord for a
separation, I have given to the Levites for a possession;
therefore have I said to them, Among the sons of Israel
you shall not possess an inheritance.

And the Lord spake with Mosheh, saying: Speak
also to the Levites, and say to them, When you take
from the sons of Israel the tenths which I have given
you of theirs, you shall set apart from them a separation
before the Lord, a tenth of the tenth. And your separation shall be reckoned to you as the corn from the
threshing-floor, and as the wine of the wine-press, so
shall you set apart the separation before the Lord of all
your tenths that you receive from the sons of Israel,
and give thereof a separation before the Lord unto
Aharon the priest. Of all that is given to you ye shall

---

[6] Sam. Vers, "for the wages of the ministry."

set apart every separation for the Lord, of all the best of it, to be the hallowed portion thereof. And say thou to them, When you have set apart the finest of it, it shall be reckoned to the Levites as the produce of the threshing-floor, and as the fruitage for the wine-press; and you may eat it in every place, you and the men of your house; for it is a remuneration to you on account of your service in the tabernacle of ordinance. And you shall not contract guilt by it in your setting apart the finest of it, nor profane the consecrated things of the children of Israel.

SECTION XXXIX.

HUKKATH.

XIX. And the Lord spake with Mosheh and to Aharon, saying: This is the decree of the law which the Lord hath commanded, saying: Speak to the sons of Israel that they bring to thee a red heifer, unblemished, with no spot in her, and upon which no yoke hath been put. And you shall give her unto Elazar the priest, that he may bring her without the camp, and (one) shall slaughter her before him. And Elazar, the priest, shall take (some) of her blood with his finger, and sprinkle of her blood against the face of the tabernacle of ordinance seven times. And (one) shall burn the heifer before his eyes; her skin, and her flesh, and her blood, with her food shall he burn. And the priest shall take cedar wood, and hyssop, and scarlet, and cast it into the midst of the burning of the heifer. And the priest shall wash his clothes, and bathe his flesh in water, and afterwards come into the camp: but the priest shall be

unclean until the evening. And he who burneth her
shall wash his clothes with water, and bathe his flesh in
water, and be unclean until evening. And a man who
is clean shall gather up the ashes of the heifer, and lay
them up without the camp in a clean place, and it shall
be for the congregation of the children of Israel to keep,
for the sprinkling with water; it is (a purification) for
sin. And he who gathereth up the ashes of the heifer
shall wash his raiment, and be unclean until the evening;
and it shall be for the children of Israel, and for the
strangers who dwell among you, a statute for ever.

Whosoever toucheth the dead of any of mankind
shall be unclean seven days. He shall sprinkle with it
on the third day, and on the seventh day shall be clean ;
but if he sprinkle it not on the third day, on the seventh
day he shall not be clean. Whoever toucheth the dead
body of a man who hath died, and sprinkleth not with
it, defileth the tabernacle of the Lord; and that man
shall be cut off from Israel : because the water of sprinkling is not sprinkled upon him, he shall be unclean, (for)
his uncleanness is yet upon him.

This is the law when a man dieth in a tent : every
one who entereth the tent, and every one who is in the
tent, shall be unclean seven days. And every open
earthen vessel which hath not a covering fastened upon
it round about is unclean. And whoever toucheth one
who is slain with the sword upon the face of the field,
or a dead body, or the bone of a man, or a grave, shall
be unclean seven days. And for the unclean person they
shall take of the ashes of the burnt sin offering, and put
spring water upon it in a vessel. And a man who is
clean shall take hyssop, and dip it in the water, and
sprinkle upon the tent, and upon every vessel, and upon
the persons who are there, and upon him who had
touched the bone, or the slain, or the dead body, or the

grave. And the clean person shall sprinkle the unclean on the third day, and on the seventh day, and on the seventh day he shall be clean; and shall sprinkle his raiment, and wash with water, and at the evening he shall be clean. But the man who is unclean, and it hath not been sprinkled upon him, shall be cut off from the congregation, because he would defile the sanctuary of the Lord. The water of sprinkling was not sprinkled upon him; he is unclean. And it shall be to them for an everlasting statute, that he who appleth the water of sprinkling shall wash his clothes, and whoever toucheth the water of sprinkling shall be unclean until the evening; and whatever may be touched by the unclean person shall be unclean, and the man who toucheth it shall be unclean until the evening.

XX. And the children of Israel, the whole congregation, came to the wilderness of Zin in the first month, and the people abode in Rekem; and Miriam died there, and was buried there.

And there was no water for the congregation; and they gathered against Mosheh and against Aharon, and the people were contentious with Mosheh, and spake, saying, Would that we had died when our brethren died [7] before the Lord! And why have you brought the congregation of the Lord into this wilderness, that we and our cattle may die here? And wherefore have you made us come up from Mizraim, to bring us into this evil place? This is not a place for sowing; here are neither fig trees, nor vines, nor pomegranates, neither is there water to drink.

And Mosheh and Aharon went up from before the congregation unto the door of the tabernacle of ordinance, and fell upon their faces; and the glory of the Lord was revealed to them. And the Lord spake with

_____

[7] Or, "with the death of our brethren"

Mosheh, saying, Take the rod, and gather the congregation together, thou and Aharon thy brother, and speak to the Rock, before their eyes, and it shall give its waters; and thou shalt bring forth water for them from the rock, and give drink to the congregation and their cattle.

And Mosheh took the rod from before the Lord, as He had commanded him. And Mosheh and Aharon assembled the congregation before the rock; and he said to them: Hear now, rebels! Are we to draw forth water for you from this rock? And Mosheh lifted up his hand, and smote the rock with the rod two times; and the waters came forth greatly, and the congregation drank and their cattle.

But the Lord spake unto Mosheh and Aharon: Because you have not believed in My Word to sanctify Me in the eyes of the sons of Israel, therefore you shall not bring this congregation unto the land that I have given them. These are the Waters of Strife,[8] because the sons of Israel strove before the Lord, and He was sanctified in them.

And Mosheh sent ambassadors from Rekem to the king of Edom:[9] Thus saith thy brother Israel, Thou knowest all the trouble we have found; that our fathers went down into Mizraim, and we dwelt in Mizraim many days, and the Mizraee badly treated us and our fathers. And we prayed before the Lord, and He accepted our prayers, and sent an Angel, and brought us out from Mizraim; and, behold, we are in Rekem, a city which is on the side of thy border. Let us now pass through thy country: we will not go through a field or through a vineyard, nor will we drink up the water of the cistern: on the king's highway will we

---

[8] *Matsutha*   Heb., *Meribah*, "contention"   LXX and Vulg., "the water of contradiction."   [9] Sam Vers., "Gabla."

travel ; we will not turn to the right hand or to the left until we have passed through thy border.

But Edomea said to him, Thou shalt not pass through my border, lest I come out against thee with the slaughtering sword. And the sons of Israel said to him, We would go up by the trodden way ; and if we drink of thy water, I and my cattle, we will give thee the price of it ; we will do nothing evil, upon my feet I will pass through. But he said, Thou shalt not pass through. And Edomea came out to meet him with great force and with a strong hand. So Edomea refused to permit Israel to go through his border ; and Israel turned away from him.

And they went forward from Rekem, and all the congregation of the children of Israel came to Mount Hor. And the Lord spake to Mosheh and to Aharon at Mount Hor, by the coast of the land of Edom, saying : Aharon shall be gathered unto his people ; for he shall not enter into the land which I have given to the children of Israel, because you rebelled against My Word at the waters of strife. Take Aharon and Elazar his son, and bring them up to Mount Hor ; and strip Aharon of his vestments, and put them upon Elazar his son ; and Aharon shall be gathered (to his people), and shall die there.

And Mosheh did as the Lord commanded, and they went up to Mount Hor before the eyes of all the congregation. And Mosheh took off his garments from Aharon, and put them upon Elazar his son. And Aharon died there, on the summit of the mount. And Mosheh and Elazar came down from the mount. And all the congregation saw that Aharon was dead ; and all the house of Israel bewailed Aharon thirty days.

XXI And when the Kenaanah, king Arad, who dwelt in the south, heard that Israel was coming by the way of the explorers, he set battle in array against Israel,

and took some of them captives. And Israel vowed a
vow before the Lord, and said: If Thou wilt surely
deliver this people into my hand, then I will destroy
their cities. And the Lord accepted Israel's prayer, and
gave up the Kenaanaah; and he destroyed them and
their cities, and he called the name of the place Charma.[1]

And they journeyed from Mount Hor by the way of
the Sea of Suph, to go round from the land of Edom:
and the soul of the people was wearied in the way. And
the people murmured (or, growled) against the Word
of the Lord, and contended with Mosheh, (saying.)
Why have you brought us up out of Mizraim to die in
the desert? for there is neither bread nor water, and
our soul is weary of manna, this light food. And the
Lord sent forth burning serpents among the people, and
much people of Israel died. And the people came to
Mosheh, and said: We have sinned, for we have murmured before the Lord, and have contended with thee.
Intercede before the Lord, that He may remove the
serpents from among us. And Mosheh prayed for the
people.

And the Lord said to Mosheh: Make thee a burning
(serpent), and uplift it on an ensign; and every one who
hath been bitten, and beholdeth it, shall live (or, be
saved). And Mosheh made a serpent of brass, and set
it upon an ensign; and when a serpent had bitten a
man, if he looked up to the serpent of brass, he lived
(or, was saved).

And the children of Israel journeyed and encamped
in Oboth. And they journeyed from Oboth, and encamped at the Ford[2] of the Passengers, which is in
the wilderness over against Moab, toward the sunrise.
And they removed from thence, and encamped by the

---

[1] Charma, *cherem*, "devoted to destruction."
[2] Peschito, "Fountain."

brook Zared. Thence they journeyed, and pitched on
the other side of Arnon, that is in the wilderness that
stretcheth out from the coasts of the Amoraah; for
Arnon is the border of Moab, between Moab and the
Amoraah. Wherefore it is said in the Book of the
Wars, That which the Lord did by the Sea of Suph, and
the great deeds which (He wrought) by the torrents of
Arnon, and at the flowing of the streams which lead
towards Leehayath, and are joined at the confine of
Moab. And from thence was given to them the well,
which is the well whereof the Lord spake to Mosheh,
Gather the people together, and I will give them water.
Therefore sang Israel this song:—Spring up, O well,
sing ye unto it. The well which the princes digged,
the chiefs of the people cut it, the scribes with their
staves; it was given to them in the wilderness. And
from (the time) that it was given to them it descended
with them to the rivers, and from the rivers it went up
with them to the height,[3] and from the height to the
vale which is in the fields of Moab, at the head of
Ramatha, which looketh towards Bethjeshimon.

And Israel sent messengers to Sihon, king of the
Amoraah, saying: I would pass through thy country ·
I will not turn aside into field or vineyard; we will not
drink of the waters of the cistern; by the king's highway will we go until we have crossed thy border. But
Sihon would not permit Israel to pass through his
coast; and Sihon gathered all his people, and came out
to prevent Israel in the wilderness, and came to Jahaz,
and arrayed battle against Israel. And Israel smote
him with the edge of the sword, and took possession of
his land from Arnon unto Jabbok, unto the Beni
Ammon; for the border of the Beni Ammon was strong.
And Israel subdued all those cities, and Israel dwelt in

---

[3] Or, "to Ramatha." Heb. text, ' Bamoth."

all the cities of the Amoraah, in Heshbon, and in all the
villages thereof.   For Heshbon was the city of Sihon,
king of the Amoraah; he had made war with the
former king of Moab, and had taken all his territory
from his hand unto Arnon.   Therefore, say the proverbs :—Come to Heshbon; let the city of Sihon be
builded and finished : for an east wind strong as fire
hath gone out from Heshbon, and the servants of war
(as) with a flame from the city of Sihon: they have
slain the people who inhabited Lechayath of Moab, the
priests who ministered in the idol-temple in the height
of Arnona.   Woe to you, Moabaee, you are undone, ye
people who have worshipped Kemosh , he hath delivered
up his besieged sons and his daughters into captivity,
unto Sihon, king of the Amoraah.   And the kingdom
hath ceased from Heshbon, the dominion hath passed
away from Dibon, they have laid waste unto Nophak
which joineth Medeba.   And Israel dwelt in the land
of the Amoraah.

And Mosheh sent to explore Jaazer; and they subdued the towns, and drave out the Amoraah who were
therein.   And they turned and went up by the way of
Mathnan; [4] and Og, king of Mathnan, came out to meet
them, he and all his people, to give battle at Edrei.
But the Lord said to Mosheh, Fear him not: for I
have delivered him into thy hand with all his people
and his country ; and thou shalt do to him as thou hast
done to Sihon, the king of the Amoraah who dwelt in
Heshbon.   And they smote him, and his sons, and all
his people, until none remained of him who were
spared ; and they took possession of his land.

XXII. And the sons of Israel moved onward, and
encamped in the plain of Moab (at some space) from
the ford of the Jordan (towards) Jericho.

[4] Sam Vers., Bataun

SECTION XL.

BALAK.

AND Balak bar Zippor saw all that Israel had done to the Amoraah. And the Moabaah feared before the people greatly, because they were many; yea, the Moabaee were in distress before the sons of Israel. And Moab said to the elders of Midian, Now will this host consume all that are round about us, as the ox licketh up the herbage of the field. And Balak bar Zippor was the king of Moab at that time. And he sent messengers to Bileam bar Beor unto Pethor [5] Aram which is upon the Phrat, the land of the sons of his people, to call him, saying: Behold, a people hath come out of Mizraim; lo, they cover the sunshine from the earth, and they are dwelling over against me. Come now, I entreat, curse this people for me, for they are stronger than I. if perhaps I may become able to fight with him, and drive him from the land: for I know that he whom thou blessest is blessed, and he whom thou dost curse is accursed.

And the elders of Moab and of Midian went, with the (price of) divinations in their hands, and came to Bileam, and told him the words of Balak. And he said to them, Lodge here for the night, and I will return you word, according as the Lord speaketh with me. And the princes of Moab tarried with Bileam.

And a word from before the Lord came unto Bileam, and said, Who are these men who are with thee? And Bileam said before the Lord, Balak bar Zippor, king of Moab, hath sent to me. Behold, a people are come out

---

[5] Sam. Vers , " Phasura " Syriac, " Bileam bar Beor, the interpreter ," (*Ph ishura,*) from *pheshar,* " to explain." *Pethar,* in Chaldee, has the same meaning

of Mizraim, and hide the glance of the sun from the earth.......Now come, curse him for me, that I may be able to fight him, and drive him away. And the Lord said to Bileam, Thou shalt not go with them : thou shalt not curse the people, for he is blessed. And Bileam arose in the morning, and said to the princes of Balak, Go back to your country; for it is not pleasing before the Lord to permit me to go with you. And the princes of Moab arose and came to Balak, and said, Bileam refuseth to come with us.

But Balak added to send princes more (in number) and nobler than those. And they came to Bileam, and said to him : Thus saith Balak bar Zippor : Be not, I beseech thee, hindered from coming to me; for I will greatly honour thee with honour, and will do all that thou shalt bid me. Come, then, curse me this people. Bileam responded, and said to the servants of Balak : If Balak would give me his house full of silver and gold, I have no power to transgress the decree of the Word of the Lord my God, to do either little or great. But now I beg you tarry here this night, that I may know what yet the Lord will speak unto me.

And word came from before the Lord unto Bileam by night, and said to him : If the men come to call thee, arise and go with them; nevertheless the word that I speak with thee, that thou shalt do.

And Bileam rose up in the morning, and saddled his ass, and went with the princes of Moab. But the displeasure of the Lord was provoked because he (so) went; [6] and the angel of the Lord stood in the road to withstand him : and he was riding upon his ass, and his two young men with him. And the ass discerned the angel of the Lord standing in the way with his sword drawn in his hand; and the ass started aside from the

---

[6] Or, "that he went of himself," *arey azel hu*, Heb., *ki holek hu*.

road, and went into the field. And Bileam struck the
ass to make her to return into the road. And the
angel of the Lord (again) stood in the way of the vineyards in a place where there was a fence here and a
fence there. And the ass discerned the angel of the
Lord, and thrust herself to the wall, and drave Bileam's
foot against the wall: and he smote her again. And
the angel of the Lord yet passed on, and stood in a
narrow place where there was no way to turn to the
right or to the left. And the ass discerned the angel
of the Lord, and fell down under Bileam ; and Bileam's
wrath was provoked, and he smote the ass with his
staff. And the Lord opened the mouth of the ass; and
she spake to Bileam, What have I done to thee that
thou hast smitten me these three times? And Bileam
said to the ass, Because thou hast mocked me: would
that there was a sword in my hand! for now would I
kill thee. And the ass said to Bileam, Am I not thy
ass, upon whom thou hast ridden from (the time that) I
have been thine unto this day? Have I ever been
used to do thus to thee? And he said, No. And the
Lord unveiled Bileam's eyes, and he saw the angel of
the Lord standing in the road with his sword
unsheathed in his hand · and he bowed, and worshipped
upon his face.

And the angel of the Lord said to him, Wherefore
hast thou smitten thine ass these three times? Behold,
I have come out to withstand thee, because it is seen
before me that thou art willing to go in a way contrary
to me. But the ass discerned me, and turned from
before me these three times : unless she had turned from
before me, now should I have slain thee, and her would
I have spared. And Bileam said to the angel of the
Lord, I knew not that thou wast standing before me in
the way. And now, if it be evil in thine eyes, I will

return. But the angel of the Lord said to Bileam, Go
with the men; only the word that I shall speak with
thee, that thou shalt say.

And Bileam went with the princes of Balak. And
Balak heard that Bileam was coming, and went forth to
meet him, at a city of Moab which is upon the border
of Arnon, on the side of the frontier. And Balak said
to Bileam, Did not I sending send for thee to call
thee? Why didst thou not come to me? Hast thou
not indeed said that I am not able to do thee honour?
And Bileam said to Balak, Behold, I have come to
thee: but even now, have I really any power to speak
anything? The word which the Lord putteth into my
mouth I will speak.

And Bileam went with Balak, and they came to a city
of his territory.[7] And Balak slaughtered oxen and sheep,
and sent to Bileam and to the princes who were with
him. And when it was morning, Balak took Bileam,
and brought him up to the high places of his idol;
and he saw from thence the extreme of the people.

XXIII. And Bileam said to Balak, Build me here
seven altars, and prepare me here seven bullocks and
seven rams. And Balak did as Bileam had spoken, and
Balak and Bileam offered up a bullock and a ram upon
every altar. And Bileam said to Balak, Remain by thy
burnt offering; and I will go, if perhaps the Word may
meet me from before the Lord; and the word that He
showeth me I will disclose unto thee. And he went
solitary.

And the Word from before the Lord[8] met Bileam;
and he said to Him, The seven altars have I set in order,
and have offered a bullock and a ram upon every altar.
And the Lord put a word upon Bileam's mouth, and

---

[7] Sam. text, "unto the city of visions." Sam Vers, "of his mysteries."

[8] Sam text, "the angel of the Lord."

said to him : Return unto Balak, and thus shalt thou
speak.   And he returned to him, and, behold, he was
standing by his burnt sacrifice, he and all the nobles of
Moab.   And he took up his parable, and said :

Balak, king of Moab, hath brought me from Aram,
From the mountains of the east :
Come, curse me, Jakob,
Come, hunt down[9] Israel for me.
How shall I curse whom God hath not cursed ?
How shall I persecute whom God hath not ?
For from the top of the mountain I discern him,
And look upon him from the heights ;
Lo, the people by themselves are to possess the world,
And among the nations they shall not be judged with
    consumption.
Who can number the dust of the house of Jakob,
Of whom it is said, They shall increase as the dust of
    the earth,
Or of one of the four camps of Israel ?
Let mine be the death of his truthful ones,
And let my end be as theirs !

And Balak said to Bileam, What hast thou done to
me ?   I brought thee to curse my enemies, and, behold,
blessing hast thou blessed them.   But he said, That
which the Lord hath put in my mouth must I not
observe to speak ?   And Balak said to him, Come now
with me to another place, from whence thou mayest see
him, where thou canst see only the outer side, but not
the whole, and curse him for me from thence.   And he
brought him to the field of the watch-tower on the top
of the hill ; and builded seven altars, and offered a bullock and a ram on every altar.   And he said to Balak,
Stand here by thy burnt offering, and I will go yonder.

___

[9] Or, "persecute."   The Syriac has, "cause to perish."   Hebrew
text, "execrate."

And the Word from before the Lord met Bileam, and
put a word in his mouth, and said, Return to Balak,
and thus speak.   And he came to him, and he was
standing by his burnt offering, and the nobles of Moab
with him.   And Balak said to him, What hath the Lord
spoken?   And he took up his parable, and said:

Arise, Balak, and hear,
Listen to my words, Bar Zippor:
The word of Eloha is not as the words of men;
The sons of men speak, but he;
Nor is it as the works of the children of flesh,
Who decree to do, but repent, and change their
counsels.
What He hath said He will perform,
And His every word is steadfast.
Behold, I have received benedictions to bless Israel,
And I may not turn my blessing from him.
I have seen that in the house of Jakob
The worshippers of idols are not,
Nor in Israel the workers of the work of lies.
The Word of the Lord their God is their helper,
And the Shekinah of their King is among them.
God, who brought them out from Mizraim,
Becomes his strength and exaltation.
For no divinations can prosper against the house of
Jakob,
Nor enchantments against the myriads of Israel.
According to the time it shall be said of Jakob and of
Israel,
What hath Eloah wrought!
Behold, the people shall dwell as a lioness,
And as a lion shall he lift himself up;
Until he hath slain with slaughter,
He will not rest in his land,
And inherit the treasures of the nations.

And Balak said to Bileam, Neither cursing curse
them, nor blessing bless them. But Bileam answered
and said to Balak, Did I not tell thee, saying, All that
the Lord speaketh, that I must do? And Balak said
to Bileam, Come now, I will take thee to another place;
perhaps it may be pleasing before the Lord, that thou
mayest curse them for me from thence. And Balak
conducted Bileam to the top of the high place that
looketh toward the face of Beth Jeshimon. And Bileam
said to Balak, Build me here seven altars, and prepare
me here seven bullocks and seven rams. And Balak
did as Bileam had said, and offered a bullock and a ram
on every altar.

XXIV. And Bileam saw that it was appointed before
the Lord to bless Israel; and he went not as at those
former times to inquire by divinations, but set his face
towards the calf that the sons of Israel had made in the
wilderness. And Bileam lifted up his eyes, and beheld
Israel dwelling by his tribes; and the Spirit of prophecy rested upon him from before the Lord. And he
took up his parable, and said:

Bileam, the son of Beor, hath said,

The man who saw the Beautiful[1] hath said,

He hath said who heard the Word from before God,

Who saw the vision of the Almighty, prostrate when
   he saw:

How goodly is thy land, O Jakob,

And the house of thy habitation, O Israel!

As rivers flowing onward; as the watered garden by
   Euphrates,

As aromatics planted by the Lord; as cedars planted
   by the waters.

The king anointed from his sons shall increase,

And have dominion over many nations;

----

[1] Or, ' who saw fairly, or clearly "

His king shall be mightier than Agag, and his kingdom be exalted.

God, who brought them from Mizraim, is mighty and
high, and by Him

Shall Israel use the wealth of the nations their foes,

Enjoy the spoils of their kings, and inherit their lands.

He reposed in his strength, as the lion and the
lioness,

And no kingdom may commove him.

They who bless thee shall be blessed,

And they who curse thee be accursed.

And the anger of Balak was roused against Bileam,
and he smote his hands together. And Balak said to
Bileam, I called thee to curse my enemies, and, behold,
blessing hast thou blessed them these three times !
And now go to thy place. I said, Honouring I would
honour thee ; but, behold, the Lord hath kept thee back
from honour. But Bileam said to Balak, Did I not
also tell the messengers whom thou sentest to me, saying, If Balak would give me his house full of silver and
gold, I have no power to transgress the decree of the
Word of the Lord, to do good or evil of my own will ;
whatsoever the Lord shall say, that will I speak ? And
now, behold, I go unto my people. Come, I will give
thee counsel what thou shouldst do ; and will show thee
what this people will do unto thy people at the end of
the days. And he took up his parable, and said :

Bileam, the son of Beor, speaketh,

The man who saw the Beautiful speaketh,

He speaks who heard the Word from before God,

And who knoweth knowledge from the Most High,

Who saw the vision of the Almighty, prostrate when
he saw.

I see him, but not now ; I behold him, but not nigh.

When a king shall arise out of Jakob,

And the Meshiha be anointed from Israel,
    He will slay the princes of Moab, and reign over all
        the children of men ;
    And Edom shall be an inheritance,
    And Seir a possession of his adversaries ;
    But Israel shall prosper in riches.
    One will descend from the house of Jakob,
    Who will destroy him that escapeth from the city of
        the peoples.

And he looked on the Amalkaah, and took up his
parable, and said :

    Amalek was the beginning of the wars of Israel,
    But in his end he shall perish for ever.

And he beheld the Shalmaah, and took up his parable,
and said ·

    Strong is the house of thy dwelling,
    And in a strong fortress thou hast set thy abode ;
    But yet Shalmaah shall be destroyed,
    For Athuria will make thee captive.

And he took up his parable, and said :

    Woe to the wicked who may live when God doeth this !
    And ships will come from the Kittace.[2]
    And afflict Athur, and subdue beyond the Phrat ;
    But they also shall perish for ever.

And Bileam arose, and went and returned to his place ;
and Balak also went upon his way.

XXV. But Israel abode in Shittin ; and the people
began to commit whoredom with the daughters of Moab ;
and they invited the people to the sacrifices of their
idols, and the people did eat and bowed down to their
idols.   And Israel was joined unto Baala Pheor, and
the anger of the Lord was kindled against Israel.   And
the Lord said unto Mosheh : Take all the chiefs of the

---

[2] Syriac   " And the legions shall come forth from the land of the
Kittoyee "   See the Palestinian Targum

people, and judge, and slay him who is guilty of death
before the Lord, over against the sun, that the fierce
anger of the Lord may be turned away from Israel.
And Mosheh said to the judges of Israel : Slay every
man his men who have joined themselves to Baala
Pheor.

And, behold, a man of the sons of Israel came and
brought to his brethren a Midianitha, in the eyes of
Mosheh, and in the eyes of all the congregation of the
children of Israel, who were weeping at the door of the
tabernacle of ordinance. And Phinehas bar Elazar bar
Aharon the priest saw, and arose from the midst of the
congregation, and took a lance in his hand; and he
went in after the man, the son of Israel, into the tent, and
thrust both of them through, the man, the son of Israel,
and the woman, through her belly ; and the pestilence was
stayed from the children of Israel. But they who had
died by the pestilence were twenty and four thousand.

SECTION XLI.

PHINEHAS.

AND the Lord spake with Mosheh, saying : Phinehas
the son of Elazar, the son of Aharon, the priest, hath
turned away My anger from the children of Israel, in
that he was zealous with My zeal among them; and I
have not consumed the children of Israel in My jealousy.
Say therefore to him (that), behold, I decree unto him
My covenant of peace; and he shall have it and his
sons after him ; a covenant of priesthood for ever,
because he hath been zealous before his God, and hath
propitiated for the children of Israel.

And the name of the man of Israel who was slain with the Midianitess was Zimri bar Salu, a chief of the house of his fathers of the house of Shemeon; and the name of the woman, the Midianitess, was Kosbé, the daughter of Zur, who was chief of the people of his father's house in Midian.

And the Lord spake with Mosheh, saying · Punish the Midianites and slay them, for they afflict you with their snares, with which they ensnare you; as by the occasion of Pheor, and by that of Kosbé, daughter of a prince of Midian, their sister, who was slain on the day of the pestilence in the matter of Pheor.

XXVI. And it came to pass after the plague, that the Lord spake to Mosheh and to Elazar bar Aharon the priest, saying : Take the account of all the congregation of the sons of Israel, from a son of twenty years and upwards by the house of their fathers, every one that goeth out with the host in Israel. And Mosheh and Elazar the priest spake with them, and directed to number them in the plains of Moab, by the Jordan (over against) Jericho, saying: From a son of twenty years and upward, as the Lord commanded Mosheh, and the sons of Israel who went forth from the land of Mizraim.

Reuben, the first-born of Israel : the sons of Reuben, Hanok, the family of Hanok; Phallu, and the family of Phallu; of Hezron, the family of Hezron; of Karmi, the family of Karmi. These are the families of Reuben, and they who were numbered of them were forty-three thousand seven hundred and thirty. And of the sons of Phallu, Eliab; and the sons of Eliab, Nemuel, and Dathan, and Abiram: these are Dathan and Abiram who called the congregation that gathered against Mosheh and Aharon in the congregation of Korach, in their gathering against the Lord, when the earth opened

her mouth and swallowed them with Korach, and the
congregation died, being devoured by the fire, two
hundred and fifty men; and they became a sign; but
the sons of Korach died not.

The sons of Shimeon by their families: of Nemuel,
the family of Nemuel; of Jamin, the family of Jamin;
of Zerach, the family of Zerach; of Shaul, the family of
Shaul. These are the families of Shemeon, twenty-two
thousand two hundred. The sons of Gad after their
families, of Zephon, the family of Zephon; of Haggi,
the family of Haggi; of Shumi, the family of Shumi;
of Aggi, the family of Aggi; of Ozni, the family of
Ozni; of Heri, the family of Heri; of Arod, the family
of the Arodi; of Areli, the family of Areli. These are the
families of the Beni Gad, the number of whom was forty
thousand five hundred.

Of the sons of Jehudah, Her and Onan: but Her
and Onan died in the land of Kenaan; of the sons of
Jehudah after their families: of Shelah, the family of
Shelah; of Pherez, the family of Pherez; of Zerach, the
family of Zerach. Of the sons of Pherez: of Hezron, the
family of Hezron; of Hamul, the family of Hamul.
These are the families of Jehudah; the number of them
seventy-six thousand five hundred.

The sons of Issakar by their families: Tola, the family
of Tola; of Phua, the family of the Phum; of Jasub,
the family of Jasub; of Shimron, the family of Shimron.
These are the families of Issakar; their number sixty-
four thousand three hundred.

The sons of Zebulon by their families: of Sared, the
family of Sared; of Elon, the family of Elon; of
Jahleel, the family of Jahleel. These are the families of
Zebulon, by their number sixty thousand five hundred.

The sons of Joseph by their families, Menasheh and
Ephraim, the sons of Menasheh: of Makir, the family of

P

Makir; and Makir begat Gilead; of Gilead, the family of Gilead. These are the children of Gilead : of Jezar, the family of Jezar; of Helck, the family of Helek ; and of Asriel, the family of Asrieli; and of Shekem, the family of Shekem ; and of Shemida, the family of She-mida ; and of Hepher, the family of Hepher. And Zelophechad [2] bar Hepher had no sons, but daughters ; and the names of the daughters of Zelophechad were Mahelah, and Nohah, Hegelah, Milchah, and Thirzah. These are the families of Menasheh, and their number fifty-two thousand seven hundred.

These are the sons of Ephraim by their families : of Shuthelah, the family of Shuthelah ; of Bekir, the family of Bekir; of Tachan, the family of Tachan. And these are the sons of Shuthelah : of Heran, the family of Heran. These are the families of the Beni-Ephraim, the number of whom was thirty-two thousand five hundred. These are the sons of Joseph by their families.

The sons of Benjamin by their families : of Bela, the family of Bela; of Ashbal, the family of Ashbal; of Ahiram, the family of Ahiram ; of Shefuphim, the family of Shefuphim ; of Hupham, the family of Hupham. And the sons of Bela, Arede and Naaman ; the family of the Aredi; and of Naaman, the family of Naaman. These are the sons of Benjamin after their families, and their number forty-five thousand six hundred.

These are the children of Dan, after their families : of Shuham, the families of Shuham. These are the families of Dan after their families, and the number of the families of Shuham sixty-four thousand four hundred.

The sons of Asher, after their families : of Jimna, the families of Jimna ; of Jeshvi, the families of Jeshvi ; of Beriah, the family of Beriah. Of the sons of Beriah : of Heber, the family of Heber ; of Malkiel, the family

[2] Or, Zelophchad.

of Malkiel. But the name of the daughter of Asher was Sarach. These are the families of the Beni Asher, by their number fifty-three thousand four hundred.

The sons of Naphtali, after their families: of Jahziel, the families of Jahziel; of Gunni, the families of Gunni; of Jezer, the family of Jezer; of Shelem, the family of Shelem. These are the families of Naphtali by their families, and their number forty-five thousand four hundred.

These were the numbered of the sons of Israel, six hundred and one thousand seven hundred and thirty.

And the Lord spake with Mosheh, saying: Unto these thou shalt divide the land for a possession, according to the number of their names. To the many thou shalt make large their possession, and to the few thou shalt make their possession small; to each according to his number shalt thou give his inheritance. Nevertheless the land shall be divided by lot, according to the names of the tribes of their fathers they shall inherit. By the lot shall their inheritance be divided among the many and the few.

And these are the sons of Levi, after their families: of Gershon, the families of Gershon; of Kehath, the family of Kehath, of Merari, the families of Merari. These are the families of Levi: the family of Libni, the family of Hebron, the family of Machli, the family of Mushi, the family of Korach. And Kehath begat Amram. And the name of Amram's wife was Jokebed, a daughter of Levi, who was born to Levi, in Mizraim; and she bare unto Amram Aharon, and Mosheh, and Miriam their sister. And unto Aharon were born Nadab and Abihu, Elazar and Ithamar. But Nadab and Abihu died in their offering strange fire before the Lord. And the numbered of them were twenty-three thousand of all the males from a month old and upwards: for they were

not numbered among the children of Israel, because no
possession was given to them among the children of Israel.

These (are they whom) Mosheh and Elazar the priest
numbered of the sons of Israel, in the plains of Moab,
by Jordan, (over against) Jericho. But among these
there was not a man of them whom Mosheh and Aharon
the priest numbered when they counted the children of
Israel in the wilderness of Sinai. For the Lord had
said to them that dying they should die in the wilderness; and not a man of them remained, except Kaleb
bar Jephuneh and Jehoshua bar Nun.

XXVII. And the daughters of Zelophechad bar
Hepher, bar Gilead, bar Makir, bar Menasheh, of the
families of Menasheh, bar Joseph,—and these are the
names of his daughters, Mahelah, Nohah, and Hegelah, and
Milchah, and Thirzah,—came and stood before Mosheh
and Elazar the priest, and before the princes, and all the
congregation, at the door of the tabernacle of ordinance,
saying Our father died in the wilderness; but he was
not among the company which gathered against the
Lord in the congregation of Korach, but died through
his (own) sin; and he had no sons. Why should the
name of our father be taken away from among his
kindred, because he had no son? Give us an inheritance among the brethren of our father.

And Mosheh brought their cause before the Lord.
And the Lord spake with Mosheh, saying: The daughters
of Zelophechad have spoken properly. Give thou to them
the possession of an inheritance among the brethren of
their father, and transfer to them their father's inheritance. And speak with the children of Israel, saying:
If a man die, having no son, you shall make over his
inheritance to his daughter; and if he have no daughter,
you shall give his inheritance to his brethren; but if
he have no brothers, you shall give his inheritance to

the brethren of his father; and if his father have no
brothers, then shall you give his inheritance to his
relative who is next (of kin) to him of his family, and
he shall inherit it.   And this shall be to the children of
Israel for a decree of judgment, as the Lord hath commanded Mosheh.

And the Lord said unto Mosheh, Go up to this
mountain of the Abaraee, and see the land which I have
given to the children of Israel; and thou shalt see it,
and be gathered to thy people, thou also, as Aharon
thy brother was gathered.   As ye rebelled against My
Word in the desert of Zin, in the strife of the congregation, to sanctify Me at the waters before their eyes:
these are the waters of strife, at Rekem, in the desert of
Zin.

And Mosheh spake before the Lord, saying · Let the
Lord, the God of the spirits of all flesh, appoint a man
over the congregation who may go out and go in before
them, and may lead them out and bring them in, that
this congregation may not be as a flock which hath no
shepherd.   And the Lord said to Mosheh, Take to thee
Jehoshua bar Nun, a man in whom is the spirit of prophecy, and lay thy hand upon him.   And make him
stand before Elazar the priest, and before all the congregation, and give him charge in their sight.   And thou
shalt confer some of thy honour upon him, that all the
congregation of the children of Israel may obey him.
And he shall stand before Elazar the priest, that he may
ask (counsel) for him by the judgment of Uraia before
the Lord   upon his word shall they go out, and upon his
word shall they come in, he and all the sons of Israel
with him, even all the congregation.

And Mosheh did as the Lord commanded him, and
took Jehoshua, and made him to stand before Elazar the
priest, and all the congregation; and he laid his hands

upon him, and gave him charge, as the Lord spake by
Mosheh.

XXVIII. And the Lord spake with Mosheh, saying :
Instruct the children of Israel, and say to them : My
oblation, the ordained bread for My oblations to be
received with acceptance, shall you observe to offer in
its time. And thou shalt say to them : This is the
oblation which you shall offer before the Lord ; two
lambs of the year unblemished daily, for a perpetual
burnt offering. The one lamb shalt thou perform in the
morning, and the second lamb between the suns. And
with one tenth of three seahs of flour for the mincha
sprinkled with the fourth of a hin of beaten oil. It is
a perpetual burnt offering, which was made in the
mountain of Sinai, to be received with acceptance (as)
an oblation before the Lord. And its libation shall be
the fourth of a hin for each lamb ; in the sanctuary
shall the libation of old wine be poured out before the
Lord. And the second lamb shalt thou perform between
the suns, as the morning offering ; and thou shalt make
its libation (in like manner) an oblation to be received
with acceptance before the Lord.

But on the Sabbath day two lambs of the year unblemished, and two tenths of flour for the mincha
sprinkled with oil, and its libation. It is the Sabbath
burnt offering which shall be performed on the Sabbath,
together with the perpetual burnt offering and its
libation.

And in the beginnings of your months you shall offer
a burnt offering before the Lord ; two young bullocks,
and one ram, lambs of the year, seven, unblemished.
And three tenths of flour sprinkled with oil for each
bullock, and two tenths of flour for a mincha sprinkled
with oil for the one ram, and a tenth of flour for a
mincha sprinkled with oil for each lamb : it is a burnt

offering to be received with acceptance as an oblation
before the Lord. And their libations a half hina of
wine shall be for the bullock, and the third of a hina
for the ram, and a quarter of a hina for a lamb: this is
the burnt offering for the beginning of the month, at its
renewal; so shall it be for all the beginnings of the
months of the year. And one kid of the goats for a
sin offering before the Lord, beside the perpetual burnt
offering, shalt thou make with its libation.

And in the first month, on the fourteenth day of the
month, is the Pascha before the Lord. And on the
fifteenth day of this month is the feast: seven days you
shall eat unleavened (bread). On the first day shall be
a holy convocation; you shall not do any servile work;
but offer the oblation of a burnt offering before the
Lord; two young bullocks and one ram, and seven
lambs of the year without blemish shall you have; and
their mincha of flour mingled with oil, three tenths for
the bullock and two tenths for the ram you shall make:
a tenth shall you make for one lamb, so for the seven
lambs. And one goat for a sin offering to make atonement for you; besides the burnt sacrifice of the morning
which is the perpetual burnt sacrifice, you shall make
these. After the manner of these you shall do by the
day for seven days; it is the bread of the oblation
to be received with acceptance before the Lord; (with)
the perpetual burnt offering and its libation shall it be
made. And on the seventh day there shall be a holy
convocation, (when) you may do no servile work.

But on the day of the First Fruits, when you bring the
new thank offering before the Lord in your expletion,[3]
there shall be a holy convocation; no servile work

---

[3] *Beatsrathekun.* Qu., "When your time of threshing and wine-
making is out." Heb. text, *Beshabuothekem*, rendered by Mendelssohn, " *Wenn eure Wochen zu ende sind.*"

shall you do, but offer a burnt offering to be received
with favour before the Lord; two young bullocks, one
ram, seven lambs of the year; and their mincha of flour
mingled with oil, three tenths for one bullock, two tenths
for the ram, a tenth for each lamb of the seven lambs;
one kid of the goats to make an atonement for you;
beside the perpetual burnt sacrifice and its mincha you
shall (make) them unblemished, and their libations.

XXIX. And in the seventh month, on the first of the
month, you shall have a holy convocation, and do no
servile work; it shall be a day of the sounding of the
trumpet to you.   And you shall make a burnt sacrifice
to be received with favour before the Lord: one young
bullock, one ram, lambs of the year seven, unblemished,
and their mincha of flour mingled with oil, three tenths
for the bullock, two tenths for the ram, and one tenth
for each of the seven lambs; and one kid of the goats
for a sin offering to make an atonement for you; beside
the offering of the month, and its mincha, and the perpetual sacrifice and its mincha, and their libations, as
proper for them, to be received with favour, an oblation
before the Lord.

And on the tenth of this seventh month you shall
have a holy convocation, and afflict your souls; [4] you
shall do no labour, but offer a burnt offering before the
Lord to be received with favour: one young bullock,
one ram, lambs of the year seven, unblemished shall you
have; and their mincha of flour mingled with oil; three
tenths for the bullock, two tenths for the ram, and a
single tenth for each of the seven lambs; one kid of the
goats for a sin offering, beside the sin offering of the
expiations,[5] and the perpetual sacrifice, its mincha and
their libations.

And on the fifteenth day of the seventh month you

---

* Sam Vers, " You shall fast."   5 This being the day of atonement

shall have a holy convocation; no servile labour shall you do, but celebrate a festival before the Lord seven days; and offer a burnt sacrifice, an oblation to be received with favour before the Lord; thirteen young bullocks, two rams, lambs of the year fourteen, unblemished shall they be; and their mincha of flour mingled with oil, three tenths to one bullock for the thirteen bullocks, two tenths for each ram, and one tenth for each of the fourteen lambs, and one kid of the goats for a sin offering, beside the perpetual sacrifice, its mincha and libation.

And on the second day you shall offer twelve young bullocks, two rams, fourteen unblemished lambs of the year, and the minchas and libations for the bullocks, for the rams and the lambs, as is proper for their number; and one kid of the goats, a sin offering, beside the perpetual sacrifice, its mincha and libation.

And on the third day eleven bullocks, two rams, fourteen unblemished lambs of the year; and their minchas and libations for the bullocks, the rams, and the lambs, as befitteth their number; and one kid for a sin offering, beside the perpetual sacrifice, its mincha and libation.

On the fourth day ten bullocks, two rams, lambs of the year unblemished fourteen; their minchas and libations for the bullocks, rams, and lambs by their number, as it is proper; and one kid of the goats for a sin offering, beside the perpetual sacrifice, its mincha and libation.

And on the fifth day nine bullocks, two rams, lambs of the year unblemished fourteen; the minchas and libations for the bullocks, rams, and lambs after their number, as it is proper; and one kid for a sin offering, beside the perpetual sacrifice and its libation.

And on the sixth day eight bullocks, two rams, lambs of the year unblemished fourteen; the minchas and libations for the bullocks, rams, and lambs by their number, as is proper; and one kid for the sin offering, beside the perpetual sacrifice, its mincha and libation.

And on the seventh day seven bullocks, two rams, fourteen lambs of the year unblemished; the minchas and libations for the bullocks, rams, and lambs by their number, as is proper; and one kid for the sin offering, beside the perpetual sacrifice, its mincha and libation.

On the eighth day you shall have an assembly; no servile work shall you do, but offer a sacrifice, an oblation to be received with favour before the Lord; one bullock, one ram, seven lambs of the year unblemished; the minchas and libations for the bullock, the ram, and the lambs, as proper, according to their number; and one kid for a sin offering, beside the perpetual sacrifice, its mincha and libation.

These shall you offer before the Lord in your solemnities, beside your vows and your free-will offerings with your burnt sacrifices, their minchas and their libations, and with your sanctified victims. XXX. And Mosheh spake to the sons of Israel according to all that the Lord commanded Mosheh.

SECTION XLII.

MATTOTH.

AND Mosheh spake with the heads of the tribes of the Beni Israel, saying : This is the word which the Lord hath commanded : When a man shall make a vow before the Lord, or swear an oath to bind a bond upon his soul, he shall not make void his word; according to all

that hath come out of his mouth he shall perform. And
if a woman make a vow before the Lord, and bind (herself) with a bond in her father's house, (being) in her
youth, and her father shall hear her vow, and the obli-
gation·she hath bound upon her soul, and her father be
silent to her, then all her vows shall stand, and every
bond that she hath bound upon her soul shall be confirmed. But if her father prohibit (or undo) them on
the day that he heareth, all the vows and the bonds
that she hath bound upon her soul shall not stand, and
she shall be forgiven before the Lord, because her father
undid them. And if she hath a husband, and taketh a
vow upon her, or if her lips pronounce that which becometh binding upon her soul, and her husband heard and
was silent to her on the day that he heard, her vows shall
stand, and the obligation she hath bound upon her soul
be confirmed: but if her husband on the day that he
heareth shall prohibit them, the vows which are on her
and the utterance of her lips which became binding
on her soul shall be void, and be forgiven her before the
Lord.

But every vow of the widow, or of one divorced,
which she hath bound upon her soul, shall be confirmed
upon her. And if (while in her husband's house) she
had vowed, or had bound aught upon her soul with an
oath, and her husband heard and was silent to her, and
did not prohibit them, all her vows shall be confirmed,
every bond with which she hath bound her soul shall
be confirmed. But if indeed her husband shall make
them void in the day that he heard, that which her lips
expressed in her vow and in the binding of her soul shall
not be confirmed; her husband hath made them void,
and she shall be absolved before the Lord. Every vow
and every covenant (oath) to chastise the soul, her husband may confirm it, or her husband may make it void.

But if her husband was entirely silent to her from day
to day, then he hath confirmed all her vows, or whatever bonds (she taketh) upon her, he confirmeth them,
because he was silent to her on the day that he heard.
But if he shall indeed make them void after (the day
that) he had heard, then he shall bear her sin.   These
are the statutes which the Lord commanded Mosheh
between a man and his wife, (and) between a father and
his daughter, in her youth in her father's house.

XXXI. And the Lord spake with Mosheh, saying:
Avenge the children of Israel of the Midianites; afterward thou shalt be gathered to thy people.   And
Mosheh spake with the people, saying: Arm, of you,
men for the host against Midian, to avenge this people
of the Lord upon Midian: a thousand of a tribe, a
thousand of a tribe, of all the tribes of Israel shall you
send to the host.

And from the thousands of Israel there were chosen
a thousand of a tribe, twelve thousand armed for the
host.   And Mosheh sent them one thousand of a tribe
to array them, and Phinehas bar Elazar the priest, with
the host, and the holy vessels, and the Jubela trumpets
in his hand.   And the host gathered against Midian, as
the Lord had commanded Mosheh; and they slaughtered
every male.   But the kings of Midian they killed with
their slain, Evi, and Rekem, and Zur, and Chur, and
Reba, five kings of Midian, and Bileam bar Beor, they
killed with the sword.   And the sons of Israel took the
women of Midian captives, with their children and all
their cattle, and all their flocks and all their goods they
despoiled.   And all their cities where they dwelt, and
their houses of worship, they burned with fire.   And
they took all the spoil, and all the prey of man and of
cattle, and brought the captives, and the prey, and the
spoil, to Mosheh, and to Elazar the priest, and to all the

congregation of the Beni Israel, to the camp in the
fields of Moab, by the Jordan, over against Jericho.

And Mosheh and Elazar the priest and all the princes
of the congregation went out to meet them, without the
camp.   But Mosheh was angry with those who had
been appointed over the host, the captains of thousands
and the captains of hundreds, who came from the battle.
And Mosheh said to them, Have you spared every
woman?   Behold, these it was (who caused) the sons of
Israel, through the counsel of Bileam, to do wickedly
before the Lord in the matter of Peor, and the plague
came upon the congregation of the Lord.   But now,
slay every male among the children, and every woman
who hath known a man you shall slay.   But all the
females who have not known a man ye may preserve
alive unto you.   And you, abide without the camp seven
days; whoever have destroyed life or touched the dead,
sprinkle yourselves on the third day, and on the seventh
day yourselves and your captives.   And every garment,
and whatever is made of skin, and every work of goat's
hair, and every vessel of wood you shall sprinkle.

And Elazar the priest said to the men of war who
came from the battle, This is the decree of the law which
the Lord hath commanded Mosheh: Only the gold, and
the silver, the brass, iron, tin, and lead, everything that
can abide in the fire, you shall make to go through fire,
and it shall be clean; nevertheless it shall be sprinkled
with the water of sprinkling; and whatever may not
abide the fire you shall make to pass through water.
And cleanse your garments on the seventh day; purify
yourselves, and afterwards come into the camp.

And the Lord spake with Mosheh, saying: Take the
account of the spoil of the captives, man and beast;
thou, Elazar the priest, and the chief fathers of the
congregation.   And divide the spoil among the men

who fought the battle, who went forth in the host, and
among all the congregation : and separate a portion
before the Lord from (that of) the men who fought the
battle, who went forth in the host, one living thing in
five hundred, of man and beast, oxen, asses, and sheep.
Take it of their half, and give it to Elazar the priest,
for a separation before the Lord. And of the half (belonging) to the children of Israel, take one of every fifty,
of man, of oxen, sheep, and all cattle, and give them to
the Levites who keep charge of the tabernacle of the
Lord.

And Mosheh and Elazar the priest did as the Lord
commanded Mosheh ; and the booty, the rest of the prey
which the people who went forth to the war had taken,
was, sheep six hundred and seventy-five thousand, oxen
seventy-two thousand, asses sixty-one thousand, persons,
women who had not known man, every soul thirty-two
thousand. And the half portion of the men who had
gone out to the war, the number was, sheep three hundred and thirty-seven thousand five hundred ; and that
which was brought up before the Lord, of the sheep
six hundred and seventy-five ; and of the thirty-six
thousand oxen, the portion brought before the Lord
seventy-two. And the asses, thirty thousand five hundred, of which the portion brought before the Lord
sixty-one. And the persons sixteen thousand, those of
them brought before the Lord thirty-two persons. And
Mosheh gave the separation brought up before the Lord
to Elazar the priest, as the Lord had commanded
Mosheh. And of the children of Israel's half, which
Mosheh divided from (that) of the men who had gone
out in the host,—and the half part for the congregation
was, sheep three hundred and thirty-seven thousand
five hundred, oxen thirty-six thousand, and asses thirty
thousand five hundred, and persons sixteen thousand :

and Mosheh took from the children of Israel's half one portion of fifty of man and beast, and gave them to the Levites who kept charge of the Lord's tabernacle, as the Lord had commanded Mosheh.

And they who had been appointed over the thousands of the host, the captains of thousands, and the captains of hundreds, came to Mosheh, and said to Mosheh, Thy servants have taken the account of the men who went forth to the war with us, and there is not wanting one man of us. And we bring an oblation before the Lord of what each man hath found, vessels of gold, chains, bracelets, rings, amulets, and brooches, to make atonement for our souls before the Lord. And Mosheh and Elazar the priest took the gold of them, every fabricated vessel. And all the gold of the separation which the captains of thousands and of hundreds separated before the Lord was sixteen thousand seven hundred and fifty shekels; for the men of the host had taken spoil, every man for himself. And Mosheh and Elazar the priest took the gold from the captains of thousands and of hundreds, and brought it into the tabernacle of ordinance, a memorial of the sons of Israel before the Lord.

XXXII. Now the sons of Reuben and the sons of Gad possessed much cattle, exceedingly many; and they saw the land of Jazer and the land of Gilead, and, behold, the region was a place fit for folds of cattle. And the sons of Gad and the sons of Reuben came and spake to Mosheh and to Elazar the priest, and to the heads of the congregation, saying: Maklelta and Malbasta and the Priests of Beth-Nemrin,[6] and Beth-Heshbena, and Baale Debaba, and Seath, (the sepulchre of Mosheh,)[7] and Beon, the land which the Lord smote before the congregation of Israel, is a country fitted for

---

[6] *Kumerin de beth Nimrin*
[7] *Seath beth keburta de Mosheh.*

cattle folds, and thy servants have cattle. And they said, If we have found grace in thine eyes, let this land be given to thy servants for a possession, and let us not go over the Jordan.

But Mosheh said to the sons of Gad and to the sons of Reuben, Shall your brethren go in to fight, and you sit down here? And why turn you away the heart[8] of the sons of Israel from going over to the land which the Lord hath given to them? Thus did your fathers when I sent them from Rekem Giah to survey the land. They went up to the stream of Ethkela, and saw the land, and subverted[9] the heart of the sons of Israel, that they might not go in unto the land that the Lord had given to them; and the Lord's anger was kindled that day, and He sware, saying: If the men who have come out of Mizraim, from twenty years old and upward, shall see the land which I covenanted to Abraham, to Izhak, and to Jakob; for they have not been wholly after my fear. Only Kaleb bar Jephunneh, the Kenezite, and Jehoshua bar Nun, for they have been wholly after the fear of the Lord. And the Lord's anger was strong against Israel, and he made them linger in the wilderness forty years, until all the generation that did wickedly before the Lord had been consumed. And, behold, you have risen up after your fathers, the disciples of the men of sin, to add yet to the fierce displeasure of the Lord against Israel. For if you turn again from (following) after His service, He will yet make you remain in the wilderness, and you will destroy all this people.

And they came near to him, and said: We will build here sheepfolds for our cattle and cities for our families, and we will go forth eagerly, armed, before the sons of Israel, to bring them into their place; and our families

---

[8] Syr., "break."   Sam Vers, "bring down the heart"
[9] Syr. "broke"

shall abide in cities defenced against the inhabitants of
the land: nor will we return to our homes till the sons
of Israel shall possess every man his inheritance. For
we will not inherit with them over the Jordan and
beyond; for we receive our possession on the eastward
side of the Jordan.

And Mosheh said to them: If you will do this; if
you will go armed before the people of the Lord to war,
and (a host) of you all armed will pass the Jordan
before the people of the Lord, until He shall have
driven out the enemy before Him, and the land have
been subdued before the Lord's people, then afterward
you shall return, and be guiltless before the Lord and
with Israel, and this land shall be to you for an inheritance before the Lord. But if you do it not, behold,
you have sinned before the Lord; and know, that your
sin will find you. Build you cities for your families,
and folds for your sheep, and do that which hath come
from your mouth. And the tribe of the Beni Gad and
of the Beni Reuben spake to Mosheh, saying: Thy
servants will do as my lord commandeth. Our little
ones, our wives, our flocks, and all our cattle shall be
here in the cities of Gilead; but thy servants, a host all
armed, will pass over before the people of the Lord to
war, as our lord speaketh.

And Mosheh commanded concerning them Elazar
the priest, and Jehoshua bar Nun, and the chief fathers
of the tribes of the Beni Israel. And Mosheh said to
them, If the sons of Gad and of Reuben pass over the
Jordan with you, all armed for war, before the Lord's
people, and the land be subdued before you, then shall
you give them the land of Gilead for a possession. But
if they go not over armed with you, they shall inherit
among you in the land of Kenaan. But the sons of
Gad and of Reuben answered, saying: As the Lord

hath spoken to thy servants, so will we do. We will
pass over armed before the people of the Lord into the
land of Kenaan, that the possession of our inheritance
may be on the other side Jordan.   And Mosheh gave
to them, to the sons of Gad, and to the sons of Reuben,
and to the half tribe of Menasheh bar Joseph, the kingdom of Sihon king of the Amoraah, and the kingdom
of Og the king of Mathanan,[1] the land with the cities
thereof in the coasts, (even) the cities of the country
round about.

And the sons of Gad built Dibon, and Ataroth, and
Aroer, and Ataroth Shophan, and Jazer, and Jag-
beha, and Beth-nimra, and Beth-haran, fenced cities and
sheepfolds.   And the sons of Reuben built Heshbon, and
Elhala, and Kirjathaim, and Nebo,[2] and Baal Meon,
changing their names, and Sibama ; and they called by
their names the names of the cities which they built.

And the sons of Makir bar Menasheh went unto Gilead,
and subdued it, and cast out the Amoraah who were in
it.   And Mosheh gave Gilead to Makir bar Menasheh,
and he dwelt therein.   And Jair bar Menasheh went
and subdued their villages, and called them the villages
of Jair.   And Nobach went and subdued Kenath and
its villages, and called it Nobach after his name.

SECTION XLIII.

MASEY.

XXXIII. These are the journeys of the Beni Israel
who went forth from the land of Mizraim in their hosts,
by the hand of Mosheh and Aharon. And Mosheh
wrote their goings out, and by their journeys by the

---

[1] Sam. Vers., " Batania "   [2] Syr., "Jabok and Nobu."

Word of the Lord; and these are their journeys according to their goings out.

And they went forth from Ramesis in the first month, on the fifteenth day of the first month, after the day of the Pascha, the children of Israel went out in full view of the eyes of all the Mizraee. And the Mizraee buried all the firstborn which the Lord had slain among them, and upon their idols had the Lord wrought judgments.

And the children of Israel proceeded from Ramesis, and encamped in Succoth. And they went on from Succoth, and encamped in Etham, which is on the side of the wilderness. And they removed from Etham, and returned upon Pum-Hiratha, before Baal-Zephon, and pitched before Migdol. And they departed from Pum-Hiratha, and went through the midst of the sea into the wilderness, and went, going three days in the wilderness of Etham, and pitched in Marah. And they removed from Marah, and came to Elim; and in Elim were twelve wells of water and seventy palm trees, and they encamped there. And they removed from Elim, and pitched by the Sea of Suph. And they removed from the Sea of Suph, and pitched in the wilderness of Sin. And they departed from the wilderness of Sin, and pitched in Dapheka; and they removed from Dapheka, and encamped in Alush. And they removed from Alush, and pitched in Rephidin; and there was no water for the people to drink. And they removed from Rephidin, and encamped in the wilderness of Sinai.

And they removed from the wilderness of Sinai, and encamped at the Sepulchres of Desire. And they removed from the Sepulchres of Desire, and pitched in Hazeroth; and they removed from Hazeroth, and pitched in Rithema. And they removed from Rithema, and pitched in Rimmon-pharez. And they removed from Rimmon-pharez, and encamped in Libnah. And

they removed from Libnah, and pitched in Resah.   And
they removed from Resah, and pitched in Kehelatha.
And they removed from Kehelatha, and encamped at
Mount Shapher.   And they removed from Mount
Shapher, and encamped in Harada.   And they removed
from Harada, and pitched in Makheloth.   And they
removed from Makheloth, and pitched in Tachath.   And
they removed from Tachath, and pitched in Tharah.
And they removed from Tharah, and pitched in Mitheka.
And they removed from Mitheka, and encamped in
Hashmona.   And they removed from Hashmona, and
pitched in Moseroth   And they removed from Moseroth, and encamped in Beni Jaakan.   And they
removed from Beni Jaakan, and pitched at Mount
Hagidgad.   And they removed from Mount Hagidgad,
and pitched in Jetbatha.   And they removed from
Jetbatha, and pitched in Ebrona.   And they removed
from Ebrona, and pitched in Ezion-Geber.   And they
removed from Ezion-Geber, and encamped in the wilderness of Zin, which is Rekem.   And they removed
from Rekem, and encamped at Mount Hor, on the
borders of the land of Edom.   And Aharon the priest
went up on Mount Hor by the Word of the Lord, and
died there in the fortieth year of the outgoing of the
children of Israel from the land of Mizraim, in the fifth
month, on the first of the month.   And Aharon was a
son of one hundred and twenty-three years when he
died on Mount Hor.

And the Kenaanite, king of Harad, who dwelt in the
south, in the land of Kenaan, heard of the coming of
the Beni Israel.

And they removed from Mount Hor, and encamped
in Zalmona.   And they removed from Zalmona, and
pitched in Phnnon.   And they removed from Phunon,
and pitched in Aboth.   And they removed from Aboth,

and encamped at the Passing Fords on the border of
Moab. And they removed from the Fords, and pitched
at Dibon Gad. And they removed from Dibon Gad,
and pitched in Elmon Diblathaimah. And they removed
from Elmon Diblathaimah, and pitched at the mountains
of Abaraee, which are before Nebo. And they removed
from the mountains of Abarace, and encamped in the
plains of Moab by Jordan (over against) Jericho. And
they encamped by the Jordan from Beth Jeshimoth unto
the vale of Sittin in the fields of Moab.

And the Lord spake with Mosheh in the fields of
Moaba by the Jordan (near) Jericho, saying · Speak
with the sons of Israel, and say to them : When you
have passed over Jordan to the land of Kenaan, you
shall cast out all the inhabitants of the land from before
you, demolish all the houses of their worship, destroy
all their molten images, and lay waste all their high
places. And you shall cast out the inhabitants of the
land, and dwell in it; for I have given you the land to
inherit. And you shall possess the land by lot, according to your families; to the many you shall make their
possession large, and to the few diminish the possession : where the lot falleth to any one, there shall he be ;
according to the tribes of your fathers you shall possess.
But if you will not drive out the inhabitants of the
country from before you, it will be that those who
remain of them, combining, will take arms against you,
and surrounding you with camps they will distress you
in the land wherein you dwell. And it shall be that
what I had thought to do unto them, I will do unto you.

XXXIV. And the Lord spake with Mosheh, saying :
Command the sons of Israel, and say to them : When
you have entered into the land of Kenaan, that land
which shall be divided to you for a possession, the land
of Kenaan by its coasts, then your south border shall

be from the wilderness of Zin on the frontier of Edom, and your south border shall be from the extremities of the Sea of Salt eastward.

And your border shall turn from the south to the going up of Akrabbim, and shall pass over to Zin ; and the going out of it shall be from the south unto Rekem Giah, and go on to Hazar-Adar, and pass over to Azemon.

And the border shall turn from Azemon to the stream of Mizraim, and its goings out shall be toward the west, (Heb., the sea,) and for the western border you shall have the Great Sea ; this shall be your western border.

And this shall be your northern border· from the Great Sea you shall appoint for you Mount Hor ; from Mount Hor you shall appoint to the entrance of Hamath, and the goings forth of the border shall be unto Zedad. And the border shall be unto Zaphron, and its goings forth to Ezarenan ; this shall be your north border.

And you shall appoint your eastern border from Ezarenan to Shepham ;[3] and the border shall go down from Shepham unto Riblah, eastward of the fountain, and the border shall go down and come to the bank of the Sea of Genesar on the east. And the border shall go down to the Jordan, and its going out be at the Sea of Salt. This shall be your land with its confines round about.

And Mosheh commanded the sons of Israel, saying : This shall be the land which you are to possess by lot, which the Lord hath commanded to give to the nine tribes and to the half tribe. For the tribe of the Beni Reuben by the house of their fathers, and the tribe of the Beni Gad by the house of their fathers, and the half tribe of Menasheh, have received their inheritance.

[3] Sam Vers , " Apamea."

The two tribes and the half tribe have received their inheritance across the Jordan by Jericho towards the east.

And the Lord spake with Mosheh, saying: These are the names of the men who shall apportion the land to you: Elazar the priest, and Jehoshua bar Nun. And you shall take of each tribe one prince to apportion the land, and these are the names of the men: of the tribe of Jehudah, Kaleb bar Jephuneh; of the tribe of the Beni Shemeon, Shemuel bar Ammihud; of the tribe of Benjamin, Elidad bar Kiselon; of the tribe of the Beni Dan, Rabba Bokki bar Jagli; of the Beni Joseph, of the tribe of the Beni Menasheh, Rabba Haniel bar Ephod; of the tribe of the Beni Ephraim, Rabba Kemuel bar Shiphtan; of the tribe of the Beni Zebulon, Rabba Elizaphan bar Parnak; of the tribe of the Beni Issakar, Rabba Peltiel bar Ezar; and of that of the Beni Asher, Rabba Ahihud bar Shelomi; and of that of the Beni Naphtali, Rabba Phadael bar Ammihud. These are they whom the Lord commanded to divide the inheritance of the children of Israel in the land of Kenaan.

XXXV. And the Lord spake with Mosheh in the plains of Moab, on the Jordan-Jericho, saying: Command the sons of Israel that they give to the Levites of the inheritance of their possession cities to inhabit, and a space (suburb) with the cities round about shall they give to the Levites. And the cities they shall have to inhabit, and their spaces, shall be for their cattle, and for their possessions, and for all their animals. And the spaces of the cities which you give to the Levites (shall extend) from the wall of the city outward, a thousand cubits round about. And you shall measure without the city, on the east side [4] two thousand cubits, and on

---

[4] "The suburbs of the cities are said in the law to be three thousand cubits on every side, from the wall of the city and outwards. The first

the south side two thousand cubits, and on the west
side two thousand cubits, and on the north side two
thousand cubits, and the city in the midst ; this shall
be for you the spaces of the cities.

And (of) the cities which you give to the Levites, six
shall be cities of refuge, which you shall appoint for the
(man) slayer [5] to flee thereunto, and to them you shall
add forty-two cities. All the cities that you give to
the Levites shall be forty-eight cities, they and their
suburbs. And the cities that you give shall be of the
inheritance of the Beni Israel ; of those who have many
you shall give many, and of the few you shall give few ;
each according to his possession he inherits shall he
give of his cities to the Levites.

And the Lord spake with Mosheh, saying : Speak
with the sons of Israel, and say to them : When you
have passed the Jordan to the land of Kenaan, then
shall you appoint to you cities, cities of refuge shall
they be for you, that the slayer who hath killed a life
unawares may flee thither. And they shall be for you
cities of refuge from the avenger of blood, that the
slayer may not die until he hath stood before the congregation for judgment. And of those cities that you
give you shall have six cities of refuge : three cities you
shall give beyond Jordan, and three cities in the land
of Kenaan ; cities of refuge shall they be. For the
sons of Israel, and for the sojourner among you, there
shall be these six cities of refuge, that thither may flee
every one who hath slain a person unawares.

But if he hath smitten him with a weapon of iron and
killed him, he is a murderer ; and the murderer is to be

thousand cubits are the suburbs. and the two thousand which they
measured without the suburbs were for fields and vineyards."—MAI-
MONIDES.

[5] Syr., "who hath killed his neighbour without willing it."

surely put to death. Or, if with a stone which he carried in his hand, that he who was struck with it should die, he who killed him is a murderer, and the murderer is to be surely put to death. Or, if with a weapon of wood which he carried in his hand that he who was struck with it might die, and he killeth him, he is a murderer, and the murderer shall be verily put to death. The avenger of blood himself shall kill the murderer, when condemned by the judgment he shall kill him. And if he smote him in enmity, or threw at him in concealment and killed him, or in enmity smote him with his hand and killed him, the smiter is a murderer, he shall be surely put to death : the avenger of blood shall slay the slayer when he is condemned.

But if he have struck him suddenly without enmity, or have thrown anything upon him without lying in wait for him, or struck him with a stone sufficient to kill him, but cast it upon him without seeing, and have killed him without hating him or seeking to do him evil, then the congregation shall judge between the smiter and the avenger of blood, according to these judgments. And the congregation shall deliver the slayer from the avenger of blood, and return him to the city of his refuge to which he had fled, and he shall dwell in it until the death of the high priest who was anointed with the holy oil.

But if the slayer shall come out of the boundary of the city of his retreat to which he hath fled, and the avenger of blood find him outside of the bounds of the city of his retreat, and the avenger of blood slay the slayer, he shall not be guilty of blood. Because he should have abode within the city of his retreat until the death of the high priest : but after the death of the high priest the slayer may return to the land of his inheritance.

And these shall be to you a decree of judgment for

your generations in all your dwellings. Whosoever
killeth a person shall die, by the mouth of witnesses;
but one witness shall not testify against a man to put
(him) to death. Neither may you take money on account
of a manslayer who is guilty of death, for dying he shall
die. Nor may you take money for him who hath fled to
his city of refuge, so that he may return to dwell in the
land till the high priest shall die. But you shall not
make guilty the land in which you are; for blood
maketh the land guilty; and the land is not expiated
for innocent blood that is shed therein but by the blood
of him who shed it. Defile not then the land in which
you dwell, for My Shekinah dwelleth in the midst of it;
for I, the Lord, by My Shekinah dwell among the children of Israel.

XXXVI. And the chief fathers of the families of the
Beni Gilead, bar Makir, bar Menasheh, of the family of
the Beni Joseph, came and spake before Mosheh, the
princes and chief fathers of the Beni Israel, and said:
The Lord commanded Rabboni to give the land an
inheritance by lot to the children of Israel; and Rabboni
was commanded by the Word of the Lord to give the
inheritance of Zelophechad our brother to his daughters.
But if they become wives to any of the sons of the
(other) tribes of the Beni Israel, then will their inheritance be taken away from the inheritance of our fathers,
and added to the inheritance of the tribe which will
have become theirs, and be (thus) diminished from the
portion of our inheritance. And when the Jubela of
the children of Israel come, their inheritance will be
added to the possession of the tribe that hath become
theirs, and our possession will pass away from the inheritance of our father's tribe.

And Mosheh commanded the sons of Israel by the
Word of the Lord, saying: The tribe of the sons of

Joseph have spoken well.   This is the thing which the
Lord hath commanded for the daughters of Zelophechad,
saying : Let them become the wives of those who are
proper in their eyes, only of (men) of their father's
tribe may they become wives.   And the inheritance of
the children of Israel shall not turn from tribe to tribe ;
for every man of the Beni Israel shall keep himself to
the inheritance of his father's tribe.

And every daughter inheriting a possession (in one)
of the tribes of the children of Israel shall be wife of one
of the families of her father's tribe : that the sons of
Israel may each man inherit the possession of his fathers.
And the inheritance shall not pass from one tribe to
another tribe, but every one of the tribes of the Beni
Israel shall keep to its own inheritance.

As the Lord commanded Mosheh, so did the daughters
of Zelophechad : and Maalah, and Thirzah, and Hegela,
and Milchah, and Nohah, the daughters of Zelophechad,
became wives of sons of their father's brethren.   They
were married into the family of the Beni Menasheh bar
Joseph, and their inheritance (remained) with the tribe
of their father's family.

These are the commandments and judgments which
the Lord commanded by the hand of Mosheh to the
children of Israel, in the plains of Moab, by Jordan, near
Jericho.

END OF THE TARGUM OF ONKELOS ON THE
SEPHER BEMIDBAR.

THE PALESTINIAN TARGUM

ON

THE BOOK OF NUMBERS.

SECTION OF THE TORAH XXXIV.

BEMIDBAR

I. AND the Lord spake with Mosheh in the wilderness
of Sinai, in the tabernacle of ordinance, on the first of
the month Ijar, which was the second month of the
second year from the time of their coming forth from
the land of Mizraim, saying: Take the account of the
whole congregation of the Beni Israel, according to the
families of their fathers' house, by the number of the
names of all the males by their capitations. From each
son of twenty years and upwards, every one going out
in the host in Israel; thou and Aharon number them
by their hosts. And let there be with you a man of
each tribe, a chief of his father's house. And these are
the names of the men who shall stand with you. Of
Reuben, Elizur bar Shedeur: of Shemeon, the leader,[1]
Shelumiel bar Zuri-Shaddai: the prince of Jehudah,
Nachshon bar Amminadab: the prince of Issakar,
Nathaniel bar Zuar: the prince of Zebulon, Eliab bar
Chelon. the prince of the Beni Joseph, of Ephraim,
Elishama bar Ammihud: the prince of Menasheh,
Gamliel bar Pedazur: the prince of Benjamin, Abidan

---

[1] *Amarkol.* See Glossary

bar Gideoni: the prince of Dan, Achiezer bar Ammi-
shadai: the prince of Asher, Pagiel bar Achran: the
prince of Gad, Eljasaph bar Dehuel: the prince of
Naphtali, Achira bar Enan. These (were) the notables
of the congregation of the people, chiefs of their fathers'
tribes, heads of thousands in Israel these. And Mosheh
and Aharon took these men who are expressed by their
names: and they assembled all the congregation on
the first day of the month Ijar, which is the second
month, and recensed them by the families of their
fathers' house, by the number of their names, from
twenty years old and upward by their capitations. As
the Lord commanded Mosheh, they numbered them in
the wilderness of Sinai.

And the sons of Reuben, the first-born of Israel by
the families of the generations of their fathers' house,
in the number of their names by their polls, every male
from twenty years old and upward, all going forth in
the host, the sum of the tribe of Reuben, forty-six
thousand five hundred. [JERUSALEM. Their sum.] Of
the families of the Beni Shemeon, after the generations
of their fathers' house in the number of their names by
their polls, every male from twenty years and upward,
every one going forth in the host, the sum of the tribe
of Shemeon, fifty-nine thousand three hundred: of the
family of the Beni Gad, after the generation of their
fathers' house, in the number of their names by their
polls, every male from twenty years and upward, forty-
five thousand six hundred and fifty. The sum of the
tribe of Jehudah seventy-four thousand six hundred:[2]
of Issakar, fifty-four thousand four hundred: of Zebulon,
fifty-seven thousand four hundred: of Ephraim, forty thousand five hundred: of Menasheh, thirty-two thousand two

[2] The same form of words is given with each tribe, in the remaining
ones I have omitted the preamble, and rendered the numbers only.

hundred : Benjamin, thirty five thousand four hundred :
Dan, sixty-two thousand seven hundred : Asher, forty-
one thousand five hundred : Naphtali, fifty-three thousand four hundred.

These are the sums of the numbered ones which
Mosheh and Aharon, and the princes of Israel, twelve
men, a man for each house of their fathers, did number.
And all the sums of the numbered of the Beni Israel
were six hundred and three thousand five hundred and
fifty.   But the Levites after their father's tribe were not
numbered among them.   For the Lord had spoken with
Mosheh, saying : Nevertheless, the tribe of Levi thou
shalt not number, nor take their sum among the children of Israel : but thou shalt appoint the Levites over
the tabernacle of the testimony, and over all its vessels,
and whatever things pertain unto it.   They shall carry
the tabernacle and all its vessels, and do service in it ;
and round about the tabernacle shall they dwell.   And
when the tabernacle is to go forward, the Levites shall
take it apart ; and when the tabernacle is to be stationary,
the Levites are to uprear it : the common person who
draweth near will be slain by a flaming fire from before
the Lord.

And the sons of Israel shall encamp every one by the
place of his own company, every one under his standard
according to their hosts.   But the Levites shall encamp
round about the tabernacle of the testimony, that there
may not be wrath upon the congregation of the children
of Israel; and the Levites shall keep charge of the
tabernacle of testimony.   And the sons of Israel did
according to all that the Lord commanded Mosheh, so
did they.

II. And the Lord spake with Mosheh and with Aharon,
saying: Every man of the Beni Israel shall encamp by his
standard, by the ensign which is signified upon the stand-

ards of their fathers' house over against the tabernacle of ordinance shall they encamp round about. The length of the camp of Israel shall be twelve miles, and its breadth twelve miles. And they who encamp eastward to the sunrise shall be of the standard of the camp of Jehudah by their hosts, spreading over four miles. And his standard shall be of silk, of three colours, corresponding with (those of) the precious stones which are in the breastplate,—sardius, topaz, and carbuncle ; and upon it shall be expressed and set forth the names of the three tribes of Jehudah, Issakar, and Zebulon ; and in the midst shall be written : *Arise, O Lord, and let Thine enemies be scattered, and Thine adversaries be driven away before Thee ;* and upon it shall be set forth the figure of a young lion. And the Rabba of the Beni Jehudah shall be Nachshon bar Amminadab. And the sum of the hosts of that tribe was seventy-four thousand six hundred.

And they who encamp next by him shall be the tribe of Issakar, and the Rabba appointed over the host of the Beni Issakar, Nathaniel bar Zuar : and the sum of the host of the tribe fifty-four thousand four hundred. The tribe of Zebulon,—the Rabba, Eliab bar Chelon ; the number, fifty-seven thousand four hundred. All the numbered ones of the camp of Jehudah, one hundred and eighty-six thousand four hundred, by their hosts ; they shall go forward in front.

(By) the standard of the camp of Reuben they shall encamp southward by their hosts, spreading over four miles. And his standard shall be of silk, of three colours, corresponding with (those of) the precious stones that are in the breastplate, azmorad, sapphire, and adamant: on it shall be expressed and set forth the names of the three tribes of Reuben, Shemeon, Gad ; and in the midst of it be written, *Hear, Israel, the Lord our God is One ;* and upon it shall be set forth the figure of a stag.

Some would have thought there should have been upon it the figure of a young ox; but Moshch the prophet altered it, that the sin of the calf might not be remembered against them. And the Rabba set over the host of the tribe Reuben was Elizur bar Shedeur. And his host and the numbered of his tribe were fifty-nine thousand three hundred. The tribe of Gad: the Rabba set over the host of the tribe of the Beni Gad was Eljasaph bar Dehuel. And his host and the number of his tribe, forty-five thousand six hundred. All the sum of the numbered ones of the camp of Reuben, one hundred and fifty one thousand four hundred and fifty by their hosts; and they went forward secondly.

But the tabernacle shall go with the host of the Levites, in the midst of their host; and their camp spreadeth over four miles, in the midst are they to be: as they encamp, so shall they go, every man going in his appointed place, by their standard.

The camp of Ephraim by the standard of their hosts shall pitch on the west; their camp spreadeth over four miles; and their standard is of silk of three colours, corresponding with the precious stones in the breast-plate, ligure, agate, and amethyst; and upon it expressed and set forth the names of the three tribes, Ephraim, Menasheh, and Benjamin, having written in the midst, *And the Cloud of the Lord was over them, in the going forward of the host;* and upon it was set forth the figure of a young man. And the Rabba set over the tribe of Ephraim, Elishama bar Ammihud; and the sum of his host, forty thousand five hundred. And next to him were the tribe of Menasheh: the Rabba, Gamliel bar Pedashur; their number, thirty-two thousand two hundred. Of the tribe of Benjamin the Rabba was Abidan bar Gideoni, and the number of his host thirty-five thousand four hundred. The sum of the camp of

Ephraim was one hundred and eight thousand one hundred; and they went forward thirdly.

The standard of the camp of Dan shall be to the north with their hosts; and the space of their camp shall spread over four miles. His standard shall be of silk of three colours, corresponding with the stones in the breastplate, chrysolite, beryl, and jasper; in it shall be expressed and set forth the names of the three tribes, Dan, Naphtali, and Asher; and upon it shall be expressed: *And in his encampment shall he say, Return, O Lord, and dwell in Thy glory in the midst of the myriads of Israel;* and upon it shall also be set forth the figure of a basilisk serpent. (Gen. xlix. 17.) The Rabba set over the hosts of Dan was Achiezer bar Amini-shaddai, and the number of his tribe sixty-two thousand seven hundred. They who encamp next to him shall be the tribe of Asher; the Rabbi was Paghiel bar Achran, and the numbers forty-one thousand five hundred. Of the tribe Naphtali, the Rabba, Achira bar Enan; and the numbers, fifty-three thousand four hundred. The sum of the hosts of Dan was one hundred and fifty-seven thousand six hundred: and these went forward last with their ensigns.

This is the amount of the numbers of the Beni Israel, according to the house of their fathers; all the sums of the camps by their hosts were six hundred and three thousand five hundred and fifty. But the Levites were not numbered among the sons of Israel, as the Lord commanded Mosheh. And the sons of Israel did according to all that the Lord commanded Mosheh; so did they encamp by their standards, and so went they forward, every man with his family by the house of his fathers.

III. These are the generations of Aharon and Mosheh, who were genealogized in the day that the Lord spake with Mosheh in the mountain of Sinai. And these are

the names of the Beni Aharon the priests, the disciples
of Moses, the Rabbi of Israel; and they were called by
his name in the day that they were anointed to minister
in offering their oblations.   But Nadab and Abihu died
by the flaming fire at the time of their offering the
strange fire from their own tents; and they had no
children.   And Elazar and Ithamar ministered before
Aharon their father.

And the Lord spake with Mosheh, saying: Bring the
tribe of Levi near, and appoint them before Aharon the
priest to minister with him, (or, to do him service;) and
let them be divided into twenty and four parties, and
they shall keep his charge, and the charge of all the
congregation before the tabernacle of ordinance, to perform the work of the tabernacle; and they shall have
charge of all the vessels of the tabernacle of ordinance,
and the charge of the sons of Israel to do the service of
the tabernacle.   And I have given the Levites unto
Aharon and his sons; a gift are they given and delivered
to him from among the sons of Israel; and number
thou Aharon and his sons, that they may keep their
priesthood; and the stranger who cometh near shall be
slain by the flame from before the Lord.

And the Lord spake with Mosheh, saying: And I,
behold, I have brought nigh the Levites from among the
sons of Israel, instead of all the first-born who open the
womb among the sons of Israel; and the Levites shall
minister before Me.   For every first-born among the sons
of Israel is Mine, from the day when I slew every first-
born in the land of Mizraim; I have sanctified before
Me every first-born in Israel; from man to animal, they
are Mine: I am the Lord.

And the Lord spake with Mosheh in the wilderness
of Sinai, saying: Number the sons of Levi according to
the house of their fathers and their families; every male

from a month old and upward shalt thou number them.
Moses therefore numbered them according to the
mouth of the Word of the Lord, as he had been commanded. And these were the sons of Levi by their
names : Gershon, Kehath, and Merari. And these are the
names of the Beni Gershon, according to their families,
Libni and Shemei. And the Beni Kehath by their
families, Amram, Jizhar, Hebron, and Uzziel. And the
Beni Merari by their families, Machli, and Mushi : these
are the families of the Levites after the house of their
fathers.

Of Gershon, the family of Libni, and the family of
Shemei; these are the families of Gershon. The sum
of them, by the numbers of all the males from a month
old and upward, seven thousand five hundred. The two
families who spring from Gershon shall encamp after the
tabernacle westward; and the Rab of the house of the
fathers set over the two families shall be Eljasaph bar
Lael. And the charge of the Beni Gershon in the
tabernacle of ordinance shall be the tent, and the covering
that overspreadeth, and the hanging of the door of the
tabernacle of ordinance, and the curtains of the court,
and the hanging which is at the gate of the court by the
tabernacle, and the altar round about, and the cords of
it, for all the service thereof.

Of Kehath was the family of Amram, and the family
of Izhar, and of Hebron, and Uzziel : these are the
families of Kehath, the numbers eight thousand six
hundred, keeping the charge of the sanctuary. The
four families that spring from Kehath shall encamp by
the south side of the tabernacle; the Rab shall be
Elizaphan bar Uzziel, and their charge, the ark, the
table, the candelabrum, the altars, the vessels of the
sanctuary wherewith they minister, and the veil, and
that which pertaineth to its service. And the Amarkol

set over the chiefs of the Levites shall be Elazar bar Aharon the priest, who inquireth by Uraya and Thumaya; and under his hand shall they be appointed who keep the charge of the sanctuary.

Of Merari, the families of Machli and Mushi, their number six thousand two hundred, and the Rab Zeruel bar Abichael : they shall encamp by the tabernacle northward ; and that delivered to their charge shall be the boards of the tabernacle, its bars, pillars, and sockets, and all (that pertains to) the service thereof. The pillars of the court also round about, their sockets, pins, and cords.

But they who encamp before the tabernacle of ordinance eastward (shall be) Mosheh and Aharon, and his sons ; keeping charge of the sanctuary and of Israel , and the stranger who draweth near shall be slain by flaming fire from before the Lord. The sum of the Levites whom Mosheh and Aharon numbered by the mouth of the Word of the Lord was twenty-two thousand.

And the Lord said unto Mosheh, Number all the first-born males among the sons of Israel, from a month old and upward, and take the number of their names. And bring near the Levites before me—I am the Lord —instead of all the firstborn among the sons of Israel, and all the cattle of the Levites instead of all the firstling cattle of the children of Israel. And Mosheh numbered, as the Lord commanded him, all the firstborn of the sons of Israel : the sum of their number was twenty-two thousand two hundred and seventy-three.

And the Lord spake with Mosheh, saying. Bring near the Levites instead of every first-born among Israel, and the cattle of the Levites instead of their cattle, that the Levites may minister before me : I am the Lord. And for the redemption of the two hundred and seventy and three of the first-born of the Beni Israel, who are

more (than the number of) the Levites, thou shalt take
of each five shekels by poll, in the shekel of the sanctuary shalt thou take, twenty mahin to the shekel.   And
thou shalt give the shekel unto Aharon, and to his sons,
as the redemption of them who are more than they.
And Mosheh took the redemption (money) of them who
were above those who were released by the Levites, one
thousand three hundred and sixty-five shekels; and
Mosheh gave the redemption silver to Aharon, and to
his sons, according to the mouth of the Word of the
Lord, as the Lord commanded Mosheh.

IV. And the Lord spake with Mosheh, saying : Take
the account of the sons of Kehath from among the
Beni Levi, from thirty years and upwards to fifty years,
every one who cometh by the hand to do the work in
the tabernacle of ordinance.   This is the service of the
Beni Kehath, in the tabernacle of ordinance (with) the
most holy things.   But whenever the camp is to be
removed, Aharon and his sons shall enter, and unloose
the veil that is spread, and cover up the Ark of the Testimony, and put over it the covering of hyacinthine
skin, and overspread it with a wrapper of twined work,
and inset its staves.   And over the table of the presence
bread they shall spread a wrapper of purple, and set
upon it the vials, and the spoons, and the vases, [JERU-
SALEM. Vials,] and the libation cups; but the bread shall
be upon it evermore.   And they shall spread upon it a
wrapper of scarlet, and cover it with a covering of hyacinthine skin, and inset its staves.   And they shall take a
purple wrapper, and cover the candelabrum that lighteth,
and its lamps, its tongs, its snuff-dishes, and all the
vessels of service by which they attend it. [JERUSALEM.
Snuffers.]   And they shall put it and all its vessels in a
covering of hyacinthine skin, and place it upon a rest.
[JERUSALEM. Upon a beam.]   And upon the golden

altar they shall spread a purple vest, and cover it with a
covering of hyacinthine skin, and inset its staves.   And
they shall take all the vessels of the service with which
they minister in the sanctuary, and wrap them in
a covering of hyacinthine skins, and place it upon a
beam.

And they shall remove the cinders from the altar,
and overspread it with a covering of crimson.   [JERU-
SALEM. And they shall take away from the altar,] and
put upon it all its vessels with which it is served, the
cinder-holders, flesh-hooks, prongs, and basins, even all
the vessels of the altar, and spread upon it a covering
of hyacinthine skin, and inset its staves.

And after Aharon and his sons have completed to
cover the sanctuary, and all the vessels thereof, when
the camp is to go forward, then the sons of Kehath may
enter in to carry : but they shall not touch any holy thing,
lest they die by the flaming fire.   This is the burden of
the sons of Kehath in the tabernacle of ordinance.   And
that delivered to Elazar bar Aharon the priest shall be
the oil for the light, the aromatic incense, the perpetual
mincha, the oil of anointing, and the custody of all the
tabernacle, and whatever is in it in the sanctuary and its
vessels.

And the Lord spake with Mosheh, saying : Thou
shalt not give occasion for the tribe of the family of
Kehath to perish among the Levites.   But this appointment make thou for them, that they may live the life of
the just, and die not by the flaming fire ; they shall turn
away their eyes from the Most Holy Place at the time
they approach thither.   Aharon and his sons shall enter,
and appoint them man by man to his service and his
burden.   But they shall not go in to gaze, when the
priests go in to cover the vessels of the sanctuary, that
they die not by the flaming fire.   [JERUSALEM. And

the Levites shall not go in to gaze when the priests
cover the vessels of the holy house, lest they die.]

SECTION XXXV.

NASA

AND the Lord spake with Mosheh, saying : Take the
account of the Beni Gershon also, from thirty years to
fifty years, of all who come by bands to do the work of
the tabernacle of ordinance.   And this is the service
of the family of Gershon, to serve and to carry.   They
shall carry the curtains of the tabernacle, the tabernacle
of ordinance, its covering, and the hyacinth covering
which is upon it above ; and the hanging of the gate
of the tabernacle of ordinance ; and the curtains of the
court, and the hanging for the gate of the court which
is by the tabernacle round about, and their cords and
all the vessels of their service, and all that is delivered
to them to serve with.   Upon the word of Aharon and
his sons shall be all the service of the Beni Gershon,
for all their burdens and service, and of their whole
work shalt thou ordain the charge upon them.   This is
the ministry of the family of the Beni Gershon, in the
tabernacle of ordinance ; and the care of them shall be in
the hand of Ithamar bar Aharon the priest.

The sons of Merari shalt thou number, from thirty
years to fifty years, every one who cometh with the band
to minister in the work of the tabernacle of ordinance.
And this shall be the charge of the burdens of all their
service in the tabernacle of ordinance, the boards of the
tabernacle, its bars, pillars, and bases ; the pillars of the
court also round about, their pins and their cords, with

all the instruments of their whole service, and all those
of the charge of their burdens, thou shalt number by
their names. This is the work of the family of Merari,
according to all their service in the tabernacle of ordinance, under the hand of Ithamar bar Aharon the priest.

And Mosheh and Aharon numbered the sons of
Kehath by their families, and by the house of their
fathers, from thirty years to fifty years; every one who
came with the band to serve in the tabernacle of ordinance; and the sums of them were two thousand seven
hundred and fifty. These are the numbers of the
family of Kehath, of all who ministered in the tabernacle of ordinance; whom Mosheh and Aharon numbered
upon the mouth of the Word of the Lord by Mosheh.

The numbers of the Beni Gershon, after the families
of their father's house from thirty years to fifty years,
every one who who came with the band to serve in the
tabernacle of ordinance; the sums of them were two
thousand six hundred and thirty. These are the numbers of the Beni Gershon, of all who ministered in the
tabernacle of ordinance, whom Mosheh and Aharon
numbered upon the mouth of the Word of the Lord by
Mosheh.

And the numbers of the Beni Merari, by the families
of their father's house, from thirty to fifty years, every
one who came with the band to the service of the tabernacle of ordinance, were three thousand two hundred.
These are the numbers of the Beni Merari, whom Mosheh
and Aharon numbered upon the mouth of the Word of
the Lord by Mosheh.

The whole sum of the Levites whom Mosheh and
Aharon and the princes of Israel numbered, from thirty
to fifty years, all coming by bands to fulfil the charge
and service of the porterage of the tabernacle of ordinance, was eight thousand five hundred and eighty. By

the mouth of the Word of the Lord were they numbered by Mosheh, every man according to his service and burden; and the numbering of them was as the Lord commanded Mosheh.

V. And the Lord spake with Mosheh, saying: Command the sons of Israel to send away from the camp every one who is leprous, or who hath an issue, or is unclean by having defiled himself (by touching) the dead. From a male to a female thou shalt send them away, and separate them without the camp, that they may not defile their tents; for the Shekinah of My Holiness dwelleth among you. And the sons of Israel did so, and sent them away from the camp; as the Lord had commanded Mosheh, so did the sons of Israel.

And the Lord spake with Mosheh, saying: Say to the children of Israel: A man or a woman who committeth any human sin, in acting perversely before the Lord, and hath become guilty; they shall make confession of their sins which they have committed. If he hath extorted money from his neighbour, he shall restore (the amount of) his sin in the principal thereof, and add to it a fifth of its value, and give (both) principal and fifth to him against whom he hath sinned. And if the man (hath died and) hath no kinsman to whom the debt may be rendered, the debt to be restored (shall he render) before the Lord; he shall give it to the priest, besides the ram for his atonement, by which atonement is to be made for him. And every separation of all consecrated things of the children of Israel which they bring to the priest shall be his. The consecrated tithe, also, of any man shall be his, that his substance may not fail; whatever a man giveth unto the priest shall be his.

And the Lord spake with Mosheh, saying: Speak

with the sons of Israel, and say to them : If the wife of
any man go astray and commit wrongness against him,
and another man lie with her, and it be hidden from
her husband's eyes, and be concealed, and she be contaminated; or, if the testimony be not clear which is
witnessed against her, and she be not convicted; or,
if the spirit of jealousy come upon him, and he be
jealous of his wife, that she hath been defiled, or the
spirit of jealousy come upon him, and he be jealous of
his wife, though she hath not been defiled ; and though
that man may have not brought separation or tythe,
there is constraint upon him to bring his wife unto the
priest.   Now, because she may have brought delicacies
to the adulterer, she ought to bring an appointed oblation of her own, a tenth of three sata of barley flour,
that being the food of beasts : he shall not pour oil, nor
'put frankincense thereon ; for it is a mincha (on account)
of jealousy, a mincha of a memorial which calleth guilt
to mind.

And the priest shall bring her near, and cause her to
stand before the Lord.

And the priest shall take holy water from the laver
with an ewer, and pour it into an earthen vessel ; because
she may have brought the adulterer sweet wine to drink
in precious vases; and he shall take of the dust that
is upon the ground of the tabernacle,—because the end
of all flesh is dust,—and put it into the water.   And the
priest shall cause the woman to stand before the Lord,
and bind a cord over her loins and upon her breast,—
because she should have bound her loins with a girdle ;
and he shall uncover the woman's head, because she had
tied a fillet upon her hair.

And he shall put the mincha of memorial, the mincha
of jealousy, into her hand ; while in the hand of the
priest shall be the bitter water of the trial.

And the priest shall adjure her by the adjuration of the Great and Glorious Name, and shall say to the woman :

If thou hast not turned aside, to defile thyself by acting against the right of thy husband, be thou unhurt by these bitter waters of trial. [JERUSALEM. Be thou made innocent by these waters of trial by their probation.] But if thou hast turned aside against the right of thy husband, and art defiled in having shared the bed with a man against thy husband's right :—Then shall the priest adjure the woman by the oath of malediction, and say to the woman,—The Lord make thee a curse and an execration among the children of thy people, in causing thy thigh to corrupt, and thy belly to swell; and may these waters of trial enter into thy bowels, to cause thy belly to swell, and thy thigh to corrupt.

And the woman shall answer and say : Amen, if I was polluted when betrothed; Amen, if I have been polluted since my marriage. [JERUSALEM. And the woman shall answer, Amen, because I have not been unclean; Amen, if ever I shall have wrought uncleanness.]

And the priest shall write these maledictions upon a parchment, and wash it out with the water of trial, and cause the woman to drink the bitter trial water: the trial water of malediction shall be received by her. But the priest shall (first) take from the woman's hand the mincha of jealousy, and uplift the mincha before the Lord, and lay it on the side of the altar. And the priest shall take a handful of the portion for its memorial, and burn it at the altar; and after that the woman shall drink the water.

And when he hath caused her to drink the water, it will be that if she hath been defiled by adultery, and hath acted with wrongness against her husband, those proving waters will enter into her with a curse, and her belly will swell, and her thigh become corrupt, and the woman will be an execration among the children of her people. The adulterer as well will be detected by these waters of probation, in whatever place he may be. But if the woman hath not been defiled by adultery, but is innocent, they will enter without harm, and her brightness will shine forth, and she will find affection before her husband, and become the mother of a son.

This is the declaration of the law of jealousy, when a woman hath fallen away from the right of her husband, and become defiled by adultery; or when the spirit of jealousy cometh upon a man, that he be so jealous of his wife as to make her stand before the Lord, then shall the priest perform all this law But if the man be innocent of transgressions, then let that woman bear her iniquity.

VI. And the Lord spake with Mosheh, saying: Speak with the children of Israel, and say to them: When a man or woman, seeing her who had gone astray in her corruption, shall (resolve to) become abstinent from wine, or for any other cause shall make the vow of a Nazir in separating one's-self unto the Name of the Lord, he shall abstain from wine, new and old, he shall drink neither vinegar of old wine or new; neither may he drink liquor in which grapes have been crushed, nor eat of grapes either fresh or dried. [JERUSALEM. From wine, new or old, he shall abstain, (keep apart,) and vinegar of old wine he may not drink, nor any liquor of grapes.] All the days of his vow he shall not eat of the tree which maketh wine, from the husks of grapes even to the kernels within them. All the days of his nazir-vow the razor shall not pass upon his head until the time when the days of his separation to the Name of the Lord be fulfilled; he shall be consecrate, letting the hair of his head grow. All the days of his separation to the Name of the Lord he shall not go in where there is a dead man. For his

father, or his mother, his brother, or his sister, he shall
not make himself unclean through their decease; for
the crown of Eloah is upon his head; all the days
in which he is a Nazir he shall be sacred before the
Lord.

But if a person die near him suddenly, and he unawares defile the head of his vow, let him shave his head
on the day of his purification; on the seventh day let
him shave it. And on the eighth day let him bring
two turtle doves, or two young pigeons, unto the priest
at the door of the tabernacle of ordinance. And the
priest shall make one a sin offering, and one a burnt
offering, and atone for him on account of that in which
he hath sinned, in defiling himself by the dead: and he
shall consecrate his head on that day. And let him
dedicate before the Lord the days of his nazirate (afresh),
and bring a lamb of the year for a trespass offering;
but the former days will have been in vain, because he
had defiled his nazirate.

And this is the law of the Nazir on the day when his
separation days are fulfilled : Let him present himself at
the door of the tabernacle of ordinance, and bring his
oblation before the Lord, one lamb of the year unblemished for a burnt offering, and one ewe lamb of
the year unblemished for a sin offering, and one ram
unblemished for the consecrated oblation, and a basket
of unleavened cakes of flour with olive oil, and unleavened wafers anointed with olive oil, their minchas
and libations. And the priest shall offer before the
Lord, and perform the sin offering, and the burnt sacrifice ; and make the ram a consecrated victim (peace
offering) before the Lord, with the basket of unleavened ;
and the priest shall make its mincha and its libation.
And the Nazir shall shave his consecrated head, without,
after the offering of the holy oblations at the door of

the tabernacle of ordinance, and take the hair of his consecrated head, and lay it on the fire that is under the cauldron of the peace offering. And the priest shall take the shoulder that is boiled, entire from the ram, and one unleavened cake from the basket, and one unleavened wafer, and put upon the hands of the Nazirite, after he hath shaved his head of the consecration. And the priest shall uplift them for an elevation. It is sacred; it belongeth to the priest, with the breast of the elevation, and the separated shoulder. And after that the Nazirite may drink wine.

This is the declaration of the law of the Nazir who shall have vowed his oblation before the Lord for his separation, besides what may come into his hand according to the rule (or measure) of his vow, to bring that which he had vowed; so shall he do according to the law of his nazirate.

And the Lord spake with Mosheh, saying. Speak with Aharon and his sons, saying: Thus shall you bless the children of Israel, while spreading forth the hands from the high place,[4] in this tongue.[5] The Lord bless thee and keep thee. The Lord make His face to shine upon thee, and be gracious unto thee. The Lord lift up His countenance upon thee, and grant thee peace. The Lord bless thee in all thy business, and keep thee from demons[6] of the night, and things that cause terror, and from demons of the noon[7] and of the morning, and from malignant spirits and phantoms. The Lord make His face to shine upon thee, when occupied in the law, and reveal to thee its secrets, and be merciful unto thee. The Lord lift up His countenance upon thee in thy

---

[4] Or, " place of speaking."

[5] The Hebrew, which the Targumist gives textually, and then paraphrases in Chaldee. See the Glossary.

[6] *Liliths.*   [7] Psalm xci. 6. Vulg. et Sept.

prayer, and grant thee peace in thy end. And they shall bestow the benediction of My Name upon the children of Israel, and I, by My Word, will bless them.

VII. And it was on the day which begins the month of Nisan, when Mosheh had finished to uprear the tabernacle, he took it not in pieces again, but anointed and consecrated it and all its vessels, the altar and all the vessels thereof, and he anointed them and hallowed them; then the leaders of Israel, who were the chiefs of the house of their fathers, brought their offerings. These were they who had been appointed in Mizraim chiefs over the numbered, and they brought their offering before the Lord; six waggons covered and fitted up, and twelve oxen; one waggon for two princes and one ox for each. [JERUSALEM. Six waggons yoked.] But Mosheh was not willing to receive them, and they brought them before the tabernacle. And the Lord spake with Mosheh, saying: Take them, and let them be used for the need of the appointed (work), and let the oxen and the waggons be for the work of the service of the tabernacle of ordinance, and give them to the Levites, to each according to the measure of his work. And Mosheh took the waggons and the oxen, and gave them to the Levites. Two waggons and four oxen he gave to the sons of Gershon, according to the amount of their service, and four waggons and eight oxen gave he to the sons of Merari, according to the measure of their service, by the hand of Ithamar bar Aharon the priest. But to the sons of Kehath he gave neither waggons nor oxen, because on them was laid the service of the sanctuary, to be carried on their shoulders. And the princes offered at the dedication of the altar by anointing, on the day that he anointed it did the princes present their oblations before the altar. And the Lord said unto Mosheh, Let the princes offer each, one prince on one day, their oblations at the dedication of the altar by anointing.

He who on the first day presented his oblation was Nachshon bar Amminadab, prince of the house of the fathers of the tribe Jehudah : and his oblation which he offered was one silver bowl, thickly embossed, (or, crusted,) in weight one hundred and thirty shekels, in shekels of the sanctuary; one silver vase, slightly embossed, of seventy shekels, in shekels of the sanctuary; both of these vessels he brought filled with flour of the separation, sprinkled with olive oil for a mincha; one pan (censer) weighing ten silver shekels, but it was itself of good gold; and he brought it full of good sweet incense of the separation ; one young bullock of three years, one ram of two years, and one lamb of the year. These three did the chief of the tribe Jehudah bring for a burnt offering; one kid of the goats brought he for a sin offering; and for consecrated victims, two oxen, five rams, five goats, lambs of the year five. this is the order of the oblation which Nachshon bar Amminadab offered of his wealth. [JERUSALEM. And the oblation which he offered was one silver dish, &c , in the same words as above.]

On the second day, Nethanel bar Zuar, chief of the house of the fathers of the tribe Issakar, brought his oblation. He brought his oblation after Jehudah by commandment of the Holy: one silver dish thickly embossed, one hundred and thirty shekels, &c., as the first.[8]

On the third day, Eliab bar Helon, prince of the Beni Zebulon, offered. On the fourth, Elizur bar Shedeur, prince of the Beni Reuben; on the fifth, Shelumiel

---

[a] The oblation of each of the twelve princes was precisely the same I have therefore omitted the details after the first, and given only the name of the offerer. The Targumist abridges here, also.

bar Zurishaddai, prince of Shemeon; on the sixth, Eljasaph bar Dehuel, prince of the Beni Gad; on the seventh, Elishama bar Ammihud, prince of the Beni Ephraim; on the eighth, Gamaliel bar Pedazur, prince of Menasheh; on the ninth, Abidan bar Gideoni, prince of Benjamin; on the tenth, Achiezer bar Amishaddai, prince of the Beni Dan; on the eleventh, Pagiel bar Achran, prince of Asher; and on the twelfth day, Achira bar Enan, prince of the Beni Naphtali, offered.

This is the oblation at the anointing of the altar, on the day that they anointed it, from the riches of the princes of Israel: twelve silver bowls, answering to the twelve tribes; twelve silver vases, answering to the twelve princes of the Beni Israel; twelve golden pans, answering to the twelve signs (*mazalia*[9]). One hundred and thirty shekels was the weight of each silver bowl, answering to the years of Jokebed when she bare Mosheh; and seventy shekels was the weight of each vase, answering to the seventy elders of the great Sanhedrin: all the silver vessels, two thousand four hundred shekels, in shekels of the sanctuary. The golden pans were twelve, answering to the princes of Israel, full of good sweet incense; the weight of ten shekels was the weight of each pan, answering to the Ten Words; all the gold of the pans, one hundred and and twenty (shekels), answering to the years lived by Mosheh the prophet. All the bullocks for the burnt offering, twelve, a bullock for a prince of the house of the fathers; twelve rams, because the twelve princes of Ishmael would perish; twelve lambs of the year, because the twelve princes of Persia would perish; and their minchas, that famine might be removed from the world; and twelve kids of the goats for the sin offering, to atone for the sins of the twelve tribes. And all the

---

[9] Signs of the Zodiac.

oxen for consecrated victims, twenty-four, answering to
the twenty-four orders (of the priests); the rams, sixty,
answering to the sixty years which Izhak had lived
when he begat Jakob; the goats, sixty, answering to
the sixty letters in the benediction of the priests; lambs
of the year, sixty, to atone for the sixty myriads of
Israel. This was the dedication of the altar by anoint-
ment on the day that they anointed it.

And when Mosheh entered into the tabernacle of
ordinance to speak with Him, he heard the voice of the
Spirit who spake with him descending from the heaven
of heavens upon the Mercy Seat which was upon the
Ark of the Testimony between the two Cherubim, and
from thence was the Oracle speaking with him.

SECTION XXXVI.

VIII. And the Lord spake with Mosheh, saying:
Speak with Aharon, and say to him: At the time when
thou dost kindle the lamps upon the candelabrum, (all)
the seven lamps shall be alight; three on the western
side, and three on the eastern side, and the seventh in
the midst. And Aharon did so; at the face of the
candelabrum he lit the lamps thereof, as the Lord commanded Mosheh. And this was the work of the candelabrum, which was of beaten gold, from its foundations unto its lilies, the work of the artificer, with the
hammer was it wrought: according to the vision which
the Lord had showed Mosheh, so did Bezalel make the
candelabrum.

And the Lord spake with Mosheh, saying: Bring

the Levites out from among the sons of Israel, and
purify them.   And this shalt thou do to purify them.
Sprinkle upon them the water for uncleanness through
sin (*chattatha*), and let the razor pass over all their
flesh, and let them wash their raiment, and wash
themselves in forty savan of water.   And they shall
take a young bullock, and his mincha of flour sprinkled
with olive oil; and take thou a second young bullock
for a sin offering.   And thou shalt bring the Levites
before the tabernacle of ordinance, and gather together
also all the congregation of the sons of Israel.   Thou
shalt bring the Levites before the Lord, and the sons of
Israel shall lay their hands upon the Levites.   And
Aharon shall present the Levites, (as) an elevation before
the Lord from the sons of Israel, and they shall be for
the work of the service of the Lord.   And the Levites
shall lay their hands upon the head of the bullocks, and
make one a sin offering, and one a burnt offering before
the Lord, to atone for the Levites.   And thou shalt
place the Levites before Aharon and his sons, and present
them (as) an elevation before the Lord; and thus shalt
thou separate the Levites from among the sons of Israel,
that the Levites may be ministers before Me.   And
afterward the Levites may enter to fulfil the service of
the tabernacle of ordinance, when thou shalt have purified them and presented them (as) an elevation; for separated they are separate before Me from among the
sons of Israel, instead of every one who openeth the
womb; the first-born of all who are of the sons of Israel
have I taken (to be) before Me.   For every first-born
of the sons of Israel is Mine, whether of man or of
beast: in the day that I slew all the first-born in the
land of Mizraim, I sanctified them before Me; and I
have taken the Levites instead of all the first-born of
the sons of Israel, and have given the Levites (as) gifts

unto Aharon and to his sons from among the sons of
Israel, to minister the service of the children of Israel
in the tabernacle of ordinance, and to atone for the children of Israel, lest there be mortality among the children
of Israel at the time when they approach the sanctuary.

And Mosheh and Aharon and all the congregation of
the Beni Israel did unto the Levites according to all
that the Lord had commanded Mosheh concerning the
Levites, so did the sons of Israel to them.   And the
Levites were purified, and they washed their raiment; and
Aharon presented them as an elevation before the Lord.
And Aharon made atonement for them to purify them.
And afterward the Levites went in to fulfil their ministry
in the tabernacle of ordinance, before Aharon and his
sons : as the Lord had commanded Mosheh concerning
the Levites, so did they unto them.

And the Lord spake with Mosheh, saying : This is
the instruction for the Levites who are not disqualified
(profaned) by their blemishes : from one of twenty-five
years and upward, he shall come, according to his
company, to the service of the tabernacle of ordinance ;
and from fifty years of age he shall return from the
band of the service, and serve no more.   Yet he may
minister with his brethren at the tabernacle of ordinance
in keeping the watch ; but he shall not do any of the
service.   So shall the Levites act in their charge.

IX. And the Lord spake with Mosheh in the wilderness
of Sinai, in the second year from the time of their going
forth from the land of Mizraim, in the first month,
saying : Let the children of Israel perform the sacrifice
of the Pascha between the suns at its time.   On the
fourteenth day of this month, between the suns, they
shall perform it in its time ; according to all its rites
and all its statutes shall they do it.   And Mosheh spake
with the children of Israel to perform the sacrifice of the

Pascha. They performed the Pascha, therefore, on the fourteenth day of the month, between the suns, in the wilderness of Sinai; after all that the Lord had commanded Mosheh, so did the children of Israel.

But certain men, who were unclean, having been defiled by the body of a man who had died near them suddenly; as the commandment (of the Pascha) came upon them, could not perform it on that day, which was the seventh of their uncleanness. And they came before Mosheh and Aharon on that day; and these men said to him, We are unclean, on account of a man who died with us: therefore we are hindered from killing the Pascha, and shedding the blood of the Lord's oblation upon the altar at its time, that we may eat its flesh, being clean, among the children of Israel.

This is one of four matters of judgment brought before Mosheh the prophet, which he decided according to the Word of the Holy One: in some of which Mosheh was deliberate, because they were judgments about life; but in the others Mosheh was prompt, they being (only) judgments concerning money: but in those (the former) Mosheh said, I have not heard; that he might teach the princes of the Sanhedrin who should arise after him to be deliberate in judgments regarding life, but prompt in judgments about money; and not to be ashamed to ask counsel in things too hard for them, inasmuch as Mosheh himself, the Rabbi of Israel, had need to say, I have not yet heard. Therefore, said Mosheh to them, Wait until I have heard what will be commanded from before the Lord concerning your case. [JERUSALEM. This is one of four matters of judgment brought before Mosheh, in two of which Mosheh was prompt, and in two was he slower. Concerning the unclean who could not perform the Pascha in its time, and concerning the daughters of Zelophehad,

was Mosheh prompt, hecause the [latter] judgment was
about money; but concerning the blasphemer who had
reviled the sacred Name, and the gatherer of wood, who
wickedly profaned the Sabbath, Mosheh was deliberate,
they being decisions involving life; and in them he said,
I have not heard; that he might teach the judges who
were to come after Mosheh to be prompt in cases of
mammon, but deliberate in those of life; and not to be
ashamed to say, I have not heard, because Mosheh our
Rabbi himself said, I have not heard.   Therefore, spake
he, Arise, and listen to what the Word of the Lord will
prescribe to you.]

And the Lord spake with Mosheh, saying: Speak
with the sons of Israel, saying: A man, whether young
or old, when unclean by defilement from the dead, or an
issue, or the leprosy, or who is hindered in the way of
the world by the accidents of the night, or who shall
be at a distance from the threshold of his house: if
such things happen to you, or to your generations,
then may he defer to perform the Pascha before the
Lord.   But in the second month, which is the month
of Ijar, on the fourteenth day of the month, between
the suns they shall perform it; with unleavened bread and
with bitters they shall eat it.   They shall not leave of
it till the morning, and a bone in it shall not be broken;
according to every instruction in the decree of the Pascha
in Nisan, they shall perform it.   In the Pascha of Nisan
(such persons) may eat unleavened bread, but not perform the oblation of the Pascha on account of their
defilement; but in the Pascha of Ijar being purified
they shall offer it.   But the man who, being clean and
undefiled by the way of the world, and not at a distance
from the threshold of his home, neglecteth to perform
the oblation of the Pascha of Nisan, that man shall be
cut off from his people, because he hath not offered the

Lord's oblation in its season ; that man shall bear his
sin. And if the stranger who is sojourning with you
will perform the Pascha before the Lord, he shall do
it after the proper manner of the Paschal decree,
according to its form so shall he do it. You shall have
one statute, both for the sojourner and for the native of
the land.

And on the day on which the tabernacle was reared
the Cloud of Glory covered the Tabernacle; it overspread the Tabernacle of Testimony by day, and at
evening it was over the Tabernacle like a vision of Fire
until the morning. So was it continually, a Cloud of
Glory covering it by day, and a vision of Fire by night.
And what time the Cloud of Glory was uplifted from
the Tabernacle, then the children of Israel went forward ;
and at the place where the Cloud rested, there did the
children of Israel rest. By the mouth of the Word of
the Lord the children of Israel went forward, and by
the Word of the Lord they rested. All the days that
the Cloud of Glory abode upon the Tabernacle, (so long)
did they abide. And if the Cloud tarried over the
Tabernacle many days, the children of Israel observed
the watch of the Word of the Lord, and did not proceed.
If for the time of a number of days, suppose the seven
days of the week, the Cloud of Glory was upon the
Tabernacle, by the mouth of the Word of the Lord they
rested, and by the mouth of the Word of the Lord they
went forward. Or, if the Cloud of Glory (rested only)
from evening until morning, and was uplifted in the
morning, then went they onward ; whether by day or by
night, when the Cloud was lifted up they went forward ;
whether it was two days, or a month, or a year complete, while the Cloud of Glory made stay over the Tabernacle, abiding on it, the children of Israel abode,
and journeyed not, and at the time of its uplifting they

went forward. By the mouth of the Word of the Lord they encamped, and by it they journeyed; they kept the observance of the Word of the Lord, by the mouth of the Word of the Lord through Mosheh.

X. And the Lord spake with Mosheh, saying: Make for thee, of thine, two trumpets of silver of solid material, the work of the artificer shalt thou make them; and let them be thine, with which to convoke the assembly, and for the removing of the camps. And thou shalt blow upon them, and bring together to thee all the congregation at the door of the tabernacle of ordinance. If they blow upon one (only), the princes of the heads of the thousands of Israel shall assemble to thee. But when you blow an alarm, then the camps which are on the east are to go forward; and when they blow a second alarm, the camps on the south shall go forward; they shall blow the alarm for their journeys. And at the time of assembling the congregation you shall blow, but not an alarm. The sons of Aharon, the priests only, shall blow with the trumpets, which shall be to you for a perpetual statute for your generations.

And when you enter upon the order of the line of battle for your country, with oppressors who oppress you, then shall you blow the alarm on the trumpets, that the remembrance of you may come up for good before the Lord your God, that you may be delivered from your enemies. And in the day of your rejoicings, and in your solemnities, and at the beginning of your months, you shall blow with the trumpets over your burnt offerings and your consecrated victims, and they shall be for a good memorial to you before the Lord your God; for Satana shall be troubled at the sound of your jubel notes: I am the Lord your God.

And it was in the second year, the second month, which is the month of Ijar, the twentieth day of the month, that the Cloud of Glory was uplifted from above the Tabernacle of Testimony; and the children of Israel went forward upon their journeys from the wilderness of Sinai, and the Cloud of Glory rested in the wilderness of Pharan. And they went forth at the first by the mouth of the Word of the Lord through Mosheh.

The standard of the camps of the Beni Jehudah went forward by their hosts, and the Rabba who was appointed over the host of the tribe of the Beni Jehudah was Nachshon bar Amminadab; the Rabba of the Beni Issakar was Nethanel bar Zuar; and the Rabba of the Beni Zebulon, Eliab bar Chelon. And the tabernacle was taken down, and the sons of Gershon and of Merari went forward, carrying the tabernacle.

The standard of the camps of Reuben went forward by their hosts. The Rabba set over the hosts of the tribe of the Beni Reuben was Elizur bar Shedeur; the Rabba of the Beni Shemeon, Shelumiel bar Zurishaddai; and the Rabba of the Beni Gad, Eljasaph bar Dehuel.

And the family of Kehath went forward, carrying the sanctuary; and they (the men of Gershon) reared up the tabernacle against their coming.

The standard of the camps of the Beni Ephraim went forward by their hosts: the Rabba set over the host of the tribe of Ephraim was Elishama bar Ammihud; the Rabba of that of Menasheh, Gamaliel bar Pedazur; and the Rabba of Benjamin, Abidan bar Gideoni.

And the standard of the camps of the Beni Dan went forward, completing all the camps according to their hosts; and the Rabba set over his host was Ahiezer bar Ammishaddai; the Rabba of the tribe of Asher, Pagiel bar Achran; and the Rabba of the Beni Naphtali, Ahira bar Enan. These are the journeys of the children of Israel by their hosts; the Cloud of Glory was lifted up from above the tabernacle, and they went forward.

And Mosheh said unto Hobab bar Reuel the Midianite, father-in-law of Mosheh, We are journeying from hence to the place of which the Lord hath said, I will give it to you: come with us, and we will do thee good; for the Lord hath spoken to do good unto the sojourner with Israel. But he answered him, I will not go (with you), but to my (own) land and to my kindred will I go. But he said, Do not now leave us; for when we were encamped in the wilderness, thou knewest how to judge, and didst teach us the method (or business) of judgment, and thou art dear to us as the apple of our eyes. And it shall be that if thou wilt go on with us, with the good that the Lord shall benefit us will we benefit thee, in the division of the land.

And they went forward from the mountain on which the glory of the Shekinah of the Lord had been revealed, going three days; and the Ark of the Lord's covenant went before them. Thirty and six miles it went that day; it preceded the camp of Israel, going three days, to provide for them a place to encamp in. And the Cloud of the Lord's Shekinah overshadowed them by day in their going out from the encampment. And it was when the ark should go forward, the Cloud gathered itself together and stood still, not going on, until Mosheh, standing in prayer, prayed and supplicated mercy from before the Lord, and thus spake: Let the Word of the Lord be now revealed in the power of Thy anger, that the adversaries of Thy people may be scattered; and let not the banner of those who hate them be uplifted before Thee. But when the ark should rest, the Cloud gathered itself together and stood, but did not overspread, until Mosheh, standing in prayer, prayed and besought mercy from before the Lord, thus speaking: Return now, Thou Word of the Lord,[1] in the goodness of Thy mercy, and

[1] Observe, Moses prays to the Memra Compare the Glossary, pp. 14–17.

lead Thy people Israel, and let the glory of Thy Shekinah
dwell among them, and (Thy) mercy with the myriads of
the house of Jakob, and with the multitudes of the
thousands of Israel. [JERUSALEM. It was when the ark
went forward Mosheh stood, with hands (outstretched)
in prayer, and said, Arise now, O Word of the Lord, in
the power of Thy might, and let the adversaries of Thy
people be scattered, and make Thine enemies flee before
Thee. But when the ark rested, Mosheh lifted his hands
in prayer, and said, O Word of the Lord, turn from the
strength of Thy anger, and return unto us in the goodness of Thy mercy, and bless the myriads and multiply
the thousands of the children of Israel.

XI. But there were wicked men of the people, who,
being discontent, devised and imagined evil before the
Lord; and it was heard before the Lord, whose displeasure was moved; and a flaming fire was kindled among
them from the Lord, which destroyed some of the wicked
in the outskirts of the house of Dan, with whom was a
graven image. And the people cried to Mosheh to pray
for them; and Mosheh did pray before the Lord, and
the fire was extinguished where it was. And he called
the name of that place Enkindlement, because the
flaming fire had been enkindled there from before the
Lord.

And the strangers who had gathered together among
them demanded with demand, and they turned and wept;
and the sons of Israel said, Who will give us flesh to
eat? We remember the fish which we had to eat in
Mizraim freely, without (being restricted by prohibitory)
precept, the cucumbers and melons, the leeks, onions,
and potherbs. [JERUSALEM. We remember the fish
that we ate freely in Mizraim, the cucumbers and melons,
leeks, onions, and potherbs.] But now our life is dried
up; there is not anything; we see only the manna, as

the pauper who looks upon a morsel (bestowed) by the hands. Alas for the people whose food is bread from the heavens! And so murmured they, because the manna was like coriander-seed, round, when it came down from the heavens, and when it had been sanctified its appearance was as the likeness of Bedilcha. And the wicked people looked about, and collected, and ground it in the mill. But he who would, bruised it in the mortar, or dressed it in the pot, or made cakes of it; and the taste of it was like the taste of cream covered with oil. [JERUSALEM. And the people were scattered abroad, and collected and ground it in mills, or crushed it in the mortar, or dressed it in the pan, and made cakes of it. And the taste of it was like the taste of pastry with honey.] And when the dew came down on the camp by night, the manna descended upon it.

And Mosheh heard the people lamenting with their neighbours, who had gathered every man at the gate of his tent, and the displeasure of the Lord was strongly moved, and in the eyes of Mosheh it was evil; and Mosheh said before the Lord, Why hast Thou done ill with Thy servant, or I have not found mercy before Thee, that Thou shouldst have laid the toil of this people upon me? Have I made or borne all this people as from the womb? are they my children, that Thou saidst to me in Mizraim, Bear the toil of them with thy strength, as the instructor of youth beareth, until they be carried into the land which Thou hast sworn unto their fathers? [JERUSALEM. Have I made all this people, have I begotten them, that Thou hast said to me, Carry them in thy bosom, as the nurse[2] carrieth the sucklings, unto the land which thou didst swear unto their fathers?] Whence am I to find meat to give all this people? for they are crying to me, saying, Give us flesh that we may

---

[2] Or, "the conductor of children."

eat. I am not able to bear all this people, for it is too
weighty for me. But if Thou do this with me, to leave
all the labour of them upon me, let me now die with the
death in which the just have repose, if I have found
mercy before Thee, that I may not see mine evil.
[JERUSALEM. That I may not see the evil of them who
are Thy people.] Then spake the Lord unto Mosheh,
Gather together in My name seventy righteous men of
the elders of Israel, whom thou knowest to be elders of
the people, and who were set over them in Mizraim, and
bring them to the tabernacle to stand there with thee.
And I will be revealed in the glory of My Shekinah, and
will speak with thee there, and will amplify the spirit of
prophecy that is upon thee, and bestow it upon them;
and they shall sustain with thee the burden of the people,
that thou mayest not bear it alone. And say thou to
the people, Make ready against the morrow that you may
eat flesh; because you have lamented before the Lord,
saying, Who will give us flesh to eat? for it was better
with us in Mizraim. The Lord therefore will give you
flesh that you may eat. You shall not eat it one day,
nor two days, nor five, nor ten, nor twenty days; for a
month of days, until the smell of it cometh forth from
your nostrils, and it become a loathing to you; because
you have been contemptuous against the Word of the
Lord, whose glorious Shekinah dwelleth among you, and
because you have wept before Him, saying, Why should
we have come out from Mizraim?

But Mosheh said, Six hundred thousand footmen are
the people among whom I dwell, and Thou hast said, I
will give them flesh to eat for a month of days! Shall
the flocks of Araby or the cattle of Nabatea be killed
for them to satisfy them, or all the fishes of the Great
Sea be collected, that they may have enough? And
the Lord said to Mosheh, Can any thing fail before the

Lord? Now shalt thou see whether what I have said
to thee shall come to pass or not. Then Mosheh went
forth from the tabernacle, the house of the Shekinah,
and told the people the words of the Lord. And he
called together the seventy men, the elders of Israel, and
placed them around the tabernacle. And the Lord was
revealed in the glorious Cloud of the Shekinah, and
spake with him. And He made enlargement of the
(Spirit of) prophecy that was upon him, so that Mosheh
lost nothing thereof, but He gave unto the seventy men,
the elders: and it was that when the Spirit of prophecy
rested upon them, they prophesied, and ceased not.

But two men had remained in the camp; the name
of the one Eldad, and the name of the second Medad,
the sons of Elizaphan bar Parnak, whom Jokebed the
daughter of Levi bare to him when Amram her husband had put her away; and to whom she had been
espoused before she gave birth to Mosheh. And the
Spirit of prophecy resting upon them, Eldad prophesied, and said: Behold, Mosheh shall be gathered from
the world; and Jehoshua bar Nun, the minister of the
camps, will be established after him, and will lead the
people of the house of Israel, and bring them into the
land of Kenaan, and make it their inheritance.

Medad prophesied, and said. Behold, quails come up
from the sea, and cover all the camp of Israel; but they
will be to the people (a cause of) an offence. And
both of them prophesied together, and said: Behold, a
king will arise from the land of Magog, at the end of
the days, and will assemble kings crowned with crowns,
and captains wearing armour, and him will all nations
obey. And they will set battle in array in the land of
Israel against the children of the captivity; but already
is it provided that in the hour of distresses all of them
shall perish by the burning blast of the flame that

cometh forth from beneath the Throne of Glory; and
their carcases shall fall upon the mountains of the land
of Israel, and the wild beasts of the field and the fowls
of the sky shall come and consume their dead bodies.
And afterward will all the dead of Israel live (again),
and be feasted from the ox which hath been set apart
for them from the beginning, and they shall receive the
reward of their works.

And they were of the elders who stood in the
registers among them; but they had not gone forth to
the tabernacle, but had hidden, to escape from the dignity; yet they prophesied in the camp. [JERUSALEM.
And there remained two men in the camp: the name of
one of them Eldad, the name of the second Medad,
upon whom rested the Holy Spirit. Eldad prophesied,
and said: Lo, Mosheh, the prophet, the scribe of Israel,
will be gathered from the world, and Jehoshua bar
Nun, his disciple, minister of the camps, will succeed.
Medad prophesied, and said: Behold, quails come up
from the sea; but they will be an offence to the
children of Israel. Both of them prophesied together,
and said: At the end, the end of the days, will Gog and
Magog and his host come up against Jerusalem; but
by the hand of the King Meshiha they will fall, and
seven years of days will the children of Israel kindle
their fire with their weapons of war, not going into the
wilderness, nor cutting down the trees. And they
were of the seventy sages, who went not from the tabernacle, while Eldad and Medad prophesied in the camp.]

And a certain young man ran, and told to Mosheh,
and said: Eldad and Medad are prophesying thus in
the camp. And Jehoshua bar Nun, the minister of
Mosheh, answered and said: Ribboni Mosheh, pray for
mercy before the Lord, that the Spirit of prophecy may
be withheld from them. But Mosheh said to him,

Because they prophesy concerning me that I am to be gathered from the world, and that thou art to minister after me, art thou jealous for my sake? I would that all the Lord's people were prophets, and that He would bestow the Spirit of prophecy upon them.

And Mosheh proceeded to the camp, he and all the elders of Israel. And the wind of a tempest went forth, and came violently from before the Lord, so as to have swept the world away, but for the righteousness of Mosheh and Aharon. and it blew over the Great Sea, and made the quails fly from the Great Sea, and settle wherever there was place in the camp, as a day's journey northward and southward, and at the height as of two cubits; they flew upon the face of the ground, and went upon their bellies, so that (the people) were not wearied while they collected them. And they who had been wanting in faith arose : and all that day, and all the night, and all the day that followed, they gathered the quails; even he who was lame and infirm gathered ten korin, [JERUSALEM. Ten korin,] and they spread them abroad round about the camps.

The wicked ate of the flesh, yet offered no thanksgiving to Him who had given it to them : but while the flesh was between their teeth, and not consumed, the anger of the Lord waxed strong against the evil people, and the Lord slew the people with a very great mortality. And he called the name of that place, The Graves of the Desirers of Flesh; for there they buried the people who had desired flesh. And from the Graves of the Desirers the people journeyed to Hatseroth, and they were in Hatseroth.

XII. And Miriam and Aharon spake against Mosheh words that were not becoming with respect to the Kushaitha whom the Kushaee had caused Mosheh to take when he had fled from Pharoh, but whom he had

sent away because they had given him the queen of
Kush, and he had sent her away. [JERUSALEM. And
Miriam and Aharon spake against Mosheh about the
Kushaitha whom he had taken. But observe, the
Kushite wife was not Zipporah, the wife of Mosheh, but
a certain Kushaitha, of a flesh different from every
creature : whereas Zipporah, the wife of Mosheh, was
of a comely form and beautiful countenance, and more
abundant in good works than all the women of her
age.] And they said, Hath the Lord spoken only
with Mosheh, that he should be separated from the
married life ? Hath He not spoken with us also ?
And it was heard before the Lord. But the man
Mosheh was more bowed down in his mind than all
the children of men upon the face of the earth ; neither
cared he for their words.

And the Lord said to Mosheh, to Aharon, and to
Miriam, Come forth, you three, to the tabernacle. And
those three went forth. And the Glory of the Lord was
revealed in the Cloud of Glory, and He stood at the door
of the tabernacle, and called Aharon and Miriam : and
those two came forth. And He said, Hear now My
words, while I speak. Have any of the prophets who
have arisen from the days of old been spoken with as
Mosheh hath been ? To those (prophets) the Word of
the Lord hath been revealed in apparition, speaking with
them in a dream. Not so is the way with Mosheh My
servant ; in all the house of Israel My people he is
faithful. [JERUSALEM. Not so is My servant Mosheh
among all the company (of the prophets), the chief of
the chiefs of My court, faithful is he.] Speaker with
speaker have I spoken with him, who hath separated
himself from the married life ; but in vision, and not
with mystery, revealed I Myself to him at the bush, and
he beheld the likeness of My Shekinah. And why have

you not feared to speak such words of My servant
Mosheh?   And the glory of the Lord's Shekinah ascended, and went.   And the glorious Cloud of the
Lord's Shekinah went up from above the tabernacle ;
and, behold, Miriam was seized with the leprosy.   And
Aharon looked upon Miriam, and, behold, she had
been smitten with leprosy.   And Aharon said to
Mosheh, I beseech of thee, my lord, not to lay upon
us the sin we have foolishly committed, and by which
we have transgressed.   I entreat thee that Miriam,
our sister, may not be defiled with leprosy in the
tent, as the dead, for it is with her as with the infant [3] which, having well fulfilled the time of the womb,
perishes at the birth : so Miriam was with us in the
land of Mizraim, seeing us in our captivity, our dispersion, our servitude ; but now, when the time hath come
for our going forth to possess the land of Israel, behold,
she is kept back from us.   I entreat thee, my lord, to
pray for her, that her righteousness may not come to
nought among the congregation.   [JERUSALEM. 11.
That we have sinned.   12. Let not Miriam, our sister,
be a leper, polluted in the tent as one dead.   For it is with
her as with the infant who hath passed nine months in its
mother's womb, in water and in heat, without injury, but
which after all perishes at the birth.   So was Miriam, our
sister, carried away with us into the desert, and with us
in our trouble ; but now the time hath come that we
may enter into the land of Israel, why should she be
kept from us?   Pray now for the dead body that it
may live, and that her righteousness may not fail.]
And Mosheh did pray, and seek mercy before the Lord,
saying : I pray through the compassions of the merciful
God, O Eloha, who hast power over the life of all flesh,
heal her, I beseech thee.   [JERUSALEM. O Eloha, who

---

[3] I have translated freely just here.

healest all flesh, heal her.] And the Lord said to
Mosheh, If her father had corrected her, would she not
have been disgraced, and secluded seven days? But
to-day, when I correct her, much more right is it that
she should be dishonoured fourteen days: yet shall it
suffice to seclude her seven days without the camp;
and for thy righteousness will I make the Cloud of My
Glory, the tabernacle, the ark, and all Israel, tarry until
the time that she is healed, and then re-admitted. And
Miriam was kept apart without the camp for seven days,
and the people went not forward until the time that
Miriam was healed.

XIII. But though Miriam the prophetess had made
herself liable to be stricken with leprosy in this world,
the doctrine is ample that in the world to come (there
remaineth a reward) for the just, and for them who keep
the commandments of the law. And because Miriam
the prophetess had watched for a little hour to know
what would be the fate of Mosheh; (Exod. i.;) for the
sake of that merit all Israel, numbering sixty myriads,
being eighty legions, and the Cloud of Glory, the tabernacle, and the well, went not, nor proceeded, till the
time that she was healed: and afterward the people
journeyed from Hatseroth, and encamped in the wilderness of Pharan. [JERUSALEM. But though Miriam the
prophetess had become liable to leprosy, we have ample
doctrine that by keeping the commandments and precepts a man who doeth even a little shall receive
a great reward. Thus, because Miriam the prophetess had stood on the river bank for a little hour,
to know what would be the end of Mosheh, the
sons of Israel, being sixty myriads, and eighty legions
in number, and the Cloud of Glory and the well, now
moved not, nor went forward from their place, till the
time that she was healed of her leprosy; but after she

was healed the people journeyed from Hatscroth, and encamped in the wilderness of Pharan.

SECTION XXXVII.
SHALACH.

AND the Lord spake with Mosheh, saying: Send thou keen-sighted men who may explore the land of Kenaan, which I will give to the children of Israel; one man for each tribe of their fathers, thou shalt send from the presence of all their leaders. And Mosheh sent them from the wilderness of Pharan, according to the mouth of the Word of the Lord; all of them acute men, who had been appointed heads over the sons of Israel. And these are the names of the twelve men, the explorers: the messenger of the tribe of Reuben, Shamua bar Zakkur; of the tribe of Shemeon, Shaphat bar Hori; for Jehudah, Kaleb bar Jephunneh; for Issakar, Yiggeal bar Joseph; for Ephraim, Hoshea bar Nun; for Benjamin, Palti bar Raphu; for Zebulon, Gadiel bar Zodi; for Menasheh, Gaddi bar Susi; for Dan, Ammiel bar Gemmalli; for Asher, Sether bar Michael; for Naphtali, Nachbi bar Vaphsi; and for Gad, Geuel bar Machi. These are the names of the men whom Mosheh sent to explore the land; and when Mosheh saw his humility, he called Hoshea bar Nun Jehoshua.

And Mosheh sent them to survey the land of Kenaan, and said to them, Go up on this side by the south, and ascend the mountain, and survey the country, what it is, and the people who dwell in it; whether they be strong or weak, few or many; what the land is in which they dwell, whether good or bad; what cities they inhabit, whether they live in towns that are open or walled; and what the reputation of the land, whether its productions are rich or poor, and the trees of it fruitful or not. And do valiantly, and bring back some of the fruit of the land. [JERUSALEM. And what the land is, whether the fruits of it are rich : or trees.]

And the day on which they went was the nineteenth of the month of Sivan, (about) the days of the first grapes. They went up, therefore, and explored the country, from the wilderness of Zin, unto the roads by which thou comest unto Antiochia. They went up from the side of the south and came to Hebron, where were Achiman, Sheshai, and Talmai, sons of Anak the giant. Now Hebron was built seven years before Tanis in Mizraim. They came then to the stream of the grapes (or bunches, *ethkala*), and cut down from thence a branch, with one cluster of grapes, and carried it on a staff on the shoulders of two of them, and also took they of the pomegranates and the figs. [JERUSALEM. And they came to the stream of the grape clusters, and cut down from thence a branch with one cluster of grapes, and carried it on a rod between two men ; and also of the pomegranates and of the figs.] Now that place they call the stream of the cluster, from the branch which the sons of Israel cut down there ; and wine was dropping from it like a stream.

And they returned from exploring the land on the eighth day of the month Ab, at the end of forty days. And they came to Mosheh and Aharon, and all the congregation of the children of Israel in the wilderness of Pharan, at Rekem, and returned them word, to them and the whole congregation, and showed them the fruit of the land.

And they recounted to him, and said : We went into the country to which thou didst send us ; and it indeed produceth milk and honey, and this is the fruit of it. But the people who inhabit the country are strong, and the fortified cities they inhabit very great ; and we saw

also there the sons of Anak the giant. The Amalekites
dwell in the south, the Hittites, Jebusites, and Amorites
in the mountains ; but the Kenaanites dwell by the
sea, and by the bank of the Jordan.

And Kaleb stilled the people, and made them listen
to Mosheh, and said · Let us go up and possess it, for
we are able to take it. [JERUSALEM. And he stilled.]
But the men who had gone up with him said, We are
not able to go up to the people, for they are stronger
than we. And they brought out an evil report about
the land which they had surveyed, to the sons of Israel,
saying, The country through which we have passed to
explore it is a land that killeth its inhabitants with
diseases ; and all the people who are in it are giants,
masters of evil ways. And there we saw the giants, the
sons of Anak, of the race of the giants ; and we appeared to ourselves to be as locusts ; and so we
appeared to them.

XIV. And all the congregation lifted up and gave
forth their voice, and the people wept that night : and
it was confirmed (as a punishment) that they should
weep on that night [4] in their generations. And all the
sons of Israel murmured against Mosheh and Aharon,
and said : Would that we had died in the land of
Mizraim, or that we may die in this wilderness ! Why
is the Lord bringing us into this land, to fall by the
sword of the Kenaanaah, and our wives and little ones
to become a prey ? Will it not be better to return into
Mizraim ? And one man said to his brother, Let us
appoint a king over us for a chief, and return to
Mizraim. [JERUSALEM. Let us set a king over us,
and go round to Mizraim.]

And Mosheh and Aharon bowed upon their faces before

[4] The ninth of Ab, a day remarkable for a succession of calamities in
the history of the Jews.

all the congregation of the sons of Israel ; and Jehoshua
bar Nun and Kaleb bar Jephunneh of the explorers of
the land rent their clothes, and spake to the congregation, saying : The land we went to see is an exceedingly good land.   If the Lord hath pleasure in us, He
will bring us into this land, and give it us, a land producing milk and honey.   Only do not rebel against the
commandments of the Lord, and you need not fear the
people of the land, for they are delivered into our hands ;
the strength of their power hath failed from them, but
the Word of the Lord will be our helper ; fear them
not.   But all the congregation said they would stone
them with stones.

And the glorious Shekinah of the Lord was revealed
in bright clouds at the tabernacle.   And the Lord said
to Mosheh, How long will this people provoke Me to
anger ?   How long will they disbelieve in My Word,
for all the signs I have wrought among them ?   I will
strike them with deadly plague and destroy them, and will
appoint thee for a people greater and stronger than
they.   But Mosheh said, The children of the Mizraee,
whom Thou didst drown in the sea, will hear that
Thou didst bring up this people from among them by
Thy power, and will say with exultation to the people
of this land, who have heard that Thou art the Lord,
whose Shekinah dwelleth among this people, in whose
eyes, O Lord, the Glory of Thy Shekinah appeared on the
mountain of Sinai, and who there received Thy law ;
and over whom Thy Cloud hath shadowed, that neither
heat nor rain might hurt them ; and whom in the pillar
of the Cloud Thou hast led on by day, that the mountains and hills might be brought low, and the valleys
lifted up, and hast guided in the pillar of Fire by night :
and after all these miracles wilt Thou kill this people as
one man ?   Then the nations who have heard the fame

of Thy power will speak, saying: Because there was no
(more) strength with the Lord to bring this people into
the land which swearing He had promised to them, He
hath killed them in the wilderness! And now, I
beseech Thee, magnify Thy power, O Lord, and let
mercies be fulfilled upon us, and appoint me for (this) great
people, as Thou hast spoken, saying : The Lord is long-
suffering, and nigh in mercy, forgiving sins and covering
transgressions, justifying such as return to His law ;
though them who turn not He will not absolve, but will
visit the sins of wicked fathers upon rebellious children
unto the third and fourth generation.   JERUSALEM.
The Lord is long-suffering, far from anger, near in
mercy, multiplying the exercise of goodness and truth ;
though the Lord will not justify sinners, but will remember, in the day of judgment, the guilt of wicked fathers
upon rebellious children.]   Pardon now the sin of this
people according to Thy great goodness, even as Thou
hast forgiven them from the time that they came out
from Mizraim until now. And the Lord said, I have
forgiven, according to thy word. [JERUSALEM. And
the Word of the Lord said, Behold, I have absolved
and pardoned, according to thy word.] Nevertheless,
by oath have I sworn that the whole earth shall be filled
with the glory of the Lord. Because all the men who
have beheld My glory, and My signs, which I have
wrought in Mizraim and in the Desert, have tempted
Me now ten times, and have not obeyed My Word : by
oath have I said this, That they shall not see the land
which I covenanted to their fathers ; and the generation
which have been provokeful before me shall not behold
it. [JERUSALEM. For I have uplifted My hand with
an oath.] But My servant, Kaleb, because there is in
him another spirit, and he hath entirely followed (in)
My fear, him will I bring into the land to which he

went, and his children shall possess it. But the Amalekites and Kenaanites dwell in the valley: to-morrow turn you and go into the wilderness by the way of the Red Sea.

And the Lord spake with Mosheh and Aharon, saying: How long (shall I bear with) this evil congregation who gather together against Me? The murmurs of the sons of Israel which they murmur against Me are heard before Me. Say to them, By oath I decree that according to (what) you have spoken, so will I do to you. In this wilderness your carcasses shall fall, the whole number of all who were counted from twenty years old and upward, who have murmured against Me, By a fast oath (have I sworn) that you shall not enter into the land which I covenanted in My Word to give you to inhabit, except Kaleb bar Jephunneh and Jehoshua bar Nun. But your children, who you said would be a prey, them will I bring in, and they shall know the land which you rejected; but your carcasses shall fall in this wilderness. Yet your children will have to wander in this wilderness forty years, and bear your sins until the time that your carcasses are consumed in the wilderness. According to the number of the days in which you were exploring the land, forty days, a day for a year, a day for a year, you shall receive for your sins, forty years, and shall know (the consequence) of your murmuring against Me. I the Lord have decreed in My Word,—if I have not made a decree in My Word against all this evil congregation who have gathered a rebel against Me in this wilderness, that they shall be consumed and die there.

But the men whom Mosheh had sent to explore the land, and who returning had made the whole congregation murmur against him, by bringing forth an evil report of the land, (even those) men who had brought forth the

evil of the report of the land died, on the seventh day of
the month of Elul, with worms coming from their navels,
and with worms devouring their tongues; and were
buried in death from before the Lord.   Only Jehoshua
bar Nun and Kaleb bar Jephunneh survived of those
men who had gone to explore the land.

And Mosheh spake these words with all the sons of
Israel, and the people mourned greatly.   And they
arose in the morning and went up to the top of the
mountain, saying : Behold, we will go up to the place
of which the Lord hath spoken; for we have
sinned.   But Mosheh said, Why will you act against
the decree of the Word of the Lord?   But it will not
prosper with you.   Go not up, for the Lord's Shekinah
dwelleth not among you; and the ark, the tabernacle,
and the Cloud of Glory proceed not; and be not
crushed before your enemies.   For the Amalekites and
Kenaanites are there prepared for you, and you will fall
slaughtered by the sword.   For, because you have turned
away from the service of the Lord, the Word of the
Lord will not be your Helper.   But they armed themselves in the dark before the morning, to go up to the
height of the mountain : but the ark, in which was the
covenant of the Lord, and Mosheh, stirred not from the
midst of the camp.   And the Amalekites and Kenaanites
who dwelt in that mountain came down and slaughtered
and destroyed them, and drave them hard to destruction.

XV. And the Lord spake with Mosheh, saying :
Speak with the sons of Israel, and say to them : When
you have entered into the land of your habitation which
I will give you, and you may make an oblation upon
the altar before the Lord, burnt offering or consecrated
sacrifice for release of a vow, or by free-will offering; or
at the time of your feasts you offer what is acceptable

to the Lord of the world, to be received with approval
before the Lord from the herd or from the flock : let
the man who offers his oblation before the Lord bring
a mincha of a tenth of flour mingled with the fourth of
a hina of olive oil ; and wine of grapes for a libation, the
fourth of a hina, to be made upon the burnt offering or
hallowed sacrifice for one lamb.　Or for a ram, let him
perform a mincha of two tenths of flour mingled with the
third of a hin of olive oil, and wine of grapes let him offer in
a vase for the libation, the third of a hin, to be received
with acceptance before the Lord.　But when he maketh
a bullock a burnt offering, or a sacrifice for release from
a vow, or a hallowed sacrifice before the Lord, let him
bring for the bullock a mincha of three tenths of flour
mixed with half of a hin of olive oil, and wine of grapes
half a hin, for a libation to be received with acceptance
before the Lord.　So let him do with each bullock, with
each ram, and each lamb, whether it be from the lambs
or the kids : according to the number of the bullocks
or lambs or goats with which the oblation is made so
shall you do, each according to their number.　All who
are native born in Israel, and not of the sons of the
Gentiles, shall so make these libations in offering an
oblation to be received with acceptance before the
Lord.　And when a sojourner who sojourneth with
you, or whoever is among you now, or in your generations, will bring an oblation to be received with
favour before the Lord, as you do so shall he.　For the
whole congregation there is one statute, for you and the
sojourner who sojourneth ; it is an everlasting statute
for your generations ; as with you, so shall it be with
the sojourner before the Lord.　One law and one judgment shall be for you and for the sojourner who
sojourneth with you.

　　And the Lord spake with Mosheh, saying : Speak

c 2

with the sons of Israel, and say to them: When you
have entered the land into which I will bring you, and
you eat the bread of the produce of it, (not rice, nor
millet, nor pulse,) you shall set apart a separation before
the Lord. Of the first of your dough one cake of
twenty-four you shall set apart as a separation for the
priest, as with the separation from the threshing floor,
so shall you set it apart. Of the first of your dough
you shall give a separation before the Lord in your generations. [JERUSALEM. Of the first of your dough you
shall give a separation unto the Name of the Lord.]

And should you have erred, and not performed some
one of all these commandments which the Lord hath
spoken with Mosheh, whatsoever the Lord hath commanded you by Mosheh, from the day He commanded it,
and thenceforth unto your generations—if without the
knowledge of the congregation sin hath been committed
through ignorance, let all the congregation make one
young bullock a burnt offering to be received with
acceptance before the Lord, with his mincha and libation as are proper; and one kid of the goats without
mixture for a sin offering; and let the priest make
atonement for all the congregation of the sons of Israel,
and it shall be forgiven them; for it was an error, and
they have brought their oblation, an offering before the
Lord, even an offering for their sin have they presented
before the Lord for their error; and all the congregation of Israel shall be forgiven before the Lord, and
the sojourners who sojourn among them; for an error
hath occurred to the people.

And if any one man sin through ignorance, let him
bring one goat of the year without mixture for a sin
offering, and let the priest make atonement for the man
who hath erred in sinning through ignorance before the
Lord to atone for him, that it may be forgiven him; as

well for the native-born of the children of Israel, and for
the strangers who sojourn among you, there shall be one
law for him who transgresseth through ignorance: but a
man who transgresseth with presumption, whether of the
native-born or strangers, and who turneth not away
from his sin before the Lord,—he causeth anger, and
that man shall perish from among his people; for, the
primal word which the Lord commanded on Sinai he
hath despised, and hath made the commandment of
circumcision vain; with destruction in this world shall
that man be destroyed; in the world that cometh shall
he give account of his sin at the great day of judgment.
[JERUSALEM. Because he hath despised the Word of
the Lord, and broken His commandments, that soul
shall perish, and shall bear his sin]

And while the sons of Israel were dwelling in the
wilderness, the decree of the Sabbath was known to
them, but the punishment (for the profanation) of the
Sabbath was not known. And there arose a man of the
house of Joseph, and said with himself :[5] I will go and
pull up wood on the Sabbath day; and witnesses saw
it, and told Mosheh; and Mosheh sought instruction
from the presence of the Lord, that he might teach me
judgment, and make known the discipline of all the
house of Israel. And the witnesses of the man who
pulled up and collected wood came, and, after they had
monished him, and he had wounded the witnesses who
had found him pulling up wood, [JERUSALEM. Stealing wood,] brought him to Mosheh and Aharon, and all
the congregation. This is one of four judgments which
were brought before Mosheh the prophet, which he
adjudged according to the Word of the Holy. Of these
judgments some related to money, and some to life. In
the judgments regarding money Mosheh was prompt,

----

[5] *Be memrieh*, "in his word,—his inmost self, or personality."

but in those affecting life he was deliberate, and in each
he said, I have not heard,—to teach the princes of the
future Sanhedrin to be prompt in decisions on mammon,
and deliberate in those that involved life, nor to be
ashamed to inquire for counsel in what may be difficult,
forasmuch as Mosheh the Rabbi of Israel himself had
need to say, I have not heard. Therefore put they him
in confinement, because they had not yet heard the
explanation of the judgment they should execute upon
him. [JERUSALEM. This is one of four cases which
are written above, on that of the blasphemer, and they
who were defiled by the dead. And they put him in
ward till the time when it should be plainly showed to
them from before the Lord, with what judgment they
were to deal with him.]

And the Lord said to Mosheh : The man shall be
surely put to death; the whole congregation shall stone
him with stones without the camp; and the congregation led him forth without the camp, and stoned him with
stones that he died, as the Lord had commanded Mosheh.

And the Lord said unto Mosheh : Speak with the
sons of Israel, and bid them make for themselves fringes,[6]
not of threads, nor of yarns, nor of fibres, but after a
manner of their own (*lesumhon*) shall they make them,
and shall cut off the heads of their filaments, and suspend
by five ligatures, four in the midst of three,[7] upon the
four corners of their garment in which they enwrap
themselves, unto their generations; and they shall put
upon the edge of their robes an embroidery of hyacinth
(*shezir de-thikela*). [JERUSALEM. And let them make
to themselves fringes for the edges of their robes, through-

[6] *Tsitsith*, either a fringe or a tassel, probably the latter. *Tsits*
sometimes means a flower. In the similar precept, Deut. xxii. 12, the
word employed is *gedilim*, tufts or tassels of a conical form, like a flower
bud   Onkelos has *keruspidin*, "borderings."
[7] *Arbea bego telatha*   (Query)

out their generations, and put upon the fringes of their
robes an embroidery of hyacinth.] And this shall
be to you a precept for fringes, that you may look
upon them at the time when you dress yourselves daily,
and remember all My commandments to do them, and
not go aside to wander after the imaginations of your
heart and the sight of your eyes, after which you have
gone astray. To the end that you may remember and
perform all My precepts, and be holy, like the angels
who minister before the Lord your God. I am the Lord
your God who have delivered and brought you free out
of the land of Mizraim, to be to you Eloha. I am the
Lord your God.

SECTION XXXVIII.

KORACH.

XVI. But Korach bar Jizhar bar Kehath, bar Levi,
with Dathan and Abiram the sons of Eliab, and On bar
Peleth, of the Beni-Reuben, took his robe which was all
of hyacinth, and rose up boldly, and in the face of
Mosheh appointed a (different) observance in the matter
of the hyacinth. [JERUSALEM. And Korach took
counsel, and made division.] Mosheh had said, I have
heard from the mouth of the Holy One, whose Name be
Blessed, that the fringes are to be of white, with one
filament of hyacinth ; but Korach and his companions
made garments with their fringes altogether of hyacinth,
which the Lord had not commanded ; and two hundred
and fifty men of the sons of Israel, who had been made
leaders of the congregation at the time when the
journeys and encampments were appointed, by expres-

sion of their names, supported him. And they gathered
together against Mosheh and Aharon, and said to them :
Let the authority you have (hitherto had) suffice you,
for all the congregation are holy, and the Lord's
Shekinah dwelleth among them ; and why should you
be magnified over the church of the Lord ?

And Mosheh heard, as if every one of them was
jealous of his wife, and would have them drink of the
trial-water on account of Mosheh ; and he fell on his
face for shame.   And he spake with Korach and all the
company who supported him, saying : In the morning
the Lord will make known him whom He hath approved,
and hath consecrated to approach unto His service, and
who it hath pleased Him should come nigh in ministering unto Him.   Do this : Let Korach and all the
company of his helpers take censers, put fire in them,
and lay incense upon them before the Lord, to-morrow ;
and the man whom the Lord shall make known, he it is
who is consecrated.   Let it suffice to you, sons of Levi.

And Mosheh said to Korach and his kindred : Hear
now, ye sons of Levi : Is it too little for you that the
God of Israel hath set you apart from the congregation
of Israel to draw near to do His service, to fulfil the
ministry of the Lord's tabernacle, and to stand before
the congregation to minister to them ?   But so hath he
brought nigh thee and all the sons of Levi with thee ;
and now, do ye demand the high-priesthood also ?
Therefore art thou and all the company of thy helpers
gathered together against the Word of the Lord : and
Aharon, what is he, that you murmur against him ?

And Mosheh sent men to summon Dathan and Abiram,
the sons of Eliab, to the house of the great judgment,
but they said, We will not come up.   Is it a little
thing, that thou hast brought us from Mizraim, a land
that produceth milk and honey, to kill us in the

wilderness, that ruling thou mayest domineer over us?
Neither hast thou brought us into the land producing
milk and honey, to give us an inheritance of fields and
vineyards. Wilt thou blind the eyes of the men of that
land, that thou mayest overcome them? We shall not
go up thither. And Mosheh was very wroth, and said
before the Lord: I beseech thee, look not upon their
offering, the portion of their hands; for not an ass have
I taken from one of them, nor to any of them done an
injury. [JERUSALEM. And it was very grievous to
Mosheh, and he said before the Lord: Regard not the
portion of their hands; for not an ass have I taken from
one of them, nor to one of them done wrong]

And Mosheh said to Korach, Thou, and all the company of thy helpers, come together to the house of
judgment before the Lord to-morrow, thou, they, and
Aharon. And take every one his censer, and put
incense upon them; and let each offer his censer before
the Lord, two hundred and fifty censers; thou also,
and Aharon, each man his censer. And they took
every one his censer, and put fire in them and sweet
incense with it, and stood at the door of the tabernacle
of ordinance on one side; but Mosheh and Aharon on
the other side. And Korach gathered to them the
whole congregation at the door of the tabernacle. And
he had brought forth, from his riches, two treasures
which he had found among the treasures of Joseph
filled with silver and gold, and sought with them to
drive the riches of Mosheh and Aharon out of the
world; but the glory of the Lord revealed itself to all
the congregation.

And the Lord spake with Mosheh and Aharon,
saying: Separate yourselves from among this congregation, that I may destroy them quickly. But they bowed
down upon their faces in prayer, and said: El Eloha,

who hast put the spirit of life in the bodies of the
children of men, and from whom is given the spirit of
all flesh,—if one man hath sinned, wilt Thou be angry
with all the congregation? [JERUSALEM. And they
bowed on their faces, and said: O God, who rulest over
the spirit of all flesh,—if one man hath sinned, wilt
Thou be wroth against all the people?] And the Lord
spake with Mosheh, saying. I have accepted thy prayer
for the congregation. Now speak thou with them,
saying: Remove away from the tents of Korach,
Dathan, and Abiram.

And Mosheh arose, and went to remonstrate with
Dathan and Abiram; and the elders of Israel followed.
And he said to the congregation, Remove now away
from the tents of these men of sin, who have been
worthy of death from (the days of) their youth in
Mizraim, for they betrayed my secret when I slew the
Mizraite; they provoked the Lord at the sea; at Alush
they profaned the Sabbath, and now are they gathered
together against the Word of the Lord; and therefore
is it fit that their wealth should be scattered abroad and
destroyed. Touch not, then, anything that is theirs,
nor be smitten on account of their sins. And they
went apart from the tents of Korach, Dathan, and
Abiram round about. But Dathan and Abiram came
out, with reviling words, and arose and provoked
Mosheh at the door of their tents, with their wives,
their sons, and their little ones.

And Mosheh said, By this you shall know that the
Lord hath sent me to do all these works, and that (I do
them) not from the thoughts of my heart. If these
men die after the manner of dying in which all men
die, and the (common) account of all men be accounted
upon them, the Lord hath not sent me. [JERUSALEM.
For not with my own heart have I devised them. If

XVI.]   ON NUMBERS.   395

these die by the death with which the sons of men die,
and the account of all men be accounted upon them,
the Lord hath not sent me.]   But if a death which
hath not been created since the days of the world be
now created for them, and if a mouth for the earth,
which hath not been made from the beginning, be
created now, and the earth open her mouth and swallow
them and all they have, and they go down alive into
Sheul, you will understand that these men have
provoked the Lord to anger.

And it came to pass, when he had finished speaking
these words, the earth beneath them clave asunder ;
and the earth opened her mouth and swallowed them
up, and the men of their houses, and all the men who
adhered to Korach, and all their substance.   And they
went down with all that they had alive into Sheul ; and
the earth closed upon them, and they perished from the
midst of the congregation.   And all Israel who were
round about them fled from the terror of their voice, as
they cried and said, Righteous is the Lord, and His
judgment is truth, and the words of His servant
Mosheh are truth ; but we are wicked who have
rebelled against him : and the children of Israel fled
when they heard ; for they said, Lest the earth swallow
us up.   And a fire came out in wrath from before the
Lord, and devoured the two hundred and fifty men who
offered the incense.

And the Lord spake with Mosheh, saying : Bid
Elazar bar Aharon the priest to take away the censers
from among the burnings, and scatter the fire hither
and thither ; for the censers of these guilty men who
have been punished by the destruction of their lives are
consecrated ; and make of them broad plates for the
covering of the altar, because they bare them before the
Lord, therefore they are consecrate ; and they shall be

for a sign to the children of Israel. [JERUSALEM. For a sign.]   And Elazar the priest took the brasen censers which they who had been burned had carried, and beat them out for a covering for the body of the altar, as they had before used them for the service of the altar: for a memorial to the sons of Israel, that no common man, who is not of the sons of Aharon, may offer incense before the Lord; and that no man should behave himself factiously to obtain the priesthood, as did Korach and the company of his helpers; and whose end would be to perish, not (indeed) with a death like that of Korach and his company, by being burned by fire, and being swallowed up by the earth, but punished with leprosy :[8]—as when the Lord said to Mosheh, Put thy hand into thy bosom, and his hand was stricken with leprosy; so would it be with him.

But on the following day the whole congregation murmured against Mosheh and Aharon, saying: You have been the occasion of the judgment of death against the people of the Lord. And it was, that when the congregation had gathered against Mosheh and Aharon to kill them, they looked towards the Tabernacle of Ordinance, and, behold, the Cloud of the Glory of the Shekinah covered it, and the Glory of the Lord was revealed there. And Mosheh and Aharon went from the congregation to the door of the tabernacle.

And the Lord spake with Mosheh, saying: Separate from the midst of this congregation, and I will consume them at once. But they bowed themselves on their faces in prayer. [JERUSALEM. Separate from the people of this congregation, and I will destroy them in a brief moment. But they bowed down on their faces in prayer.]

And Mosheh said to Aharon, Take the censer, put

---

[8] Compare the case of King Uzziah.

fire in it from the altar, and sweet incense on the fire;
bear it quickly into the congregation, and make atonement for them : for a destruction like that which consumed them in Horeb, whose name is Burning, hath
begun by commandment to kill, from the presence of
the Lord. And Aharon took, as Mosheh had said, and
ran into the midst of the congregation, and, behold, the
destructive burning had begun to destroy the people :
but he put on incense, and made atonement for the
people. And Aharon stood in the midst, between the
dead and the living, with the censer, and interceded in
prayer; and the plague was restrained. But the
number who had died by the plague was fourteeen
thousand and seven hundred, beside those who had died
in the schism of Korach. And Aharon returned to
Mosheh at the door of the tabernacle; and the plague
was stayed.

XVII. And the Lord spake with Mosheh, saying :
Speak with the sons of Israel, and take of them severally a rod, according to the house of their fathers;
twelve rods; and upon each rod thou shalt inscribe
its (tribe) name. But on the rod of Levi thou shalt
write the name of Aharon : for there is but one rod for
each head of their father's house. And thou shalt lay
them up in the tabernacle before the testimony, where
My Word is appointed to meet you And the man
whose rod germinateth shall be he whom I approve to
minister before Me; and I will make the murmurings
of the sons of Israel with which they have murmured
against you to cease from Me.

Mosheh spake, therefore, with the sons of Israel, and
the chiefs of them gave him severally their rods, according to the house of their fathers, twelve rods; and
Aharon's rod was among theirs. And Mosheh laid up
the rods before the Lord in the tabernacle of ordinance.

And it came to pass, the day after, when Mosheh went
into the tabernacle of the testimony, that, behold, the
rod of Aharon had germinated ; it had shot forth
branches, blossomed with flowers, and, in the same
night, produced and ripened almonds. [JERUSALEM.
And the day following Mosheh went into the tabernacle
of testimony, and, behold, the rod of Aharon, of his house
of Levi, had germinated, put forth buds, bloomed with
flowers, and ripened almonds, the fruit of the almond.]

And Mosheh brought out all the rods from before
the Lord to all the sons of Israel, who recognised and
took severally their rods. And the Lord said to Mosheh,
Take back the rod of Aharon, before the testimony, to
be kept for a sign for the rebellious children, that
their murmurings may cease from before Me, lest they
die. And Mosheh did so ; as the Lord commanded so
did he.

And the sons of Israel spake with Mosheh, saying :
Behold, some of us have been consumed with the flaming
fire ; some of us have been swallowed up by the earth,
and have perished ! Behold, we are accounted as if all
of us are to be destroyed. Any one who approaches the
tabernacle must die : are we not doomed to destruction ?
[JERUSALEM. And the sons of Israel spake, saying :
Behold, we are consumed, and are all of us as if
destroyed. Some of us have died of the plague, and
some of us the earth, opening her mouth, hath swallowed up.]

XVIII. And the Lord said unto Aharon, Thou, and
thy sons, and the house of thy fathers with thee, shall
bear the iniquity of the consecrated things, when you
nave not been heedful in offering them ; and thou and
thy sons with thee shall bear the iniquity of your priesthood, when you have not been heedful of their separations. And thy brethren also of the tribe of Levi, who

are called by the name of Amram thy father, shalt thou bring near to thee, that they may consociate with and minister to thee. But thou, and thy sons with thee, (only) shall stand before the tabernacle of the testimony. And they shall keep thy charge, and have charge of all the tabernacle; yet to the vessels of the sanctuary and to the altar they are not to come near, lest both they and you die. And they shall have appointment from thee without, and keep charge of the tabernacle of ordinance for all its service; and a stranger shall not come near you. And you shall keep the charge of the sanctuary and of the altar, that there may be no more the wrath that hath been upon the children of Israel. And, behold, I have taken your brethren the Levites from among the sons of Israel; to you they are given, a gift before the Lord, to perform the work of the tabernacle of ordinance. But thou, and thy sons with thee, shall keep the charge of your priesthood in all things that pertain to the altar, and (those) within the veil, and shall minister by lots, according to the service. So, provision of food have I given you, on account of the anointing of your priesthood; and the stranger who cometh near shall die.

And the Lord said to Aharon, And I have been pleased to give you the charge of My separated offerings; the cakes of the firstfruits, and all the consecrated things of the children of Israel, to thee have I given them, on account of the anointing, and to thy sons, by an everlasting statute. They shall be to thee most sacred; whatsoever remaineth of the sheep offered by fire, all their oblations, of all their minchas, of all their sin offerings, and of all their trespass offerings which they present before Me, they are most sacred for thee and for thy sons. Thou mayest eat it in the sanctuary; every male may eat thereof; on account of the holy anointing

it shall be thine. And this is what I have set apart to
thee of their separated minchas, and of all the uplifted
things of the sons of Israel, to thee have I given them,
and to thy sons and thy daughters with thee by an everlasting statute. Whoever is clean in thy house may eat
of it. All the best of the olive oil, of the grape wine,
and of the wheat of their firstfruits which they present
before the Lord, I have given unto thee. [JERUSALEM.
All the best of the wheat, of the wine, and of the oil of
their firstfruits.] The firsts of all the trees of their
ground which they present before the Lord shall be
thine; every one who is clean in thy house may eat
them. Every devoted thing in Israel shall be thine.
Whatever openeth the womb, of all flesh among animals
which they offer before the Lord, as the regulation concerning men, so the regulation concerning cattle, it is
to be thine : only thou art to redeem the firstborn of
man by the five shekels, and the firstlings of the unclean
animal thou shalt redeem with lambs. And the redemption of a man child of a month old thou shalt make,
according to thy estimation of him, by five shekels of
silver in the shekel of the sanctuary, which is twenty
meahs. But the firstlings of oxen, of sheep, or of
goats thou mayest not redeem, for they are sacred ; but
thou shalt sprinkle their blood upon the altar, and burn
their fat for an oblation to be accepted before the Lord.
And their flesh shall be thine, for food ; as the breast of
the elevation, and as the right shoulder, it shall be thine.
Every thing set apart of the sacred things which the sons
of Israel consecrate to the Lord have I given to thee, to
thy sons and thy daughters with thee, by a perpetual
statute not to be abolished ; as the salt which seasoneth
the flesh of the oblation, because it is an everlasting
statute before the Lord, so shall it be for thee and for
thy children.

And the Lord said to Aharon, Thou wilt not receive
a possession in their land as the rest of the tribes, nor
wilt thou have a portion among them : I am thy Portion
and thy Inheritance in the midst of the children of
Israel. And, behold, I have given to the sons of Levi
all the tenths in Israel for a possession, on account of
their service with which they serve in the work of the
tabernacle of ordinance. And the sons of Israel shall
no more come near the tabernacle to incur the sin unto
death ; but the Levites shall minister in the work of the
tabernacle, and shall bear their sin if they be not diligent in their work. It is an everlasting statute for
your generations ; but among the sons of Israel they
shall have no possession. Therefore the tenths of the
children of Israel, which they set apart for a separation
before the Lord, have I given to the Levites for a possession, because I have said to them that among the sons
of Israel they shall possess no inheritance.

And the Lord spake with Mosheh, saying : Speak to
the Levites, and bid them take from the sons of Israel
the tenth which I have given them for their possession ;
and (then) shall you separate from it a separation before
the Lord, a tenth from the tenth , and your separation
shall be reckoned to you as the corn from the threshing-
floor, and as the wine from the fulness of the wine-
press ; so shall you set apart your separation before the
Lord from all your tenths, which you may receive from
the sons of Israel, and give thereof a separation before
the Lord unto Aharon the priest. Of all your gifts you
shall set apart a separation before the Lord, of all the
finest and the best therein. And say thou to the priests,
When you have set apart the finest and the best of it
and in it, then shall it be reckoned to the Levites as the
setting apart of corn from the threshing-floor, and of
wine from the wine-press. And you may eat it, you,

the priests, in any place, you and the men of your house; for it is your remuneration for your service in the tabernacle of ordinance. And you shall not contract guilt by it, at what time you set apart the finest and best of it, by any one eating of it who is unclean; neither shall you profane the consecrated things of the children of Israel, lest you die.

SECTION XXXIX.

HUKKATH.

XIX. And the Lord spake with Mosheh and Aharon, saying: This is the decree, the publication of the law which the Lord hath commanded, saying; Speak to the sons of Israel, that they bring to thee from the separation of the fold a red heifer, two years old, in which there is neither spot nor white hair, on which no male hath come, nor the burden of any work been imposed, neither hurt by the thong, nor grieved by the goad or prick, nor collar (band) or any like yoke. And thou shalt give her unto Elazar, the chief of the priests, who shall lead her alone without the camp, and set round about her a railing (border) of the branches of fig trees; and another priest shall slay her with the two signs before him, after the manner of other animals, and examine her by the eighteen kinds of divisions. And Elazar, in his priestly dress, shall take of her blood with the finger of his right hand, without (first) containing it in a vessel, and shall sprinkle the border of fig branches, and (afterwards) from the midst of a vessel on one side towards the tabernacle of ordinance, with one dipping, seven times (shall he sprinkle). And they shall bring her

out from the midst of the railing, and another priest,
while Elazar looketh on, shall burn the heifer, her skin,
flesh, and blood, with her dung shall he burn. And
another priest shall take a piece of cedar wood and
hyssop, and (wool) whose colour hath been changed to
scarlet, and throw them into the midst of the burning of the heifer; and he shall enlarge the burning,
that the ashes may be increased. [JERUSALEM. And
throw into the midst of the ashes of the burning
heifer.] And the priest who slew the heifer shall
wash his dress in forty satas of water, and afterwards
he may go into the camp; but the priest before his
ablution shall be unclean until the evening. And the
priest who was employed in the burning shall wash his
dress in forty satas of water, and his flesh in forty satas,
and before his ablution shall be unclean until the
evening.

And a man, a priest who is clean, shall gather up the
ashes of the heifer in an earthenware receptacle, its
opening covered round about with clay; and shall divide
the ashes into three portions, of which one shall be
placed within the wall (of Jerusalem), another in the
Mount of Olives, and the third portion be in the custody of the Levites; and it shall be for the congregation
of Israel, for the Water of Sprinkling : it is the heifer
(immolated) for the remission of sins.

And the priest who gathered up the ashes of the
heifer shall wash his clothes, and before his ablution be
unclean till the evening. And this shall be for the
cleansing of the children of Israel, a statute for ever.

Whoever toucheth the body of a dead man, or of a
child of some months old, either his body or his blood,
shall be unclean seven days. He shall sprinkle himself
with this water of the ashes on the third day, and on
the seventh day he shall be clean. But if he sprinkle

not himself on the third day, his uncleanness will remain
upon him, and he will not be clean on the seventh day.
Whoever hath touched the body of a dead man, or of a
child nine months old, either the body or the blood, and
will not sprinkle himself, he hath defiled the tabernacle
of the Lord, and that man shall be cut off from Israel ;
forasmuch as the water of sprinkling is not sprinkled
upon him, he is unclean, his uncleanness is yet on him,
until he shall sprinkle himself; yet may he sprinkle and
make ablution on the seventh evening. This is the
indication of the law concerning a man when he hath
died under the outspread tent : every one who entereth
into the tent by the way of the door, but not from its
side, when its door is open, (or when one hath opened
its door,) and whatever is in the tent, its floor, stones,
wood, and vessels, shall be unclean seven days. And
every earthen vessel which hath no covering fastened
upon its mouth, which would have kept it separate from
the uncleanness, is defiled by the uncleanness of the air
which toucheth its mouth, and its interior, and not the
outside of it (only). [JERUSALEM. And every open vessel
which hath no covering of stone upon it shall be unclean.] And whoever shall touch not one who hath
died in his mother's womb, but who hath been slain
with the sword on the face of the field, or the sword
with which he was slain, or the dead man himself, or a
bone of his, or the hair, or the bone of a living man
which hath been separated from him, or a grave, or a
shroud, or the bier, shall be unclean seven days. And
for him who is unclean, they shall take of the ashes of
the burnt sin offering, and put spring water upon them in
an earthen vessel. And let a man, a priest, who is clean,
take three branches of hyssop bound together, and dip
(them) in the water at the time of receiving the uncleanness, and sprinkle the tent and all its vessels, and

the men who are in it, or upon him who hath touched
the bone of a living man that hath been severed from
him, and hath fallen, or him who hath been slain with
the sword, or hath died by the plague, or a grave, or a
wrapper, or a bier.　And the priest who is clean shall
sprinkle upon the unclean man on the third day, and on
the seventh day, and shall make him clean on the
seventh day ; and he shall sprinkle his clothes, and wash
himself with water, and at eventide be clean.

But the unclean man who will not be sprinkled, that
man shall be cut off from among the congregation, because he hath defiled the sanctuary of the Lord ; the
water of sprinkling hath not been sprinkled upon him,
he is unclean.　And it shall be unto you an everlasting
statute.　The priest, also, who sprinkleth the water of
sprinkling shall sprinkle his clothes, and he who toucheth
the water of sprinkling shall be unclean until evening.
And whatever the unclean person hath touched, though
he carry it not, shall be unclean ; and the clean man
who toucheth him shall be unclean till evening.

XX. And the whole congregation of the children of
Israel came to the desert of Zin on the tenth day of the
month Nisan.　And Miriam died there, and was buried
there　And as on account of the innocency of Miriam
a well had been given, so when she died the well was
hidden, and the congregation had no water.　And they
gathered against Mosheh and Aharon, and the people
contended with Mosheh, and said, Would that we had
died when our brethren died before the Lord !　And
why hast thou brought the congregation of the Lord
into this desert, that we and our cattle may die here ?
And why didst thou make us come up out of Mizraim,
to bring us to this evil place, a place which is not fit
for sowing, or for planting fig trees, or vines, or pomegranates, and where there is no water to drink ?　And

Mosheh and Aharon went from the face of the murmuring congregation to the door of the tabernacle of ordinance, and bowed upon their faces, and the Glory of the Lord's Shekinah was revealed to them.

And the Lord spake with Mosheh, saying : Take the rod of the miracles, and gather the congregation, thou, and Aharon thy brother, and both of you adjure the rock, by the Great and manifested Name, while they look on, and it shall give forth its waters : but if it refuse to bring forth, smite thou it once, with the rod that is in thy hand, and thou wilt bring out water for them from the rock, that the congregation and their cattle may drink.

And Mosheh took the rod of the miracles from before the Lord, as He had commanded him. And Mosheh and Aharon gathered the congregation together before the rock. And Mosheh said to them, Hear now, rebels : is it possible for us to bring forth water for you from this rock ? And Mosheh lifted up [JERUSALEM. And Mosheh lifted up] his hand, and with his rod struck the rock two times : at the first time it dropped blood ; but at the second time there came forth a multitude of waters.   And the congregation and their cattle drank.

But the Lord spake to Mosheh and Aharon with the oath, Because ye have not believed in My Word,[9] to sanctify Me in the sight of the children of Israel, therefore you shall not bring this congregation into the land that I will give them. These are the Waters of Contention, where the sons of Israel contended before the Lord on account of the well that had been hidden ; and He was sanctified in them, in Mosheh and Aharon, when (the waters) were given to them.

Then Mosheh sent messengers from Rekem unto the

---

[9] From this expression some of the Jewish commentators consider the sin of Moses to have lain in his *doubting* whether the water would come from the rock at the word spoken, though God had said it should.

king of Edom, saying, Thus saith thy brother Israel.
Thou hast known all the trouble that hath found us;
that our fathers went down into Mizraim and dwelt in
Mizraim many days, and the Mizraee afflicted us and
our fathers.　And we prayed before the Lord, who heard
our prayers, and sent one of the ministering angels to
lead us out of Mizraim : and, behold, we are in Rekem,
a city built on the side of thy border.　Let us now pass
through thy land : we will not seduce virgins, nor carry
off the betrothed, nor commit adultery : on the king's
highway, under the heavens, we will go forward, and
turn not to the right or to the left, to do any injury in
the public way while we pass through thy border.
[JERUSALEM. Let us now pass through thy country.
We will do no kind of mischief, neither seduce virgins,
nor seek the wives of the men ; by the highway of the
king we will proceed, nor turn to the right or the left
till we have passed through thy coast.]　But Edomea
answered him, You shall not go through my coast, lest I
come to meet thee with the unsheathed sword.　And
Israel said to him, We would go by the king's highway;
if we drink thy waters, I and my cattle, I will give thee
the price of their value.　I will only pass through, without doing wrong.　But he said, You shall not pass
through.　And Edomea came out to meet him with a
large army and with a strong hand.　So Edomea would
not suffer Israel to pass through his coast; and Israel
turned away from him, because it was commanded from
before the Word of the Heavens that they should not set
battle in array against them, forasmuch as the time was
not yet come when the punishment of Edom should be
given into their hands. [JERUSALEM. And Israel turned
away from them ; for so was the commandment of their
Father who is in heaven, that they should not set against
them the array of war.]

And the whole congregation of the children of Israel journeyed from Rekem, and came unto Mount Umanom. And the Lord spake unto Mosheh in the Mount Umanom, on the coast of the land of Edom, saying : Aharon shall be gathered unto his people; for he shall not enter into the land which I have given unto the children of Israel, because you were rebels against My Word at the Waters of Contention. Take Aharon and Elazar his son, and make them come up to Mount Umanom. And thou shalt strip Aharon of his vestments, the adornment (glory) of the priesthood, and put them on Elazar his son; but Aharon shall be gathered, and die there. And Mosheh did as the Lord commanded him.

And they ascended Mount Umanom, in the view of all the congregatoin. And Mosheh stripped Aharon of his vestments, [JERUSALEM. And Mosheh drew off from Aharon] the priestly decoration, and put them on Elazar his son; and Aharon died there on the summit of the mountain, and Mosheh and Elazar came down from the mount.

And when the soul of Aharon was at rest, the Cloud of Glory was lifted up on the first day of the month Ab; and all the congregation beheld Mosheh come down from the mountain with rent garments; and he wept and said, Woe unto me, for thee, my brother Aharon, the pillar of Israel's prayers! And they too wept for Aharon thirty days, the men and the women of Israel. [JERU-SALEM. And all the congregation beheld Mosheh come down from the height of the mountain, with garments rent and dust upon his head, weeping and saying, Woe unto me, for thee, my brother Aharon, the pillar of the prayers of the sons of Israel, who madest atonement for them once every year! In that hour the sons of Israel believed that Aharon was dead; and all the congregation of the children of Israel wept for Aharon thirty days.]

XXI. And Amalek, who had dwelt in the south, and changed, and came and reigned in Arad, heard that the soul of Aharon was at rest, that the pillar of the Cloud which for his sake had led the people of the house of Israel had been taken up, and that Israel was coming by the way of the explorers to the place where they had rebelled against the Lord of the world. For, when the explorers had returned, the children of Israel abode in Rekem, but afterward returned from Rekem to Motseroth, in six encampments during forty years, when they journeyed from Motseroth, and returned to Rekem by the way of the explorers, and came unto Mount Umanom, where Aharon died, (and,) behold, he came and arrayed battle against Israel, and captured some of them with a great captivity. [JERUSALEM. And when the Kenaanite, king Arad, who dwelt in the south, heard that Aharon was dead, that holy man on account of whose merit the Cloud of Glory had protected Israel; that the pillar of the Cloud had been taken up; and that the prophetess Mizraim was dead, on whose account the well had flowed, but had (since) been hidden; he answered and said, Ye servants of war, come and let us set battle in line against Israel; for we shall find the way by which the explorers came up. Therefore they set battle in line against Israel, and carried away some of them with a great captivity.]

And Israel vowed a vow before the Lord, and said: If Thou wilt indeed deliver this people into my hand, I will destroy their cities. And the Lord heard Israel's prayer, and delivered up the Kenaanites, and he destroyed them and their cities. And he called the name of the place Hormah.[1]

And they journeyed from Mount Umanom, by the way of the Sea of Suph, that they might compass the land of Edom; and the soul of the people was wearied in the

[1] "Destruction."

way. And the people thought (wickedly) in their heart, and talked against the Word of the Lord, and contended with Mosheh, saying: Why didst thou bring us up from Mizraim to die in the wilderness; for there is neither bread nor water, and our soul is weary of manna, this light food?

And the bath-kol fell from the high heaven, and thus spake: Come, all men, and see all the benefits which I have done to the people whom I brought up free out of Mizraim. I made manna come down for them from heaven, yet now turn they and murmur against Me. Yet, behold, the serpent, whom, in the days of the beginning of the world, I doomed to have dust for his food, hath not murmured against me: but My people are murmuring about their food. Now shall the serpents who have not complained of their food come and bite the people who complain. Therefore did the Word of the Lord send the basilisk serpents, and they bit the people, and a great multitude of the people of Israel died. [JERUSALEM. The bath-kol came forth from the midst of the earth, and a voice was heard from the heights, See, all men, and listen and hear, all ye children of flesh. The serpent, whom I cursed at the beginning, and said to him, Dust shall be thy food, hath not complained about his food. I led forth My people from Mizraim free, and caused the manna to descend for them from heaven; I made the quails to come over to them, and the well to spring up from the deep; yet now they again complain before Me on account of the manna, saying, Our soul is aggrieved by this light bread: therefore shall the serpent who hath not complained of his food come and bite this people who have murmured about their food. So the Word of the Lord sent fiery serpents among the people, and they bit the people, and a great multitude of Israel died.]

And the people came to Mosheh, and said: We have sinned, in thinking and speaking against the glory of the Lord's Shekinah, and in contending with thee. Pray before the Lord to remove the plague of serpents from us. And Mosheh prayed for the people.

And the Lord said to Mosheh, Make thee a serpent of brass, and set it upon a place aloft;[2] and it shall be that when a serpent hath bitten any one, if he behold it, then shall he live, if his heart be directed to the Name of the Word of the Lord. And Mosheh made a serpent of brass, and set it upon a place aloft; and it was, when a serpent had bitten a man, and the serpent of brass was gazed at, and his heart was intent upon the Name of the Word of the Lord, he lived. [JERU-SALEM. And Mosheh made a serpent of brass, and set it upon a high place; and it was that when any one had been bitten by a serpent, and his face was uplifted in prayer unto his Father who is in heaven, and he looked upon the brasen serpent, he lived.]

And the children of Israel journeyed from thence, and pitched in Oboth; and they journeyed from Oboth, and encamped in the plain of Megistha, in a desert place which looketh toward Moab from the rising of the sun. Thence they journeyed and encamped in a valley abounding in reeds, osiers, and mandrakes.[3] And they journeyed from thence, and encamped beyond the Arnon, in a passage of the desert that stretcheth from the coast of the Amoraah; for Arnon is the border of Moab, situate between Moab and the Amoraah; and therein dwelt a priesthood of the worshippers of idols. Therefore it is said in the book of the Law, where are recorded the wars of the Lord: Eth and Heb, who had been smitten with the blast of the leprosy, and had been banished beyond the confine of the camp, made known to Israel

---

[2] Or, "a place of suspension." [3] Or, "lilies."

that Edom and Moab were concealed among the mountains in ambush, to destroy the people of the house of Israel. But the Lord of the world made a sign to the mountains, which pressed one to another, so that they died · and their blood flowed through a valley on the brink of the Arnon (or, a valley adjoining Arnon). And the effusion of the streams of their blood flowed to the habitations of Lechaiath, which were, however, delivered from this destruction, because they had not been in their counsels ; and, behold, it was unto the confine of Moab.

And from thence was given to them (the Israelites) the living well, the well concerning which the Lord said to Mosheh, Assemble the people and give them water. Then, behold, Israel sang the thanksgiving of this song, at the time that the well which had been hidden was restored to them through the merit of Miriam : Spring up, O well, spring up, O well ! sang they to it, and it sprang up : the well which the fathers of the world, Abraham, Izhak, and Jakob, digged : the princes who were of old digged it, the chiefs of the people : Mosheh and Aharon, the scribes of Israel, found it with their rods ; and from the desert it was given to them for a gift.

⌈JERUSALEM. Therefore it is said in the Book of the Law of the Lord, which is likened to a Book of Wars : The miracles and mighty acts which the Lord-wrought for His people, the sons of Israel, when they stood by the Red Sea, so did He with them when they were at the fords of the vale of Arnona. When the children of Israel were passing through the vale of Arnona, the Moabites were hidden in the caverns of the valley, saying : When the Beni Israel are coming through, we will go forth to prevent them, and will slay them. But the Lord of all the world, the Lord, who knew what was in their hearts,—for before Him that which is within the reins is manifest,—the Lord signed to the

mountains, and their heads here and there were brought
together, and the chiefs of their mighty ones were crushed,
and the valleys were overflowed with the blood of the
slain. But Israel walked above upon the top of the
hills, and knew not the miracle and mighty act which
the Lord was doing for them in the valley of Arnon.
But Lechaiath, the city which took no part in their
counsel, was delivered from them ; and, behold, it is by
the confines of the Moabites   17. Behold, then sang
Israel this song of praise: Spring up, O well ! they
sang to it, and it sprang up . the well which Abraham,
Izhak, and Jakob, the princes of the world, at the
beginning did see, the sages of the world, the Sanhedrin,
the seventy wise men who were appointed by name
beheld it : Mosheh and Aharon, the scribes of Israel,
found it with their rods, and from the desert it was
given to them as a gift.]

And from thence it was given to them in Mattana ;
turning, it went up with them to the high mountains,
and from the high mountains it went down with them
to the hills surrounding all the camp of Israel, and
giving them drink, every one at the door of his tent.
And from the high mountains it descended with them
to the lower hills, but was hidden from them on the
borders of Moab, at the summit of the hill looking
toward Bethjeshimon, because there they neglected the
words of the Law. [JERUSALEM. And from thence
the well was given to them at Mattana, turning it became
strong overflowing streams, and again it ascended to the
top of the mountains, and went down with them to the
ancient valleys ; but the well was hidden from them
when on the borders of Moab, on the head of the height
which overlooketh toward Abeth Jeshimon.]

Then sent Israel messengers to Sihon, king of the
Amorites, saying : I would pass through thy country.

We will not carry off the betrothed, nor seduce virgins, nor have to do with the wives of men; by the highway of the King who is in the heavens we will go, until we have passed through thy border. But Sihon would not permit Israel to pass through his limit, but constrained all his people, and came out to Jahaz, and made war against Israel. And Israel smote him with the anathema of the Lord, that he would destroy (him) with the edge of the sword; and he took possession of his country, from Arnon unto the Jabbok, unto the border of the children of Ammon; because Rabbath, which is the limit of the children of Ammou, was strong; and so far was their boundary.

And Israel took all those cities, and dwelt in all the cities of the Amorites, in Heshbon, and in all her villages. For Heshbon was the city of Sihon, king of the Amorites; for he had beforetime made war with the King of Moab, and had taken all his country from his hand unto the Arnon. Therefore, say the young men, (or the chosen ones,) using proverbs: The righteous who rule their passions say, Come let us reckon (Heshbon) the strength [4] of a good work by the recompense, and the recompense of an evil work by the strength; for whoso is watchful and diligent [5] in the law is builded up and perfected; for mighty words like fire go forth from the lips of the righteous, the masters of such thought, (calculation, *heshbona*,) and powerful merit like flames from those who are read and devoted in the law: their fire devoureth the foe and the adversary, who are reckoned before them as the worshippers of the idol altars in the valley of Arnona. Woe to you, ye haters of the just! ye have perished, ye people of Kemosh, haters of the words of the law, in whom there is no

[4] Or, "the weapon, instrument."
[5] Or, "devoted," literally, "anointed."

righteousness, unless he waste you to bring you captive
unto the place where they teach the law, and their sons
and daughters be removed by captivity of the sword to
be near them who consult in its counsels the instructors
and those anointed with the law. The wicked have
said, In all this there is nothing lofty to the sight; but
your numbers shall perish until the falsehood of your
souls be ended, and the Lord of the world destroy them
till their lives have expired, and they have come to
nothing, as the cities of the Amorites have perished, and
the palaces of their princes from the great gate of the
house of the kingdom to the street of the smiths which
is nigh to Medeba.

[JERUSALEM. 27. Therefore say they who speak in
proverbs, Ascend. 28. Because the men of their
people like fire come out of Heshbon, making war as
flames of fire from the city of Sihon: the kings of the
Amoraee are slain, the villages of the Moabite cities are
destroyed, and the priests are slaughtered who sacrificed
before the idols of Arnona. Woe to you of Moab!
ye are consumed, destroyed, O worshippers of the idol
of Kemosh; your sons and daughters bound by the collar
are carried into the captivity of Sihon, king of the
Amorites. And the kingdom hath ceased from Heshbon, and the ruler from Dibon, and his ways are made
desolate unto the smithies which are nigh to Medaba.]

And Israel, after they had destroyed Sihon, dwelt in
the land of the Amorites. And Mosheh sent Kaleb and
Phineas to examine Makbar, and they subdued the
villages, and destroyed the Amorites who were there.
Then they turned, and went up by the way of Mathnan;
and Og, the king of Mathnan, came out to meet us,
he and all his people, to give battle at Edrei. And it
was, when Mosheh saw Og, he trembled before him,
stricken with fear: but he (soon) answered and said,

This is Og the Wicked, who taunted Abraham our
father and Sarah, saying: You are like trees planted
by the water channels, but bring forth no fruit : therefore
hath the Holy One, blessed be He, spared him to live
through generations, that he might see the great multitude of their children, and be delivered into our hands.
Then spake the Lord unto Mosheh: Fear him not, for
I have delivered him into thy hand, and all his people
and country ; and thou shalt do to him as thou hast
done to Sihon, king of the Amorites, who dwelt in
Heshbon.

Now it was, after Og the Wicked had seen the camp
of Israel spreading over six miles, he said with himself,
I will make war against this people, that they may not
do to me as they have done to Sihon : so went he and
tare up a mountain six miles in size, and brought it
upon his head to hurl it upon them. But the Word of
the Lord forthwith prepared a reptile [6], which ate into
the mountain and perforated it, and his head was
swallowed up within it ; and he sought to withdraw it,
but could not, because his back teeth and his front
ones were drawn hither and thither. And Mosheh
went and took an axe of ten cubits, and sprang ten
cubits, and struck him on the ankle of his foot, and he
fell, and died beyond the camp of Israel. Thus it is
written. And they smote him and his sons and daughters, and all his people, till none of them remained to
escape ; and they took possession of his land. [JERU-
SALEM. And Israel dwelt in the land of the Amorites.
And Mosheh sent to explore Makvar, and they took the
villages, and destroyed the Amorites who were there.
34 And when Mosheh saw Og, he said, Is not this Og
the Wicked, who taunted Abraham and Sarah, and said,

---

[6] " Grasshopper," *zechila* The Targumist here draws the long bow of
the Hagadistic method of paraphrase.

They are like fair trees by fountains of water, but give
no fruit? Therefore the Holy One, blessed be He, hath
kept him alive for many years, till the time that he
should see their children and children's children, and
fall by their hands. Therefore the Lord said to Mosheh,
Fear him not, for I have delivered him into thy hand,
and all his people, and all his land; and thou shalt do to
him as thou hast done to Sichon, king of the Amorites,
who dwelt in Heshbon.]

XXII. And the children of Israel journeyed, and
encamped in the plains of Moab, near the passage of the
Jordan (toward) Jericho.

SECTION XL.

BALAK.

AND Balak bar Zippor saw what Israel had done to
the Amoraee. And the Moabaee feared before the people
greatly because they were many, and they were distressed
in their life before the sons of Israel. And they said
to the elders of the Midianee, for the people had been
one and the kingdom one unto that day: Now will
this congregation consume all that is about them, as the
ox eateth up the grass of the field. And Balak bar
Zippor, a Midianite, was the king of Moab at that time;
without (a Midianite) being such at another time; for so
was the tradition among them, to have kings from this
people and from that, by turns.

And he sent unto Laban the Aramite, who was Bileam,
(so called because he it was) who sought (*Bilvva*) to
swallow up (*Amma*) the people of the house of Israel:
the son of Beor, who was insane [7] from the vastness of
his knowledge; and would not spare Israel, the descend-

[7] Or, "gross."

ants of his sons and daughters : and the house of his habitation in Padan was at Pethor, a name signifying an interpreter of dreams. It was built in Aram upon the Phrat, in a land where the children of the people worshipped and adored him. (To him did Balak send) to call him, saying : Behold, a people hath come out of Mizraim, and, lo, they cover the face of the earth, and are encamped over against me. But now, I entreat, come, curse this people for me, for they are stronger than I, if I may but be able to meet them, though smaller than they, and drive them from the land. For I know that he whom thou dost bless is blessed, and he whom thou dost curse is cursed.

And the elders of Moab and of Midian went, with the price of divinations sealed up in their hands, and came to Bileam, and told him the words of Balak. [JERUSALEM. And the sages of the Moabites and of the Midianites went, with sealed letters in their hands, and came to Bileam, and spake with him the words of Balak.] And he said to them, Abide here to-night, and I will return you word as the Lord shall speak with me. And the princes of Moab stayed with Bileam. And the Word from before the Lord came to Bileam, and He said, What men are these who are now lodging with thee ? And Bileam said before the Lord, Balak bar Zippor, king of the Moabaee, hath sent messengers to me, saying : Behold, a people hath come out of Mizraim, and cover the face of the land : now therefore, come, curse them for me, so that I may be able to fight and drive them away. And the Lord said unto Bileam, Thou shalt not go with them, nor curse the people, for they are blessed of Me from the day of their fathers. And Bileam rose up early, and said to the princes of Moab, Go unto your country, for it is not pleasing before the Lord to permit me to journey with you. And the princes of Moab arose and came to Balak, and said, Bileam hath refused to come with us.

But Balak added to send (other) princes more, and nobler than they ; and they came to Bileam, and said to him : Thus saith Balak bar Zippor, Let not anything hinder thee from coming to me ; for honouring I will honour thee greatly, and whatever thou biddest me I will do.   Come therefore now, and curse this people for me. And Bileam answered the servants of Balak, and said, If Balak would give me out of his treasury a house full of silver and gold, I have no power to transgress the decree of the Word of the Lord my God, to fabricate a word either small or great.   But I entreat you to remain here this night also, that I may know what the Word of the Lord may yet speak with me.

And the Word came from before the Lord [s] unto Bileam in the night, and said to him, If these men come to call thee, arise, go with them ; only, the word that I will speak with thee, that shalt thou do.

And Bileam arose in the morning, and saddled his ass, and went with the princes of Moab. [JERUSALEM. And Bileam arose in the morning, and made ready his ass, and went with the princes of Moab.]   But the anger of the Lord was provoked, because he would go (that he might) curse them ; and the angel of the Lord stood in the way to be an adversary to him.   But he sat upon his ass, and his two young men, Jannes and Jambres, were with him.   And the ass discerned the angel of the Lord standing in the way with a drawn sword in his hand, and the ass turned aside out of the road, to go into the field.   And Bileam smote the ass to make her return unto the way.   And the angel of the Lord stood in a narrow path that was in the midst between vine-yards, [JERUSALEM. And the angel of the Lord stood

[s] Glossary, p. 16

between the vineyards, a hedge (being) on this and on
that side,] in the place where Jacob and Laban raised
the mound, the pillar on this side and the observatory
on that side,[9] which they raised, that neither should pass
that limit to do evil (to the other).   And the ass discerned the angel of the Lord, and thrust herself against
the hedge, and bruised Bileam's foot by the hedge, and
he smote her again; for the angel was invisible to him.
And the angel of the Lord yet passed on, and stood in
a distant place, where there was no way to turn either to
the right or left.   And the ass saw the angel of the
Lord, and fell under Bileam; and Bileam's wrath was
strong, so that he smote the ass with his staff.—Ten
things were created after the world had been founded at
the coming in of the Sabbath between the suns,—the
manna, the well, the rod of Mosheh, the diamond, the
rainbow, the cloud of glory, the mouth of the earth, the
writing of the tables of the covenant, the demons, and
the speaking ass.   And in that hour the Word of the Lord
opened her mouth, and fitted her to speak : and she
said to Bileam, What have I done to thee, that thou hast
smitten me these three times ?   And Bileam said to the
ass, Because thou hast been false to me; if there was
now but a sword in my hand, I would kill thee.   And
the ass said to Bileam, Woe to thee, Bileam, thou want-
ing-in-mind, when me, an unclean beast, who am to die
in this world, and not to enter the world to come, thou
art not able to curse; how much less (canst thou
harm) the children of Abraham, Izhak, and Jakob, on
account of whom the world hath been created, but whom
thou art going to curse !   So hast thou deceived these
people, and hast said, This is not my ass, she is a loan
in my hand, and my horses remain in the pasture.   But
am I not thine ass upon whom thou hast ridden from

<hr>

[9] Gen. xxxi. 51

thy youth unto this day? and have I been used to do
thus with thee? And he said, No. [JERUSALEM. And
the ass said to Bileam, Woe to thee, Bileam the wicked,
wanting in understanding and wisdom! Behold, me, an
unclean beast, who am to die in this world and not to
enter the world to come, thou hast not power with all
thy skill to curse; how much less the children of
Abraham, Izhak, and Jakob, on whose account the world
was created at the beginning! And why art thou going
to curse them? For thou hast deceived the people,
saying to them, This is not my ass: she is a loan in my
hand. But am I not thy ass, upon whom thou hast ridden
from thy youth unto this day? Did I indeed intend to
do thus with thee? And he said to her, No.] And the
Lord unveiled the eyes of Bileam, and he beheld the angel
of the Lord standing in the way, his sword unsheathed in
his hand; and he bowed, and worshipped on his face.

And the angel of the Lord said to him, Why hast
thou smitten thine ass these three times? Behold, I
have come out to withstand thee, and the ass, fearing,
saw, and turned from the way. It is known before me
that thou seekest to go to curse the people, a thing that
is not pleasing to me. But the ass discerned me, and
turned away from me these three times: had she not
turned from me, surely now I should have slain thee,
and spared her alive. And Bileam said to the angel of
the Lord, I have sinned, because 1 knew not that thou
wast standing against me in the way. But now, if it
displease thee, I will go back. But the angel of the
Lord said to Bileam, Go with these men; but the word
that I will tell thee that thou shalt speak. And Bileam
went with the princes of Balak.

And Balak heard that Bileam was coming, and came
out to meet him at a city of Moab on the border of
Arnon, which is on the side of the frontier. And Balak

said to Bileam, Did I not send to call thee? Why camest thou not to me? Didst thou not indeed say that I could not do thee honour? And Bileam said to Balak, Behold, I have come to thee; yet now am I able to say any thing to thee? But the word that the Lord shall ordain for my mouth, that I must speak. And Bileam went with Balak, and they came to a city surrounded with walls, to the streets of the great city, the city of Sihon, which is Berosha. And Balak slew oxen and sheep, and sent to Bileam and the princes, and those who were with them. And at the time of the morning Balak took Bileam, and brought him up to the high place of the idol Peor; and he saw from thence the camp of Dan, which went at the rear of the people; and they were discovered under the Cloud of Glory.

XXIII. And Bileam, as he looked upon them, knew that strange worship was among them, and rejoiced in his heart; and he said to Balak, Build here seven altars, and prepare me here seven bullocks and seven rams. And Balak did as Bileam had said, and Balak and Bileam offered a bullock and a ram upon an altar. And Bileam said to Balak, Stand by thy burnt offering, and I will go, if peradventure the word of the Lord may come to meet me; and the word that shall be discovered to me, that I will declare to thee. And he went, bending as a serpent. [JERUSALEM. And Bileam went with a humbled heart.]

And the Word from before the Lord met with Bileam, who said before Him, The seven altars I have set in order, and have offered a bullock and a ram upon every altar. And the Lord put a word in Bileam's mouth, and said, Return to Balak, and thus speak. And he returned to him, and, behold, he was standing by his burnt-offering, he and all the nobles of Moab. And he took up the parable of his prophecy, and said:

From Aram on Euphrates hath Balak king of the
Moabaee brought me; from the mountains of the east:
Come, curse for me the house of Jakob; come, for me
make Israel small. [JERUSALEM. And he took up the
parable of his prophecy, and said: Balak, the king of the
Moabaee, hath brought me from Aram, from the mountains of the east: Come, curse for me the house of Jakob;
come, diminish for me the tribes of the house of Israel.]
How shall I curse, (while) the Word of the Lord
blesseth them? and whom shall I diminish, when the
Word of the Lord increaseth them? For, said Bileam
the wicked, I look on this people who are led on for the
sake of their righteous fathers, who are like the mountains, and of their mothers, who are like the hills: behold,
this people alone are to possess the world, because they
are not led by the laws of the nations. And when
Bileam the sinner beheld the house of Israel, a circumcised people, hidden in the dust of the desert, he said,
Who can number the merits of these strong ones, or
count the good works of one of the four camps of Israel?
Bileam the wicked said: If the house of Israel kill me
with the sword, then, it is made known to me, I shall
have no portion in the world to come: nevertheless if I
may but die the death of the true! O that my last end
may be as the least among them! [JERUSALEM. Wherewith shall I curse the house of Jakob, when the Word
of the Lord blesseth them? and how shall I diminish the
house of Israel, when the Word of the Lord doth multiply
them? I see this people, who are conducted through
the merit of their righteous fathers, Abraham, Izhak,
and Jakob, who are like the mountains, and of their four
mothers, Sarah, Rivekah, Rahel, and Leah: behold, this
people shall dwell alone, and not be mixed with the laws
of the Gentiles. Who can number the youth of the
house of Jakob, of whom it is said, They are to be like the

stars of the skies? Bileam the wicked said, in the parable of his prophecy, If Israel do kill him with the sword,
Bileam himself declareth that he hath no portion in the
world to come: but if Bileam may die as the faithful
die, may his last end be as one of the least among them.]

And Balak said to Bileam, What hast thou done to
me? I brought thee to curse my enemies, and, behold,
blessing, thou hast blessed them. But he answered and
said, That which the Lord hath put in my mouth shall
I not be careful to speak? And Balak said to him,
Come now with me where thou mayest see him from
another place. Thou shalt see only the camp that
goeth in his rear, but not all their camps; and curse
him for me there. And he brought him to the field of
the observatory on the top of the hill, and builded seven
altars, and offered a bullock and a ram on every altar.
And he said to Balak, Stand thou here by thy burnt
offering, and I will meet (Him) yonder. And the
Word from before the Lord met Bileam, and put a
word in his mouth, and said, Return to Balak, and thus
speak. And he came to him, and, behold, he was standing by his burnt offering, and the princes of Moab with
him. And Balak said to him, What hath the Lord
spoken? And he took up the parable of his prophecy,
and said:

Arise, Balak, and hear; listen to my words, Bar Zippor.
The Word of the living God is not as the words of men:
for the Lord, the Ruler of all worlds, is the unchangeable;
(but) man speaketh and denieth. Neither are His works
like the works of the children of flesh, who consult, and
then repent them of what they had decreed. But when the
Lord of all worlds hath said, I will multiply this people
as the stars of the heavens, and will give them to possess
the land of the Kenaanites, is He not able to perform
what He hath spoken? and what He hath said, can He

not confirm it? Behold, from the mouth of the Holy
Word I have received the benediction, and their
appointed benediction I cannot restrain from them.
[JERUSALEM. 15. And I with My Word will honour
thee. 19. Not as the word of the sons of men is the
Word of the living God, nor are the works of God as
the works of men. Men say, and do not; they decree,
but do not confirm; but God saith and performeth, He
maketh decree and confirmeth it, and His decrees are
established for ever. Behold, I have received to
bless Israel, and I cannot restrain the blessings from
them.]

Bileam the wicked said, I see not among them of the
house of Jakob such as worship idols: they who serve
false idols are not established among the tribes of the
sons of Israel. The Word of the Lord their God is
their help, and the trumpets of the King Meshiha
resound among them. Unto Eloha, who redeemed and
led them out of Mizraim free, belong power and exaltation, glorification and greatness. They of the house of
Jakob who use divination are not established, nor the
enchanters, who enchant among the greatness (multitudes) of Israel. At this time it is said to the house
of Jakob and Israel, How glorious are the miracles and
wonder-works which God hath wrought! This people
reposeth alone, and dwelleth strong as a lion, and
reareth himself as an old lion. They sleep not till with
great slaughter they have slain their adversaries, and
taken the spoils of the slain. [JERUSALEM. I have
not seen the worshippers of a lie, nor those who offer
strange service, among the tribes of the sons of Israel.
The Word of the Lord is with them, and the trumpet of
their glorious King protecteth them. Unto God who
redeemed, and brought them out from Mizraim free,
belong power, and praise, and exaltation. For I see not

those who perform divination in the house of Jakob,
nor them who enchant with enchantments among
the tribes of Israel.   At this time it is said to Jakob,
What bounties and comforts are prepared of the Lord
to bestow upon you of the house of Jakob !   Then said
he in the parable of his prophecy, O happy saints, how
goodly is the reward prepared for you by your Father in
heaven, in the world to come!   Behold, these people
dwell as a lion, like the strong lion ; as the lion resteth
not, nor is quiet, until he hath taken and eaten flesh and
drunk up blood, so this people will rest not, nor be in
quiet, till they have slain their enemies, and have shed
the blood of their slaughtered foes like water.]

And Balak said to Bileam, Neither curse them nor
bless them.   But Bileam answered and said to Balak,
Did I not tell thee at the beginning, Whatsoever the
Lord speaketh, that must I do?   And Balak said to
Bileam, Come, and I will now take thee to another
place, if so be it may be pleasing before the Lord, that
thou mayest curse him for me from thence.   And Balak
led Bileam to the high place of the prospect which
looketh toward Beth Jeshimoth.   And Bileam said to
Balak, Erect here for me seven altars, and prepare me
seven bullocks and seven rams.   And Balak did as
Bileam had said, and offered a bullock and a ram upon
every altar.

XXIV. And Bileam, seeing that it was good before
the Lord to bless Israel, went not, as once and again
before, in quest of divinations, but set his face toward
the wilderness, to recall to memory the work of the calf
which they had there committed.   And Bileam lifted up
his eyes, but beheld Israel dwelling together by their
tribes in their schools, and (saw) that their doors were
arranged so as not to overlook the doors of their companions : and the Spirit of prophecy from before the

Lord rested upon him. [JERUSALEM. And Bileam saw that it was pleasing before the Lord to bless Israel, so that he went not, as he had gone from time to time, to seek for divinations, or to provide enchantments; but went and set his face toward the wilderness to recall to memory their work of the calf, (still) being desirous to curse Israel.] But he took up the parable of his prophecy, and said:

Bileam, son of Beor, speaketh; the man speaketh who is more honourable than his father, (because) the dark mysteries hidden from the prophets have been revealed to him; and who, because he was not circumcised, fell upon his face when the angel stood over against him: he hath said who heard the Word from before the living God; who beheld the vision before God the Almighty, and, seeking that it might be discovered to him, fell upon his face, and the secret mysteries hidden from the prophets were revealed to him.

How beautiful your houses of instruction, in the tabernacle where Jakob your father ministered; and how beautiful this tabernacle of ordinance which is found among you, and the tents that surround it, O house of Israel! As tides of waters, so are the house of Israel, dwelling like flocks made strong by the doctrine of the law; and as gardens planted by the flowing streams, so are their disciples in the fellowships of their schools. The light of their faces shineth as the brightness of the firmament which the Lord created on the second day of the creation of the world, and outspread for the glory of the Shekinah. They are exalted and lifted up above all the nations, like cedars of Lebanon planted by fountains of waters. From them their King shall arise, and their Redeemer be of them and among them, and the seed of the children of Jakob shall rule over many nations. The first who will reign over them

will make war with the house of Amalek, and will be
exalted above Agag their king; but because he had
spared him his kingdom will be taken from him.   Unto
Eloha, who brought them out free from Mizraim, belong
might, and exaltation, and glory, and power.   He will
destroy the nations of their adversaries, and break down
their strength, and will send forth the plague-arrows of
His vengeance among them, and destroy them.   They
shall repose and dwell as a lion, and as an old lion, that
sleeping who will (dare to) awake?   They who bless
them are blessed, as Mosheh the prophet, the scribe of
Israel; and they who curse them are accursed, as Bileam
son of Beor.

And Balak's wrath grew strong against Bileam, and,
smiting his hands, Balak said to Bileam, I brought thee
to curse my enemies, and, behold, in blessing thou
hast blessed them these three times.   [JERUSALEM.
3.   And he took up in parable his prophecy, and said :
Bileam the son of Beor saith ; the man saith who is
more honourable than his father, for what hath been
hidden from all prophets is revealed to him ; the man
saith who heard the Word from before the Lord, and
who saw the vision before the Almighty ; when, in-
quiring, prostrate on his face, the mysteries of prophecy
were disclosed to him, and of himself he did prophesy that
he shall fall by the sword, a prophecy to be confirmed at
the end !

How goodly were the tabernacles in which Jakob
their father did pray; and the tabernacle of ordinance
which you have made to My name, and your own tabernacles, O house of Israel ! As torrents that prevail, so
shall Israel overpower their adversaries ; and as gardens
planted by fountains of water, so shall be their cities,
giving forth scribes and teachers of the law ; and as the
heavens which the Memra of the Lord spread forth for

the dwelling of His Shekinah, so shall Israel live, and
endure unto eternity, beautiful and renowned as cedars
by the waters which grow up on high. Their King will
arise from among their children, and their Redeemer
will be of them and among them; and He will gather
their captives from the cities of their adversaries, and
their children shall have rule among the peoples. And
the kingdom of the King Meshiha shall be made great:
stronger is He than Shaul who vanquished Agag the
king of the Amalkaah. Unto God who redeemed, and
brought them out free from the land of Mizraim, belong
power, and praise, and exaltation. The sons of Israel
will prevail over their enemies, will divide their cities,
slay their heroes, and disperse their residue. Behold,
these people will dwell as a lion, and be as the strong
lions. He who blesseth you, O Israel, shall be blessed,
as Mosheh the prophet, the scribe of Israel, and he who
curseth you will be accursed, as Bileam, the son of Beor.

And Balak's anger grew strong against Bileam, and
Balak smote his hands, and said to Bileam, I brought
thee to curse my enemies, and thou hast only blessed.]
And now flee to thy place. I had said that honouring
1 would honour thee; but, behold, the Lord hath kept
back Bileam from honour. But Bileam said to Balak,
Did I not tell thy messengers whom thou sentest to me,
saying, If Balak would give me the fulness of his treasures of silver and gold, I have no power to transgress
the decree of the Word of the Lord, to do good or evil
of my own will: what the Lord saith shall I not speak?
And now, behold, I return to go to my people. Come,
I will give thee counsel: Go, furnish tavern houses,
and employ seductive women to sell food and drinks
cheaply, and to bring this people together to eat and
drink, and commit whoredom with them, that they
may deny their God; then in a brief time will they be

delivered into thy hand, and many of them fall. Never-theless, after this they will still have dominion over thy people at the end of the days.

And he took up the parable of his prophecy, and said : Bileam the son of Beor speaketh ; the man speaketh who is more honourable than his father, because the mysteries hidden from prophets have been revealed to him ; he speaketh who heard the Word from before the Lord, and who knoweth the hour when the Most High God will be wroth with him ; (he speaketh) who saw the vision before the Almighty, seeking, prostrate on his face, that it should be revealed to him ; the secret, concealed from the prophets, was disclosed unto him.

I shall see Him, but not now ; I shall behold Him, but it is not near. When the mighty King of Jakob's house shall reign, and the Meshiha, the Power-sceptre of Israel, be anointed, He will slay the princes of the Moabaee, and bring to nothing all the children of Sheth, the armies of Gog who will do battle against Israel, and all their carcases shall fall before Him. And the Edomaee will be utterly driven out, even the sons of Gabela from before Israel their foes, and Israel will be strengthened with their riches and possess them. And a prince of the house of Jakob will arise and destroy and consume the remnant that have escaped from Con-stantina the guilty city, and will lay waste and ruin the rebellious city, even Kaiserin, the strong city of the Gentiles.

And he looked on the house of Amalek, and took up the parable of his prophecy, and said : The first of the nations who made war with the house of Israel were those of the house of Amalek ; and they at last, in the days of the King Meshiha, with all the children of the east, will make war against Israel ; but all of them together will have eternal destruction in their end.

And he looked upon Jethro, who had been made proselyte, and took up the parable of his prophecy, and said : How strong is thy habitation, who hast set thy dwelling in the clefts of the rocks ! Yet so is it decreed that the children of the Shalmaia must be despoiled, but not until Sancherib the king of Athur shall come and make thee captive.

[JERUSALEM. And now, behold, I go to my people. Come now, I will counsel thee how thou art to act with this people. Lead them into sin ; for else thou canst have no power against them. Nevertheless, these people are to prevail over thy people at the end of the days. And he took up the parable of his prophecy, and said :

Bileam the son of Beor saith ; the man who is more honourable than his father saith, for what hath been hid from all the prophets is revealed unto me : the man speaketh who heard the Word from before the Lord, and learned knowledge from the Most High ; who saw the vision in the presence of the Almighty, seeking, prostrate on his face, when the visions of prophecy were disclosed to him, and he was made to foreknow of himself that he will fall by the sword, but that his prophecy will be confirmed.

I shall see Him, but not now ; I shall behold Him, but He is not nigh. A King is to arise from the house of Jakob, and a Redeemer and Ruler from the house of Israel, who will slay the strong ones of the Moabaee, and bring to nothing and consume all the children of the east. And Edom may inherit Mount Gabela from their enemies, but Israel will be stronger with a mighty host. A King will arise from the house of Jakob, and destroy what shall remain of the strong city. And he beheld the Amalkaah, and took up the parable of his prophecy, and said : The house of Amalek was the first of the peoples to make war with Israel, and at last in the

end of the days they will array battle against them; but
their end is to perish, and their destruction to be for
ever. And when he looked upon the Shalmaia, taking
up the parable of his prophecy, he said, How strong is
thy abode, who hast set the house of thy dwelling in the
clefts of the rock! But the Shalmaia will not be spoiled,
until Athuria shall arise, and take thee captive.]

And he took up the parable of his prophecy, and said:
Woe to them who are alive at the time when the Word
of the Lord shall be revealed, to give the good reward
to the righteous, and to take vengeance on the wicked,
to smite the nations and the kings, and bring these
things upon them! And ships (lit., sails) armed for war
will come forth with great armies from Lombarnia, and
from the land of Italia,[1] conjoined with the legions that
will come forth from Constantina, and will afflict the
Athuraee, and bring into captivity all the sons of Eber;[2]
nevertheless the end of these and of those is to fall by
the hand of the King Meshiha, and be brought to everlasting destruction. [JERUSALEM. Woe to him who is
alive when the Word of the Lord setteth Himself to give
the good reward to the just, and to take vengeance on
the wicked! And great hosts in Livernia will come from
the great city, and will conjoin with them many legions
of the Romaee, and subjugate Athuria, and afflict all the
children beyond the river. Nevertheless the end of
these and of those is to perish, and the destruction to be
everlasting. And Bileam rose up and went to return to
his place; and Balak also.]

And Bileam rose up and went to return to his place,
and Balak also went upon his way, and appointed the
daughters of the Midianites for the tavern booths at
Beth Jeshimoth, by the snow mountain, where they sold

[1] Vulgate, *Veniat in trieribus de Italiá*
[2] Peschito, "and subjugate all the Hebrews"

sweetmeats cheaper than their price, after the counsel of Bileam the wicked, at the dividing of the way.

XXV. And Israel dwelt in the place which is called Shittim, on account of the (*Shetutha*) foolishness [3] and depravity which were among them. And the people began to profane their holiness, and to strip their bodies to the image of Peor, and commit fornication with the daughters of the Moabites, who brought out the image of Peor, concealed under their bundles. And they invited the people to the sacrifices of their idols; and the people ate in their feasts, and bowed themselves to their idols And the people of the house of Israel joined themselves to Baala-Peor, like the nail in the wood, which is not separated but by breaking up the wood (or, with the splinters). And the anger of the Lord was kindled against Israel.

And the Lord said to Mosheh, Take all the chiefs of the people, and appoint them for judges, and let them give judgment to put to death the people who have gone astray after Peor, and hang them before the word of the Lord upon the wood over against the morning sun, and at the departure of the sun take them down and bury them, and turn away the strong anger of the Lord from Israel. And Mosheh said to the judges of Israel, Slay every one a man of his tribe of those who have joined themselves to the idol of Peor. [JERUSALEM. And Israel abode in Shittim; and the people began to commit fornication with the daughters of the Moabites. And they invited the people to the sacrifices of their idols. And Israel were united with the worshippers of the idol of Peor; and the anger of the Lord was strong against Israel. And the Word of the Lord said to

---

[3] *Shoteh*, in Chaldee, is "a fool or sot." The above derivation seems fanciful. The place took its name probably from the Acacia trees which may have abounded there, the Shittah, *Mimosa Nilotica.*

Mosheh, Take all the chiefs of the people and set them
for a Sanhedrin before the Lord, and let them hang all
who are worthy of death; and at sunset take down their
bodies and bury them, that so may be averted the strong
anger of the Lord from Israel. And Mosheh said to the
princes of Israel, Slay each one a man of his house of
them who have joined themselves to the idol of Peor.]

And, behold, a man of the sons of Israel came, holding
a Midianitess, and brought her to his brethren, in the
sight of Mosheh and all the congregation of the children
of Israel. He answered and said to Mosheh, What is
it (that is wrong) to have company with her? If thou
sayest, It is forbidden, didst thou not thyself take a
Midianitess, the daughter of Jethro? When Mosheh
heard, he trembled and swooned. But they wept, and
cried, Listen! And they stood at the door of the tabernacle of ordinance.   And Phinehas bar Elazar bar
Aharon, the priest, saw, and, remembering the ordination,
answered, and said: He who ought to kill, let him kill!
Where are the lions of the tribe of Jehudah? When
they saw, they were quiet.   And he arose from among
his Sanhedrin, and took a lance in his hand. [JERUSALEM.
And, behold, a man of the sons of Israel came and
brought to his brethren a Midianitha, before Mosheh
and all the congregation of the children of Israel; and,
behold, they were weeping at the door of the tabernacle.
And Phinehas bar Elazar bar Aharon, the high priest, saw,
and arose from among the assembly, and took a lance.]

Twelve miracles were wrought for Phinehas at the
time that he went in after the man of Israel with the
Midianitha.   The first sign was, He would have parted
them, but could not.   2. Their mouth was closed,
that they could not cry out; for, had they cried out, they
would have been rescued. 3. He drave the lance
through both of them.   4. The lance remained fixed

in the wound. 5. When he bare them aloft, the lintel was uplifted for him until he had gone forth. 6. He carried them through the whole camp, six miles, without fatigue. 7. He held them up by his right arm, in sight of their kindred, who had no power to hurt him. 8. The lance was made strong, so as not to be broken with the load. 9. The iron transpierced them, but was not withdrawn. 10. An angel came and made bare their corpses in sight of the people. 11. They lingered alive till they had been carried through the entire camp, lest the priest in the tabernacle should be defiled by the dead. 12. Their blood thickened so as not to flow upon him, but when he had borne them through the camp, it brake forth, and they died.

Answering, he said before the Lord of the world, Can it be that, on account of these, twenty and four thousands of Israel shall die? Immediately the compassions of Heaven were moved, and the plague was stayed from the children of Israel. [JERUSALEM. And he went in after the man of Israel into the tent, and thrust both of them, the man and the woman, through the body; and the plague was stayed from the children of Israel.] And the number who died by the pestilence was twenty and four thousand. [JERUSALEM. And those who died by that plague were twenty and four thousand.]

SECTION XLI.

PHINEHAS.

AND the Lord spake with Mosheh, saying: Phinehas the zealous, the son of Elazar bar Aharon, the priest, hath turned away mine anger from the children of Israel, in that, when zealous with My zeal, he hath slain the

sinners who were among them ; and for his sake I have
not destroyed the children of Israel in My indignation.
Swearing by My Name, I say to him, Behold, I decree
to him My covenant of peace, and will make him an
angel of the covenant, that he may ever live, to announce
the Redemption at the end of the days. [JERUSALEM.
With the oath went Mosheh, and said unto Phinehas,
Behold, I give to him] And because they defamed
him, saying, Is he not the son of Phuti, the Midianite?
behold; I will make him to possess the high priesthood ;
and because he took the lance with his arm, and struck
the Midianitess in her body, and prayed with his mouth
for the people of the house of Israel, the priests shall
be held worthy of the three gifts of the shoulder, the
cheek-bone, and the inwards ; and it shall be to him,
and to his sons after him, an everlasting covenant of
consecration, because he was zealous for the Lord, and
propitiated for the children of Israel. Now the name
of the man of Israel who was slain with the Midianitha
was Zimri bar Salu, a chief of the house of his fathers
of the tribe of Shemeon. And the name of the Midianite
woman who was killed was Kosbi, daughter of Zur, who
was called Shelonae, a daughter of Balak, the prince of
the people of Moab, whose dwelling-place was in
Midian.

And the Lord spake with Mosheh, saying : Trouble
the Midianites and slay them, because they troubled you
by their deceitful counsels when they beguiled you in
the matter of Peor, and of Kosbi their sister, the
daughter of the prince of Midian, who was slain in the
day of the plague for the matter of Peor. [JERUSALEM.
For their false dealings.]

XXVI. And it came to pass after the plague, that
the compassions of the heavens were turned to avenge
His people with judgment. And the Lord spake to

Mosheh and Elazar bar Aharon the priest, saying: Take
the sum of the account of the whole congregation of the
Beni Israel, from twenty years old and upward, according to the house of their fathers, of every one who
goeth forth with the host in Israel. And Mosheh and
Elazar the priest spake with the leaders, and commanded
that they should number them in the plain of Moab, by
the Jordan (over against) Jericho, saying, (You are to
number them) from a son of twenty years and upward,
as the Lord commanded Mosheh and the sons of Israel
when they came out of the land of Mizraim.

Reuben, the first-born of Israel: the sons of Reuben,
Hanok, the family of Hanok; of Phallu, the family of
Phallu; of Hezron, the family of Hezron; of Karmi.
the family of Karmi. These are the families of Reuben,
and their numbers were forty-three thousand seven
hundred and thirty. And the sons of Phallu Eliab;
the sons of Eliab, Nemuel, and Dathan, and Abiram.
The same were Dathan and Abiram who brought together the congregation that gathered and made the
division against Mosheh and Aharon in the congregation of Korach, when they gathered together and made
division against the Lord, and the earth opened her
mouth and swallowed them and Korach, when the congregation of the wicked died, when the fire devoured
the two hundred and fifty men, and they were made an
example. But the sons of Korach were not in the
counsel of their father, but followed the doctrine of
Mosheh the prophet; and therefore they died not by the
plague, nor were smitten by the fire, nor engulphed in
the yawning of the earth. [JERUSALEM. But the sons
of Korach, who were not in the counsel of their father,
did not die.]

The Beni Shemeon,[1] Nemuel, Jamin, Jakin, Zerach,

---

[1] I have omitted the form of words recited under the name of the

Shaul, with their families, twenty-two thousand two hundred.

Of Gad, the families of Zephon, Haggi, Suni, Ozni, Heri, Arod, Areli, forty thousand five hundred.

Of Jehudah, Her and Onan. But Her and Onan died, on account of their sins, in the land of Kenaan. Of the Beni Jehudah, the families of Shela, Pherez, Zerach. The sons of Pherez, Hezron, Amul. The numbers of the families of Jehudah, seventy-six thousand five hundred.

Of Issakar, the families of Thola, Puah, Jashub, Shimron, sixty-four thousand three hundred. Of Zebulon, the families of Sered, Elon, Jahleel, sixty thousand five hundred. Of Joseph, the Beni Menasheh, Makir, Gilead, Thezar, Helek, Asriel, Shekem, Shemida, Hepher. But Zelophehad bar Hepher had no sons, but daughters only; and the names of the daughters of Zelophehad were, Mahelah, Nohah, Hogelah, Milchah, and Thirzah. These are the families of Menasheh, and their number fifty-two thousand seven hundred.

The Beni Ephraim, Shuthelah, Bekir, Tachan, Heran the son of Shuthelah, their numbers thirty-two thousand five hundred.

The families of Benjamin, Bela, Ashbel, Ahiram, Shephuphia, (the sons of Bela, Ared and Naaman,) forty-five thousand six hundred.

The Beni Dan, the families of Shuham, sixty-four thousand four hundred.

Those of Asher, Jimnah, Jishvah, Beriah, and of the sons of Beriah, Heber and Malkiel. The name of the daughter of Asher was Sarach, who was conducted by six myriads of angels, and taken into the Garden of Eden alive, because she had made known to Jacob

first tribe, and repeated in the other eleven, and have given the names and the numbers without it.

that Joseph was living. The numbers of Asher, fifty-
three thousand four hundred. The Beni Naphtah,
according to their families, Jaczeel, Guni, Jezer, Shillem,
forty-five thousand four hundred. These are the numbers of the sons of Israel, six hundred and one thousand
seven hundred and thirty.

And the Lord spake with Mosheh, saying: Unto
these tribes shall the land be divided by inheritances
according to their names. To that tribe whose people
are many thou shalt make their inheritance large, and
to the tribe whose people are few thou shalt give a
smaller inheritance; to each his heritage shall be given
according to the number of his names. Yet the land
shall be divided by lots; according to the names of
their fathers' tribes they shall inherit. Their heritage
shall be divided by lots, whether great or small.

But these are the names of the Levites after their
families, the families of Gershon, Kehath, Merari. These
are the families of the Levites: the family of Lebni,
Hebron, Maheli, Mushi, Korach. And Kehath begat
Amram; and the name of Amram's wife was Jokebed,
a daughter of Levi, who was born to Levi when they
had come into Mizraim, within the walls; and she bare
to Amram Aharon, and Mushe, and Miriam their sister.
And to Aharon were born Nadab and Abihu, Elazar
and Ithamar. But Nadab and Abihu died when they
offered the strange fire from the hearth-pots before the
Lord. And the number of them (the Levites) was
twenty-three thousand, every male from a month old,
and upward; for they were not reckoned among the
children of Israel, as no possession was given them
among the sons of Israel. These are the numbers when
Mosheh and Elazar the priest numbered the sons of
Israel in the plains of Moab, by Jordan, (over against)
Jericho. And among them was not a man of the

numbers when Mosheh and Aharon the priest took the sum of the children of Israel in the wilderness of Sinai, because the Lord had said that dying they should die in the wilderness; and none of them remained except Kaleb bar Jephunneh, and Jehoshua bar Nun.

XXVII. And the daughters of Zelophehad bar Hepher, bar Gilead, bar Makir, bar Menasheh, of the family of Menasheh bar Joseph, when they heard that the land was to be divided to the males, came to the beth din, trusting in the compassions of the Lord of the world. And these are the names of the daughters, Mahelah, Nohah, Hogela, Milelah, and Thirzah. And they stood before Mosheh, after that they had stood before Elazar the priest, the princes, and all the congregation, at the door of the tabernacle of ordinance, saying · Our father died in the wilderness, but he was not among the congregation who murmured and gathered to rebel against the Lord in the congregation of Korach, but died for his own sin; nor made he others to sin; but he had no male children. Why should the name of our father be taken away from among his family because he had not a male child? If we are not reckoned as a son, and our mother claim (or observe) the Jebam,[2] our mother will take the portion of our father and of our father's brother. But if we be reckoned as a son, give us an inheritance among our father's brethren.

This is one of the four cases of judgment brought before Mosheh the prophet, and which he resolved in the manner above said. Of them some were judgments, &c.[3] And Mosheh brought their cause before the Lord.

And the Lord spake with Mosheh, saying : The daughters of Zelophehad have fitly spoken : this hath been written before Me : but they are worthy that it

---

[2] *Vide* Glossary, p. 69.   [3] The same words as recited before, p 389.

be said of them, Give them possession and inheritance
among the brethren of their father, and make over their
father's possession unto them. And when a son of
Israel shall speak, and say, A man hath died without
having a male child, then you shall make over his
inheritance to his daughter: if he have no daughter,
you shall give his possession to his brothers : if he have
no brothers, you shall give his possession to the
brethren of his father : but if his father had no
brothers, then you shall give his possession to his kinsman who is nearest to him of his father's family to
inherit. And this shall be the publication of a decree
of judgment to the children of Israel, as the Lord
hath commanded Mosheh.

And the Lord said to Mosheh, Go up to this mount
of Abaraee, and survey the land which I have given to
the children of Israel. And thou shalt see it, but thou
thyself shalt be gathered to thy people, as Aharon thy
brother hath been gathered : because you were dis-
obedient against My Word in the desert of Zin, in the
congregation at the Waters of Strife, to sanctify Me at
the waters in their sight : these are the Waters of Strife
in the desert of Zin.

And Mosheh spake before the Lord, saying : May
the Word of the Lord, who ruleth over the souls of
men, and by whom hath been given the inspiration
of the spirit of all flesh, appoint a faithful man over
the congregation, [JERUSALEM. The Word of the Lord,
the God who ruleth over the spirit of all flesh, appoint
a praiseworthy man over the people of the congregation,] who may go out before them to set battle in
array, and may come in before them from the battle ;
who may bring them out from the hands of their
enemies, and bring them into the land of Israel ; that
the congregation of the Lord may not be without the

wise, nor go astray among the nations as sheep who go
astray, having no shepherd. And the Lord said to
Mosheh, Take to thee Jehoshua bar Nun, a man upon
whom abideth the Spirit of prophecy from before the Lord,
and lay thy hand upon him, and make him stand before
Elazar the priest and the whole congregation, and
instruct him in their presence. And thou shalt confer a
ray of thy brightness upon him, that all the congregation
of the sons of Israel may be obedient to him. And he
shall minister before Elazar the priest; and when any
matter is hidden from him, he shall inquire for him
before the Lord by Uraia. According to the word of
Elazar the priest they shall go forth to battle, and come
in to do judgment, he, and all the sons of Israel with
him, even all the congregation. And Mosheh did as
the Lord commanded him, and took Jehoshua and
caused him to stand before Elazar the priest and all the
congregation; and he laid his hands upon him and
instructed him, as the Lord commanded Mosheh.

XXVIII. And the Lord spake with Mosheh, saying:
Instruct the children of Israel, and say to them: The
priests may eat of My oblation the bread of the order of
My table; but that which you offer upon My altar may
no man eat. Is there not a fire that will consume it?
And it shall be accepted before Me as a pleasant smell.
Sons of Israel, My people, be admonished to offer it from
the firstlings on the Sabbath, an oblation before Me in
its time. [JERUSALEM. Instruct the children of Israel,
and say to them, My oblation, the bread of the order of
My table. That which you offer upon the altar. Is
there not a fire that will consume it? To be received
from you before Me for a pleasant smell. Sons of
Israel, My people, be admonished to offer it before Me
in its season.]

And say to them: This is the order of the oblations

you shall offer before the Lord; two lambs of the year,
unblemished, daily, a perpetual burnt offering. The one
lamb thou shalt perform in the morning, to make atonement for the sins of the night; and the second lamb
thou shalt perform between the suns to atone for the
sins of the day; and the tenth of three seahs of wheaten
flour as a mincha mingled with beaten olive oil, the
fourth of a hin. It is a perpetual burnt offering, such
as was (ordained to be) offered at Mount Sinai, to be received with favour as an oblation before the Lord. And
its libation shall be the fourth of a hin for one lamb;
from the vessels of the house of the sanctuary shall it be
outpoured, a libation of old wine. [JERUSALEM. From
the vessels of the house of holiness, it shall be poured
out a libation of choice wine unto the Name of the
Lord.] But if old wine may not be found, bring wine
of forty days to pour out before the Lord. And the
second lamb thou shalt perform between the suns,
according to the presentation of the morning, and
according to its oblation shalt thou make the offering,
that it may be accepted with favour before the Lord;
but on the day of Shabbatha two lambs of the year
without blemish, and two-tenths of flour mixed with
olive oil for the mincha and its libation. On the
Sabbath thou shalt make a Sabbath burnt sacrifice in
addition to the perpetual burnt sacrifice and its libation.

And at the beginning of your months you shall offer
a burnt sacrifice before the Lord; two young bullocks,
without mixture, one ram, lambs of the year seven,
unblemished; and three tenths of flour mingled with
oil for the mincha for one bullock; two tenths of flour
with olive oil for the mincha of the one ram; and one
tenth of flour with olive oil for the mincha for each
lamb of the burnt offering, an oblation to be received
with favour before the Lord. And for their libation to

be offered with them, the half of a hin for a bullock, the
third of a hin for the ram, and the fourth of a hin for a
lamb, of the wine of grapes. This burnt sacrifice shall
be offered at the beginning of every month in the time
of the removal of the beginning of every month in the
year ; and one kid of the goats, for a sin offering before
the Lord at the disappearing (failure) of the moon, with
the perpetual burnt sacrifice shalt thou perform, with its
libation.

And in the month of Nisan, on the fourteenth day of
the month, is the sacrifice of the Pascha before the Lord.
On the fifteenth day of this month is a festival ; seven
days shall unleavened be eaten. On the first day of the
festival a holy convocation ; no servile work shall ye do ;
but offer an oblation of a burnt sacrifice before the Lord,
two young bullocks, one ram, and seven lambs of the
year, unblemished, shall you have. And their minchas of
wheat flour, mingled with olive oil, three tenths for each
bullock, two tenths for the ram, and for a single lamb a
tenth, so for the seven ; and one kid of the goats, to
make an atonement for you : beside the burnt sacrifice
of the morning, the perpetual burnt sacrifice, you shall
make these offerings. According to these oblations of
the first day you shall do daily through the seven days
of the festival. It is the bread of the oblation which is
received with favour before the Lord ; it shall be made
beside the perpetual burnt offering, with its libation.
And on the seventh day you shall have a holy convocation ; no servile work shall you do.

Likewise on the day of your firstlings, when you offer
the gift from the new produce before the Lord in your
ingatherings, after the seven weeks are completed, you
shall have a holy convocation, no servile work shall you
do ; but offer a burnt sacrifice to be received with favour
before the Lord, two young bullocks, one ram, seven

lambs of the year; also their mincha of wheaten flour mingled with olive oil, three tenths for each bullock, two tenths for the ram, a tenth to a lamb; so for the seven lambs one kid of the goats to make an atonement for you; beside the perpetual burnt offering you shall make these; they shall be unblemished, with their libation of wine.

XXIX. And in the seventh month, the month of Tishri, on the first of the month you shall have a holy convocation, you may not do any servile work; it shall be to you a day for the sounding of the trumpet, that by the voice of your trumpets you may disturb Satana who cometh to accuse you. And you shall make a burnt sacrifice to be received with favour before the Lord; one young bullock, one ram, lambs of the year seven, unblemished; and their mincha of wheaten flour mingled with olive oil, three tenths for the bullock, two tenths for the ram, and one tenth for each of the seven lambs; and one kid of the goats for a sin offering to make an atonement for you; besides the sacrifice for the beginning of the month and its mincha, and the perpetual sacrifice and its mincha; and their libations according to the order of their appointments, an oblation to be received with favour before the Lord.

And on the tenth of the seventh month, the month of Tishri, you shall have a holy convocation, and chasten your souls (by abstaining) from food and drink, the bath, friction, sandals, and the marriage bed; and you shall do no servile labour, but offer a sacrifice before the Lord to be received with favour; one young bullock, one ram, lambs of the year seven, unblemished, shall you have; and their mincha of wheat flour mingled with olive oil, three tenths for the bullock, two tenths for one ram, a single tenth for a lamb, so for the seven lambs, one kid of the goats for a sin offering; beside the sin offering of the expiations, (Lev. xvi.,) and the perpetual sacrifice and their minchas, and the wine of their libations.

And on the fifth day of the seventh month you shall have a holy convocation, no servile work shall you do; but shall celebrate the Feast of Tabernacles before the Lord seven days, and offer a sacrifice, an oblation to be received with favour before the Lord: thirteen young bullocks proceeding daily and diminishing their number, (in all) seventy for the seventy nations, and offering them by thirteen orders;[4] two rams, which you shall offer by two orders; lambs of the year fourteen, unblemished, to be offered by eight orders, offering six of them, by two and two, and two of them one by one, they shall be perfect. Their mincha also of wheat flour, with olive oil, three tenths for each bullock of the thirteen, two tenths for each ram, a single tenth for each of the fourteen lambs, and one kid of the goats for a sin offering, which shall be offered by one order, beside the perpetual sacrifice, the wheat flour for the mincha, and the wine of the libation.

On the second day of the Feast of Tabernacles you shall offer twelve young bullocks, by twelve orders; two rams, by two orders; fourteen lambs of the year unblemished by nine orders, five of them shall offer two by two, and four of them one by one. And their mincha of wheat flour, and the wine of their libation which shall be offered with the bullocks, rams, and lambs, by their number according to the order of their appointment; and one ram by one order, a sin offering, beside the perpetual sacrifice, and the wheat flour of their minchas, and their libations of wine.

On the third day of the Feast of Tabernacles you shall

---

[4] *Mattarta*. thirteen of the twenty-four orders or classes of priests. *Vide Mishna, Succah,* 5, § 6.

offer twelve bullocks by twelve orders; two rams by two orders, fourteen unblemished lambs of the year, by ten orders; four of them shall offer two and two, and six of them one by one; and their mincha of wheat flour, and their libations of wine, you shall offer with the bullocks, rams, and lambs, by the number in their appointed order; and one kid of the goats for a sin offering by one order; beside the perpetual sacrifice, the wheat flour for the mincha, and its libation of wine.

On the fourth day of the Feast of Tabernacles, ten young bullocks by ten orders; two rams by two orders; fourteen unblemished lambs of the year by twelve orders; three of them shall be offered at two times, and eight of them singly; their mincha of wheaten flour, and their libations of wine, which you shall offer with the the bullocks, rams, and lambs by their number, after their appointed order, and one kid for a sin offering, by one order; beside the perpetual sacrifice, the wheat flour for the mincha, and its libation of wine.

On the fifth day of the Feast of Tabernacles, nine young bullocks by nine orders; two rams by two orders; lambs of the year fourteen, perfect by twelve orders; two of them in a pair, twelve singly; and the wheat flour for their mincha, and the libation wine for the bullocks, the rams, and lambs by their number after the order of their appointment; and one kid for a sin offering by one order; beside the perpetual sacrifice and the wheat flour for the mincha, and the wine of its libation.

On the sixth day of the Feast of Tabernacles, eight young bullocks by eight orders; two rams by two orders; fourteen unblemished lambs of the year by thirteen orders; a pair of them together, and twelve of them singly. Their mincha of wheat flour, and their libation of wine, you shall offer with the bullocks, rams, and lambs, by their number in the order appointed; and

one kid for a sin offering by one order, besides the perpetual sacrifice, the wheat flour for the mincha, the wine
of its libation, and a vase of water to be outpoured
on the day of the Feast of Tabernacles in grateful
acknowledgment (for a good memorial) of the showers
of rain.

On the seventh day of the Feast of Tabernacles you
shall offer seven bullocks by seven orders; two rams
by two orders; fourteen unblemished lambs of the year
by fourteen orders: the number of all these lambs ninety-
eight, to make atonement against the ninety-eight maledictions. And their mincha of wheat flour and libations
of wine you shall offer with the bullocks, rams, and lambs,
by their number, according to the order appointed;
and one kid by one order, beside the perpetual sacrifice, the wheat flour for the mincha, and its libation of
wine.

And on the eighth day you shall gather together joy-
fully from your tabernacles, in your houses, a gladsome
company, a festal day, and a holy convocation shall you
have, no servile work shall you do, but offer a sacrifice,
an oblation to be received with favour before the Lord;—
light oblations; one bullock before the one God, one
ram for the one people, lambs of the year unblemished,
seven, for the joy of the seven days. Their mincha of
wheat flour, and their libations of wine which you shall
offer with the bullocks, rams, and lambs, by their number,
after the order of their appointment; and one kid for a sin
offering, beside the perpetual sacrifice, the flour for its
mincha, and the wine for its libation. These you shall
offer before the Lord in the time of your festivals,
beside your vows which you vow at the festival, and
which you shall bring on the day of the feast, with
your free-will oblation for your burnt sacrifice, your
mincha, libations, and consecrated victims.

XXX. And Mosheh spake to the sons of Israel, according to all that the Lord had commanded Mosheh.

SECTION XLII.

MATTOTH.

AND Mosheh spake with the chiefs of the Tribes of the Beni Israel, saying: This is the Word which the Lord hath spoken, saying: A man, a son of thirteen years, when he shall have vowed a vow before the Lord, or have sworn an oath, saying, I will withhold from such a thing which is permitted to me, shall not be allowed to relax his word (at his own will): nevertheless, the house of judgment (beth dina) can absolve him; but if they absolve him not, whatsoever hath gone out of his mouth he shall perform.

And a female who hath not passed twelve years when she hath vowed a vow before the Lord, and hath bound herself in her father's house until her thirteenth year; and her father hear her vow, and whatever bond she hath bound upon her soul, and her father be acquiescent, and speak not to her; then every vow and every bond which she hath bound upon her soul shall be confirmed. But if her father prohibit her on the day that he heareth, or, not being prepared to confirm, annulleth after he hath heard, (then) no vow or bond that she hath bound upon her soul shall be confirmed, but is remitted and forgiven her before the Lord, because her father hath made her free from the authority of the vow, (or, nullified to her the power of the vow.) And if when she hath been taken by a husband a vow be upon her, or her lips have expressed that which is binding upon her soul while in her father's house, and her father had not absolved her while unmarried, then, when she hath been married, it shall be confirmed. But if after she is married she make a vow, and her husband hear it, and on the day that he heareth it he is minded to confirm it, and is silent to her, then the vow and the bond which she hath bound upon her soul shall be ratified. But if her husband prohibit her on the day that he heareth, then the vow which is upon her, and the utterance of her lips which bound her soul, are remitted and forgiven her. Yet the vow of a widow, or a divorced, whatever hath bound her soul, shall be confirmed upon her. But if, while she was in her husband's house, or while she had not attained to marriage years, she had vowed, or bound her soul with the bond of an oath which her husband had heard of, and had neither spoken nor prohibited her, or had died before she was married, then all her vows shall be confirmed, and all the obligations with which she had bound her soul be ratified, and her father shall have no power to absolve her. But if her husband released her [JERUSALEM. Her husband released her] on the day that he heard, then, whatever her lips had pronounced to be a vow, or a bond upon her soul, shall not be confirmed, and if her husband had annulled them, [JERUSALEM. Her husband had released them,] and she, not knowing, had performed, it shall be forgiven her before the Lord. Every vow, every oath-bond to chasten the soul, her husband may ratify or annul. But if her husband was silent and consented when he heard from one day to the next, then all her vows and all the bonds upon her are ratified; by his silence he hath confirmed them; for he was silent to her on the day, and consented, and absolved her not on the day that he heard. But if, absolving, he would absolve her one day after he had heard, there is no force in the absolution; and if he then nullify the word, her husband or her father shall bear her sin. These are the

publications of the statutes which the Lord commanded
Mosheh (on these matters) between a man and his wife,
and a father and his daughter in the day of her youth
in her father's house; [JERUSALEM. In the time of
her youth in her father's house;] but not in the time
of her youth, and she be in the house of her husband.

XXXI. And the Lord spake with Mosheh, saying:
Take retribution for the children of Israel from the
Midianites; and afterward thou shalt be gathered to
thy people. And Moses spake with the people, saying:
Arm of you men, [JERUSALEM. Arm of you,] for the host
to make war against Midian, to give the people of the
Lord avengement upon Midian; a thousand of each tribe
of all the tribes of Israel send ye to the war. And of
the thousands of Israel fit men were chosen who gave
up themselves, a thousand of a tribe, twelve thousand,
armed for the war. And Mosheh sent them, a thousand of each tribe to the war, them and Phinehas bar
Elazar the priest unto the war, with the Uraia and
Thummaia consecrated to inquire for them, and the
Jubilee trumpets in his hand for assembling, encamping,
and ordering forward the host of Israel. And they
warred against Midian, circumventing them from three
corners, as the Lord had instructed Mosheh, and they
killed every male; and they slew the kings of the
Midianites with the slain of their armies, Evi, Rekem,
Zur, who is Balak, and Hur and Reba, five kings of
Midian; and Bileam bar Beor they killed with the
sword. And it was when Bileam the guilty saw
Phinehas the priest pursuing him, he made use of his
magical arts, (lit., made words of enchantment,) and
flew in the air of the heavens; but Phinehas forthwith
pronounced the Great and Holy Name, and flew after
him, and seized him by his head, and bringing him
down drew the sword, and sought to kill him; but he

opened his mouth with words of deprecation, and said
to Phinehas : If thou wilt spare my life, I swear to thee
that all the days I live I will not curse thy people.
He answered him, and said : Art thou not Laban the
Aramite, who didst seek to destroy Jakob our father,
who wentest down into Mizraim, to destroy his children,
and, after they had come out of Mizraim, didst send the
wicked Amalek against them ; and hast thou not now
been sent to curse them ? But after thou hadst seen
that thy works did not prosper, and that the Word of
the Lord would not hear thee, thou didst give the evil
counsel to Balak to set his daughters in the way to
make them go wrong, when there fell of them twenty-
four thousand. Therefore, it cannot be that thy life may
be spared ; and at once he drew the sword and slew him.

And the sons of Israel led captive the wives of the
Midianites, their children, their cattle, and all their
flocks, and destroyed all their goods ; and all their
towns, the houses of their rulers, and the high places of
their houses of worship, they burned with fire ; but they
took all the spoil and the prey both of men and beasts,
and brought to Mosheh, Elazar the priest, and all the
congregation of Israel, the captives, the prey, and the
spoils, at the camp in the fields of Moab, by the Jordan,
near Jericho.

And Mosheh and Elazar the priest, with all the
heads of the congregation, went forth to meet them
without the camp. But Mosheh was angry with the
leaders appointed over the host, the chiefs of thousands
and of hundreds who came from the war with the host ;
and Mosheh said to them, Why have you spared all
the women ? These are they who caused the offence of
the sons of Israel, by the counsel of Bileam, to do
wrongly before the Lord in the matter of Peor, so that
pestilence came upon the congregation of the Lord.

Now, therefore, slay every male among the children, and every woman who hath known a man; but every female child you shall stand before the Crown of Holiness, (the priest's tiara,) and look upon her: she who is not a virgin will be pallid in the face, but she who is a virgin child will blush in the face, like fire; them you shall spare. But as for you, abide without the camp seven days; whoever hath slain a man, or touched the dead, you shall sprinkle on the third; and on the seventh day, both you and your captives, and every garment, and whatever is made of skin, goats' hair, horn, or bone, and every vessel of wood, you shall sprinkle.

And Elazar the priest said to the men of the host who had returned from the war: This is the manifestation of the decree of the law which the Lord hath commanded to Mosheh. Nevertheless, these (articles) without their rust, the gold, silver, brass, iron, tin, and lead, [JERUSALEM. Tin and lead,] their vessels, but not the unformed and simple (metals), every thing whose nature it is to abide the fire, of the pans, pots, spits, and gridirons, you shall make to pass through fire to purify them, and afterward (sprinkle them) with water such as is used to purify the unclean; but whatever will not abide the fire, coverlids, cups, flagons, and utensils, you shall make to pass through forty sata of water; and you shall wash your raiment on the seventh day to be clean, and afterwards come into the camp.

And the Lord spake with Mosheh, saying: Take the sum of the prey of the captives, both of man and beast, and take their amount, thou and Elazar the priest, and the chiefs of the fathers of the congregation; and divide the spoil between the men of war who took the spoil in the conflict of battle, having gone forth with the host, and between all the congregation; and separate that which is to be given up to the Name of the Lord by the

men of war who went forth with the host: one woman
out of five hundred; so, likewise, of oxen, asses, and
sheep.   From their half, the portion of the men of war,
shalt thou take them, and give to Elazar the priest, as a
separation unto the Name of the Lord, but of the half
(falling to) the children of Israel thou shalt take one
out of fifty of the women, and of the oxen, the asses,
and of all the cattle, and give them to the Levites who
keep charge of the Lord's tabernacle; and Mosheh and
Elazar the priest did as the Lord commanded Mosheh.

And the amount of the prey, the rest of the spoil
which had been taken by the people who went forth in
the host,—the number of the sheep was six hundred
and seventy-five thousand; oxen, seventy-two thousand;
asses, sixty-one thousand; persons, the women who had
not known man, all the persons thirty-two thousand.
And the half of the portion for the men who had gone
to the war, the number of the sheep was three hundred
and thirty-seven thousand five hundred; and the amount
of that brought up for the Name of the Lord was of sheep
six hundred and seventy-five; oxen thirty-six thousand,
those for the Name of the Lord seventy-two; asses
thirty thousand five hundred, for the Name of the Lord
sixty-one; persons sixteen thousand, for the Name of
the Lord thirty-two.   And Mosheh gave the number
separated to the Name of the Lord unto Elazar the
priest, as the Lord commanded Mosheh.   And the half
part for the children of Israel which Mosheh divided
from the men's who went forth to the war, the amount
was three hundred and thirty-seven thousand five hundred
sheep, thirty-six thousand oxen, thirty thousand five
hundred asses, and sixteen thousand women.   And
Mosheh took from the half part for the children of
Israel of that which had been captured, one out of fifty,
whether of man or beast, and gave it to the Levites who

kept charge of the tabernacle of the Lord, as the Lord commanded Mosheh.

And the officers who had been appointed over the thousands of the host, the captains of thousands and of hundreds, drew near to Mosheh, and they said to Mosheh, Thy servants have taken the account of the men of war who have been with us, and not any of them are wanting. And we have brought a gift unto the Name of the Lord, forasmuch as the Lord hath delivered the Midianites into our hands, and we have been able to subdue their land and their cities. And we entered into their chambers, and there saw their daughters, fair, tender, and delicate; and every man who found on them jewels of gold, loosened the coronets from their heads, the earrings from their ears, the necklaces from their necks, the bracelets from their arms, the rings from their fingers, and the brooches from their bosoms;—but in all this we abstained from lifting our eyes upon themselves, or gazing on one of them, lest we should sin with any one of them, and die the death which the wicked die in the world to come. And may this be had in memorial for us in the day of the great judgment, to make propitiation for our souls before the Lord. [JERUSALEM. And we have brought the oblation of the Lord. When we entered into the houses of the Midianite kings, and into their sleeping-chambers, and saw there the fair and delicate daughters of the Midianite kings, we took from their heads their golden coronets, the earrings from their ears, the rings from their fingers, the bracelets from their arms, and the jewels from their bosoms; yet, Mosheh our master! far was it from us,—not one of us was united with any one of them, neither will he be companion with her in Gehinnom. In the world to come may it stand to us, in the day of the great judgment, to propitiate for our souls before the Lord.]

And Mosheh and Elazar the priest took the gold
from them, every article fabricated , and the sum of all
the gold of the separation which they had separated unto the Name of the Lord was sixteen thousand
seven hundred and fifty shekels, from the captains of
thousands and of hundreds. For the men of the host
had taken spoil, every man for himself. And Mosheh
and Elazar the priest took the gold from the captains of
thousands and of hundreds, and brought it into the
tabernacle of ordinance, a good memorial of the sons of
Israel before the Lord.

XXXII. Now the sons of Reuben and of Gad possessed
much cattle, exceeding much : and they surveyed the
land of Mikvar and of Gilead, and, behold, it was a
region suitable for cattle folds. [JERUSALEM. And they
saw the land of Mikvar and of Gilead, and, behold, it was
a place of wealth.] And the sons of Gad and Reuben
came and spoke to Mosheh, Elazar, and the princes of
the congregation, saying : Makelta, Madbeshta, Mikvar,
Beth Nimre, Beth Hoshbane, Maalath Meda, Shuan,
Beth Kebureth, de Moshe, and Behon, [JERUSALEM.
Makalta, Madbeshta, Mikvar, Beth Nimrin, Heshbon,
Elhala, Shebam, Nebo, and Behan,] the land which
the Lord hath subdued, and whose inhabitants he hath
smitten before the congregation of Israel, is a land
suitable for cattle, and thy servants have cattle. [JERU-
SALEM. Wealth.] They said therefore, If we have
found grace before thee, let this land be given to thy
servants for a possession, and let us not pass over
Jordan.

But Mosheh said to the sons of Gad and Reuben,
Shall your brethren go to the war, and you sit down
here ? And why should you enfeeble [JERUSALEM.
And why do you break] the will of the sons of Israel
from going over to the land which the Lord hath given

to them? So did your fathers when I sent them from
Rekem Giah to survey the land: they went up to the
brook of Ethkela, and saw the land, [JERUSALEM. They
went unto Segola, and saw the land,] but enfeebled the
will of Israel's heart, that they would not enter into the
land which the Lord had given to them. And the
anger of the Lord was that day moved, and He sware,
saying, If these men who came out of Mizraim from
twenty years old and upward shall see the land which I
covenanted to Abraham, Izhak, and Jakob, because they
have not fully (walked) according to My fear; except
Kaleb bar Jephunneh the Kenezite, and Jehoshua bar
Nun, for they have fully (walked) after the fear of the
Lord. And the anger of the Lord was moved against
Israel, and He made them wander in the wilderness forty
years, until all that generation which did evil before the
Lord have been consumed. And, behold, you are risen up
after your fathers, disciples of wicked men, to increase
yet the anger of the Lord against Israel. [JERUSALEM.
You have multiplied the men of sin yet to increase the
strength of His displeasure.] For if you go back from
fearing Him, He will still make them abide in the
wilderness, and so will you destroy all this people.

And they drew near to him, and said, We will build
sheepfolds for our flocks, and towns for our families; but
we will go armed among the sons of Israel until we have
brought them into their place: but our families shall dwell
in towns defended against the inhabitants of the land.
[JERUSALEM. In cities fortified against the (former) masters
of the land.] We will not return to our homes until the
sons of Israel possess every one his inheritance. For we
will not inherit with them over the Jordan and beyond;
for our inheritance cometh to us beyond Jordan eastward.

And Mosheh said to them, If you will perform this
thing; if you will go forth armed before the people of

the Lord to the war, if some of you armed will pass
over Jordan before the Lord's people to go on with the
war until He hath driven out the enemy before Him,
and the land be subdued before the people of the Lord,
then afterwards you shall return, and be acquitted
before the Lord and by Israel ; and this land shall be
yours for an inheritance before the Lord.   But if you
will not perform this, behold, ye will have sinned before
the Lord your God, and know that your sin will meet you.
Build (then) cities for your little ones and folds for
your sheep, and do that which hath proceeded from
your mouth. [JERUSALEM. Build cities for your little
ones and folds for your sheep, and do that which hath
come out of your mouth.]

And the sons of Gad and Reuben spake to Mosheh
with one consent, saying, Thy servants will do whatever my lord hath commanded : our children, wives,
flocks, and all our cattle shall be here in the cities of
Gilead ; but thy servants will go over, every one armed
for the host, before the people of the Lord to the war, as
my lord hath said.

And Mosheh commanded concerning them Elazar
the priest, and Jehoshua bar Nun, and the heads of the
tribes of the Beni Israel, and said to them : If the sons
of Gad and of Reuben go over the Jordan with you,
every one armed for the war, before the people of the
Lord, and the land be subdued before you, then shall
you give to them the land of Gilead for a possession.
But if they will not pass over armed with you, then they
shall receive an inheritance among you in the land of
Kenaan. But the sons of Gad and Reuben answered and
said : Whatsoever the Lord hath spoken to thy servants
so will we do. We will go over armed before the Lord's
people into the land of Kenaan, that our inheritance
may be on this side the Jordan.

And Mosheh gave to them, the sons of Gad and of
Reuben, and to the half tribe of Menasheh bar Joseph,
the kingdom of Sihon king of the Amoraee, and
the kingdom of Og king of Mathnan, the land with
its cities by the limits of the cities of the land round
about. And the sons of Gad built (rebuilt) Madbashta
and Maklalta and Lechaiath, [JERUSALEM. And the sons
of Gad built Debeshta, and Maklalta, and Lechaiath,]
and Maklelath, Shophena, and Mikvar Geramatha,
[JERUSALEM. And Maklalta of Shophan, and Makvar,
and Jegbeha,] and the strong city of Beth Nimrin,
and Beth Haran, fenced cities (with) folds for sheep.
And the sons of Reuben built (rebuilt) Beth Heshbon
and Mahalath Mera, and the city of the two streets
paved with marble which is Beresha, and the place of
the sepulchre of Mosheh, and (rebuilt) the city of Balak,
destroying out of it the idol of Peor, in the house
of his high places, and the city whose walls surrounded
it, inscribed with the names of his heroes, and Shiran.
And after they had built them they called their names
after the names of the men who had built them.

And the sons of Makir bar Menasheh went to Gilead
and subdued it, and drave out the Amoraee who were
therein. And Mosheh gave Gilead to Makir bar
Menasheh, and he dwelt in it. And Jair bar Menasheh
went and subdued their villages, and called them the
villages of Jair. And Nobach went and subdued
Kenath and its villages, and called it Nobach, after his
own name.

SECTION XLIII.

MASEY.

XXXIII. THESE are the journeys of the Beni Israel
who came out from Mizraim by their hosts, after the

miracles had been wrought for them by the hand of
Mosheh and Aharon.   And Mosheh recorded their outgoings by their journeys by the Word of the Lord ; and
these are their journeys by their goings forth.

They departed from Pelusin in the month of Nisan, on
the fifteenth day of the month ; after they had eaten the
sacrifice of the Pascha did the children of Israel go
forth, with uncovered head, in sight of all the Mizraee.
[JERUSALEM. And they went out from Pelusin in the
first month.]   And the Mizraee buried those whom the
Lord had killed among them, even all the first-born ;
and upon their idols did the Word of the Lord do judgments ; their molten idols were dissolved, their idols of
stone were mutilated, their idols of earthenware broken
in pieces, their wooden idols turned to ashes, and their
cattle gods were slain with death.

And the sons of Israel went forth from Pelusin, and
encamped in Sukkoth, a place where they were protected by seven glorious clouds.   And they removed
from Sukkoth, and encamped in Etham, on the side of
the wilderness. They removed from Etham, and returned
unto Pumey Hiratha, which he in front of the idol of
Zephon, and encamped before Migdol.   [JERUSALEM.
And removing from Etham they returned to the caravansaries of Hiratha, which are in front of the idols.]
And from the caravansaries of Hiratha they removed,
and passed through the midst of the sea, and went upon
the shore of the sea, collecting onyx stones and pearls.
Afterwards they proceeded three days' journey in the
wilderness of Etham, and encamped in Marah.   And
they removed from Marah, and came to Elim ; in Elim
were twelve fountains of water for the twelve tribes, and
seventy palm trees, answering to the seventy sages ; and
they encamped there by the waters.   [JERUSALEM. And
they removed from Marah and came to Elim : in Elim

were twelve fountains of water, answering to the twelve
tribes of Israel, and seventy palm trees, answering to
the seventy elders of the Sanhedrin of Israel; and they
encamped there.]   And they removed from Elim, and
camped on the banks of the Sea of Suph; and they
removed from the banks of the sea, and encamped in the
wilderness of Sin; thence [5] to Dopheka, Kerak Takiph
(the strong tower), Rephidim, where, because their
hands were (*raphin*) neglectful of the words of the
law, there was no water for the people to drink;
thence to the wilderness of Sinai; thence to the Graves
of those who desired flesh; thence to Hazeroth, where
Miriam the prophetess was struck with leprosy; thence
to Rithema, the place of many juniper trees; thence to
Rumana, whose fruit is hard; [6] thence to Libnah, whose
borders are built of bricks (*libnetha*); thence to Beth
Rissa; thence to Kehelath, where Korach and his companions banded together against Mosheh and Aharon; thence
to the mountain whose fruit is good; thence to Harada,
where they were confounded by the evil plague; thence
to Makheloth, the place of congregation; thence to the
lower Makheloth; thence to Tharach, and Muka, whose
waters were sweet; thence to Hasmona; thence to
Meredotha, the place of rebellion (or chastisement);
thence to Bere-Haktha, Gudgad, at the Rocks, Jote-
bath, a good and quiet place; thence to the Fords;
thence to Tarnegolla, the tower of the cock; thence to
the wilderness of Zin; at the Iron Mount, which is
Rekem; thence to Mount Umano, on the borders of
the Land of Edom.   And Aharon the priest went up
to Mount Umano by the Word of the Lord, and died

---

[5] The expression "and they removed from" such a place occurs in
the recital of all these stages.   I have henceforward omitted it, and
given only the place of each encampment in succession

[6] From *rimmon*, "a pomegranate." (?)

there, in the fortieth year from the going out of the
children of Israel from Mizraim, in the fifth month, on
the first of the month. And Aharon was one hundred and
twenty-three years old when he died on Mount Umano.

And Amalek the wicked, who was combined with the
Kenaanites, and reigned in Arad,—the house of his
abode was in the land of the south,—heard that the
sons of Israel were coming to wage war against them,
and utterly to destroy their cities.

And they removed from Mount Umano, and encamped
in Zalmona, a place of thorns, and narrow (or squalid),
in the land of the Edomaee; and there the soul of the
people was distressed on account of the way; thence to
Punon, where the Lord sent burning serpents among
them, and their cry went up to heaven. And they
removed to Oboth; thence to the passage of the Fords,
on the border of the Moabaee; thence to Dibon, the
place of fortune;[7] thence to Almon Diblathaimah, where
the well was hidden from them, because they had forsaken the words of the law, which are as delicious as
figs (*diblatha*); thence to the Mount Ibraee, in front
of the place of the burial of Mosheh; thence they
removed and encamped in the fields of Moab, by Jordan,
near Jericho; and they encamped by the Jordan, from
Bethjeshimon unto the plain of Sillan in the fields of
Moab.

And the Lord spake with Mosheh, in the fields of
Moab, at the Jordan, by Jericho, saying: Speak with
the sons of Israel, and say to them: When you have
passed over the Jordan into the land of Kenaan, you
shall drive out all the inhabitants of the country from
before you, and lay waste all the houses of their worship, destroy all their molten images, and overthrow all
their high places. [JERUSALEM. You shall destroy all

---

[7] *Beth Mazala*, "the house of the planet."

the inhabitants of the land from before you, make an
end of all their idols, break their molten images, and
overthrow all their high places.] And you shall drive
out the inhabitants of the land, and dwell therein, for I
have given you the land to possess it. And you shall
inherit the land by lots, according to your families; to
the tribe whose people are many you shall enlarge, and
to the tribe whose people are few, you shall diminish.
According to the place where one's lot falleth, there
shall his place be; you shall inherit by the tribes of
your fathers.

But if you will not drive out the inhabitants of the
land from before you, it will be that the residue whom
you have spared looking at you with an evil eye will
surround you as shields (*terisin*) on your sides, and
afflict you in the land wherein you dwell; and it shall
be that as I had thought to do to them I will do to you.

XXXIV. And the Lord spake with Mosheh, saying :
Command the sons of Israel, and say to them : When
you have entered into the land of Kenaan, this shall be
the land that shall be divided to you for an inheritance,
the land of Kenaan by its limits. Your south border
(shall be) from the Wilderness of Palms, by the iron
mountain, at the confines of Edom, even the south
border at the extremities of the Sea of Salt, eastward.
And your border shall turn from the south to the ascent
of Akrabbith, and pass on to the palms of the mountain
of iron, and the going forth thereof shall be southward
of Rekem Giah, and shall go onward to the tower of
Adar, and pass over to Kesam. And the border shall
wind round from Kesam unto Nilos, of the Mizraee, and
its outgoings shall be to the west.

And for the western border you shall have the Great
Ocean Sea ; its limits are the waters of the beginning,[8]

[8] Or, "the creation."

with the waters of old which are in its depth; its capes
and havens, its creeks and its cities, its islands and
ports, its ships and its recesses:[9] this shall be your
border westward.

And this shall be your northern border;—from the
Great Sea you shall appoint to you unto Mount Umanis.[1]
From Mount Umanis you shall appoint to you (a line)
as thou goest up to the entrance of Tebaria, and the
outgoings of the border at its two sides, unto Kadkor
of Bar Zahama, and to Kadkoi of Bar Samgora, and
Divakinos and Tarnegola unto Kesarin, where thou goest
up to Abelas of Cilicia. And the border shall go on
unto Keren Zekutha, and to Gibra Hatmona, and its
outgoings shall be at Keria Bethsekel, and to the midst
of the great court (*dareta rabtha*), which is at Mizeha,
between the towers of Hinvetha and Darmeshek: this
shall be your northern limit.

And you shall appoint your eastern border from the
towers of Hinvetha unto Apamea; and the border shall
descend from Apamea to Dophne, eastward of Hinvetha;
thence the border shall go down to the cavern of Panias,
and from the cavern of Panias to the mountain of snow,
and from the mountain of snow to Henan, and from
Henan the border shall go down and encompass the
plain of the river of Arnon, and arrive at the wilderness
and the palms of the mountain of iron, take in the
Waters of Contention, and rest at Ginesar, a city of the
kings of the Edomites, the inheritance of the tribes of
Reuben and Gad, and the half tribe of Menasheh; and
the border shall descend and encompass the Sea of
Genesar on the east.

[JERUSALEM. And your border shall be southward,
from the wilderness of Rekem, over against the frontier
of the Edomaee, and southward shall it be to you unto

---

[9] Or, "interior"   [1] This name is here given to Mount Lebanon.

the extremity of the Sea of Salt, eastward.   And your
south border shall go round from the ascent of Akrabim,
which passeth over by the mountain of iron, and its
outgoings shall be from the south unto Rekem Giah,
and proceed to the buildings of the threshing floors, and
pass on to Kesam.   And the border shall wind round
from Kesam unto Nilos Mizraim,[2] and the going out
of it shall be at the sea.

And the (west) border shall be the Great Ocean Sea;
its isles, ports, and ships, with the ancient waters that are
in it, the waters of the beginning; this shall be your
western border.

And this shall be your northern limit: from the
Great Sea you shall appoint to you unto Mount Manos.
From Mount Manos you shall extend to the entrance of
Antiochia, and the outgoing shall be unto Abelas of the
Cilicians; and the border shall go to Zapherin, and
its outgoing be at the dwellings of Hainutha, unto
Apamea, unto Dophne, east of Hainutha, and shall
descend and come down upon the Sea of Ginesar at the
west.]   And the border shall descend to the Jordan,
and its outgoing be at the Sea of Salt.   Rekem Giah
on the south, Mount Umanos on the north, the Great
Sea on the west, the Sea of Salt on the east,—this shall
be your country, the Land of Israel, by the extent
of its borders round about.   [JERUSALEM. And it shall
descend to Jordan, and have its outgoings at the Sea of
Salt.   This shall be your land by its limits round about.]

And Mosheh commanded the sons of Israel, saying:
This is the land which you are to inherit by lot, which
the Lord hath commanded to give to the nine tribes and
the half tribe.   For the tribe of the children of Reuben,
according to the house of their fathers, and tribe of Gad,

---

* Not the Nile, but a small river falling into the Mediterranean, a
little below Gaza. Compare Joshua xv. 47.

and the half tribe of Menasheh have received their inheritance beyond the Jordan on the eastern side.   [JERU-
SALEM. The two tribes and the half tribe have received
their inheritance beyond Jordan-Jericho first.   Their
border goeth forth on the east from the plain of the Salt
Sea to Kinnereth, the city of the kingdom of the Amorites, and thence to the mountain of snow, and to Hamatha
of Lebanon; thence to Hoba, on the northern side of
Hainutha, of Damasek, and from Hoba to Divakinos, at
the snowy mount of Kisarion, eastward of (the town of)
Dan, on the west, and from thence to the Great River,
the river Phrat, upon which is the order of the victories
of the wars of the Lord, which are to be wrought there.
And from the Great River, the Phrat, their border
goeth forth to the cities of Zavatha, beyond all the
Tarkon (Trechonites), unto Zimra, the royal house of
Sihon, king of the Amoraee, and the royal house of Og,
king of Mathnan, going to Raphiach and to Shokmezai,
until thou comest to the shore of the Salt Sea.   This
is the portion of the two tribes and the half tribe.]

And the Lord spake with Mosheh, saying: These
are the names of the men who shall make to you the
inheritance of the land: Elazar the priest, and Jehoshua
bar Nun, and one prince from each of the tribes you
shall choose to give you the inheritance of the land.
And these are the names of the men. Of the tribe of
Jehudah, Kaleb bar Jephunneh; for *Shemeon*, Shemuel
bar Amminhud; *Benjamin*, Elidad bar Kiselon; *Dan*,
Buki bar Jageli; *Joseph*,—*Menasheh*, Haniel bar
Ephod; *Ephraim*, Kemuel bar Shiphtan; *Zebulon*,
Ehzaphan bar Parnak; *Issakar*, Paltiel bar Azan;
Asher, Ahihud bar Shelomi; *Naphtali*, Pedahael bar
Amminhud. These are they whom the Lord commanded
to divide the inheritance of the land of Kenaan to the
children of Israel.

XXXV. And the Lord spake with Mosheh in the plains of Moab, by Jordan-Jericho, saying: Command the sons of Israel that they give to the Levites from their inheritance cities to dwell in, and suburbs (open spaces) to the cities round about shall you give to the Levites. [JERUSALEM. And suburbs to the cities round about them shall you give to the Levites.] And the cities shall be for them to dwell in, and the suburbs for their cattle, their property, and all their needful things. But of the cities which you give to the Levites the suburbs round the city shall be one thousand cubits without the city round about. [JERUSALEM. But the suburbs.] And you shall measure outside the city, on the east side, two thousand cubits; on the south two thousand, on the west two thousand, and on the north two thousand cubits, with the city in the midst; these shall be to you the suburbs of the cities. And of the cities you give to the Levites, six shall be for refuges to manslayers, that the manslayer may escape thither. Beside these you shall give them forty-two other cities. All the cities that you give to the Levites shall be forty-eight cities with their suburbs. But when you give the cities from the inheritance of the Beni Israel, from the tribe whose people are many you shall give many, and from the tribe whose people are few you shall diminish; every one shall give of his cities to the Levites, according to the inheritance he possesses.

And the Lord spake with Mosheh, saying: Speak with the sons of Israel, and say to them, When you have passed over Jordan unto the land of Kenaan, you shall provide you cities with streets and houses of living (boarding houses), cities of refuge shall they be to you, that thither the manslayer may flee who hath killed a man inadvertently. And they shall be to you for cities of refuge for the manslayer from the avenger of blood,

that the man may not be put to death till he shall have
stood before the congregation for judgment. And these
cities which you give shall be six cities of refuge for the
manslayer; three you shall appoint beyond Jordan, and
three in the land of Kenaan; cities of refuge shall they
be.   For the sons of Israel and the sojourners among
you shall be these six cities of refuge, that thither
whoever hath killed a man through ignorance may flee.

But if he smote him with an instrument of iron and
killed him, he is a murderer; and the murderer shall be
surely put to death.   Or if, filling his hand with a stone
large enough to kill any one, he struck him, and killed
him, he is a murderer, and the murderer dying shall die.
Or if, filling his hand with an instrument of wood
sufficient to kill any one, he struck him, and killed him,
he is a murderer; the murderer shall be put to death.
The avenger of blood may himself kill the manslayer, if
he meet him outside of these cities; he may kill him in
judgment.

But if (the manslayer) had assaulted in enmity and
intentionally with a club or staff, or thrown stones
upon him with purpose of heart, and killed him; or
cherishing enmity had struck him with his hand and
killed him; he is a murderer; dying he shall die.   The
avenger of blood may slay the homicide when he hath
been condemned.   But if in ignorance, without keeping
of malice, he let any thing fall upon him, having no
intention to kill; or if without intention he let a stone
sufficient to kill any one, or any other thing, fall upon
him, and kill him, without having hated, or purposed to
do him harm, then the congregation shall judge between
him who had smitten him, and the avenger of blood,
according to these judgments; and the congregation
shall release the manslayer from the hand of the avenger
of blood, and make him return to his city of refuge

whither he had fled; and he shall dwell there until the time that the high priest die, whom the multitude (*sagia*) had anointed with the oil of anointing;—because he did not pray on the Day of Atonement in the Holy of Holies concerning the three great transgressions, that the people of the house of Israel might not be smitten for strange worship, or impure connexions, or the shedding of innocent blood, when it was in his power to obviate them by his prayer, and he prayed not, therefore hath he been condemned to die in that year.

But if, while the high priest is yet alive, the man-slayer goeth out indeed from the bounds of his city of refuge whither he had fled, and the avenger of blood find him without the bounds of his city of refuge, he may kill the manslayer, without being guilty of death, for he should have abode in his city of refuge until the death of the high priest; but after the high priest is dead he may return to the land of his inheritance.

And these indications shall be to you a decree of judgment for your generations in all your dwellings: Whosoever killeth a man, according to the word of witnesses fit to give testimony against him, the avenger of blood, or the house of judgment, shall put him to death. But one witness only shall not testify against a man to put him to death. You may not take a ransom for the release of a murderer who is guilty of death, for dying he shall die. Neither may you take ransom for him who hath fled to his city of refuge, so as that he may return to dwell in the land before the time of the high priest's decease. Nor contaminate ye the land in which you are, because innocent blood which hath not been avenged will overflow the land, and there is no atonement made for the land upon which innocent blood hath been shed, but by the shedding of the blood of him who shed it. Therefore defile not the land in which you are; for My Shekinah dwelleth in the midst of it; for I am the Lord whose Shekinah dwelleth among the children of Israel.

XXXVI. And the heads of the fathers of the family of the Beni Gilead bar Makir bar Menasheh, even the family of the Beni Gilead bar Joseph, came to the house of judgment, and spake before Mosheh and the princes, the chief fathers of the Beni Israel, and said: The Lord commanded Rabboni to give the land an inheritance by lot to the children of Israel, and Rabboni was commanded before the Lord to give the inheritance of our brother Zelophehad to his daughters. But if these marry into any of the tribes of the children of Israel, their inheritance will be withdrawn from that of our fathers, and will be added to the inheritance of the tribe which will have become theirs, and our lot will be diminished. And at the Jubilee of the Beni Israel their inheritance will be added to that of their tribe in which they will be; and their possession will have been withdrawn from the inheritance of our father's tribe.

Then Mosheh commanded the children of Israel by the Word of the Lord, saying: The tribe of the Beni Joseph have said well. This is the thing which the Lord hath commanded,—not for the generations that shall arise after the division of the land, but for the daughters of Zelophehad, saying: They may be the wives of them who are proper in their eyes, only such must be of the families of their father's tribe. That the inheritance of the children of Israel may not pass about from one tribe to another: for the children of Israel shall every one keep to the inheritance of their father's tribe. (Verses 9 and 10 are wanting.) As the Lord commanded Mosheh, so did the daughters of Zelophehad; and Mahalah, Thirzah, Hogelah, Milchah, and Nobah, the daughters of Zelophehad, became wives

of sons of their kindred; of the family of the children
of Menasheh bar Joseph were they wives, and their
inheritance was with the tribe of their father's family.

These are the commandments and orders of judgments
which the Lord commanded the children of Israel, by
Mosheh, in the plains of Moab by the Jordan near
Jericho.

END OF THE PALESTINIAN TARGUM ON THE
SEPHER BEMIDBAR.

THE TARGUM OF ONKELOS

ON THE

SEPHER ELLEH HADDEBARIM,

OR

BOOK OF DEUTERONOMY.

SECTION OF THE TORAH XLIV.

TITLE DEBARIM.

I. THESE are the words which Mosheh spake with all Israel beyond the Jordan, reproving them because they had sinned in the wilderness, and had provoked (the Lord) to anger on the plains over against the Sea of Suph, in Pharan, where they scorned the manna; and in Hazeroth, where they provoked to anger on account of flesh, and because they had made the golden calf. It is a journey of eleven days from Horeb by the way of Mount Seir unto Rekem Giah.

And it came to pass in the fortieth year, in the eleventh month, in the first day of the month, Mosheh spake with the sons of Israel according to all that the Lord had commanded him for them. After he had slain Sihon, king of the Amorites, who dwelt in Heshbon, and Og, king of Mathnan, who dwelt at Ashtaroth in Edrehi; on this side Jordan in the land of Moab began Mosheh to explain the doctrine of this law, saying:

The Lord our God spake with us at Horeb, saying: It is sufficient for you to have dwelt at this mountain: turn, and proceed, and go unto the mountain of the

Amoraah, and to all its habitable places in the plains, the mountain, the valleys, and in the south, and by the side of the sea; the land of the Kenaanah and Lebanon, unto the river, the great river Phrat; behold, I have set the land before you; go in and possess the land which the Lord covenanted to your fathers, to Abraham, to Izhak, and to Jakob, to give it to them, and to your children after them.

And I spake to you at that time, saying: I am not able to bear you myself alone. The Lord your God hath multiplied you; and, behold, you are this day as the stars of the heavens for multitude. The Lord God of your fathers make you a thousand times more than you are, and bless you, as He hath said to you! How can I bear alone your labour, your business, and your adjudgments? Provide (then) for yourselves prudent and sagacious men of your tribes, and I will appoint them to be chiefs over you. And you answered me, and said: The thing that thou hast spoken it is right that we should do.

And I took the heads of your tribes, wise men and masters of knowledge, and appointed them chiefs over you, captains of thousands, of hundreds, of fifties, and of tens, and officers [1] of your tribes. And I charged your judges at that time, saying: Hear between your brethren, and judge rightly [2] between a man and his brother, or the sojourner. You shall not have respect to persons in the judgment; you shall hear little words (matters) as well as great; nor be afraid of the face of man, for the judgment is of the Lord; and the matter that is too hard for you bring to me, and I will hear it; and I commanded you at that time all the things that you should do.

And we departed from Horeb, and went through all that great and fearful desert which you saw by the way

---

[1] Sam. Vers., "scribes."   [2] Sam. Vers., "the truth."

of the mountain of the Amoraah, as the Lord our God
commanded us, and we came unto Rekem Giah. And I
said : You are come to the mountain of the Amoraah,
which the Lord our God will give to us. See, the Lord
thy God hath set the land before thee : arise, possess (it),
as the Lord the God of thy fathers hath bid thee ; fear
not, nor be broken. And all of you came to me and
said : We will send men before us, to explore the land for
us, and bring us word about the way to go up to it, and
to what cities we shall come. And the thing was good
in my eyes, and I took from you twelve men, one man
for a tribe. And they turned and went up to the mountain, and came to the brook of Ethkela, and explored it.
And they took in their hands some of the produce of
the land and brought to us, and returned us word,
saying : The land which the Lord will give us is good.
But you were not willing to go up, but were rebellious
against the Word of the Lord your God, and murmured
in your tents, and said : Because the Lord hath hated
us, He hath brought us from the land of Mizraim to
deliver us into the hand of the Amoraah to destroy us.
To what shall we go up ?   Our brethren have broken [3]
our heart, saying : The people are greater and stronger
than we ; vast are the cities, and walled to the height of
heaven, and we saw there also the sons of the giants.
But I said to you : Be not broken (hearted), fear them
not ; the Word of the Lord, who leadeth on before you,
will fight for you, according to all that He did for you
in Mizraim in your sight ; and in the wilderness, where
thou hast seen that the Lord thy God carrieth thee,
as a man carrieth his child, in all the way you have
journeyed until your coming to this place. But in this
thing you did not believe in the Word of the Lord your
God, who led on before you in the way to prepare for

[3] Sam. Vers., "have brought down."

you (each) place of encampment for your sojournings, in the pillar of fire by night to show you in which way to go, and in the pillar of the cloud by day. But the voice of your words was heard before the Lord, and He was angry, and made oath, saying: If a man of the men of this evil generation shall see the good land which I sware to your fathers, save Kaleb bar Jephunneh. He shall see it, and I will give to him the land on which he hath trodden, and unto his children, because he hath been upright in the fear of the Lord. Also against me was there displeasure before the Lord on your account, (He) saying: Thou too art not to go in thither; Jehoshua bar Nun, who standeth before thee, he shall go in thither; strengthen him, for he is to make Israel to inherit; but your little ones, who you said would be for prey, your children, who to-day know not good and evil, they shall enter therein, to them will I give it, and they shall possess it; but you, turn you, and go into the wilderness by the Weedy Sea.

Then you answered, and said : We have sinned before the Lord; we will go up and wage war according to all that the Lord our God commanded; and you girded on every man his weapons of war, and began to go up to the mountain. But the Lord said to me: Tell them, You shall not go up, neither wage war; for My Shekinah is not among you, lest you be crushed before your enemies. And I told you, but you hearkened not, but rebelled against the Word of the Lord, and dared, and went up to the mountain; but the Amoraah who dwelt in that mountain came out against you, and pursued you as bees are dispersed, and smote you in Seir unto Hormah. And you returned, and wept before the Lord; but the Lord would not receive your prayer, nor hearken to your words; and you dwelt in Rekem many days, according to the days that you abode.

II. And we turned, and journeyed to the wilderness by the way of the Sea of Suph, as the Lord had told us; and we encompassed the mountain of Seir many days. And the Lord spake to me, saying: You have been about this mountain enough for you: turn you northward; and command the people, saying: You are going through the coasts of your brethren, the sons of Esau, who dwell in Seir; and they will be afraid of you. Take great heed, quarrel not with them; for I will not give you of their land, not so much as you may tread upon with the sole of the foot; for the inheritance of Mount Seir I have given to Esau. You shall buy provision of them with silver, that you may eat; and water, with silver, that you may drink; for the Lord thy God hath blessed thee in all the works of thy hands; He hath given thee sufficient for thy need in thy going about in this great wilderness; these forty years the Word of the Lord thy God hath been thy helper, thou hast not wanted any thing. And we passed by from our brethren, the sons of Esau, who dwelt in Seir, by the way of the plain from Elath, and from Ezion Geber; and turned and passed by the way of the wilderness of Moab.

And the Lord said to me, Distress not the Moabaee, nor stir thyself to make war with them; for I will not give thee any of their land to inherit, for I have given Le- chiath unto the children of Lot for an inheritance. The Emethanee in old times dwelt in it; a people great and many, and strong as the giants. They were reputed as giants, and like giants also they were; but the Moabites called them Emethanee.[4] And in Seir dwelt the Horaee in former times; but the sons of Esau drave them out, and destroyed them, and dwelt in their places, as Israel did [6] in the land of his inheritance which the Lord gave to them.

---

[4] The Formidable.   [5] Past for the future, compare *aber* in verse 17

Now arise, (said I,) and go over the stream of Zared. And we passed over the stream of Zared. And the days in which we were journeying from Rekem Giah until we crossed the stream of Zared were thirty and eight years, till all the generation of the men of war were consumed from the camp, as the Lord had sworn to them. For the plague stroke from before the Lord was upon them to destroy them from among the host till they were consumed.

When all the men of war had been consumed, and had died away from among the people, the Lord spake with me, saying: Thou art to-day to pass by Lechaiath, the frontier of Moab. But when thou comest nigh over against the Beni Ammon, be not troublesome to them, nor provoke thyself to make war with them; for I have not given to thee of the land of the Beni Ammon any inheritance; for I have given it to the children of Lot to inherit.—That also was reputed a land of giants; in old times giants did dwell in it, and the Ammonites called them Hashbanee; a people great and many, and strong as giants, but the Lord destroyed them before them, and cast them out, and they dwelt in their places. As did the sons of Esau who dwelt in Seir, when He destroyed the Horaee from before them, and drave them out, and they have dwelt in their places unto this day. And the Avaee, who dwelt in Pheziach unto Hazah, destroyed the Kaphutkaee, who came out of Kaphutkaia, and dwelt in their place.

Arise, remove, and pass over the river of Arnon: behold, I have delivered into thy hand Sihon, king of Heshbon, the Amorite, and his land; begin to cast him out, and rouse thyself to make battle with him. This day will I begin to put dread of thee and fear of thee upon the face of the peoples which are under the whole heavens, who shall hear thy fame, and be broken before thee.

And I sent ambassadors from the wilderness of Kedemoth unto Sihon king of Heshbon with words of peace,
saying, May I pass through thy land by the way? I
will go by the way, nor turn to the right or the left :
thou shalt sell me provision for silver, and I will eat ;
and give me water for silver, and I will drink ; I will
only go through on my feet : as the Beni Esau who
dwell in Seir, and the Moabaee who dwell in Lechaiath,
did to me, until I pass over Jordan to the land which
the Lord our God shall give to us.   But Sihon king of
Heshbon was not willing to permit us to pass through
his coasts ; for the Lord thy God hardened his spirit
and strengthened his heart, that He might deliver him
into thy hand, as at this day.   And the Lord said to me,
See, I have begun to deliver to thee Sihon and his
country ; begin thou to drive him out, that thou mayest
inherit his land.   And Sihon came forth to meet us,
he and all his people, to give battle at Jahaz ; and the
Word of the Lord our God delivered him up before us,
and we smote him, and his sons, and all his people.
And we subdued all his cities at that time, and consumed
all the towns, and the men, women, and children, and
left none to escape.   Only the cattle was a booty to us,
and the spoil of the cities which we subdued.   From
Aroer which is upon the bank of the river of Arnon, and
the city that is by the river, even unto Gilead, there
was no city too strong for us ; for the Lord our God
delivered all before us.   Only to the land of the Beni
Ammon thou didst not come near, nor to all the side of
the river Jubeka, nor the cities of the mountain, nor to
any of which the Lord our God had commanded us.

III. And we turned, and went up the way of Mathnan ; [6] and Og king of Mathnan came out to meet us,
he and all his people, to give battle at Edrehi.   And

---

[6] Sam. Vers., *Batanæa.* Heb., *Bashan.*

the Lord said to me, Fear him not ; for I have delivered
him into thy hand, with all his people and his land ; and
thou shalt do to him as thou hast done to Sihon king
of the Amoraah, who dwelt at Heshbon.   And the Lord
our God delivered Og the king of Mathnan into our
hand with all his people, and we smote him until not a
remnant of him escaped.   And we subdued all his cities
at that time, there was not a city which we took not
from them, sixty cities, all the region of the territory of
the kingdom of Og in Mathnan.   All those strong cities
were fortified with gates and bars, beside unwalled towns
very many.   But we consumed them as we did Sihon
king of Heshbon : we destroyed in all the cities the men,
women, and children ; but all the cattle and the spoil of
the cities were a prey to us.   And we took at that time
from the hand of the two kings of the Amoraah, the
country on this side of Jordana, from the river of Arnon
unto the mountain of Hermon.   The Zidonaee call
Hermon Sirion, but the Amoraee call it the Mount of
Snow.[7]   All the cities of the plain, all Gilead, and
all Mathnan, unto Salka and Edrehi, cities of the
kingdom of Og in Mathnan.   For only Og king of
Mathnan remained of the remnant of the giants. Behold,
his bedstead was a bedstead of iron: is it not in Rabbath
of the children of Ammon, nine cubits its length, and
four cubits its breadth, in the cubit of the king ?   And
their land (which) we took into possession at that time,
from Aroer, upon the river Arnon, and half Mount
Gilead, and the cities thereof, I have given to the
tribe of Reuben, and to the tribe of Gad.   And the rest
of Gilead, and all Mathnan, the kingdom of Og, I have
given to the half tribe of Menasheh ; all the surrounding country, even all Mathnan, which was called the
Land of the Giants.   Jaer bar Menasheh took all the

[7] *Tor Talega.*

territory of Terakona,[8] unto the border of Geshurah and Aphkiros, and called it after his name, Mathnan Kapharne-Jair, unto this day. And to the tribe of Reuben, and of Gad, I have given from Gilead unto the river of Arnou (to) the middle of the river [9] and its bound, unto the river Jubeka, which is the border of the children of Ammon. And the plain, and the Jordan, and the border thereof, from Genezar unto the Sea of the Plain, the Sea of Salt, under the declivity of the height, eastward. And I instructed you at that time, saying: The Lord your God hath given you this land to possess it; you shall pass over armed before your brethren the sons of Israel, all armed for the host. Only your wives, and little ones, and your cattle,—for I know that you have much cattle,—shall abide in your cities which I have given you, until the Lord hath given rest to your brethren as well as to you, and they also possess the land which the Lord your God hath given to them on the other side of Jordana : and you shall return every man to his inheritance which I have given you. And I charged Jehoshua at that time, saying · Thine eyes have seen all that the Lord your God hath done unto these two kings; so shall the Lord do to all the kingdoms to which thou art going over. Fear them not, for the Word of the Lord your God will fight for you.

SECTION XLV.

VAETHCHANNAN.

And I prayed before the Lord at that time, saying : O Lord God, Thou hast begun to show Thy servant Thy

---

[8] Heb., *Argob*. Sam. Vers., *Rigoblaah*.   [9] Or, " valley."

greatness and Thy mighty hand; for Thou art God, whose
Shekinah is in the heavens above, and Thou rulest in the
earth, and none can do according to Thy greatness or
Thy might.　Let me, I pray, go over and see the good
land that is beyond Jordan, that goodly mountain, and
the place of the sanctuary.　But there was displeasure
with the Lord against me on your account, and He heard
me not; but said to me, It is enough for thee; add not
to speak again before Me of this thing: go up to the
summit of the height, and lift up thy eyes to the west,
the north, the south, and the east, and see with thy eyes;
for thou shalt not pass over this Jordan.　But instruct
Jehoshua, and fortify, and make him strong; for he shall
go over before this people, and put them in possession
of the land which thou wilt see.　And we dwelt in the
valley over against Beth Peor.

　IV. And now, Israel, hear the statutes and the
judgments which I am to teach you to do, that you may
live, and go in to inherit the land which the Lord God
of your fathers hath given you.　Ye shall not add to
the word that I command you, nor diminish from it, to
keep the commandments of the Lord your God which I
command you.　Your eyes have seen what the Lord
hath done with the worshippers of Baala Peor; for
all the men who went after Baala Peor the Lord
thy God hath destroyed from among you.　But you
who have cleaved to the fear of the Lord your God, are
alive all of you this day.　Behold, I have taught you
statutes and judgments, as the Lord my God commanded
me, that you may so do in the land to which you go to
possess it.　And observe, and perform; for this is your
wisdom and understanding in the eyes of the nations
who will hear all these statutes, and say, Most surely
this great people is a wise and understanding people.
For what people so great who hath God so nigh unto it

Y

to hearken to their prayer in the time of their tribulation, as the Lord our God (is to us) in every time that
we pray before Him? Or what people so great which hath
statutes and judgments so true as all this law which I
set before you this day? Only take heed to thyself, and
diligently keep thy soul, all the days of thy life, lest
thou forget the things which thy eyes have seen, and
they pass away from thy heart. But make them known
to thy children, and to thy children's children, (as was
said) on the day when thou stoodest before the Lord
thy God at Horeb, when the Lord said to me, Gather
the people together before Me, and I will make them
hear My words, that they may learn to fear Me all the
days which they live on the earth, and may teach their
children. And you came near, and stood at the lower
parts of the mountain, and the mount burned with fire
to the height of the heavens, in darkness, clouds, and
shadow. And the Lord spake with you from the midst
of the fire; you heard a voice of words, but you beheld
no similitude; (there was) only the Voice. And He
proclaimed to you His covenant which He commanded
you to do, (even) the Ten Words; and He wrote them
upon two tables of stone.

And the Lord commanded me at that time to teach
you statutes and judgments for you to perform in the
land whither you pass over to possess it. But take
heed to your souls; for you saw no likeness in the day
that the Lord spake with you from the midst of the
fire; lest you corrupt yourselves, and make you an
image, or the likeness of any form, the likeness of male
or female, of any beast on the ground, or of any bird
which flieth in the air of the expanse of the skies, of
any reptile of the earth, or any fish of the waters, under
the earth; and lest thou lift up thine eyes to the
heavens, and behold the sun, or moon and stars, all the

host of the heavens, and go astray and worship them, and serve them, which the Lord thy God hath not appointed for any of the nations that are under the whole heavens. But you hath the Lord drawn nigh unto His service, and brought you out from the iron furnace, (even) from Mizraim, to be unto Him a people of inheritance, as at this day. But towards me the Lord had displeasure, on account of your words, and He sware that I should not go over Jordan, nor enter the good land which the Lord your God giveth you to inherit. For I must die in this land; I am not to pass over the Jordan; but you are to pass over, and inherit that good land. Take heed to yourselves, lest you forget the covenant of the Lord your God, which He hath concluded with you, and you make an image for you, the likeness of anything about which the Lord thy God hath commanded thee. For the Word of the Lord thy God is a consuming fire: He is a jealous God.

When thou shalt have begotten sons and daughters, and have grown old in the land, and thou become corrupt, and make an image, the likeness of anything, or do what is evil before the Lord thy God, to cause displeasure before Him; I call, this day, the heavens and earth to witness that you will surely perish from off the land whither you go over the Jordan to possess it: you will not prolong days upon it, for with destruction you will be destroyed. And the Lord will scatter you among the nations, and you will remain a numbered people [1] among the nations whither the Lord shall lead you. And there will you serve the peoples who are worshippers of idols, the work of men's hands, wood and stone, which see not, nor hear, nor eat, nor smell.

---

[1] *Am deminyan,* "a people of (small) number." (°) Heb. text, *mithe mispar,* "men of number." Peschito Syriac, *kalil be-menyono,* "small in number."

Yet if from thence thou seek the fear of the Lord thy God, thou shalt find, if thou seek for Him with thy heart, and with all thy soul. When thou wilt be in trouble, and all these words will have found thee, in the end of the days, and thou wilt turn unto the fear of the Lord thy God, and be obedient to His Word, because the Lord thy God is a merciful God ; He will not forsake thee, nor destroy thee, nor forget the covenant of thy fathers which He sware unto them. For ask now of the ancient days that have been before thee, from the day that the Lord created man upon the earth, and (ask) from one end of the heavens to the other, if there hath been so great a thing as this, or any heard like it, whether a people have heard the voice of the Word of the Lord speaking from the midst of the fire as thou didst hear, and have lived. Or (if any have seen) like miracles which the Lord hath wrought, in being revealed to redeem to Himself a people from among a people, by miracles, signs, and wonders, and with war, and by a mighty hand and uplifted arm, and by grand visions, according to all that the Lord your God hath done for you in Mizraim before your eyes. Unto thee hath it been shown, that thou mayest know that the Lord He is God, there is none beside Him. From the heavens thou didst hear the voice of His Word, that He might teach thee, and upon earth He showed thee His great fire, and thou heardest His words from the midst of the fire. And because He loved thy fathers, and had pleasure in their children after them, He brought thee out by His Word, by His mighty power, from Mizraim, to drive out nations greater and stronger than thou from before thee, to bring thee in, to give thee their land to inherit, as at this day.

Know then, this day, and revolve it in thy heart, that the Lord He is God, whose glory is in the heavens above, and who ruleth upon the earth beneath, (and that) there is none but He; and keep His statutes and His commandments that I teach thee this day, that it may be well with thee, and thy sons after thee, and thou mayest prolong days on the land which the Lord thy God giveth thee, all the days.

Then Mosheh separated three cities on the other side of the Jordan (toward) the sunrise, that the slayer may escape thither who may kill his neighbour unawares, not having hated him yesterday, or before it; and that, escaping to one of those cities, he may live :—Bezer, in the wilderness, in the plain land of the tribe of Reuben; Ramoth, in Gilead, of the tribe Gad; and Golan, in Mathnan, of the tribe of Menasheh.

And this is the law which Mosheh set in order before the children of Israel : these are the testimonies, statutes, and judgments, which Mosheh spake to the children of Israel, on their coming forth from Mizraim; on the other side of Jordan, in the vale over against Beth Peor, in the land of Sihon king of the Amoraah, who dwelt in Heshbon, whom Mosheh and the children of Israel smote when they had come out of Mizraim. And they took possession of his land, and the land of Og king of Mathnan, two kings of the Amoraah, who were beyond Jordan, toward the sunrise; from Aroer, upon the bank of the river Arnon to the mountain of Siaon, which is Hermon; and all the plain beyond Jordan eastward unto the sea of the plain at the declivity of the heights.

V. And Mosheh called all Israel, and said to them : Listen, Israel, to the statutes and judgments which I speak before you this day, and learn them, and keep them to do them. The Lord our God confirmed a covenant with us at Horeb. The Lord confirmed not this covenant with our fathers, but with us who are

here all of us living this day: word with word hath the
Lord spoken with you at the mountain from the midst
of the fire, (I stood between the Word of the Lord
and you, to announce to you at that time the word
of the Lord; for you were afraid in presence of the
fire, and went not up to the mountain,) saying: I
am the Lord thy God, who hath brought thee out of
the land of Mizraim, from the house of bondage; there
shall not be with thee another god beside Me. Thou
shalt not make to thee an image or any likeness of that
which is in the heavens above, or on the earth below, or
in the waters under the earth; thou shalt not worship
them or serve them: for I, the Lord thy God, am a
jealous God, visiting the guilt of fathers upon rebellious
children, upon the third generation and upon the fourth
of them that hate Me, when the children complete the
sins of their fathers; but doing good unto (thousands
of) generations of those who love Me, and keep My
commandments. Thou shalt not swear by the Name
of the Lord thy God in vain; for the Lord will
not acquit him who shall swear by His Name falsely.
Keep the day of Shabbatha to sanctify it, as the Lord
thy God hath commanded thee. Six days thou shalt
work, and do all thy labour; but the seventh day is the
Sabbath before the Lord thy God: thou shalt not perform any work, thou, nor thy son, nor thy daughter,
thy servant, thy handmaid, thy ox, thy ass, nor any of
thy cattle, nor thy sojourner who is in thy gates; that
thy servant and handmaid may rest as well as thou.
And remember that thou wast a servant in the land of
Mizraim, and that the Lord brought thee out from
thence with a mighty hand and uplifted arm; therefore
the Lord thy God hath commanded thee to observe the
Sabbath day. Honour thy father and mother, as the
Lord hath commanded, that thou mayest prolong thy

days, and it may be well with thee in the land which
the Lord thy God shall give thee. Thou shalt not kill
life, nor commit adultery, nor steal, nor bear false
witness against thy neighbour. Nor shalt thou desire
thy neighbour's wife, nor covet thy neighbour's house,
his field, or his servant, or his handmaid, his ox, or his
ass, or any thing that is thy neighbour's.

These words spake the Lord with all your congregation at the mount, from the midst of the fire, the
clouds and the darkness, with a great voice, and hath not
ceased.[2] And He wrote them upon two tables of
stone, and gave them to me. But it was, when you
heard the voice from the midst of the fire and darkness,
the mount burning with fire, all the chiefs of your tribes
and your elders drew near to me ; and you said, Behold,
the Lord our God hath showed to us His glory and His
greatness, and we have heard the voice of His Word out
of the midst of the fire; this day have we seen that the
Lord speaketh with a man,[3] and he liveth. But now
why should we die? For this great fire will consume
us : if we go on to hear the voice of the Word of the
Lord our God, we shall die. For who is there of all
flesh who can hear the voice of the Word of the Living
God speaking from the midst of fire (in the manner)
that we have, and can live? Go thou near, and hear all
that the Lord our God shall say, and speak thou with us
all that the Lord our God shall speak with thee, and we
will hearken and will do. And the voice of your words
was heard before the Lord when you spake with me, and
the Lord said to me, The voice of the words of this
people which they have spoken with thee is heard before
Me; all (the words) they have spoken are right. O that

---

[2] Pesch. Syriac, " a great voice which hath no limit."   Hebrew text
" and He added not."

[3] I. e , Moses : *vide* the Palestine, *in loco.*

they may have such a heart to fear Me and keep all My
commandments all days, that it may be well with them
and their children for ever. Go, and say to them,
Return to your tents. But thou, stand here before Me,
and I will tell thee all the commandments, the statutes,
and the judgments, which thou shalt teach them, that
they may do them in the land that I will give them to
possess it.

And you shall observe to do as the Lord your God
hath commanded you, nor decline to the right hand or
to the left. In all the way which the Lord your God
hath commanded you shall ye walk, that you may live,
and it may be well with you, and you may lengthen out
your days in the land which you are to inherit.

VI. And this is the commandment, (these are) the
statutes and the judgments, which the Lord your God
hath commanded (me) to teach you to perform in the
land to which you go over to possess it, that thou
mayest fear before the Lord thy God, and keep all His
statutes and His commandments which I command thee;
thou, thy sons, and thy sons' son, all the days of thy
life, that thy days may be prolonged. And thou, Israel,
shalt receive, and keep, and perform, that it may be
well with thee, and thou mayest increase greatly, as the
Lord God of thy fathers hath said to thee, (in) the land
which produceth milk and honey.

HEAR, ISRAEL;[4] THE LORD OUR GOD IS ONE LORD:
and thou shalt love the Lord thy God with all thy heart,
and with all thy soul, and with all thy substance. And
these words that I command thee this day shall be upon
thy heart. And thou shalt deliver them to thy children,
and talk of them when thou art sitting in thy house, and

---

[4] Verses 4-9 form the first part of what in the Hebrew liturgy is
called the *Shema* (" Hear "). The other parts are Deut. xi. 13-21, and
Num. xv. 37-41.

when thou goest in the way, and in thy lying down, and thy rising up. And thou shalt bind them for a sign upon thy hand, and they shall be for tephillin[5] between thine eyes; and thou shalt write them upon the door-posts, and affix them to the lintels[6] of thy house, and upon thy gates.

And it shall be, when the Lord thy God will have brought thee into the land which He covenanted to thy fathers, to Abraham, Izhak, and Jakob, to give thee great and goodly cities which thou buildedst not, and houses full of goods that thou didst not fill, and cisterns hewn which thou hewedst not, vineyards and olive trees which thou didst not plant, and thou have eaten and be full, beware, lest thou forget the fear of the Lord who brought thee out from the land of Mizraim, from the house of bondage. Thou shalt fear the Lord thy God, and serve before Him, and swear by His Name. You shall not go after the idols of the Gentiles, the idols of the peoples who surround you, (for the Lord thy God is a jealous God, His Shekinah dwelleth in the midst of thee,) lest the anger of the Lord thy God be kindled against thee, and He destroy thee from off the face of the earth. You shall not tempt the Lord your God as you tempted Him in the temptation : keeping you shall keep the commandments of the Lord your God, His testimonies, and His statutes He hath commanded thee, and do what is right and well ordered before the Lord, that it may be well with thee, and thou mayest enter in and possess the good land which the Lord sware unto thy fathers to break all thy enemies before thee, as He hath said.

When thy son shall ask thee in time to come, (mehar, to-morrow,) saying, What are the testimonies, statutes,

---

[5] Heb , totaphoth. LXX , ἀσάλευτα New Test , φυλακτήρια.

[6] Or, "in the ends,"—besiphey.

and judgments, which the Lord our God hath commanded you? then thou shalt say, We were servants
to Pharoh in Mizraim; and the Lord brought us out of
Mizraim with a mighty hand, and put forth miracles
great and sore upon Pharoh, and all the men of his
house, before our eyes; and He brought us out from
thence, to bring us in, to give us the land which He
sware to our fathers.   And the Lord commanded us to
perform all these statutes, to fear the Lord our God, that
all days it may be well with us, (and) that He may
preserve us alive as at this day.   And it shall be our
righteousness to observe to do all these commandments
before the Lord our God, as He hath commanded us.

VII. When the Lord thy God shall bring thee into
the land into which thou goest to possess it, and cast
out many peoples from before thee, the Hittites,
Girgashites, Amorites, Kenaanites, Pherizites, Hivites,
and Jebusites, seven nations, greater and mightier than
thou, and shall deliver them up before thee; then thou
shalt smite and utterly consume them; thou shalt make
no covenant with them, nor show mercy upon them.
Neither shalt thou intermarry with them; thou shalt not
give thy daughter to his son, nor take his daughter for
thy son.   For they will cause thy son to go astray from
serving Me, and they will worship the idols of the Gentiles, and the anger of the Lord will be kindled against
you, and He will destroy thee speedily.   But thus shall
you do to them: you shall pull down their altars, break
their statues in pieces, cut down their (sacred) groves,
and burn their images with fire.   For thou art a people
consecrated before the Lord thy God, thee hath the Lord
thy God chosen to be to Him a people more beloved
than all peoples upon the face of the earth.   Not because
you were greater than any of the peoples, hath the Lord
chosen and befriended you, for you were smaller than

any of the peoples; but because the Lord had mercy on
you, and that He would keep the covenant He sware to
your fathers, hath the Lord brought you out with a
mighty hand, and redeemed thee from the house of
bondage, out of the hand of Pharoh, the king of
Mizraim. Know, then, that the Lord thy God, He is
God, a faithful God, keeping covenant and mercy for
them who love Him and keep His commandments to a
thousand generations, but repaying them who hate Him
the good which they have done before Him in their lives,
to destroy them (in the life to come?). He delayeth not
to do good to His enemies for the good they may have
wrought before Him in their lives, to repay them.
Thou shalt therefore observe the commandments, statutes, and judgments, which I command thee this day, to
do them.

SECTION XLVI.

EKEB.

And it shall be that because thou wilt have obeyed
these judgments, and have observed and performed
them, the Lord thy God will keep with thee the covenant and the mercy which He sware to thy fathers.
And He will love thee, and bless thee, and multiply
thee, and will bless the offspring of thy womb, the fruit
of thy land, thy corn, wine, and oil, the herds of thy
oxen, and the flocks of thy sheep, on the land which He
sware to thy fathers to give thee. Blessed shalt thou
be above all peoples; there shall not be among thee a
barren male or a barren female, neither among thy
cattle. And the Lord thy God will remove from thee
all diseases, and all the plagues of Mizraim; the
evil things that thou knowest He will not lay upon thee,

but will put them on all that hate thee. And thou shalt
consume all the peoples that the Lord thy God will give
up to thee; thine eye shall not have pity upon them,
nor shalt thou serve their idols, for that will be a
stumbling-block to thee.

If thou say in thy heart, These nations are greater
than I am: how can I drive them out? thou shalt not
be afraid of them; remembering thou shalt remember
what the Lord thy God did to Pharoh and all Mizraim;
the great miracles which thine eye beheld, and the signs
and wonders, the mighty hand and uplifted arm, by
which the Lord thy God led thee forth; so shall the
Lord thy God do to all the nations before whom thou
art afraid. And moreover, the Lord thy God will stir
up the hornet among them, until they who remain and
who hid themselves from before thee have perished.
Thou shalt not be broken down before them; for the
Lord thy God dwelleth in the midst of thee, the Great
and fearful God. And the Lord thy God will put away
those nations before thee by little and little; for
thou mayest not consume them instantly, lest the wild
beast of the field multiply against thee. Yet will the
Lord thy God deliver them up before thee, and destroy
them with a great destruction, till they be consumed;
and He will deliver their kings into thy hand, and
destroy their names from under the heavens, and not a
man will stand before thee till thou wilt have destroyed
them. The images of their idols thou shalt burn with
fire; thou shalt not desire the silver or the gold upon
them, nor take (it) to thyself, lest thou offend through
it, for it is an abomination before the Lord thy God.
Nor shalt thou bring what is abominable into thy house,
and thou be accursed as that is; but with loathing thou
shalt loathe it, and with abhorrence abhor it, for it is a
thing accursed.

VIII. Every mandate that I command thee this day,
you shall observe to do, that you may live and multiply,
and go in and possess the land which the Lord did
covenant unto your fathers. And thou shalt remember
all the way that the Lord thy God hath led thee these
forty years in the wilderness, that He might humble
thee, to prove thee, to know what was in thy heart,
whether thou wouldst keep His commandments or not:
and He humbled (or afflicted) thee, and let thee hunger,
and fed thee with the manna which thou knewest not,
nor did thy fathers know; that He might make thee to
know, That not by bread only is man sustained, but by
every forth-coming word from before the Lord shall man
live. Thy raiment faded not away from thee, and thy
shoes wore not out these forty years; and know thou
with thy heart, that as a man instructeth his son, (so)
the Lord thy God instructeth thee. Keep then the commandments of the Lord thy God, to walk in the ways
which are right before Him, to fear Him for the Lord
thy God bringeth thee into the good land; a land
streaming with brooks of water, with fountain-springs,
and depths (of water) gushing from valleys and hills; a
land of wheat and barley, vines, figs, and pomegranates;
a land of olives yielding oil, and which produceth
honey; a land where, without poverty, thou mayest eat
bread, and have want of nothing; a land whose stones
are iron, and out of whose hills thou mayest cast brass:
and thou shalt eat and be satisfied, and shalt bless the
Lord thy God in the good land.

Beware, lest thou forget the fear of the Lord thy God,
in not keeping His commandments, His judgments,
and His statutes, which I command thee this day. Lest,
when thou hast eaten and art full, and hast built goodly
houses and inhabited (them), and when thy oxen and
sheep have multiplied to thee, and silver and gold have

increased, and whatever thou hast is increased with thee, thy heart should be lifted up, and thou shouldest forget the fear of the Lord thy God, who brought thee up from the land of Mizraim, from the house of bondage; who led thee through the great and terrible desert, the place of burning serpents and scorpions, the place of thirsting, where there is no water, who brought out water for thee from the hard rock ; who fed thee in the wilderness with manna which thy fathers knew not, that he might humble thee, and prove thee, to do thee good in thy latter end. And (lest) thou say in thy heart, My power and the might of my hand have gathered to me these possessions . but remember the Lord thy God, for He it is who giveth thee power to acquire riches, that He may confirm his covenant which He sware to thy fathers, as at this day.

But it will be that if thou forget the fear of the Lord thy God, and walk after the idols of the Gentiles to serve and worship them,—I testify against you this day that perishing you will perish. As the nations which the Lord destroyeth from before you, so shall you perish, because you would not obey the Word of the Lord your God.

IX. Hear, Israel : thou art this day (about) to pass over the Jordana, to enter, to drive out nations greater and stronger than thou, and (to take possession of) cities, great and fortified to the height of heaven ; a people great and mighty, the sons of the giants whom thou knowest, and (of whom) thou hast heard (it said), Who can stand before the sons of the giants ? But know this day that the Word of the Lord thy God, He it is who goeth over before thee, He who is a burning fire, He will consume them, He will break them down before thee, and thou wilt soon drive them out, as the Lord hath told thee. Thou shalt not (therefore) speak in thy

heart when the Lord thy God hath broken them before
thee, saying : For the sake of my righteousness hath
the Lord brought me in to inherit this land ; but for
the wickedness of these nations the Lord driveth them
out before thee. Not for thy righteousness or the
integrity of thy heart dost thou go in to possess their
land, but for the guilt of these nations the Lord thy
God doth drive them out before thee, and that He may
confirm the word which he sware to thy fathers, to
Abraham, to Izhak, and to Jakob. Know, then, that
not for thy righteousness will the Lord thy God give
thee this good land to possess it, for thou art a hard-
necked people. Be mindful, and forget not that thou
didst provoke the Lord thy God to wrath in the wilderness ; from the day that thou camest out from the land of
Mizraim until thou hast come to this place, ye have been
rebellious before the Lord. And in Horeb (itself) you
provoked the Lord, and aroused the Lord's anger to
destroy you. When I had gone up to the mountain to
receive the tables of the stones, the tables of the covenant which the Lord had made with you, and I abode
in the mount forty days and forty nights—I ate no
bread, I drank no water—And the Lord gave to me
the two tables of stones, written upon by the finger of
the Lord, according to all the words which the Lord had
spoken with you on the mount from the midst of the
fire, on the day of the convocation. It was at the end
of forty days and nights, when the Lord gave to me the
two tables of the stones, the tables of the covenant, that
the Lord said to me, Arise, go down quickly from hence ;
for thy people whom I brought out from Mizraim are
corrupted ; they have soon turned from the way that I
commanded them, and have made them a molten image.
And the Lord spake to me, saying : This people are disclosed before me, and, behold, it is a hard-necked people.

Cease from thy prayer before me, and I will destroy
them, and blot out their name from under the heavens,
and I will make thee for a people stronger and greater
than they.

And I turned and descended from the mount; and
the mountain burned with fire, and the two tables of the
covenant were upon my two hands. And I looked, and,
behold, you had sinned before the Lord your God; you
had made you a molten calf; you had turned quickly
from the way which the Lord had commanded you.
And I took the two tables, and cast them away from
my two hands, and brake them before your eyes. And I
fell down before the Lord as at the first, forty days and
forty nights, bread I ate not, water I drank not, for all
your sins which you sinned to do evil before the Lord,
to provoke to anger before Him; for I was afraid before
the anger and indignation wherewith the Lord was
angry against you to destroy you; but the Lord
hearkened to my prayer on that day also. And against
Aharon was there great displeasure before the Lord to
destroy him; but I prayed for Aharon also at that time.

And your sin which you had made, the calf, I took
and burned it in fire, and ground it to a fine grinding
till it was small as powder, and I threw the dust of it
into the stream that descended from the mount.

And at the Burning, and at the Temptation, and at
the Graves of Desire, you were rebellious before the
Lord; and when the Lord sent you from Rekem Giah,
saying. Go up and possess the land I have given, then
rebelled you against the decree of the Word of the Lord
your God, and would not believe Him, nor be obedient
to His Word. You have been contumacious before the
Lord from the day that I have known you; but I fell
down before the Lord the forty days and the forty
nights that I was prostrate, for the Lord had spoken to

consume you. And I prayed before the Lord, and
said: O Lord God, destroy not Thy people, and Thine
inheritance, which Thou hast redeemed by Thy power,
and brought out from Mizraim with a mighty hand.
Remember Thy servants Abraham, Izhak, and Jakob;
regard not the stubbornness of this people, nor their
wickedness, nor their sin: lest the inhabitants of the
land from whence Thou hast led us should say: Because
there was no power before the Lord to bring them into
the land which He had told them of, or because He
hated them, He led them forth to kill them in the
wilderness. But they are Thy people, and Thy inheritance, which thou hast led forth with Thy great power
and Thy uplifted arm.

X. At that time the Lord said to me: Hew thee two
tables of stones like the first, and come up before Me
on the mount, and make thee an ark of wood; and I
will write upon the tables the words that were upon the
former tables which thou brakest, and thou shalt put
them into the ark. And I made an ark of sittin wood,
and hewed two tables of stones like the former, and
went up to the mountain, and the two tables were in
my hand; and He wrote upon the tables according to
the former writing, the Ten Words which the Lord
spake with you on the mount from the midst of the fire
on the day of the assembly; and the Lord gave them to
me. And I returned and descended from the mount,
and put the tables into the ark which I had made, and
they are there, as the Lord commanded me.

And the children of Israel went forward from Bearith
of the Beni Jaakan unto Moserah; there Aharon died,
and was buried there, and Elazar his son hath ministered in his stead. From thence they journeyed unto
Gudgod, and from Gudgod unto Jatbath, a land flowing
with streams of water.

At that time the Lord had set apart the tribe of Levi, to bear the ark of the Lord's covenant, to stand before the Lord to minister unto Him, and to bless in His Name, unto this day. Wherefore, Levi hath no portion or inheritance with his brethren; the gifts which the Lord shall give him are his inheritance, as the Lord thy God hath told him. And I stood on the mountain as in the former days, forty days and nights; and the Lord received my prayer at that time also, that He would not destroy thee. And the Lord said to me: Arise, go, to proceed before the people, that they may be brought in to possess the land which I sware unto their fathers to give them.

And now, Israel, what doth the Lord thy God require of thee, but to fear before the Lord thy God, to walk in all the ways that are right before Him, and to love Him, and to serve before the Lord thy God with all thy heart, and with all thy soul; to keep the commandments of the Lord, and His statutes which I command thee this day, that it may be well with thee? Behold, the heavens, the heavens of the heavens, are the Lord's thy God, and all that is therein; only the Lord did choose thy fathers to love them, and He hath taken pleasure in their children after them, even in you, above all people, as at this day. Put away, therefore, the foolishness of your hearts, and harden your neck no more; for the Lord your God is the God of judges, and the Lord of kings, the Great God, mighty and terrible, before whom is no respect of persons, nor doth He accept a reward.[6] He executeth judgment for the orphan and the widow, and hath pity on the stranger to give him food and raiment. Be loving then to the stranger, for you were sojourners in the land of Mizraim. Thou shalt fear the Lord thy God, and serve before

---

[6] Sam. Vers., "money"

Him; to His fear thou shalt keep close, and shalt swear by His Name; He is thy glory, and He is thy God, who hath done for thee these vast and mighty acts which thy eyes have seen. With seventy souls went thy fathers down into Mizraim, and now the Lord thy God hath set thee as the stars of the heavens for multitude.

XI. And thou shalt love the Lord thy God, and keeping keep His word, His statutes, His judgments, and His commandments all days. And you know this day what your children have not known or seen, the discipline of the Lord your God, His greatness, His mighty hand and uplifted arm, His miracles, and His works which He did in Mizraim, to Pharoh king of Mizraim, and to all his land; and what He did to the host of the Mizraee, to their horses and their chariots, when he made the waters of the Sea of Suph to overflow their faces as they followed after you, and the Lord destroyed them unto this day; and what He did to you in the wilderness until your coming unto this place; and what He did unto Dathan and Abiram, the sons of Eliab bar Reuben, when the earth opened her mouth, and swallowed them up with the men of their house, their tents, and all the substance they had, in the midst of all Israel; for your eyes have seen all the great acts of the Lord which He hath wrought.

You shall observe all the precepts which I command thee this day, that you may be strengthened, and go in and possess the land unto which you are going over to inherit, and may prolong your days upon the land which the Lord sware to your fathers to give them and their children, a land producing milk and honey; for the land into which thou art going to possess it, is not as the land of Mizraim from which thou hast come out, where thou sowedst thy seed, and didst water it with thy feet as a garden of herbs (or a green garden); but the

land to which thou goest over to possess is a land of
hills and valleys, drinking water of the rains of heaven ;
a land which the Lord thy God looketh after ; (inquireth
for ;) the eyes [7] of the Lord thy God are evermore upon
it, from the beginning unto the end of the year.

And it shall be, if you will be diligently obedient to
My commandments which I command you this day to
love the Lord your God, and to serve before Him with all
your heart, and with all your soul, I will give you the
rain of your land in its season, the early and the latter ,
and thou shalt gather in thy corn, thy wine, and thy oil ;
and I will give herbage in thy field for thy cattle, and
thou shalt eat and be satisfied.

Take heed to yourselves lest your heart be deceived,
and you turn aside to serve the gods of the Gentiles and
worship them , and the anger of the Lord be aroused
against you, and He shut up the skies that there be no
rain, and the earth yield not her fruit, and you perish
soon from off the good land which the Lord will give
you : but lay these my words upon your heart, and
upon your soul, and bind them for a sign upon your
hand, and let them be for tephilin between your eyes ;
and teach them to your children, speaking of them
when thou sittest in thy house, and when thou walkest
in the way, when thou liest down, and when thou
risest up ; and write them upon the posts, and fix them
to the entrance of thy house, and upon thy gates ; [8] that
your days and the days of your children may be multiplied on the land which the Lord sware unto your
fathers to give them, as the days of heaven upon the
earth.

For if you surely keep all this precept that I command you to perform it, to love the Lord your God, to

---

[7] Sam. Vers , " the favourable eye."

[8] Sam. Vers., " thy cities."

walk in all the ways that are right before Him, and
keep close unto His fear, then will the Lord drive out
all these nations from before you, that you may possess
(the lands) of nations greater and stronger than yourselves.   Every place on which the sole of your foot
shall tread shall be yours, from the wilderness and
Lebanon, from the river. the river Phrat, unto the utter-
most sea shall be your border.   There shall not a man
stand before you ; for the Lord your God will put the
fear and dread of you upon the face of all the land that
you tread upon, as the Lord hath said unto you.

SECTION XLVII.

REEH.

BEHOLD, I set before you this day blessings and
curses : blessings, if you obey the precepts of the Lord
your God, which I command you this day ; but curses,
if you obey not the precepts of the Lord your God, and
turn aside from the way that I teach you this day, to
go after the idols of the peoples whom you have not
known.   And it shall be, when the Lord your God
hath brought thee into the land which thou goest to
possess, thou shalt set the blessings upon the Mount of
Gerizim, and the curses upon the Mountain of Ebal.
Are they not beyond Jordan, after the way of the sun-
setting, in the land of the Kenaanites, which dwell in
the plains over against Gilgala, by the side of the plain
of Moreh ?[9] For you are to pass over the Jordan to
enter in to inherit the land which the Lord your God
will give you ; and you will possess, and dwell therein.

[9] Sam. Vers., " the Valley of Vision."

And you shall observe to do all the statutes and judgments which I have set before you this day.

XII. These are the commandments and judgments you shall observe to do in the land that the Lord the God of your fathers will give to thee to inherit all the days that you subsist upon the earth. You shall destroying destroy all the places wherein the peoples (whose lands) you will inherit have served their idols, upon the high mountains, and the hills, and under every leafy tree. And you shall lay their altars in ruin, break their statues,[1] burn their groves with fire, cut the images of their idols in pieces, and blot out their names from that place.

Not so shall you do before the Lord your God; but, to the place which the Lord your God will choose that His Shekinah may dwell there, unto the house of His Shekinah you shall seek, and thither come to offer there your burnt offerings, your consecrated victims, your tenths, and the separations of your hands, your vows and freewill gifts, and the firstlings of your oxen and sheep. And there shall you eat before the Lord your God, and rejoice in all that you have set your hand unto, you and your households, for that the Lord thy God hath blessed thee. You shall not (then) do as we are doing here this day, every man as (seemeth) proper in his own eyes; for you are not come as yet to the place of quietness, and to the inheritance which the Lord thy God will give thee. But (when) you go over the Jordan, and dwell in the land which the Lord your God giveth you to inherit, and He hath given you rest from all your enemies round about, and you dwell in safety, then there will be a Place which the Lord your God will choose, to make His Shekinah to dwell there; thither shall you bring all that I command you, your

[1] Or, " columns."

burnt offerings and consecrated oblations, your tenths
and the separations of your hands, and all the goodly
things of your vows which you may vow before the
Lord.   And you shall rejoice before the Lord your God,
you and your sons and daughters, your servants and
handmaids, and the Levite who is among you, for he
hath no part or inheritance with you.

Take heed to thyself that thou offer not thy burnt
offerings in every place that thou seest; but in the
Place which the Lord will choose out of one of thy
tribes thou shalt offer thy sacrifices, and there do all
that I command thee.   Though in any place where thy
soul may desire thou mayest kill and eat flesh, according to the blessing of the Lord thy God, which He will
give thee in all thy cities; the unclean and the clean
may eat thereof, as the flesh of the gazelle and the deer.
Only of blood you may not eat; thou shalt pour it upon
the ground like water.   It is not lawful for thee to eat
in thy cities of the tythe of the produce of thy wine or
oil, or the firstlings of thy bullocks or thy sheep, or of
any vow which thou hast devoted, or of thy freewill
offerings, or separations of thy hands; but before the
Lord thy God shalt thou eat it, in the place which the
Lord thy God will choose; thou and thy son and
daughter, thy servant and handmaid, and the Levite
who is in thy cities, and you shall rejoice before the
Lord thy God in all that thou settest thy hand unto.
Take heed to thee that thou forsake not the Levite all
thy days upon thy land.

When the Lord thy God shall have enlarged thy
border, as He hath said to thee, and thou sayest, I will
eat flesh, when thy soul desireth to eat flesh, of all the
desire of thy soul thou mayest eat flesh.   If the place
which the Lord thy God will choose for His Shekinah
to dwell there, be too far from thee, thou mayest kill of

thy oxen and sheep which the Lord will give thee, as I
have commanded thee, and eat in thy cities of all the
desire of thy soul.   As the flesh of the gazelle and the
deer so shalt thou eat it, the unclean and the clean may
eat it alike.   Only, be steadfast in not eating the blood,
for blood is life, and thou mayest not eat the life with
the flesh: thou shalt not eat it, thou shalt pour it like
water upon the ground; thou shalt not eat it,—that it
may be well with thee and with thy children after thee,
when thou doest that which is right before the Lord.
Only thy consecrated things which thou hast, and thy
vows, thou shalt take and bring to the place that the
Lord will choose; and make thy burnt sacrifices, the
flesh and the blood, upon the altar of the Lord thy God;
and the blood of thy consecrated victims thou shalt
pour out at the altar of the Lord thy God, but of the
flesh thou mayest eat.   Observe and obey all these
commandments which I command thee, that it may go
well with thee, and with thy children after thee for ever,
when thou doest that which is meet and right before
the Lord thy God.

When the Lord thy God shall have destroyed the
nations (of the land) whither thou art going to cast
them out from before thee, and He cast them out, and
thou dwell in their land,—take heed to thyself that
thou stumble not after them when they shall have been
dispersed before thee, and that thou seek not to their
idols, saying, How did these nations serve their idols?
for so will I do also.   Thou shalt not do so before the
Lord thy God; for all that is abominable before the
Lord, and that He hateth, have they done to their
idols.   For even their sons and daughters they have
burned in the fire.   Every word I command you, that
shall you observe to perform; you shall not add to it
nor diminish from it.

XIII. If there shall arise among you a prophet, or a
dreamer of dreams, and he give a sign or a wonder, and
the sign or wonder cometh to pass, (yet,) should he
speak with thee, saying, Let us go after the gods of the
Gentiles whom thou hast not known, and let us worship them ; thou shalt not hearken to the words of that
prophet or dreamer of dreams ; for the Lord your God
is proving you, to know whether you will love the Lord
your God with all your heart and with all your soul.
You shall walk after the Lord your God; Him shall ye
fear, and keep His commandments, and be obedient to
His Word, and serve Him, and keep close to His fear.
And that prophet, or dreamer of dreams, shall be put
to death; for he hath spoken perversions against the
Lord your God, who brought you out from the land of
Mizraim, and delivered you from the house of bondage,
to make you go astray from the path in which the Lord
thy God hath commanded thee to walk; and so shalt
thou put away the evil doer from the midst of thee.

If thy brother, the son of thy mother, or thy son, or
thy daughter, or the wife of thy covenant,[2] or thy friend
who is as thy soul, shall persuade thee in secret, saying :
Let us go and worship the gods of the Gentiles whom
thou hast not known, nor thy fathers, gods of the
nations round about you, nigh thee, or far off, from one
end of the earth to the other ; thou shalt not consent to
him, nor listen to his word, nor must thy eye have pity
on him; thou shalt neither compassionate nor conceal
him, but killing thou shalt kill him; thy hand shall be
upon him the first to kill him, and afterwards the hand
of all the people ; and thou shalt stone him with stones
that he die, because he sought to lead thee astray from
the fear of the Lord thy God who brought thee out of
the land of Mizraim, from the house of bondage ; and

---

[2] Sam. Vers., " of thy love."

all Israel will hear and be afraid, and not add to do this evil thing among thee.

If thou hear in one of the cities which the Lord thy God will give thee to dwell in, saying: Men, sons of wickedness, have gone forth from among thee, and led away the inhabitants of their city, saying: Let us go and worship the gods of the nations which you have not known; then shalt thou seek and search out, and fairly inquire; and, behold, such a thing is the truth, and this abomination is being done among thee, thou shalt smite the inhabitants of that city with the edge of the sword, and destroy it and all that is therein and its cattle by the edge of the sword; and thou shalt gather all the spoil of it together into the midst of its street, and burn the city and the whole spoil thereof with fire entirely before the Lord thy God, and it shall be a desolate heap for ever, it shall be builded no more; and nought of the accursed thing shall cleave to thy hand, that the Lord may turn away His anger from thee, and show mercy upon thee, and be loving towards thee, and increase thee, as He sware unto thy fathers; when thou shalt be obedient to the Word of the Lord thy God, to observe all His commandments which I command thee this day, to do that which is right before the Lord thy God.

XIV. Children are you before the Lord your God. You shall not lacerate yourselves, nor make baldness between your eyes for the dead; for thou art (to be) a holy people before the Lord thy God, chosen to be unto Him a people more beloved than all the nations upon the face of the earth. Thou shalt not eat any thing that is abominable. These are the cattle that you may eat: oxen, lambs of the flock, and kids of the goats. The hart, and the antelope, the forest deer, and the wild goat, the pygarg, the buffalo, and the chamois; and any animal that hath the hoof cloven, and that divideth the hoof into two parts, and ruminateth the cud, among cattle, that you may eat. Nevertheless, you shall not eat of those that (only) chew the cud, or of them that (only) separate the hoof into divided parts : the camel, the hare, and the coney, for they bring up the cud, but divide not the hoof, they are unclean to you ; and the swine, because it divideth the hoof, but doth not rumi-nate, shall be unclean to you; of their flesh you may not eat, nor touch their carcases.

Of all that are in the waters these you may eat : all that have fins and scales you may eat; but any (fish) that hath not fins and scales you may not eat; it is unclean to you. You may eat any clean bird ; but of these you shall not eat : the eagle, ossifrage, osprey, gleed, vulture, and kite after his kind, and every raven after his kind ; the owl, nightbird, gull, and hawk after his kind ; the heron, swan, and stork, the cormorant, pelican, and owl; the bittern and ibis after his kind ; the lapwing and the bat : and no reptile may you eat whose flesh is unclean to you; but you may eat any fowl (or winged thing) that is clean.

You shall not eat of any thing that dieth of itself thou mayest give it to the uncircumcised stranger who is in thy city, and he may eat it ; or thou mayest sell it to the outward people; for thou art to be a holy people to the Lord thy God. Thou shalt not eat flesh with the milk.

Thou shalt tythe all the produce of thy seed, and all that thy field may bring forth from year to year; and be-fore the Lord thy God in the place which He will choose to make His Shekinah dwell there, thou shalt eat the tythe of thy corn, wine, and oil, and the firstlings of thy herd and flock, that thou mayest learn to fear before the Lord thy God all days. But if the way be too great for thee, so that thou art not able to bring it, if the way be too

7 2

distant from the place which the Lord thy God may
choose to make His Shekinah to dwell there, when the
Lord thy God shall have blessed thee, then thou shalt
put (change) it into silver, and bind the silver in thy
hand, and go to the place which the Lord thy God will
choose, and shalt give the silver for whatever thy soul
may please, for oxen, sheep, wine, new or old, or any
thing thy soul may desire, and shalt eat there before
the Lord thy God, and rejoice, thou, the men of thy
house, and the Levite who is in thy cities; thou shalt
not forsake him, for he hath no portion or inheritance
with thee.

At the end of three years thou shalt bring forth all
the tithes of thy produce in that year, and lay it up in
thy cities; and the Levite, because he hath no part or
inheritance with thee, and the stranger, the orphan, and
the widow who are in thy cities, shall come and eat and
be satisfied, that the Lord thy God may bless thee in all
the work of thy hand which thou shalt do.

XV. At the end of seven years thou shalt make the
Release,[3] and this is the sentence (word) of the Release:
—That every man who is a creditor[4] shall give release
to him who oweth to his neighbour; he shall not exact
it from his neighbour or his brother, because the release
is proclaimed before the Lord. From a son of the
Gentiles thou mayest demand; but that which is with
thy brother, thou shalt release by thy hand. Save when
there shall not be the poor among thee, for the Lord in
blessing will bless thee in the land which the Lord thy
God will give thee for a possession to inherit. Only if
thou wilt indeed be obedient to the Word of the Lord
thy God, and observe to do all these precepts which I
command thee this day; for the Lord thy God doth

[3] *Shemittha,* " *remissio.*"
[4] *Mari-rasho,* " a lord or master of rent."

bless thee, as He hath said to thee: and thou shalt
lend to many peoples, but thou shalt not take a loan;
and thou shalt have rule over many peoples, but they
shall not have rule over thee.

If there be with thee a poor man of thy brethren, in
one of the cities in the land which the Lord thy God
will give thee, thou shalt not harden thy heart, nor
shut up thy hand from thy poor brother; but thou shalt
open thy hand to him, and lend, according to the measure of his want, of that which he may need.   Beware,
lest there be a word with thy wicked heart, saying, The
year of release draweth near, and thine eye be evil toward thy poor brother, and thou give not to him, and he
cry against thee before the Lord, and there be guiltiness
in thee.   Giving thou shalt give to him, and thy heart
shall not be evil when thou givest to him: because for
this thing the Lord thy God will bless thee in all thy
works, and in all thou puttest thy hand unto.   For the
poor will not cease (to be) in the midst of thy land;
therefore I command thee, saying, Thou shalt verily
open thy hand to thy brother, to thy afflicted, and to
thy poor in thy land.

If thy brother, a son of Israel, or a daughter of Israel,
be sold to thee, and shall have served thee six years, in
the seventh year let him go, a son of liberty, from thee.
And when thou lettest him go free from thee, thou shalt
not send him away empty.   But thou shalt separate to
him from thy flock, and thy floor, and thy wine-press,
and give to him of that which the Lord thy God hath
blessed thee.   And thou shalt remember that thou wast
a servant in the land of Mizraim, and the Lord thy God
set thee free: therefore I command thee this thing
to-day.

But if he say to thee, I will not go out from being
with thee, because he loveth thee, and the men of thy

house, (and) because it is good for me to be with thee,
then thou shalt take an awl, put it through his ear, and
into the door, and he shall be a ministering servant to
thee evermore.   And also likewise shalt thou do to thy
handmaid.

It shall not be a hardship in thy eyes when thou dost
send him from thee to be a son of freedom, for he hath
been doubly worth a hireling, serving thee six years; and
the Lord thy God will bless thee in all that thou shalt do.

Every firstling male which cometh of thy cattle or
thy sheep, thou shalt consecrate before the Lord thy
God : thou shalt not work with the firstling of thy herd,
nor shear the firstling of thy flock.   Thou shalt eat it
before the Lord thy God from year to year in the place
which the Lord will choose, thou and the men of thy
house.   And if there be any blemish (spot) in it, (if
it be) lame, or blind, or have any evil spot, thou shalt
not sacrifice it before the Lord thy God : thou mayest
eat it in thy cities, unclean (persons) and clean alike
(may eat it), as the antelope and the hart.   Only thou
shalt not eat the blood, but pour it out upon the ground
like water.

XVI. Observe the month of Abiba, and perform the
pascha before the Lord thy God; for in the month of
Abiba the Lord thy God brought thee out of Mizraim,
and wrought signs for thee in the night.   And thou
shalt sacrifice the pascha before the Lord thy God, with
the lambs (young) of thy flock, and with consecrated
victims from thy herd, in the place which the Lord
will choose to make His Shekinah dwell there.   Thou
shalt not eat leaven with it.   Seven days shalt thou eat
unleavened bread with it, the bread of humiliation; for
in haste didst thou come out of the land of Mizraim :
that thou mayest remember the day of thy coming from
the land of Mizraim all the days of thy life.   And there

shall not be leaven seen with thee within all thy borders
seven days; neither shall any of the flesh of that which
thou didst sacrifice in the evening of the first day
remain until the morning.   Thou hast not liberty to
sacrifice the pascha in any one of thy cities which the
Lord thy God will give thee; but in the place which
the Lord thy God will approve to make His Shekinah
dwell, there thou shalt sacrifice the pascha, in the
evening, at the going away of the sun; the time of thy
coming out of Mizraim.   And thou shalt dress and eat
it in the place which the Lord thy God shall favour,
and in the morning turn and go to thy tent.   Six days
thou shalt eat unleavened, and on the seventh day
gather together before the Lord thy God: thou shalt do
no work.

Seven weeks number to thee from the beginning (of
the harvest); when the omer of the elevation [5] is reaped
with the sickle, shalt thou begin to number the seven
weeks.   And thou shalt perform the festival of the
weeks before the Lord thy God, with a tribute of the
free-will offering of thy hand, which thou shalt give as
the Lord thy God will have blessed thee.   And thou
shalt rejoice before the Lord thy God, thou, thy son,
thy daughter, thy man-servant, thy handmaid, the Levite
who is in thy cities, the sojourner, the orphan, and the
widow who are among you, in the place which the Lord
thy God will choose to make His Shekinah to dwell
there.   And thou shalt remember that thou wast a
servant in Mizraim, and keep and perform these statutes.

The Feast of Tabernacles thou shalt make to thee
seven days, when thou hast gathered in from thy threshing-floor, and from thy wine-press.   And thou shalt
rejoice in thy feast, thou, thy son, thy daughter, thy
servant, thy handmaid, the Levite, the stranger, the

[5] Glossary, page 57

orphan, and the widow, who are in thy cities. Seven days shalt thou hold the festival before the Lord thy God in the place the Lord shall choose, because the Lord thy God will have blessed thee in all thy produce, and in all the work of thy hands, and therefore shalt thou rejoice.

Three times in the year all thy males are to appear before the Lord thy God in the place that He will choose; at the Feast of the Unleavened, the Feast of Weeks, and the Feast of Tabernacles; and they shall not appear before the Lord empty; but every man with the gift of his hand, according to the blessing of the Lord thy God which He hath given thee.

SECTION XLVIII.

SHOPHETIM.

Judges and officers [6] shalt thou appoint to thee in all thy cities which the Lord thy God will give thee throughout thy tribes, and they shall judge the people with true judgment. Thou shalt not pervert judgment, nor have respect to persons, nor receive a gift; [7] for a gift blindeth the eyes of the wise, and depraveth right words. Thou shalt follow that which is surely true, that thou mayest live and inherit the land which the Lord thy God will give thee. Thou shalt not plant thee a grove, nor any tree beside the altar of the Lord thy God that thou makest thee, nor erect a statue which the Lord thy God abhorreth.

XVII. Thou shalt not sacrifice before the Lord thy

---

6 Sam. Vers., " scribes."   7 Sam. Vers., " mammona."

God a bullock or ram which hath blemish in it, nor anything that is evil; for that is abomination before the Lord thy God.

If, in any one of the cities which the Lord thy God will give thee, there be found a man or woman who hath done evil before the Lord thy God in transgressing his covenant, and going to do service to the idols of the Gentiles, or to the sun, moon, or all the host of the heavens, in worshipping them, which I have not commanded; and it be told thee, and thou hast heard, thou shalt inquire fairly, and if such word be true that this abomination hath been wrought in Israel, thou shalt bring forth that man or woman, and stone them with stones that they die. On the word of two witnesses or of three shall he die who is guilty of death: he shall not die on the word of one witness. The hands of the witnesses shall be upon him first to kill him, and the hands of all the people afterward; and thou shalt put down the doer of evil from among you.

If a matter for judgment be extraordinary [a] to thee, between blood and blood, between cause and cause, or between plague and plague, of leprosy, they being matters of divided judgment in thy cities,—then thou shalt arise and go up to the place which the Lord thy God shall choose, and come to the priests, the Levites, and to the judge who may be in those days, and inquire; and they will show thee the sentence of decision. And thou shalt do according to the word of the sentence which they will show thee from the place which the Lord will choose, and thou shalt observe to do according to all that they will teach thee. Upon the word of the law which they teach thee, and upon the judgment they tell thee, thou shalt act; thou shalt not swerve from the word they will

[a] *Iithpharash*: other copies have *ithkasi*, " be hidden from thee."

have shown thee, to the right or the left. And
the man who doeth wickedly in not receiving from the
priest who standeth there to minister before the Lord
thy God, or from the judge, that man shall die; and
thou shalt put down the evil doer from Israel. And all
the people will hear and be afraid, and do wickedly no
more.

When thou art come into the land which the Lord
thy God will give thee, and dost possess and dwell in
it, and thou mayest say, I will appoint a king over me,
like the nations who are about me; thou mayest verily
appoint over thee a king whom the Lord thy God will
choose, from among thy brethren thou shalt appoint the
king over thee. Thou shalt not have power to set over
thee a foreign man, who is not thy brother. Only he
shall not multiply to him horses, nor cause the people
to return to Mizraim for the purpose of multiplying
horses; for the Lord hath said to you, Ye shall no
more return by that way. Neither shall he multiply
wives to him, that his heart be not turned away; nor
shall he increase silver and gold for himself greatly.
And it shall be, when he sitteth upon the throne of his
kingdom, he shall write for himself a copy of this Law
in a book, out (of that which is) before the priests, the
Levites. And he shall have it with him, to read in it
all the days of his life, that he may learn to fear before
the Lord his God, to keep all the words of this law, and
these statutes, to perform them: that his heart may not
be lifted up from his brethren, nor swerve from the precepts of the Lord to the right or to the left, and may
prolong (his days) in his kingdom, he and his sons in
the midst of Israel.

XVIII. For the priests and Levites, (even) all the
tribe of Levi, there shall be no part or inheritance with
Israel; they shall eat the oblations of the Lord and

his inheritance, but have no heritage among their
brethren : the gifts presented unto the Lord they are
his heritage, as the Lord hath said to him.

And this is what shall appertain to the priests from
the people, from them who offer a sacrifice, whether
bullock or lamb; they shall give to the priest the
shoulder, the cheeks, and the maw. The first of thy
corn, wine, and oil, and the first of the fleece of thy sheep,
thou shalt set apart for him. For the Lord thy God hath
chosen him out of all thy tribes to stand to minister in
the Name of the Lord, he, and his sons, all the days.

And if a Levite come from one of thy cities out of
all Israel, where he hath dwelt, and come with all the
desire of his soul, to the place which the Lord will
choose, then he shall minister in the Name of the Lord
his God with his brethren the Levites who minister
there before the Lord. Portion for portion shall they
eat, beside the accustomed allotment which cometh on
the Sabbath, as the fathers have appointed.[9]

When thou hast entered into the land which the
Lord thy God will give thee, thou shalt not learn to do
after the abominations of these peoples. No one shall
be found among thee who maketh his son or his
daughter to pass through the fire, using enchantments,
observing times or augury or witchcraft, nor an incan-
tator, or a consulter at a heathen oracle, or a wizard, or
an inquirer from the dead : for all who do these things
are an abomination to the Lord; and because of these
abominations the Lord thy God driveth them out from
before thee. Thou shalt be perfect in the fear of the

---

[9] Or, "beside the order which cometh on the Sabbath." Heb.,
"beside his sellings according to the fathers" (query, "patri-
mony?"). Vulg., *excepto eo quod in urbe sua ex paterná et suc-
cessione debetur.* Syr., "beside the sale of the father's (property)."
The Levites could purchase real property. Comp. 1 Kings ii. 26,
Jerem. xxxii. 7, 8.

Lord thy God. For these nations which thou shalt
possess hearkened to diviners and enchanters; not so
hath the Lord given thee to do. A PROPHET from
among thee, of thy brethren, like me, will the Lord thy
God raise up unto thee, to him shall ye hearken.
According to all that thou didst ask before the Lord
thy God at Horeb on the day of the assembly, saying:
Let me not again hear the voice of the Word of the
Lord my God, and let me not see the great fire any
more, lest I die. And the Lord said to me, That
which they have spoken is right: I will raise up to
them a Prophet from among them like unto thee, and I
will put My words of prophecy upon his lips, and he
will speak to them all that I shall command him. And
the man who will not hearken to My words which he
will speak in My Name, My Word will require it of him.

But a prophet who shall do wickedly in speaking in
My Name a word which I had not commanded him to
speak, or who shall speak in the name of the gods of
the Gentiles, that prophet shall die. And if thou say
in thy heart, How shall we know the word which the
Lord hath not spoken? When a prophet speaketh in
the Name of the Lord, if the word come not to pass,
neither be confirmed, that is a word which the Lord
hath not spoken: of the prophet who hath spoken in
wickedness thou shalt not be afraid.

XIX. When the Lord thy God hath destroyed the
nations whose land the Lord thy God will give thee,
and you possess it, and dwell in their cities and houses;
three cities shalt thou set apart to thee within thy land,
which the Lord thy God will give thee to inherit. Thou
shalt prepare for thee a way, and divide into three parts
the boundary of thy land which the Lord thy God
giveth thee to possess, for any manslayer to escape
thither. And this shall be the case of the manslayer

who fleeth thither that he may live: he who shall have
slain his neighbour unwittingly, he not having hated
him yesterday or before. As, when a man goeth with
his neighbour into the thicket to cut wood, and his hand
with the iron is driven aside in cutting the wood, and
the iron flieth off from the handle and striketh (findeth)
his neighbour, and he be killed, he shall flee to one of
these cities that he may live; lest the avenger of blood
pursue him while his heart is hot, and overtake him,
because the way is long, and destroy his life; he not
being guilty of death, because he had not hated him in
time past. Wherefore, I command thee, saying: Thou
shalt set apart to thee three cities. And when the Lord
thy God shall enlarge thy border, as He sware to thy
fathers, and give thee all the land which He said to thy
fathers He would give, if thou wilt keep all this commandment which I command thee this day, to perform
it, to love the Lord thy God, and to walk in the ways
that are right before Him all the days; then thou
halt add yet three cities to those three, that innocent
blood may not be shed within thy land which the Lord
thy God will give thee to inherit, and that the guilt of
murder may not be upon thee.

But if a man bear hatred to his neighbour, and lie
in wait for him,[1] and rise up against him, and destroy
his life, and he die, and he flee to one of these cities, then
the elders of his city shall send and take him from
thence, and deliver him into the hand of the avenger of
blood, and he shall die. Thine eye shall not have pity
upon him, and thou shalt do away with the shedding of
innocent blood from Israel, that it may be well with
thee.

Thou shalt not remove the boundary of thy neighbour
which he hath set for a limit in the inheritance which

---

[1] Sam. Vers., "contend with him."

thou shalt possess in the land the Lord thy God will give thee to inherit.   .

One witness shall not rise up (alone) against a man for any iniquities or sins, or any sin by which he (may have) transgressed; but upon the word of two or of three witnesses shall the case be confirmed. If a false witness stand up against a man to testify against him [2] with perversity, then the two men to whom the cause belongeth shall stand in the presence of the Lord before the priests and judges who shall be in those days; and the judges shall make inquest fairly, and, behold, he hath testified falsely, and the testimony is false that he hath witnessed against his brother, then you shall do to him as he had designed to do to his brother, and so shall you put away the evil doer from among you. And the rest shall hear and be afraid, and not do any more like this evil thing among thee. And thine eye shall not have pity: life for life; eye for eye; tooth for tooth; hand for hand; foot for foot.

XX. When thou goest out to war with thy adversaries, and seest horses, and chariots, and more people than thou, be not afraid of them; for thy helper is the Word of the Lord thy God, who brought thee up from the land of Mizraim. And it shall be when you draw nigh to battle, that the priest shall approach, and speak with the people, and say to them, Hear, Israel · you come this day to do battle with your enemies: let not your heart waver, neither be afraid, or confounded, or broken before them; for the Lord your God (is He) who goeth before you to fight for you against your enemies, to save you. And the officers shall speak before the people, saying: What man is there who hath built a new house, and hath not dedicated it? let him go and return to his house, lest he be slain in the battle, and

---

[1] Sam. Vers., "to afflict him."

another man dedicate it. And what man who hath
planted a vineyard, but hath not made it common (for
use)? let him go and return to his house, lest he be
slain in the battle, and another man make it common,
(or partake of it). And what man hath betrothed a
wife, and not taken her? let him go and return to his
house, lest he be slain in the battle, and another man
take her. And the officers shall yet speak to the people,
and say: What man is there who is afraid and broken-
hearted? Let him return to his house, and not make
the heart of his brethren to be broken as his heart.
And it shall be, when the officers have finished to speak
with the people, they shall appoint captains of the host
at the head of the people.

When thou drawest nigh to a city to make war
against it, then proclaim to it words of peace. And if
it be that it make thee an answer of peace, and open to
thee, then all the people who dwell in it shall be tributaries to thee and serve thee. But if it will not make
peace with thee, but will have war with thee, then thou
shalt besiege it: and when the Lord thy God hath
delivered it into thy hand, thou mayest smite all the
males thereof by the sentence of the sword; but the
women, children, cattle, and all that is in the city, even
all the spoil, thou shalt make booty for thyself; and
thou shalt eat the spoil of thy enemies, which the Lord
thy God will have given thee. Thus shalt thou do to all
cities which are remote from thee, but are not of the
cities of these nations; for of the cities of these nations
which the Lord thy God giveth thee, thou shalt not
spare alive any breathing thing, but utterly destroy
them, Hittites and Amorites, Kenaanites and Phere-
sites, Hivites and Jebusites, as the Lord thy God hath
commanded thee; that they may not teach you to do
according to all their abominations which they have

done to their idols, and you sin against the Lord your God.

When thou layest siege to a city many days in making war against it to subdue it, thou shalt not destroy the trees (that are about) it, nor lift up the iron against them : for of them thou mayest eat ; thou shalt not cut them down, for the tree of the field is not like a man, to come against thee in the siege.   Only a tree which thou knowest is not for food, thou mayest destroy and cut down ; and thou shalt build bulwarks (palisades) against the city which maketh war with thee, until thou subdue it.

XXI. When in the land which the Lord thy God giveth thee to inherit there may be found one who is slain, lying in the field, and it is not known who hath killed him, then thy elders and judges shall come forth and admeasure unto the cities that surround the dead man ; and the elders of the city that is nearest to the dead man shall take an heifer of the herd which hath not been worked with, nor hath drawn on the yoke. And the elders of that city shall bring the heifer down to an uncultivated valley (or field) which is not tilled nor sown, and there cut off the heifer in the field.   And the priests the sons of Levi shall go near,—for them the Lord thy God hath chosen to minister to Him, and to bless in the Name of the Lord, and on their word shall every controversy or stroke of leprosy (be adjudged); —and all the elders of that city which is nearest to the dead man shall wash their hands over the heifer which hath been cut off in the field ; and shall answer and say, Our hands have not shed this blood, and our eyes have not seen.   And the priests shall say, Forgive Thy people Israel whom Thou, O Lord, hast redeemed, and let not the guilt of innocent blood be among Thy people Israel.   And it shall be forgiven them concerning the

blood : so shalt thou put away the guilt of innocent
blood from among you, when thou shalt do that which
is right before the Lord.

SECTION XLIX.

TITSE.

WHEN thou goest out to war against thy enemies, and
the Lord thy God doth deliver them into thy hand,
and thou takest them captive; and thou seest among the
captives a woman of fair countenance, and hast a desire
for her, and wouldst take her unto thee to wife; then thou
shalt bring her into thy house, and she shall shave her
head, and pare her nails, and take off from her the dress
of her captivity, and dwell in thy house, and mourn for
her father and mother a month of days; and afterward
thou mayest go to her and marry her, and she shall be
thy wife.

But if it be that thou hast no pleasure in her, then
thou mayest send her away by herself: thou shalt in no
wise sell her for money, nor make merchandise of her, for
thou hast afflicted her.

If a man have two wives, the one beloved and the
other hated, and they have borne sons, the beloved one
and the hated one, and the firstborn son belong to the
hated ; then in the day that he maketh his sons to
inherit what he hath, he shall not make the son of the
beloved to be (as) the firstborn over the head (face) of
the son of the hated, the (actual) firstborn. For he shall
distribute to the firstborn the son of the hated by
giving him two parts of all his possession; for he is the
beginning of his strength, and to him pertaineth the
birthright.

If a man hath a son perverse and rebellious, who will

not obey the word of his father or his mother, and, though
they instruct him, will not hearken to them; then his
father and mother shall lay hold of him, and bring him
forth before the elders of his city at the gate of the
judgment house of his place, and shall say to the elders
of the city, This our son is perverse and rebellious; he
will not obey our words, he is a devourer of flesh and
a taker of wine: then all the men of the city shall
stone him with stones, that he die; and thou shalt put
away the evil doer from among you, and all Israel will
hear, and be afraid.   When a man guilty of the judgment of death is put to death, and thou hast hanged
him on a gibbet; his body shall not remain upon the
gibbet, but thou shalt surely bury him on that day: for
he was hanged because he had sinned before the Lord;[3]
and thy land which the Lord thy God hath given thee
to inherit shall not be defiled.

XXII. Thou shalt not see thy brother's ox or his
lamb going astray, and turn thyself aside from them;
thou shalt surely bring them back to thy brother.   And
if thy brother be not near to thee, or if thou know him
not, then thou shalt bring it into thy house, and it shall
be with thee until thou make inquiry for thy brother, and
then thou shalt restore it to him.   In like manner shalt
thou do with his ass, and with his garment, and with any
lost thing of thy brother's which thou mayest have found;
it is not lawful for thee to conceal it.   Thou shalt not see
thy brother's ass or his ox fallen in the way, and turn
thyself away from them; thou shalt surely lift them up
for him.

The adorning of a man shall not be upon a woman,
nor shall the apparel of a man be like the apparel of a
woman; for every one who doeth these things is abominable before the Lord thy God.

----

[3] Heb., "For the hanged one is a malediction of God."

If thou find the nest of a bird before thee on the way, in any tree, or upon the ground, with young ones, or eggs, and the mother lying over the young ones, or upon the eggs, thou shalt not take the mother with the off-spring. Thou shalt send away the mother, and take the young ones with thee; that it may be well with thee, and thou mayest prolong thy days.

When thou buildest a new house, then thou shalt make a parapet to thy roof, that thou mayest not bring the guilt of the blood of the slain upon thy house, by the falling of any one who may fall there-from.

Thou shalt not sow thy vineyard with mixed (seeds), lest what cometh from the seed which thou sowest, and the produce of thy vineyard, be unclean. Thou shalt not plough with an ox and an ass together. Thou shalt not dress with a contexture of woollen and of linen joined together. Thou shalt make thee fringes (or tassels) upon the four corners of thy garment with which thou coverest thyself.

If a man take a wife, and go unto her, and dislike her, and lay an occasion of words about her, or bring out an evil name upon her, and say, I took this woman and came to her, and I have not found her to be a virgin: then shall the father and mother of the damsel bring forth the tokens of the damsel's virginity before the elders of the city, at the gate of the judgment house of the place; and the father of the damsel shall say to the elders, I gave my daughter to this man to wife, and he hateth her; and, behold, he hath set an occasion of words, saying, I have not found the virginity of thy daughter; but these are the tokens of my daughter's virginity. And he shall spread the cloth before the elders of the city. And the elders of the city shall take that man and scourge him, and fine him a hundred shekels

of silver, and give to the father of the damsel, because
he brought out an evil name upon a virgin of the house
of Israel. And she shall be his wife, he hath no power
to put her away all his days. But if this word be true,
and the tokens of virginity are not found unto the
damsel, then they shall bring out the damsel to the door
of her father's house, and the men of that city shall
stone her with stones that she die; for she hath wrought
shame in Israel in playing whoredom in her father's
house, and thou shalt put away the evil doer from
among you.

If a man be found lying with a woman, the wife of
(another) man, they shall be both of them put to death,
the man who lay with the woman, and the woman; and
thou shalt put away the evil doer from Israel. If a man
find in the city a damsel, a virgin, who is betrothed to
a man, and lie with her, then shall you bring them both
out to the gate of that city, and stone them with stones
that they die, the damsel because she cried not out in
the city, and the man because he humiliated his neighbour's wife; and thou shalt put away the evil doer from
among you. But if a man find the betrothed damsel in
the field, and prevail against her, and lie with her, then
only the man who lay with her shall be put to death;
but unto the damsel thou shalt not do anything; there
is not with the damsel guilt of the judgment of death;
for as when a man riseth up against his neighbour and
killeth him, even so is this matter; he found her in the
field, the betrothed damsel cried, but there was none to
deliver. If a man find a damsel, a virgin who is not
betrothed, and lay hold of her and lie with her, and they
be found, then the man who lay with her shall give to
the damsel's father fifty shekels of silver, and she shall
be his wife; because he had humbled her, he shall not
have power to send her away all his days. A man shall

not take his father's wife, nor uncover the skirt of his father.

XXIII. He who is castrated or ruptured shall not be clean so as to enter into the congregation of the Lord.[4] A bastard or mixed person (*mamzer*)[5] shall not be clean, so as to enter into the congregation of the Lord;[4] his offspring also to the tenth generation shall not be clean, so as to enter into the congregation of the Lord. An Ammonite or a Moabite shall not be clean, so as to enter into the congregation of the Lord; neither to the tenth generation shall they be clean ever to enter the congregation of the Lord; because they met you not with bread and water in the way, when you came up from Mizraim; and because they hired Bilaam bar Beor from Pethor Aram, upon the Phrat, to curse thee. But the Lord thy God would not hearken to Bileam, and the Lord thy God turned the curses into blessings, because the Lord thy God loved thee. Thou shalt not seek their peace nor their prosperity all thy days for ever. Thou shalt not abhor an Edomite, for he is thy brother; thou shalt not abhor a Mizraite, for thou wast a sojourner in his land. The children that are begotten of them of the third generation shall be clean, so as to enter into the congregation of the Lord. When thou goest forth a host against thy enemies, then beware of every wicked thing. If there be among thee a man who is not clean, by an accident of the night, let him go forth without the camp, let him not enter into the midst of the camp, but at eventide let him wash with water, and at sunset he may come into the camp. And a place shall be appointed for thee outside of the camp, that thou mayest

[4] That is, according to the Talmud, shall not be permitted to marry an Israelitish woman.

[5] According to the Rabbins, a person born from the illicit connexions forbidden in Leviticus.

go thither without. And thou shalt have a blade upon thy weapon, that when thou sittest abroad thou mayest dig with it, and cover that which cometh from thee. For the Shekinah of the Lord thy God walketh amid thy camp to save thee and deliver up thy enemies before thee, and thy camp shall be sacred, that nothing that offendeth may be seen among thee, lest His Word turn away from doing thee good.

Thou shalt not deliver up a slave of the Gentiles into the hand of his master, when he hath escaped to thee from his master; he shall dwell with thee in thy midst in the place that he may choose in one of thy cities where it may be best for him; thou shalt not oppress him. No woman of the children of Israel may be the wife of a man who is a slave; neither shall any man of the sons of Israel take a bondwoman to wife. Thou shalt not bring the hire of fornication nor the price of a dog into the house of the sanctuary of the Lord thy God, for any vow; for even both of them are an abomination before the Lord thy God. Thou shalt not make usury[6] of thy brother; the usury of money, of corn, or of any thing that produceth usury. From a son of the Gentiles thou mayest take usury, but from thy brother thou shalt not take it; for the Lord thy God will bless thee in all that thou puttest thy hand unto in the land to which thou goest to possess it.

When thou vowest a vow before the Lord thy God, thou shalt not delay to fulfil it; for the Lord thy God requiring will require it of thee, and it would become sin in thee. Yet if thou shouldst forbear to vow, it will not be sin in thee. What hath gone forth from thy lips thou shalt observe and perform; as thou hast vowed before the Lord thy God, (thou shalt perform) freely what thou hast spoken with thy lips.

[6] Sam. Vers., "double"

If thou comest for hire into thy neighbour's vineyard, thou mayest eat grapes for the satisfying of thy life; but thou shalt not put (them) into thy vessel. If thou comest into thy neighbour's ripe corn, thou mayest pluck the full ears with thy hand, but not put in the sickle upon thy neighbour's corn.

XXIV. When a man shall have taken a wife, and become her husband, and she hath not found favour in his eyes, because he hath found something wrong in her, then he may write for her a bill of divorcement, and give it into her hand, and send her from his house. And when she hath departed from his house, she may go and become (the wife) of another man. And if the latter husband dislike her, and write her a bill of divorce, and put it into her hand, and dismiss her from his house; or if the latter husband who had taken her to be his wife shall die, the first husband who had put her away hath no power to return to take her to be his wife, after that she hath been defiled; for that is an abomination before the Lord; and thou shalt not cause the land to sin, which the Lord thy God giveth thee to inherit. When a man hath taken a new wife, he shall not go forth with the army, nor shall any transaction be (laid) upon him; he shall be free in his house for a year, that he may cheer (or, may enjoy himself with) his wife whom he hath taken.[7]

No man shall take as a pledge the millstones (either lower) or upper; for by them is made the subsistence of every living man. If a man be found stealing a person of his brethren of the sons of Israel, to make merchandise of him, or to sell him, that man shall be put to death, and thou shalt put away the evil doer from among thee. Take heed, in the plague of leprosy, to observe and perform entirely all that the priests, the Levites,

7 Sam. Vers., " may rejoice with his wife."

shall teach you; as I have commanded them, you shall observe to do. Remember what the Lord thy God did unto Miriam, in the way when you came out of Mizraim.

When thou hast lent the use of anything to thy neighbour, thou shalt not enter into his house to take his pledge. Thou shalt stand without, and the man to whom thou hast lent shall bring out the pledge to thee. And if the man be poor, thou shalt not sleep with his pledge; thou shalt return him his pledge at sunset, that he may sleep in his garment, and may bless thee, and it shall be righteousness before the Lord thy God. Thou shalt not oppress an hireling who is needy and poor, (whether he be) of thy brethren, or of thy sojourners who are in thy land or thy cities. In his day thou shalt give him his hire; thou shalt not let the sun go down upon it, for he is needy, and to it he delivereth his life (soul); that he cry not against thee before the Lord, and it be sin in thee. The fathers shall not die for the children, nor shall children die for the fathers; a man shall die for his own sin. Thou shalt not wrest the judgment of the stranger or the orphan, nor take the garment of the widow for a pledge; but thou shalt remember that thou wast a bondman in Mizraim, and that the Lord thy God redeemed thee from thence; therefore I command thee to do this thing.

When thou art harvesting thy harvest in thy field, and hast forgotten a sheaf in the field, thou shalt not return to take it; let it be for the stranger, the orphan, and the widow, that the Lord thy God may bless thee in all the work of thy hands. When thou beatest thy olive (trees), thou shalt not make search for what thou hast left behind thee; let it be for the stranger, the orphan, and the widow. When thou art gathering thy vineyard, thou shalt not glean the grapes that are left behind thee; let them be for the stranger, the orphan, and the widow; and remember that thou wast a bondman in the land of Mizraim; therefore have I commanded thee to do this thing.

XXV. If there be (a case for) judgment between men, let them bring it to the judges, that they may adjudicate; and they shall justify the innocent, and condemn the guilty. And if the guilty be condemned to be scourged, the judge shall cause him to lie down, and have him scourged before him (with stripes), in number according to the measure of his guilt. Forty (times) he may smite him, not more, lest he should go on to smite him above these with many stripes, and thy brother be made vile in thy eyes. Thou shalt not muzzle the mouth of the ox while he treadeth out (the corn). If brothers dwell together, and one of them die, having no son, the wife of the deceased shall not marry another man without; her husband's brother shall go to her, and take her to him to wife, and marry her for his brother. And the first-born that she beareth shall keep up the name of his deceased brother, that his name be not blotted out from Israel. But should the man be unwilling to take the wife of his brother, his brother's wife shall go up to the gate of the house of judgment, and say before the elders, My husband's brother refuseth to keep up a name to his brother in Israel; he is not willing to marry me. Then the elders of his city shall call him, and speak with him; and if he rise up and say, It is not my pleasure to take her; then shall his brother's wife approach him in the presence of the elders, and loose his shoe from off his foot, and spit in his face, and answer, and say, Thus let it be done to the man who will not build up the house of his brother. And his name shall be called in Israel, The house of the loosed shoe.

If men strive together, a man and his brother,

and the wife of one (of them) come nigh to save her husband from the hand of him who smiteth him, and put forth her hand and seize the place of his shame, then thou shalt cut off her hand, thine eye shall have no pity on her.

Thou shalt not, have in thy bag weight and weight, great and small. Thou shalt not have in thy house measure and measure, great and small: perfect weights and true shalt thou have, perfect measures and true shalt thou have, that thy days may be prolonged upon the land which the Lord thy God giveth thee: for every one who doeth these things, every one who acteth falsely, is an abomination before the Lord thy God.

Remember what Amalek did to thee in the way, when thou camest up out of Mizraim; how he overtook thee in the way, and slew of thee all who were following behind thee [8] when thou wast faint and weary, [9] and he was not afraid before the Lord. Therefore when the Lord thy God shall have given thee rest from all thy enemies round about, in the land which the Lord thy God giveth thee for a possession to inherit, thou shalt blot out the memory of Amalek from under the heavens: thou shalt not be forgetful.

SECTION L.

THABO.

XXVI. And when thou hast entered into the land which the Lord thy God will give thee for possession, and thou inherit and dwell in it, thou shalt take of the first of all the produce of the earth which thou shalt bring up from the land the Lord thy God will give thee, and put it into a basket, and go to the place which the Lord thy God will choose to make His Shekinah to

---

[8] Sam. text, "the infirm."   [9] Sam. Vers., "hungry."

dwell there. And thou shalt come unto the priest who
will be in those days, and say to him : I profess this
day before the Lord thy God, that I have come into the
land which the Lord did covenant to our fathers to give
them. And the priest shall take the basket from thy hand,
and lay it down before the altar of the Lord thy God ;
and thou shalt answer and say before the Lord thy God :

Laban the Aramite sought to destroy my father,[1] and
he went down to Mizraim, and dwelt there with a few
people, but became there a people great and strong.
But the Mizraee maltreated and afflicted us, and laid
hard labour upon us. And we prayed before the Lord,
the God of our fathers ; and the Lord heard our prayer,
and our travail, weariness, and oppression were manifest
before Him ; and the Lord brought us out of Mizraim
with a mighty hand and uplifted arm, with great visions,
signs, and wonders, and brought us to this place, and
gave us this land, a land producing milk and honey.
And now, behold, I have brought the first fruits of the
land which Thou, O Lord, hast given me.

And thou shalt set it down before the Lord thy God,
and worship before the Lord thy God. And thou shalt
rejoice in all the good which the Lord thy God hath
given thee, with the men of thy house, the Levite and
the stranger who is among you.

When thou hast made an end of tything all the tythe
of thy produce in the third year, the year of the tythes,
and hast given it to the Levite, the stranger, the orphan,
and the widow, that they may eat within thy cities and
be satisfied, then thou shalt say before the Lord thy God :

I have set apart the consecrated tenth from my house,

---

[1] Heb. text, "A perishing Aramite was my father." Vulgate, "A
Syrian persecuted my father." Septuagint, "My father abandoned
Syria.' Peschito Syriac, "My father was led to Aram, and he went
down to Mizreen."

and have given also to the Levite, the stranger, the
fatherless, and the widow, according to all Thy commandment which Thou hast commanded me. I have not
transgressed Thy commandment, nor been forgetful. I
have not eaten of it in my mourning, nor exchanged any
of it for what is unclean, nor given of it for the dead.
I have been obedient to the Word of the Lord my God,
and have done according to all that Thou hast commanded me. Look down from the heavens, the habitation of Thy holiness, and bless Thy people Israel, and
the land which Thou hast given us, as Thou didst swear
to our fathers, a land producing milk and honey.

This day doth the Lord thy God command thee to do
these statutes and judgments, and to keep and perform
them with all thy heart, and with all thy soul. This
day hast thou declared (or avouched) the Lord to be
thy God, and to walk in the ways that are right before
Him, and to keep His statutes, His commandments, and
His judgments, and to be obedient to His word. And
the Lord hath declared thee this day to be His beloved
people, as He hath said unto thee, that thou mayest
observe all His commandments, and that He may set
thee above all the nations whom He hath made, in praise,
and in name, and in greatness, and that thou mayest be a
holy people before the Lord thy God, as He hath spoken.

XXVII. And Mosheh and the elders of Israel instructed the people, saying: Observe all the commandments which I command you this day. In the day that
you pass over the Jordan to the land which the Lord
thy God giveth thee, thou shalt set thee up great stones,
and cover them with plaster (or lime), and write upon
them all the words of this law, when thou hast passed
over to go into the land which the Lord thy God giveth
thee, a land producing milk and honey, as the Lord
God of thy fathers hath said to thee. When you have

passed the Jordan, you shall set up those stones which I
command you this day, on the mountain of Ebal, and
plaster them with lime; and thou shalt build an altar
before the Lord thy God, an altar of stones: thou
shalt not lift up iron upon it. With perfected stones
shalt thou build the altar of the Lord thy God, and offer
sacrifices thereon before the Lord thy God. And thou
shalt sacrifice consecrated victims, and eat there, and
rejoice before the Lord thy God; and thou shalt write
upon the stones all the words of this law, distinctly and
beautifully.

And Mosheh, and the priests, the Levites, spake to all
Israel: Listen and hear, O Israel: To-day art thou a
people before the Lord thy God; and thou shalt hearken
to the Word of the Lord thy God, and do His commandments and His statutes which I command thee this
day. And Mosheh charged the people on that day,
saying: These shall stand to bless the people on the
mountain of Gerizim, when you have passed the Jordan,
Shemeon and Levi, Jehudah, Issakar, Joseph, and
Benjamin. And these shall stand to accurse upon the
mountain of Ebal; Reuben and Asher, Zebulon, Dan,
and Naphtali. And the Levites shall answer and say to
all the men of Israel, with a high voice:

Accursed be the man who shall make an image or
molten (one), an abomination before the Lord, the work
of an artificer's hand, and place it in secret. And all
the people shall respond and say, Amen. Accursed be
he who contemneth his father or his mother. And
all the people shall say, Amen. Accursed he who
changeth the boundary of his neighbour. And all the
people shall say, Amen. Accursed he who maketh the
blind wander in the way. And all the people shall say,
Amen. Accursed he who perverteth the judgment of
the stranger, the orphan, or the widow. And all the

people shall say, Amen. Accursed he who lieth with his father's wife : he uncovereth the skirt of his father. And all the people shall say, Amen. Accursed is he who lieth with any beast. And all the people shall say, Amen. Accursed is he who lieth with his sister, the daughter of his father or the daughter of his mother. And all the people shall say, Amen. Accursed is he who lieth with his mother-in-law. And all the people shall say, Amen. Accursed is he who smiteth his neighbour in secret. And all the people shall say, Amen. Accursed is he who receiveth hire to kill the life, and (shed the) blood of the innocent. And all the people shall say, Amen. Accursed is he who confirmeth not the words of this law to do them. And all the people shall say, Amen.

XXVIII. And if thou wilt indeed be obedient to the Word of the Lord thy God, to observe and to do all His commandments which I command thee this day, the Lord thy God will set thee on high above all the peoples of the earth ; and all these blessings shall come upon thee and keep with thee, if thou wilt be obedient to the Word of the Lord thy God. Blessed (shalt) thou (be) in the city, and blessed in the field. Blessed shall be the offspring of thy womb, and the produce of thy land, the increase of thy cattle, the oxen of thy herd, and the flocks of thy sheep. Blessed shall be thy basket and thy store.[2] Blessed shalt thou be in thy coming in, and blessed in thy going out. The Lord shall cause thy adversaries that rise up against thee to be shattered before thee ; they will come out to thee in one way, but in seven ways shall they flee from before thee. The Lord will command a blessing upon thee in all thy storehouses, and on all that thou settest thy hand unto, and will bless thee in the land which the Lord thy God

---

[2] Sam. Vers., " thy grinding and thy kneading."

giveth to thee. The Lord shall confirm thee for Himself to be a holy people, as He hath sworn to thee, if
thou wilt keep the commandments of the Lord thy God,
and walk in the ways which are right before Him.
And all the nations of the earth shall see that the Name
of the Lord is invoked upon thee, and they will be
afraid of thee. And the Lord will make thee to abound
in good, in the offspring of thy womb, and of thy cattle,
and in the produce of thy ground, in the land which
the Lord sware to thy fathers to give thee. The Lord
will open for thee His good treasure, the heavens, to
give rain to thy land in its season, and to bless all the
works of thy hand; and thou shalt lend unto many
nations, but not borrow; and the Lord will make thee
strong and not weak, and thou shalt evermore be upper
and not under, if thou wilt obey the commandments of
the Lord thy God which I command thee this day to
keep and to perform. And you shall not go astray from
any of the things I command you this day, right or left,
to walk after the gods of the Gentiles to serve them.

But if thou wilt not obey the Word of the Lord thy
God to observe and do all His commandments, and His
statutes which I command you this day, all these curses
shall come upon thee and cleave to thee. Accursed shalt
thou be in the city, and accursed in the field; accursed
thy basket and thy store; accursed the generation of thy
womb, the produce of thy ground, the oxen of thy herd,
and the folds of thy sheep. Accursed shalt thou be in
thy coming in, and accursed in thy going out. The
Lord shall send upon thee malediction and trouble and
rebuke (or menace) in all that thou settest thine hand
unto for to do, until thou art consumed and perish
quickly, on account of the wickedness of thy works, when
thou hast forgotten to fear Me (or, whereby thou hast
forgotten My fear). The Lord shall make the pestilence

cleave to thee, until He have destroyed thee from off the
land into which thou art going to possess it. The Lord
will smite thee with wasting, with fever, with inflammation, with dryness, and with the sword, and with
jaundice (or mildew ?). And they shall follow thee till
thou art destroyed. And the heavens over thy head will
be obdurate as brass in withholding rain, and the ground
under thee obstinate as iron in producing no fruit.
The Lord will give thee ashes for the rain of thy land,
and dust will come down from the heavens upon thee,
until thou be consumed. The Lord will deliver thee up
to be broken before thy enemies; thou wilt go out to
them by one way, but by seven ways shalt thou flee
before them, and thou shalt be dispersed in all the
kingdoms of the earth. And thy carcase shall be cast
out for food for all the fowls of the heaven, and for the
beasts of the earth, and there shall be none to drive
(them) away. And the Lord will smite thee with the
ulcer of the Mizraee, with emerods, soreness, and the dry
scurvy, from which thou canst not be healed. And the
Lord will smite thee with distraction, and blindness, and
with bewilderment of heart; and thou shalt grope in the
noonday as the blind gropeth in darkness; and thou
shalt not prosper in thy way, but be only oppressed and
despoiled always, and no man will be able to save.
Thou wilt betroth a wife, but another man shall have
her; thou wilt build a house, but not dwell in it, and
plant a vineyard, but have no use thereof. Thy ox will
be killed in thy sight, but thou shalt not eat of it; thy
ass shall be taken away from thee, and not be returned to
thee; thy sheep will be delivered to thy enemies, and
thou wilt have no one to rescue them; thy sons and
daughters will be given up to another people, and thy
eyes look and fail (with longing) for them all the day,
and there shall be no power in thy hand. The produce

of thy land and all thy labours a people whom thou knowest not shall devour, and thou wilt only be oppressed and crushed all the days. And thou wilt be mad through the sight of thy eyes which thou seest. The Lord will smite thee with an evil ulcer upon thy knees and thy thighs, from which thou wilt not be able to be healed from the sole of thy foot unto thy brain.

The Lord will make thee and thy king whom thou mayest have set over thee to be captive to a people whom thou and thy fathers have not known; and there shalt thou serve a people, worshippers of idols of wood and stone; and thou wilt become a ruin, a proverb, and a history, among all nations whither the Lord shall make thee go.

Much seed wilt thou carry out into the field, but little shalt thou gather in, for the locust will consume it; thou wilt plant and till vineyards, but wilt not drink the wine, nor gather in, for the worm shall eat it; thou wilt have olive trees in all thy borders, but with the oil thou wilt not anoint, for thy olive trees shall waste; thou wilt beget sons and daughters, but wilt not have them (with thee), for they shall go into captivity. The locust will consume all the fruitage and the trees of thy land. The uncircumcised stranger who is among thee will rise up high above thee, but thou shalt be brought down very low: he shall lend to thee, but thou wilt not lend to him; he will be strong, and thou wilt be weak. And all these curses shall come upon thee, and follow thee, and cleave to thee till thou art consumed, because thou wast not obedient to the Word of the Lord thy God, to keep His commandments and His statutes which He hath commanded thee. And they will be upon thee for a sign and a wonder, and upon thy children for ever; because thou wouldst not worship before the Lord thy God with cheerfulness and comeliness of heart for the

abundance of all (His benefits): but thou shalt serve
thy enemies whom the Lord will send against thee, in
hunger, thirst, nakedness, and want of all things; and
He will put a yoke of iron upon thy neck until He hath
destroyed thee.   And the Lord will bring upon thee a
nation from afar, from the ends of the earth, like the
flying eagle, a people whose language thou wilt not
understand, a people of mighty presence, who will not
regard the old man, nor have mercy on the infant. And
he will eat up the increase of thy cattle, and the
fruitage of thy ground, until he hath consumed thee;
for he will not leave thee corn, wine, nor oil, the oxen
of thy herd, nor the sheep of thy flock, until he hath
brought thee to ruin.   And he will shut thee up in all
thy cities, till he hath brought down thy high and
fenced walls, wherein thou didst confide to be saved by
them throughout all thy land; and he will besiege thee
in all thy cities in all thy land which the Lord thy God
did give thee.   And thou wilt eat the offspring of thy
womb, the flesh of thy sons and daughters whom the
Lord thy God had given thee, in the siege and straitness
with which thy enemies shall straiten thee.   The man
who is gentle among you, and very delicate, will look
with an evil eye upon his brother, and upon the wife of
his covenant, and upon the remnant of his children
whom he will leave; he will not give to one of them of
the flesh of his children which he shall eat, for that
nothing remaineth to him of all, in the siege and the
straitness with which thy enemies shall straiten thee
in all thy cities.   She who is tender among you, and
delicate, who had not (been used to) put the sole of her
foot upon the ground under her, from delicateness and
tenderness, will look with an evil eye upon the husband
of her covenant, and upon her son and her daughter,
and against her little children who have been brought

forth of her, and against her children whom she hath
borne; for she will eat them in secret, in the want of
all things, in the siege and the straitness with which thy
enemies shall straiten thee in thy cities:—if thou wilt
not observe to perform all the words of this law which
are written in this book, to reverence this glorious and
fearful Name, THE LORD THY GOD.[3]   And the Lord
will make thy plagues to be manifest (distinguished),
and the plagues of thy children, great plagues and continuous, afflictions evil and abiding.   And He will lay
upon thee all the strokes of Mizraim of which thou wast
afraid, and they shall cleave to thee.   All the diseases
also and all the plagues that are not written in the book
of this law, will the Lord lay upon thee till He hath
destroyed thee.   And you, who had been as the stars of
heaven for multitude, will be left a small people, because
you would not be obedient to the Word of the Lord
your God.   And as the Lord rejoiced over you to do
you good and to multiply you, so will the Lord rejoice
over you to destroy and consume you, and to carry you
away from off the land which you are entering to possess
it.   And the Lord will scatter thee among all nations
unto the ends of the earth; and thou shalt there serve
peoples who worship idols of wood and stone, which
neither thou nor thy fathers have known.   But among
those nations thou wilt have no repose, nor will the sole
of thy foot have rest, but the Lord will give thee there
a timorous heart, darkness of eyes, and feebleness of
mind; and thou wilt hold thy life in suspense, and be
afraid by night and day, for thou wilt be never sure of
thy life.   In the morning thou wilt say, O that it were
evening! but in the evening thou wilt say, O that it
were morning! from the fearfulness of thy heart with
which thou wilt fear, and the sight of thy eyes which

[3] Heb., *Yehovah Eloheika.*

thou shalt see.   And the Lord will cause thee to return
to Mizraim, in ships, by the way of which I spake with
thee, Thou shalt see it no more: and there shall you be
offered for sale for bondmen and bondwomen, but none
shall buy.

These are the words of the covenant which the Lord
commanded Mosheh to ratify with the children of Israel
in the land of Moab; besides the covenant which He
ratified with them at Horeb.

XXIX. And Mosheh called unto all Israel, and said
to them : You have seen all that the Lord wrought
before your eyes in the land of Mizraim on Pharoh, and
all his servants, and on all his land; the great temptations, the signs and grand portents which thy eyes
beheld; yet the Lord hath not given you a heart to
understand, nor eyes to discern, nor ears to hear, unto
this day.   And I have led you forty years in the wilderness; your raiment hath not become old upon you, and
thy shoes have not worn away from off thy feet; you
have not eaten bread, nor drunk wine, either new or old,
that you may know that I am the Lord your God.

And you came to this place; and Sihon the king of
Heshbon and Og the king of Mathnan came out to
meet us, to wage battle ; and we smote them, and subdued their land, and gave it for an inheritance to the tribe
of Reuben and Gad, and the half tribe of Menasheh.
Keep ye the words of this covenant, and perform them,
that you may prosper in all that you do.

SECTION LI.

NITSTSABIM.

You stand this day all of you before the Lord your
God, the princes of your tribes, your elders, and your

officers, every man of Israel; your children, your wives, and thy sojourner who is within thy camp, from the hewer of thy wood to the filler of thy water; to enter into the covenant of the Lord thy God, and into His oath which the Lord thy God doth ratify with thee this day, that He may establish thee this day to be a people before Him, and that He may be a God unto thee, as He promised thee, and as He sware unto Abraham, and to Izhak, and to Jakob.

And I ratify this covenant and oath not with you only, but with him who is standing here with us this day before the Lord our God, and with him also who is not here with us this day. For you know how we dwelt in the land of Mizraim, and how we came through the midst of the nations by whom we have passed. And you have seen their abominations, and their idols of wood and stone, silver and gold, which (were found) among them; lest there should be among you a man, woman, family, or tribe whose heart is turned away this day from the fear of the Lord our God, to go after the worship of these Gentiles; lest there should be with you a man who imagineth wickedness or pride, that, when he heareth the words of this oath, he should reckon in his heart, saying, I shall have peace, though I go on in the imagination of my heart to multiply sins of ignorance with (sin of) presumption. The Lord will not absolve him, but now will the anger and indignation of the Lord break forth against that man, and all the curses which are written in this book will cleave to him, and his name will be blotted out from under the heavens. And the Lord will separate him from all the tribes of Israel unto evil, according to all the curses of the covenant which are written in the book of this law. And the generation that cometh after, and your children who will arise after you, and the son of the Gentiles who

may come from a land afar off, when they see the plagues
of that land, and the afflictions with which the Lord
will afflict it, the whole land, brimstone and salt and
burning, with no sowing, or growth, or any herbage
springing up therein, even as the overthrow of Sedom and
Amorah, Admah and Zeboim, which the Lord overthrew
in His anger and indignation, even all the nations will
say, Why did the Lord thus to this land? What caused
the fury of this wrath? Then shall they say, Because
they have forsaken the covenant of the Lord, the God
of their fathers, which He ratified with them when He
brought them out of the land of Mizraim. For they
went and served the idols of the Gentiles, and worshipped
fearful things which they knew not, and which could do
them no good. And the anger of the Lord waxed
strong against this land to bring upon it all the curses
that are written in this book. And the Lord cast them
away from off their land in anger, indignation, and
great violence, and drave them captive into another land
as at this day. The things which are secret are before
the Lord our God; and those which are revealed are
ours, and our children's for ever, that we may do all the
words of this law.

XXX. And it will be that when all these words of
blessings or of maledictions which I have set before thee
have come upon thee, and thou turn unto thy heart
among all the nations whither the Lord thy God will
have led thee captive, and return to the fear of the Lord
thy God, and obey His Word, according to all that I
command thee this day, thou and thy children, with all
thy heart and all thy soul, that the Lord thy God will
turn thy captivity,[4] and have mercy upon thee, and will
return, and gather thee from all the nations among

---

[4] Sam. Vers., "that the Lord thy God may return with thy conversion."

which the Lord thy God hath dispersed thee.   If any of
thy dispersed be (scattered) unto the ends of the heavens,
from thence will the Lord thy God gather thee, and lead
thee.   And the Lord thy God will bring thee into the
land which thy fathers did inherit, and thou shalt possess
it: and he will do thee good, and multiply thee above
thy fathers.   And the Lord thy God will take away the
foolishness of thy heart, and the foolishness of thy children's heart, to love the Lord thy God with all thy
heart and all thy soul, that thou mayest live.   And the
Lord thy God will put all these curses upon thy enemies
and upon them who hated and persecuted thee; but
thou shalt return and be obedient to the Word of the
Lord, and do all the commandments which I command
thee this day.

And the Lord thy God will make thee to abound in
all the works of thy hand, the offspring of thy womb,
the increase of thy cattle, and the produce of thy land,
unto good; for the Lord will return to rejoice [5] over
thee for good, as He rejoiced over thy fathers; when
thou shalt be obedient to the Word of the Lord thy
God, to keep His commandments and statutes which are
written in the book of this law, if thou return unto the
fear of the Lord thy God with all thy heart and all thy
soul.

For this commandment which I command thee this
day is not apart [6] from thee, nor is it far away.   It is
not in the heavens, that thou shouldst say, Who shall
ascend for us into heaven, that he may bring it to us,
that we may hear and do it? nor is it beyond the sea,
that thou shouldst say, Who will go over for us beyond
the sea, and bring it to us, that we may hear and do it?

---

[5] Sam. Vers., " to be kind to thee, as to thy fathers "

[6] Or, " separated," *mepharash*.   Hebrew text, *nephleeth*, " too won-
derful for thee."   Vulg., *non supra te.*   Syr., *lo kasé*, " is not hidden."

For the word is very nigh thee, in thy mouth and in thy heart, that thou mayest do it.

Behold, I have set before thee this day life and good, and death and evil; for I command thee this day to love the Lord thy God, to walk in the ways that are right in His presence, and to keep His commandments, statutes, and judgments, that thou mayest live and multiply, and the Lord God may bless thee in the land into which thou art going, to possess it. But if thy heart be averse, and thou wilt not obey, but wilt go astray, and worship the idols of the Gentiles, and serve them, I have shown you this day that perishing you shall perish. You will not prolong your days upon the land whither thou passest over Jordan to enter in and possess it. I call heaven and earth to attest in you this day that I have set before thee life and death, blessings and curses: but choose for life, that thou mayest live, thou and thy children, to love the Lord thy God, to be obedient to His word, and to keep close unto His fear, for He is thy life, and the prolonger of thy days, to abide upon the land which the Lord sware to thy fathers, to Abraham, Izhak, and Jakob, to give unto them.

SECTION LII.

VAIYELECH

XXXI. AND Mosheh went and spake these words with all Israel. And he said to them, I am the son of a hundred and twenty years this day. I am no more able to go out and to come in; and the Lord hath said to me, Thou shalt not pass over this Jordan. The Lord thy God, He goeth over before thee; He will destroy

these nations from before thee, and thou shalt inherit
them. Jehoshua, he goeth over before thee, as the
Lord hath said. And the Lord will do to them as He
did to Sihon and to Og, kings of the Amorites, and to
the lands of them whom He destroyed. The Lord will
deliver them up, and you shall do to them according
to all the commandments that I have commanded you.
Be strong and of good courage, fear not, nor be broken
before them ; for the Word of the Lord thy God will be
the leader before thee, He will not forsake thee, nor be
far off from thee.

And Mosheh called Jehoshua, and said to him before
the eyes of all Israel, Be strong and of good courage ;
for thou art to go in with this people to the land which
the Lord hath sworn to their fathers to give it to them,
and thou shalt cause them to inherit. But the Lord,
He is the leader before thee ; His Word shall be thy
helper, for He will not forsake thee, nor be far from
thee ; fear not, nor be dismayed.

And Mosheh wrote this law, and gave it to the
priests, the sons of Levi, who bare the Ark of the
Covenant of the Lord, and to all the elders of Israel.
And Mosheh commanded them, saying : At the end of
seven years, at the time of the year of release, at the
Feast of Tabernacles, when all Israel cometh to appear
before the Lord thy God, in the place that He will
choose, thou shalt read this law before all Israel, and
make them hear. Gather the people together, the men,
the women, and children, and thy sojourners who are in
thy cities, that they may hear, and learn, and fear before
the Lord your God, and observe and perform all the words
of this law, and that their children who have not known
may hear and learn to fear before the Lord all the days
that you abide upon the land to which you pass over
the Jordan to possess it.

And the Lord said to Mosheh, Behold, the days are
drawing near for thee to die: call Jehoshua, and let
him stand in the tabernacle of ordinance, and I will
give him commandment.   And Mosheh and Jehoshua
went and stood in the tabernacle of ordinance.   And
the Lord was revealed at the tabernacle in the pillar of
the cloud, and the pillar of the cloud stood over the
door of the tabernacle.   And the Lord said to Mosheh,
Behold, thou art to sleep with thy fathers; and this
people will rise up and go astray after the idols of the
peoples of the land among whom they are going, and
will forsake My fear, and remove (or change) from My
covenant [7] which I have made with them.   And my
anger will be kindled against them at that time, and I
will drive them afar off, and remove My Shekinah [8] from
them to consume them,[9] and many evils and troubles
shall befall them.   And they will say in that day, Is it
not because the Shekinah of my God is not among me,
that these evils have befallen me?   But I will remove
My Shekinah from them at that time on account of the
evils they had done; for they will have turned away
after the idols of the nations.

And now, write for you this hymn, and teach it to
the children of Israel; put it upon their lips, that this
hymn may be a witness for Me against the children of
Israel.   For when they will have entered into the land
which I promised to their fathers, (a land) producing
milk and honey, and they have eaten and been satisfied,
and have become luxurious, they will turn away after
the idols of the nations, and serve them, and provoke
to anger before Me, and change from My covenant.
And when many evils and troubles have fallen on them,

[7] Heb. text, "and will violate My covenant,"—*vehepher Berithi*
[8] Sam Vers., "My favour."
[9] Other copies, "to cast them away."

this song shall answer against them, for it will not be
forgotten from the mouth of their children, because
their imagination which they will do is manifest before
Me this day, while (as yet) I have not brought them
into the land which I have promised.

And Mosheh wrote this hymn on that day, and
taught it to the children of Israel. And he commanded Jehoshua bar Nun, and said, Be strong, and
of good courage; for thou shalt bring the sons of Israel
into the land which I have promised to them, and His
Word shall be thy helper. And it was, when Mosheh
had finished to write the words of this law upon a book
until they were completed, that Mosheh commanded
the Levites who bare the Ark of the Covenant of the
Lord, saying, Take this book of the law, and put it in
the side of the Ark of the Covenant of the Lord, and it
shall be there for a witness against thee. For I know
thy rebelliousness, and the stiffness of thy neck: behold,
while I am alive with you this day, you have rebelled
against the Lord; but (how much) also after that I am
dead? Gather to me all the elders of your tribes, and
your officers, and I will speak these words before you,
and will call the heavens and earth to witness: for I
know that after I am dead you will corrupt yourselves,
and decline from the way which I have commanded you,
and that evil will befall you at the end of the days; for
you will do evil before the Lord to provoke Him to
anger by the works of your hands. And Mosheh spake
before all the congregation of Israel the words of this
hymn, until he had finished it.

SECTION LIII.

HAAZINU.

XXXII. LISTEN, ye heavens, and I will speak; give ear, O earth, to the words of my mouth. My doctrine shall be soft as rain; let it be received as the dew, and my word be as the breath of the rain that breathes upon the grass, and as the showers of the latter rain upon the herbage. For in the Name of the Lord do I invoke :—Ascribe ye greatness unto our God; the Mighty One whose works are perfect, for all His ways are justice; a faithful God from whom no iniquity proceedeth, just and true is He.

They have corrupted themselves, and not Him;[1] children who worship idols, a generation that changeth its work, and maketh it another. Behold, render you this before the Lord, ye people who have received the law, but have not become wise? Is He not thy Father, and thou art His who made thee and bought thee? Remember the days of old, consider the years of generation and generation; ask thy fathers, and they will show thee, thy elders, and they will tell thee. When the Most High gave the nations their inheritance, when He made the distribution of the children of men, He ordained the boundaries of the nations after the numbers of the sons of Israel.[2] For the Lord's portion is His people, Jakob is the lot of His inheritance. He satisfied their wants in the land of the wilderness, in the dry place where there was no water; He placed them round about His Shekinah; He taught them the words of His

---

[1] The meaning seems to be, "Their wickedness is from themselves, not from the Holy God."

[2] "He limited the boundaries of the nations that Keuaan should belong to the people of Israel."—HERDER.

law; He kept them as the apple of His eye. As the
eagle which hasteneth to his nest, and spreadeth himself
over his young ones, stretching out his wings, taketh
them, upbeareth them with the strength of his pinions,[3]
so did the Lord alone prepare them to dwell in the
world which He will renew (set right), while the worship
of idols shall not be established before Him. He made
them to dwell in the strong places of the earth, to eat
the spoil of their enemies: He gave them the spoil of
the rulers of cities, and the wealth of them who dwelt in
strong defences. He gave them the spoil of their kings
and sultans, with the riches of their princes, and the
strength of the people of their lands, their possessions,
the booty of their hosts and camps, and the blood of
their heroes was poured out like water.

But Israel waxed fat and kicked, he prospered, grew
strong and got rich, and forgat the worship of Eloha who
made him, and provoked the Almighty who redeemed
him. They provoked Him by the worship of idols, by
abominations they made Him angry. They sacrificed to
demons in whom there is no help, (nothing that is
needed,) and fearful things that they had not known,
new (gods) that were lately made, with which your
fathers had no dealings; of the Awful One and the Omnipotent who created thee, thou art forgetful; thou hast
forsaken the worship of Eloha who made thee.

And it was seen before the Lord, and His anger was
kindled by the provocation of His sons and daughters
before Him. And He said: I will take away (take up)
My Shekinah from among them; what will be their
latter end is manifest to Me; for they are a perverse
generation, children in whom is no faith. They have
moved Me to jealousy by that which is not worshipful,
they have angered Me by their idolatries; and I will

---

[3] *Ebarohi,* "his limbs."

make them jealous by what hath not been a people, by a foolish nation will I provoke them. For a burning, strong as fire, shall go forth before Me in fury consuming unto the lowest hell, to make an end of the earth and its produce, and to destroy the mountains to the end; and I will multiply calamities upon them, My plagues will I send forth among them; they shall be swollen with hunger, and be eaten by the fowl, and be vexed with evil spirits; and the teeth of wild beasts will I appoint among them with the venom of serpents that crawl in the dust. Without will the sword devour, and within the chambers be the slaughter-work of death, the youths and the maidens, the sucklings with the aged. I said I would make My anger to remain upon them and consume them; I will abolish their memorial from (among) the children of men: only that the wrath of the enemy would be condensed,[4] and the adversary make himself great, and would say: Our hand hath prevailed, and all this is not from the Lord. For they are a people that letteth counsel go, and there is no understanding in them. O that they were wise, that they had understanding in this, and would consider what will be in their end! How would one pursue a thousand, and two put ten thousand to flight, unless the Mighty One had delivered them up, and the Lord had requited them!

For their strength is not as our Strength, and our enemies are the judges. For as the punishment of the people of Sedom will their punishment be, and their stroke like (that) of the people of Amorah; their plagues will be evil as the heads of serpents, and the retribution of their works like their venom. As the poison of dragons is the cup of their punishment, and as the heads of the cruel basilisks. Are not all their

----

* Or, "gathered together."

works manifest before Me, laid up in My treasures
against the day of judgment? Their punishment is
before Me, and I will repay; in the time of their dispersion from their land; for the day of their ruin draweth
near, and that which is prepared for them maketh haste.

For the Lord shall decide the judgment of His people,
and the avengement of His righteous servants shall be
avenged; for it is seen before Him, that in the time
when the stroke of their enemies would prevail against
them, they will be wavering (as those who) are forsaken.
And He will say: Where are their idols, the mighty
things in which they had trusted, which did eat the fat of
their sacrifices, and drink the wine of their libations?
Let them now rise up and help you, let them be a shield
over you.   See, now, that I, even I, am He, and there is
no God beside Me.   I kill and make alive, I wound
but also heal, and there is none who can deliver out of
My hand.   For I have prepared in the heavens the
abode of My Shekinah, and have said, I live for evermore.   When My sword is revealed like the sight of
twofold lightning from one end of the heavens to
another, and My hand taketh hold on judgment, I will
render vengeance on My enemies, and My adversaries
will I repay; I will make My arrows drunk with blood,
and My sword shall slay the peoples, that by the blood
of the slain, and the captives, I may take the crowns from
the head of the foe and the enemy.

Give praise, ye Gentiles, with His people, because
the avengement of His righteous servants will have been
made; for He will bring retribution on them who hate
Him, and will show mercy unto His land and His
people.

And Mosheh came and spake all the words of this
hymn before the people, he and Jehoshua bar Nun.
And Mosheh concluded to speak all these words with

all Israel, and said to them, Set your heart upon all
the words that I have witnessed to you this day, that
you may instruct your children to observe and perform
all the words of this law. For the word is not (given)
in vain to you ; it is your life, and by this word will
you prolong your days upon the land which you pass
over Jordan to inherit.

And the Lord spake with Mosheh the same day,
saying : Go up to this mountain of Abaraee, the mountain of Nebo, which is in the land of Moab, over against
Jericho, and see the land of Kenaan which I have given
to the sons of Israel for possession ; and, dying on the
mountain to which thou goest up, thou shalt be
gathered to thy people, as Aharon thy brother died on
Mount Hor, and was gathered to his people ; because
thou wast perverse with My Word in the midst of the
children of Israel, at the Waters of Contradiction, at
Rekem, in the desert of Zin, and because thou didst not
sanctify Me among the children of Israel. For, though
thou mayest see the land, yet from thence thou shalt
not go in unto the land which I have given to the
children of Israel.

XXXIII. And this is the benediction wherewith
Mosheh, the prophet of the Lord, blessed the children
of Israel before his death ; and he said :

The Lord was revealed from Sinai, and the brightness of His glory appeared to us from Seir. He was
revealed in His power upon the mountain of Pharan,
and with Him were ten thousand saints ; He gave us,
written with His own right hand, the law from the
midst of the fire.

He loved the tribes, all the holy ones of the house of
Israel ; with power He led them out of Mizraim, and
they were conducted under Thy Cloud, they journeyed
by Thy Word.

Mosheh gave to us the law, and delivered it an inheritance to the congregation of Jakob. And he was the king in Israel, when the heads of the people were gathered with the tribes of Israel.

Let Reuben live in life eternal, and not die the second death; and let his children receive their inheritance according to their numbers.

And of Jehudah he said this: Hear, O Lord, the prayer of Jehudah when he goeth forth to battle, and let him return to his people in peace; let his hands do vengeance upon his enemies, and be Thou to him a help against his foes.

And of Levi he said: With perfections and lights [4] clothe Thou the man who is found holy before Thee; whom Thou didst try in the temptation, and he was upright, and whom Thou didst prove at the Waters of Contention, and he was faithful. Who, when they had sinned, had no mercy in the judgment upon his father or his mother, and no respect to his brother or his children; for they have kept the charge of Thy word, and Thy covenant have they not altered. These are worthy to teach Thy judgments unto Jakob, and Thy law unto Israel. They shall set the sweet incense before Thee, and the full free will offerings upon Thy altar. Bless, Lord, his substance, and the oblation of his hands receive Thou with favour; break the loins of his enemies and of his adversaries, that they may not arise.

Of Benjamin he said: The beloved of the Lord shall dwell in safety by Him: the shield will be over him all the days, and the Shekinah will dwell in his land.

And of Joseph he said: Blessed be his land from before the Lord; let it make fruit [5] by the dew of the

---

[4] *Tummaia ve-uraia.*   [5] *Magdanin,* " rich fruit."

heavens from above, and from the fountain springs, and
the depths which flow from the abysses of the earth
beneath, let it make fruit and produce which the sun
causeth to grow; let it make fruit from the beginning
of month after month; and first fruits from the mountain tops, and goodly things from the unfailing hills,
with the good of the earth and its fulness, and the
favour of Him whose glory is in the heavens, and
who was revealed unto Mosheh at the Bush: let
all these come upon the head of Joseph, and upon
the man who was separated from his brethren. The
greatness of his children will be his beauty, and
the mighty works wrought for him from before the
Omnipotent and the Most High, by whose strength
he will slay nations together unto the ends of the
earth; and these are the myriads of the house of
Ephraim, and these are the thousands of the house of
Menasheh.

And unto Zebulon he said: Rejoice, Zebulon, when
thou goest out to war against thy adversaries, and thou,
Issakar, when thou goest to compute the time of the
festivals in Jerusalem. They shall assemble the tribes
of Israel at the mountain of the sanctuary, to offer there
the holy sacrifices with free will; for they will eat the
victims of the Gentiles, and the treasures hidden in the
sand shall be disclosed for them.

And of Gad he said: Blessed is He who enlargeth
Gad. He dwelleth as a lioness; he will kill sultans with
kings: and he shall receive his own at the beginning:
for there, in his inheritance, Mosheh the scribe-prince of
Israel is (to be) buried; he who came out and went
in at the head of the people, who hath wrought
righteousness before the Lord and His judgments with
Israel.

And of Dan he said: Dan is strong as a lion's whelp;

his land is watered by the streams that flow from Mathnan.

And of Naphtali he said: Naphtali, satisfied with favour and full of blessings from the Lord, shall inherit from the western sea, Genesar, unto the south.

And of Asher he said: Blessed shall be Asher with the blessings of children: let him be acceptable to his brethren, and be nourished with the dainties of kings: strong shalt thou[6] be as iron and brass, and as the days of thy youth shall be thy strength.

There is no God like the God of Israel, whose Shekinah in the skies is thy help, and whose power is in the heaven of heavens. The habitation of Eloha is from eternity, and the world was made by His Word; and He will drive out thy enemies from before thee, and will say, Destroy.

And Israel shall dwell securely by themselves, according to the benediction with which Jakob their father blessed them in the land producing corn and wine; the heavens also above them shall drop down with dew.

Happy art thou, Israel; none is like unto thee, a people whose salvation is from the Lord, who is the strength of thy help, and from whom is the might of thy victory: thy enemies shall be liars unto thee, and thou shalt tread upon the necks of their kings.

XXXIV. And Mosheh went up from the plains of Moab to the mountains of Nebo, to the summit of the height which is over against Jericho; and the Lord showed him all the land of Gilead unto Dan, and all Naphtali, and the land of Ephraim and Menasheh, and all the land of Jehudah to the hinder sea, and the south, and the country of the plain of Jericho, the city of palm trees, unto Zoar.

And the Lord said to him, This is the land which I

---

[6] Some copies, "Strong shall be thy dwelling, or seat," *mothabaka*.

covenanted unto Abraham, Izhak, and Jakob, saying, To thy children will I give it; thou hast seen it with thine eyes, but unto it thou art not to pass over.

And Mosheh the servant of the Lord died there, in the land of Moab, by the Word of the Lord.

And He buried him in a valley (or cavity, *becheltha*) in the land of Moab, over against Bethpeor: but no man knoweth his sepulchre unto this day.

And Mosheh was a son of a hundred and twenty years when he died: his eye had not dimmed, neither was the radiance of his face changed.

And the children of Israel wept for Mosheh in the fields of Moab thirty days; and the days of the mourning for Mosheh were completed.

And Jehoshua bar Nun was filled with the spirit of wisdom; for Mosheh had laid his hands upon him, and the children of Israel obeyed him, and did as the Lord had commanded (by) Mosheh.

But no prophet hath arisen in Israel like unto Mosheh, unto whom the Lord revealed Himself face to face, in all the signs and wonders which the Lord sent him to perform in the land of Mizraim upon Pharoh, and on all his servants, and on all his land, and all the Mighty Hand, and all the great manifestations which Mosheh wrought in the eyes of all Israel.

END OF THE TARGUM OF ONKELOS
ON THE TORAH.

THE PALESTINIAN TARGUM

SEPHER HADDEBARIM,

DEUTERONOMY.

SECTION OF THE TORAH XLIV.

TITLE DEBARIM.

I. THESE are the words of admonition[1] which Mosheh spake with all Israel. He gathered them together to him while they were beyond the Jordan, and answered and said to them:

Was it not in the wilderness at the mountain of Sinai that the law was given to you? and in the plains of Moab you were made to understand how many miracles and signs the Holy One, blessed be He, had wrought for you, from the time that you passed over the border of the Weedy Sea, where He made for you a way for every one of your tribes. But you declined from His word, and wrought provocation before Him, in Pharan, on account of the words of the spies, and put together lying words against Him, and murmured about the manna which He had made to come down for you, white from the heavens; in Hazeroth you demanded flesh, and made

---

[1] Or, "reproof."

yourselves deserving to perish from the midst of the
world, but for the memory, on your behalf, of the merit
of your righteous fathers, the tabernacle of ordinance,
and the ark of the covenant, and the holy vessels which
you had covered with pure gold, and made atonement
for you on account of the sin of the golden calf. It is a
journey of eleven days (only) from Horeb by the way of
Mount Gebal unto Rekem Giah; but because you
declined and provoked the Lord to displeasure, you have
been retarded forty years.

And it was at the end of forty years, in the eleventh
month, the month of Shebat, on the first of the month,
that Mosheh spake with the sons of Israel according to
all that the Lord had given him commandment for them.

[JERUSALEM. These are the words which Mosheh
spake with all Israel, reproving them, while as yet they
were situate beyond the Jordan. Mosheh answering
said to them: Was it not in the wilderness at Mount
Sinai, that the law was given to you? and on the plains
of Moab was shown you what miracles and mighty acts
the Word of the Lord had wrought on your behalf.
When you stood by the Weedy Sea, the sea was divided
before you, and there were made twelve ways [2] of one
way, (a path) for each tribe. Yet you provoked Him at
the sea, and rebelled at the Sea of Suph. On account
of the matter of the spies who had been sent from the
wilderness of Pharan, the decree (came forth) against
you, that you should not enter into the land of Israel;
and for that of the manna, of which you said, Our soul
is afflicted with this bread, whose eating is too light, the
serpents were let loose upon you; and in Hazeroth,
where your carcasses fell on account of the flesh, and
concerning the calf that you had made, He would have
spoken in His Word to destroy you, had He not been

---

[2] Or, "streets."

mindful of the covenant which He sware to your fathers,
Abraham, Izhak, and Jakob, and of the tabernacle of
ordinance which you had made unto His name, and the
ark of the covenant of the Lord, and of your burnt
sacrifices in the midst (of the tabernacle and the ark)
which you covered with purified gold. A journey of
eleven days is it from Mount Horeb by way of Mount
Gebal unto Rekem Giah; yet, because you sinned and
provoked anger before Him, you have been delayed, and
have been journeying for forty years. And it was at the
end of forty years.]

After He had smitten Sihon king of the Amorites,
who dwelt in Heshbon, and Og the king of Mathnan,
who dwelt at Astarvata in Edrehath, beyond Jordan, in
the land of Moab, began Mosheh to speak the words of
this law, saying: The Lord our God spake with us (and
not I, of my own mind) in Horeb, saying: It is enough
for you, and hath been profitable for you until this time
(during) which you have received the law, and have
made the tabernacle and its vessels, and appointed your
princes over you; but now it would be evil for you to
tarry longer at this mount. Turn you, and journey to
Arad and Hormah, and go up to the mountain of the
Amorites; and to the dwelling-places of Ammon, Moab,
and Gebala, in the plains of the forests, in mountain
and valley, and by the south on the shore of the sea,
Ashkelon and Kiserin, the land of the Kenaamite unto
Kaldohi, and Lebanon, the place of the mountain of the
sanctuary, to the great river, the River Phrat. See, I
have given up the inhabitants of the land before you;
nor shall it be needful to carry arms; go in and possess
the land, and appoint the allotters, and divide it, even as
the Lord sware to your fathers, to Abraham, Izhak, and
Jakob, that He would give it unto them and their sons
after them.

And I spake to you at that time, saying: We will not leave you with but one judge, for I am not able to bear you alone. The Word of the Lord our God hath multiplied you; and, behold, you are to-day as the stars of heaven for multitude. The Lord God of your fathers increase you a thousand fold on account of this my benediction, and bless you beyond numbering, as He hath said unto you. But how can I alone sustain the labour, your sensuality, your evil thoughts, your words of strife, your offering one shekel for two? Present, then, from among you wise men, prudent in their thinking, men of wisdom, by your tribes, and I will appoint them to be chiefs over you. And you answered me and said: The thing that thou hast spoken it is right for us to do. So I took the chiefs of your tribes, and moved them kindly with words; wise men, masters of knowledge, but prudent in their thoughts, I found not;[3] and I appointed them chiefs over you, rabbans of thousands, of hundreds, of fifties; twelve thousand rabbans of tens, six myriads, officers of your tribes. And I charged your judges at that time with the orders of judgments, saying: So hear your brethren that one may not (be permitted to) speak all his words, while another is compelled to cut his words short; and so hearken to their words, as that it may be impossible for you not to judge them, and deliver judgment in truth, and to resolve (a matter) completely between a man and his brother, and between him who hireth words of litigation. You shall not have respect to persons in a judgment; you shall hear little words as well as great ones, nor be afraid before the rich man and the ruler; for a judgment is from before the Lord, and He seeth every secret. But the thing that is too hard for you bring to me, and I will hear it. And at that time

[3] *Lo ashkachith.*

I taught you all the Ten Words which you are to prac-
tise about judgments of money, and judgments of life.

And we journeyed from Horeb, and came through all
that great and fearful desert, where you saw serpents
like boughs, and loathsome scorpions darting at you like
arrows, on the way of the mountain of the Amoraah, as
the Lord our God had commanded us, and came to
Rekem Giah. And I said to you, Ye are come to the
mountain of the Amoraah, which the Lord our God will
give to us. Behold, the Lord our God hath given you
the land; arise and possess it, as the Lord your God hath
told you; fear not, nor be dismayed (broken). And all
of you came to me in a body, and said, We will send
men before us to examine the land for us, and bring us
back word by what way we shall go up to it, and the
cities we should enter. And the thing was proper in my
eyes; and I took from you twelve chosen men, one man
for a tribe, and they turned and went up into the mountain, and came to the stream of Ethkela, and explored
it. [JERUSALEM. And they prepared and went up into
the mountain, and came to the stream of the Grapes, and
surveyed it.] And they took in their hands of the produce
of the land and brought to us. And they returned us
word; and Kaleb and Jehoshua said, The land which the
Lord our God hath given us is good. But you were not
willing to go up, but believed the words of the ten
wicked ones, and rebelled against the Word of the Lord
your God. And you cried in your tents, taking your
sons and your daughters to your breasts, saying, Woe to
you, ye stricken ones! to-morrow ye will be slain. Why
hath the Lord hated us, to have brought us out of the
land of Mizraim, to deliver us into the hand of the
Amorites to destroy us? How shall we go up? Our
brethren have dissolved our hearts, saying, The people
are greater and mightier than we; their cities are vast,

and walled to the height of heaven, and we saw there
also the sons of Ephron the giant.

And I said to you, Be not broken down, nor be afraid
of them : the Word of the Lord your God who goeth
before you will Himself fight for you, according to all
that He did for you in Mizraim before your eyes.   And
in the desert, where thou sawest burning serpents full of
deadly venom, the Lord thy God bare thee with the
glorious clouds of His Shekinah, as a man carrieth his
child, all the way that you went, until you have come to
this place.   But in this thing you believed not in the
Word of the Lord your God, who led before you in the
way[3] to prepare for you the place of your encampments,
in the pillar of fire by night to light you in the way you
should go, and in the pillar of the cloud by day.   And
the voice of your words was heard before the Lord, and
He was displeased, and did make oath, saying, If any one
of the men of this evil generation shall see the good land
which I covenanted to give unto their fathers, except
Kaleb bar Jephunneh, who shall see it, and to whom I
will give the good land, the land of Hebron through
which he walked, and to his children, because he hath
followed with integrity the fear of the Lord.   Against
me also was there displeasure before the Lord on your
account, saying, Thou too art not to go in thither ;
Jehoshua bar Nun, who ministereth in thy house of
instruction, he is to go in thither : strengthen him, for
he is to make Israel possess it.   But your little ones, of
whom you said, They will be for prey, and your children,
who as yet know not between good and evil, they shall
go in thither : I will give it to them, and they shall
possess it for an inheritance.   As for you, turn, and go
(back) into the wilderness by the way of the Weedy Sea.
Then answered you, and said to me, We have sinned

[3] Compare Glossary, p. 16.

before the Lord; we will go up and fight, according to all that the Lord our God commanded us. And you girded on every man his arms, and began to ascend the mountain. But the Lord said to me, Say to them, Go not up, nor prepare for battle, for My Shekinah goeth not among you; that you be not crushed before your enemies. And I spake with you, but you would not obey, but were rebellious against the Word of the Lord, and did wickedly, and went up to the mountain. And the Amoraah who dwelt in that mountain came out to meet you, and pursued you, as they drive away and destroy hornets, and smote you from Gebal unto Hormah. [JERUSALEM. And they chased you as bees are chased, and slew you in Gebal unto destruction.] And you returned, and wept before the Lord: but the Lord would not receive your prayers, nor hearken to your words. So you abode in Rekem many days, according to the days that you abode.

II. And turning we journeyed into the wilderness, by the way of the Sea of Suph, as the Lord had bidden me, and we compassed Mount Gebal many days. And the Lord spake to me, saying: It is enough for you to have dwelt about this mountain: turn you to the north, and command the people, saying, You are to pass by the border of your brethren, the children of Esau, who dwell in Gebala, and they will be afraid of you; be very heedful therefore; provoke them not; for of their land I have not given you as much as the sole of the foot; for I have given Mount Gebal an inheritance unto Esau on account of the honour which he did unto his father. You shall buy fresh provision of them for silver, that you may eat, and water shall you buy with silver, to drink. Be careful that you vex them not: for the Lord your God hath blessed you in all the works of your hands, he hath supplied your wants in thy journeying in the great wilderness; these forty years hath the Word of the Lord your God been your helper; you have not wanted anything.

So we passed by our brethren the sons of Esau, who dwell in Gebala, from Elath and the fortress of Tarnegola, and turned and went by the way of the wilderness of Moab. [JERUSALEM. So we passed by our brethren the sons of Esau, who dwell in Gebala, by the way of the plain from Elath and from the fortress of Tarnegola, and we turned and went by the way of the wilderness of Moab.] And the Lord spake to me, saying: Thou shalt not aggrieve the Moabaee, nor make war against them; for I have not given you their land to inherit, because I have given Lachaiath for a possession to the children of Lot. The Emthanaia dwelt in it of old, a people great and many, and mighty as the giants. The giants[4] who dwelt in the plain of Geyonbere were also reputed as the giants who perished in the Flood; but the Moabites called them Emethanee.[5] And in Gebala dwelt the Genosaia in old times, and the Beni Esau drave them out and destroyed them, and dwelt in their place; as did Israel in the land of their inheritance, which the Lord gave to them. Now arise, and pass over the stream of Tarvaja. And we crossed the stream of Tarvaja. And the days in which (from the time) we came from Rekem Giah till we crossed the stream of Tarvaja, were thirty and eight years, until all the generation of the men of war were wasted out from the camp, as the Lord had sworn to them. But a plague also from the Lord had scourged them to consume them from the host, until they were brought to an end.

And when all the men of war, the makers of the high places, were consumed by dying out of the host, the Lord spake with me, saying: You are this day to pass

---

[4] *Gibbaraia* Heb., *Rephaim.*   [5] Or, *Emthanee,* "Formidable."

the border of Moab towards Lechaiath. But coming
near over against the children of Ammou, you are not
to vex, nor provoke them to war; for I have not given
you the land of the Beni Ammon for a possession : I
have given it an inheritance to the children of Lot, for
the sake of Abraham's righteousness. That also was
accounted a land of giants; in old time the giants
dwelt in it, and the Ammonites called them Zimthanee,
a people great and mighty as giants : but the Word of
the Lord destroyed them, and drave them out before
them, and they dwelt in their place ; as He did for the
Beni Esau who dwell in Seir : for He destroyed the
Horaee before them, and drave them out, and they
dwell in their place to this day. And the rest of the
escaped of the Kenaanah which dwelt in the cities of
Dephia to Gaza, the Kapotkaee who came out of Kapot-
kaia destroyed them, and dwelt in their place. Arise,
take your journey, and pass over the river Arnona ;
behold, I have delivered into your hands Sihon the
king of Heshbon and the Amoraah, and his land :
begin to drive them out, and to provoke him to wage
war. To-day I will begin to put thy terror and fear
upon the faces of all the peoples which are under the
whole heavens, who shall hear the report of thy virtue,
that the sun and moon have stood still, and have ceased
from speaking (their) song for the space of a day and a
half, standing still in their habitation until thou hadst
done battle with Sihon ; and they will shiver and tremble
before thee.

And I sent messengers from Nehardea, which is by
the wilderness of Kedemoth, to Sihon king of the
Amorites, with words of peace, saying, I would pass
through thy land ; by the way which is the beaten road
will I go ; I will not turn aside to do thee harm on the
right hand or the left. I will buy fresh provision with

silver, to eat, and thou shalt give me water for silver,
to drink; I will only pass through : as the Beni Esau,
who dwell in Gebal, and the Moabaee, who dwell in
Lechaiath, have done to me, until the time that I pass
over the Jordan into the land which the Lord our God
giveth us. But Sihon the king of Heshbon was not
willing to allow us to pass through his borders; for the
Lord our God had hardened the form of his spirit, and
made his heart obstinate, to deliver him into thy hand
as at this day. And the Lord said to me, See, within
the space of a sun and a moon I have begun to deliver
Sihon and his country into thy hand, begin thou to
cast him out, to inherit his land.

And Sihon came out to meet us, he and all his people,
to do battle at Jehaz. And the Lord our God delivered
him up before us, and we smote him, and his children,
and all his people. And we subdued all his cities at
that time, and destroyed all the towns, the men, women,
and children, we left none to escape; only the cattle
took we for prey, and the spoil of the towns which we
subdued. From Aroer, on the bank of the river Arnona,
and the city which is built in the midst of the river,
even unto Gilead, there was no city too strong for us,
the Lord our God gave all of them up before us. Only
to the land of the children of Ammon we went not
nigh, nor to any place on the river Jobeka, nor to the
cities of the mountain, according to all that the Lord
our God had commanded us.

III. And turning, we went up by the way of Mathnan :
and Og the king of Mathnan came out to meet us, he
and all his people, to give battle in Edrehath. And the
Lord said to me, Fear him not; for into thy hand I
have delivered him, and all his people, and his land;
and thou shalt do to him as thou hast done to Sihon
king of the Amoraah, who dwelt in Heshbon. [JERU-

SALEM. When Mosheh saw that wicked one, he trembled
before him, and said, Is not this he who did scoff at our
father Abraham and Sarah, and said to them, Ye are
like trees planted by a fountain of water, but ye bear no
fruit ?   Therefore did the Holy One, blessed be He, and
let His Name be glorified, cause him to wait, and prolong him many years alive, to show to him the generations,
because He would deliver him into the hands of his
(Abraham's) children : therefore the Word of the Lord
said to Mosheh, Be not afraid of him, for into thy hand
have I given him up, and all his people, and his land,
and thou shalt do to him as thou hast done to Sihon
king of the Amoraee, who dwelt in Heshbon.]   And
the Lord our God gave up into our hands Og the king
of Mathnan, and all his people ; and we smote him till
no remnant remained to him.   And we subdued all his
cities at that time, there was no city which we took not
from them, sixty cities, the whole boundary of Targona,[6]
the kingdom of Og in Mathnan.   All these cities were
fortified, surrounded with high walls, shut up with gates
and bars ; besides open towns very many.   [JERU-
SALEM. All these cities were fortified, surrounded with
high walls, with gates and bars.]   And we utterly
destroyed their cities : as we did to Sihon king of
Heshbon, so destroyed we with every city the men,
women, and children.   But all the cattle, and the prey
of the cities, we made a spoil for ourselves.   And at
that time we took from the power of the two kings of
the Amorites the land beyond the Jordan, from the
streams of Arnona unto Mount Hermon.   The Sidonaee
call Hermon the fruit-producing Mount,[7] but the
Amoraee call it the Snowy Mountain,[8] because the snow

---

[6] Trachonitis, from τραχύς, "rough or rocky"

[7] Or, "the mount whose productions are fruits."

[8] *Tor Talga.* So the present Arab name, *Jebel Thelj.*

never ceases from it either in summer or winter. [JE-
RUSALEM. The Sidonaee call Hermon the fruit-producing
land, but the Amoraee call it the land which multiplies
the fruits of the tree.] All the cities of the plain, and
all Gilead, and all Mathnan, unto Selukia and Edrehi,
cities of the kingdom of Og in Mathnan. For only Og
king of Mathnan remained of the remnant of the giants
who perished in the deluge. Behold, his bedstead was a
bedstead of iron; behold, it is placed in the archive-house
in Rabbath, of the Beni Ammon, nine cubits its length,
and four cubits its breadth, in the cubit of his own
(stature). [JERUSALEM. Is it not placed in the citadel
of the Beni Ammon?] And this land which we took in
possession at that time, from Aroer unto the border of
the river, and half of Mount Gilead, and the cities, I
have given to the tribe of Reuben and Gad; but the
remaining part of Gilead, and all Mathnan, the kingdom of Og, I have given to the half tribe of Menasheh;
all the limit of the region of Targona, and all Mathnan,
which is called the land of the giants.

And Jair bar Menasheh took the whole limit of the
region of Targona, unto the limit of Korze and Anti-
kiros, [JERUSALEM. All the limit of Atarkona, unto
the limit of the city of Aphikeras,] and called them by
his own name Mathnan, the towns of Jair, unto this
day. But I gave Gilead to Makir. To the tribe
Reuben and the tribe Gad have I given from Gilead to
the river Arnona, half of the valley and its limit, unto
the stream of Jubeka on the limit of the children of
Ammon, the plain also, the Jordan, the boundary from
Genesar to the sea of the plain, and the city of Tebaria,
which is by the Sea of Salt, the limit of the outflow of
waters from the heights of the east. [JERUSALEM. The
plain, the Jordan, and the limit from Ginosar to the
sea of the plain, the Sea of Salt, under the place of the

pouring forth of ashes from the east.] And I commanded you, the tribe of Reuben, and of Gad, and the
half tribe of Menasheh, at that time, saying : The Lord
your God hath given this land to you to possess it; but
you are to go over armed before your brethren, every
one girded for the host. Only your wives, your children,
and your cattle, (for I know that you have much cattle,)
shall abide in your cities which I have given you, until
the time when the Lord will have given rest to your
brethren as to you, that they also may possess that land
which the Lord your God hath conferred upon you;
then shall you return every one to his inheritance which
I have given you.

And I instructed Jehoshua at that time, saying :
Thine eyes have seen all that the Lord thy God hath
done to these two kings; so will the Lord do unto all
the kingdoms to which thou art passing over. Fear
them not, for the Word of the Lord your God fighteth
for you.

SECTION XLV.

VAETHCHANAN.

AND I sought mercy at that time from before the Lord,
saying : I supplicate compassion before Thee, O Lord
God : Thou hast begun to show unto Thy servant Thy
greatness, and the power of Thy mighty hand; for Thou
art God, and there is none beside Thee; for Thy glory
dwelleth in the heavens on high, and Thou rulest upon
the earth; there is none who can work according to Thy
working or Thy power. [JERUSALEM. And I prayed
and sought mercy in that hour, said Mosheh, saying :

I supplicate compassion before Thee, O Lord God;
Thou hast begun.]   Let me, I pray, pass over and see
the good land that is beyond Jordan, that goodly mountain on which is builded the city of Jerusalem, and
Mount Lebanon, where the Shekinah will dwell.   But
the Lord was displeased with me on your account, and
received not my prayer; but the Lord said to me · Let
it be enough for thee; speak not before Me again of
this matter: go up to the head of the mountain, and lift
up thine eyes to the west, to the north, to the south,
and to the east, and behold with thy eyes, for thou shalt
not pass over this Jordan.   But instruct Jehoshua,
strengthen and confirm him; for he shall go over before
this people, and give them the inheritance of the land
which thou seest.   And we dwelt in the valley, weeping
for our sins, because we had been joined with the
worshippers of the idol of Peor. [JERUSALEM.   And we
dwelt in the valley weeping for our guilt, and confessing
our sins, for that we had been joined with the worshippers
of the idol of Baal Peor.]

IV. And now, Israel, hear the statutes and judgments
which I teach you to do, that you may live, and go in
and inherit the land the Lord God of your fathers giveth
you.   Ye shall not add to the words that I teach you
nor diminish them, but keep the commandments of the
Lord your God which I command you.

Your eyes have seen what the Word of the Lord hath
done to the worshippers of the idol Peor: for all the
men who went astray after the idol Peor, the Lord thy
God hath destroyed from among you; but you who have
cleaved to the worship of the Lord your God are alive
all of you this day.   See, I teach you statutes and
judgments, as the Lord God hath taught me, that you
may so do in the land which you are entering to possess
it.   So shall you observe and perform the law; for it is

your wisdom and understanding in the sight of the peoples, who will hear all these statutes, and will say : How wise and intelligent is this great people ! For what people so great, to whom the Lord is so high in the Name of the Word of the Lord ?   But the custom of (other) nations is to carry their gods upon their shoulders, that they may seem to be nigh them ; but they cannot hear with their ears, (be they nigh or) be they afar off ; but the Word of the Lord sitteth upon His throne high and lifted up, and heareth our prayer what time we pray before Him and make our petitions. [JERUSALEM. For what people is so great, who hath God so nigh to it as the Lord our God is, in every hour that we cry unto Him, and He answereth us ?]   And what people have statutes and right judgments according to all this law which I order before you this day ? Only take heed to yourselves and diligently keep your souls, lest you forget the things which you beheld with your eyes at Sinai, and that they depart not from thy heart all the days of thy life, and you may teach them to your children, and to your children's children ; and that you may make yourselves pure in your transactions thereby, as in the day when you stood before the Lord your God at Horeb, at the time when the Lord said to me : Gather the people before Me, that they may hear My words, by which they shall learn to fear before Me all the days that they remain upon the earth, and may teach their children.   And you drew near, and stood at the lower part of the mount, and the mountain burned with fire, and its flame went up to the height of the heavens, with darkness, clouds, and shadows. And the Lord spake with you on the mountain from the midst of the fire : you heard the voice of the word, but you saw no like-ness, but only a voice speaking. And He proclaimed to you His covenant which He commanded you to per-

form; Ten Words which He wrote upon sapphire
tablets.

And the Lord commanded me at that time to teach
you the statutes and judgments, that you may do them
in the land which you pass over to possess.   Keep then
your souls diligently; for you saw no likeness on the day
when the Lord spake with you in Horeb from the midst
of the fire. Be admonished, lest you corrupt your
works, and make to you an image or likeness of any
idol, the likeness either male or female of any beast
of the earth, of any winged bird that flieth in the
air in the expanse of heaven, of any reptile on the
ground, or of any fish in the waters under the earth.
[JERUSALEM.   The likeness of any fishes which are in
the waters under the earth.]   And lest, when you lift
up your eyes to the height of the heavens, and gaze at
the sun, or the moon, and the principal stars of all the
hosts of the heavens, you go astray, and adore and serve
them; for the Lord your God hath by them distributed
(or divided) the knowledge of all the peoples that are
under the whole heavens.[9]   For you hath the Word of
the Lord taken for His portion, and hath brought you
out from the iron furnace of Mizraim to be unto Him a
people of inheritance as at this day.   [JERUSALEM.   To
be a people beloved as a treasure in this day.]

But against me was displeasure before the Lord on
account of your words, because you had murmured for
the water; and He sware that I should not pass the
Jordan, nor go into the land which the Lord your God
giveth you to inherit.   But I must die in this land; I
am not to pass over Jordan; but you will pass over and
possess the inheritance of that good land.   Beware, then,

---

[9] That is, according to some Jewish commentators, He has revealed
Himself to the Gentiles *mediately*, by the display of His works, but to
Israel *immediately* by His Word   Compare the next clause.

that you forget not the covenant of the Lord your God
which He hath confirmed with you, or make to you an
image, the likeness of any thing of which the Lord your
God hath commanded that you should not make it.
For the Word of the Lord your God is a consuming
fire; the jealous God is a fire, and He avengeth Himself in jealousy. [JERUSALEM. For the Lord your God
is a consuming fire; the jealous God is a fire, and He
avengeth Himself in jealousy.]

If, when thou wilt have begotten children and children's children, and wilt have grown old in the land,
you corrupt your works, and make to you an image or
any likeness, and do that which is evil before the Lord
to provoke Him; I attest against you this day the
sworn witnesses of the heavens and the earth, that
perishing you will perish swiftly from the land to
possess which you pass the Jordan: you will not
lengthen out days upon it, but will be utterly destroyed.
And the Lord will scatter you among the Gentiles, and
you will remain as a little people with the nations among
whom the Lord will disperse you in captivity. And
there will you be constrained to serve the worshippers of
idols, the work of men's hands, of wood and stone,
which see not, nor hear, nor eat, nor smell. But if
there you seek to return to the fear of the Lord your
God, you shall find mercy, when you seek before Him with
all your heart and with all your soul. When you suffer
oppression, and all these things come upon you in the
end of the days, and you be converted to the fear of the
Lord your God, and obey His Word; for the Lord our
God is a merciful God; He will not forsake you, nor
destroy you, nor forget the covenant of your fathers
which He sware unto them.

For ask now the generations which have been from the
days of the beginning, which have been before thee from

the day when the Lord created man upon the earth, from
one end of the heavens to the other, whether so great a
thing as this hath been, or any like to it hath been
heard?   Hath it ever been that a people should hear
the voice of the Word of the Lord, the Living God,
speaking from the midst of fire, as you heard, and
remained alive?   Or, as the wonder which the Lord
hath wrought, revealing Himself to separate a people to
Himself from among another people, by signs, by
miracles, by portents, by the victories of ordered battles,
by an uplifted arm, and by great visions, like all that
the Lord our God hath done for us in Mizraim, and
your eyes beholding?   [JERUSALEM. Or what is the
people or kingdom that hath heard?...... Or the signs
which the Word of the Lord hath wrought, coming to
announce (that He would separate) to Himself a people
from among a people?]   Unto thee have these wonders
been shown, that thou mayest know that the Lord is
God, and there is none beside Him.   He made you
hear the voice of His Word from the heavens on high,
to give you discipline by His doctrine, and showed thee
upon earth His great fire, and made thee hear His words
from the midst of the flame.   And because He loved
thy fathers Abraham and Izhak, therefore hath He pleasure in the children of Jakob after him, and hath
brought you in His lovingkindness and power from
Mizraim, to drive out nations greater and stronger than
you from before you, and give you their land to inherit
as at this day.   Know therefore to-day, and set your
heart upon it, that the Lord is God, whose Shekinah
dwelleth in the heavens above, and reigneth on the
earth beneath, neither is there any other beside Him.
Therefore observe His covenant, and the commandments
which I command you this day, that He may do good
to you and to your children after you, and that you

may have continuance upon the land which the Lord
your God giveth you for all days.

And now, behold, Mosheh set apart three cities
beyond the Jordan toward the sunrise, that the manslayer who had killed his neighbour without intention,
not having hated him yesterday or before, may flee,
and escape into one of those cities, and be spared alive.
[JERUSALEM. Who had slain his neighbour unawares,[1]
but had not entertained enmity toward him yesterday or
before.]   Kevatirin in the wilderness, in the plain
country, for the tribe of Reuben, and Ramatha in Gilead
for the tribe of Gad, and Dabera in Mathnan for the
tribe of Menasheh. This is the declaration of the law
which Mosheh set in order before the sons of Israel,
[JERUSALEM. This is the declaration of the law which
Mosheh set before the sons of Israel,] and the statutes
and judgments which Mosheh spake with the sons of
Israel at the time when they had come out of Mizraim.
And Mosheh delivered them beyond Jordan over against
Beth Peor, in the land of Sihon king of the Amoraee,
who dwelt in Heshbon, whom Mosheh and the sons of
Israel smote when they had come out of Mizraim. And
they took possession of his land and the land of Og
king of Mathnan, the two kings of the Amoraee, who
were beyond the Jordan, eastward, from Aroer on the
bank of the river Arnon to the mountain of Saion, which
is the Snowy Mount ; [JERUSALEM. From Lechaiath,
on the side of the river Arnona, unto the mountain whose
fruits are delivered, which is the Snowy Mount ;] and
all the plain beyond Jordan, eastward, unto the sea that
is in the plain under the spring of the heights.

V. And Mosheh called all Israel, and said to them :
Hear, Israel, the statutes and judgments that I speak
before you this day, to learn them, and observe to per-

---

[1] *Beketuph*, " by, or over, the shoulder."

form them. The Lord our God confirmed a covenant
with us in Horeb : not with our fathers did the Lord
confirm this covenant, but with us, who are all of us
here this day alive and abiding. Word to word did the
Lord speak with you at the mountain from the midst of
the fire. I stood between the Word of the Lord and
you at that time, to declare to you the Word of the Lord,
because you were afraid before the voice of the Word of
the Lord, which you heard from the midst of the fire ;
neither did you go up to the mountain while He said :
Sons of Israel, My people, I am the Lord your God, who
made and led you out free from the land of Mizraim,
from the house of the bondage of slaves. Sons of Israel,
My people, no other god shall you have beside Me.
You shall not make to you an image or the likeness of
anything which is in the heavens above, or in the earth
below, or in the waters under the earth : thou shalt not
worship them or do service before them ; for I am the
Lord your God, a jealous and avenging God, taking
vengeance in jealousy ; remembering the sins of wicked
fathers upon rebellious children to the third generation and to the fourth of them that hate Me, when
the children complete to sin after their fathers; but
keeping mercy and bounty for a thousand generations
of the righteous who love Me and keep My mandates
and My laws. Sons of Israel, My people, no one of you
shall swear by the Name of the Word of the Lord your
God in vain : for the Lord, in the day of the great
judgment, will not acquit any one who shall swear by
His Name in vain. Sons of Israel, My people, observe
the day of Sabbath, to sanctify it according to all that
the Lord your God hath commanded. Six days you
shall labour and do all your work, but the seventh day
(shall be for) rest and quiet before the Lord your God ;
ye shall do no work, neither you, nor your sons, nor

your daughters, nor your servants, nor your handmaids,
nor your oxen, your asses, nor any of your cattle, nor
your sojourners who are among you ; that your servants
and handmaids may have repose as well as you. And
remember that you were servants in the land of Mizraim,
and that the Lord your God delivered and led you out
with a strong hand and uplifted arm ; therefore the Lord
thy God hath commanded thee to keep the Sabbath day.
Sons of Israel, My people, be every one mindful of the
honour of his father and his mother, as the Lord your
God hath commanded you, that your days may be prolonged, and it may be well with you in the land which
the Lord your God giveth you. Sons of Israel, My
people, you shall not murder, nor be companions or par-
ticipators with those who do murder, nor shall there be
seen in the congregations of Israel (those who have part)
with murderers; that your children may not arise after
you, and teach their own (to have part) with murderers;
for because of the guilt of murder the sword cometh
forth upon the world.

Sons of Israel, My people, you shall not be adulterers,
nor companions of, or have part with, adulterers ; neither
shall there be seen in the congregations of Israel (those
who have part) with adulterers, and that your children
may not arise after you, and teach theirs also to be with
adulterers ; for through the guilt of adulteries the
plague cometh forth upon the world. Sons of Israel,
My people, you shall not be thieves, nor be companions
nor have fellowship with thieves, nor shall there be seen
in the congregations of Israel (those who have part) with
thieves ; for because of the guilt of robberies famine
cometh forth on the world. Sons of Israel, My people,
you shall not bear false witness, nor be companions or
have fellowship with the bearers of false testimony;
neither shall there be seen in the congregations of Israel

c c

those who (have part) with false witnesses; for because
of the guilt of false witnesses the clouds arise, but the
rain does not come down, and dearth cometh on the
world. Sons of Israel, My people, you shall not be
covetous, nor be companious or have fellowship with the
covetous; neither shall there be seen in the congregation.
of Israel any who (have part) with the covetous; that
your children may not arise after you, and teach their
own to be with the covetous. Nor let any one of you
desire his neighbour's wife, nor his field, nor his servant,
nor his handmaid, nor his ox, nor his ass, nor anything
that belongeth to his neighbour; for because of the guilt
of covetousness the government (*malkutha*) seizeth upon
men's property to take it away, and bondage cometh on
the world.

These words spake the Lord with all your congregation at the mount, from the midst of the fiery cloud and
tempest, with a great voice which was not limited; and
the voice of the Word was written upon two tables of
marble, and He gave them unto me. But when you had
heard the voice of the Word from the midst of the darkness, the mountain burning with fire, the chiefs of your
tribes and your sages drew nigh to me, and said, Behold,
the Word of the Lord our God hath showed us His
glorious Shekinah, and the greatness of His excellency,
(*tushbachteih*, His magnificence,) and the voice of His
Word have we heard out of the midst of the fire. This
day have we seen that the Lord speaketh with a man in
whom is the Holy Spirit, and he remaineth alive. But
now why should we die? For this great fire will devour
us; if we again hear the voice of the Word of the Lord
our God, we shall die. For who, of all the offspring of
flesh, hath heard the voice of the Word of the Living
God speaking from amid the fire as we, and hath lived?
Go thou nigh, and hear all that the Lord our God shall

say, and speak thou with us all that the Lord our God
will say to thee, and we will hearken and will do.   And
the voice of your words was heard before the Lord
when you spake with me, and the Lord said to me, All
the words of this people which they have spoken with
thee are heard before Me ; all that they have said is
good.   O that the disposition of their heart were perfect
as this willingness is to fear Me and to keep all My
commandments all days, that it may be well with them
and with their children for ever !   [JERUSALEM. O that
they may have this good heart !]   Now therefore be
separate from thy wife, that with the orders above thou
mayest stand before Me, and I will speak with thee the
commandments, statutes, and judgments, which thou
shalt teach them to perform in the land that I give you
to inherit.   And now observe to do as the Lord your
God hath commanded you ; decline not to the right
hand or to the left.   Walk in all the way which the
Lord your God commandeth you, that you may live and
do well, and lengthen out days in the land you shall
inherit.

   VI. And this is the declaration of the commandments,
the statutes, and the judgments which the Lord your
God hath commanded (me) to teach you to perform in the
land to which you pass over to inherit; that thou mayest
fear the Lord thy God, and keep all His statutes and precepts which I command thee; thou, thy son, and the son
of thy son, all the days of thy life ; and that thou mayest
prolong thy days.   Hearken then, Israel, to keep and to
do, that it may be well with thee, and you may increase
greatly, as the Lord God of thy fathers hath spoken to
thee, (that) He will give thee a land whose fruits are
rich as milk, and sweet as honey. [JERUSALEM. A land
producing good fruits, pure as milk, sweet and tasty as
honey.]

It was, when the time came that our father Jakob should be gathered out of the world, he was anxious lest there might be an idolater among his sons. He called them, and questioned them, Is there such perversity in your hearts? They answered, all of them together, and said to him: HEAR, ISRAEL OUR FATHER: THE LORD OUR GOD IS ONE LORD! Jakob made response, and said, Blessed be His Glorious Name for ever and ever. [JERUSALEM. When the end had come to our father Jakob, that he should be taken up from the world, he called the twelve tribes, his sons, and gathered them round his conch. Then Jakob our father rose up, and said to them, Do you worship any idol that Terah the father of Abraham worshipped? do you worship any idol that Laban (the brother of his mother) worshipped? or worship you the God of Jakob? The twelve tribes answered together, with fulness of heart, and said, Hear now, Israel our father: The Lord our God is one Lord. Jakob responded and said, May His Great Name be blessed for ever!]

Mosheh the prophet said to the people of the house of Israel, Follow after the true worship of your fathers, that you may love the Lord your God with each disposition of your hearts, and also that He may accept your souls, and the (dedicated) service of all your wealth; and let these words which I command you this day be written upon the tables of your hearts. And thou shalt unfold them to thy children, and meditate upon them when thou art sitting in your houses, at the time when you are occupied in secret chambers, or in journeying by the way; at evening when you lie down, and at morn when you arise. And you shall bind them as written signs upon thy left hand, and they shall be for tephillin upon thy forehead over thine eyes. And thou shalt

write them upon the pillars, and affix them in three
places, against the cupboard,[2] upon the posts of thy
house, and on the right hand of thy gate, in thy going
out.

And when the Lord thy God hath brought thee into
the land which he promised to Abraham, Izhak, and
Jakob, thy fathers, to give thee cities great and goodly
which thou didst not toil in building, houses also,
filled with all good, which thou wast not occupied in
filling, and hewn cisterns in hewing which thou didst not
labour, vineyards and olives with planting which thou
wast not wearied; and when thou hast eaten and art
satisfied, beware lest you forget the fear of the Lord
your God, who delivered and led you out free from the
land of Mizraim, from the house of the affliction of
slaves; but fear the Lord your God, and worship before
Him, and swear by the Name of the Word of the Lord
in truth.   You shall not go after the idols of the
Gentiles, the idols of the peoples who are round about
you: for the Lord our God is a jealous God, and an
Avenger, whose Shekinah dwelleth in the midst of you;
lest the anger of the Lord your God be kindled against
you, and He quickly destroy you from the face of the
earth.   Sons of Israel, my people, be warned not to
tempt the Lord your God as you tempted Him in the
ten temptations; keeping keep the commandments of
the Lord your God, and His testimonies and statutes
which He hath commanded you; and do what is good
and right before the Lord, that it may be well with you,
and ye may go in, and possess by inheritance the good
land which the Lord covenanted to your fathers; that
He may drive out all thy enemies before thee, as the
Lord hath said.

When thy son, in time to come, shall ask thee, say-

---

[2] Or, "repository," *tekey, i. e., theca.*

ing, What are the testimonies, statutes, and judgments
which the Lord our God hath commanded you? then
shall you say to your sons, We were servants to Pharoh
in Mizraim, and the Word of the Lord brought us out
of Mizraim with a mighty hand; and the Word of the
Lord wrought signs, great wonders, and sore plagues
on Mizraim and on Pharoh and all the men of his
house, which our eyes beheld; but us He led forth free
to bring us in and give us the land which He sware to
our fathers.   And the Lord commanded us to perform
all these statutes, that we may fear the Lord our God
for good to us in all days, that He may preserve us alive
as at the time of this day; and (the reward of) righteousness will be reserved for us in the world to come, if we
keep all these commandments to perform them before
the Lord our God, as He hath commanded us.

VII. When the Lord thy God shall bring thee into
the land to which thou wilt come to possess it, and He
will make many peoples to go out from before thee, the
Hittites, Girgashites, Amorites, Kenaanites, Perizites,
Hivites, and Jebusites, seven nations more numerous
and strong than thou, and the Lord your God will
deliver them up before you, then shall you blot them
out and utterly consume them by the curse of the Lord.
You shall strike no covenant with them, nor have pity
upon them.   You shall not intermarry with them; your
daughters you shall not give to their sons, nor take
their daughters for your sons; for whosoever marrieth
with them is as if he made marriage with their idols.
[JERUSALEM. You shall not be commixed with them.]
For their daughters will lead your sons away from My
worship to serve the idols of the Gentiles; so will the
anger of the Lord be kindled against you, and He will
destroy you suddenly.   But this shall you do to them:
you shall destroy their altars, break their statues in

pieces, cut down their groves for worship, and burn the images of their idols with fire. For you shall be a holy people before the Lord your God, as the Lord your God hath taken pleasure in you, that you may be a people more beloved before Him than all the peoples who are on the face of the earth. Not because you were more excellent than all other peoples hath the Lord had pleasure in you and chosen you, but because you were poor in spirit, and more humble than all the nations. Therefore, because the Lord had mercy on you, and would keep the covenant He had sworn with your fathers, He led you out free with a mighty hand, and redeemed you from the house of the affliction of slaves, from the hand of Pharoh king of Mizraim. Know therefore that the Lord your God is a Judge, strong and faithful, keeping covenant and mercy with them who love Him and keep His commandments unto a thousand generations, and who repayeth to them who hate Him the reward of their good works in this world, to destroy them (for their evil works) in the world to come; neither delayeth He (to reward) His enemies, but while they are alive in this world He payeth them their recompense. [JERUSALEM. And he repayeth them who hate Him for their little deeds of good which are in their hands in this world, to destroy them in the world to come; nor doth He delay to render to them that hate Him the reward of the slight works that are in their hands in this world.] Observe therefore the mandates, the statutes, and judgments which I command you, to perform them.

SECTION XLVI.

EKEB.

If you receive these judgments, and observe and perform them, then will the Lord your God keep with you the covenant and the lovingkindness which He sware to your fathers. And He will love, bless, and multiply you, and will bless the children of your wombs, the fruit of your ground, your corn, wine, and oil, the herds of your oxen, and the flocks of your sheep, on the land which He sware to your fathers to give you. More blessed will you be than all peoples; there shall not be among you barren men or women, nor thy cattle (be wanting) in wool, or milk, or offspring. And the Lord will put away from thee all the diseases and evil plagues that He sent upon Mizraim which thou hast known; He will not put them upon you, but will send them forth upon all your enemies. And thou shalt consume all the nations which the Lord thy God giveth up to thee; thine eye shall not spare them nor their idols, because they would be a stumbling-block to thee. Neither say in thy heart, These nations are greater and stronger than I am : how shall I be able to drive them out? Be not afraid of them; remember the work of power which the Lord thy God wrought upon Pharoh and all the Mizraee; the great miracles which thou didst see with thine eyes, the signs and wonders, the strength of the mighty hand, and the victory of the uplifted arm, when the Lord your God led you out free : so will the Lord your God do unto all the peoples before whom thou art afraid. Moreover, the Lord your God will send the plague of biting hornets among you, until they who have remained shall perish and disappear before you. Therefore be not down-broken before them, for the Shekinah of the Lord your God is among you, the Great and Fearful God.

But the Lord your God will make these nations depart from before thee by little and little. You may not destroy them at once, lest the beasts of the field multiply against you, when they have come to devour their carcases. But the Lord your God will give them up before you, and will trouble them with great trouble, until they shall be consumed. [JERUSALEM. And shall trouble them with great trouble, till the time that they shall be destroyed.] And He will deliver their kings into your hands, and you shall destroy their names from remembrance under the whole heavens : not a man shall stand before you until you have destroyed them. You shall burn their images with fire, nor desire the silver and gold that may be upon them, nor take them, lest through them you offend, for they are an abomination before the Lord your God. Neither may you bring their abominable idols or their service-vessels into your houses, that you be not accursed as they : but you shall utterly loathe them as a loathsome reptile, and abhor them altogether, because they are accursed.

VIII. Every commandment which I command you this day, observe ye to do, that you may live, and multiply, and go in and inherit the land which the Lord sware to your fathers. And remember all the way by which the Lord your God hath led you these forty years in the wilderness, to humble and try you, to know whether you will keep His commandments or not. And He humbled thee and let thee hunger, and fed thee with the manna which thou knewest not, nor thy fathers had known, that He might make thee to know that man liveth not by bread only, but by all that is created by the Word of the Lord doth man live.

[JERUSALEM. That by manna only.] Your raiment
hath not waxen old upon your bodies, and your feet
have not gone without covering these forty years. But
you know with the thoughts of your hearts, that as a man
regardeth his child, so the Lord your God hath regarded
you. Keep, therefore, the commandments of the Lord
your God, to walk in the ways that are right before
Him, and to fear Him. For the Lord your God
bringeth you into a land whose fruits are celebrated, a
land whose streams flow in clear waters, from sweet
fountain springs, and depths that dry not up, issuing
forth among the vales and mountains; a land producing
wheat and barley, and growing vines from which cometh
out wine sweet and ripe, and a land which yieldeth
figs and pomegranates, a land whose olive trees make
oil, and whose palms give honey; a land where, without poverty, you may eat bread and want nothing; a
land whose sages will enact decrees unalloyed as iron,
and whose disciples will propound questions weighty as
brass. [JERUSALEM. A land from whose olive trees
they make oil, and from whose palms they make honey
......whose stones are pure as iron, and whose hills are
firm as brass.]

Be mindful, therefore, in the time when you will have
eaten and are satisfied, that you render thanksgiving
and blessing before the Lord your God for all the fruit
of the goodly land which He hath given you, lest you
forget the fear of the Lord your God, and keep not His
commandments, His judgments, and His statutes, which
I command you this day, lest, when you shall have
eaten and are satisfied, and you have builded pleasant
houses to dwell in, and your oxen and sheep are multiplied, and silver and gold are increased to you, and all
things you have are multiplied, your heart be lifted up,
and you forget the fear of the Lord your God, who

brought you out free from the land of Mizraim, from
the house of the affliction of slaves; who led thee in
mercy through that great and fearful desert, a place
abounding in burning serpents and scorpions with
stings, a place where there is thirst but no water; but
(where) He brought thee forth water out of the hard rock,
and fed thee in the desert with manna which thy fathers
knew not, to humble thee and to prove thee, that He
may do thee good in thine end.

Beware that you say not in your heart, Our strength
and the might of our hands have obtained us all these
riches; but remember the Lord your God; for He it is
who giveth thee counsel whereby to get wealth; that
He may confirm the covenant which He sware to your
fathers at the time of this day. For it shall be that if
you forget the fear of the Lord your God, and go after
the idols of the Gentiles, to serve and worship them, I
testify against you this day, you will surely perish; as
the peoples which the Lord your God disperseth before
you, so will you perish, because you were not obedient
to the Word of the Lord your God.

IX. Hear, Israel: you are this day (about) to pass
Jordana to enter in and possess (the country of) nations
greater and stronger than you, and cities many, and
fortified to the height of heaven. A people (are they)
strong and tall as the giants whom you know, and of
whom you have heard (say), Who can stand before the
sons of the giants? Know, therefore, to-day that the
Lord your God, whose glorious Shekinah goeth before
you, whose Word is a consuming fire, will destroy them
and drive them out before you; so shall you drive them
out, and destroy them quickly, as the Lord your God hath
said to you. Speak not in your heart when the Lord
your God hath driven them away from before you,
saying, For the sake of my righteousness hath the Lord

brought me in to inherit this land; for on account of
the sins of these people the Lord driveth them out
before you. Not for your righteousness, or the integrity of your heart, will you be brought in to possess
their land, but for the sins of these people the Lord
your God driveth them away before you; and that the
Lord may establish the word which He sware to
Abraham, Izhak, and Jakob, your fathers. Know,
therefore, that it is not on account of your merit that
the Lord your God giveth you this glorious land to
possess it; for a hard-necked people are you. Be
mindful and forget not how you have provoked unto
anger before the Lord in the wilderness, from the
day that you went out of the land of Mizraim until you
came to this place, and have been perverse before the
Lord. (Even) at Horeb you provoked the Lord to
anger, so that there was wrath before the Lord against
you, to destroy you. When I had gone up to the
mountain to receive the tables of marble, the tables of
the covenant which the Lord had made with you, and I
tarried on the mountain forty days and forty nights, I
ate no bread, I drank no water; and the Lord gave to
me the two tables of marble inscribed by the finger of
the Lord, and upon which was written according to all
the words which the Lord spake with you on the mount
from the midst of the fire in the day of the assembling
of the congregation. But at the end of the forty days
and nights, when the Lord gave to me the two tables
of marble, the tables of the covenant, the Lord said
to me, Arise, go down quickly from hence, for the
people who are called by thy name, whom I led forth
from the land of Mizraim, have corrupted their way;
they have soon gone aside from the way that I commanded them on Sinai, saying, Make not to you a likeness or image; for they have made for themselves a

molten (form).' And the Lord spake to me saying,
the sin of this people is revealed before Me, and, behold,
this people is hard-necked: desist from thy prayer to
Me, that I may destroy them, and blot out their name
from under the heavens; and I will make of thee a
people stronger and greater than they.

And I prepared and went down from the mountain,
and the mountain burned with fire; and the two tables
of the covenant were upon my two hands. And I saw,
and, behold, you had sinned before the Lord your God;
you had made for you a molten calf, and had quickly
declined from the way which the Lord had commanded
to you. And taking the two tables, I cast them from
my two hands and broke them; and you looked on
while the tables were broken, and the letters fled away.[3]
[JERUSALEM. And I took both the tables and cast
them down.] But I prayed for mercy as at the first
before the Lord; forty days and forty nights I ate no
bread, nor drank water, for all your sin whereby you
had sinned in doing what was evil before the Lord to
provoke Him to anger.

At that time five destroying angels were sent from the
Lord to destroy Israel, Wrath, Burning, Relentlessness,
Destruction, and Indignation; but when Mosheh the
Rabban of Israel heard, he went and made memorial of
the great and glorious Name, and called. And Abraham,
Izhak, and Jakob arose from their tomb, and stood in
prayer before the Lord; and forthwith three of them
were restrained, and two of them, Wrath and Burning,
remained. But Mosheh (yet) supplicated mercy, and the
two were also restrained; and he digged a grave in the
land of Moab and buried them, in swearing by the great
and tremendous Name; for so it is written: For I was
afraid before the anger with which the Lord was angry

---

[3] *Vide* Palest. Targ. on Exodus xxxii.

with you to destroy you, and the Lord received my prayer at that time also.

But against Aharon was there great displeasure before the Lord, (so that) He would destroy him; but I prayed for Aharon also at that time. And your sin, the calf which you had made, I took, and burned it in fire, and crushed it well with crushing until I had bruised it into dust; and I threw the dust into the stream that descended from the mountain.

And at the place of Burning, and that of the Temptation, and at the Graves of Desire [JERUSALEM. And at the Graves of Desire] you provoked to anger before the Lord. And at the time when the Lord sent you from Rekem Giah, saying: Go up and take possession of the land which I have given you, then were you perverse with the Word of the Lord your God, and would not believe Him, nor be obedient to His Word. You have been perverse before the Lord from the day that I have known you.

And I bowed down in prayer before the Lord for the forty days and nights in which I was prostrate in supplication, because the Lord had said He was about to destroy you. And I prayed before the Lord, and said: I implore mercy before Thee, O Lord God, that Thou wouldst not destroy Thy people and Thy heritage which Thou hast redeemed by Thy power, and led forth from Mizraim by the strength of Thy mighty hand. Remember Thy servants Abraham, Izhak, and Jakob, nor regard Thou the hard heart of this people, nor their wickedness, nor their sin: lest the inhabitants of the land from whence Thou hast led us say, that power failed before the Lord to bring them into the land of which Thou hast told them, and that because Thou didst hate them, therefore didst Thou lead them out to kill them in the wilderness. But they are Thy people and Thy heritage, whom Thou didst bring out by Thy great power, and with Thy uplifted arm.

X. At that time did the Lord say to me: Hew thee two tables of marble according to the form of the first; and ascend before Me into the mountain, and make thee an ark of wood. And I will write upon the tables the words which were upon the former ones, which thou didst break with thy entire strength; and thou shalt put them within the ark. And I made an ark of sitta wood, and hewed two marble tables according to the form of the first, and went up into the mountain, having the two tables in my hand. And He wrote upon the tables according to the former writing, the Ten Words which the Lord spake with you from the mount in the midst of the fire on the day that the congregation was gathered together, and the Lord gave them to me. And I turned and came down from the mountain, and put the tables into the ark which I had made, and there are they laid up (hidden) as the Lord commanded me.

And the children of Israel journeyed from the villages of the wells of the Beni Jahakan to Mosera.[4] There Amalek, who reigned in Arad, and who had heard that Aharon was dead, and that the Cloud of Glory had gone up, (came and) fought with them. And those of Israel who were distressed by that war sought to go back into Mizraim, and returned (towards it) six journeys; (but) the sons of Levi followed after them, and slew eight families of them, and the remainder returned. Of the sons of Levi also four families were slain. And they said one to another, What hath been the cause of this slaughter? Because we have been remiss in the mourning for Aharon the Saint. Therefore all the children of Israel observed there a mourning for Aharon's death; and there was he buried, and Elazar his son ministered.

[4] Compare the Samaritan Text.

in his stead. Thence they journeyed to Gudgod, and
from Gudgod to Jotbath, a land flowing with streams
of water. At that time the Lord distinguished the
tribe of Levi, because they had been zealous (even)
to slay for His honour; that they should bear the
ark of the Lord's covenant, and stand before the Lord
to minister unto Him and to bless in His Name
until this day. Therefore the tribe of Levi hath not
a portion or inheritance with his brethren; the gifts
which the Lord giveth him are his inheritance, as
the Lord your God hath spoken to him. But I stood
in the mount praying and interceding as in the former
days (of the) forty days and nights, and the Lord
received my prayer at that time also, and the Lord
would not destroy you. And the Lord said to me,
Arise, go, lead forth the people, that they be brought
in, and possess the land which I promised to their
fathers to give them.

And now, Israel, what doth the Lord your God
require of you, but that you fear the Lord your God,
to walk in all the ways that are right before Him, and
that you love Him, and serve the Lord your God with
all your heart and with all your soul, to keep the commandments of the Lord and His statutes which I command you this day, that it may be well with you?
Behold, the heavens, and the heavens of the heavens, are
the Lord's your God, and the hosts of angels are in
them to minister before Him, and the earth, and whatsoever is therein. Only the Lord had pleasure in your
fathers, and because He would love you He hath had
favour to their children after them, as you, above all the
nations upon the face of the earth, at the time of this
day. Put away folly, therefore, from your heart, and be
not stiff-necked any more; for the Lord thy God is God,
the Judge, and the Monarch of kings, a Great God,

mighty and terrible, before whom there is no respect of
persons, and who taketh no bribe ; He doeth judgment
for the orphan and widow, and hath compassion upon
the stranger to give him food and raiment.　Have pity
then (yourselves) upon the stranger, for you were
strangers in the land of Mizraim.　Revere the Lord
your God, and worship before Him, and cleave closely
to His fear, and swear by His Name.　He is your
praise, and He is your God, who hath done for thee
these great and mighty acts which thou hast beheld
with thy eyes.　With seventy souls your fathers went
down into Mizraim, and now hath the Lord your God
set you as the stars of the heavens for multitude.

XI. Therefore shall you love the Lord your God, and
diligently observe His Word, His statutes, and His
judgments always.　And know you this day, for (I
speak) not with your children who have not known or
seen the instruction of the law of the Lord your God,
nor His greatness, nor His mighty hand, nor His
uplifted arm, or His signs and works which He wrought
in Mizraim, on Pharoh king of Mizraim, and on all the
inhabitants of his land; what He did also to the hosts
of Mizraim, to their horses and chariots, when He made
the waters of the Red Sea to overwhelm their faces when
they followed after you, when the Lord destroyed them
unto this day's time; and what He hath done to you
in the wilderness till the time that you came to this
place; and what He did unto Dathan and Abiram the
sons of Eliab bar Reuben, when the earth opened her
mouth and swallowed them up with the men of their
house, and all their substance, in the midst of all Israel:
for with your eyes have you seen all the great work of
the Lord which He hath wrought.　Therefore shall you
keep all the precepts which I command you this day,
that you may be strengthened, and go in, and inherit

the land to possess which you go over; and that your
days may be multiplied upon the land which the Lord
sware to your fathers to give it to them and their children; a land whose fruits are rich as milk, and sweet as
honey.   For the land to which thou goest in to possess
it is not like the land of Mizraim, from whence you have
come, in which thou didst sow thy seed, and water it
thyself as a garden of herbs; but the land which you
pass over to inherit is a land of mountains and valleys:
it drinketh water from the rain that cometh down from
the heavens; it is a land which the Lord your God
inquireth after by His Word, that He may bless it evermore; [JERUSALEM. A land which the Lord your God
inquireth after continually;] the eyes of the Lord your
God look upon it from the beginning of the year to the
year's end.   And it shall be that if you diligently obey
My commandments which I command you this day, to
love the Lord your God, and to serve Him with all your
heart, and with all your soul, then will I give you the
rain of your land in its time, the early in Marchesvan,
and the latter in Nisan, that you may gather in your
corn, your wine, and your oil.   I will give herbage also
in thy field for thy cattle, that thou mayest eat and
have enough.

Take heed to yourselves, lest you be led away by the
imagination of your heart, and turn aside to serve the
idols of the Gentiles, and worship them, and the Lord's
anger be provoked against you, and He shut up the
clouds of heaven, and let not the rain come down, and
the earth yield no provender, and you perish soon from
off the glorious land which the Lord shall give you.
But lay these my words upon your heart, and upon your
soul, and bind them, written upon tephillin, as a sign
upon the upper part (wrist?) of your left hands, and
let them be for tephillin over thy forehead between thy

eyes. And thou shalt teach them to thy children, to study them when you are sitting in your house with your kindred, and when you are walking in the way, and in the evening when you lie down, and at morning when you arise. [JERUSALEM. And when you repose, and when you rise up.] And you shall write them upon parchment,[4] upon the posts, and affix them to three (things), against thy chest,[5] against the pillars of thy house, and against thy gates: that your days and the days of your children may be multiplied on the land which the Lord sware to your fathers to give you, as the number of the days that the heavens abide over the earth.

For if you diligently keep every commandment that I command you to do it, to love the Lord your God, and walk in all the ways that are right before Him, and cleave unto His fear, then will the Word of the Lord drive out all these nations from before you, and you shall possess the heritage of nations greater and stronger than your-selves. Every place where the sole of your foot shall tread will be yours, from the wilderness and the moun-tain; (among) your mountains shall be the house of the sanctuary, and from the great river, the River Phrat, unto the ocean sea, whose waters are (old as) the creation, on the western side shall be your limit. Not a man will be able to stand before you; but the Lord your God will set the fear and dread of you upon the faces of all the inhabiters of the land that you tread upon, as it hath been told you. [JERUSALEM. Not a ruler nor a prince shall stand before you; but your terror and your fear.]

---

[4] Or "rolls," *megiltha.*　　　　[5] *Tekey, theca.*

SECTION XLVII.

REEH.

MOSHEH the prophet said: Behold, I have this day set in order before you a Blessing and its contrary :[6] the Blessing, if you will be obedient to the commandments of the Lord your God which I command you this day; and its contrary, if you will not obey the commandments of the Lord your God, [JERUSALEM. And their contraries, if you will not hearken,] but will go astray from the path which I have taught you this day, in turning aside after the idols of the nations whom thou hast not known. And it shall be, when the Lord your God will have brought you to the land into which you are going, to possess it, you shall place six tribes upon the mountain of Gerizim, and six tribes on the mountain of Ebal. They who recite the blessings shall turn their faces towards Mount Gerizim, and they who recite the curses shall turn their faces towards Mount Ebal. Are they not situated beyond Jordan by the way of the sunset, in the land of the Kenaanah, who dwell in the plain over against Gilgela by the side (of the place) of the vision of Mamre? For you are to pass over Jordan to enter and possess the land which the Lord your God giveth you, and you will hold and will dwell therein. Look well, therefore, that you perform all the statutes and judgments that I have set before you this day.

XII. These are the statutes and judgments which you are to observe to do in the land which the Lord God of your fathers giveth you to inherit all the days that you live upon the earth. You shall utterly destroy all the places in which the people (whose land) you will possess

6 *Chiluphah*, "its alternative:" root, *chalaph*, "to change"

have worshipped their idols, upon the high mountains
and hills, and under every tree of beautiful form.　You
shall lay their altars in ruin, break down their pillars,
burn their abominations with fire, and utterly destroy
the images of their gods, and abolish their names from
that place.

Not so may you do to blot out the inscription of the
Name of the Lord your God.　But in the land which
the Word of the Lord your God will choose out of all
your tribes for His Shekinah to dwell there, unto the
place of His Shekinah shall you have recourse, and come
thither, and bring your sacrifices and consecrated oblations, your tythes, the separation of your hands, your
vows, your voluntary offerings, and the firstlings of your
herds and flocks.　And you shall there eat before the
Lord your God, and rejoice in all that you put your
hand unto, you and your households, in which the Lord
your God will have blessed you.

It will not be lawful for you to do (there) as we do
here to-day, whatever any one thinks fit for himself;
for you are not yet come to the Sanctuary, to the
dwelling of Peace, and to the inheritance of the land
which the Lord your God will give you.　But when you
have passed over Jordan, and dwell in the land which
the Lord your God will give you to inherit, and He
hath given you repose from all your enemies round about,
then shall you build the house of the Sanctuary, and
afterward shall dwell securely.　And to the place which
the Word of the Lord will choose to make His Shekinah
to dwell there, shall you bring all your oblations, firstlings, and tythes, which I command you; there shall
you offer your sacrifices and hallowed victims, there eat
your tythes and the separation of your hands, and all
your goodly vows which you may have vowed before the
Lord.　And you shall rejoice before the Lord your God,

you and your sons and daughters, your servants and handmaids, and the Levite who is in your cities, for he hath no portion or inheritance with you.

Beware lest you offer your sacrifices in any place which thou mayest see; but in the Place which the Lord will choose in the inheritance of one of your tribes, there shall you offer your sacrifices and do whatever I command you. Nevertheless, after every wish of your soul, you may kill and eat flesh according to the blessing of the Lord your God, which He will give you in all your cities; they who are unclean so as not to be able to offer holy things, and they who are clean that they may offer holy things, may eat of it alike, as the flesh of the antelope or of the hart. Only be careful to pour out the blood upon the ground like water. It will not be lawful for you to eat the tenths of your corn, or wine, or oil, or the firstlings of your herd or flock, nor any of the vows that you have vowed, or freewill offerings, or the separation of your hands in your cities; but you shall eat it before the Lord your God, in the place which the Lord your God will choose; you, and your sons and daughters, and your handmaids, and the Levites who are in your cities; and you shall rejoice before the Lord your God, in all that thou puttest thine hand unto. Beware that thou aggrieve[7] not the Levite all your days in which you dwell in your land.

When the Lord your God will have enlarged your border, as He hath said unto you; and thou sayest, I would eat flesh, because thy soul may desire to eat flesh, thou mayest eat flesh according to all thy desire. But if the place which the Lord your God will have chosen that His Shekinah may dwell there be too far off, then may you eat of your herds and flocks which the Lord your God shall give you, as I have com-

[7] *Mehal,* "to injure, be false or perverse with."

manded you, in your cities you may eat, according to
all the desire of your soul : as the flesh of the antelope
or hart so may you eat it; he who is unclean that he
may not offer holy things, and he who is clean that he
may offer them, may eat of it alike. [JERUSALEM. He
who is restrained from holy things, and he who is clean
for holy things, may eat alike.]   Only put a strong
restraint upon your desires, that you eat no blood; for
the blood is the subsistence of the life.   You may not,
with the flesh, eat blood, in which is the subsistence of
life: you shall not eat it, you shall pour it out upon
the ground like water : eat it not, that it may be well
with you, and with your children after you, while you
do that which is right before the Lord.   Nevertheless,
animals which are your consecrated tenths, and your
votive offerings, you shall take and bring to the place
which the Lord will choose; and thou shalt do (with
them) according to the rite of thy burnt offerings, (and
offer) the flesh and the blood upon the altar of the
Lord thy God: the blood of the rest of thy holy oblations shall be poured out at the altar of the Lord thy
God, but of the flesh it is lawful to eat.

Observe and obey all these words that I command you,
that it may be well with you and with your children after
you for ever, while you do that which is good and right
before the Lord your God.   When the Lord your God
shall have cut off the nations among whom you go, and
have expelled them from before you, and you inherit
and dwell in their land, beware that you stumble not
after their idols when they shall have been destroyed
before you, or lest you seek after their idols, saying,
How did these peoples worship their gods, that we may
worship as they did ?   So shall you not do in serving
the Lord your God; for whatever is abominable and
hateful to Him have they done to their idols ; for even

their sons and daughters they have bound and burned
with fire unto their idols.   Whatsoever I command you,
that shall you observe to do; ye shall not add to it nor
diminish from it.

XIII. When there may arise among you a false prophet, or a dreamer of a profane dream, and he give
you a sign or a miracle, and the sign or the miracle
come to pass, (yet) because he spake with you, saying,
Let us go after the gods of the peoples whom thou hast
not known, and worship them, you shall not hearken to
the words of that lying prophet, or his who hath dreamed
that dream; for the Lord your God (thereby) trieth you,
to know whether you will love the Lord your God with
all your heart and with all your soul.   You shall walk
after the service of the Lord your God, and Him shall
you fear, and keep His commandments, hearken to His
word, pray before Him, and cleave unto His fear.   And
that prophet of lies, or that dreamer of dreams, shall be
slain with the sword, because he had spoken perversity
against the Lord your God,—who brought you out
from the land of the Mizraee, and redeemed you from
the house of the affliction of slaves,—to make you to go
astray from the path which the Lord your God hath
commanded you to walk in : so shall you bring down
the doers of evil among you.

When thy brother, the son of thy mother, when even
the son of thy father, or thy own son, or thy daughter,
or thy wife who reposeth with thee, or thy friend who
is beloved as thy soul, shall give thee evil counsel, to
make thee go astray, speaking out and saying, Let us
go and worship the gods of the Gentiles, which neither
thou nor thy fathers have known ; of the idols of the
seven nations who are near you round about, or of the
rest of the nations who are far away from you, from one
end of the earth to the other ; you shall not consent to

them, nor hearken to him, neither shall your eye spare
him or have compassion, nor shall you hide him in
secret; but killing you shall kill him; your hand shall
be the first upon him to slay him, and afterwards the
hand of all the people; and you shall stone him that he
die; because he sought to draw them away from the
fear of the Lord thy God, who brought you out free
from the land of Mizraim, from the house of the affliction of slaves. And all Israel will hear and be afraid,
and never more do according to that evil thing among
you. [JERUSALEM. When thy brother, the son of thy
mother, thy son, thy daughter, or the wife who reposeth
with thee, shall turn thee away.]

When, in one of your cities which the Lord your God
will give you to dwell in, you hear it said that (certain)
men of pride are drawing back from the doctrine of the
Lord your God, or that even sages of your rabbins have
gone forth and led away the inhabitants of their city,
saying, Let us go and worship the gods of the nations
which you have not known: then search you out, and
examine with witnesses, and make good inquiry; and,
behold, if the thing be true and certain that this abomination hath been really done among you, you shall
smite the inhabitants of that city with the edge of the
sword, to destroy it utterly and whatever is therein,
even its cattle, with the edge of the sword. You shall
gather all its spoil into the midst of the street, and
burn the city with fire, together with the whole of the
spoil, before the Lord your God; and it shall be a desolate heap for ever, never to be builded again: that the
Lord may be turned from the fierceness of His anger,
and may show His mercy upon you, and love you, and
multiply you, as He hath sworn to your fathers. So be
ye obedient to the Word of the Lord your God, to keep
all His commandments which I command you this day,

that you may do what is right before the Lord your
God.

XIV. As beloved children before the Lord your God,
you shall not make lacerations in your flesh, nor make
bare the crown of the hair over your foreheads on
account of the soul of the dead. [JERUSALEM. You are
beloved children before the Lord your God; you shall
not make divers wounds for strange worship, nor cause
baldness above your forehead to mourn for a person who
is dead.] For you are to be a holy people before the Lord
your God: the Lord your God hath chosen you to be a
people more beloved than all the peoples who are upon
the face of the earth. You may not eat of any thing
that for you is abominable.

These are the animals which you may eat: oxen, and
lambs of the ewes, such as are not blemished (unclean),
and kids of the goats unmixed with what are unclean.
Harts and antelopes and fallow deer, rock goats and
reems, wild oxen and pygargs;[8] and every animal that
hath the divided hoof, and horns, and that cleaveth the
cleft, bringing up the cud among animals, that you may
eat. [JERUSALEM. Which bringeth up the cud among
animals, that may you eat.] But of these you may not
eat that bring up the cud, or of those who (only) have
the hoof divided, the cast thing (embryo) which hath
two heads or a double back, things which are not to be
perpetuated in the same species (*i. e.*, as a species); nor
the camel, the hare, or the coney, because they chew the
cud, but do not divide the hoof; they are unclean to
you. [JERUSALEM. Because they bring up the cud,
but have not the hoof divided.] The swine, because,
though he hath the hoof divided, and there is none produced that like him divideth (the hoof), and yet cheweth
not the cud, is unclean to you; of their flesh you shall

---

[8] *Ditzin*, " springers."

not eat, nor touch their dead bodies. But this you
may eat, of all that are in the waters, whatever hath fins
to move, as by flying, and scales upon its skin; and
though (some of which) may fall away, yet if there
remain one under its jaw, another under its fin, and
another under its tail, that you may eat.[9] But whatever hath neither fins nor scales you may not eat; it is
unclean to you. Every bird which hath a vesicle or crop
which may be picked away,[1] and which (bird) is longer
than a finger, and not of the rapacious kind, you may
eat. But these are they which you may not eat: the
eagle, the ossifrage, the osprey, the daitha (lammer
geyer?) white or black, which is a bird of prey, a kind
of vulture.[2] [JERUSALEM. 12. And these are they of
which you may not eat; the eagle, and the sea eagle
(ossifrage), and the osprey. 13. And the rook, the
heron also, and the vulture after his kind.] And every
raven after his kind; and the owl, and nighthawk, and
the cuckoo, and the falcon after his kind; the great
owl, and the sea gull (catcher of fish from the sea), and
the night owl, (?) and the cormorant[3] white or black,
and the pica, and the stork white or black after its kind,
and the heathcock, and the bat, [JERUSALEM. And
the white daitha, and the ibis according to his kind, and
the heathcock, and the bat,] and all flies (bees) and
wasps, and all worms of vegetables and pulse, which
come away from (materials of) food and fly as birds, are
unclean to you, they may not be eaten; but any clean
beast you may eat. You shall not eat of anything that
is unclean through the manner of its death;[4] you may

---

[9] Fishes are clean when they have at least two scales and one fin.—
Mishna, Cholin, iv.

[1] Every bird which hath a crop, and of which the internal coat of the
stomach may be readily peeled off, is clean.—*Ib*., iii, 6

[2] Or, "which is an *ibu*, a daitha after its kind."   [3] Query, pelican.

[4] Or, "that is corrupted in the slaughtering of it."

give it to the uncircumcised stranger who is in your
cities to eat it, or sell it to a son of the Gentiles; for
you are a holy people before the Lord your God. It
shall not be lawful for you to boil, much less to eat,
flesh with milk when both are mixed together.

Be mindful to tythe your fruitage of whatsoever
cometh forth, and which you gather in from the field
year by year; not giving the fruit of one year for the
fruit of another. [JERUSALEM. My people of the house
of Israel, tything you shall tythe all the produce of your
seed, of that which you sow upon the face of the field
and gather in the produce of each year. Israel, My
people, it is not lawful for you to tythe and eat the fruit
of one year along with the fruit of (another) year.]
And the second tythe you shall eat before the Lord
your God in the place which He will choose to make
His Shekinah to dwell there; the tenths of your corn,
your vines, and your oil, and likewise the firstlings of
your oxen and sheep, that you may learn to fear the
Lord your God all the days. And if the way be too
great for you to be able to carry the tenth, because the
place which the Lord thy God will choose for His
Shekinah to dwell there is too distant from you, when
the Lord thy God shall have blessed thee, then thou
mayest make exchange for it into silver, and bind the
sum in thy hand, and proceed to the place which the
Lord thy God shall choose, and give the silver for any
thing that thy soul pleaseth, of oxen, sheep, wine new or
old, or whatever thy soul desireth; and you shall eat
there before the Lord your God and rejoice, you and the
men of your house. And the Levite who is in your
cities forsake not, for he hath not a portion or a heritage
with you. At the end of three years you shall bring
forth all the tenths of your produce for that year, and
lay them up in your cities. And the Levite, because

he hath no part or heritage with you, and the stranger, the orphan, and the widow who are in your cities, shall come and eat and be satisfied; that the Lord your God may bless you in all the works of your hands that you do.

XV. At the end of seven years you shall make a Release. And this is the indication of the custom of the Release. Every man who is master of a loan, who lendeth to his neighbour, shall give remission. He shall not have power to coerce his neighbour in demanding his loan, nor of his brother, a son of Israel; because the beth din hath published the Release before the Lord. From a son of the Gentiles thou mayest exact, but the lawful right (*dina*) which is thine with thy brother thou shalt release with thine hand. If you will only be diligent in the precepts of the law, there will be no poor among you; for, blessing, the Lord will bless you in the land which the Lord your God will give you for a possession to inherit; if, obeying, you will only obey the Word of the Lord your God, to observe and do all these commandments which I command you this day. For the Lord your God blesseth you, as He saith to you (that) you shall take from many nations, but they will not take from you; and you will have power over many nations, but they shall not have power over you. But if you be not diligent in the precepts of the law, and there be among you a poor man in one of thy cities of the land which the Lord thy God giveth thee, thou shalt not harden thy heart, nor hold back thy hand from thy poor brother; but thou shalt open thy hand to him, and lend to him according to the measure of his want through which he is in need. Beware lest there be a word in thy proud heart, saying: The seventh year, the year of release, is at hand, and your eye become evil toward your poor brother, so as to be not willing to

give to him, and he cry against you to the Lord, and
there be guilt upon you. Giving you shall give to him,
nor shall your heart be evil when you give to him; for
on account of this matter the Lord your God will bless
you in all your works that you put your hands unto.
But forasmuch as the house of Israel will not rest in
the commandments of the law, the poor will not cease
in the land: therefore I command you, saying: You
shall verily open your hands toward your neighbours,
to the afflicted around you, and to the poor of your
country. [JERUSALEM. Giving thou shalt give to him,
nor let your looks be evil at the time you give to him.
If Israel would keep the precepts of the law, there would
be no poor among them; but if they will forsake the
precepts of the law, the poor shall not cease from the
land . therefore I command you, saying · You shall
verily open your hands to your poor brethren, and to
the needy who will be in your land.]

If your brother, a son of Israel, or if a daughter of
Israel, be sold to you, he shall serve you six years; and
when the seventh comes, thou shalt send him from you
free.   And when thou lettest him go away from thee at
liberty, thou shalt not send him away empty.   Comfort-
ing thou shalt comfort him out of your flocks, your
floors, and your wine presses; as the Lord hath blessed
you ye shall give to him. [JERUSALEM. Thou shalt
furnish him.]   And be mindful that you were servants in
the land of Mizraim, and that the Lord your God set
you free; therefore I command you to-day that you do
this thing.

But if he say to thee, I will not go out from thee,
because I love thee and the men of thy house, and because
it hath been good for him to be with thee, then thou shalt
take an awl, and bore (or apply) it through his ear, and
that to the door of the house of judgment, and he shall

be thy serving servant until the Jubilee.　And for thy handmaid also thou shalt write a certificate of release, and give it to her.　It must not be a hardship in thy eyes when thou sendest him away from thee; for double the hire of an hireling hath he been of service to thee six years; and on his account the Lord thy God hath blessed thee in all that thou hast done.

Every firstling male that cometh of thy herd and flock thou shalt consecrate before the Lord thy God. Thou shalt not work with the firstlings of your herd, nor shear the firstlings of your flocks; you shall eat thereof before the Lord your God from year to year, in the place which the Lord will choose, you and the men of your houses.　But if there be any spot in it, if it be lame or blind, or have any blemish, you shall not sacrifice it before the Lord your God: you may eat it in your cities; he who is unclean, (so) that he may not approach to holy things, and he who being clean may approach the holy, may alike (eat), as the flesh of the antelope or hart.[4]　Only you shall not eat the blood; you shall pour it out upon the ground like water.

XVI.　Be mindful to keep the times of the festivals, with the intercalations of the year, and to observe the rotation thereof: in the month of Abiba to perform the pascha before the Lord your God, because in the month of Abiba the Lord your God brought you out of Mizraim; you shall eat it therefore by night.　But you shall sacrifice the pascha before the Lord your God between the suns; and the sheep and the bullocks on the morrow,[5] on that same day to rejoice in the feast at the place which the Lord will choose to make His Shekinah to dwell there.　You shall not eat leavened bread

---

[4] That is, as any of the clean animals which were not permitted to be sacrificed at the altar.

[5] Num. xxviii 19.

with the pascha; seven days you shall eat unleavened
bread unto His Name, the unleavened bread of humiliation; for with haste you went forth from the land of
Mizraim; that you may remember the day of your outgoing from the land of Mizraim all the days of your
life. Take heed that in the beginning of the pascha
there be no leaven seen among you within all your
borders for seven days; and that none of the flesh which
you sacrifice in the evening of the first day remain till
the morning. It will not be allowed you to eat the
pascha in (any) one of your cities which the Lord your
God giveth to you; but in the place which the Lord
your God will choose to make His Shekinah to dwell,
there shall you sacrifice the pascha; and in the evening
at the going down of the sun you may eat it until the
middle of the night, the time when you began to go out
of Mizraim. And you shall dress and eat it in the
place which the Lord your God will choose, and in the
early morn (if need be) thou mayest return from the
feast, and go to thy cities. On the first day thou shalt
offer the omer, and eat unleavened cakes of the old
corn; but in the six remaining days you may begin to
eat unleavened cakes of the new corn,[6] and on the
seventh day you shall assemble with thanksgiving
before the Lord your God; no work shall you perform.

Seven weeks number to you; from the time when you
begin to put the sickle to the harvest of the field after
the reaping of the omer you shall begin to number the
seven weeks. And you shall keep with joy the Festival
of Weeks before the Lord your God, after the measure
of the freewill offerings of your hands, according as the
Lord your God shall have blessed you. And you shall
rejoice with the joy of the feast before the Lord your

* The consecrated harvest sheaf having been offered on the preceding
day.

God, you and your sons, your daughters, your servants
and handmaids, the Levites who are in your cities, and
the stranger, the orphan, and the widow who are among
you, at the place which the Lord your God will choose
where to make His Shekinah to dwell.   Remember that
you were servants in Mizraim; so shall you observe and
perform these statutes.

The Feast of Tabernacles you shall make to you seven
days, when you will have completed to gather in the corn
from your threshing floors, and the wine from your
presses.   And you shall rejoice in the joy of your feasts
with the clarinet and flute, you and your sons and
daughters, your handmaids, the Levite, the stranger, the
orphan, and the widow, who are in your cities.   Seven
days you shall keep the feast before the Lord your God
in the place which the Lord will choose, because the
Lord your God will have blessed you in all your provision, and in all the work of your hands, and so shall
you be joyful in prosperity.

Three times in the year shall all your males appear
before the Lord your God in the place that He will
choose; at the Feast of the Unleavened, at the Feast of
Weeks, and at the Feast of Tabernacles; nor must you
appear before the Lord your God empty of any of the
requirements; every one after the measure of the gifts
of his hands, according to the blessing which the Lord
your God hath bestowed upon you.

SECTION XLVIII.

SHOPHETIM.

Upright judges and efficient administrators[7] you
shall appoint in all your cities which the Lord your God

[7] *Dayanin kashilin ve Sarekin alemin.*

will give you for your tribes, and they shall judge the
people with true judgment. [JERUSALEM. Judges and
administrators.] You shall not set judgment aside, nor
respect persons, nor take a gift, because a gift blindeth
the eyes of the wise who take it; for it perverteth them
to foolishness, and confuseth equitable words in the
mouth of the judges in the hour of their decision.
[JERUSALEM. You shall not go astray in judgment,
nor respect persons, nor take the wages of mammon;
for a bribe blindeth the eyes of the wise, and depraveth
their right words in the hour of their judgment.]
Upright and perfect judgment in truth shalt thou follow,
that you may come to inherit the land which the Lord
your God will give you. As it is not allowed you to
plant a grove by the side of the Lord's altar, so is it not
allowed you to associate in judgment a fool with a wise
judge to teach that which you are to do. As it is not
for you to erect a statue, so are you not to appoint to be
a governor a proud man, whom the Lord your God
doth abhor.

XVII. You shall not sacrifice before the Lord your
God a bullock or lamb which hath any blemish or evil
in it, or which is torn or rent; for that is abominable
before the Lord your God.

If there be found among you in one of your cities
that the Lord your God will give you a man or woman
who doth what is evil before the Lord your God in
transgressing His covenant, and, following after evil
desire, shall serve the idols of the Gentiles, and worship
them, or the sun, or the moon, or all the host of the
heavens, which 1 have not commanded; and it be told
you, and you hear and make inquiry by witnesses fairly;
and, behold, if this word be true and certain, that such
abomination is wrought among you, then you shall bring
forth that man or woman who hath done this evil thing,

unto the gate of your house of judgment, the man or
the woman, and you shall stone them that they die.
Upon the word of two witnesses or of three he shall die
who is guilty of death; they shall not be put to death on
the word of one witness. The hands of the witnesses
shall be first upon him to kill him, and afterward the
hands of all (any of) the people; and so shall you bring
down the evil doer among you.

If there be with you an extraordinary matter for
judgment between unclean and clean blood, cases of life
or of money, or between a plague of leprosy or of the
scall, with words of controversy in your beth din, then
you shall arise and go up to the place which the Lord
your God will choose; and you shall come to the priests
of the tribe of Levi, and to the judge who will be in
those days, and inquire of them, and they will show you
the process of judgment. Then shall you do according
to the word of the custom of the law that they will show
you at the place the Lord will choose, and observe to do
whatsoever they teach you. [JERUSALEM. When a
matter is too occult for you, in setting judgment in order
between the blood of murder and innocent blood,
between leprosy and the scall, with words of contention
in your cities, then shall you arise and go up to the
place which the Lord your God will choose.] According
to the word of the law that they will teach you, and the
manner of judgment they pronounce, you shall do. You
shall not turn aside from the sentence they will show
you, to the right or to the left. And the man who will
act with presumption, and not obey the judge or the
priest who standeth there to minister before the Lord
your God, that man shall be put to death; so shall you
put down the doer of evil from Israel, and all the people
will hear, and be afraid, and not do wickedly again.

When you enter the land which the Lord your God

giveth you, and possess, and dwell in it, and you say,
Let us appoint a king over us, like all the nations about
me, you shall inquire for instruction before the Lord,
and afterward appoint the king over you: but it will
not be lawful to set over you a foreign man who is not
of your brethren. Only let him not increase to him
more than two horses, lest his princes ride upon them,
and become proud, neglect the words of the law, and
commit the sin of the captivity of Mizraim; for the
Lord hath told you, By that way ye shall return no
more. Neither shall he multiply to him wives above
eighteen, lest they pervert his heart; nor shall he increase
to him silver or gold, lest his heart be greatly lifted up,
and he rebel against the God of heaven. And it shall
be that if he be steadfast in the commandments of the
law, he shall sit upon the throne of his kingdom in
security. And let the elders write for him the section
(*pharasha*) of this law in a book before the priests of
the tribe of Levi; and let it be at his side, and he shall
read it all the days of his life, that he may learn to fear
the Lord his God, to keep all the words of this law, and
all these statutes to perform them: that his heart may
not be arrogant toward his brethren, nor decline from
the precepts to the right or the left, and that his days
may be prolonged over his kingdom, his and his sons'
among Israel.

XVIII. The priests of the tribe of Levi will have no
part or inheritance with their brethren: they shall eat
the oblations of the Lord as their portion, but an
inheritance in field or vineyard they will not have
among their brethren. The twenty and four gifts of the
priesthood which the Lord will give to him are his
heritage; as He said to him, And this shall be the
portion belonging to the priest from the people, from
them who offer sacrifices, whether bullock or lamb:

they shall give to the priest the right shoulder, the
lower jaw, the cheeks, and the maw; the firsts of your
corn, wine, and oil, the first of the fleece of your sheep,
as much as a girdle measureth shall you give to him :
because the Lord thy God hath chosen him out of all
thy tribes to stand and minister in the Name of the
Lord, him, and his sons, all the days.

And when a Levite may come from one of your cities
out of all Israel where he hath dwelt, and come with all
the obligation of his soul's desire to the place which the
Lord will choose, then he shall minister in the Name of
the Lord his God as all his brethren the Levites who
minister there before the Lord. Portion for portion
equally shall they eat, besides the gifts of the oblations
which the priests do eat, which Elazar and Ithamar
your fathers have given them to inherit. [JERUSALEM.
And the allowance of his sale which they sell to him
according to the fathers.]

When you have entered the land which the Lord
your God giveth you, ye shall not learn to do after the
abominations of those nations. None shall be found
among you to make his sons or daughters pass through
the fire, nor who enchant with enchantments, or inspect
serpents, nor observe divinations and auguries, or make
(magical) knots [8] and bindings of serpents and scorpions
or any kind of reptile, or who consult the oba,[9] the
bones of the dead [1] or the bone Jadua, or who inquire
of the manes. [JERUSALEM. No one shall be found
among you to make his son or daughter pass through
the fire, to enchant with enchantments, to inspect
serpents, or to observe divinations and auguries; or any
who use (magical) knots, or are binders of snakes,

---

[8] Or, " combinations."   [9] Python. Glossary, p 25.
[1] " Bones of the dead," lit., " the unclean." *Tamya, i. e, " immundi,
polluti, Sanhedrin*, cxui., 1, *per synecdoch.: cadavera, ossa cadaverum.*"
—CASTEL.

scorpions, or any kinds of reptiles, or are consulters of
oba, or who bring up the manes, or seek to learn from
the dead.]   For every one who doeth these is an abomination before the Lord; and because of these abominations the Lord driveth them out before you.   Ye shall
be perfect in the fear of the Lord your God.   For these
nations which thou art about to dispossess have listened
to inspectors of serpents and enchanters.   [JERUSA-
LEM. To inspectors of serpents and to users of enchantments have they hearkened.]   But you are not to be
like them: the priests shall inquire by Urim and
Thummim; and a Right Prophet [2] will the Lord your
God give you; a Prophet from among you of your
brethren like unto me, with the Holy Spirit will the
Lord your God raise up unto you; to Him shall you be
obedient.   According to all that you begged before the
Lord your God in Horeb on the day of the assembling
of the tribes to receive the law, saying, Let us not again
hear the Great Voice from before the Lord our God,
nor behold again that great fire, lest we die: and the
Lord said to me, That which they have spoken is right;
I will raise up unto them a Prophet from among their
brethren in whom shall be the Holy Spirit, as in thee;
and I will put My Word of prophecy in his mouth, and
he shall speak with them whatsoever I command him;
and the man who will not hearken to the words of My
prophecy which shall be spoken in My Name, My Word
shall take vengeance upon him.   But the false prophet
who doeth wickedly in speaking a thing in My Name,
when I have not commanded him to speak, or who
shall speak in the name of the gods of the Gentiles,
that prophet shall be slain with the sword.   And if
thou shalt say in your thoughts, How shall we know
the word which the Lord hath not spoken?   When a

[2] Or, " a Prophet of Righteousness."   *Vide* Glossary, p. 19.

false prophet speaketh in the Name of the Lord, and
the thing doth not come to pass, or be not confirmed,
it is a word which the Lord hath not spoken; the false
prophet spake it in presumption; fear him not.

XIX. When the Lord your God shall have destroyed
the nations whose land the Lord your God giveth you,
and you possess them, and dwell in their cities and
houses, three cities shall you set apart within your land
which the Lord your God giveth you to inherit. You
shall prepare a high road, and divide your limit which the
Lord your God bestoweth upon you, that any manslayer
may flee thither. And this is the regulation for the
manslayer who fleeth thither that he may live: Whoever shall have killed his brother without intention, he
not having kept enmity against him yesterday, or the
day before, (as for example) if any one goeth with his
neighbour into the thicket to cut wood, and he driveth
his hand with the axe to cut wood, and the iron flieth
apart from the haft and lighteth on his neighbour that
he die, he may flee to one of those appointed cities, and
save his life. [JERUSALEM. He who may go with his
neighbour into the thicket to cut wood, and exerting
himself with the axe to cut the wood, the iron separate
from the handle, and fall upon his neighbour that he
die, he may flee into one of those cities, and live.]
Lest the avenger of blood follow after him, his heart
boiling within him on account of his grief, and appre-
hend him, if the way be long, and take his life, though
he is not guilty of the judgment of death, because he
had not enmity against him in time past. [JERUSALEM,
Because his heart is boiling, and he meeteth.] Therefore I command you to-day that you set apart for you
three cities.

And if the Lord your God enlarge your border, as
He hath sworn to your fathers, and give you all the

land which He hath sworn to your fathers to give, then shall you keep all this commandment which to-day I command you to do, that thou mayest love the Lord thy God, and walk in the ways which are right before Him all days; and you shall add yet three cities to those three; that innocent blood may not be shed in your land which the Lord your God giveth you to inherit, and the guilt of the judgment of death may not be upon you.

But if a man with enmity against his neighbour shall lay wait for him in secret, to destroy his life, and he die, then should he flee into one of those cities, the sages of his cities shall send aud take him thence, and give him up into the hand of the pursuer for blood, and he shall be put to death. Your eye shall not spare him, but you shall put away shedders of innocent blood from Israel, that it may be well with you.

You shall not remove the boundary mark of your neighbours which the predecessors did set for the limit in your possession of inheritance in the land which the Lord your God giveth you to inherit.

The testimony of one (witness) shall not be valid against a man for any crime (regarding the taking) of life, or guilt concerning money, or any sin with which one may be charged with sinning; but, by the Word of the Lord, (to insure) retribution upon secret crimes, (while) one witness may swear to deny what hath been attested against him, the sentence shall be confirmed upon the mouth of two witnesses, or of three.

When false witnesses stand up against a man to testify wrong things against him, then the two men between whom lies the subject of contention shall stand in the presence of the Lord, before the priests and judges who will be in those days: and the judges shall question the witnesses of their times fairly; and,

behold, false testimony is in the mouth of the witnesses;
they have borne false witness against their brother.
And so shall you do unto them as they had devised to
do against their brother, and you shall put down the
doers of evil from among you. And the wicked who
remain will hear and be afraid, and not add to repeat
an evil thing like this among you. Your eye shall not
spare; life for life, the value of an eye for an eye, the
value of a tooth for a tooth, the value of a hand for a
hand, the value of a foot for a foot.

XX. When you go forth to battle against your
enemies, and see horses and chariots, and peoples proud,
overbearing, and stronger than you, fear them not; for
all of them are accounted as a single horse and a single
chariot before the Lord your God, whose Word will
be your Helper; for He brought you free out of the
land of Mizraim. And at the time that you draw nigh
to do battle, the priest shall approach and speak with
the people, and say to them, Hear, Israel, you draw
near this day to fight against your adversaries; let not
your heart be moved, be not afraid, tremble not, nor be
broken down before them: for the Shekinah of the
Lord your God goeth before you to fight for you against
your enemies, and to save you.

And the officers shall speak with the people, saying:
Who is the man who hath builded a new house, and
hath not set fast its door-posts to complete it? let
him go and return to his house, lest through sin he be
slain in the battle, and another man complete it. Or,
what man hath planted a vineyard, and hath not redeemed it from the priest [JERUSALEM. And hath not
redeemed it] to make it common? let him go and
return to his house, lest sin be the occasion of his not
redeeming it, but he be slain in the battle, and another
make it common. And what man hath betrothed a

wife, but not taken her? let him go and return to his
house, lest sin prevent him from rejoicing with his wife,
and he be slain in the battle, and another take her.
Yet more shall the officers speak to the people, and say,
Who is the man who is afraid on account of his sin,
and whose heart is broken? let him go and return to his
house, that his brethren be not implicated in his sins, and
their heart be broken like his. And when the officers
shall have finished to speak with the people, they shall
appoint the captains of the host at the head of the people.

When you come nigh to a city to make war against
it, then you shall send to it certain to invite it to
peace; and if they answer you with words of peace,
and open their gates to you, all the people whom you
find therein shall be tributaries, and serve you. [JERU-
SALEM. And if it answer thee with words of peace, and
open the gates to you, all the people whom you find.]
But if they will not make peace, but war, with you,
then you shall beleaguer it. And when the Lord your
God will have delivered it into your hand, then may
you smite every male thereof with the edge of the
sword. But the women, children, and cattle, and whatever is in the city, even all the spoil, you shall seize,
and eat the spoil of your enemies which the Lord your
God giveth you. Thus shall you do to all cities that are
remote from you, which are not of the cities of these
seven nations; but of the cities of these peoples, which
the Lord your God giveth you to inherit, ye shall
not spare alive any breathing thing: for destroying ye
shall destroy them, Hittites, Amorites, Kenaanites,
Pherizites, Hivites, and Jebusites, as the Lord your
God hath commanded you; that they may not teach
you to do after their abominations with which they
have served their idols, and you sin before the Lord
your God.

When you beleaguer a city all the seven days to war
against it, to subdue it on the Sabbath, you shall not
destroy the trees thereof by bringing against them (an
instrument of) iron; that you may eat its fruit, cut it
not down; for a tree on the face of the field is not as a
man to be hidden (put out of sight) before you in the
siege.   But the tree that you know to be a tree not
making fruit to eat, that you may destroy and cut down.
And you shall raise bulwarks against the city which
maketh war with you, until you have subdued it.

XXI. If a man be found slain upon the ground, un-
buried, in the land which the Lord your God giveth you
to inherit, lying down, and not hanged on a tree in the
field, nor floating on the face of the water; and it be
not known who did kill him: then two of the sages shall
proceed from the chief court of judgment, and three of
thy judges, and shall measure to the surrounding cities
which lie on the four quarters from the (spot where) the
dead man (is found); and the city which is nearest to
the dead man, being the suspected one, let the chief
court of justice take means for absolution (or discul-
pation). Let the sages, the elders of that city, take an
heifer from the herd, not commixed, an heifer of the
year, which hath not been wrought with, nor hath drawn
in the yoke: and the sages of that city shall bring the
heifer down into an uncultivated field, where the ground
hath not been tilled by work, nor sowed; and let them
there behead the heifer from behind her with an axe (or
knife, dolch) in the midst of the field.   And the priests
the sons of Levi shall draw near; for the Lord your God
hath chosen them to minister to Him, and to bless Israel
in His Name, and according to their words to resolve
every judgment, and in any plague of leprosy to shut
up, and pronounce concerning it; and all the elders of
the city lying nearest to the dead man shall wash their

hands over the heifer which hath been cut off in the field, and shall answer and say : It is manifest before the Lord that this hath not come by our hands, nor have we absolved him who shed this blood, nor have our eyes beheld. [JERUSALEM. Nor have our eyes seen who it is who hath shed it.] And the priests shall say : Let there be expiation for thy people Israel, whom Thou, O Lord, hast redeemed, and lay not the guilt of innocent blood upon Thy people Israel ; but let him who hath done the murder be revealed. And they shall be expiated concerning the blood ; but straightway there will come forth a swarm of worms from the excrement of the heifer, and spread abroad, and move to the place where the murderer is, and crawl over him : and the magistrates shall take him, and judge him. So shall you, O house of Israel, put away from among you whosoever sheddeth innocent blood, that you may do what is right before the Lord.

SECTION XLIX.

TITSE.

WHEN you go out to war against your enemies, and the Lord your God shall deliver them into your hands, and you take some of them captive : if you see in the captivity a woman of fair countenance, and you approve of her, and would take her to you to wife ; then thou shalt take her into thy house, and let her cut off the hair of her head, pare her nails, and put off the dress of her captivity, and, dipping herself, become a proselyte in thy house, and weep on account of the idols of the house of her father and mother. And thou shalt

wait three months to know whether she be with child;
and afterwards thou mayest go to her, endow her, and
make her thy wife.

But if thou hast no pleasure in her, then thou
mayest send her away, only with a writing of divorce:
but thou shalt in no wise sell her for money, nor make
merchandise of her, after thou hast had intercourse with
her. [JERUSALEM. If thou hast no pleasure in her,
thou mayest send her away with power over herself;
but thou shalt in no wise sell her for money, nor make
merchandise of her; because thy power over her is
given up.]

If a man have two wives, and one is beloved and the
other hated, and they bear him sons, both the beloved
and the hated (wife), and the first-born son be of the
hated, it shall be in the day that he deviseth to his sons
the inheritance of the wealth that may be his, he shall
not be allowed to give the birthright portion to the son of
the beloved, over the head of the son of the hated wife,
to whom the birthright belongs, but (let him acknowledge) the birthright of the son of her who is disliked,
and all that belongeth to it, to give him the double
portion of all that may be found with him, because he is
the beginning of his strength, and to him pertaineth the
birthright.

If a man hath a son depraved and rebellious, who
will not obey the word of his father or of his mother,
and who, when they reprove him, will not receive
admonition from them; his father and mother shall take
him, and bring him before the sages of the city at the
door of the court of justice in that place, and say to the
sages of the city, We had transgressed the decree of the
Word of the Lord; therefore was born to us this son,
who is presumptuous and disorderly; he will not hear
our word, but is a glutton and a drunkard. And it

shall be that if he brought to fear and receive instruction,
and beg that his life may be spared, you shall let him
live; but if he refuse and continue rebellious, then all
the men of his city shall stone him with stones that he
die; and so shall you put away the evil doer from among
you, and all Israel will hear, and be afraid.

When a man hath become guilty of the judgment of
death, and is condemned to be stoned, and they afterwards hang him on a beam, [JERUSALEM. And you
hang him on a beam,] his dead body shall not remain
upon the beam, but he shall be certainly buried on the
same day; for it is execrable before God to hang a man,
but that his guilt gave occasion for it; and because he
was made in the image of God, you shall bury him at the
going down of the sun, lest wild beasts abuse him, and
lest you overspread your land, which the Lord your God
giveth you to possess, with the dead bodies of criminals.

XXII. Thou shalt not see thy brother's ox or his
lamb going astray, and estrange thy knowledge from
them; thou shalt certainly restore them to him. But if
knowledge of thy brother is not thine, if thou knowest
him not, thou shalt bring it into thy house, and it shall
be supported by thee till the time that thou hast sought
out thy brother, and thou shalt restore it to him. So
shalt thou do with his ass, with his garment, and with
any lost thing of thy brother's. If thou find, it is not
· lawful for thee to hide it from him, thou shalt cry it,
and restore it. [JERUSALEM. And so shalt thou do
with his ass, and with his robe.] Thou shalt not see
thy brother's ass nor his ox thrown on the way, and
turn thy eyes from them; thou shalt verily lift it up for
him. [JERUSALEM. Thou shalt forgive what may be
in thy heart against him, thou shalt deliver and lead it.]

Neither fringed robes nor tephillin which are the
ornaments of a man shall be upon a woman; neither

shall a man shave himself so as to appear like a woman;
for every one who doeth so is an abomination before the
Lord thy God.

If thou find the nest of a clean bird before thee in
the way, in a tree, or upon the ground, in which there
are young ones or eggs, and the mother sitting upon the
young ones or eggs, thou shalt be sure to send the
mother away, but thou mayest take the young for thyself;
that it may be well with thee in this world, and that
thou mayest prolong thy days in the world to come.

When thou buildest a new house, thou shalt make a
surrounding fence to thy roof, that it may not be the
occasion of blood guilt by the loss of life at thy house,
by any one through heedlessness falling therefrom.
[JERUSALEM. Then thou shalt make a parapet to thy
roof, that the guilt of innocent blood shedding may not
be set upon thy house.]

You shall not sow your vineyard with seeds of different kinds, lest thou be chargeable with burning the
mixed seed that you have sown and the produce of the
vine. You shall not plough with an ox and an ass, nor
with any animals of two species bound together. You
shall not clothe nor warm yourselves with a garment
combed (carded) or netted, or interwoven with woollen
and linen mixed together. Nevertheless on a robe of
linen thread you may be permitted to make fringes of
woollen upon the four extremities of your vestments with
which you dress in the day. [JERUSALEM. Fringes of
threads shall you make upon the four edges of your
vestments with which you dress.]

If a man take a wife or virgin and go unto her, but
afterwards dislike her, and bring upon her words of
calumny in an evil report against her, and say, I took
this woman, and lay with her, but found not the witnesses for her; then the father and mother of the

damsel may have licence from the court of judgment to
produce the linen with the witnesses of her virginity,
before the sages of the city, at the door of the beth din.
And the father of the damsel shall say to the sages, I
wedded my daughter to this man to be his wife; but
after lying with her he hath hated her; and, behold, he
hath thrown upon her occasion of words, saying : I have
not found the witnesses of thy daughter's (virginity);
but these are my daughter's witnesses; and they shall
spread the linen before the sages of the city; and the
sages shall take that man, scourge him, and fine him a
hundred shekels of silver, and give to the father of the
damsel, because he had brought out an evil report
against an upright virgin of Israel; and she shall be
his wife, nor shall he have power to put her away all his
days.   But if that word be true, and the witnesses of
virginity were not found with the damsel, then shall
they bring her forth to the door of her father's house,
and the men of that city shall stone her with stones that
she die; for she had wrought dishonour in Israel in
bringing the ill fame of whoredom against her father's
house; and so shall they put away the evil doer from
Israel. [JERUSALEM. But if this word be true, and
the damsel's witnesses are not found, they shall bring
that damsel from the door of her father's house, and the
people shall stone her.]

If a man be found lying with another's wife, both of
them shall be put to death; the man who hath lain
with the woman, and the woman.   Even if she be with
child, they shall not wait till she is delivered, but in the
same hour they shall put them to death by strangulation with the napkin, and cast away the evil doer from
Israel.

If a damsel a virgin is betrothed to a man, and
another man find her in the city, and lie with her, they

shall bring forth both of them to the door of the beth
din of that city, and stone them with stones that they
die; the damsel because she did not cry out in the city,
and the man because he lay with his neighbour's wife;
and you shall put away the evil doer from among you.
But if a man find a damsel in the wilderness, and do
violence to her and lie with her, the man only shall die
who lay with her, for the damsel is not guilty of death;
but her husband may put her away from him by a bill
of divorcement; for as when a man lieth in wait for his
neighbour and taketh his life, so is this matter: he
found her upon the face of the field; the betrothed damsel cried out for help, but there was no one to deliver her.

If a man find a damsel who is not betrothed, and seize
and lie with her, and they be found, then the man who
lay with her shall give to her father, as a fine for her
dishonour, fifty shekels of silver, and she shall be his
wife, because he humbled her, nor shall he have power
to put her away by divorcement all his days.

XXIII. A man should not take a wife who is bowed
down (or violated), or who hath had intercourse with
his father, much less his father's wife, nor disclose the
skirt that covereth his father. He who is castrated is not
fit to take a wife from the congregation of the Lord's
people. He who is born of fornication, or who hath
upon him the evil mark which is set upon the unclean
Gentiles, is not fit to take an upright wife from the congregation of the people of the Lord; nor unto the
tenth generation shall it be fit for him to enter into the
congregation of the Lord. Neither an Ammonite nor a
Moabite man is fit to take a wife from the congregation
of the Lord's people, nor unto the tenth generation shall
they take a wife from the congregation of the people of
the Lord, because they met you not with bread and
water in the way when you came from Mizraim, but

hired against you Bileam bar Beor from Pethor Chelmaya,[2] which is built in the land of Aram upon the Phrat, to curse you; but the Lord your God would not hearken unto Bileam, but turned in his mouth curses into blessings, because the Lord your God loveth you. Ye shall not seek their peace or their prosperity all your days, because, if even they become proselytes, they will entertain enmity in their hearts for ever. You shall not abhor an Edomite when he cometh to be a proselyte, for he is your brother; nor shall you abhor a Mizraite, because you were dwellers in their land. The children who are born to them in the third generation shall be fit to take wives from the people of the congregation of the Lord.

. When you go forth in hosts against your enemies, beware of every evil thing, of strange worship, the exposure of the shame, and the shedding of innocent blood. Should there be a man among you who is unclean from accidents of the night, let him go without the camp, and come not among the tents. But at evening time let him wash with water, and on the going down of the sun he may come within the camp. [JERU- SALEM. And at evening let him bathe with water.] Let a place be prepared for thee without the camp where thou mayest shed the water of thy feet, and insert a blade with your weapon in the place on which you bind your swords, and in thy sitting without thou shalt dig with it, and do what thou needest there, and turn and cover it. For the Shekinah of the Lord thy God walk- eth in the midst of thy camp to save you, and to deliver your enemies into your hands; therefore shall the place of your camps be holy, and nothing impure be seen in it, that His Shekinah go not up from you.

Thou shalt not deliver up a stranger into the hand of

---

[2] " Pethor of the Dreams."

the worshipper of idols; (the sojourner) who hath escaped to be among you shall be under the protection of My Shekinah; for therefore he hath fled from his idolatry. Let him dwell with you, and observe the commandments among you; teach him the law, and put him in a school in the place that he chooseth in one of your cities: employ (or, have business with) him, that he may do well, and trouble him not by words.

You shall not profane your daughters to make them harlots; nor shall any man of Israel debase himself by fornication. You shall not bring a gift of the hire of an harlot, nor the price of a dog, to offer it in the sanctuary of the Lord your God for any vow, much less as any of the oblations; for they are abominable, both of them, before the Lord your God. [JERUSALEM. There shall not be a harlot among the daughters of the house of Israel, nor a whoremonger among the sons of Israel. You shall not bring the hire of an harlot, nor the price of a dog.]

Thou shalt not make usury of that which is thine from thy neighbour upon the loan which thou lendest, either of money, or food, or any thing by which thou mayest make usury. To a son of the Gentiles thou mayest lend for usury, but to thy brother thou shalt not lend for usury; that the Lord thy God may bless thee in all that thou puttest thine hand unto, in the land into which thou art entering to possess it.

When you vow a vow before the Lord your God, delay not to fulfil it in (one of) the three festivals; for the Lord your God requiring will require it. And in the oblation there shall not be any fault or blemish, for in the prescription of the Lord of the world it is so ordained. And thou shalt not be guilty of keeping back (delaying) thy vow: though, if you refrain from vowing, it will not be sin in you, the oath which goeth from

your lips you shall confirm. The precepts of integrity
you shall verily perform, but that which is not right to do
ye shall not do; and according as you have vowed shall
you fulfil; sin offerings, trespass offerings, burnt sacrifices, and consecrated victims shall you present before
the Lord your God, and bring the libations and the
gifts of the sanctuary of which you have spoken (in
promises), and alms for the poor which your lips have
declared. When thou hast come for hire into thy
neighbour's vineyard, thou mayest eat there as thou wilt,
till thou art satisfied; but thou mayest not put any
into thy basket. When you go to work for hire in the
field of thy neighbour, thou mayest gather with thy
hands, but thou art not to put forth the sickle upon thy
neighbour's corn (for thyself).

XXIV. When a man hath taken a wife and gone
unto her, if she hath not favour in his eyes because he
findeth the thing that is wrong in her, then he may
write her a bill of divorce before the court of justice,
and put it into her power,[3] and send her away from his
house. And departing from his house she may go and
marry another man. But should they proclaim from
the heavens about her [4] that the latter husband shall
dislike her, and write her a bill of divorce, and put it
into her power to go from his house; or should they
proclaim about him that he the latter husband shall
die: it shall not be in the power of the first husband
who dismissed her at the beginning to return and take
her to be with him as his wife, after that she hath
been defiled; for that is an abomination before the
Lord: for the children whom she might bear should
not be made abominable, or the land which the Lord
your God giveth you to inherit become obnoxious to
the plague.

---

[3] *Veyitten bereshuthah.*   [4] *Veakrizu arah min shemaya.*

When a man hath taken a new wife a virgin, he shall not go forth with the army, lest anything evil befall him ; he shall be at leisure in his house one year, and rejoice with his wife whom he hath taken.

A man shall not take the millstones, lower or upper, as a pledge; for they are necessary in making food for every one. [JERUSALEM. You shall not take the upper and lower millstones for a pledge ; for the pledge is a necessary of life.] Neither shall a man join bride-grooms and brides by magical incantations; for what would be born of such would perish.[5] [JERUSALEM. Nor shall there be unlawful conjoinments of bride-grooms and brides; for what such produce is denied the life of the world to come.]

When a man is found stealing a person of his brethren of the sons of Israel, making merchandise of him, and selling him, that man shall die by strangulation with the napkin ; and you shall put away the evil doer from among thee.

Take heed that you cut not into flesh in which there is an ulcer ; but make careful distinction between the plague of leprosy and ulceration ; between the unclean and clean, according to all that the priests of the tribe of Levi shall teach you : whatever they prescribe to you be observant to perform. Be mindful that no one contemn his neighbour, lest he be smitten : remember that which the Lord your God did to Miriam, who contemned Mosheh for that which was not in him, when she was smitten with leprosy, and you were delayed in the way when coming out of Mizraim.

When a man hath lent any thing to his neighbour upon a pledge. he shall not enter into his house to take his pledge ; he shall stand in the street, and the man to

---

[5] *Arum naphesha deathid lemiphak minhun, hu mechabbel·* "For the soul that would proceed from them would perish."

whom thou hast made the loan shall bring out the
pledge to thee into the street.   If the man be poor, thou
shalt not have his pledge all night with thee; as the sun
goeth down, thou shalt return the pledge, that he may
lie in his garment and may bless thee; and to thee it
shall be righteousness, for the sun shall bear the witness
of thee before the Lord thy God.   [JERUSALEM. Thou
shalt certainly return the pledge to him as the sun
goeth down, that he may sleep in his garment, and may
bless thee; and to thee it shall be righteousness before
the Lord thy God.]

You shall not be hard upon your neighbours, or
shift (or decrease) the wages of the needy and poor
hireling of thy brethren, or of the strangers who sojourn
in your land, in your cities.   In his day thou shalt pay
him his hire.   Nor let the sun go down upon it;
because he is poor, and he hopes (for that hire) to sustain his life: lest he appeal against thee before the Lord,
and it be guilt in thee.   [JERUSALEM. You shall not
wilfully keep back the wages of the poor and needy of
your brethren.   In his day thou shalt pay his wages,
nor let the sun go down upon them; for he is poor, and
by means of his hire he sustaineth his life: that he may
not cry against thee before the Lord: so beware that it
become not guilt in you.]

Fathers shall not die either by the testimony [6] or for
the sin of the children, and children shall not die either
by the testimony [6] or for the sin of the fathers: every
one shall die, by proper witnesses, for his own sin.
Thou shalt not warp the judgment of the stranger, the
orphan, or the widow, nor shall any one of you take the
garment of the widow for a pledge, that evil neighbours
rise not and bring out a bad report against her when
you return her pledge unto her.   And remember that

[6] *Besahadutha.*

you were bondservants in the land of Mizraim, and that
the Word of the Lord your God delivered you from
thence; therefore have I commanded you to observe
this thing.

When you have reaped your harvests in your fields,
and have forgotten a sheaf in the field, you shall not
return to take it; let it be for the stranger, the orphan,
and the widow, that the Word of the Lord your God
may bless you in all the works of your hands. When
you beat your olive trees, you shall not search them
after (you have done it); for the stranger, the orphan,
and widow, let it be. [JERUSALEM. When you beat
your olive trees, search them not afterward; let them
be for the stranger, the orphan, and the widow.]
When you gather in your vineyard, you shall not glean
the branches after you; they shall be for the stranger,
the orphan, and widow. [JERUSALEM. When you
gather your vines, search not their branches afterwards;
let them be for the stranger and the widow.] So
remember that you were bondservants in the land of
Mizraim; therefore I command you to do this thing.

XXV. If there be a controversy between two men,
then they shall come to the judges, and they shall judge
them, and give the decision (or outweighing of) righteousness to the innocent, and of condemnation to the
guilty. And if the wicked deserve stripes, the judge
shall make him lie down, and they shall scourge him
in his presence by his judgment, according to the
measure of his guilt. [JERUSALEM. And if it be needful to scourge the guilty, the judge shall make him lie
down, and they shall smite him in his presence, according to the measure of his guilt, by number.] Forty
(stripes) may be laid upon him, but with one less shall
he be beaten, (the full number) shall not be completed,
lest he should add to smite him beyond those thirty and

nine, exorbitantly, and he be in danger ; and that thy
brother may not be made despicable in thy sight.

You shall not muzzle the mouth of the ox in the time
of his treading out; [JERUSALEM. Sons of Israel, My
people, you shall not muzzle the ox in the hour of his
treading;] nor the wife of the (deceased) brother, who
would be mated with one smitten with an ulcer, and
who is poorly related,[7] shalt thou tie up with him.

When brethren from the (same) father inhabit this
world at the same time, and have the same inheritance,
the wife of one of them, who may have died, shall not
go forth into the street to marry a stranger, her brother-
in-law shall go to her, and take her to wife, and become
her husband. And the first-born whom she beareth
shall stand in the inheritance in the name of the
deceased brother, that his name may not be blotted out
from Israel. But if the man be not willing to take his
sister-in-law, then shall his sister-in-law go up to the
gate of the beth din before five of the sages, three of
whom shall be judges and two of them witnesses, and
let her say before them in the holy language : My
husband's brother refuseth to keep up the name of his
brother in Israel, he not being willing to marry me.
And the elders of his city shall call him and speak
with him, with true counsel ; and he may rise up in the
house of justice, and say in the holy tongue, I am not
willing to take her. Then shall his sister-in-law come
to him before the sages, and there shall be a shoe upon
the foot of the brother-in-law, a heeled sandal whose
lachets are tied, the latchets at the opening of the sandal
being fastened ; and he shall stamp on the ground with
his foot ; and the woman shall arise and untie the
latchet, and draw off the sandal from his foot, and afterward spit before him, as much spittle as may be seen

---

[7] Or, "who hath nothing of his own."

by the sages, and shall answer and say, So is it fit to
be done to the man who would not build up the house
of his brother. And all who are standing there shall
exclaim against him, and call his name in Israel the
House of the Unshod. [JERUSALEM. And his name in
Israel shall be called the House of him whose shoe was
loosed, and who made void the law of Yeboom.[8]]

While men are striving together, if the wife of one of
them approach to rescue her husband from the hand of
him who smiteth him, and putting forth her hand layeth
hold of the place of his shame, you shall cut off her
hand; your eyes shall not pity. [JERUSALEM. If she put
forth her hand, and lay hold by the place of his shame.]

You shall not have in your bag weights that are
deceitful; great weights to buy with, and less weights
to sell with. Nor shall you have in your houses
measures that deceive; great measures to buy with, and
less measures to sell with. [JERUSALEM. You shall not
have in your houses measures and measures; great
ones for buying with, and small ones to sell with] Perfect weights and true balances shalt thou have, perfect
measures and scales that are true shall be yours, that
your days may be multiplied on the land which the
Lord your God giveth you. For whosoever committeth
these frauds, every one who acteth falsely in trade, is an
abomination before the Lord.

Keep in mind what the house of Amalek did unto
you in the way, on your coming up out of Mizraim;
how they overtook you in the way, and slew every one
of those among you who were thinking to go aside from
My Word; the men of the tribe of the house of Dan,
in whose hands were idols (or things of strange worship), and the clouds overcast them, and they of the

---

[8] Glossary, p. 69. The intricacies of this law are explained in the
Mishna, Treatise *Yebamoth*, and by Maimonides in his *Hilkoth Yeboom*.

house of Amalek took them and mutilated them, and they were cast up: but you, O house of Israel, were faint and weary from great servitude of the Mizraee, and the terrors of the waves of the sea through the midst of which you had passed. Nor were the house of Amalek afraid before the Lord. [JERUSALEM. Who overtook you in the way, and slew among you those who were thinking to desist from My Word, the cloud overcast him, and they of the house of Amalek took him and slew him. But you, people of the sons of Israel, were weary and faint; nor were they of the house of Amalek afraid before the Lord.] Therefore, when the Lord hath given you rest from all your enemies round about in the land that the Lord your God giveth you to inherit for a possession, you shall blot out the memory of Amalek from under the heavens; but of the days of the King Meshiha you shall not be unmindful.

SECTION L.

THABO.

XXVI. AND when you have entered into the land which the Lord thy God giveth you for an inheritance, and you possess and dwell in it; you shall take of the earliest first fruits which are ripe at the beginning, of all the produce of the ground which thou ingatherest from the land which the Lord your God hath given you, and put them into a basket, and go unto the place which the Lord your God will choose that His She-kinah may dwell there. And you shall put crowns upon the baskets, hampers, and paper cases, and bring them to the priest appointed to be the chief priest in those days, and shall say to him: We acknowledge this day before the Lord thy God that we have come into the land which the Lord sware unto our fathers to give us. [JERUSALEM. And thou shalt come to the priest who will be appointed the chief priest in those days, and say to him : We give glory and thanks this day before the Lord thy God, that we have come into the land which the Word of the Lord did covenant unto our fathers to give us.] And the priest shall receive the basket of early fruits from thy hand, and take, bring, uplift, and lower it, and afterward lay it down before the altar of the Lord your God. And you shall respond, and say before the Lord your God :

Our father Jakob went down into Aram Naharia at the beginning, and (Laban) sought to destroy him; but the Word of the Lord saved him out of his hands. And afterwards went he down into Mizraim and sojourned there, a few people; but there did he become a great people, and mighty and many. But the Mizraee evil-treated and afflicted us, and laid heavy bondage upon us. But we prayed before the Lord our God, and the Lord hearkened to our prayers, our affliction and our travail; and our oppression was manifest before Him. And the Lord brought us out of Mizraim with a mighty hand and uplifted arm, and with great visions, signs, and wonders, and brought us into this place, and gave us this land, a land of fruits rich as milk and sweet as honey. Now, therefore, behold, I have brought the early firsthngs of the fruit of the land which thou hast given me, O Lord.

And thou shalt lay them before the Lord thy God, and worship, and rejoice in all the good which the Lord thy God giveth thee, thou and the men of thy house, and enjoy and eat, you, the Levites and the sojourners who are among you.

When you make an end of tything all the tenths of your produce in the third year, which is the year of

release, you shall give the first tenth to the Levites, the
second tenth, which is the tythe of the poor, to the
stranger, the orphan, and widow, that they may eat in
your cities, and be satisfied. [JERUSALEM. When you
finish tything all the tenths of your produce in the
third year, which is the year of the tythe for the poor,
you shall give the first tenth to the Levites, and the
poor's tenth to the stranger, the orphan, and widow,
that they may eat in your cities, and be satisfied.] But
the third tenth you shall bring up, and eat before the
Lord thy God, and thou shalt say:

Behold, we have set apart the consecrations from the
house, and have also given the first tenth to the Levites,
the second tenth to the strangers, the fatherless, and the
widow, according to the commandment which Thou
hast commanded me. I have not transgressed one
of Thy commandments, nor have I forgotten. I have
not eaten of it in the days of my mourning, nor separated from it for the unclean, neither have I given of it
a covering for the soul of the dead:[9] we have hearkened
to the voice of the Word of the Lord; I have done
according to all that Thou hast commanded me.
[JERUSALEM. We have not eaten thereof in (our)
mourning, nor separated therefrom for the unclean, nor
given of it for the defiled soul; for we have obeyed the
voice of the Word of the Lord our God, we have done
according to all that Thou hast commanded us.] Look
down from heaven, from the habitation of the glory of
Thy holiness, and bless Thy people Israel, and the land
which Thou hast given to us, as Thou didst swear unto
our fathers, a land of fruits rich as milk and sweet as
honey. [JERUSALEM. Look down, we beseech Thee,
from the heavens, the habitation of Thy glory and Thy
holiness, and bless Thy people Israel, and the land

[9] Vide *Addenda.*

which Thou hast given us, as Thou didst swear unto
our fathers (to give us a land) producing good fruits,
pure as milk, sweet and delicious as honey.]

This day doth the Lord our God command you to
perform these statutes and judgments, which you shall
observe and do with all your heart and with all your
soul. The Lord have you confessed with one confession in the world this day; for so it is written, Hear, O
Israel: The Lord our God is one Lord; that He may be
thy God, and that thou mayest walk in the ways that
are right before Him, and keep His statutes, commandments, and judgments, and be obedient unto His Word.
And the Word of the Lord doth acknowledge (or
honour) you with one acknowledgment in the world
this day; as it is written, Who is as Thy people Israel,
a peculiar people upon the earth, to be to Him a people
beloved, as He hath said unto you, and that you may
obey all His commandments? [JERUSALEM. You have
chosen the Word of the Lord to be King over you this
day, that He may be your God. But the Word of the
Lord becometh the King over you for His Name's
sake, as over a people beloved as a treasure, as He
hath spoken to you, that you may obey all His commandments.] And He will set you on high, and exalt you
above all the peoples He hath made in greatness, and with
a name of glory and splendour, that you may be a holy
people before the Lord your God, as He hath spoken.

XXVII. And Mosheh and the elders of Israel instructed the people, saying: Observe all the commandments which I command you this day. And it shall be
on the day that you pass over the Jordana into the
land which the Lord your God giveth you, that you
shall erect for you great stones, and plaster them with
lime; and thou shalt write upon them all the words of
this law, when you go over to enter the land which the

Lord your God giveth you, a land whose fruits are rich as milk and producing honey, as the Lord God of your fathers hath said to you. When you pass over Jordana, you shall erect the stones that I command you on the mountain of Ebal, and plaster them with lime; and you shall build there an altar before the Lord your God, an altar of stone, not lifting up iron upon it. With perfect stones ye shall build an altar to the Lord your God, and offer sacrifices upon it before the Lord your God. And you shall immolate the consecrated victims, and eat there, and rejoice before the Lord your God. And upon the stones you shall write all the words of this law with writing deeply (engraven) and distinct, which shall be read in one language, but shall be interpreted in seventy languages. [JERUSALEM. And you shall write upon the stones all the glorious words of this law in writing deep and plain, to be well read, and to be interpreted in seventy tongues.]

And Mosheh and the priests, the sons of Levi, spake with all the people, saying: Listen, O Israel, and hear : This day are you chosen to be a people before the Lord your God. Hearken, therefore, to the Word of the Lord your God, and perform His commandments which I command you to-day. And Mosheh instructed the people that day, saying: These tribes shall stand to bless the people on the mountain of Gerezim when you have passed the Jordan,—Shemeon, Levi, Jehudah, Issakar, Joseph, and Benjamin ; and these tribes shall stand (to pronounce) the curses on the mountain of Ebal,—Reuben, Gad, Asher, Zebulon, Dan, and Naphtali. And the Levites proclaimed and said to every man of Israel with a high voice : Six tribes shall stand on Mount Gerezim, and six on Mount Ebal ; and the ark, the priests, and Levites in the midst. In blessing they shall turn their faces towards Mount Gerezim, and say :

Blessed shall be the man who maketh not an image or form, or any similitude which is an abomination before the Lord, the work of the craftsman's hand, and who placeth not such in concealment. In cursing, they shall turn their faces toward Mount Ebal, and say · Accursed be the man who maketh an image, figure, or any similitude which is an abomination before the Lord, the work of the craftsman's hand, or who placeth such in concealment. And all of them shall respond together, and say, Amen. Accursed is he who contemneth the honour of his father or his mother. And all of them shall answer together, and say, Amen. Accursed is he who shall transfer the boundary of his neighbour. And all of them shall answer together, and say, Amen. Accursed is he who causeth the pilgrim, who is like the blind, to wander from the way. And all of them shall answer together, and say, Amen. [JERUSALEM. Six tribes of them shall stand on Mount Gerezim, and six tribes on Mount Ebal. And the ark, with the priests and Levites in the midst. And all Israel, here and there, turning their faces towards Mount Gerezim, shall open their mouth in benediction : Blessed be the man who hath not made an image, or a figure, or any similitude which the Lord hateth, and which is an abomination before Him, (being) the work of man's hand, and who hath not hidden such. But in pronouncing the curses let them turn their faces toward Mount Ebal, and say : Accursed be the man who shall make an image, or figure, or any similitude which the Lord hateth, and which is an abomination to Him, the work of man's hands; or the man who hath concealed such. And all the people shall answer them, and say, Amen. Accursed be the man who changeth the bound mark. Accursed ʼbe the man who maketh the wayfarer, who is like the blind, to wander from the way. And all the people shall answer, and say, Amen.]

Accursed be he who perverteth the judgment of the stranger, the widow, and the fatherless. And all shall answer together, and say, Amen. Accursed is he who lieth with his father's wife, because he uncovereth his father's skirt. And all shall answer together, and say, Amen. Accursed is he who lieth with a beast. And all shall answer together, and say, Amen. Accursed is he who lieth with his sister, the daughter of his father or mother. And all shall answer together, and say, Amen. Accursed is he who shall lie with his mother-in-law. And all shall answer together, and say, Amen. [JERU-SALEM. Accursed is he who lieth with his mother-in-law. And all shall answer togther, and say, Amen.] Accursed is he who attacketh his neighbour with slander in secret. And all shall answer together, and say, Amen. Accursed is he who receiveth hire to kill and to shed innocent blood. And all shall answer together, and say, Amen.

The twelve tribes, each and every, shall pronounce the blessings altogether, and the curses altogether. In blessing, they shall turn their faces (in pronouncing) word by word towards Mount Gerezim, and shall say: Blessed is the man who confirmeth the words of this law to perform them. In cursing, they shall turn their faces towards Mount Ebal, and say: Accursed is the man who confirmeth not the words of this law to perform them. And all shall answer together, and say, Amen.

These words were spoken at Sinai, and repeated in the tabernacle of ordinance, and (again) the third time on the plains of Moab, in twelve sentences (words), as the word of every tribe; and each several commandment (was thus) ratified by thirty and six adjurations.

XXVIII. And it shall be, if you will diligently hearken to the Word of the Lord your God, to observe and perform all the commandments which I command

you this day, that the Lord your God will set you on
high, and exalt you above all the nations of the earth;
and all these blessings shall come upon you, and abide
with you, for that you will have hearkened to the Lord
your God.

Blessed shall you be in the city, and blessed in the
field.   Blessed shall be the offspring of your womb, the
fruits of your ground, the oxen of your herd, and the
flocks of your sheep.   Blessed shall be the basket of
your first fruits, and the first cakes of your flour.
Blessed shall you be in your coming in to your houses of
instruction, and blessed shall you be when you go out
to your affairs. [JERUSALEM. Blessed shall you be in the
baskets of your first fruits, and in your wheaten cakes.
Blessed shall you be when you go in to your houses of
instruction, and blessed when you go out of them.]
The Word of the Lord will cause your enemies who rise
up against you to hurt you, to be broken before you.
By one way they will come out to fight against you, but
by seven ways they shall be dispersed in fleeing before
you.   The Lord will command the blessing upon you
in your treasuries, and on all that you put your hands
unto, and will bless you in the land which the Lord
your God giveth you.   The Word of the Lord will
establish you to be a holy people before Him, as He
hath said unto you, when you keep the commandments
of the Lord your God, and walk in the ways that are
·right before Him.   And all the nations of the earth
will see that the Name is written by (His own) appointment on the tephillin that are upon thee, and will be
afraid of thee.   And the Word of the Lord will make
thee to abound in good, in the offspring of thy womb,
and the increase of thy cattle, and in the fruit of thy
ground, in the land which the Lord hath promised to
thy fathers.—Four keys are in the hand of the Lord of

all the world, which He hath not delivered into the
hands of any secondary power :[8] the key of life, and of
the tombs, and of food, and of rain; and thus did
Mosheh the prophet speak :—The Lord will open to you
His good treasure which is with Him in the heavens, and
will give you the rain of your land in its season; the
early in Marchesvan, and the latter in Nisan ; and will
bless you in all the works of your hands ; and you will
lend to many peoples, but shall have no need to borrow.
And the Word of the Lord will appoint you to be kings
and not subjects,[9] and to be ennobled and not abased,
when you have hearkened to the commandments of the
Lord your God which I command you this day to keep
and perform. Decline not from any of these words that
I teach you to-day either to the right or the left, in
walking after the idols of the Gentiles to serve them.

When Mosheh the prophet began to pronounce the
words of threatening, the earth trembled, the heavens
were moved, the sun and moon were darkened, the stars
withdrew their beams, the fathers of the world cried
from their sepulchres, while all creatures were silent, the
very trees waved not their branches. The fathers of the
world answered and said, Woe to our children should
they sin, and bring these maledictions upon them; for
how will they bear them ? lest destruction be executed
on them, and no merit of ours protect, and there be no
man to stand and intercede on their behalf ! Then fell
the Bath-kol from the high heavens, and said, Fear not,
ye fathers of the world; if the merit of all generations
should fail, yours shall not; and the covenant which I
have confirmed with you shall not be annulled, but will
(still) overshadow them.

Mosheh the prophet answered and said, Whomsoever I
threaten I threaten conditionally, saying, If you hearken

---

[8] *Tiphsera,* "a viceroy."   [9] *Hedistin,* "plebeians."

not to the Word of the Lord your God in neither observing nor doing all my commandments and statutes which I command you this day, then shall all these maledictions come upon and cleave unto you.

Accursed shall you be in the city and in the field. Accursed shall be the basket of your first fruits, and the first cakes of your flour. Accursed the children of your wombs, the fruits of your ground, the oxen of your herds, and the sheep of your flocks. Accursed shall you be in your going into the houses of your theatres, and the places of your public shows, to make void the words of the law; and accursed shall you be in your coming out to your worldly affairs. The Word of the Lord will send forth curses among you to curse your wealth, and confusion to confound your prosperity, and vexation with all that you put your hands to do, until He hath undone you, and you perish soon on account of the wickedness of your doings when you have forsaken My worship. The Word of the Lord will make the pestilence to cleave to you, to consume you from off the land which you are going to inherit. The Word of the Lord will smite you with abscess and inflammation, and fire in the bones that will burn up the marrow, and with fearful imaginations in the thoughts of the heart; and with the naked sword, and with blasting, and the jaundice of Macedonia, which shall follow you to your beds, until you are destroyed.

And the heavens above you shall be as brass which sweateth,[1] but that will not yield you any dew or rain; and the ground under you be as iron which sweateth not, nor maketh green the trees, nor yieldeth spiceries, fruits, nor herbs. After the rain which cometh down on the earth, the Lord will send a wind that shall drive

---

[1] *Mezia*, root, *zua*, *sudavit*, but also *contremuit, percussus est.* (Query.)

dust and ashes upon the herbage of your fields ; and calamity will fall upon you from the heavens, until you are consumed.

The Word of the Lord will cause you to be broken before your enemies : by one way you will go out to battle, but by seven ways shall you flee confounded before them, to become an execration in all the kingdoms of the earth. And your carcases will be cast out to be meat for all the fowls of the sky, and for the beasts of the earth, and no one will scare them away from your corpses. [JERUSALEM. And no one shall drive them away.] And the Word of the Lord will smite you with the ulcers with which the Mizraee were smitten, and with hæmorrhoids that blind the sight, and with blotches, and with erysipelas,[2] from which you will not be able to be healed. [JERUSALEM. The Word of the Lord will smite you with the ulcer of Mizraim, and with hæmorrhoids, and with the blotch, and with scurvy, which cannot be healed.] The Word of the Lord will smite you with fearfulness which bewildereth the brain, and with blindness and stupor of heart. And you will seek good counsel for enlargement from your adversities, but there will be none among you to show the truth, so that you will grope in darkness like the blind who have none passing by the road to see how to direct them in the way, nor shall you prosper in your ways, but be oppressed and afflicted all the days, without any to deliver.

Thou wilt betroth a wife, but another man will have her ; thou wilt build a house, but not dwell in it ; thou wilt plant a vineyard, but not make it common. Your oxen will be killed, you looking on, but without eating of them ; your asses will be taken away from before you, but they will not be returned ; your sheep will be

_____
[2] Or, "prurigo."

delivered over to your enemies, and there will for you be no deliverance; your sons and daughters will be given up to another people, and your eyes see it, and grow dim because of them from day to day; and in your hand will be no good work by which you may prevail in prayer before the Lord your Father who is in heaven, that He may save you. [JERUSALEM. Your sons and daughters shall be delivered unto another people, while your eyes behold and fail on account of them all the day; nor will you have the good works to give satisfaction unto God, that He might redeem you.]   The fruitage of your ground, and of all your labour, will a people whom thou hast not known devour, and thou shalt be oppressed and trodden down all the days.   And you will be maddened by the vengeance, and shaken by the sight of your eyes that you will see.   The Word of the Lord will smite you with a sore ulcer in the knees, because you bent (them) in the matter of the transgression; and in the legs, by which you ran into it; for if you be not converted to the law you cannot be saved, but will be beaten by it from the sole of your feet unto the crown of your head.

The Lord will make you and your king whom you may set over you to go away among a people that neither you nor your fathers have known; and you will carry tribute to peoples who worship idols of wood and stone.   And if the thought of your heart be to worship their idols, you shall be for astonishment, for proverbs and tales, among the sons of the Gentiles where the Lord will have scattered you.

You will carry much seed into the field, but gather in little, for the locust shall eat it.   [JERUSALEM. You will carry out, but collect little, for the locust will devour it.]   You will plant vineyards and till them, but will not drink the wine nor press out the vintage, because

the worm will have consumed it. You will have olive
trees in all your borders, but will not be anointed with
oil, for your olive trees will fail. [JERUSALEM. But
with oil you will not be anointed, for the bloom of your
olive trees shall be destroyed.] You will beget sons
and daughters, but they will yield you no advantage,
for they shall go into captivity. All the trees and fruits
of your land the locusts will destroy. [JERUSALEM.
Robbers shall take possession of the trees and the fruits
of your land.] The uncircumcised who dwelleth among
you will rise above you with ascension upon ascension,
but you will go downwards by descent after descent.
He will lend to you, but you will not lend to him; he
will be the master, and you the servant.

And all these curses will come on you, and will follow
and cleave to you until you have perished, because you
would not hearken to the Word of the Lord your God,
to observe His commandments and statutes which He
had commanded you. And they will be upon you for
signs and portents, and upon your children for ever; for
that you would not serve before the Lord your God
cheerfully, with rightness of heart for the abundance of
all good. But you will serve your enemies whom the
Word of the Lord will send against you, in hunger,
thirst, nakedness, and the want of every good; and they
will put an iron yoke upon your necks until it hath
worn you away. The Word of the Lord will cause a
people to fly upon you from afar, from the ends of
the earth, swift as an eagle flieth; a people whose
language thou wilt not understand; a people hard
in visage, who will not respect the old nor have
pity on the young. [JERUSALEM. A people hard in
visage, who will not respect the aged nor have mercy on
the children] And they will consume the increase of
your cattle and the fruit of your ground till you are

wasted away; for they will leave you neither corn, oil,
wine, herds, nor flocks, until the time that they have
destroyed you. And they will shut you up in your
cities until they have demolished your high walls
whereby you trusted to be saved in all your land; for
they shall besiege you in all your cities, in the whole
land which the Lord your God gave you. And the
children of your wombs shall be consumed; for you will
eat them in the famine, even the flesh of your sons and
daughters, whom the Lord your God did give you, by
reason of the anguish and oppression wherewith your
enemies shall oppress you. The man who is gentle and
refined among you will look with evil eyes upon his
brother, and the wife who reposeth on his bosom, and
upon the rest of his children who remain. He will not
give to one of them of the flesh of his children which
he eateth, because nothing remaineth to him in the
anguish and straitness with which I will straiten you in
all your cities. She who is delicate and luxurious among
you, who hath not ventured to put the sole of her foot
upon the ground from tenderness and delicacy, will look
with evil eyes upon the husband of her bosom, upon
her son and her daughter, and the offspring she hath
borne; for she will eat them in secret, through the want
of all things, by reason of the anguish and oppression
with which your enemies shall oppress you in your
cities. [JERUSALEM. The man who is gentle and
most tender among you will look with evil eyes upon
his brother, and on the wife of his youth, and on the
rest of his children who remain. She who is tender and
delicate among you, who hath not attempted to walk
with her feet upon the ground from delicacy and tenderness, will look with evil eyes on the husband of her
youth, and on her son and her daughter.]

If you observe not to perform all the commands of

this law written in this book, to reverence this glorious
and fearful Name, The Lord your God, the Word of
the Lord will hide the Holy Spirit from you, when the
plagues come upon you and your children, great and
continuous plagues which will not leave you, and
grievous and continual evils that will grow old upon
your bodies; and will turn upon you all the woes which
were sent upon the Mizraee before which thou wast
afraid, and they shall cleave to you; and evils also that
are not written in the book of this law will the Word
of the Lord stir up against you until you are consumed.
And you who were as the stars of heaven for multitude
will be left a few people, because you hearkened not to
the Word of the Lord your God. And as the Word
of the Lord rejoiced over you to do you good, and to
multiply you, so will He rejoice (in sending) against
you strange nations to destroy and make you desolate,
and you shall be uprooted from the land which you are
going to possess. And the Lord will disperse you
among all nations, from one end of the earth to the
other, and you shall be tributaries to the worshippers of
idols of wood and stone which neither thou nor thy
fathers have known. And if your mind be divided
to worship their idols, He will send (that) between you
and those nations that you shall have no repose or rest
for the sole of your feet, and will give you there a fearful heart which darkens the eyes and wears out the
soul. And your life will be in suspense; you will be
in dread day and night, and have no assurance of your
life. In the morning you will say, O that it were
evening! for afflictions will make the hours of the
day longer before you; and at evening you will say,
O that it were morning! for afflictions will make the
hours of the night longer before you, because of the
terror of your heart; for you will be in stupor by a

vision of your eyes, which you will see for punishment,
and be terrified.

And the Word of the Lord will bring you captive
to Mizraim in ships through the Sea of Suph, by the
way you passed over, of which I said to you, No more
shall you see it. [JERUSALEM. And the Word of the
Lord will cause you to return into Mizraim in galleys,[3]
by the way of which I said to you, Ye shall see it no
more.] And there will you be sold to your enemies, at
the beginning for a dear price, as artificers, and afterward at a cheap price, as servants and handmaids, until
you be worthless and (be consigned) to unpriced
labour, and there be none who will take you.[4]

XXIX. These are the words of the covenant which
the Lord commanded Mosheh to ratify with the children of Israel in the land of Moab, besides that
covenant which He ratified with them at Horeb.

And Mosheh called to all Israel, and said to them : You
have seen all the plagues which the Word of the Lord
wrought in the land of Mizraim on Pharoh and all his
servants, and all the inhabitants of that land ; those
great temptations, signs, and wonders which you saw
with your eyes. And the Word of the Lord hath
given you a heart not to forget, but to understand ;
eyes, not to blink, but to see ; ears, not to be stopped,
but to listen with : yet you have forgotten the law with
your heart, and have blinked with your eyes, and have
stopped your ears, unto the time of this day. And I
have led you forty years in the wilderness ; your garments have not become old upon your bodies, nor your
shoes worn away from your feet. You have not eaten
leavened bread, nor drunk wine new or old ; and My
law hath been diligently delivered in your schools, that
you might be occupied therein, and you might know

---

[3] *Be-libranaia.*   [4] Or, "and there be none to bring in."

that I am the Lord your God. And you came to this
place; and Sihon king of Heshbon and Og king of
Mathnan came out to meet us in battle array, and we
smote them, and subdued their land, and gave it for an
inheritance to the tribe of Reuben, Gad, and the half
tribe of Menasheh. Keep, therefore, the words of this
covenant and perform it, that you may have prosperity
in all that you do. [JERUSALEM. And you shall keep
the words of this covenant and perform them, that you
may prosper in all that you do.]

SECTION LI.

NITSTSABIM.

MOSHEH the prophet said: I have called you not in
secret, but while standing this day all of you before the
Lord your God; the princes of your sanhedrin, the
chiefs of your tribes, your elders and your officers, all
men of Israel, your little ones, your wives, and your
sojourners who are in your camps, from the hewer of
your wood to the filler of your water, that you may
enter into the covenant of the Lord your God, and may
have in remembrance the oath which the Lord your
God doth ratify with you this day: [JERUSALEM. Your
little ones, wives, and sojourners within your camps,
from the hewer of your wood to the filler of your water,
that you may not transgress the covenant of the Lord
your God, nor the oath which He confirmeth with you
this day:] that you may stand to-day before Him a
purified people; and that He may be a God to you, as
He hath spoken to you, and as He did swear unto
Abraham, Izhak, and Jakob.

And not with you only do I ratify this covenant, and
attest this adjuration; but all the generations which
have arisen from the days of old stand with us to-day

before the Lord our God, and all the generations which
are to arise unto the end of the world, all of them
stand with us here this day. [JERUSALEM. All the
generations which have arisen from the days of old
until now stand with thee to-day before the Lord your
God, and all the generations which are to arise after us
stand also here with us to-day.] For you know the
number of the years that we dwelt in the land of
Mizraim, and the mighty works which were wrought
for us among the nations through which you have
passed. You have seen their abominations, and their
idols of wood and stone which they have set forth in
the streets, and the idols of silver and gold that they
have placed with themselves in the houses, shutting the
doors after them lest they should be stolen.   Beware,
then, lest there be among you now or hereafter a man,
woman, family, or tribe, whose heart may be turned
away to wander any day from the service of the Lord
our God to worship the idols of those nations; or lest
there be among you the error which striketh root (in
them) whose heart wandereth after his sin; for the
beginning of sin may be sweet, but its end is bitter as
the deadly wormwood; [JERUSALEM. You have seen
their hateful things and their abominations, the idols of
wood and stone, of silver and gold; idols of wood and
stone set forth in the streets, but those of silver and
gold kept with themselves in the house because they
were afraid they would be stolen.......Lest there be
among you man or woman, family or tribe, whose heart
is turned away this day from the Lord our God to go
and worship the idols of these people, or there be a
man among you whose heart pondereth upon sin, which
is like a root struck into the earth; for its beginning
may be sweet as honey, but its end will be bitter as the
deadly wormwood;] or it be that when he heareth

2 F 2

the words of this curse he become reprobate in his heart, saying : I shall have peace, though I go on in the strength of the evil desires of my heart : so that he will add presumption to the sins of ignorance. It will not be pleasing to the Lord to forgive him ; for the Lord's anger and indignation will wax hot against that man, and all the words of the curses written in this book will rest upon him, and the Lord will blot out the memorial of his name from under the heavens. And the Lord will separate him unto evil, from all the tribes of Israel, according to all the maledictions of the covenant which are written in this book. And the generations of your children who will arise after you, and the stranger who will come from a far-off land, when they see the plagues of that land, and the afflictions which the Lord will have sent upon it, the whole land burnt with brimstone, salt, and fierce heat, no longer fit for sowing, nor productive of a blade of any springing herbage ; ruined, as Sedom and Amorah, Admah and Zeboim, were overthrown by the Word of the Lord in His wrath and indignation ; then all people will say : Why hath the Lord done so unto this land ? What meaneth the strength of this great anger ? And they will say, Because they forsook the covenant of the Lord, the God of their fathers, which He made with them when He brought them out of the land of Mizraim. But they went after their evil desires, and served the gods of the Gentiles, and worshipped gods which they had not known nor had any part with. And the anger of the Lord waxed strong against this land, to bring upon it all the curses written in this book. And the Lord hath made them to wander forth from their country with anger, indignation, and wrath, and hath cast them into captivity in another land until this day.

The secret things are manifest before the Lord our

God, and He will take vengeance for them; but the things that are revealed are delivered unto us and to our children for ever, to perform by them the thing that is right, for the confirmation of all the words of this law.

XXX. And it will be, when all these words of blessings, or their contraries, which I have set in order before you shall have come upon you, you will be converted in your hearts to return unto My fear, in all the dispersions (among) the nations where the Lord will have scattered you. The upright of you will be favoured with a blessed repentance; and though you have sinned, yet shall your repentance come up unto the glorious throne of the Lord your God, if you will hearken to His Word according to all that I hav commanded you this day, you, and your children, with all your heart and with all your soul. And His Word will accept your repentance with favour, and will have mercy upon you, and He will gather you again from all the nations whither the Lord your God had scattered you. Though you may be dispersed unto the ends of the heavens, from thence will the Word of the Lord gather you together by the hand of Elijah the great priest, and from thence will He bring you by the hand of the King Meshiha. And the Word of the Lord your God will bring you into the land which your fathers possessed by inheritance, and you shall possess it, and He will bless you and increase you more than your fathers. And the Lord your God will take away the foolishness of your heart, and of your children's heart; for He will abolish evil desire from the world, and create good desire, which will give you the dictate to love the Lord your God with all your heart and soul, that your lives may flow on for evermore. And the Word of the Lord your God will send these curses upon your enemies who have oppressed you in your captivities, and such as

have hated and persecuted, to destroy you. But you
shall return, and be obedient to the Word of the Lord,
and do all His commandments that I command you this
day. And the Lord your God will make you to abound
in good; for you shall prosper in all the works of your
hands, in the offspring of thy womb, the increase of thy
cattle, and the produce of your land, for good, for the
Word of the Lord will return, to rejoice over you, to bless
you, as He rejoiced over your fathers, if you will hearken to
the Word of the Lord your God in keeping His commandments and statutes which are written in the book of this
law, when you have returned to the fear of the Lord
your God with all your heart and with all your soul.

For this commandment which I command you to-day
is not hidden from you, nor afar off. It is not in the
heavens, that thou shouldst say, Who will ascend for us
into heaven, and bring it to us to make us hear, that we
may do it? Neither is it beyond the great sea, that
thou shouldst say, Who will go beyond the sea for us,
and fetch it for us to make us hear, that we may do it?
For the Word is nigh you, in your schools;[4] open your
mouth, that you may meditate on it; purify your hearts,
that you may perform it. Behold, I have set before you
this day the way of life, wherein is the recompense of
the reward of good unto the righteous, and the way of
death, wherein is the retribution of the wages of evil
unto the wicked. [JERUSALEM. The law is not in
the heavens, that thou shouldst say, O that we had one
like Mosheh the prophet to ascend into heaven, and bring
it to us, and make us hear its commands, that we may do
them! Neither is the law beyond the great sea, that
thou shouldst say, O that we had one like Jonah the
prophet, who could descend into the depths of the sea,
and bring it to us, and make us hear its commands, that

---

[4] *Be-beth medrashkun.*

we may do them! For the word is very nigh you, in
your mouth, that you may meditate upon it, and in your
hearts, that you may perform it. See, behold, I have
set before you this day the way of life, which is the path
of the good, and the way of death, which is the path of
the evil.] For I teach you to-day to love the Lord
your God, and to walk in the ways that are right before
Him, and to keep His commandments, statutes, and
judgments, and live and multiply; that the Lord your
God may bless you in the land into which you are
entering to possess it. But if you think in your heart
that you will not obey, but will go astray to worship the
idols of the nations, and serve them, I proclaim to you
this day, that you will perish, and will not prolong your
days on the land to which you are to pass over the
Jordan to possess it. I attest this day, not only you,
who are to pass away from this world, but the heavens
and the earth, that I have set before you life and death,
blessing and its reverse. Choose therefore the way of
life, even the law, that you and your children may live
the life of the world to come; that you may love the
Lord thy God, to obey His Word, and keep close unto
His fear; for the law in which you occupy yourselves
will be your life in this world,[5] and the prolongment
of your days in the world[5] that cometh, and you shall
be gathered together at the end of the scattering,[6] and
dwell upon the land which the Lord sware to your fathers,
to Abraham, Izhak, and Jakob, to give it unto them.

SECTION LII.

VAIYELEK.

XXXI. And Mosheh went into the tabernacle of the
house of instruction,[7] and spake these words unto all

---

[5] Or, "age."   [6] Or, "captivity."   [7] *Beth ulphana.*

Israel, and said to them : I am the son of a hundred
and twenty years this day. I am no more able to go
out and come in, and the Word of the Lord hath said
to me : Thou shalt not go over this Jordan. The Lord
your God, and His Shekinah, will go over before you.
He will destroy those nations, and you shall possess
them. Jehoshua also will go before you, as the Lord
hath said. And the Lord will execute judgment on
them, as He did on Sihon and Og kings of the Amoraee,
and the people of their land, whom He destroyed. And
the Word of the Lord will deliver them up before you,
and you shall do to them according to all the commandment that I have commanded you. Be strong,
then, and of good courage, fear not, nor be dismayed
before them ; for the Shekinah of the Lord your God
will be the Leader of you, He will not forsake nor be
far from you.

And Mosheh called Jehoshua from among the
people, and said to him · Be thou strong, and of good
courage ; for thou art appointed to go with this people
to the land which the Word of the Lord sware to your
fathers to give them, and thou art to divide it among
them. And the Shekinah of the Word of the Lord will
go before thee, and His Word will be thy helper; He
will not forsake nor be far from thee; fear not, nor be
dismayed.

And Mosheh wrote this law, and delivered it to the
priests the sons of Levi, who bare the ark of the Lord's
covenant, and to all the sages of Israel. And Mosheh
commanded them, saying : At the end of seven years in
the time of the year of remission, at the feast of Tabernacles, when all Israel cometh to appear before the
Lord your God, in the place that He will choose, you
shall read this law before all Israel while they listen.
Assemble the people, the men, that they may learn,

the women, that they may hear instruction, the
children, that they may partake the benefit (reward) of
those who bring them, and your sojourners who are in
your cities, that they may behold the majesty of the
law, and be reverent all of them before the Word of the
Lord your God, and observe to do all the words of this
law.   Let their children also, who know not, hear, and
learn to fear the Lord your God all the days that you
live in the land to inherit which you pass over Jordan.

Unto three of the just was it told that the time of
their death was drawing nigh, and that they should not
attain to the days of their fathers , and each of them
had been appointed a prince in his days; Jakob our
father, David the king, and Mosheh the prophet; for
thus it is written : And the Lord said unto Mosheh,
Behold, thy day approacheth when thou must die.
Call Jehoshua, and stand both of you in the tabernacle
of ordinance, that I may give him charge.   And
Mosheh and Jehoshua went, and stood in the tabernacle of ordinance.   And the glorious Shekinah of the
Lord revealed itself at the tabernacle in the pillar of the
Cloud, and the pillar of the Cloud stood over the door
of the tabernacle, and Mosheh and Jehoshua stood
without.   And the Lord said to Mosheh, Behold, thou
wilt lie down in the dust with thy fathers, and thy soul
shall be treasured in the treasury of eternal life with
thy fathers : but this wicked people will rise up and go
astray after the idols of the nations among whom they
come, and will forsake My worship, and change My
covenant which I have made with them. [JERUSALEM.
They will forsake, and will profane the statutes I have
confirmed with them.]   Then My anger will be kindled
against them in that day, and I shall abhor them, and
remove My Shekinah from them, and they will become
a prey, and many evils and troubles shall befall them.

And they will say at that time, with adjuration, Is it not because the Shekinah of my God dwelleth not among me, that all these evils have befallen me? But I will indeed remove My Shekinah from them at that time, until they have dwindled away, to receive the punishment of their sins for all the evil they have wrought, because they turned themselves after the idols of the nations. And now, write you this hymn, and teach the children of Israel; put it upon their lips, that this hymn may be before them, for a witness against the children of Israel. For I will bring them into the land which I promised to their fathers, (a land) producing milk and honey, and they will eat and be satisfied : but (after that they have) waxen fat they will turn away to the idols of the Gentiles and worship them; so will they provoke Me to anger, and abolish My covenant. And when these many evils and troubles shall come upon them, then will this hymn bear witness to them for a testimony; for it is revealed before Me that it will not be forgotten on the lips of their children : for their evil disposition to which they are yielding to-day, even before I bring you into the promised land, is known to Me.

And Mosheh wrote this hymn, and taught the children of Israel. And He commanded Jehoshua bar Nun, saying : Be strong and of good courage; for thou art to bring the sons of Israel into the land I have promised to them, and My Word shall be thy Helper. And when Mosheh had finished to write the words of this law upon parchment[s] to complete them, [JERU-SALEM. When Mosheh had completed to write the glorious words of this law until they were finished,] he commanded the Levites who bare the ark of the Lord's covenant, saying : Take the book of this law, and put

[s] *Gevila*, which signifies also "freestone."

it into a chest on the right side of the ark of the
covenant of the Lord your God, that it may be for a
testament to you.   For your rebellion is revealed
before me, and the obduracy of your neck.   Behold,
while I am yet alive among you to-day ye are rebellious
before the Lord; but how much more when I am dead!
[JERUSALEM. How much more when I am dead!]
Gather together to me all the sages of your tribes and
your officers, and I will speak all these words in their
hearing, and will call heaven and earth to bear witness
against them.   For I know that after my death corrupting you will corrupt your works, and go astray
from the way I have commanded you, and that evil will
befall you in the end, because you will do what is wrong
before the Lord in provoking Him to anger.   And
Mosheh spake in the hearing of all the congregation of
Israel the words of this hymn until they were ended.

SECTION LIII.

HAAZINU.

XXXII. AND when the last end of Mosheh the prophet
was at hand, that he should be gathered from among the
world, he said in his heart : I will not attest against this
people with witnesses that taste of death in this world, behold, I attest against them with witnesses which do not
taste of death in this world, and whose destination is to be
renewed in the world to come.   Isaiah the prophet, when
he prophesied in the congregation of Israel, attributed
hearing to the heavens, and attentiveness to the earth ;
because (in his case) earth was nearest and heaven more
remote: but Mosheh the prophet, when he now prophesied in the congregation of Israel, attributed hearing to
the earth, and attentiveness to the heavens; because (in

his case) heaven was nearest and earth more remote;
for. so it is written, Attend, ye heavens, and I will speak;
and hear, O earth, the words of my mouth. My doctrine shall smite the rebellious like heavy rain; but
shall be enjoyed with pleasantness by those who receive
instruction, as the dew: my words shall be like the
downfalling rain of the wind that breathes upon the
grass in the month of Marchesvan, and as the drop-
pings of the latter rain which water the springing
herbage of the earth in Nisan.

[JERUSALEM. When the end of Mosheh came, that
he should be removed from the world, he said: Behold,
I testify in this world a thing which tasteth not of
death; so will I attest against them the heavens and
earth which taste not of death in this world, but whose
end is to be consumed in the world that cometh. For
so he explained, and said: Lift up your eyes to the
heavens, and consider the earth beneath; for the
heavens shall dissolve like smoke, and the earth fade
away as a garment, but I have prepared to create new
heavens and a new earth. Isaiah the prophet, when he
prophesied in the congregation of Israel, because he was
remote from the heavens and nearest the earth, attributed hearing to the heavens, and attention to the
earth: for so he explaineth, and saith: Hear, O
heavens, and listen, O earth; for the Word of the Lord
hath spoken. Mosheh the prophet, &c. (as above.)
The doctrine of my law shall be sweet to the children
of Israel as the rain, the word of my mouth will be
received by them with pleasantness as the dew, as the
wind which breathes upon the herb, and as the drops of
the latter rain that descend and water the herbage of
the ground in Nisan.]

Woe to the wicked who make memorial of the Holy
Name with blasphemies. Wherefore Mosheh, who was

the Doctor of Israel, would not permit himself to pronounce the Holy Name until he had dedicated his
mouth at the beginning of his hymn with eighty and
five letters, making twenty and one words, and afterwards he spake: In the Name of the Lord I invoke
you, O house of Israel, to ascribe glory and greatness
before our God. [JERUSALEM. Mosheh the prophet
said: Woe to the wicked who make memorial of the
Holy Name with blasphemies. For it is not possible
even to one of the highest angels to utter that Name
rightly until that they have said, Holy, Holy, Holy!
thrice.   And from them did Mosheh learn not to utter
that Name openly until he should have dedicated his
mouth with twenty-one words which consist of eighty-
five letters;[9] and so explained he and said: Hear, ye
heavens, and I will speak; for it is the Name. of the
Lord.   Mosheh the prophet said: O people of Israel, I
invoke you, in the Name of the Lord, to give glory,
praise, and highest exaltation unto God.]

Mosheh the prophet said: When I ascended the
mountain of Sinai, I beheld the Lord of all the worlds,
the Lord, dividing the day into four portions; three
hours employed in the law, three with judgment,
three in making marriage bonds between man and
woman, and appointing to elevate or to abase, and
three hours in the care of every created thing : for so it
is written : The Mighty One whose works are perfect,
for all His ways are judgment, a faithful God before
whom no iniquity comes forth, pure and upright is He.
[JERUSALEM. (The same words to)—three hours, uniting
the marriage yoke of the husband to the wife......a
faithful God and true; falsehood is not before Him;
He is just and upright in judgment.]

The beloved children have corrupted their good

---

[9] The Hebrew text of verses 1-3, to the word *shem* inclusive.

works, a blemish is found upon them; a perverse generation which have altered their works; so shall the order of this world's judgment be altered upon them. [JERUSALEM. The children have corrupted their works, and not them only, but themselves also: they have so corrupted that the spot is upon them; a depraved and perverse generation which changeth its work, and the order of this world shall be changed upon it.]

Can you indeed so requite the Name of the Word of the Lord, O foolish people, and receive the law, yet not be made wise? Is He not your Father who bought [1] you, who created you and established you? [JER. Do you return this before the Lord, O people foolish and unwise? Is He not your Father who is in heaven, who bought you? He created and founded you.] Remember the days of old; consider the years of every generation; read the books of the law, and they will teach you, and the books of the prophets, and they will tell you. [JER. Be mindful of the days, the days of old, consider the years of one generation and another; ask your fathers who are greater in the law than you, and they will teach you, the sages, and they will tell you.] When the Most High made allotment of the world unto the nations which proceeded from the sons of Noach, in the separation of the writings and languages of the children of men at the time [2] of the division, He cast the lot among the seventy angels, the princes of the nations with whom is the revelation to oversee the city, even at that time He established the limits of the nations according to the sum of the number of the seventy souls of Israel who went down into Mizraim. [JER. When the Most High divided the nations by lot, and distinguished the languages of

[1] Or, "who possessed."
[2] "Age or generation." The dispersion at Babel

the children of men, He appointed the bounds of the
peoples according to the number of the tribes of the
Beni Israel.]

And when the holy people fell to the lot of the Lord
of all the world, Michael opened his lips and said :
Let the good portion of the Name of the Lord's Word
be with Him.   Gabriel opened his lips with thanks-
givings, and said, Let the house of Jakob be the lot of
His inheritance. [JER. Because the Lord's portion
are His people, and the house of Jakob the lot of
His inheritance.]   He found them dwelling in the
wilderness, in the solitude, the place of howling demons
and thorns, the place of thirsting ; He overspread them
with His seven glorious clouds ; He taught them His
law ; He kept them as the Shekinah keepeth the apple
of His eye. [JER. He found them wandering in a
desert land, in the solitude of a howling wilderness ;
He threw over them clouds of glory ; His Shekinah
taught them the Ten Words, watched over them, and
kept them as the apple of His eye.] As an eagle stirreth
up and careth for his nest, and hovereth over his young,
so did His Shekinah stir up the tents of Israel, and the
shadow of His Shekinah overspread them ; and as an
eagle outstretcheth his wings over his young ones,
beareth them and carrieth them upon his wings, so bare
He them and carried them, and made them dwell upon
the strong places of the land of Israel.   [JER. As
an eagle stirreth up his nest, and carefully spreadeth
out his wings, and taketh and beareth them with the
strength of his wings.]   The Word of the Lord made
them to dwell in His land, nor suffered any among
them to be the followers of strange worship. [JER.
The Lord alone caused them to dwell, and none
were among them who served with strange worship.]
He made them to dwell in the strong places of the

land of Israel, and give them to eat of the goodly
produce of His field, and nourished them with the honey
of its fruits which grow even upon the rocks, with the
oil of its olive trees, and from branches (growing) out
of the rocks. [JER. He made them ride upon the
high places of the earth, and gave them to eat of
royal delicacies, and nourished them with honey out of
the rock, and with oil from their olives (growing) out of
the flinty stone of the rock.] He gave them rich butter
of kine from the spoil of their kings, and the fat of the
firstlings of the sheep from the prey of their sultans,
with the choice rams and goats of the flocks of Mathnan.
Mosheh the prophet said : If the people of Israel will
observe the precepts of the law, it is foretold that their
wheat granary shall be like the kidneys of oxen, and
that from one bunch of grapes shall come forth a kor
of red wine. [JER. Tender oxen and choice flocks,
goodly fatlings, rams bred in Batenaia, and goats, with
the richest of the wheat. Mosheh the prophet said : If
the children of Israel will observe the precepts of the
law......from one bunch they shall drink a cup of wine.]

But the house of Israel grew rich and wicked, they
prospered much and possessed wealth, and forsook the
worship of Eloah who created them, and provoked Him
to anger who redeemed them. They moved Him to
jealousy with strange worship, by their abominations
they made Him angry. They sacrificed to idols, resem-
bling devils, in whom there is no profit, to idols which
they had not known, new gods lately made, with which
your fathers had nothing to do. But the adorable
Strong One who created you have you forgotten ; of the
Word of Eloha who strengthened you so often [3] have
you been forgetful. And when it was manifest before
the Lord, He was wroth, provoked thereto by His

---

[3] Or, "who so often gave you refuges."

beloved children who were called upon His Name
sons and daughters. [JER. But the house of Jeshu-
ron ate and kicked; they became rich, and rebelled;
they prospered, got wealth, and forsook the Word of
God who had created them, and refused to worship the
Almighty who had redeemed them. They provoked
Him to anger with their idols, by their abominations
they made Him wroth. They sacrificed to demons in
whom is no stability,[4] idols which they had not known,
lately formed, which your fathers remembered not. The
Almighty who created you ye have forgotten, and have
forsaken the Word of God who gave you to be, and
made you so many refuges. And it was manifest
before the Lord, and He was angry, because the beloved
children had provoked Him, even they who were beloved
by Him as sons and daughters.] And He said, I will
take away from them the favour of My countenance; it
will be seen what will be the end; for they are a
perverse generation, children who have not faith. They
have made Me jealous by that which is not God, they
have angered Me by their vanities : I also will provoke
them to jealousy by a people which hath not been
a people, by the foolish Babylonian people will I
provoke them. [JER. And He said, I will surely turn
away the favour of My countenance from them; I will
see what will be in their latter end; for they are a
perverse generation, children in whom is no faith. They
have moved Me to jealousy by their idols in which there
is nothing whatever, they have provoked Me by their
abominations; but I also will move them to jealousy by
a people which is not a people, by a foolish nation will
I anger them] For an east wind strong as fire shall
go out before Me, and blaze in the might of My anger,
and burn to the lowest hell; it shall consume the land

---

[4] Or, " subsistence "

with its produce, and set the foundations of the
mountains in flame. [JER. For a fire shall come
forth in the hour of My wrath, and burn to the
lowest hell, devouring the earth and its fulness, and
setting in flame the foundations of the hills.] And
when they dwell in Babel they will serve their idols; for
I have spoken in My Word to array calamities against
them, the plague-arrows of My vengeance to destroy
them. I will make them go into captivity in Media
and Elam, in the captivity of Babel, the house of Agag
who are like demons gaping with famine, and to corpses
devoured by birds, and to stricken evil spirits of the
noon, to Lillin and to spirits big with evil. And the
Javanaee (Greeks) who bite with their teeth like wild
beasts will I send against them, and will shake them by
the hand of the Syrians venomous as basilisks, the
serpents of the dust. [JER. I have spoken in My
Word to bring evil upon them, the arrows of My
vengeance will I send among them: gaping with famine,
devoured by unclean fowl, filled with evil spirits, even
the teeth of the four kingdoms, which are like wild
beasts,[5] will I send among them, with the poison of
serpents, the reptiles of the earth.] A people who will
come from beyond the land of Israel shall consume them
with the stroke of the sword, and those who are left in
the land of Israel will I throw into the terror of death,
in the chambers here and there where they sleep; their
young men shall perish, their maidens, their sucklings, with their men and their elders. [JER. In the
street the sword will devour them; in the chambers
where they sleep, the terrors of death; their young men
and maidens, their infants and aged men.] I have
spoken in My Word to withhold from them My Holy
Spirit; I will make them weak; as a man who reaps

[5] Dan. vii.

his field leaveth but one upon the ground, so will I
abolish their memory from the book of the genealogy
of mankind; [JER. I have spoken in My Word to
bring wrath upon them, and to cause their memorial to
fail from among men;] but for the wrath of the enemy,
and that their oppressors would glorify themselves
against Me, and say, Our hand hath taken vengeance
upon our adversaries, and all this hath not been decreed
by the Lord ;—for they are a people lost to good counsel
and void of understanding. O that they were intelligent
in the law, and that they understood what they will
become in their latter end ! How will one foe pursue a
thousand of them, and two put ten thousand of them
to flight, unless He who is their strength deliver
them, and the Lord avenge them ! [JER. But that
the wrath of the enemy would wax strong, that they
could not prevail against their foes; and that they may
not say, Our hand hath avenged us on our adversaries,
and it hath not been done by the Lord; for this people
perish by evil counsels, and they are void of understanding. If Israel were but wise, learning the law they would
understand what shall be in their latter end. When
Israel was diligent in the law, and observed the commandments, one of them chased a thousand, and two of
them put ten thousand to flight; but because they have
sinned and vexed the Almighty to anger, He hath left
them to the hand of their enemies.]

For the idols of the Gentiles are not as He who is the
Strength of Israel ; for the Strength of Israel, when they
have sinned, bringeth punishment upon them ; but when
they stretch forth their hands in prayer, He answereth
and delivereth them. But the idols of the peoples of
strange worships are of no use : but because we have
provoked Him, and have not returned to His service,
our adversaries are our witnesses and our judges.

[JER. For the confidence of the nations is not as our
confidence; but because we have sinned and provoked
Him to anger, our adversaries are made our judges.]
For the works of this people are like the works
of the people of Sedom, and their evil counsels
like those of the people of Amorah; their wicked
thoughts are as serpents' heads; bitter therefore to them
is their punishment which maketh desolate. Behold,
as the bitterness of serpents when they come forth from
their wines, (?) so shall be the bitter cup of the curse
which they are to drink in the day of their punishment,
and cruel as the head of asps. [JER. For the
works of this people are like those of the people of
Sedom, and their thoughts like those of the people of
Amorah: their evil works make them desolate, and become
bitter to them. For the poison of this people is like that
of serpents what time they drink wine, and their malice
like the head of asps and cruel reptiles.] Are not their
secret works all known before Me? Sealed and laid up
are they in My treasury! Vengeance lies before Me,
and I will recompense them at the time when their foot
shall move to the captivity; for the day of their destruction is coming near, and the evil which is prepared
for them maketh haste. [JER. Is not this the cup of
punishment, mixed and ordained for the wicked, sealed
in My treasuries for the day of the great judgment?
Vengeance is mine: I am He who repayeth; in the
time when the foot of the righteous is moved; for the
day of destruction for the wicked is nigh, the fire of
Gehinnam is prepared for them, and their punishment
girdeth itself to come upon them.]

For the Word of the Lord adjudgeth in His mercy
the judgment of His people Israel, and for the evil He
hath appointed upon His servants there shall be
repentance before Him; for He knoweth that in the

time when they have sinned the stroke of their enemies will be heavy upon them, and help have passed away from their hands, and the faithful will have failed with their good works and be scattered and forsaken. And the enemy will say, Where is the fear of Israel, their Strength in whom they confided, who ate the fat of their sacrifices, and drank the wine of their libations? Let Him now rise up and help you, let Him shield you by His Word. [JER. For the Lord Himself will adjudge the judgment of the people of the children of Israel, and comfort His righteous servants; for it is manifest before Him that the hand of the righteous will waver, and that they will be forsaken and cast down, with none to help or support them. For the Gentiles will say, Behold, the God of Israel is strong, in whom they put their trust; they brought before Him the fat of their sacrifices, and the wine of their libations; let Him who (once) was over them as a shield rise up now and deliver them.]

When the Word of the Lord shall reveal Himself to redeem His people, He will say to all the nations: Behold now, that I am He who Am, and Was, and Will Be, and there is no other God beside Me: I, in My Word, kill and make alive; I smite the people of the Beth Israel, and I will heal them at the end of the days; and there will be none who can deliver them from My hand, Gog and his armies whom I have permitted to make war against them. [JER. See now that I in My Word am He, and there is no other God beside Me. I kill the living in this world, and make alive the dead in the world that cometh; I am He who smiteth, and I am He who healeth; and there is none who can deliver from My hand.] I have lifted My hand with an oath to heaven, and have said, As I exist, I will not abolish My oath for ever. If I whet my sword, as lightning it

will prevail in the judgment of My hand. I will return
retribution on them who afflict My people, and repay to
their enemies the hire of their wickedness. I will make
My arrows drunk with the blood of their slain, and
the captivity of their hosts shall be the punishment
of My people's foes. [JER. For I have uplifted My
hand with an oath to heaven, and said, I live, and
My Word subsisteth for ever: If I whet My sword as
lightning, My right hand will prevail in judgment. I
will render punishment upon the adversaries of My
people, I will repay them for their evil deeds. I will
make My arrows drunk with their blood, and My sword
shall consume their flesh; with the blood of the
destroyers of My people, their captives, and the chieftains
of their hosts.]

Rejoice, ye nations, (and) ye people of Beth Israel;
for the blood of His servants which was shed, He hath
avenged. He hath kept (in mind) and returned just
vengeance upon His adversaries, and by His Word will
He make Atonement for His land, and for His people.
[JER. Let the nations give praise before Him, let
the people of Beth Israel glorify Him; for He hath
made inquisition for the trouble of His righteous
servants, and brought vengeance upon His enemies;
for the sins of His people He smote the land; but He
will make Atonement for the land, and for His people.]

And Mosheh came from the tabernacle of the house
of instruction, and spake all the words of this hymn,
in the hearing of the people, he and Jehoshua bar Nun.
And Mosheh made an end of speaking all these words
with all Israel, and said to them : Apply your heart to all
the words with which I bear witness to you this day,
that you may dictate them to your children, so that they
may observe and do all the words of this law. For
there is no vain word in the law, unless to them who

transgress it; for it is your life, and by this word you will prolong days upon the land that you pass over Jordan to inherit. [JER. And Mosheh came and spake all the praise of the words of this hymn in the hearing of the people, he and Hoshea bar Nun. And Mosheh ended speaking all these words with all Israel, and said to them: Set your heart unto all the words with which I bear witness to you this day, and which you shall teach your children, that they may observe and do all the glorious words of this law. For it is not a vain word to you, because it is your life, and by this word you will multiply days upon the land that you pass over Jordan to inherit.]

And the Lord spake with Mosheh on the seventh of the month Adar, on the same day, saying,—It was when the Word of the Lord had said to him, Go up to this mount Ibraee, the mountain of Nebo, and he thought in his heart, and said, Perhaps this up-going will be like that to Mount Sinai; and he said, I will go and sanctify the people; but the Word of the Lord said to him, Not so at all, but,—Go thou up and view the land of Kenaan, which I have given to the children of Israel for an inheritance. And thou shalt sleep in the mountain to which thou goest up, and be gathered to thy people, even thou, as Aharon thy brother hath slept in the mountain of Omanos, and hath been gathered unto his people. Mosheh at once opened his mouth in prayer, and said, Lord of all the world, I entreat that I may not be as a man who had one only son, who being in captivity, he went and redeemed him with great price; he taught him wisdom and art, espoused him to a wife, planted for him a royal bower, builded him a marriage house, prepared for him the bed, invited his companions, baked his bread, slew his victims, and mixed his wine; yet, when the time came for his son to make glad with his wife, and the guests were about to consecrate the feast; then was that man required to go to the house of judgment, before the king, and be punished with the judgment of death; neither would they delay to execute his sentence, that he might see the happiness of his son. So have I laboured for this people; I have led them by Thy Word out of Mizraim, I have taught them Thy Law, and builded for them the tabernacle to Thy Name; but now that the time hath come to pass the Jordan, I am punished with death! ' Let it please Thee to withhold from me this sentence until I have passed the Jordan, to see the good of Israel before I die. The Lord of the world answered him, and said: Because thou didst prevaricate with My Word in the midst of the children of Israel, at the Waters of Contention at Rekem, in the desert of Zin, and didst not sanctify Me among them; therefore thou mayest look over against it, but shalt not enter into the land that I give unto the children of Israel. [JER. Because you were rebellious towards the Name of My Word, among the Beni Israel, at the Waters of Contention in Rekem in the desert of Zin; forasmuch as you did not sanctify Me in the midst of them, therefore thou mayest look over against it, but shalt not enter into the land which I give to the children of Israel.]

SECTION LIV.
VEZOTH HABBERAKAH

XXXIII. AND this is the order of the Benedictions wherewith Mosheh the Prophet blessed the children of Israel before he died. And he said:

The Lord was revealed at Sinai to give the law unto His people of Beth Israel, and the splendour of the glory of His Shekinah arose from Gebal to give itself to the sons of Esau; but they received it not. It shined forth

in majesty and glory from mount Pharan, to give itself
to the sons of Ishmael; but they received it not. It
returned and revealed itself in holiness unto His people
of Beth Israel, and with Him ten thousand times ten
thousand holy angels. He wrote with His own right
hand, and gave them His law and His commandments, out of the flaming fire. [JERUSALEM. This is
the Benediction wherewith Mosheh the prophet of the
Lord blessed the children of Israel before he should be
gathered, and he said: The Lord was revealed from
Sinai to give the law unto His people of Beth Israel.
He arose in His glory upon the mountain of Seir to give
the law to the sons of Esau; but after they found that
it was written therein, Thou shalt do no murder, they
would not receive it. He revealed Himself in His glory
on the mountain of Gebala, to give the law to the sons
of Ishmael; but when they found that it was written
therein, Ye shall not be thieves, they would not
receive it. Again did He reveal Himself upon Mount
Sinai, and with Him ten thousands of holy angels; and
the children of Israel said, All that the Word of the
Lord hath spoken will we perform and obey. And He
stretched forth His hand from the midst of the flaming
fire, and gave the Law to His people.]

And whatever hath befallen to the nations (hath been
done) because He loved His people of Beth Israel, and
all of them He hath called to be saints, to stand in the
place of His sanctuary. And when they observed the
precepts of the law, they were conducted at the foot of
Thy glorious Cloud, they rested and encamped according
to the dictate of the Word. The sons of Israel said,
Mosheh commanded us the law, and gave it for an heritage to the tribes of Jakob. And he was king in Israel:
when the chiefs of the people were gathered together,
the tribes of Israel were obedient to him. [JER. Is it

not all manifest and known before Him, that neither the
sons of Esau nor of Ishmael would receive the law?
Nevertheless, because He loved His people of Beth Israel
as myriads of the holy angels, though He brought upon
them many corrections, they rested not, nor desisted
from the doctrine of the law; and, behold, they were
conducted and brought on at the foot of His Cloud, and
went forward and encamped according to His Word.
The sons of Israel said, Mosheh commanded us the law:
he gave it for an inheritance and possession to the congregation of the house of Jakob.   And a king shall arise
from the house of Jakob, when the heads of the people
are gathered together: unto Him shall the tribes of
Israel be obedient.]

Let Reuben live in this world, nor die the second
death which the wicked die in the world to come; and
let his youths be numbered with the young men of his
brethren of Beth Israel.   [JER. Let Reuben live in
this world, nor die the second death which the wicked
die in the world to come; and let his youths be with
the men in number.]

And this is the benediction of the tribe of Jehudah,—
conjoined with the portion and benediction of his
brother Shemeon; and thus he spake: Receive, O Lord,
the prayer of Jehudah when he goeth forth unto war,
and bring Thou him back from war unto his people in
peace.   Let his hand take vengeance on his enemies,
and be Thou his help and support against his foes.
[JER. And this is the benediction with which Mosheh
the prophet blessed the tribe of Jehudah, and he said:
May the Word of the Lord hearken to the prayer of
Jehudah, and bring him back to his people from battle.
May his hand avenge him upon his enemies, and be
Thou a help and a support against his foes.]

And Mosheh the prophet blessed the tribe of Levi,

and said, With Perfections and Lights hast Thou robed
Aharon, the man whom Thou didst find devout before
Thee, whom Thou didst try in the temptation, and he
was sincere, and didst prove at the Contention Waters in
Rekem, and he was found faithful. The tribe of Levi
go forth to the service of the tabernacle, and separate
themselves from their dwellings, saying of their fathers
and mothers, I have not regarded them, and of their
brethren, Since we were of thirty years we have not
known them or their children, for that they abide twenty
years in their charge according to Thy Word, and keep
the service of the holy covenant. Apt are they in
teaching the orders of Thy judgments to them of Beth
Jakob, and Thy law to them of Beth Israel. Their brethren the priests put incense on the censers to restrain the
plague in the day of Thy wrath, and offer up the burnt sacrifice with acceptance at Thy altar. Bless, Lord, the sacrifices of the house of Levi, who give the tenth of the tenth;
and the oblation of the hand of Elijah the priest, which he
will offer on Mount Karmela, receive Thou with acceptance: break the loins of Achab his enemy, and the neck
of the false prophets who rise up against him, that the enemies of Johanan the high priest [5] may not have a foot to
stand. [JER. And Mosheh the prophet blessed the tribe
of Levi, and said: With the Uraia and Tummaia hast thou
clothed Aharon the saint, whom Thou didst try, and he was
steadfast in the temptation, and whom Thou didst prove
at the Waters of Contention in Rekem, and he was found
faithful. For of the tribe of Levi it may be said, He re-
spected not the face of his own father and mother in the
judgment of Tamar, and knew not his brother in the
matter of the (golden) calf, nor towards his own children
was he moved with mercy, in the work of Zimri; for
they have kept the word of Thy mouth, and have been

[5] According to *Seder Olam*, high priest in the reign of Jehoshaphat.

2 G 2

ready (to fulfil) the decree of Thy law. Apt are they to
teach the orders of Thy judgments to them of Beth Jakob,
and the decree of Thy law to the congregation of the
tribes of Israel. They put the goodly aromatic incense
(on the censer) to restrain Thy anger, and offer the
perfect sacrifice with acceptance at Thy altar. Bless,
Lord, the substance of the tribe of Levi, and receive with
favour the oblation of his hand ; break Thou the loins of
his enemies, that his adversaries may fall, and rise no more.]

Mosheh the prophet blessed the tribe of Benjamin,
and said : The beloved of the Lord shall abide in safety
with Him, He will protect him all the days, and
His Shekinah will dwell within his borders. [JER.
Mosheh the prophet of the Lord blessed the tribe of
Benjamin, and said : The beloved of the Lord shall
abide with confidence by Him, He will protect him all
the days, and within his borders will dwell the glory of
the Shekinah of the Lord.]

And Mosheh the prophet of the Lord blessed the
tribe of Joseph, and said · The land of Joseph shall be
blessed from before the Lord. From the bounty of the
heavens shall it have goodly fruit, from the dew and
the rain that come down from above, and from the
bounty of the founts of the deep which rise up and flow
to water the herbage from beneath, and with good fruitage and produce that the earth maketh perfect by the
aid (bringing out) of the sun, and with the bounty of
the firstfruits of the trees which the ground yieldeth in
the beginning of month after month, and with the goodness of the mountain tops, through the birthright ordained
him at the beginning by the benediction of the fathers
who resemble the mountains, and with the goodness of
the hills whose produce faileth not, which was given him
in heritage by the benedictions of the mothers of old, who
resemble the hills ; and with the goodness of the excel-

lent fruits of the earth and its fulness, and the favour
towards him of Eloah who revealed Himself to Mosheh
at the bush in the glory of His Shekinah: let all these
blessings be combined, and be made a diadem of grandeur for the head of Joseph, and for the brow of the
man who was chief and ruler in the land of Mizraim,
and was the glory and honour of his brethren. The
birthright had belonged to Reuben, but was taken from
him and given to Joseph at the beginning; from thence
comes the splendour of his glory and praise. For as it
may not be that a man should work the ground with
the firstling of his herd, so are not the children of
Joseph to be reduced to servitude among the kingdoms; and as the reema pusheth with his horns the
beasts of the wilderness, so will the sons of Joseph pre-
dominate together among the peoples in all the ends of
the earth. Myriads will be slain in Gulgela by Hoshea
bar Nun who hath arisen from the house of Ephraim,
and thousands of the Midyanee by Gideon bar Yoash
who will be of the tribe of Menasheh. [JER. And
Mosheh the prophet of the Lord blessed the tribe
of Joseph, and said: Blessed be the land of Joseph
before the Lord, with the blessing of the dew and the
rain that come down from the heavens above, with the
blessings of the fountains of the deep which well up
from the earth beneath. Bounteous produce will it
yield from the good provision of the sun; and will
ripen its first fruits at the beginning of month and
month. It aboundeth in fruitfulness for the righteousness' sake of Abraham, Izhak, and Jakob, the holy
fathers who are like the mountains, and for the merit of
Sarah, Revekah, Rahel, and Leah, the four mothers who
are like the hills. It bringeth forth richly from the
excellence of the earth and its fulness, and by the good
will of Him who caused the glory of His Shekinah to

dwell in the bush. Let all these blessings come and be
a crown upon the head of Joseph, and upon the brow of
the man who ruled in the land of Mizraim, and was the
brightness of his brothers' glory. The birthright, kingdom, and honour are Joseph's: for as it may not be that
one should work with the firstling among cattle, nor bring
the horns of the reema into servitude; but as the ox and
the reema push with their horns, so this people, the
sons of the tribe of Joseph, going out to battle against
their enemies, will slaughter kings and princes.
Myriads of the Amoraah will be slain by Jehoshua bar
Nun, who is of the tribe of the Beni Ephraim; thousands of the Midyanee will be slain by Gideon bar
Yoash, who is of the tribe of the Beni Menasheh.]

And Mosheh the prophet blessed the tribe of Zebulon, and said: Rejoice, O house of Zebulon, in your
going forth for your commerce, and you, O house of
Issakar, in the tabernacles of your schools. Many
peoples shall pray at the mountain of the sanctuary,
thither will they bring their oblations of truth: for
they dwell by the side of the great sea, they are nourished with (its) dainties; and they take the shell-fish
and dye with its blood in purple the threads of their
vestments; and from the sands make mirrors and vessels of glass; for the treasures of their coasts are
discovered to them. [JER. Mosheh the prophet
of the Lord blessed the tribe of Zebulon, and said:
Rejoice, O ye of the house of Zebulon, when you go
out upon your commerce; and ye of the house of
Issakar, rejoice, when you come in unto your houses of
learning. Behold, this people of the house of Zebulon
will come up together to the mountain of the sanctuary
to offer true oblations; for they eat the revenue of the
seas, and the treasures hidden in the sands are disclosed
unto them.]

Mosheh the prophet of the Lord blessed the tribe of Gad, and said : Blessed be He who hath made wide the border of Gad. He reposeth as a lion in his habitation ; but when he goeth out to battle against his adversaries, he slayeth kings and rulers, and his slaughtered ones are known from all the slain, for he striketh off the arm with the crown (of the head). And he saw that the land was good, and took his portion among the first ; for there was a place strown with precious stones and pearls ; for there is the place where Mosheh the prophet is hidden, who, as he went in and out at the head of the people in this world, will go in and out in the world that cometh ; because he wrought righteousness before the Lord, and taught the orders of the judgments to the house of Israel his people. [JER. And Mosheh the prophet of the Lord blessed the tribe of Gad, and said : Blessed is he who hath made wide the border of Gad. He reposeth and inhabiteth as a lion and a lioness ; nor will there be any kingdom or people who can stand before him ; and when he goeth forth in war against his enemies, his slaughtered are known among the slain by the head being cut away unto the arm. And he saw at the beginning that a place had been prepared there for a sepulchre, a place strown with precious stones and pearls, where Mosheh the prophet, the scribe of Israel, was to be hidden, (who,) as he went in and out at the head of the people in this world, so will he go in and out in the world to come ; because he wrought righteousness before the Lord, and taught the orders of the judgments to the sons of Israel.]

And Mosheh the prophet of the Lord blessed the tribe of Dan, and said : The tribe of Dan is like a lion's whelp, his land is watered by the streams that flow from Mathnan, and his border cometh unto Batania. [JER. And Mosheh the prophet of the Lord blessed the tribe of Dan, and said : The tribe of Dan is like a lion's whelp, and his land is watered from Batanea.]

And Mosheh the prophet of the Lord blessed the tribe of Naphtali, and said: Naphtali is satisfied with favour, and hath delight in the fishes of the sea which falleth within his portion; and he will be replete with blessings in the fruits of the vale of Genesareth which hath been given him from the Lord; he shall inherit the water of Sopheni, and the sea of Tebaria. [JER. And Mosheh the prophet of the Lord blessed the tribe of Naphtali, and said: Naphtali shall be satisfied with favour, and be filled with blessings from the Lord; he will have possession to the west of the sea of Genesareth, and to the south.]

And Mosheh the prophet of the Lord blessed the tribe of Asher, and said: Blessed is Asher of the sons of Jakob. He will be acceptable to his brethren, and will supply them with provender in the years of release: his border will produce many olives yielding oil, enough for him to bathe in it even his feet. The tribe of Asher will be sound [6] as iron, and their feet strong as brass in walking on the stony rocks; and as the days of their youth so shall they be strong in their age. [JER. And Mosheh the prophet of the Lord blessed the tribe of Asher, and said: Asher will be blessed of the children; he will be acceptable to his brethren, in the release of the land, for his ground shall produce oil like water. Behold, this people of Beth Asher are sound as iron and strong as brass; as the days of their youth so will be the days of their age.]

There is no God like the God of Israel, whose Shekinah and Chariot dwell in the heavens. He will be your helper. He sitteth on His glorious throne in His majesty, in the expanse of the heavens above. The habitation of Eloha is from eternity; by the arm of His power beneath the world is upborne. He will

_____
[6] Or, "clear, unalloyed."

scatter your adversaries before you, and will say by His Word, Destroy them.   And Israel shall dwell safely as of old according to the benediction with which Jakob their father did bless them, for whose righteousness' sake He will cause them to inherit the good land that yieldeth corn and wine; the heavens also above them will drop with the dews of blessing, and the rains of lovingkindness.   Happy are you, O Israel : who of all the nations are like you, a people saved in the Name of the Word of the Lord?   He is the shield of your help, and His sword, the strength of your excellency.   And your enemies shall be found liars against you from terror, and you shall tread upon the necks of their kings.   [JER. There is none like the God of Israel, whose glorious Shekinah dwelleth in the heavens, and His magnificence in the high expanse.   In His abode hath His Shekinah dwelt before they were, and under His power He bringeth[7] the world; and He driveth out your enemies before you, and saith in His word, Let them be destroyed. But Israel shall dwell safely by themselves according to the benediction with which Jakob did bless them, in the land yielding wine and oil.   The heavens also above you are bidden to send down upon you the dew and the rain.   O Israel, happy are you !   Who is as you, a people saved before the Lord,—the shield of your help, the guardian of your armies, and the trusty sword of your pre-eminence ?   Your enemies are to be scattered before you; but you, O Beth Israel, while you give diligence in the law, and keep the commandments, shall tread upon the necks of their kings.]

XXXIV. And Mosheh went up from the plains of Moab to the mountain of Nebo, to the summit of the height which is over against Jericho ; and the Word of the Lord showed him all the strong ones of the land,

---

[7] Or, "conducteth."

and the mighty acts which would be done by Jeptha of
Gilead, and the victories of Shimeon bar Manoah of the
tribe of Dan; and the thousand princes of Beth Naphtali
who would gather with Barak, and the kings who would
be slain by Jehoshua bar Nun of the tribe of Ephraim,
and the deeds of strength to be wrought by Gideon bar
Yoash of the tribe of Menasheh, and all the kings of
Israel, and of the kingdom of Beth Jehudah, who would
have dominion in the land until the latter sanctuary
should be destroyed. And the king of the south who
will combine with the king of the north to destroy the
inhabitants of the land, and the Ammonites and Moabites,
the dwellers in the plain, who will oppress Israel, and
the captives of Elijah's disciples who will be dispersed
from the plain of Jericho, and the captives of Elisha's
disciples who will be dispersed from the city of palm
trees by the hand of their brethren of Beth Israel, two
hundred thousand men; and the affliction of generation
after generation, and the punishment of Armalgos the
wicked,[8] and the battle of Gog, when in the time of that
great tribulation Michael will rise up to deliver by his
arm.[9] [JER. And Mosheh went up from the plain
of Moab to the mountain of Nebo, to the summit
of the height which is over against Jericho; and the
Lord showed him the whole land of Gilead unto Dan
of Kesavan, and the whole land of Naphtali and
Ephraim and Manasheh, and all the land of Jehudah to
the outer sea, and the south, and the plain of the vale of
Jericho, the city which cultivateth palms, which is Zeir.]

  And the Lord said to him, This is the end of the
word concerning the land,[1] and this is the land which
I covenanted unto Abraham, to Izhak, and to Jacob,
saying, I will give it unto your children. I grant thee to
see it with thine eyes, but thou shalt not pass over to it.

---

[8] *Armillos, i. e.*, Antichrist. Vide the *Midrash, Sepher Zerubabel.*
[9] Ezek. xxxviii., Dan. xii.   [1] *Sepha de multha be arah.*

Mosheh, the Rabban of Israel, was born on the seventh day of the month Adar, and on the seventh day of Adar he was gathered from the world. A voice fell from heaven, and thus spake: Come, all ye who have entered into the world, and behold the grief of Mosheh, the Rabban of Israel, who hath laboured, but not to please himself, and who is ennobled with four goodly crowns :—the crown of the Law is his, because he brought it from the heavens above, when there was revealed to him the Glory of the Lord's Shekinah, with two thousand myriads of angels, and forty and two thousand chariots of fire. The crown of the Priesthood hath been his in the seven days of the peace offerings. The crown of the kingdom they gave him in possession from heaven : he drew not the sword, nor prepared the war horse, nor gathered he the host. The crown of a good name he possesseth by good works and by his humility. Therefore is Mosheh, the servant of the Lord, gathered in the land of Moab, by the kiss of the Word of the Lord.

Blessed be the Name of the Lord of the world, who hath taught us His righteous way. He hath taught us to clothe the naked, as He clothed Adam and Hava; He hath taught us to unite the bridegroom and the bride in marriage, as He united Hava to Adam. He hath taught us to visit the sick, as He revealed Himself to Abraham when he was ill, from being circumcised; He hath taught us to console the mourners, as He revealed Himself again to Jakob when returning from Padan, in the place where his mother had died. He hath taught us to feed the poor, as He sent Israel bread from heaven; He hath taught us to bury the dead by (what He did for) Mosheh; for He revealed Himself in His Word, and with Him the companies of ministering angels. Michael and Gabriel spread forth the golden bed, fastened with chrysolites, gems, and beryls, adorned with hangings of purple silk, and satin, and white linens. Metatron, Jophiel, and Uriel, and Jephephya, the wise sages, laid him upon it, and by His Word He conducted him four miles, and buried him in the valley opposite Beth Peor;—that Israel, as oft as they look up to Peor, may have the memory of their sin; and at sight of the burying-place of Mosheh may be humbled:—but no man knoweth his sepulchre unto this day.

[JER. Spake Mosheh the prophet: The Word of the Lord said unto me, This is the land which I have sworn unto Abraham, to Izhak, and to Jakob, saying, Unto the children of thy children will I give it. Behold it with thine eyes, but thou shalt not pass over unto it. And Mosheh, the servant of the Lord, died there in the land of the Moabaee, according to the mouth of the decree of the Word of the Lord. And He buried him in a valley in the land of the Moabaee, opposite to the idol Peor; nor knoweth any one his sepulchre unto this day.] Mosheh was a son of a hundred and twenty years when he died; the orbs of his eyes were not darkened, nor had his teeth passed away. [JER. Mosheh was the son of a hundred and twenty years in the time that he died; his eyes were not darkened, nor had the brightness of his face faded away.]

And the children of Israel wept for Mosheh in the plains of Moab thirty days; and the days of weeping in the mourning for Mosheh were completed on the eighth of the month of Nisan. And on the ninth of Nisan the people of Beth Israel prepared their vessels and set their cattle in order, and passed over the Jordan on the tenth of Nisan. And the manna ceased for them on the sixteenth of Nisan. They found manna to eat thirty-seven days after the death of Mosheh, for the sake of his righteousness. [JER. And the children of Israel wept for Mosheh in the plains of Moab thirty days; and so were fulfilled the days of weeping in mourning for Mosheh.]

But Jehoshua bar Nun was filled with the Spirit of wisdom; for Mosheh had laid his hands upon him; and the children of Israel received instruction from him, and did as the Lord had commanded (by) Mosheh.

But no prophet hath again risen in Israel like unto Mosheh, because the Word of the Lord had known him to speak with him word for word, in all the signs, and wonders, and manifestations which the Word of the Lord sent him to perform in the land of Mizraim upon Pharoh, and all his servants, and all the people of his land; and in all the strength of the Mighty Hand by which he bare the rod whose weight was forty savin, and that divided the sea, and smote the rock; and in all the solemn things which Mosheh did when he received the two tables of sapphire stone, whose weight was forty savin, and carried both of them in his hands in the sight of all Israel. [JER. And Jehoshua bar Nun was filled with the Spirit of Wisdom: for Mosheh had laid his hands upon him; and the children of Israel hearkened unto him, and did as the Word of the Lord had commanded Mosheh. But no prophet hath arisen yet in Israel as Mosheh, whom the Word of the Lord knew, (speaking with him word for word,) in all the miracles, and wonders, and distinguishing signs which the Word of the Lord sent him to perform in the land of Mizraim, on Pharoh, and all his servants, and all his land; and in all the Mighty Hand, and all the great manifestations which Mosheh did in the sight of all Israel.

END OF THE TARGUM OF PALESTINE ON THE TORAH.

BLESSED BE THE LORD, THE GOD OF ISRAEL, FOR EVER AND EVER, AND LET THE WHOLE EARTH BE FILLED WITH HIS GLORY.

ADDENDA.

I. *Divine Titles.* (*Glossary, p.* 3.)

In addition to the names of the Deity found in the Holy Scriptures, the ancient Jewish theologians employed several others, as descriptive epithets of the Divine perfections; such as, 1. *Matsui Rishon,* "the Primary Being." 2. *Ha-Shem,* "the Name;" a pronounceable alternative for JEHOVAH. 3. *Yechido,* "the Only One." 4. *Chai Haolamim,* "the Ever-Living One." 5. *Hakkadosh,* "the Holy One;" to which is usually added, *Baruch Hu,* "Blessed is He." 6. *Zaddiko,* "the Righteous One." 7. *Makom,* literally "Place;" an epithet used to denote the Ubiquity of God. The place or space occupied by a creature is limited to the dimensions of its own contracted being: the Place of the Creator is infinitude. 8. *Geburah,* "Power," or "Omnipotence." 9. *Ha-Boré,* "the Creator." 10. *Mi sheomar rehayah ha olam,* "Who spake, and the world was." 11. *Adon kol Haärets,* "The Supporter of the whole earth." 12. *Malko shel olam,* "King of the world." 13. *Melek malkey hammelakim,* "the King of the kings of kings." 14. *Melek shehashalom shelo,* "the King of Peace;" or, "the King with whom there is peace." 15. *Ha El hakkabod vehannorah,* "the glorious and awful God." 16. *Rachamana,* "the Merciful." 17. *Mazega de alma,* "the Distributor of good things (*lit.,* wine) to the world." 18. *Baal harachamim,* "the Lord of Mercies." 19. *Abinu shebbashamayim,* "our

Father who is in the heavens." 20. *Ha-Shamayim,* "Heaven."

II. *Amarkol amarkella.* (*Glossary, p.* 70.)

WE have said that Rashi defines this appellation as meaning a Treasurer; it should be added that others consider it an amplification of the word *Markol; i. e., mar,* "a lord," and *kol,* "all;" "a chief ruler."

III. *Nephesh.*

THIS word commonly denotes animal life, or the soul; but in some cases it is put for the body, whether animated with life or bereft of it. So both in the Bible and Targum it is used for "a dead body;" and in the Jerusalem Talmud for "a stone or monument which marks the place of the dead." In Deut. xxvi. 14, (Palest.,) I have rendered *Velo yehabith mineh takrikin lenephash de mith,* "I have not given of it a covering for the soul of the dead." But, for the reason just assigned, we might have translated thus: "I have not given from it a shroud for the body of the dead."

IV. *Numbers xxvi.* 59, *Palest., p.* 439.

READ, "And she bare unto Amram Aharon and Mosheh," instead of "Mushe."

V. *Fauna of the Pentateuch.* (*Lev. xi.; Deut. xiv.*)

To identify in every instance the exact animal or bird nominated in these chapters is an almost hopeless attempt. While about most of the names there is sufficient certainty, others of them can be rendered only tentatively. Bochart, who spent many years in the study of the natural history of the Bible, remarks truly that the old versions of these chapters only use names for some of the birds and beasts as uncertain to us as those of the original Hebrew.

VI. *Deut. xxviii.* 15, *Palest.*

Bath kol, Heb., here in Chaldee *Berath kalla*, " the daughter of the voice," *i. e.*, the resonance of the voice of God ; according to the Jews the only mode of Divine communications subsequent to the prophets. For instances in which it is affirmed to have occurred, and the rabbinical opinions about it, see VITRINGA's *Observ. Sac.*, ii., 341 ; and the *Prolegomena* to Dr. PINNER's German Translation of the Talmud, book *Berakoth.*

WORKS BY THE SAME AUTHOR.

I.

Royal 18mo. in Cloth. Price Two Shillings and Sixpence.

MISERICORDIA:

OR,

CONTEMPLATIONS ON THE MERCY OF GOD:
REGARDED ESPECIALLY IN ITS ASPECTS ON THE YOUNG.

MASON. 1842.

"An admirable work. Whoever wishes for devotional reading of the best sort, will not be disappointed if he procures this volume. It is sound and clear in doctrine, rich in feeling, impressive and argumentative, and full both of admonition and encouragement"—WATCHMAN.

"An impressive and edifying view of the mercy of God ....A most effective and stirring appeal to young people, on their immediate submission to that mercy ....An appropriate present to young persons, especially to those of education. It is eloquent, argumentative, and affectionate, and, in many places, reminds one of the energy and unction of Baxter's practical treatises."—WESLEYAN METHODIST MAGAZINE.

II.

Royal 18mo. in Cambric. Price Three Shillings

HORÆ ARAMAICÆ:

Being Outlines on, I The Shemetic Languages. II. Aramaic, as adopted by the Hebrews. III Dialects of the Aramaic. IV. Study of the Language. Bibliography. V. The Old Testament in Aramaic. VI. The Targums. VII. Aramean Versions of the New Testament, the Philoxenian. VIII. The Hierosolymitan. IX. The Peschito, or Old Syriac, its Antiquity. X. Its Relation to the Greek Text. XI. Its Relation to some other Versions. XII. Critical Uses. XIII. Sopplements to the Syrian Canon. XIV.

Editions of the Peschito. XV. The Karkaphensian Version. XVI. Translations. St. Matthew's Gospel, and the Epistle to the Hebrews.

LONGMAN.

"A very useful manual."—Church of England Quarterly Review.

"A valuable volume."—Patriot

"*Destiné à faciliter l'étude de la langue Syriaque.*"—Journal Asiatique de Paris.

III.

Demy 12*mo Cambric, pp.* 538.   *Price Seven Shillings and Sixpence.*

THE SYRIAN CHURCHES:

THEIR

EARLY HISTORY, LITURGIES, AND LITERATURE.

WITH

A LITERAL TRANSLATION OF THE FOUR GOSPELS

FROM THE PESCHITO, OR CANON OF HOLY SCRIPTURE IN USE AMONG THE ORIENTAL CHRISTIANS FROM THE EARLIEST TIMES.

LONGMAN.

"A great mass of information which will be new to most English readers   His materials are derived from the best sources of information. His work fills up an important chasm in ecclesiastical history, and is well deserving of a place in every well-assorted ecclesiastical library."—Church-of-England Quarterly Review.

"A work of interest, and one well calculated to meet with the popularity it so well merits..... The information he imparts is weighty in itself, and gracefully conveyed by the author   The sketch of the Hebrew Christian church in Jerusalem is exceedingly well detailed; and the same praise is due to the research exhibited in the traditions of early Oriental Missionaries.   The pictorial prose in which he portrays the fortunes of Antioch and Edessa, of Seleucia and Ctesiphon, deserves, too, its meed of laudatory notice.   He enters largely into questions connected with the Nestorians, Jacobites, Maronites, and the Syrian Christians of India: of the three former he discourses at length, (but at a length which never wearies,) of their founders, doctrines, controversies, vicissitudes, discipline, decadence, and present condition   The Liturgies are remarkable for their ancient beauty, and the Gospels, as here translated, are of double interest, as offering a correct representation of the evange-lical canon read, from the primeval days, by the Christians of the East, and as establishing the excellence of our own authorized version."—CHURCH AND STATE GAZETTE.

"Follows up the author's learned Horæ Aramaicæ, and investigates the canon of the Scriptures in use in the East—The translation of the Gospels is a production of much literary curiosity . ...as such we recommend it, especially to all biblical students ; but readers of every class will find in it much of a description to deserve their most anxious attention and serious consideration."—LITERARY GAZETTE

"We are deeply indebted to Mr. Etheridge for having placed within reach of the English student so much of the Peschito version as is con-tained in this present volume. We look forward with great interest to the appearance of the 'Apostolical Acts and Epistles,' by the same author, which, we are glad to find, are preparing for publication. There is a simplicity and beauty in the tone of the Gospel narrative, as here given, which is affecting in the highest degree.

"The former half of the book. consists of an introduction to the history of the Syrian churches. ..and will well repay perusal; involving dissertations. ..full of condensed information, which, we think, could scarcely be found in the same form elsewhere

"The Liturgies are translated with exactness....frequently reminding us of the more sublime portions of our own Liturgy, and of their common origin.

"The Conspectus of (Syrian) authors is extremely valuable. It con-tains a list of no less than three hundred and twenty-eight names, with the title of their works, and their dates, from A.D. 190 to A.D. 1714. It does infinite credit to the industry of the author.

"There is no better sign of the times than the production of such books , and that they meet with encouragement, is a proof that people are beginning to inquire about 'the old ways.'"—THE THEOLOGIAN, No. 7.

"The title-page of this work has the merit, which all title-pages do not possess, of being a faithful index of its real contents. The writer is evidently a person of sound judgment, of a Christian and catholic spirit, and thoroughly conversant with the subject of his work. We do not know where those who are unacquainted with the history of the Eastern churches can find a brief sketch of their origin and progress at once so full, accurate, and comprehensive, as in the opening part of this volume."—EVANGELICAL CHRISTENDOM.

"This is a volume which ought to be placed, not only in every theological library, but on the book-shelves, or book-shelf, of every biblical student."—WATCHMAN.

"The title-page tells us what it is, and the body of the work abun-dantly fulfils the promise. It is a valuable contribution to ecclesiastical history and antiquity , and the more so, because it is not only executed with ability, but on sound principles. While we particularly and earnestly recommend it to Ministers and students, we are bound to say, that general religious readers will find it to be to them a volume both interesting and serviceable."—WESLEYAN-METHODIST MAGAZINE.

IV.

Uniform with the above, pp. 508. *Price Seven Shillings and Sixpence.*

THE APOSTOLICAL ACTS AND EPISTLES,

FROM THE PESCHITO, OR ANCIENT SYRIAC ·

TO WHICH ARE ADDED,

THE REMAINING EPISTLES, AND BOOK OF REVELATION,

AFTER A LATER SYRIAN TEXT.

WITH PROLEGOMENA AND INDICES.

LONGMAN.

"Completes the New Testament. The Introduction contains a valuable body of information "—SPECTATOR.

"Dr. Etheridge has conferred no ordinary obligation on students in biblical literature, by the publication of this volume It is pleasing to see the close agreement of the text from which our authorized version was rendered, with that which the Syriac translators must have had before them."—WESLEYAN-METHODIST MAGAZINE.

"In an earlier volume the learned author gave a translation of the Gospels; the present one completes his design of presenting a translation of the entire Syriac New Testament. We are gratified with the opportunity of repeating an opinion of the admirable manner in which the task has been executed. To unquestionable competence on the score of learning, Dr. Etheridge adds a profound reverence for the sacred records, and the zeal of an enlightened theologian His Prolegomena contain much valuable information, well digested, which cannot but be of great advantage to the biblical student and the young divine."
—EVANGELICAL CHRISTENDOM.

"Completes an undertaking which all intelligent biblical students will know how to prize, a literally exact translation of the venerable Peschito. ......The Prolegomena evince learning combined with modesty: much research, little show. The style throughout is succinct, elegant, and scholarly. There is a livingness about even the scholastic parts," &c.—WATCHMAN.

"We had occasion, some time since, to notice with commendation the translation of the Gospels by Dr. Etheridge. We have now to award equal commendation to the translation he has accomplished of the remaining books of the New Testament ... We must not conclude without especially praising the Prolegomena, a critical, historical, and philosophical introduction to this volume, which reflects great credit upon its able and painstaking author."—CHURCH AND STATE GAZETTE.

(See also the CHURCH OF ENGLAND QUARTERLY REVIEW, for April, 1849.)

"By this work we are enabled to compare the sacred text, as read in the Eastern churches for sixteen or seventeen centuries, with that which

during the same lapse of time has been received in the West. Such a
comparison will tend to confirm our belief in the integrity and incorrupt
transmission of the inspired documents of the Christian dispensation.
......The Prolegomena will be found extremely valuable. We know
not any single work in which so much rare information could be found
upon ancient translations. We earnestly commend the volume to the
notice of all Ministers and Missionaries."—EVANGELICAL MAGAZINE.

"His high-toned, beautiful, and elaborate works on the Syrian
Churches and Hebrew Literature entitle him to the warm thanks of all
Christian scholars."—LONDON QUARTERLY REVIEW.

V.

Demy 12mo. Cambric. Price Seven Shillings and Sixpence.

JERUSALEM AND TIBERIAS;
SORA AND CORDOVA.

A SURVEY OF THE RELIGIOUS AND SCHOLASTIC LEARNING
OF THE JEWS: DESIGNED AS AN INTRODUCTION
TO THE STUDY OF HEBREW LITERATURE.

LONGMAN. 1856.

"A useful work on the History of Jewish Literature has been recently
published by the Syriac scholar, Dr Etheridge"—PROFESSOR FARRAR.
Sermons before the University of Oxford.

"A work, from the perusal of which we have derived pleasure and
information. We do not know any other book in the English language
which comprises an equal amount of instruction on Hebrew literature."
—JEWISH CHRONICLE.

"It is quite unnecessary to point out the utility of such a work, the
want of which must have been felt by every one desirous of obtaining
information on these matters .. We have given a sort of descriptive
catalogue of the treasures to be found in the volume, and we doubt not
that many of our readers will be tempted to become possessors of it."—
CLERICAL JOURNAL.

"In the acquisition of such knowledge this work will be found a most
valuable handbook "—RECORD.

"We welcome the work "—LITERARY CHURCHMAN.

"The manual will prove useful and acceptable. Where it fails to
communicate instruction it directs us to its sources nor will we withhold from Dr Etheridge the praise due to his industry and manifest
acquaintanceship with Jewish writings, both in their original and in the
works of his German predecessors."—ATHENÆUM.

"Dr Etheridge is a painstaking scholar, and well known by his many
labours on the Syriac New Testament. As the result of the study of
many years he has produced the volume now before us, which supplies
a want in our literature which has long been felt."—JOURNAL OF SACRED
LITERATURE.

"Dr. Etheridge is by birth a Hebrew of the Hebrews,* but in spirit

---

* The writer here was misinformed.

6

and in faith he is now a Christian of the Christians, and in the purity
and beauty of his style an Englishman of the Englishmen.   He
is evidently a great master of his recondite subject, and it was the
absolute absence of any treatise of the kind in our language, which hap-
pily compelled him to become its author."—METHODIST QUARTERLY
REVIEW. (American.)

VI.

Post 8vo. Cambric   Price Six Shillings.

THE LIFE OF THE
REV. ADAM CLARKE, LL.D.
MASON. 1858.

"The very cordial thanks of the Conference are given to the Rev.
Dr. Etheridge for the valuable service rendered in his deeply interesting
Life of the Rev. Dr Clarke. The Conference record their high approval
of the spirit, judgment, taste, and general ability which mark the work,
and hail this addition to our literature as a memorial at once just and
beautiful, honourable to departed excellence, and faithful to the great
cause which Dr Clarke lived to serve."—MINUTES OF THE METHODIST
CONFERENCE, 1858.

"It was most proper that the Christian church, and especially the
communion to which he belonged, should possess such a record of his
life and character as is now supplied.'—EVANGELICAL CHRISTENDOM.

"We should find it difficult to select from the whole of our biographical literature of the bygone generation, anything of the same magni-
tude making a nearer approach to completeness. The book abounds
with every excellence"—CHRISTIAN WITNESS.

"Free from any ungenial bias, he enters fully into the spirit of his
work, and has produced a book worthy of taking its place beside the best
biographical writings of the age"—CHRISTIAN TIMES

"We are here presented with the picture of patient industry and un-
flagging zeal, gradually overcoming the greatest obstacles, and rising
superior to their besetting difficulties,—the picture of a great mind in
circumstances adverse to its own development, at length shining forth
with its own brilliance, an object for admiration, and an example for
imitation."—CLERICAL JOURNAL

VII.

Post 8vo. Cambric.   Price Six Shillings.

THE LIFE OF THE
REV. THOMAS COKE, D.C.L.
MASON 1860

"Those who have read the masterly and captivating 'Life of Dr.
Adam Clarke,' by the same author, will be prepared for the rich treat
which is here set before them.'—CHRISTIAN WITNESS.

"For nearly half a century there has been a yearning in the Methodist mind for a volume that should exhibit Dr. Coke as he really was..... Such a volume we have now before us."—WESLEYAN MAGAZINE.

"The pleasant biography before us, we may venture to say, will be a long-lived book."—LONDON REVIEW.

———

VIII.

Demy 12mo. Cambric. Price Eight Shillings and Sixpence.

THE TARGUMS OF ONKELOS AND JONATHAN BEN UZZIEL ON THE PENTATEUCH:

WITH THE FRAGMENTS OF THE JERUSALEM TARGUM, TRANSLATED FROM THE CHALDEE. GENESIS AND EXODUS.

LONGMAN. 1862.

"Among the most valuable contributions to the history of Jewish literature, we ought to notice the interesting works of Dr Etheridge, well known as the translator of the New Testament from the Peschito Syriac. Dr. Etheridge's last volume, containing the Targums of Onkelos and Jonathan Ben Uzziel on the Pentateuch, deserves the careful attention of biblical scholars."—EDINBURGH REVIEW.

"This is the first attempt which has been made to translate the Chaldee paraphrases on the Pentateuch into the English language The author has done his work well, and given a good literal version."—ATHENÆUM.

"This is a work which has been long needed, and Mr Etheridge is perfectly equal to the translation he has accomplished"—THE CRITIC

"A volume of great and lasting interest to all biblical students, and especially to those who love the language and literature of the Jewish people. Dr. E. has earned a new title to our esteem and gratitude by this contribution to our too scanty stock of translations of books of this class, and for bringing within the reach of all what has been, until now, the exclusive property of the learned."—WATCHMAN.

"The volume has a superior charm for the general reader, and especially for the commentator on the Old Testament"—BRITISH STANDARD.

"Mr. Etheridge deserves well of biblical literature by his former publications.... .The present volume will add much to the usefulness of his labours"—CLERICAL JOURNAL

"The translation has been made with fidelity and accuracy"—JOURNAL OF SACRED LITERATURE.

"The introduction will be welcome to the biblical student."—BRITISH QUARTERLY REVIEW.

"To few, even among students, are the originals familiar, hence the greater is the debt to Dr. Etheridge."—WESLEYAN MAGAZINE.

"A literal and trustworthy translation. A good service has been rendered to Bible students by this volume. It enables Englishmen of the present day to appreciate the forms of thought prevalent in the times of the apostles, and will account to them for the use of words and phrases in the New Testament which have seemed hard to understand. In this way it will confirm the faith of many, and be accepted by all intelligent readers as a valuable contribution towards a history of the interpretation of the Holy Scriptures."—BAPTIST MAGAZINE.

"It is no common service which he has rendered in the publication of this very valuable volume. To the unlearned, and the scholar, too, this translation will be welcome. The version has been carefully executed by the author, who is a competent scholar for that purpose."—EVAN-GELICAL MAGAZINE

———

Preparing for the Press

THE TARGUM OF JONATHAN BEN UZZIEL ON THE PROPHECIES OF ISAIAH, JEREMIAH, AND EZEKIEL.

TRANSLATED FROM THE CHALDEE.

LONDON ·

PRINTED BY WILLIAM NICHOLS,

46, HOXTON SQUARE.

Printed in the USA
CPSIA information can be obtained
at www.ICGtesting.com
LVHW081024071123
763276LV00004B/18